Faith and Science

Joined by God, Separated by Man

Second Edition

By Allen E. Hillegas

Edited By Allen E. and Mary M. Hillegas

Cover By: Joyce Herreid and Mary Hillegas

Order this book online at www.trafford.com
or email orders@trafford.com

Most Trafford titles are also available at major online book retailers.

Print information available on the last page.

ISBN: 978-1-4120-7627-2 (sc)

Trafford rev. 06/12/2023

 www.trafford.com

North America & international
toll-free: 844-688-6899 (USA & Canada)
fax: 812 355 4082

Acknowledgements

I have a long list of people I would like to thank for their support and encouragement. It is highly likely I will miss someone. So, in advance, I would like to apologize if you are someone who has encouraged my work on this book and I have somehow forgotten your support over the many years this book has taken to develop. First and foremost I give thanks to our Savior and Lord Jesus Christ. What can a Christian say about the Lord? We can never praise the Lord Jesus Christ enough for all He has given to each of us. This book is the result of a continual prayer for the Lord to guide my path and teach me His ways. It is also the result of asking the Lord to guide how I can best serve Him. My life has had many twists and turns since it began in 1963. Even the circumstances around my conception and birth have many interesting components I will not discuss at this time. I accepted the Lord at an early age, five years old, and have asked for His guidance nearly every day, in prayer. What brought me to the Lord was the fear of a bolt of lightening that struck close to where I was standing. My wife and I plan to write a book about the many aspects of fear in the near future. In this case, through attending the First Baptist Church in Troy Kansas, I understood that the Lord was under control of everything. The only thing to fear is the Lord and this is the beginning to wisdom. – Proverbs 9:10. Soon after this lighting bolt incident, I attended vacation bible school and accepted Jesus Christ as Lord and savior. This was the beginning of my life as a Christian and my desire to understand this power in the lightening bolt which struck the tree next to me. Over the years, I have grown in the Lord and in a desire to share my faith. There have been numerous church services, conventions and rally's in which I felt the call of the Holy Spirit to "come forward" and profess a re-dedication to the Lord. On one such occasion at a Youth for Christ rally, I followed with consultations with Pastor Leroy Davis who performed my baptism. There are many times in my life in which I felt pulled to either ministry or towards teaching science at a university or high school. However, there have been many times I have strayed from these desires and have fallen into the sin of procrastination. But, with the Lord's help I have repented of my sin and focused on finishing this book, to aid in the spread of the gospel of Jesus Christ. This book represents my desire to share some of the things I have learned throughout my life in the study of science. The Introduction will explain how the desire I have to serve God is intimately tied with my quest for understanding more about science. I pray this book will encourage & strengthen the Christian reader. If you are not a Christian and are reading this book, realize that it was designed from a Christian perspective. There are many phrases that may offend a non-Christian reader. This is not my intention! The book was intended to help Christians to better equip themselves in responding to legitimate questions about their faith. If you are not a Christian, please bear this in mind and excuse some of the ways I trivialize the non-Christian perspective. My wife and I plan to write other books which will be more sensitive to other perspectives in the near future. These books will not compromise the gospel, but reach out to a lost world with a loving hand. It is always very difficult to express your convictions on a controversial topic without offending someone who has an opposing view. I pray that my efforts to examine the controversial topics of faith and science challenge or encourage the convictions you already have on the subject. Thank You, the reader very, very much for your attention.

I decided to list the names of those who have impacted my life with inspiration and encouragement in basically chronological order. This section is from family members who have encouraged my efforts. First, the love of my life, my best friend, my honey bear and wife Mary. Next, my three wonderful children Allene, Charlene & Melissa. I thank my adopted parents Uncle Raymond & Aunt Lela Hillegas. My birth mother Betty Jane (Wykert) Losson. Next, I would like to thank Pastor Leroy Davis of Troy Baptist Church, who helped me grow in the ways of our Lord Jesus Christ and provided for me a wonderful example of a Christian. Thank the Lord for the inspiration of many family members, especially: Grandpa Carl Caine, Grandma Mernie (Abel) Caine, Aunt Ana Caine & her family, Uncle George & Aunt Florine Caine & their son Jimmie & daughter Sharon, Uncle Charlie & Aunt Gene Caine & their five daughters, Aunt Hazel Caine & here family in Georgia & Tennessee, Uncle Bill & Aunt Leona

Abel & their family, Uncle Burl Abel & his family, Uncle Herbert Abel, Aunt Eva Stephans & her four daughters, Aunt Ruth Green & Aunt Emma Louis Newbarth in Oregon, Helen Wykert who was like a sister to me. Billy Boos & others of Aunt Edith Pergamo's Family. You might take notice that indeed in my family the Caine and Abel families got together had a wonderful life and shared their faith in Jesus Christ with as many people as there lives permitted. I often share more about this wonderful union in my lecture series. Special thanks goes to Robert & Connie Lantz & their family, & Ralph & Pat Lantz & their family of Nebraska. And many other relatives that inspired me to reach "higher ground". I Thank You All.

Next, I would like to deeply appreciate my extended family. It is so wonderful to have friends who support your dreams with encouragement. There are far too many people that ridicule others because someone plans to accomplish something different or out-of-the-ordinary. Like the title of a popular book said, Don't Let Anybody Steal Your Dream! So many people have good intentions, yet discourage you from achieving great things without realizing that they are doing more harm than good. This situation is perfectly described in a best selling book called, The Dream Giver by Bruce Wilkinson. This book describes the journey of a person by the name of Ordinary who leaves the Land of Familiar to pursue a Big Dream given to him by the Dream Giver, God our Father. Along the way he encounters "Border Bullies" that try to keep him in the Land of Familiar. Ordinary also encounters "Champion" who had previously left the Land of Familiar to achieve success. Our number one champions who have encouraged us to succeed are Dr. David & Melissa Hullender, Ph.D. M.I.T. Mechanical Engineering. Their friendship has meant more to us than words can express. They are truly the "salt of the earth". In the Kansas area, my appreciation goes out to: David & Patricia Meadows, Joyce Herreid for all her hard work putting our ideas on the book cover together, Kent Otott & family, Dean & Kara Revell & their family, and Larry Stringer & his family. Also, Pastor Mark Webb of the Miltonvale Christian Church, Jim & Judy Nelson, Dick & Deanna Phelps, David & Marilyn Benfer, Larry & Glenda Cyr & family, Ken & Janet Fuller & family, Bill & Fran Garrison, Alan Gilmore, Steve & Jo LaBarge & family, Glenn Lee & Janice Lacy, Dr. Ken Lacy, Roger & Barbara Mikels, Jason & Marilee Paillet, Waine Turner, Fern & Dorothy Turner, Lucile Vanek, Dee Warren, Peggy Wilkins, & Mike & Sharon Stepter & family. In the Texas area I would like to give special recognition to the following: former Pastor Dr. Charles Wade & his family, especially Mark & Pam Wade, Pastor Dr. Dennis Wiles, Don & Debbie McLeod & their family, Miller & Ellen Bunkley, Harvey & Jane Burns, & many other members of the First Baptist Church of Arlington Texas. The members of the First Baptist Church of Arlington who have offered encouragement and shown a kind heart are too numerous to mention in a complete list. Also from Texas: Gary Williams, Bill & Linda Lair, Mario & Kelly Reyes, Susan Fredrick, and Feng Ying Guo. Also, from North Dakota, Darrell and Lorna Abbey & their family. From Nebraska, George and Jan Cheek & their family, and the Ministry of Lloyd Spear and his family. Others who have had a profound impact on my life include Josh McDowell, and the Reverend Billy Graham. Meeting Josh McDowell in a 1983 conference greatly encouraged me to peruse and finally complete this book.

Last, but certainly not least, I would like to thank the many co-workers who have encouraged my dreams over the years. There are so many, I know I will miss mentioning many friends. Again, please forgive my absent memory. In roughly chronological order, Steve Rogers and Richard Noll of Topeka, Kansas. Jackie Bradford & family of Arlington, Texas. Linda Travoilli of Arlington, Texas. Dale James, and Rick Van Meter of Texas. Thanks to my "pitch playing pals" Linda Pahls, Patricia Landry, Jerry Stout, Craig Meadows, Derrick Reinerio and Bret Snyder. My thanks and prayers for blessings especially go out to all the church members of the Miltonvale Christian Church and the Christian Church of Clay Center Kansas. Finally, I sincerely appreciate the encouragement and friendship from Pastor Doug Wallace and his family. Thank you all and I deeply appreciate you the reader of this book. I sincerely pray that this work will draw you even closer to understanding the wondrous gifts we have received from God.

Sincerely,

Allen E. Hillegas.

Contents

Introduction

Wisdom of God, by God, and for God
All Paths of Wisdom lead to Glorify God

This book is intended to be used by Christians to strengthen their faith in Jesus Christ as savior and Lord. One of the greatest challenges to the Christian faith is in the area of science. This introduction is designed to clarify the relationship between faith and science. Science can be defined as the collective works of studying the universe or an effort to acquiring wisdom. If science is simply a pursuit to acquire truth, understanding, and wisdom, there is no conflict between science and the Bible. In fact, the quest for wisdom is highly regarded in the scripture. This book will cover many facts in the various disciplines of science and how they support the Christian faith. Numerous verses will be included throughout the chapters to share some spiritual truths that can be applied to the various scientific disciplines. Some of the subjects carefully covered include: Astronomy, Biology, genetics, fossil dating methods, classical physics, sub-atomic physics, theoretical physics and the theories of relativity. Many of my ideas and beliefs have been challenged and changed throughout the years as I have conducted many hours of research for the writing of this book. The result is that I am more convince in the accuracy of the Holy Scriptures than ever before in my life! The greatest research tool for any subject is the Holy Bible. Through years of prayer and study, the Lord has revealed to me how all things work together for the glory of God. "I pray also that the eyes of your heart may be enlightened in order that you may know the hope to which he has called you, the riches of his glorious inheritance in the saints, and his incomparably great power for us who believe. That power is like the working of his mighty strength, which he exerted in Christ. ... And God placed all things under his feet." Ephesians 1:18-20, 22. The scripture has something to say on every subject. Science is no different than other subjects discussed in scripture. Just as there are guidelines in scripture for inter-personal relationships, there are also numerous references to the value and purpose of scientific studies. I believe there are many verses that can help us understand the nature of seeking wisdom and the ability to have faith. I pray that this book will be useful in understanding many scientific principles. Also, I pray it will help clarify how the Lord intends us to love Him with all our heart and mind. "Jesus replied: Love the Lord your God with all your heart and with all your soul and with all your mind. This is the first and greatest commandment." Matthew 22:37. Just because you take a High School biology class, doesn't mean you are allowed to disregard this command and no longer honor the Lord with your thoughts. I hope this book will help you to follow the great commandment of loving the Lord under the pressure to ignore the word of God in areas of apparent conflict with scientific studies. "And we know that in all things God works for the good of those who love him who have been called according to his purpose." Romans 8:28.

According to the Bible: "The fear of the Lord is the beginning of wisdom, and knowledge of the Holy One is understanding." Proverbs 9:10. What does this mean? To understand this profound statement we must go back to the beginning and look at the laws of God. First, what does it mean to "fear the Lord"? To "fear the Lord" we must recognize the one true God as ruler of our lives and maker of the universe. He alone is our righteous judge and will convict our hearts of our sin. You must keep in mind the fact that God is the ultimate giver of wisdom when you begin a discussion into any subject. You must then submit yourself to His will and give God praise for His gifts of love. God made us for the purpose of worshiping Him. It is God's first commandment. "I am the Lord your God, who brought you out of Egypt, out of the land of slavery. You shall have no other gods before me." Exodus 20:2-3. This is the first of the Ten Commandments. First we must praise the Lord our God. Who is this? After all, we are commanded to "have no other gods before me." One of the practices of men was to worship an object made of stone. This is a type of worship is forbidden in God's second commandment. "You shall not make for yourself an idol in the form of anything in heaven above or on the earth beneath or the waters below. You shall not bow down to them or worship them." Exodus 20:4-5. In modern times, the worship of stone idols seams strange to most people. However, there are other religions that oppose the Christian faith and worship other things made by man. One such religion that will be discussed extensively is the religion of atheism. We will not compare other religious doctrines; this is a study unto itself. We will simply work with the opposing views of biblical Christianity and atheism. If you do an Internet search you will finds a recent surge in the beliefs of atheism. Also, you will find that there is a great difficulty among those who support this theology to form a consensus. Atheism can be thought as the belief that there is no God or believing that there is not anything beyond what is explainable by the physical sciences. They have great difficulty presenting their ideas without using the word "belief". They claim that the physical sciences support their convictions when in fact there is overwhelming evidence from scientific investigations that there is a God. One of the simplest, yet most effective examples is that nearly all of the physical sciences deal with cause and effect relationships. If any event occurs, there must be a pre-existing event causing this new event to take place. If you go back to the beginning of the universe, science has shown that something that can not be defined by natural science, and hence a super-natural event, must have created the universe. These ideas and a multitude of other issues will be discussed in great detail in this book.

There are many references to the attributes of God through out the Old and New Testament. Some of the attributes of God can be found in various references in the Old Testament to the name of God. "Whenever God wanted to reveal himself in a special way, he used the name Yahweh. We use the English name, Jehovah, for the name Yahweh, and it means 'I am that I am' or 'Self-existent One.[0.1]'" This second definition for Jehovah, "Self-existent One" is the most relevant to the field of science. The laws of physics clear state that nothing in the universe is created or destroyed but only changes form. The laws of conservation of mass, energy and other properties are based on the universal truth that nothing is created or destroyed since the universe began. This fact will be closely explored in this book. This means that whatever made the universe must have always existed and still exists because it can never be destroyed. The Lord has declared He is the God of eternity always existing. An eternal God is exactly what science requires for a reasonable explanation for the beginning of the universe. Some additional insights into the character of God are given with various attachments to the name Jehovah. Jehovah-Tsidkenu - The Lord Our Righteousness - Jeremiah. 23:5, 6, 33:16, Jehovah-M'keddesh - The Lord Who Sanctifies - Leviticus. 20:8, Jehovah-Shalom - The Lord Our Peace -Judges 6:24, and Jehovah-Rohi, - The Lord our Shepherd. [0.2] The scriptures also describe God as one being, but also existing in three separate persons, refereed to by the church as the Holy Trinity. It is through the writing of John that we receive a clear picture of the Holy Trinity, God the Father, The Son and the Holly Spirit. To obey the first commandment and worship God requires a clear understanding of the object of your worship. God in the Biblical record is one who is constantly reaching down from heaven trying to reveal His character to men through revelations.

There is just one true God who has revealed himself through the historical records given in the Holy Bible. How did God identify himself to Moses? "Then he said, 'I am the God of your father, the God of Abraham, the God of Isaac and the God of Jacob." Exodus 3:6. God identifies Himself as the God of eternity and the God who has revealed Himself through history as described in the book of Genesis. In order to center your worship on God and obey the first commandment you must have some knowledge of who God is and the history of his relationship with mankind. Wisdom and worship are inseparable; you must know what you believe and why you believe it. What is God's name? "Moses said to God, 'Suppose I go to the Israelites and say to them, 'The God of your fathers has sent me to you, and they ask me, 'What is his name? Then what shall I tell them? God said to Moses, Say to the Israelites 'I AM WHO I AM. This is what you are to say to the Israelites: 'I AM' has sent me to you. God also said to Moses, Say to the Israelites, The God of your fathers – the God of Abraham, the God of Isaac and the God of Jacob – has sent me to you. This is my name forever, the name by which I am to be remembered from generation to generation." Exodus 3:13-15. God was simply refereed to as the I AM. God calls his name "Jehovah" or "Lord" as translated from the Hebrew in Exodus 6:3. The name "Jehovah" was considered so holy by the early Jews that it was seldom mentioned in the Old Testament. God was therefore simply referred to as the Lord or Lord of your fathers. Again, this required knowledge of the biblical record and the history of Jews to know about God. In the New Testament we identify the Lord as Jesus. "I tell you the truth, Jesus answered, before Abraham was born, I AM!" John 8:58. "I am the Alpha and the Omega, says the Lord God, 'who is, and who was, and who is to come, the Almighty." Revelation 1:8. The Bible is a complete record about the nature of God that tells the history of creation to the end of this world and the start of a new world described in Revelation.

There are many books written about the Orthodox Christian belief of the Holy Trinity. It is the probably the most controversial and most misunderstood of all the Orthodox Christian beliefs. I have been asked numerous times about my personal beliefs. I have often re-examined my faith in a variety of areas of theology, which I believe is a healthy part of a Christian's life. Bible studies and discussions help us grow spiritually, test our convictions, as well as help us find new ways to apply Biblical truth to a modern world. To summarize a lifetime of discussions with church leaders and cult members: I believe in a very conservative so called "Orthodox Christian view". My beliefs closely follow the teachings and writings of my two favorite heroes of faith: Josh McDowell and Billy Graham. The quickest way to identify a cult or a religion that differs from Orthodox Christian beliefs is their view of the trinity. It is a difficult subject to explore and this book is intended to be primarily a book about science with a secondary emphasis in theology. Many people are confused by my combining these two subjects because there are only a handful of authors that make the attempt. I hope I have clarified my position in many areas throughout this book. Now, concerning the trinity, I offer this reference. "The doctrine of the Trinity is not 'irrational'; what is irrational is to suppress the biblical evidence for Trinity in favor of unity, or the evidence for unity in favor of Trinity. ... A close analogy to the theologian's procedure here lies in the work of theoretical physicist: Subatomic light entities are found ... to possess wave properties [W], particle properties [P], and quantum properties [h]. Though these characteristics are in many respects incompatible ... physicists 'explain' or 'model' an electron as PWh. They have to do this in order to give proper weight to all the relevant data." [0.3]. We will extensively study the dual nature of light, (light as a particle and as a wave function), and the many biblical references to light in chapters 8 & 9. We will discover that the analogy of the properties of light to the Holy Trinity is a profound and a far reaching concept.

Now that we have briefly explored the identity of God the Father and His son Jesus Christ, how should we pray to God to give proper respect to Him? "This, then, is how you should pray: Our Father who is in heaven, hallowed be your name, your kingdom come, your will be done on earth as it is in heaven. Give us today our daily bread."- Mathew 6:9-11. First we are to seek Him in prayer to worship Him. We give Him praise for what He has already provided, and then we make our requests known to Him. The proper way to pray is therefore to praise God for His past blessings, then make a request for something that will aide our lives. God wants to help provide for our needs and thereby give us a greater ability to worship God for His blessings. What prayer request makes God happiest? It seams that God most appreciates the prayer asking for wisdom. "At Gibeon the Lord appeared to Solomon during the night in a dream and God said, 'Ask for whatever you want me to give you. ... O Lord my God, you made your servant king in place of my father David. But I am only a little child and do not know how to carry out my duties. ... So give your servant a discerning heart to govern your people and to distinguish between right and wrong. ... THE LORD WAS PLEASED THAT SOLOMON HAD ASKED FOR THIS." 1 Kings 3:5, 7, 9-10. There are many requests made of God by Holy men and women mentioned in scripture. There are many times God has granted their requests. God's response "The LORD answered his prayer", or similar responses, is recorded frequently, showing God answering a specify prayer. But where else in the Bible does it state God was pleased with a prayer request? What does it mean for God to be our Lord? It is when God is directing our lives, thereby our will is place on hold and His leadership is implemented. Naturally, it is most pleasing to God when you submit to the will of God by giving Him control of your life. This means to ask for wisdom in discerning right from wrong in our daily lives is

God's favorite request. Solomon followed the proper steps for making a prayer request. First he hallowed God's name, "O Lord my God." Then Solomon praised God for making him king. Next he made a request that God most wanted to hear, He asked for wisdom. "So God said to him, 'Since you have asked for this and not for long life or wealth for yourself, nor have asked for the death of your enemies but for discernment in administering justice, I will do what you have asked. I will give you a wise and discerning heart, so that there will have never have been anyone like you, nor will there ever be. Moreover, I will give you what you have not asked for – both riches and honor – so that in your lifetime you will have no equal among kings. And if you walk in my ways and obey my statues and commands as David your father did (not perfectly), I will give you a long life." 1 Kings 3:11-14. God was so pleased with Solomon that he didn't just make him wise but the wisest of the wise. Also, the Lord gave Solomon riches and honor because He was so pleased with Solomon's prayer. God showered King Solomon with many blessings because he asked God for guidance and wisdom. Albert Einstein had nothing in the way of wisdom in comparison. We have the book of Proverbs as the result of God's blessing of wisdom on King Solomon. Jesus states that if we focus on learning about the kingdom of God and doing the will of God we will receive a great reward. "But seek first His kingdom and His righteousness, and all these things will be given to you." Matthew 6:33. King Solomon received great wealth as the result of his request for wisdom. Salvation comes from a fundamental change in your life as the result of your faith. This faith is in what you have learned about God from the Holy Scripture. "I tell you the truth; no one can see the kingdom of God unless he is born again." John 3:3. To be saved we must become like children with a desire to learn about the kingdom of God. "I tell you the truth, unless you change and become like little children, you will never enter the kingdom of heaven." Mathew 18:3. As children learn from parents and follow their direction so we must follow God.

The Holy Trinity; Father, Son, Holy Spirit (Word of God)

Nothing is more important than the word of God. But, what is the word of God? It is a collection of writings that describe God and the history of His dealings with mankind. We must learn as much as we can from the Word of God. This implies gaining wisdom. You can either read the word of God, which implies ability to acquire wisdom through reading, or listen to the word spoken by others. Either way, to be saved you must be able to understand the word of God. Incidentally, there are provisions listed in the scripture, which we will not explore at this time, concerning people who have comprehension difficulties due to a physical condition. There are some very clear ideas expressed in the Holy Scripture. We may be able to identify the word of God as the third person of the Holy Trinity called the Holy Spirit. The Holy Spirit might be the same as the wisdom of God. We can see that at the very least the primary function of the Holy Spirit is to communicate the word of God. See how perfectly these verses fit together describing the Holy Trinity. "In the beginning was the Word, and the Word was with God, and the Word WAS God. He was with God in the beginning. Through him all things were made that have been made; without him nothing was made that has been made. ... The Word became flesh and made his dwelling among us. We have seen his glory, the glory of the one and only, who came from the Father, full of grace and truth." John 1:1-3, 14. "Does not wisdom call out? Does not understanding raise her voice? ...You who are simple, gain prudence; you who are foolish, gain understanding. ... All the words of my mouth are just; none of them is crooked or perverse. To the discerning all of them are right; they are faultless to those who have knowledge. Choose my instruction instead of silver, knowledge rather than choice gold, for wisdom is more precious than rubies and nothing you desire can compare with her. I, wisdom, dwell together with prudence; I possess knowledge and discretion." Proverbs 8:1-2, 5, and 8-12. What is this voice mentioned in Proverbs 8:1. Is this not the voice of wisdom? "The heavens declare the glory of God; the skies proclaim the work of his hands. Day after day they pour forth speech; night after night they display knowledge. There is no speech or language where their voice is not heard. Their voice goes out into all the earth, their words to the ends of the world. In the heavens he has pitched a tent for the sun."

Psalms 19:1-4. No where is this verse made clearer than in modern Astronomy. Today we study the stars using the principles of modern physics. In the language of mathematics we see the glory of God. What other language "goes out into all the earth" but the language of mathematics. Since the tower of Babel, mankind has not had a single unifying language, except the language of mathematics. Those who studied the heavens in ancient times, as today, understood the science of mathematics. The message of mathematics is clear; the universe has a harmony that can only be explained by the presence of God. This conclusion will be explained in great depth in several chapters of this book. A tent is a structure made for a home or shelter for people. The tent, mentioned in the previous verse for the sun, could be the force of gravity. There is also the subject of "dark matter" which we will address in this book. Everyone can appreciate the power of God as it is displayed in the universe as we study Astronomy.

Studying the word of God, I began to realize that the Holy Spirit might be the same as the word of God. Remember John 1 says "And the Word was with God and the Word was God." This makes perfect sense. It was through the influence of the Holy Spirit that the word of God was formed. "All Scripture is God breathed and is useful for teaching, rebuking, correcting and training in righteousness." 2 Timothy 3:16. "Above all, you must understand that no prophecy of Scripture came about by the prophet's own interpretation. For prophecy never had its origin in the will of man, but men spoke from God as they were carried along by the Holly Spirit." 2 Peter 1:20-21. "For the word of God is living and active. Sharper than any double-edged sword, it penetrates even to dividing soul and spirit, joints and marrow; it judges the thoughts and attitudes of the heart. Nothing in all creation is hidden from God's sight. Everything is uncovered and laid bare before the eyes of him to whom we must give account." Hebrews 4:12-13. The word of God loves those who seek to bow down and worship God. Again, Proverbs chapter 8 describes the attributes of wisdom. "I love those who love me, and those who seek me find me. With me are riches and honor, enduring prosperity. … The Lord brought me forth as the first of his works, before his deeds of old; I was appointed from eternity, from the beginning, before the world began. … I was there when He set the heavens in place, when He marked out the horizon on the face of the deep, when He established the clouds above and fixed securely the foundations of the deep (the fundamental forces of nature?) … And when He marked out the foundations of the earth. Then I was the craftsman at His side. I was filled with delight day after day, rejoicing always in his presence. … Listen to my instruction and be wise; do not ignore it. Blessed is the man who listens to me, watching daily at my doors, waiting at my doorway. For whoever finds me finds life and receives favor from the Lord. But whoever fails to find me harms himself; all who hate me love death." Proverbs 8:17-36. Remember John's account once more. "In the beginning was the Word, and the Word was with God, and the Word WAS God. He was with God in the beginning. Through him all things were made that have been made; without him nothing was made that has been made. . … The Word became flesh and made his dwelling among us. We have seen his glory, the glory of the one and only, who came from the Father, full of grace and truth." John 1:1-3, 14. Many Christians have assumed that the person who was in the beginning and made all things was the Lord Jesus Christ since we understand that He is referred in the statement: and the "Word became flesh". However, doesn't the above reverence in Proverbs 8 say that wisdom was "the craftsman at his side" and "the first of His works"? Could it be the third person in the Holy Trinity, the Holy Spirit, which brought forth the universe? Do we not believe that the Trinity implies God expressed in three persons all equal with God? The Holy trinity is an infinite mystery: God the Father, God the Son, and God the Holy Spirit. Sometimes the roles each play is clear sometimes not. Wisdom: the first of God's works the craftsman at God's side as He "marked out the horizon on the face of the deep".

Studying Astronomy is to study the power of God and should be a calling for all Christians to explore to some degree. The previous verses describe how God created the universe by wisdom. "By wisdom the Lord laid the earth's foundations, by understanding he set the heavens in place; by his knowledge the deeps were divided, and the clouds let drop the dew." Proverbs 3:19-20. To seek wisdom, as a Christian, is to obey God. The beginning of the book of Proverbs clearly describes the purpose of the book. "The proverbs of Solomon son of David king of Israel; for attaining wisdom and discipline; for understanding words of insight; for acquiring a disciplined and prudent life, doing what is right and just and fair; for giving prudence to the simple, knowledge and discretion to the young - let the wise listen and add to their learning, and let the discerning get guidance – for understanding proverbs and parables, the sayings and riddles of the wise." Proverbs 1:1-6. With this kind of introduction, you can expect that the next 30 chapters of Proverbs to have a high regard for acquiring wisdom. Many of the verses in proverbs describe wisdom as a means to guide you on the path of righteousness. "My son, if you keep my words and store up my commandments within you, turning you ear to wisdom and applying your heart to understanding, and if you call out for insight and cry aloud for understanding, and if you look for it as for silver and search for it as hidden treasure, then you will understand the fear of the Lord and find the knowledge of God. For the Lord gives wisdom, and from his mouth come knowledge and understanding." Proverbs 2:1-6. All wisdom can be considered a "hidden treasure" and a gift from God, unless it is used to take away glory from God. Knowledge about perverse acts for example is detestable and forbidden by God. The simple rule applies: Any wisdom that gives glory to God is to be praised. Any wisdom that takes away from God's glory should be discredited and shunned. With this in mind, the search for wisdom through science brings glory to God unless the studies have been manipulated with the sole intent to discredit God as creator and Lord. This can be a considerable concern as we receive scientific information from scientists who add their own interpretations to the data collected.

Why does the scripture have such a high regard for finding wisdom? Simple, all wisdom and all knowledge lead us back to Jesus Christ. When we seek "the truth" we inevitably are supported in our faith that Jesus Christ is Lord. "Jesus answered, 'I am the way, and the truth, and the life. No one comes to the Father but by me.'" John 14:6. "For this reason I was born, and for this I came into the world, to testify to the truth. Everyone on the side of truth listens to me. What is truth? Pilate asked." John 18:37, 38. There is no record if Jesus answered Pilate's question in private or not. Today, society asks the same question: What is truth? Some believe that truth is relative to the situation and changes. The Bible is clear that there is an absolute "truth" and it is the word of God. All paths that follow truth lead us to recognize that the Holy Bible is truth and everything that does not recognize this fact is a lie. Lies do not always begin with blatant falsehoods, but usually lies start by telling a partial truth. Jesus affirms that He is the truth, and from other references, we know that all scripture is about Jesus Christ. From the scripture we know He is the Son of God and King of all things. "These are the Scriptures that testify about me, yet you refuse to come to me to have life. ... But do not think that I will accuse you before the Father. Your accuser is Moses, on whom your hopes are set. If you believed Moses, you would believe me, for he wrote about me." John 5:39, 45-46. This passage is where Jewish leaders mistakenly believed that the scripture of the Old Testament is all that is needed for salvation. "Consider Abraham: 'He believed God, and it was credited to him as righteousness.' ... The scripture foresaw that God would justify the Gentiles by faith, and announced the gospel in advance to Abraham: 'All nations will be blessed through you.' ... All who rely on observing the law are under a curse, for it is written: 'Cursed is everyone who does not continue to do everything written in the book of the law'. ... Christ redeemed us from the curse of the law ... He redeemed us in order that the blessing given to Abraham might come to the Gentiles through Christ Jesus, so that by faith we might receive the promise of the spirit." Galatians 3:6-14.

The Great Lie: Wisdom and Christianity are Opposites.

There is a popular belief that in order to be a Christian you must be very lacking in wisdom and simply have faith in the principles of the Bible. This is a lie propagated constantly. The truth of the matter is that Christians deeply enjoy learning more things on a wide variety of subjects. "Wisdom calls aloud in the street, she raises her voice in the public squares; at the head of the noisy streets she cries out, in the gateways of the city she makes her speech. How long will you simple ones love your simple ways? How long will mockers delight in mockery and fools hate knowledge?" Proverbs 1:20-22. How long will you hate knowledge? Do you fear that God's word is a lie? Where is you faith in God if you believe this blasphemy? There is no "down side" to seeking wisdom. You simply need to test the accuracy of the information you receive when it comes to various subjects such as science. There is a large supply of books of the subject of science that can support your faith in Jesus Christ as Lord. Never rest in your search for wisdom. "For wisdom will enter your heart, and knowledge will be pleasant to your soul. Discretion will protect you, and understanding will guard you. Wisdom will save you from the ways of wicked men, from men whose words are perverse." Proverbs 2:10-12. "Blessed is the man who finds wisdom, the man who gains understanding, for she is more profitable than silver and yields better returns than gold. She is more precious than rubies; nothing you desire can compare with her. Long life is in her right hand; in her left are riches and honor. Her ways are pleasant ways, and all her paths are peace. She is a tree of life to those who embrace her; those who lay hold of her will be blessed." Proverbs 3:13-18. "Get wisdom, get understanding; do not forget my words or swerve from them. Do not forsake wisdom, and she will protect you; love her, and she will watch over you. Wisdom is supreme; therefore get wisdom. Though it cost all you have, get understanding. Esteem her, and she will exalt you; embrace her, and she will honor you. She will set a garland of grace on your head and present you a crown of splendor." Proverbs 4:5-9. "Hold on to instruction, do not let go; guard it well, for it is your life." Proverbs 4:13. "Say to wisdom, 'You are my sister,' and call understanding your kinsman." Proverbs 7:4. "I, wisdom, dwell together with prudence; I possess knowledge and discretion. ... With me are riches and honor, enduring prosperity. My fruit is better than fine gold; what I yield surpasses choice silver. I walk in the ways of righteousness, along the paths of justice, bestowing wealth on those who love me and making their treasuries full." Proverbs 8:11, 18-21. "Leave your simple ways and you will live; walk in the way of understanding. ... Instruct a wise man and he be wiser still; teach a righteous man and he will add to his learning. The fear of the Lord is the beginning of wisdom, and knowledge of the Holy One is understanding. For through me your days will be many, and years will be added to your life. If you are wise, your wisdom will reward you; if you are a mocker, you alone will suffer." Proverbs 9:6, 9-12. "The wise in heart accept commands, but a chattering fool comes ruin. ... Wisdom is found on the lips of the discerning, but a rod is for the back of him who lacks judgment. The wise man stores up knowledge but the mouth of a fool invites ruin." Proverbs 10:8, 13-14. "The mouth of the righteous brings forth wisdom, but a perverse tongue will be cut out." Proverbs 10:31.

Sometimes pride becomes a part of a person's character when they have acquired a great deal of knowledge. "When pride comes, then comes disgrace, but with humility comes wisdom." Proverbs 11:3. We must reverently and humbly search the universe for the wisdom of God. It is when a man has pride in his heart and wants to credit himself for discovering the wisdom of God, that person becomes a fool. The wisdom that scientists discover often has a lot of value in our daily lives. We must recognize these technological achievements as gifts from God through the talents God has bestowed on engineers and scientists. We must analyze each new discovery, every theory, to see if it is the product of truth or a lie being made to resemble truth. Again, whither our knowledge is of value or not depends on the attitude of the heart. What comes first? Is it pride which perverts the knowledge or does knowledge create pride? Wisdom only gives glory to God. Pride comes from a person who is not in right relationship with the Lord and twists knowledge and wisdom to suit his own purpose. Pride is a part of mankind's rebellion against God. The solution to ridding the pride found in a person's heart is to gain more wisdom about the sovereignty of God, and the grace and Love He has shown towards us through the sacrifice of Jesus on the cross. We then realize that we must be grateful for God's gifts of wisdom and humble ourselves before God as the source of all true wisdom, pride is relinquished. There are many scientists that have great pride in their accomplishments. Sometimes this pride gets in the way of these individuals recognizing a need for the savior. Do they need less knowledge? Of course not, they need to open their minds and hearts to the gospel. People are lost because they lack an understanding of the plan of salvation. "This is why I speak to them in parables: "Though seeing, they do not see; though hearing, they do not hear or understand. In them is fulfilled the prophecy of Isaiah: 'You will be ever hearing but never understanding; you will be ever seeing but never perceiving. For this people's heart has become calloused; they hardly hear with their ears, and they have closed their eyes. Otherwise they might see with their eyes, hear with their ears, understand with their hearts and turn, and I would heal them.' But blessed are your eyes because they see, and your ears because they hear." Mathew 13:13-16. A scientist is a person like any other person. Sometimes they can not "see the forest because of the trees". To deal with the issue of pride, each person must understand his limitations and that God does indeed exist and rules all of creation. By understanding the need to submit to the power of God, because He alone is worthy to be praised, selfish pride is destroyed. All must bow to the Lord. "As surely as I live, says the Lord, every knee will bow before me; every tongue will confess to God. So then each of us will give an account of himself to God." Romans 14:11-12. "That at the name of Jesus every knee should bow, in heaven and on earth and under the earth, and every tongue confess that Jesus is Lord, to the glory of God the Father." Philippians 2:10-11

The honest search for wisdom will always lead to establish the truth of the gospel in the heart of mankind. It is foolish to think that wisdom leads a person away from God. We serve the God of all creation. Throughout the Old Testament God refers to His acts of creation and deliverance that demonstrate His great power. God knows that because of sin we often lack faith and need constant reassurance that God is real and is Lord of all. This is why Jesus performed so many miracles in the presence of his disciples, who still doubted his power over death. People who say that there is no need for evidence for faith are greatly misled. This type of thinking is from warped minds that attempt to convince people that a lie is actually truth. To them, the Bible is merely a bunch of stories. They try to convince everyone, with a religious zeal, that in fact there is no God except the one mankind has invented. "A man is praised according to his wisdom, but men with warped minds are despised." Proverbs 12:8. "Wisdom reposes in the heart of the discerning and even among fools she lets herself be known." Proverbs 14:33. Even when "uneducated" Christians are among people "preaching" other philosophies, the truth the Christians speak is recognized by the crowd. Often those who oppose the Christian perspective are made to look like a fool when confronted by only a few verses of scripture. When you share undeniable self-evident facts i.e. axioms of science, that support the gospel, even the most educated person is convicted of the truth you have shared. Do not be dismayed if your testimony is not well received, you will have an impact from the seed of wisdom you planted into someone's mind. "The heart of the discerning acquires knowledge; the ears of the wise seek it out." Proverbs 18:15. "He who gets wisdom loves his own soul; he who cherishes understanding prospers." Proverbs 19:8. "Gold there is, and rubies in abundance, but the lips that speak knowledge are a rare jewel." Proverbs 20:15. "A man who strays from the path of understanding comes to rest in the company of the dead." Proverbs 21:16. "Apply your heart to instruction and your ears to words of knowledge." Proverbs 23:12. "My son, if your heart is wise then my heart will be glad; my inmost being will rejoice when your lips speak what is right." Proverbs 23:15-16. "By wisdom a house is built, and through understanding it is established; through knowledge its rooms are filled with rare and beautiful treasures. A wise man has great power, and a man of knowledge increases strength." Proverbs 24: 3-5. "Know also that wisdom is sweet to the soul; if you find it, there is a future hope for you, and your hope will not be cut off." Proverbs 24:14. "It is the glory of God to conceal a matter; to search out a matter is the glory of kings. As the heavens are high and the earth is deep, so the hearts of kings are unsearchable." Proverbs 25:2-3. In modern times, Christian scientists search for truth and bring glory to God. With their many discoveries we acknowledge them for their dedication to the Lord.

Misconception of some Christians:
Wisdom in Proverbs Only Refers to Studying the Bible.

Could it be possible that the wisdom praised in proverbs is restricted to only learning about the Bible and the laws of God? We have already read how it seams clear that by wisdom God brought forth the creation of the universe. A Christian studying God's creation is seeking the wisdom described in Proverbs. Remember we are commanded to, "Seek wisdom". We do not worship the author of confusion, which is Satan. Satan wants us to remain ignorant so he can control you! It is by the ignorance of scientific principles that Satan has planted in the hearts of Christians doubts about the reliability of the scripture. Do not be deceived into thinking that a Christian should simply avoid the subject of science! If we were to merely restrict our education to only the Bible, the Bible would have clearly stated this instruction. It would specify it is the study of the law that brings all the treasures of wisdom. Another reference that helps dispenses the myth that scientific wisdom should be somehow forbidden for a Christian is found in the account of the life of Solomon. "God gave Solomon wisdom and very great insight, and a breadth of understanding as measureless as the sand on the seashore. Solomon's wisdom was greater than the wisdom of the men of the East, and greater than all the wisdom of Egypt. He was wiser than any other man, including Ethan the Ezrahite – wiser than Herman, Calcol and Darda, the sons of Mahol. And his fame spread to all the surrounding nations. He spoke three thousand proverbs and his songs numbered a thousand and five. He described plant life (Botany) from the cedar of Lebanon to the hyssop that grows out of walls. He also taught about animals (Zoology) and birds, reptiles and fish (Marine Biology). Men of all nations came to listen to Solomon's wisdom, sent by all kings of the world, who had heard of his wisdom." 1 Kings 4:29-34. We all know about the sophisticated mathematics and architecture of ancient Egypt and the nations of the East including China. Yet all these great societies had no one who could compare with King Solomon's wisdom as given to him by God. It was God's gift of wisdom that all the kings of his time were drawn to learn from King Solomon. This gave glory to God and provided King Solomon an opportunity to tell everyone about the history of the Jewish people. In New Testament times the subject of science gives Christians numerous opportunities to share their testimony about their faith in God. Remember, many other nations are recorded in the Bible as having allegiance with Israel. As a result of a common worship of the Lord, these other nations received blessings from God. King Solomon is not the only man of God who was blessed by the wisdom of God, but he is the most blessed as we have already read from scripture. Other people of God who have benefit from the wisdom of God include Daniel. "Then the king ordered Aspenaz, chief of his court officials, to bring in some of the Israelites from the royal family and the nobility – young men without any physical defect, handsome, showing aptitude for every kind of learning, well informed, quick to understand, and qualified to serve in the king's palace. … Among these were some from Judah: Daniel, Hananiah, Mishael, and Azariah. The chief official gave them new names: to Daniel, the name Belteshazzar, to Hananiah, Shadrack, to Mishael, Meshac, and to Azariah, Abedego. … To these four young men God gave knowledge and understanding of all kinds of literature and learning. And Daniel could understand visions and dreams of all kinds. … In every matter of wisdom and understanding about which the king questioned them, he found them ten times better than all the magicians and enchanters in his whole kingdom." Daniel 1:3-4, 6-7, 17. We see Daniel and the others given wisdom by God in all matters of understanding. Daniel, in particular, was given a gift to understand visions and dreams. Daniel used this gift thankfully and wholeheartedly in serving the Lord. Many Christian scientists have gifts of understanding in a particular area of science and they give God the glory for their gifts. "Praise be the name of the Lord for ever and ever, wisdom and power are his. He changes times and seasons; he sets up kings and deposes them. He gives wisdom to the wise and knowledge to the discerning, He reveals deep and hidden things; he knows what lies in dreams, and light dwells with him. I thank and praise you, O God of my fathers: You have given me wisdom and power, you have made known to me what we have asked of you, you have made known to us the dream of the king." Daniel 2:20-23. When you need direction, just ask God in prayer. God's nature is the same forever, but He does change how he deals with His people. God does not just "sit on his hands" all day long. God answers the prayers of his people. "Jesus Christ is the same yesterday and today and forever." Hebrews 13:8. "The prayer of a righteous man is powerful and effective." James 5:16.

Christians, in some cases, have lost their faith as they have begun to believe the lie that science has proven we came from random natural forces or from the power of mutations instead of God. Therefore, many Christian groups have attempted to separate Science and the Bible, just as schools have attempted to remove the Bible from the school. Discussions about a persons' faith should be encouraged in every setting, especially in a place of learning. Science is a necessary part of our every day life. Every time you get in a car, watch a television program; even turn on a light switch you are reminded of the blessings of technology. Imagine the reaction of ancient people in modern times. You can prepare meals in seconds in a microwave, type and edit books easily on a computer, cure numerous diseases and many more "modern miracles". Some would believe we are in the millennial kingdom with this heaven-like lifestyle here in America, until they saw the pollution of sin remaining and growing in our society. We should openly discuss science in Churches and schools to present a clear understanding of why our faith in Jesus Christ is reasonable. We must denounce the lie that it is unreasonable to believe the scripture. There are not enough Christians speaking out on this subject. "I thought, 'Age should speak; advanced years teach wisdom.' But it is the spirit in a man, the breath of the Almighty that gives him understanding. It is not only the old who are wise, not only the aged who understand what is right." Job 32:7-9. Wisdom comes from God. There are some who are young in years but are given great wisdom from studying the word, praying for wisdom and allowing the Holy Spirit to teach this person the ways of knowledge. We need more teachers who are called by God. "Who endowed the heart with wisdom or gave understanding to the mind?" Job 38:36. "Wisdom, like an inheritance is a good thing and benefits those who see the sun. Wisdom is a shelter as money is a shelter, but the advantage of knowledge is this: that wisdom preserves the life of its possessor," Ecclesiastes 7:11-12. Share the knowledge of God's grace; it is the only thing can save your life and your soul.

"When I applied my mind to know wisdom and to observe man's labor on earth … then I saw all that God has done. No one can comprehend what goes on under the sun. Despite all his efforts to search it out, man cannot discover its meaning. Even if a wise man claims he knows, he cannot really comprehend it." Ecclesiastes 8:16-17. There is a limit to our ability to comprehend the wisdom of God. We will never fully understand God's power until we are forever in his presence and have an eternity to ask Him our many questions. This should not discourage us to pursue understanding. "Wisdom is better than weapons of war, but one sinner destroys much good." Ecclesiastes 9:18. Sometimes it just takes "one bad apple", as the saying goes, to spoil the efforts of Christians to spread the gospel. There are many opportunities to share the gospel by discussing subjects of science. There is, however, a general lack of knowledge on the subject of science among Christians. This is why this book was written. This book is intended as a tool, one of many; to assist Christians in sharing their faith about God's word with others. Christians need to be prepared to answer questions in science and take the discussion back to references in scripture. This is one reason there are so many scriptural references in this book. We must always be on the alert and prepared to share the gospel with anyone at anytime. "But in your hearts reverence Christ as Lord, always be prepared to make a defense to any one who calls you to give an account for the hope that is in you."- 1 Peter 3:15. RSV "The Lord is exalted, for he dwells on high; he will fill Zion with justice and righteousness. He will be the sure foundation for your times, a rich store of salvation and wisdom and knowledge; the fear of the Lord is the key to this treasure." Isaiah 33:5-6.

Where the Scientific Quest for Wisdom Goes Wrong.

With all the verses in Proverbs praising the quest for wisdom, why isn't every scientist praising God? There is wisdom gained by science that gives praise to God. However, there are scientists who study science with the express intention to take away from the glory of God. They begin their investigation with an attitude of rebellion against God. The Bible describes these people as ones not seeking wisdom but fools attempting to refute the existence of God. "The fool says in his heart, 'There is no God.' They are corrupt, they do abominable deeds; there is none that does good. The Lord looks down from heaven upon the children of men, to see if there are any who act wisely, that seek after God." Psalm 14:1-2 RSV. This verse equates someone acting wisely, seeking wisdom or understanding, with seeking after God. Scientists who do not understand this principle that all wisdom ultimately comes from God, eventually are made to look like the fool they are by believing in their heart that there "is no God". "The fear of the Lord is the beginning of knowledge, but fools despise wisdom and discipline." Proverbs 1:7. The term "fear the Lord" is used many times in the scripture. It is always used to describe the necessity of worshiping the Lord God of Israel. In the New Testament we discover this is our Lord and friend Jesus the Son of God. This is God in the flesh. "For since the creation of the world God's invisible qualities – his eternal power and divine nature – have been clearly seen, being understood from what has been made, so that men are without excuse. For although they knew God, they neither glorified him as God nor gave thanks to him, but their thinking became futile and there foolish hearts were darkened. Although they claimed to be wise, they became fools, and exchanged the glory of the immortal God for images made to look like mortal man and birds and animals and reptiles." Romans 1:20-23. This verse simply states that if anyone were to examine God's creation carefully, they would know God exits and should be worshiped. It is by the studies of science that God makes one of his most powerful cases for a person to believe in God and turn to the scripture for wisdom. Science has turned more than one person to the Lord Jesus Christ. The case of scientists who believe in evolution is also described in this powerful verse. They worship "unknown natural forces", the dinosaurs, and the fossils of what they accept are from pre-historic man, fulfilling this verse. They "claim to be wise" but are really fools believing and teaching a lie. They desperately try to convince even Christians to become atheists. "For the time will come when men will not put up with sound doctrine. Instead, to suit their own desires, they will gather around them a great number of teachers to say what their itching ears want to hear. They will turn their ears away from the truth and turn aside to myths." 2 Timothy 4:3-4. Wisdom by itself is nothing. The most important thing is the attitude of your heart. Even Solomon with all of his wisdom lost his way and turned from God. "The lord became angry with Solomon because his heart had turned away from the Lord, the God of Israel, who had appeared to him twice. Although he had forbidden Solomon to follow other gods, Solomon did not keep the Lord's command." 1 Kings 11:9-10. Wisdom alone is not enough to guide you or save your soul. You must daily pray that the Lord will guide you. "I devoted myself to study and to explore by wisdom all that is done under heaven. ... I have seen all the things that are done under the sun all of them are meaningless, a chasing of the wind. ... For with much wisdom comes much sorrow; the more knowledge, the more grief." Ecclesiastes 1:13-14,18. Does this verse cancel out the entire book of Proverbs? Do we now consider wisdom something to be avoided? Like so many things in scripture, we need to consider the background and circumstances of the writing. You can not gain a full understanding of scripture by plucking out one or two verses. The first part of the book of Ecclesiastes often makes me depressed. It leaves the impression that everything is meaningless. However, the entire book is about the struggles we all face and everything must be taken in moderation, including seeking wisdom. There are many times that our work seams to be a burden and this takes away the joy we should experience when we are doing what God called us to do. "So, I hate life, because the work that is done under the sun was grievous to me. All of it is meaningless, a chasing after the wind." Ecclesiastes 2:17. Should we continuously hate to live? Of course not. When the above verse is quoted to build an argument that too much knowledge is not a good thing, consider the context and the source. Recall, even later in this book we see the following verse: "Wisdom, like an inheritance is a good thing and benefits those who see the sun. Wisdom is a shelter as money is a shelter, but the advantage of knowledge is this: that wisdom preserves the life of its possessor," Ecclesiastes 7:11-12. "Wisdom brightens a man's face and changes its hard appearance." Ecclesiastes 8:1. Wisdom is definitely a good thing, but too much of anything is not good. We must not be totally consumed with information and knowledge. We must only focus on serving our Lord and savior Jesus Christ. This is the only thing that you can never overdo.

No one can live a perfect life. No, not one person, except the Lord Jesus Christ. "There is no one who does good." Psalms 14:1 "But how can a mortal be righteous before God?" Job 9:2. However, many

Christian destroy their usefulness by dwelling on their battle with sin. It is an ongoing struggle, but there can be long periods of time without sin, with God's help. This is what we are commanded to strive for. "Be perfect, therefore, as your heavenly Father is perfect." Matthew 6:48. "To them God has chosen to make known among the Gentiles the glorious riches of this mystery, which is Christ in you, the hope of glory. We proclaim him, admonishing and teaching everyone in all wisdom, so that we may present everyone perfect in Christ." Colossians 1:27-28. To strive for perfection requires constantly being filled with the wisdom found in God's word. "Aim for perfection, listen to my appeal, be of one mind, live in peace. And the God of love and peace will be with you." 2 Corinthians 13:11. "Not that I have already obtained all this, or have already been made perfect, but I press on to take hold of that for which Christ Jesus took hold of me." Philippians 3:12. "Trust in the Lord with all your heart and lean not on your own understanding; in all your ways acknowledge him, and he will make your paths straight. Do not be wise in your own eyes; fear the Lord and shun evil." Proverbs 3:5-7. When men of science who are Christians debate scientists who are Atheists, the true picture of the heart is revealed. The Christian will list the facts supporting the presence and creation of God. The Atheist will avoid an intelligent debate on the subject and simply accuse the Christian of being "religious". "Since they hated knowledge and did not choose to fear the Lord, since they would not accept my advice and spurned my rebuke, they will eat the fruit of their ways and be filled with the fruit of their schemes." Proverbs 1:29-31. "The wise in heart accepts commands, but a chattering fool comes to ruin." Proverbs 10:8. Scientists, who do not begin their investigation into the nature of the universe with a fear of the Lord, merely become "chattering fools". In this book we will discuss in detail various theories in Astronomy, Chemistry, Biology, Archeology, Genetics, Physics, Modern Physics, History and Theology. What facts are accurate and verifiable? Which theories are reasonable? What is a theory? A scientific theory is ideas that a scientist believes will successfully explain a situation under investigation. If the scientist accepts that it is the best possible explanation, he accepts it as true on the basis of faith. To prove the theory, the theory must be tested in a laboratory under controlled conditions. If it is proven to be true, the theory sometimes becomes a law of science. It is assumed that this principle of science will be true at all times under a given set of explicit control conditions. There is no conflict with any of the scientific laws and the word of God. There are, however, a number of ill-conceived theories that do conflict with God's word. We will explore a number of these theories and detailed reasons why these ideas are not reasonable and should not be blindly accepted as fact, just because a "famous" scientist said it was true.

Anyone who proposes science can prove that the Bible is "just a story book" lacks wisdom and scientific knowledge. To suggest that the subject of faith and science can be completely severed from one another is the result of lies and a complete lack of understanding of the scientific method of investigating events. They are the ones who "claim to be wise", but are in fact fools with wisdom that will trap them in the lies they have created. "The wise will be put to shame; they will be dismayed and trapped. Since they have rejected the word of the Lord, what kind of wisdom do they have?" Jeremiah 8:9. "For the wisdom of this world is foolishness in God's sight. As it is written: He catches the wise in their craftiness'; and again, 'The Lord knows that the thoughts of the wise are futile.'" 1 Corinthians 3:19-20. This wisdom, again, is the attempt to exclude God from the explanation of the creation of the universe. It is the "craftiness" of men who attempt to make a lie truth and the truth a lie. A good example is the lie that anyone who doubts evolution is automatically not a "true" scientist. As more scientific evidence against evolution is discovered each day, the more the atheists reveal their foolish desperate plea for the public to remain faithful to the "gospel" of evolution. Today, it is the evolutionist that must rely on a "blind faith" that evolution is true. The evolutionist has lost so many debates concerning the facts of evolution that they can only depend on a faithful devotion to sin to keep alive the myth that evolution is scientifically based. They are constantly using censorship to prevent serious questions to be introduced in the public class rooms. Ultimately, all the debates concerning evolution and creation bring to light each individual's convections. What does your life stand for? What are your convictions and beliefs? Perhaps this book will challenge those convictions as it has in my life. "'Let not the wise men boast of his wisdom or the strong man boast of his strength or the rich man boast of his riches. But let him who boasts boast about this: that he understands and knows me, that I am the Lord, who exercises kindness, justice and righteousness on earth, for in these I delight,'" Jeremiah 9:23-24. "It is because of him that you are in Christ Jesus, who has become for us wisdom from God, that is, our righteousness, holiness and redemption. Therefore, as it is written: 'Let him who boasts boast in the Lord.' When I came to you, brothers, I did not come with eloquence or superior wisdom as I proclaimed to you the testimony about God. For I resolved to know nothing while I was with you except Jesus Christ and Him crucified." 1Corintians 1:30-2:1. What should any person be known for? A scientist, an athlete? No, there is just one thing for a person to be known for; being a Christian. You can have all the academic titles you can poses, and still amount for nothing in the eyes of God. First make your heart right with God, then he will help you understand any problem; answer any question you may have. "Praise be to the name of God for ever and ever; wisdom and power are his. … He gives wisdom to the wise and knowledge to the discerning. He reveals deep and hidden things; he knows what lies in darkness, and light dwells with him." Daniel 2:20-22.

We are entering, I believe, a church age of unparalleled wisdom. The great theologians and scientists who are devoted to the Lord are revealing wonderful truths about the wondrous power and glory of God. "As you do not know the path of the wind, or how the body is formed in a mother's womb, so you cannot understand the work of God, the maker of all things." Ecclesiastes 11:5. But are we not uncovering many of these mysteries? Are we not come closer to understanding the wisdom of God? "We do, however, speak a message of wisdom among the mature, but not the wisdom of this age or the rulers of this age, who are coming to nothing. No, we speak of God's secret wisdom, a wisdom that has been hidden and that God destined for glory before time began. … However, as it is written: No eye has seen, no ear has heard, no mind has conceived what God has prepared for those who love him. But God has revealed it to us by his Spirit. The Spirit searches all things, even the deep things of God. For who among you know the thoughts of a man except the man's spirit within him? In the same way no one knows the thoughts of God except the Spirit of God. We have not received the spirit of the world but the Spirit who is from God, that we understand what God has freely given us. … For who has known the mind of the Lord that we may instruct him? But we have the mind of Christ." 1 Corinthians 2:6-7, 9-12, 16. "We have the mind of Christ." What has God hidden from Christ? Nothing! If we have the mind of Christ shouldn't we expect to be gaining wisdom and stature as he did? Shouldn't the mysteries of the human body be revealed to us over time? This verse implies that we should be learning the "secrets of God." How do we do this? By science! We will explore this view more carefully in chapter 7. In chapter 7: Calculus and Modern Mathematics, I not only discuss mathematical principles but the religious and theological convictions of some of the world's greatest mathematicians and scientists. In my most recent research for this second edition, I have discovered more about the Christian faith and theological convictions of Sir Isaac Newton. The results shocked me! Newton's theology and mine appears more alike than I previously believed. It is amazing that God revealed this perspective to Newton and independently revealed this same way of looking at science to me. This somewhat controversial view that scientific discovery is as an extension of our desire to know more about the creator. In this manner, everything we learn from science should be based on the desire to add just one more detail to the long list of things we praise God as a gift of grace from Him to his creation. The heavens do indeed "declare the glory of God". Psalm 19:1. How wondrous our Father God, His Son Jesus and the Holy Spirit are as they reveal to us His calling and purpose to spread the gospel and plan of redemption.

It is the calling of all leaders in the church to seek God's wisdom. One of the most obvious declarations to this calling is found in the Old Testament book of Hosea, the next book after Daniel. "My people are destroyed from lack of knowledge. Because you have rejected knowledge, I also reject you as my priests; because you have ignored the law of your God, I also will ignore your children." Hosea 4:6 The Christian Church today is not well versed in the scientific knowledge that supports their Christian faith. This "lack of knowledge" is destroying the Christian faith. Every day new discoveries in particle physics, genetics, and the ability to understand the human mind can be interpreted to support the Christian faith. Church leaders should be called to study these areas in addition to detailed analysis in the accuracy of the Holy Scriptures. Pastors should continue with messages of hope, understanding and love to a troubled world. In order to be effective in their ministries, church leaders must continually learn to relate to the needs of others. This includes the ability to converse on a wide variety of subjects, including science. This is the "common ground" we can use to witness to the atheist viewpoint. Throughout this book, we will explore how the ***ATHEIST FAITH*** is based on a misunderstanding of scientific principles. Pastors need to address these issues with the help of books, films and staff members well versed in science. We need to expose misconceptions about science with the truth of God's word. This is the only way to save our children from the deadly ignorance of God's gift of grace through the sacrifice of his one and only begotten Son, Jesus Christ, on the cross at Calvary.

Faith: Going Beyond Earth-Bound Human Wisdom.

The purpose of faith is to bring us closer to God. "By faith Abraham, when called to go to a place he would later receive as his inheritance, obeyed and went. ... By faith Abraham, even though he was past age- and Sarah herself was barren – was enabled to become a father ... By faith Abraham, when God tested, offered Isaac as a sacrifice. ... By faith Isaac blessed Jacob and Esau in regard to their future. By faith Jacob, when he was dying, blessed each of Joseph's sons. ... By faith Joseph, when his end was near, spoke about the exodus of the Israelites from Egypt and gave instructions about his bones. ... By faith Moses' parents hid him for three months after he was born ... These were all commended for their faith, yet none of them received what had been promised. God had planned something better for us so that only together with us would they be made perfect." Hebrews 11:8, 11, 17, 20-21, 22-23, 39-40. The entire chapter 11 of Hebrews is about the importance of faith. This is leading to the explanation that the Holy Spirit had come down from God at Pentecost. The book of Hebrews describes how the Holly Spirit becomes a part of our lives by faith. These examples of faith in the Old Testament are only a preview of the great reward of joining with God through the indwelling of the Holy Spirit. In this way faith brings us closer to God. Faith has always been a means of bringing man into a right relationship with God, even in the Old Testament. But how do we define faith? The answer is found just a few verses before the listed examples of faith from the Old Testament written down in Hebrews. "Now faith is being sure of what we hope for and certain of what we do not see. This is what the ancients were commended for. By faith we understand that the universe was formed at God's command, so that what is seen was not made out of what was visible." Hebrews 11:1-2. Some interpret this as we are expected to believe in God with out a reason to believe. This "blind faith" has never been a requirement by God. There is a union of faith and reason. Faith is a means to go beyond what we see with our eyes, and accept what we do not see but have been given evidence to its existence. One way to explain the relationship between faith and reason is by memory. For example, you may say: "I know that after the attack on pear harbor on December 7th 1941, FDR said that it was a 'DATE which will leave in infamy.'" Someone may ask, "Are you sure he didn't say it was a DAY that will live in infamy?" Then you may doubt your wisdom and say, "I BELIEVE he said date." Then you verify if you conviction was reasonable by checking historical files. You discover you were right and FDR did indeed say that December 7th 1941 was a date which will live in infamy. This is how faith and reason work together and are affected by each other and the surrounding evidence. Wisdom and knowledge is when you are sure something is true. If you doubt your wisdom you may still believe your information is true. As the scripture has said, faith is being certain of what we do not see. If it is something you can repeatedly check, and test under laboratory conditions, it is a scientific fact, or simply reliable information. The empirical data found in science supports the Christian faith in every way. There is absolutely no physical law that conflicts with a single passage of scripture! In science, we have been bombarded by lies that have weakened the Christian faith. These lies are in the form of theories that are believed to be true by some scientists. They are not proven facts but theories, ideas presented as if they were established facts. It is time that more Christians have their faith restored by being exposed to the facts that science offers which support our faith in Jesus Christ as Lord.

We discussed that faith can be defined as the ability to go beyond presently known facts to an accepted truth not yet proven. But, where does faith come from? "So then faith comes by hearing, and hearing by the word of God." Romans 10:17 NKJ. In order to have faith we must be exposed to the word of God. The wisdom found in the word of God convicts the spirit that these words are true. Some people need a lot of evidence in various forms in order to accept that the word of God is true. "Now Thomas, one of the twelve, was not with the disciples when Jesus came. So the other disciples told him, 'We have seen the Lord!' But he said to them, 'Unless I see the nail marks in his hands and put my finger where the nails were, and put my hand into his side, I will not believe it.' ... Then he said to Thomas, 'Put your finger here; see my hands. Reach out your hand and put it into my side. Stop doubting and believe.' Thomas said to him, 'My Lord and my God!' Then Jesus told him, 'Because you have seen me, you have believed; blessed are those who have not seen and yet believed." John 20:24-25, 27-29. The above explanation of faith and facts are inseparably linked can be applied to any belief. Your faith is built around a set of information you believe to be true. In other words, the information you have received effects your individual faith in a set of information you accept as true because you trust the source as accurately giving you "truthful" information. Each person's set of beliefs are constantly being stretched, grown and to some degree changed as new information is presented. Consequently, sometimes you doubt your convictions with new information, and other times you are more convinced that your decision of faith was a "wise" decision. A little doubt is okay, I think, but how much evidence do you need? Evidence for the truth of the gospel has many sources. Since we do not have Jesus physically walking with us, we need other sources to convince us that the gospel is true. There is personal testimony, archeology studies, historical records and all other areas of scientific research, which can present convincing evidence for the gospel of Jesus Christ. This is why true scientific research testifies to the glory of God manifested in nature. This testimony is of great importance to strengthen the Christian faith. There are a wide variety of different faiths accepted by individuals around the world. Many of these ideas, philosophies and religions have convincing arguments for their perspective. The Bible warns us that ultimately every person will give account for his or her faith before the Lord Jesus Christ. "But I tell you that men will have to give account on the day of judgment for every careless word they have spoken. For by your words you will be acquitted, and by your words you will be condemned." Mathew 12:36-37.

Conclusions About Science.

The main purpose for this book is for Christians to be prepared for challenges to their faith. "Preach the Word; be prepared in season and out of season; correct, rebuke and encourage – with great patience and careful instruction." 2 Timothy 3:2. "But in your hearts reverence Christ as Lord, always be prepared to make a defense to any one who calls you to give an account for the hope that is in you."- 1 Peter 3:15-RSV. "Take the helmet of salvation and the sword of the Spirit, which is the word of God. And pray in the Spirit on all occasions with all kinds of prayers and requests. With this in mind, be alert and always keep on praying for all the saints." Ephesians 6:17-18. We need to fill our minds with the evidence supporting God's power and authority. Like the saying goes, garbage in, garbage out. Again, the opposite is true. Put the Holly Scriptures continuously in your mind, and live a life pleasing to God. The helmet of salvation is to know that your heart is pure in worshiping God. With the scriptures assuring you of your salvation, you can then boldly take the word of God to a lost world. The word of God is always true, and can not be compromised. "I keep asking the God of our Lord Jesus Christ, the glorious Father, may give you the Spirit of wisdom and revelation, so that you may know him better." Ephesians 1:17. "His intent was that now, through the church, the manifold wisdom of God should be made known to the rulers and authorities in the heavenly realms, according to his eternal purpose which is accomplished in Christ Jesus our Lord." Ephesians 3:10-11. We are commanded by God to take what you know to be true and teach the word of God to all those in authority. "Let the word of Christ dwell in you richly as you teach and admonish one another with all wisdom, and as you sing psalms, hymns and spiritual songs with gratitude in your hearts to God." Colossians 3:16-17. "If any of you lacks wisdom, he should ask God, who gives generously to all without finding fault, and it will be given to him." James 1:5 "But the wisdom that comes from heaven is first of all pure; then peace-loving, considerate, submissive, full of mercy and good fruit, impartial and sincere. Peacemakers who sow in peace raise a harvest of righteousness." James 3:17. In everything you do, do it as a peacemaker. Do not compromise, but do not confront violence with violence but with wise words that calls attention to the word of God.

The Holly Spirit will guide you in all maters concerning wisdom and understanding. "I have much more to say to you, more than you can now bear. But when he, the Spirit of truth, comes, he will guide you into all truth. He will not speak on his own; he will speak only what he hears, and he will tell you what is yet to come. He will bring glory to me by taking from what is mine making it known to you. All that belongs to the Father is mine. That is why I said the Spirit will take from what is mine and make it known to you." John 16:12- 15 What is the Spirit sharing? The Holly Spirit is sharing what Jesus has learned from the Father, which is everything. When the Spirit shares it with us, we give glory to Jesus Christ and the Father for the source of this wisdom. "You are my friends if you do what I command. I no longer call you servants, because a servant does not know his master's business. Instead, I have called you friends, for everything that I learned from my Father I have made known to you. ... Go and bear fruit – fruit that will last. Then the Father will give you whatever you ask in my name. This is my command: Love each other." John 15:14-17. In all these things, remember we serve a God who desires peace. "For God is not a God of disorder but of peace." 1 Corinthians 14:33. While we learn from each other and share our faith, let us do everything in accordance with the love of Christ. "Do not let any unwholesome talk come out of your mouths, but only what is helpful for building others up according to their needs, that it may benefit those who listen. And do not grieve the Holy Spirit of God, with whom you were sealed for the day of redemption. Get rid of all bitterness, rage and anger, brawling and slander, along with every form of malice. Be kind and compassionate to one another, forgiving each other, just as in Christ God forgave you. Be imitators of God, therefore, as dearly loved children and live a life of love, just as Christ loved us and gave himself up for us." -Ephesians 4:29-5:2. Let us join together and support each other for the cause of sharing the gospel of our Lord. I was reminded recently that there are many possible interpretations to the Bible. There are 100's of verses in this book. Some verses are repeated, but I believe they are essential verses with little room for "miss-interpretation." I realize that the very mentioning of the correlation between faith and science can bring heated debates. Throughout this book I will remind the reader that all interpretations to any subject are acts of reason. The very act of making a decision is the process in which the *individual accepts by faith* a certain concept, idea, or theory is true. I pray that I am not offending any reader that disagrees with my view as I express my convictions.

References for Introduction

0.1   Brian Sprung, Pastor Miltonvale Wesleyan Church, Miltonvale Kansas, Sermon Notes, Reviewed October 15, 2004.

0.2   Brian Sprung, The Names of God, II, Sermon Notes, Reviewed October 22, 2004.

0.3   Josh McDowell and Don Stewart, Handbook of Today's Religions, Understanding the Cults, Campus Crusade for Christ, Published by Here's Life Publishers, Inc., San Bernardino, Ca, 1982, p. 34.

Astronomy Part 1: Theories about Universal Origin

Astronomy Today and Yesterday

Our first controversial subject will be in the field of Astronomy. It is ironic that some Christians have a problem with the field of Astronomy since it can create the greatest amount of evidence to support the Christian faith. When someone thinks about Astronomy, they usually think of the Big Bang Theory. The Big Bang Theory, as we will discover in the next three chapters, supports the Biblical accounts of creation. The controversy begins when scientists use natural forces alone to explain the creation of the universe. For instance, the Big Bang Theory proposes that the universe originated with an explosion around 12-14 billion years ago. Scientists have discovered that the universe is expanding outwardly in all directions. They postulate from this data that the entire universe originated from what is called a point of singularity. After a massive explosion, fundamental forces of nature developed the first atoms. By using gravity, the sun developed in a nebula region and the earth out of the interstellar matter. After millions of years, evolutionary forces on earth created amino acids, the building blocks of the first living organisms. These yet undiscovered forces took over and life evolved from a single cell to humans over a 4.5 billion-year earth history, according to the theory of evolution. Thus the big bang theory has become a supporting structure for the theory of evolution. Because the theory of evolution is such an adversary to the Christian faith, Christians begin to mistrust any scientific principle, which might even remotely support the theory evolution. Thus many of the discoveries in Astronomy have been unjustly dismissed as conflicting with the Christian faith. This chapter will review many astronomical discoveries and examine if these observations actually conflict with the Christian faith or not. This chapter will also cover the most fundamental scientific ideas explaining the origin of the universe. If you examine the facts closely, you will find that most theories and observations support the scripture instead of contradicting the word of God. Also, we will careful examine scientific laws throughout this book. As the book progresses, you will see increasingly more details to scientific methods and findings. By Chapter 9 on modern physics, you should be aware of most of the bedrock principles in a variety of scientific fields. We will discover that the principles of modern physics exactly match the Genesis account of creation.

A Pastor friend of mine once told me "A big problem with Astronomy is that it is 90% speculation and 10% observation. [1.1]" This statement might have been true in the days of Galileo but now this statement is approximately 100 years out of date! Today Astronomy is 90% precisely detailed information obtained from observations and instrument readings from a wide variety of sources. There are basically only two fundamental theories in Astronomy, which may directly conflict with the Christian faith. 1) The size of the universe absolutely determines the age of the universe. 2) Natural forces working over a long period of time is the "true" power of creation. We will discuss the physical laws supporting the accuracy of these two theories and the possibility that these two theories simply do not apply in the creation of the universe. If we can find an instantaneous creation acceptable, all other conclusions based on observations and measurements from instruments have no conflict with the Christian faith. One thing that is remarkable is how scientists propose that natural laws are somehow apart from the works of God. As Sir Isaac Newton and many other great scientists of history propose, natural forces are merely the day-to-day workings of God. We will study in chapter 9 the principles of quantum physics and the origin of all so called "natural forces". In summation, all natural forces are derived from an exchange of energy or particles. Where did all this energy come from? This simple question represents a profound question of origin, which we will later describe in detail. Do you accept, entirely by faith, that natural forces have given us all of creation? The same question has been asked throughout all of human history. Is there a God? If so, what is his nature? Is there something beyond our understanding which created these natural forces? Do we simply worship nature as the origin of life? These questions will be explored, along with some of the most precise details of scientific study.

Theories Defined: The Importance of Faith in Science

First, we need to discuss the differences between scientific theories and scientific laws. Scientific theories are simply a set of ideas a scientist, or group of scientists, believe to accurately explain current observations. The dictionary definition of a theory is quote, "A merely speculative or an ideal circumstance, principle, mode of action ... A body of fundamental or abstract principles underlying science ... A proposed explanation or hypothesis designed to account for any phenomenon.[1.2]" Scientific laws, on the other hand, are regulations found to exist throughout the universe. For example, the universal law of gravity, which states that any object that has mass, exerts a force called gravity on every other mass in the universe. The larger the mass, the stronger the force of gravity. This is why if you let go of a hammer on earth it falls down on your foot (ouch), instead of the earth going up to your hammer. Also, on the moon, which has considerably less mass than the earth, the same hammer weighs much less. Scientific laws begin as theories, which usually seek to explain a set of observations. A theory is proposed to explain these observations and the parameters for the explanation. Sir Isaac Newton proposed the theory of gravity, mentioned above, to explain why objects fall toward the center of the earth. The theory is that there are a number of natural forces present in every material object. We call the force pulling two objects together, due to their mass, gravity. Through repeated laboratory experiments, under controlled conditions, precise measurements are taken. In the case of gravity, it is found that the amount of force due to gravity is proportional to the mass of the two objects attracted by gravity and the distance between the bodies. This is represented by the expression $F_g = G(m_1 m_2 / D)$ where F_g is the magnitude of the force of gravity, G is the universal gravitational constant, m_1 is the mass of object one, m_2 is the mass of object two and D is the distance between the two objects. Experiments continue to test the accuracy of this relationship until it is widely accepted by the scientific community as a proven universal truth. Then the theory of gravity became known as the universal law of gravity. If any theory can be proven to be universally true, then it becomes a scientific law. One thing that is expected from a scientific theory is that in addition to explaining a group of observations it is able to make predictions about other events. In the case of gravity, we determine the property of how much a body weighs by the above description of gravity. We know the mass of the earth is approximately 5.98×10^{24} kg, the universal gravitational constant (G) is approximately 6.67259×10^{-11} N*m^2/kg^2. We know, from another theory of Sir Isaac Newton, that the amount of force is defined as equivalent to mass times acceleration (F=ma). Using both equations, F=ma and $F_g = G(m_1 m_2 / D)$, we solve for acceleration and get 9.80m/s^2. This is the amount of acceleration due to gravity on every object free falling on the earth, 9.8 meters per second per second. Acceleration is given by a change in speed per second. (Please be patient we will explain these terms more precisely later in this book.) Many experiments have been done to prove this value is correct. For example, drop any two objects off a tall building and, if there is no wind resistance, they will reach the ground at the same time. Why? Because of the acceleration due to gravity. Even if there is an enormous difference in the weights of the two objects, they will still reach the ground simultaneously. For example, drop a bowling ball and a base ball and they will both hit the ground at the same time. Weight is determined by the mass of an object times this constant of acceleration, W=mg. If you were on the moon, you would weigh less, even though you haven't lost any mass. The constant of acceleration has changed because the mass of the moon is significantly smaller than the mass of the earth. Thereby, the pull of gravity on your body is less on the moon than on the earth.

First mass is a rather arbitrary concept. We simply know that anything that takes up space has a certain amount of mass associated with the object. Wither the object in question is a rock, a gas molecule or a person makes no difference. We compare the mass of one object in relationship to a standard unit of mass in order to meaningfully evaluate the physical quantity of mass. In the International System, (SI), of units, the basic unit for mass is the kilogram. "The SI unit of mass, the kilogram, is defined as the mass of a specific platinum-iridium alloy cylinder kept at the International Bureau of Weights and Measures at Sevres, France. This mass standard was established in 1887, and there has been no change since that time because platinum-iridium is an unusually stable alloy. The Sevres cylinder is 3.9 centimeters in diameter and 3.9 centimeters in height. A duplicate is kept at the National Bureau of Standards in Gaithersburg, Md. [1.3]" Likewise, there are two other quantities that are considered "fundamental" in the study of mechanics. "In mechanics, the three fundamental quantities are Length (L), Time (T), and mass (M). All other physical quantities in mechanics can be expressed in terms of these. [1.4]" The standards have changed over time. They are all approximately the same value as their original quantities, but some are now more accurate. "Before 1960, the standard of time was defined in terms of the mean solar day for the year 1900. Thus, the mean solar second, representing the basic unit of time, was originally defined as $(1/60)(1/60)(1/24)$ of a mean solar day. ... In 1967, the second was redefined to take advantage of the high precision that could be obtained using a device known as an atomic clock. ... Thus, in 1967 the SI unit of time, the second, was redefined using the characteristic frequency of a particular kind of cesium atom as the 'reference clock'. [1.5]" The same change in the standard of length has occurred over time. "When the metric system was first established in France in 1792, the meter was defined to be 10^{-7} time the distance from the equator to the North Pole through Paris. ... Until 1960, the standard for length, the meter, was defined as the distance between two lines on a specific platinum-iridium bar stored under controlled conditions. ... In October 1983, the meter was redefined as follows: One meter- the distance traveled by light in vacuum during a time of $1/299\ 792\ 458$ second. In effect, this latest definition establishes the speed of light in vacuum is $299\ 792\ 458$ meters per second. [1.6]" All of physical science is a comparison of two or more quantities. It is interesting to note that to make sense out of observations in the universe you must compare properties to a reference or point of origin. As Christians, we know our point of origin is the Lord Jesus Christ. So, we can say, science in essence proves the need to reference a creator to make sense of our observations. There will be many more examples of this truth in nature throughout this book.

Sometimes scientific laws must be modified to illustrate they are not always true, but only true under certain circumstances. Like the experiment mentioned previously, the test of the gravitational constant of acceleration fails if you drop a rock and a feather. The feather is lifted up by the wind, and does not reach the ground as quickly as the rock. Thereby, we can say that the above equation can estimate the force due to gravity in an "isolated system" where, for example, there is no effect of wind resistance. The best example of the fact that all physical principles have limitations is in the observations of nuclear physics experiments. From Einstein's theory of relativity, we now know that all the classical laws must be modified when you are dealing with objects moving at speeds near the velocity of light. An example of this type of modification can be found in the formula for kinetic energy, K.E. $= \frac{1}{2}mv^2$ and applies to matter moving at velocities much slower than light. When we calculate the kinetic energy of a mass in a particle accelerator moving at relativistic speeds, we need to modify this equation. We know for a fact that by the equation $M_f = M_i \div \sqrt{[1-(v^2/c^2)]}$, derived from E$=mc^2$, mass increases with velocity. Therefore, the equation for kinetic energy must be modified to take into account this effect K.E. $= \frac{1}{2}m_0v^2 + \frac{3}{8} m_0v^2(v^2/c^2) + \ldots$.[1.7] Theories are ideas, which are unproved and open for debate. The theory of evolution is certainly filled with ideas which can be challenged on a scientific basis. Scientific laws are ideas representing consistent relationships in the nature of the universe. Even scientific laws must be accompanied by specific conditions in which the laws are true. When describing the conditions at the beginning of the universe, we find that the physical laws do not apply, and fail to explain the conditions at the moment of creation. The physical laws are only true under specific controlled conditions. Theories are even more susceptible to errors than laws and are not proven to be true under any circumstances. Otherwise, by definition, these ideas would no longer be considered a theory but a scientific law. If you accept a certain theory as true, you are accepting it solely on your personal interpretation of the evidence and with your faith in the theory. Despite many teaching practices to the contrary, accepting the theory of evolution as true requires an act of faith. Therefore, in essence, any teacher presenting ideas based on the theory of evolution as absolutely true is not merely explaining scientific ideas, but promoting a type of religion. Evolutionary theories, to a large degree, are merely an attempt to re-write universal history, and leave God out of the picture. To be a truly accurate teacher, there should be constant reminders that the theory of evolution is only one possible explanation to the origin of the universe, the world, and life. Evolution is not the only scientific explanation to life. This fact should be made clear as often as possible to be scientifically accurate. This concept will be explored in more detail in Chapters 4-6.

In the final analysis, I believe, these theories are irrelevant around the fact that Jesus Christ is Lord and God has created the universe. I say this is a fact because I accept it as fact through faith. "For what does the Scripture say? Abraham believed God, and it was accounted to him for righteousness. ...For with the heart one believes unto righteousness, and with the mouth confession is made unto salvation." Romans 4:3, 10:10. NKJ More about faith in science will be discussed in Chapter 9 when we discuss the concepts of Modern Physics. The world of quantum physics is filled with moving from one position to another, without apparently crossing the distance between. Accepting the events have taken place is similar to the concept of having a leap of faith, as we will discuss. God could have made the universe in any manner that suited him. I believe that it is good to continually re-evaluate your personal convictions. I have done so many times throughout the writing of this book. I urge you who are my brothers and sisters in Christ, not to allow debates over astronomical principles, or other scientific theories, divide you within the family of God. My theories are not necessarily the correct ones, but I feel that one should keep an open mind to the evidence presented. My final conclusions are based on the belief that the glory of God is revealed through the study of Astronomy. "The heavens are telling the glory of God; and the firmament declares his handiwork." Psalms 19:1 RSV I hope that my message will be understood, even if there are disagreements with my conclusions. It is important to take note that details to our faith are constantly changing as we learn more about God's Holy word. In this sense, new information always effects our convictions and our faith. Sometimes our faith is challenged, sometimes it is uplifted. I pray that the information present in this book will uplift the Christian faith. My faith has never been stronger in the Lord since completing this work. May the principles we will cover redirect your attention to the one and only one thing that is important in life: Worship the Lord Jesus Christ.

Current information about the universe has no conflict with any Biblical record! We have many instruments to study the size and composition of the universe, stars, galaxies and nebulas regions. All of this information can be accepted without any conflict with the Scripture. The HR diagram of star formation will be discussed in chapter 3, as well as the shape of the universe described by general relativity. I, personally, believe the classifications of the differences in stars are completely reliable and consistent with nuclear physics. Verification of nuclear activity in stars has several sources. One is the necessity of nuclear reactions to supply the observed power and radiation coming from the stars, in particular the sun. The sun is the closest star and has been closely examined. We will discuss the nuclear properties of the sun and how the emission of light, heat, power, and sub-atomic particles is in complete agreement with the current theory of nuclear reactions in the stars. To verify the nuclear process in different stars, we can use spectral analysis. Spectroscopic observation involves principles of quantum mechanics and proven laws of optics. The work to determine the elements within a particular star is perfectly acceptable. However, I will disagree with scientists who conclude that the present state of the universe proves that the evolutionary theory is correct. Sudden and unexplainable events, which defy scientific explanation, have definitely occurred. These events are sometimes commonly referred too as miracles. We will examine the evidence in a sudden creation act of God to explain the beginning to the universe. There is no need to believe in the slow gradual changes proposed by evolution as the source of universal creation.

The Naturalist View vs. Creationist View

To begin our discussion, we need to clarify the two approaches to the study of universal origin: the naturalist view and the creationist view. The naturalist view is represented by a belief that all things are created by natural forces alone. The naturalist's theory is derived from the idea that given enough applied force, random motion and an unlimited amount of time, there is a probability that a set of circumstances will exist to produce all life and all matter in the universe. The theory states that there must have been, at the beginning of the universe, a law of nature that produced successively more complex organizations. There are some really serious problems with this theory. First, scientific research continually shows that the circumstances needed for even the simplest atomic and chemical inter-actions are highly complex. The naturalist believes that this problem is resolved by the continuous improvement of the circumstances through great amounts of time. This is a primary principle to the theory of evolution, i.e. things are continually improving, going from a lower order to a higher order form. Thus over billions of years, anything is possible. Evolutionists have a lot of faith in the belief random chance and time working together. However, their faith is unsubstantiated by scientific evidence. "One has only to contemplate the magnitude of this task to concede that the spontaneous generation of a living organism is impossible. Yet here we are- as a result, I believe, of spontaneous generation. It will help to disagree for a moment to ask what one means by 'impossible'. With every event one can associate a probability- the chance that it will occur. ... To give an example: Every Physicist knows that there is a very small probability, which is easily computed, that the table upon which I am writing will suddenly and spontaneously rise into the air. The event requires no more than that the molecules of which the table is composed, ordinarily in random motion in all directions, should happen by chance to move in the same direction. ... Time is in fact the hero of the plot. The time with which we have to deal with is of the order of two billion years. What we regard as impossible on the basis of human experience is meaningless here. Given so much time, the 'impossible' becomes possible, the possible probable, and the probable virtually certain. One has only to wait: time itself performs the miracles. [1.8]" This quote accurately describes the thinking of scientists who believe in the naturalistic view of creation. We will discuss in great depth where this faith in the power of evolution originates. Be assured our battle is not with science but with false beliefs, religions, and teachings against the Word of God. We will discuss further about how science is progressing towards the opposite conclusion. That is to say, scientific studies are making it increasingly clear that the universe must have originated by intelligent design. There doesn't scam to be enough time for these incredible events of life beginning from simple chemical reactions, to have taken place on earth.

Does Random Chance and Time Work Together?

The biggest problem to the naturalist view of the universe is in proving that random chance and time work together to produce a successively greater complexity. This concept of increasing order with time is a direct violation of many fundamental principles of physics, including the second law of thermodynamics. This law states that physical systems tend to go from a higher order to a lower one, not from a lower order to a higher one. This principle is often stated that entropy, the amount of disorder in the universe, increases with time. Stephen Hawking, one of the most brilliant theoretical physicists and astronomers of the twentieth century, puts the problem this way: "There also is the matter of entropy. This measure of perpetually increasing decay and chaos is controlled by the second law of thermodynamics, which declares that any change in the universe will lead to a slightly more disorderly place. Entropy always goes up. Order always goes down. Evidence of this universal tendency toward disintegration is everywhere. ... This leads to a dilemma: If the universe is a place that is like a watch slowly running down, how, in the face of this natural tendency, did it get wound up in the first place? In defiance of the second law of thermodynamics, order has risen out of chaos. ... Is our universe an enormous, accidental reversal of entropy? Or is it-literally- a miracle? [1.9]" Which theory is more reasonable to believe? 1) God created the universe and thus we follow the laws of thermodynamics from a higher, perfect order to a less perfect order, us. 2) Or, we evolved from amoebas to apes to humans by evolution, in violation of the laws of thermodynamics? Which is more reasonable believe? Creation, which is in complete agreement with scientific laws or evolution which conflicts with scientific laws? In particular, here are just four areas in which the creation model best represents the scientific description of the origin to the universe. 1) The laws of thermodynamics previously explained. 2) There is no ability for a force of nature to save beneficial changes and reject the misfits to create the complex structures in the universe, like the structure of the atom. 3) The universe is so incredibly vast and complex, that there seams to be no limit to the mysteries yet to be solved. This testifies to the presence of an infinite mind of God. 4) The amount of faith it requires for a person to accept each of the theoretical explanations to the origin of the universe. When we compare the Christian and the evolutionary view side by side, we see that the Christian view, in my opinion, is easier to accept on the basis of the scientific evidences.

Random motion never creates complexity, according to all the known laws of physics. The evolutionists have a profound belief that this does occur, despite the laws of thermodynamics. Their basis is on applying the uncertainty principle of quantum mechanics and over-emphasizing the probability equations. It is a fact that there is a chance that random motion can create a single part to an overall structure, given an unlimited amount of time. However, how can these parts accumulate through natural forces alone? What are the limitations to the ability of nature to constructively build things out of random chance and time? The naturalists believe that there are virtually no limits to this ability of nature to organize constructively. This is scientifically and philosophically impossible. However, scientists worldwide attempt to justify their profound convictions and their religious faith in evolution. They accomplish this task by confusing the general public with long speeches and with complex mathematical equations. In short, the general public has been duped. Most people are overwhelmed with scientific jargon that makes the evolutionary view plausible, when in fact science does not support most of their conclusions. However, you usually receive only one side of the argument.

What Natural Force is a Craftsman?

One example to illustrate the naturalist position is by taking a house and blowing it up with dynamite. There is a definite probability, according to the naturalistic theories, that out of the rubble, the random motion of the wind will eventually re-build the house. With the use of probability equations and imaginative uses of mathematics and principles of forces, many scientists attempt to prove that there exists a method in which nature can form order out of chaos. The naturalist attempts to prove how the house in our example, could be totally rebuilt by the wind and the debris. The first step would be a single board blown around and eventually made to stand upright. In time, there is again a probability that another board is blown close to the first board and again made to stand upright. By sifting the dirt on the ground the boards are supported in the upright position. Then the wind could eventually pick up a nail and blow it into the two boards with enough force to connect them together. This process of random wind motion constructing substances from a complex series of events continues until the entire house is rebuilt, including the glass windows and the porch. I wonder how the glass, in our example, was put back together by the force of the wind. But, according to the naturalistic view of the universe, nature has incredible abilities to construct order out of chaos. Naturalistic theories will even admit that these methods and abilities are beyond our understanding of science and physics. However, they BELIEVE these forces were used to construct every organizational structure in the universe. Millions and billions of dollars are spent each year to research what exact conditions were taking place at the origin of the universe. The original creation of the universe is far beyond our understanding of physical principles and laws, as we will discuss in the next chapter. The creation of the universe apparently violates many fundamental scientific laws. Any event that can not be explained by science and is beyond our present understanding of the laws of physics, but the evidence conclusively proves that the event did happen; I would define as a miracle. Scientist have practically proven that the origin of the universe and, as we shall see in chapters four, five and six, the creation of life was a miracle. Scientists simply refuse to call it a miracle and prefer a long-winded explanation of a complex series of events, which took place "billions" of years ago. Just like the resurrection of Jesus Christ from the dead and the miracles of Jesus during his ministry on earth, the creation of the universe was a one-time miracle made by the Word of God. You can not prove any of these events took place "scientifically" because they can not be repeated under controlled laboratory conditions.

Let us examine some of the problems with the view that everything can be scientifically explained, and the naturalistic theory. The most obvious problem is this mysterious ability of nature to take random forces and create an organized structure. For example, the two boards in our previous illustration. Let us assume that the wind had indeed propped a single board upright. This would take a strong force from the wind. Then let us say that the wind started to pick up a second board and blow it towards the first board. Experience tells us that the first board is likely to blow over on the ground as the second board approaches the first board. If the second board didn't by some "miracle" knock over the first board, as it was moving towards the first, the force of the wind would be so great as to knock over the first board. This would leave the final conditions the same as the original, chaos. It seams inconceivable that there is some mysterious force with the ability to constructively increase the order to the universe. This is one reason why it is my belief that it requires more unrealistic faith to believe in the naturalistic and evolution principles, than is required to accept the Christian faith. We will see throughout this book how the naturalistic and evolutionary prospective continually contradicts itself and violates fundamental physical laws. The Christian view, on the other hand, violates no laws of physics, science, or rules of logical reasoning. Chapter 9 on modern physics, which includes relativity and quantum mechanics, should provide a new appreciation to the sophisticated design God has created in the universe. The whole theory of natural forces as the source of creation is based on the existence of a mechanism which can save beneficial changes and withstand forces which tend to destroy any previously made progress. This is an unrealistic faith by evolutionists in a non-existent process.

The most famous illustration of the theory of order resulting from random motion is the monkey typist. First you have a monkey randomly type on a typewriter, or computer keyboard. The theory states that eventually the monkey would type out one of Shakespeare's plays. No natural force can accomplish this goal. Any progress towards a sophisticated structure is usually, not always, canceled by the next set of random events. If our monkey somehow typed a small intelligible word, it is highly likely that the next bit of random typing would be nonsense. How would the monkey ever get a complete sentence, little alone the entire Shakespeare play? After completing even a small three-letter word, the next set of random typing would eliminate any progress for completing the Shakespeare play. However, evolutionists would have us believe that this is possible with natural forces. We will explore the monkey typist theory in more detail along with the subject of the chemical origin of life. They teach that on the large scale of universal creation, gravity pulls particles together to organize the structure. They suppose that, by the power of gravity alone, all the planets and the stars in the universe were formed. However, the smaller the particle, the less gravity affects the object. At the atomic level, gravity has essentially no effect on the sub-atomic particle interactions. The other three fundamental forces, electromagnetism, weak and strong force, are dominant in interactions at the sub-atomic level. To this day, the best scientists in the world can not explain the precise conditions that brought the universe into existence. How or when did gravity become the dominant force? Could a sudden creation of the entire universe explain the evidence more understandably? We will discover that indeed the literal interpretation of Genesis does fit perfectly into the scientific information. Random chance and the force of wind can not build a house, but a good carpenter can do the job. Similarly, the Good Carpenter, Jesus Christ, is the reason for our existence. "For every house is built by someone, but the builder of all things is God." Hebrews 3:4. What makes the universe operate with a clock-like perfection? Many philosophers point to the complexity of the universe as undeniable proof in the existence of God. "It is impossible to account for the creation of the universe without agency of a Supreme Being." George Washington (1732-1799) "The visible order of the universe proclaims a supreme intelligence." J.J. Rousseau (1712-1178) "All things speak of God" Edward Young (1683-1765) "The visible marks of extraordinary wisdom and power appear so plainly in all the works of the creation that a rational creature who will but seriously reflect on them, cannot miss the discovery of a deity." John Locke (1632-1704). 'As a house implies a builder, and a garment a weaver, and a door a carpenter, so does the existence of the Universe imply a Creator.' Akiba (c.140-c.185) in Midrash [1.10]" It is through Jesus Christ that we have life everlasting. It is by the power of the spoken Word of God that we exist today. Life is a miracle; treat each breath you take as a gift from God, always giving thanks to God.

Figure 1.1

As Easy as Baking a Cake

Another illustration explaining the naturalistic theory is found in mixing cake batter. According to the big bang theory, the entire universe was organized by a random mixing of forces, particles, and chemical elements. Supposedly, that out of the random displacement of this "soup" from the "primeval fireball" developed all the stars, planets, galaxies, and galactic clusters. How, exactly, is all this possible? The theoretical reconstruction of what took place at the big bang is a source of continual research and development from scientists around the world. Back to our cake batter comparison, the organized structures of the universe were supposedly constructed by a "lumping" effect. Given the substances in the batter, and applying probability equations, you could establish the likelihood of a small clump of matter forming. The naturalistic viewpoint will state that with the random motion generated by the forces from a mixer, a single clump will form within a certain amount of time. If you continue the mixing process, a whole bunch of clumps will form. This is supposedly how all matter in the universe was created. The forces continued to clump matter and energy until the stars, galaxies and galactic clusters all formed. Out of this clumping, due to the random application of forces, our sun was formed. Out of material from either the sun or the nebula which formed the sun, our solar system developed, see figure 1.1. Out of random displacement of chemicals, life began on the earth. And eventually man evolved from amino acids and proteins in the "primordial soup". This is the naturalistic view of origins. The "clumping" started from gravity holding things together. Next in biological evolution, it was DNA that was the hero of saving beneficial changes. Many aspects of this theory will be discussed throughout the remainder of this book. The crucial point of this section is that random motion does not naturally tend to produce "lumps". This is explained in precise detail with the science of thermodynamics. In practical, every-day experience you know that the cake batter theory is not logical. If you continue mixing the cake batter, you don't get an increasing number of lumps. Of course, just the opposite takes place. The batter may start out lumpy, but by continuing the mixing process, the lumps disappear. Just ask any baker and you know this is an absolute truth! Once again, evolutionists expect us to believe a lie!

What is the reasoning behind the theories of nature having the ability to organize structures? Many scientists rely on the force of gravity for controlling the movement of large amounts of matter and the strong and weak nuclear forces for atomic construction. Scientists who support a naturalistic view of the universe overlook the structural and physical limitations of the universe. For example, in our chapters concerning evolution we will discuss biological changes and their limitations. Evolutionists attempt to prove that there are no limitations to biological change and they are absolutely wrong. A close examination of the probability equations essentially rules out the structure of the universe coming from anything other than the power of God. The events, which created the universe, are those described in the Genesis account. What are the forces, which bridge the gap, between elements in the nuclear fusion of the stars, to the production of life? Scientists rely on many theories and still search for ways to understand the origin of life from a naturalistic view. A recent article in Scientific American listed the top ten mysteries of science left to be explored. Eight out of the ten dealt with either the origin of life or the origin to the universe. [1.11] For the Christian, the mystery is solved. God is the source of all things, the center of all things. Through a personal relationship with Jesus Christ we can have a truly fulfilled and abundant life. "I have come that they might have life and that they might have it more abundantly". John 10:10

The creationist viewpoint is considerably different from the naturalistic view. We believe all the natural laws of physics and chemistry to be consistencies in the nature of God. All laws of physics and scientific principles are merely the daily manner in which the universe operates as established by God in his creation. As we have said, the main lack of evidence for the naturalistic view is the lack of evidence for natural forces to have the ability to save beneficial changes and organize in a positive way. This is primarily based on the laws of thermodynamics. The creationist view properly attributes the underlying nature of the universe to the power of God. The power to construct the universe, to "wind up our universal clock", comes from a God with infinite power and presence. You are following the laws of thermodynamics by having an infinite God create a finite universe. You are going from the highest order of all to a much lesser order. Some believe that the creationist theory leads to a discouragement of the study of science. Nothing could be farther from the truth. "In its most extreme form, 'scientific creationism' strikes at the heart of science not by citing faulty evidence, but by proposing a 'scientific' study in which evidence means nothing at all! [1.12]" This description was taken from an Astronomy textbook used in classes at the University of Texas at Arlington, 1992. The quotation is directed at an unreasonable plea to turn students away from books about scientific creationism. I feel there is a problem with many Christian books. Many of the books which have been published are severely out of date. However, this "religious" conviction that evolution is the only possible explanation to universal origin is unfounded. This statement shows how atheistic teaching has no basis in fact, but is a belief that there is no God and constantly bombards students with this lie. They accuse the Christians and other students who believe in a deity of being ignorant. We will see many evidences to the contrary in this book. In fact, if a person does not accept the biblical view, I believe it is a clear indication they do not understand the principles of science!

Universal Expansion: From a Big Bang or God's Creation?

All the stars and other objects of the universe seam to be moving away from each other at a certain rate, confirming that the universe is expanding. However, this does not mean all the principles of the big bang theory are correct. Just because the universe is expanding does not necessarily mean it was created from a point of singularity becoming unstable as the big bang theory suggests. The big bang theory teaches that we come from an explosion. This is not true. Order does not come from chaos. The Bible says that the stars were made by God and placed in a position that would allow their light to be seen by earth. "And God said, 'Let there be lights in the firmament of the heavens to separate the day from night; and let them be for signs and seasons and for days and years, and let them be for lights in the firmament of the heavens to give light upon the earth. And God set them in the firmament of the heavens to give light upon the earth." Genesis 1:14-15, 17 Notice that God placed the stars in the firmament. This suggests that God made the stars and then placed them at a certain location from the earth. I believe that the location of these stars has changed very slightly from the time of creation. God placed the stars, relatively speaking, where they exist today. The forces theorized in the big bang theory could be the exact conditions God used on the first day of creation. We will discuss the discoveries in astronomy, theoretical physics, sub-atomic physics and other disciplines of science. All these scientific studies point to a nearly instantaneous creation and a beginning to time. The next stage of how the universe arrived at its present state can be debated. If we see planets forming in a nebulas region, does this mean that all planets must have originated this way? If there is even the slightest possibility that the early universe could have looked much like it does today, I presently feel I must believe this as a fact of history by faith. This should in no way discourage any scientific study of the universe. We can still reconcile every scientific investigation into the nature of the universe with a belief that God did not want to wait billions of years to let the stars shine their light on the earth. He did not want to wait millions of years for people to be created to worship His glory. Why should God need to wait for worshipers? So, God created Adam and Eve fully mature. Similarly, why should wait for the stars to form or give light on the earth? Let us explore the facts.

Principles of Universal Expansion

There are many evidences which support the theory of universal expansion. The Doppler Effect explains the astronomical red shift which has been detected in the universe. The astronomical red shift is used extensively as conclusive proof of the naturalist theory of the big bang theory and the evolution of the universe. The expanding universe was verified in the 1920's by Edwin Hubble. His observations from the 100-inch telescope at Mount Wilson observatory in California confirmed the expansion of the universe. "Hubble discovered that distant galaxies are distributed evenly across the heavens and, more important, confirm that they are all flying apart from one another like spray from a shotgun. Hubble announced in 1929 that his data showed the galaxies were moving apart at a rate directly proportional to their distance from the Milky Way. [1.13]" The expanding universe was first verified by the observed separation between the galaxies. Other observations have confirmed the expansion. The astronomical red shift, later discovered, allowed astronomers to accurately calculate the rate of expansion. In recent years the Hubble telescope, named after the famous astronomer, has made some startling discoveries about the expansion of the universe. According to an episode on 60 minutes I watched, the Astronomers and Astrophysicists were surprised to learn that the expansion of the universe was not slowing down as predicted but speeding up. There are a few theories attempting to explain this phenomena but nothing as yet gives a clear explanation of why the universe is expanding more rapidly in violation of the laws of thermodynamics which states that everything winds down. "Until a few years ago, it was the conventional wisdom that the expansion of the universe that began with the big bang was slowing down. Dr. Ed Weiler, the head of science for NASA and the person in charge of the Hubble, says that, in fact, it's speeding up. 'It means that we don't understand gravity,' he says. 'This implies there's some negative energy force, some anti-gravity, that's actually pushing things apart. We don't understand it. It's not supposed to be there.' He says it's something that wasn't known before Hubble. According to Livio, the discovery that the expansion of the universe is accelerating flies in the face of what everyone thought was happening. He says it is one of the most amazing and important discoveries in the history of science. He explains: 'Suppose I'll take my keys from here, and I throw them up. They come back to my hand. Why did that happen? The gravity of the Earth was able to slow these keys down, and then finally even reverse the motion. So what we naturally thought was that this expansion ought to slow down in the same way as these keys slow down. What we discovered is that this expansion is, in fact, speeding up, accelerating. It would be like, I throw these keys up, and instead of falling back into my hand, they actually speed up upwards.' This extraordinary phenomenon was confirmed by a 32-year-old astrophysicist, Dr. Adam Riess. Riess' calculations on an exploding star in a small section of the Hubble deep field confirm that the universe has picked up speed. One astronomer says that many years from now, our direct descendants won't see the sky as we see it today. It will appear as though we are sort of alone on an island, because all the lights around us will blink out. [1.14]" Let us explore possible reasons for this acceleration of the universal expansion.

If the universe was created by the big bang, then the expansion of the universe should be slowing by the combined force of gravity of the stars and galaxies. This has been taught in high schools and colleges for many years and makes sense. To explain how the universe behaves, the term "dark matter" was created. When there does not appear to be enough regular matter to control the expanding universe and maintain galactic clusters, dark matter is proposed. Originally suggested as anti-matter, now scientists are puzzled by the properties of dark matter since we have learned how to detect anti-matter. Dark Matter is defined as: "Unseen matter, inferred to exist in galactic halos and in space between galaxies that is thought to make up at least 90% of the mass of the universe. It could exist in various forms, such as black holes, brown dwarfs, or unknown atomic particles, all of which are termed cold dark matter; or it could be in the form of a 'sea' of fast-moving neutrinos, known as hot dark matter, or a mixture of both. [1.15]" The debate over the existence of dark matter continues today. Even through daily research and discoveries, we learn more about the universe, we still have more questions than answers. Just about the only possible explanation is that God created the Universe and he is still using the universe for His great purpose. The continual expansion can be compared with the word of God in which God sends us as missionaries to share the endless love he has toward his creation. "Again, it will be like a man going on a journey, who called his servants and entrusted his property to them. To one he gave five talents of money, to another two talents and to another one talent, each according to his ability. Then he went on his journey. The man who had received the five talents went at once and put his money to work and gained five talents more. So also, the one with two talents gained two talents more. But the man who had received the one talent went off, dug a hole in the ground and hid his master's money. After a long time the master of those servants returned and settled accounts with them. The man who had received the five talents brought the other five. 'Master,' he said, 'you entrusted me with five talents. See, I have gained five more.' His master replied, 'Well done good and faithful servant! You have been faithful with a few things; I will put you in charge of many things. Come and share your master's happiness!' The man with the two talents also came. 'Master,' he said, 'you entrusted me with two talents; see, I have gained two more.' His master replied, 'Well done good and faithful servant! You have been faithful with a few things; I will put you in charge of many things. Come and share your master's happiness!' Then the man who received the one talent came. 'Master,' he said. 'I knew that you are a hard man, harvesting where you have not sown and gathering where you have not scattered seed. So I was afraid and went out and hid your talent in the ground. See, here is what belongs to you.' His mastered replied, 'You wicked, lazy servant! So you knew that I harvest where I have not sown and gathered where I have not scattered seed? Well then, you should have put my money on deposit with bankers, so that when I returned, I would have received it back with interest. Take the talent from him and give it to the one who has ten talents. For everyone who has will be given more, and he will have an abundance. Whoever does not have, even what he has will be taken from him. And throw that worthless servant outside, into the darkness, where there will be weeping and gnashing of teeth." Mathew. 25:14-30 NIV "Then he said to his disciples, the harvest is plentiful but the workers are few. Ask the Lord of the Harvest, therefore, to send out workers into his harvest field." Mathew 9:37-38. These passages are often referenced when speaking about missionary work. There are many other references to encouraging growth physically, mentally, spiritually, and financially in all of His creation. We will discuss this in further detail in later chapters. The point I wish to make in this section is that God has always encouraged growth and development. "Be fruitful and multiply." Genesis 1:28 is His constant command. Why should any Christian debate an expanding universe? God's word makes it abundantly clear that we should grow in His service. If 'the heavens are telling of the glory of God' shouldn't they also be changing, growing, expanding? What is disturbing is when scientists attempt to explain this growth as the "power of nature" instead of the power of God.

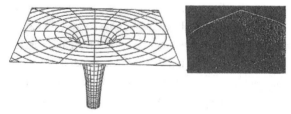

Figure 1.2

Background or 3-K Radiation

Another evidence for universal expansion is the so called background microwave radiation which appears throughout the entire universe. It has been upheld that this discovery provides the clearest evidence for the big bang theory. As early as 1948, predictions were made concerning the exact set of conditions which resulted in the big bang. It was then first speculated that a residual radiation from the big bang, could be detected on earth. It was predicted that when radiation was separated from matter, as a result of a sudden temperature change, a universal background radiation was produced. The predictions indicated that the high density radiation was reduced to temperatures of 1 to 5 degrees Kelvin. Discoveries since this prediction have confirmed the existence of such a background radiation. "The radiation was observed exceedingly accurately in 1989-1990 from a new satellite, as shown in figure 27-4 (Figure. 1.2). It corresponds exactly to radiation from material with temperature of 2.735 K. For convenience it has been labeled the 3-degree radiation. [1.16]" This discovery is considered good evidence for the big bang model of creation. Some even say it provides conclusive evidence that the big bang theory is correct. Despite the great support the background radiation gives the big bang theory, there were some unexpected problems with the discovery. It was predicted that the radiation would be relatively uniform, but it was suspected the radiation would have a few cold spots, which corresponds to the big bang theory's explanation of galaxy formation. Strangely enough, this evidence was lacking in the discovery. "But the original big bang theory predicted that by the time the universe reached these conditions, different regions would have had different temperatures and densities, consistent with the filamentary pattern of galaxy clusters. The theory would thus predict a spotty 3-K glow in the sky, and this is not observed! [1.17]" One approach to explain this inconsistency was the inflammatory big bang theory, or bubble theory, which proposes adjustments to the original big bang theory. The bubble theory was created to explain the uncanny uniformity to the universe. The bubble theory is another futile attempt to explain the creation of the universe by natural forces. "For one thing, during the universe's inflationary era, the bubbles developed more slowly than in the Big Bang format. This allowed the matter developing inside time to mix evenly, come to the same temperature, and thus produce a uniform radiation throughout the universe. [1.18]". The bubble theory does provide a natural explanation to the uniformity of the universe, which it was designed to do. However, it also creates new unresolved problems in physics. More about the bubble theory and Hawking's work will be discussed in Chapter 2. In conclusion, the observation of the universal 3-k radiation supports the creation model more than the big bang theory. The only thing that the 3-k radiation proves is that there was a drop in the temperature of the entire universe to a point that was necessary for the first hydrogen atoms to form. The fact that this drop in temperature is evenly throughout the universe suggests a sudden temperature drop by the word of God. Again, all the scientific evidence supports a sudden and complete creation of the universe as described in Genesis.

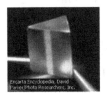

Figure 1.3

Should We Accept the Doppler Effect to Explain Universal Expansion?

There should be no reason to reject the concept of the Doppler Effect as the proper explanation of the astronomical red shift. Other explanations of the astronomical red shift have been proposed, but none of them seams to be reasonable. It is almost universally accepted that the astronomical red shift does occur, but there is still a debate among Christian theologians over what causes the red shift in the stars. It is well established that the spectroscopy red shift occurs with changing speeds of objects on earth, but could the same spectral change be due to another source where the stars are concerned? Dr. Donald B. DeYoung in his book, God's Universe, lists four explanations for the astronomical red shift. 1) Stellar motion away from the earth. The most widely accepted explanation for the red shift. 2) The effect of the object's gravitational field on the light leaving the stellar form. This is a doubtful explanation of the observed red shift because it is well established that gravity merely bends light. 3) The "second order Doppler effect". This is an interesting proposal by DeYoung, which assumes that Astronomers are correct in explaining the red shift by stellar movement, but are incorrect about the direction, the stars are traveling. DeYoung suggests that the universe is moving in a circle rather than outward in all directions. However, again this is unsupported by observations. 4) Photon interaction. This last explanation of stellar red shift is concerned with a concept of light waves having one part faster than another part. Quote, "It is possible that light waves exchange energy during their movement across space and lose some energy in the process. A loss of light energy is equivalent to a 'Redding effect' of its light. A theoretical understanding of this proposed 'tired light' process has not yet been developed. [1.19]" It is commonly known that passing through a medium, like a prism effects the light spectrum. When light is passed through a prism, a rainbow appears. When light goes through the prism, the coherent white light is separated into a collection of light with different wavelengths, see figure 1.3. In order for DeYoung's proposed photon interaction to cause the red shift effect, the collective gravitational field of the universe must act, somewhat, like a prism and create the red shift appearance as light travels through space and comes to earth. This proposal is also disproved by the nature of gravitational fields described by general relativity. The "second- order Doppler effect" described in DeYoung's book proposes that the universe is moving in a circular manner instead of outward in all directions. Quote, "A light source moving at right angles (tangentially) to an observer will always be red shifted. This can be observed in a laboratory by using a high speed turntable. A detector is placed in the center and a gamma radiation source is placed on the outside edge. The gamma energy is seen to decrease or 'red-shift' as the turntable speed increases. This is an intriguing explanation for stellar red shift. When applied to stars, it implies that the universe may be in circular motion instead of radial expansion. [1.20]" I have not seen data concerning this proposal, but I wonder what speed it would require the universe to be turning in order to produce the observed red shift? In either picture of the universe, circular or radically outward, the universe does appear to be expanding. I can not understand how many Christians fight so hard against any proposal which might be linked with an opposing view of creation. Often, Christian scientists discredit themselves by not being more careful on determining which theories directly violated the Christian faith and which theories do not. The fight against the expanding universe is primarily based on the importance it plays with the big bang theory and the theories of an evolving universe. There is really no reason why we can not accept the expanding universe theory and reject the concept of a universe made by natural forces. Despite years of research, there is no way to explain the creation of the universe by natural forces. This is the only fact of any importance.

The Doppler Effect

The Doppler Effect is a fundamental principle of physics. The effect of a spectral line red or blue shifted has been used to determine speeds of objects leaving each other or approaching one another for many years. Another situation in which the principles of the Doppler Effect are used is in a device commonly held by Highway Patrol Officers. It is called a radar gun. The radar gun works extremely well to measure the speed of vehicles traveling either toward or away from a patrol car; some people will say it works too good. The radar gun sends out radar signals which bounce off the target vehicle. The radar gun has circuitry that will take into account the Doppler Effect to determine the speed of the vehicle. It is necessary to determine the direction as well as the speed of the vehicle when the patrol officers are approaching the speeding vehicle. Therefore, accepting that the universe is expanding outward in all directions seams reasonable. However, I feel scientists rely too heavily on this one piece of information to make a wild determination as to the origin of the universe. I find no conflict with the idea of the universe having a great deal of movement and the Biblical references to the heavens and the stars established by the power of God. I believe that when the Bible speaks of establishing the stars in the heavens it is in the same context as the references to God establishing the moon and the earth. "When I consider your heavens, the work of your fingers, the moon and the stars, which you have set in place, what is man that you are mindful of him?" Psalms 8:3-4. Does the moon move? Does the earth? Of course they do. So why debate how the universe is moving and changing? All these things give glory to the power of God's creation. Why argue about the details concerning the movements of celestial objects? The ideas presented in modern Astronomy theory in no way conflicts with the biblical record.

Established by God and Moving Strong

Many Christians have a misinterpretation of the term "established", and the message of the gospel has been adversely affected. Establishment means that God made these things and put them in a place which has a purpose for man. The moon has the purpose of shining light on the earth and the stars to show signs for the seasons. Yet, the moon moves, so why don't the stars? The stars have always appeared to move. In the past, astronomers believed that the sun, moon and the stars moved around the earth. The position of the stars, relative to the earth, is how we can determine the seasons during the year. "And God said, let there be lights in the firmament of the heavens to separate the day from the night; and let them be for signs and for seasons and for days and years:" Genesis 1:14 In order for the stars to be signs for the changing seasons, the stars must appear to move thorough space. However, as we know the great constellations appear to be fixed. Today, we realize that the earth rotates about its axis and revolves around the sun. The stars are relatively fixed in space, but the stars are still having a small amount of movement through empty space due to the expanding universe. Einstein once rejected the idea of an expanding universe, even though his calculations in general relativity predicted it. He invented a "cosmological constant" that he incorporated into his theory to support the concept of a static universe. Einstein later had this to say about the cosmological constant: "It was the greatest blunder of my life. [1.21]" The expanding universe is a tremendous testimony to the power of God. It represents a harmony in the universe for the stars to move in a uniform expansion and to change in well defined patterns. Think about it, the entire universe expanding with amazing uniformity. Each object maintaining basically the same change in distance as the expansion is distributed uniformly throughout the universe. As stated earlier, a recent discovery by the Hubble telescope shows not only is the universe expanding, but also the rate of expansion is accelerating. This shocks the scientific community who accepted predictions that universal expansion should be slowing down. Just like after a shotgun blast, eventually the pellets slow down and stop scattering in all directions. There are many other problems uncovered by the Hubble telescope causing scientists to re-think their conclusions about the nature of the universe.

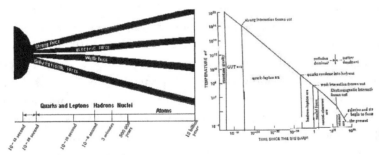

Figure 1.4

What is the Big Bang Theory?

What exactly is the big bang theory? The big bang theory attempts to explain the creation of the universe by natural forces. The following principles of physics must be taken under consideration when discussing any theory about the origin of the universe: 1) The law of conservation of mass and energy. This is the first law of thermodynamics. Simply stated, nothing can be created or destroyed but simply changing form. From this principle, it is assumed that the universe was not actually created by the big bang. Inside the primeval fireball was the collection of energy and elementary particles which contained all the substances of the universe concentrated in a single point of the space time continuum. Where did all the stuff come from? Scientists don't know. Some recent theories have proposed an oscillating universe to explain the origin of this material. Basically, this simply states that the universe recycles itself. It dies in a universal collapse and is reborn in a big bang. In the big bang, the collection of energy and mass became unstable for some unknown reason, exploded, and from the debris, the universe was created. Eventually, the expansion stops, the universe collapses in on itself, and the universe is reborn from the same material. With the discovery that the universe is increasing its rate of expansion, this theory has lost some support. 2) The second law of thermodynamics. The second law of thermodynamics states that entropy constantly increases with time. "Isolated systems tend toward disorder and entropy is a measure of this disorder. ... The entropy of the universe increases in all natural processes. [1.22]" This means that all isolated systems increase in entropy, or increase in their amount of disorder, as we have discussed. 3) The law of mass and energy equivalence. This is based on laws of thermodynamics and Einstein's famous formula of $E=mc^2$. There is a definite amount of energy in any material body. This amount does not change but matter can be turned into energy and back to matter again. 4) The principle of universal expansion. The expanding universe theory suggests that the universe began at a definite center and currently is expanding in all directions. The current expansion rate of the universe is called Hubble's constant. It has approximately the value of 100 kilometers per second for each mega parsec. (Mega -parsec is a measure of distance with 1 parsec = 3.26 times the distance light travels in one year {a light year}). [1.23] The big bang theory describes the origin of the universe to begin with an intensely hot fireball containing matter and radiation, see figure 1.4. The universe began as a radiation dominated universe and ended as a matter dominated universe. Physicists describe the process with a complex series of transitions from particle interactions and the unification of four fundamental forces: electromagnetism, gravity, strong and weak force. The number of fundamental forces was reduced to three with the unification of the weak and electromagnetic forces. Sheldon Glashow, Abdus Salam and Steven Weinberg won the 1979 Nobel Prize in physics for their theory of weak interactions. Work towards a Grand Unified Field Theory (GUT theory) began with Albert Einstein in the late 1920's. This work continues today and is considered the "missing piece" of the puzzle to uncovering how the universe began.

Fundamental Forces

According to the most recent explanations of the big bang, the original dominant forces inside the fireball were electro-weak forces, and the strong force. The theory states that once matter and energy were separated, gravity became the dominate influence organizing the structure of the universe. The step-by-step process is formulated from a study of subatomic physics. "From 10^{-43} to 10^{-35} s the universe cooled from 10^{28} to 10^{23} eV. At energies like theses the strong, electromagnetic, and weak interactions merge into a single interaction mediated by extremely heavy field particles, the X and Y bosons. ... At 10^{-35} s, however, particle energies become two low for free X and Y bosons. ... Quarks and leptons now become independent. ... From 10^{-35} to 10^{-10} s the universe consisted of a soup of quarks and leptons whose behavior was controlled by the strong, electroweak, and gravitational interactions. ... Somewhere around 10^{-6} s the quarks condensed into hadrons. At about 1s neutrino energies fell sufficiently for them to be unable to interact with the hadron-lepton soup. ... Nuclear reactions synthesis stopped at T = 3 min when the ratio of protons to alpha particles should have been, according to theory, about 3:1, which is indeed the ratio found in most of the universe today. ... From 3 min to around 100,000 y after the big bang, the universe consisted of a plasma of hydrogen and helium nuclei and electrons in thermal equilibrium with radiation. Once the temperature fell below 13.6eV, the ionization energy of hydrogen, hydrogen atoms could form and not be disrupted. [1.24]" Look at figure 1.4 and follow the sequence of events, which was to occur. The fireball was created by some unknown force. Temperature was unimaginably high due to the highly excited state of the universe. No matter existed yet, but the fundamental forces and energy, which would eventually create all the matter in the universe, existed at a highly excited state. The first force on the scene was quantum gravity. This is a theorized force which might have existed at the beginning of the universe. It is a combination of quantum mechanical principles and general relativity. Next is the GUT era (grand unified field theory). This is where the four fundamental forces of nature (electromagnetism, gravity, strong and weak force) existed as a single unit. Next is the quark-lepton era. Here is where fundamental components of matter develop for the first time. Theoretically, all matter is composed of quarks, which make up, protons, neutrons and all subatomic particles except electrons, (electrons are completely unique). Leptons are a group of particles, which are affected by the weak force. Next is the hadron-lepton era. Hadrons are particles that interact with the strong nuclear force. The weak force and the strong force dominate subatomic particles. The weak force is responsible for instability in certain nuclei like in natural radio-active decay. The strong force binds the neutrons and protons in the nucleus. All these stages theoretically take place before one second has elapsed from the beginning of the universe. More about these stages will be discussed in the next chapter as we review the works of Stephen Hawking and in chapter nine when we take more time to unravel the sequence of events in the big bang theory. The formation of matter takes considerably longer than the formation of the building blocks of atoms. The diagram shows a considerable long and gradual development of matter, stars and galaxies. The Big Bang Theory states that it took approximately 100,000 years for the first atoms to appear after the sub-atomic parts were made during the first 3 minutes of creation. The reason for this long waiting period was due to the highly energetic state of the universe. In essence, the universe had to "naturally" cool off before atoms could be formed. If you can believe that God created the universe, why would he wish to wait 100,000 years to finish his work of universal creation? It seams the Big Bang Theory has the sequence of events up to the first 3 minutes correct. However, we have good reason that God stepped into the "natural" process and departed from a long cooling period. What are natural forces anyway? We will explore this question in great detail in the coming chapters. The Big Bang Theory does not explain why the fundamental forces were organized in the manner scientists present or where the energy for the forces to create matter came from, just that for some reason it always existed. There continues to develop much speculation about the circumstances forming the big bang. The simplest atom is incredibly complex, as we will study in later chapters. Scientists are still wondering if they have reached the end of elemental parts of the atom when they discovered quarks. What are quarks? What is the strong nuclear force (mediated by gluons) that holds individual quarks together? Is it simply a manifestation of the power of God? The scripture says: "He is before all things, and in him all things hold together." Collisions 1:17 NIV There is yet to be a clear- cut explanation to the origin of the universe from a naturalistic perspective. Each theory requires a leap of faith to accept or reject their proposals. Is natural forces our creator of is it the power of God? After reading the rest of this book, you decide.

Christian Response to Universal Origin

Christians already know the answer to the age old question: "Where did we all come from?" It is found in the word of God. "In the beginning was the Word, and the Word was with God, and the Word was God. He was in the beginning with God; all things were made through him, and without him was not anything made that was made. In him was life, and the life was the light of men. ... The true light that enlightens every man was coming into the world. He was in the world, and the world was made through him, yet the world knew him not. ... And the Word became flesh and dwelt among us, full of grace and truth; we have beheld his glory, glory as of the only Son from the Father." John 1:1-14 Many scientists around the world have searched for a single formula, which explains all the basic forces in the universe, the Grand Unified Field Theory. However, the answer to the origin of the universe is in these verses. It was by God 'speaking' that the entire universe was formed. We can not fully comprehend what occurred, even modern science is baffled by what took place at the beginning of the universe, but there are a few comparisons we can make. Human speech is caused by the vocal cords. The vocal cords vibrate and mechanical energy is transformed into electromagnetic energy. The energy has a definite pattern described by its frequency, wavelength, and power. When it reaches a person's ear, it is converted to an impulse that travel to the brain and is interpreted. In the creation of the universe, God's word was the power source of the highly organized energy form. God created all things directly from His 'spoken' word. Now whether or not God spoke and the result was the fireball mentioned in the big bang theory is unimportant. The fact is that the "mysterious" source of power for the creation of the universe is the word of God. It is unclear if the modern theories about the exact forces used or types of particle action that took place in the beginning, but the solution to the seemingly endless research to what caused the universe to form is simple. God spoke and the universe was made. "And God said, 'Let there be light,' and there was light." Genesis 1:3 Now, there are a number of theories reconstructing specific events which possibly occurred in the big bang. Again, this study should provide no alarm to the Christian. "If you continue in my word, you are truly my disciple, and you will know the truth, and the truth will make you free." John 8:31-32 The Christian relishes in the truth and does not fear it. Modern theories describe the origin of the universe as a fireball at the center of the universe. The fireball was intensely hot. In time, the fireball followed the second law of thermodynamics and cooled off. Thus, the original state of the fireball was pure energy, and then slowly matter formed as the energy became less excited. The concept of converting energy into matter in this form is derived from concepts in Einstein's special theory of relativity. Einstein gave us the image that mass was "frozen" energy and energy was "excited" matter. One thing that is a continuing dilemma to scientists who attempt to explain the existence of the universe without God is to explain the origin of the energy. According to the first and second laws of thermodynamics, the laws of conservation of mass and energy, nothing can be created, but must have always existed in some form. So you have two choices to decide the source of power for the universe. 1) There existed a fireball, containing the energy equivalent of all the mass in the universe, since the beginning of time. For some unknown reason at a particular point in time the fireball exploded, sending energy throughout the universe. The dominant forces were originally the electromagnetic and electro-weak forces. Eventually gravity and the strong force (which dominates in subatomic interactions) took over and produced elements, stars, planets, and galaxies. 2) God created the universe through the power of his word. The Lord our God was what had existed from the beginning of time. "I am the Alpha and the Omega, the first and the last, the beginning and the end." Revelation 22:13. Then, at God's chosen time, he created the universe. Neither theory describing the origin of the universe can be proven scientifically. It requires a leap of faith as to which theory you accept as true and which theory you reject as false. I would rather accept the timeless nature of God than a more abstract form of forces always existing. As we will see later, Steven Hawking showed that time itself had a beginning. Therefore, something before time had to exist and created the universe, including the creation of time itself! I am much more comfortable accepting God as this source than a point of undefined singularity.

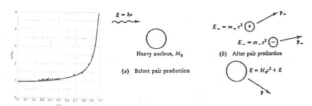

Figure 1.5

How Do You Convert Energy Into Matter?

In order to understand some of the naturalistic theories about the origin of the universe, we need to examine the process of converting matter into energy and energy into matter. To turn matter into energy is fairly simple. According to mass and energy equivalence law of Einstein, mass becomes pure energy when it has been accelerated to the speed of light. Experiments' converting small particles into energy is done routinely in particle accelerator laboratories, like the one at Fermi Lab just outside of Chicago. Particle accelerator experiments accelerate particles at near the speed of light. Due to the laws of physics described in Einstein formula, it is impossible to reach the speed of light by acceleration alone. On the left side of figure 1.5 we see an asymptote. This is a graph were the quantity increase towards a point but never reaches a certain value. In this case, mass is increasing with velocity as the velocity of the object approaches light speed. If an object reaches the speed of light, it is instantaneously converted to pure energy. Experiments in particle accelerators involve tiny projectiles striking a target nucleus, causing small particles to "jump" to light speed. These objects are considered massless particles. The particle wave duality of these objects will be described in our chapter on modern physics. The conversion of energy to matter simply involves the opposite to occur. You start with an accelerated massless particle (a beam of light), when it collides with a target nucleus the beam of light sometimes produces tiny particles. When mater is made in this manner, there is always a pair of particles produced i.e. matter and anti-matter. The principle of matter production, described by quantum mechanics, makes it difficult to believe that gravitational forces are the sole source of matter creation at the time the universe began. According to Einstein's theory of general relativity, gravity bends a beam of light; it does not convert light energy into matter. According to quantum mechanics, light can only be converted to matter when it strikes a relatively stationary target. So, in the beginning of the universe where was the original mass to allow other matter to be created from energy? Another theory we have somewhat discussed is the production of "temporary" particles that lead to the development of matter. This theory seams more reasonable than ones scientists previously have made. We will discus more details in chapter nine. The production of "virtual" particles will be explored as well as their role in creating mater components like the neutron. When converting energy into matter there is always an anti-particle created. They usually find each other again and are quickly annihilated, producing energy again. So again, how did we get all this matter in the universe? Where is all the anti-matter that must have been produced by converting energy into matter? There are a number of theories to explain this problem, but are we sure any one of these theories is correct?

One proposal explaining the abundance of matter at the beginning of the universe involves black holes where it is believed pair creation was abundant at the outer edge of the singularity of the big bang, see figure 1.2. The outer edge is called the event horizon. It is believed that, at random, some of the anti-mater fell into the singularity due to the incredible gravitational forces at work. Large amounts of matter were supposedly created by this process which eventually formed all the stars and planets today. This would be similar to radiation predicted, and discovered to be coming from the event horizon of black holes. But is the radiation from the event horizon the result of gravity or light striking particles in the event horizon? There are some inconsistencies with this proposal. Where is the energy coming from to be skirting around the outer edge of the singularity that created the universe? It is well known that the pair creation and annihilation from photons is nearly instantaneous. Even taking into account the incredible properties of the time-dilatation effect of a singularity how are the matter and anti-matter pulled apart so quickly? We know that normal gravity only bends light and has essentially no effect of subatomic particles. Other forces, such as the gluon force influence particles as small as electrons and neutrons. Can even the gravitational force of this singularity separate the electron-positron pair? At the point of creation, we have more questions than answers. Every astronomer and theoretical physicist today should have no argument with that statement. The universe was created by an event in the past that can not be completely explained by science, yet. However, significant progress has been made in experiments at the Relativistic Heavy Ion Collider, or RHIC (pronounced "Rick") at Long Island, N.Y. The results were published in the February, 2007 issue of the Discover magazine. I believe that this article explaining the results of the experiments at RHIC one of the most significant articles in all of the history of science! We will explore some of the findings from these monumental achievements in Chapter 2 and Chapter 9 of this the book.

Why Does Matter Exist at All?

When energy strikes an atom, matter can form but it is always in the form of pair creation. Quote, "A photon collides with a nucleus and only the electron and positron comes out. In either case, we refer to the occurrence as pair creation and speak of the electron- positron pair. It is important to realize that in this process the electron and positron are both created from energy, and that neither is part of the nuclear debris. [1.25]" In the laboratory experiments, after the creation of an electron-positron pair, the positron usually quickly finds an electron and is annihilated, forming a photon of energy once again. So, there remains a mystery to how matter was formed in the beginning of the universe. If there was only energy in the beginning of the universe, how was it converted to matter without a collision? If it did collide with matter where did the matter come from? Where did the energy come from? What prevented the matter and anti-matter created by the collision to annihilate each other to form energy again? How did we wind up with so much matter and don't have a lot of anti- matter floating around? These are not trivial questions. An article in the August 2004 edition of Discover Magazine attempts to answer this very question. The article states that neutrinos once thought to be massless particles not only have some mass but also can increase or decrease their amount of mass at random. The article attempts to explain the apparent abundance of matter and lack of anti-matter from this theory. It speculates that "heavy" neutrinos existed in the early universe and thus explain how matter won the battle between pair annihilation and matter left over. Every Astronomer in the world should agree that the beginning of the universe can not currently be explained by natural laws. Do you accept the theory of creation by yet undiscovered natural forces, or the power of God? Either theory is plausible. The question is, do you have faith in the existence of God or not? Do you believe in God having supernatural powers? It is amazing how scientists deal with areas of science that can not be explained by scientific laws. They use terms like hypothesis or theorem. From these terms, the field of theoretical physics is formed. It is amazing that theoretical physics is considered a legitimate field of science. Even the term meta-physics, to describe situations beyond ordinary science, is sometimes acceptable. Why then is the term super-natural not considered scientific? All these terms merely describe research into events, which can not be explained by natural laws. Each day, science brings a better understanding of the intricate workings of the universe. However, with each answered question there are a thousand new questions formed. Anything occurring that can not be explained by natural forces is by definition, a supernatural event. Therefore, why is there any controversy over the universe being created by a supernatural act of God? Why deny the importance of faith in scientific research? Faith is present all the time in the scientific process. If you accept a theory as true, you are accepting it entirely based on faith. You believe that a particular theory is the best possible explanation of the scientific data currently gathered. "Now faith is the substance of things hoped for, the evidence of things not seen." Hebrews. 11:1.

Dark Matter and the Missing Mass Problem

What is Dark Matter? How is it formed? Dark Mater is more of a term to describe the need for some source of the unexplainable amount of uniformity in the universe. "Dark Matter is "unseen matter", inferred to exist in galactic halos and in space between galaxies that is thought to make up at least 90% of the mass of the universe. [1.26]" Dark matter could be some other kind of matter or simply doesn't exist at all, since we have no way of detecting it, presently. Another possible description of this "missing mass" is from an abundance of black holes. However, black holes can give radiation along their event horizon. Thus black holes are not entirely invisible. Nothing has confirmed the presence of Dark Matter. However, when there are problems explaining how the universe can operate in an orderly fashion, dark matter is presented as the only answer. In the August 2006 issue of the Discover magazine, Dr. Mordehai Milgrom describes his radical new theory of gravity that could explain away the need for dark matter. One thing is for certain, there is a huge unsolved mystery to the way the universe operates. For example, there are cases when galactic clusters are predicted to have long since vanished due to the amount of time astronomers believe have elapsed since the big bang. What keeps these objects moving through space together? When there is not enough gravitational force for such events, the theory of dark matter is brought into play. The missing mass problem can be summarized by the following statement: "Analysis of the rotation of our Galaxy strongly suggests that the galactic halo is embedded in an enormous corona that is roughly 600,000 light years in diameter and contains at least 10^{12} solar masses of low-luminosity matter. Other galaxies have similar rotation curves, so they too are presumed to be surrounded by large, massive coronae. In addition, clusters of galaxies must contain a substantial amount of non-luminous matter. Otherwise there would not be enough gravity to hold the clusters together. ... Estimates of the cosmic deceleration indicate that the average density of matter is near the critical density of 5×10^{-30} g/cm^3. ... But the average density of matter that astronomers actually see in space is about 3×10^{-31} g/cm^3. Thus, the observed matter is less than one-tenth that needed to account for the behavior of the Universe. [1.27]" What is causing these gravitational forces? Does the force of gravity have some yet undiscovered properties to explain these observations? The research into this complex harmony of the universe continues today. Remember: "He is before all things, and in him all things hold together." Collisions 1:17.

Can Miracles Occur?

There is enormous debate on what event can be defined as a miracle. One possible definition of a miracle could be a unique event that can not be explained by normal physical laws. To conclude this chapter, we can state that the creation of the universe was a miracle. Every scientist on Earth should agree that the exact circumstances beginning the universe are still somewhat a mystery. In the next chapter we will go into further details of this fact. Therefore, we can conclude by definition, the birth of the universe was a miracle. Obviously, the event occurred and yet, we can not scientifically explain how the event took place. There is no law of science or physics to prove that miracles can not take place. Miracles are events which take place during a certain point of time and can not be explained by a current state of knowledge. Someday, in the presence of the Lord Jesus, we may find the answers to all our questions about Miracles and why God has used them throughout history. Until then, we can only make a few theories about how God has performed past miracles by using His super-natural power. The bottom line is this: miracles can and do exist at times when God commissions someone to perform them. Miracles are simply conditions, made by God, which allow events to take place which can not be explained by physical laws. Physical explanations can only be assured in controlled conditions in which the events can be repeated. Certain events can never be repeated. For example, the death of Jesus Christ on the cross, or the first day the universe was created. The bottom line does indeed come down to the amount of faith you have in the evidences of a particular event taking place. There is plenty of room for faith in science. As we shall see, it is very similar to establishing the probability of events taking place as outlined in quantum mechanics. The Christian perspective merely states that you must make a decision concerning whether or not an event, which can not be repeated, actually occurred. Again, your decision is made by examining the evidences and then individually deciding by faith, what took place. For example, a Christian's view over the death and resurrection of Jesus Christ is that Christ died for my sins and was raised on the third day. The Christian accepts this fact by faith. We are presented with facts concerning the life, teachings, death, and resurrection of Jesus Christ. The evidence comes from both external evidence and evidence in the Holy Scriptures. For a more complete examination of the evidences for the reliability of the scripture, I recommend the works of Josh McDowell. Christ also offered everlasting life to anyone who would accept Him as Lord of their life. "For God so loved the world that he gave his only Son, that whoever believes in him should not perish but have eternal life." John 3:16.

References for Chapter 1

1.1   Pastor of Tabernacle Baptist Church, 1991, Quotation.

1.2   Sidney I. Landau- Editor in Chief, Webster Illustrated Contemporary Dictionary, Garden City, New York, Doubleday & Company, Inc., J. G. Ferguson Publishing Company, 1982, p. 763.

1.3   Raymond A. Serway, Physics For Scientists & Engineers with Modern Physics Third edition, Philadelphia, Saunders College Publishing, 1990, p. 4.

1.4   Ibid p. 4.

1.5   Ibid p. 5.

1.6   Ibid p. 6.

1.7   Ronald Gautreau, William Savin, Schaum's Outline of Theory and Problems of Modern Physics, McGraw-Hill Book Company, 1978, p 45.

1.8   A Scientific American book, The Physics and Chemistry of Life, New York N.Y., Simon And Schuster Inc, 1955, p. 9-12.

1.9   John Boslough, Stephen Hawking's Universe: The Man and the Theories Behind the Bestseller, A BRIEF HISTORY OF TIME, New York, Avon Books, 1985, p. 111-112.

1.10 Tom Morris, Philosophy For Dummies, Hungry Minds, Inc., 1999, p. 248-258.

1.11 Scientific American - May 1993.

1.12 William K. Hartmann, Astronomy: The Cosmic Journey, Belmont California, Wadsworth Publishing, 1991, p.643.

1.13 John Boslough, Stephen Hawking's Universe: The Man and the Theories Behind the Bestseller, A BRIEF HISTORY OF TIME, New York, Avon Books, 1985, p. 38-39.

1.14 June 2, 2003 CBS News 60 Minutes Hailing The Hubble. http://www.cbsnews.com/stories/2003/05/30/60minutes/main556337.shtml.

1.15 Firefly Astronomy Dictionary. Firefly Books Inc., Buffalo, New York, 2003, p.56.

1.16 William K. Hartmann, Astronomy: The Cosmic Journey, Belmont California, Wadsworth Publishing, 1991, p.606.

1.17 Ibid. P.607.

1.18 John Boslough, Stephen Hawking's Universe: The Man and the Theories Behind the Bestseller, A BRIEF HISTORY OF TIME, New York, Avon Books, 1985, p. 93.

1.19 Donald B. Deyoung, God's Universe, New York, Dell Publishing Co., Crown Publishers MCMLIV, p. 100.

1.20 Ibid. P.100.

1.21 John N. Clayton, Einstein's "Greatest Blunder", Does God Exist? 1991, Vol. 18, No. 4, p.6.

1.22 Raymond A. Serway, Physics For Scientists & Engineers with Modern Physics Third edition, Philadelphia, Saunders College Publishing, 1990, p. 600.

1.23 Meir H. Degani, Astronomy Made Simple, Garden City, New York Made Simple Books, Doubleday & Company, 1976, p. 112.

1.24 Arthur Beiser, Concepts of Modern Physics Fourth Edition, McGraw-Hill Book Company, 1987, p. 549-552.

1.25 James S. Trefil, From Atoms To Quarks: An Introduction to the Strange World of Particle Physics, New York, Charles Scribner's Sons, 1980, p.63.

1.26 Firefly Astronomy Dictionary. Firefly Books Inc., Buffalo, New York, 2003, p.56.

1.27 Ibid. p.147.

Illustrations for Chapter 1

1.1   William K. Hartmann, Astronomy: The Cosmic Journey, Belmont California, Wadsworth Publishing, 1991, p. 301.

1.2   Left side: William J. Kaufmann, III, Black Holes and Warped Spacetime, W.H. Freeman and Company, San Francisco, 1979, p. 196. Right side: William K. Hartmann, Astronomy: The Cosmic Journey, Belmont California, Wadsworth Publishing, 1991, p. 607.

1.3   Microsoft Encarta Encyclopedia Standard, 2002 edition, David Parker/Photo Researchers, Inc.

1.4   Left side: Raymond A. Serway, Physics For Scientists & Engineers with Modern Physics Third edition, Philadelphia, Saunders College Publishing, 1990, p.1435. Right Side: Arthur Beiser, Concepts of Modern Physics Fourth Edition, McGraw-Hill Book Company, 1987, p. 550.

1.5   Left side: Dudley Williams, John Spangler, Physics for Science and Engineering, D. Van Nostrand Company, New York, 1981, p. 922. Right Side: Ronald Gautreau, William Savin, Schaum's Outline of Theory and Problems of Modern Physics, McGraw-Hill Book Company, 1978, p. 69.

Chapter 2: Astronomy Part 2:
Big Bang Theory from Einstein to Hawking
The Accomplishments of Stephan Hawking

In a September 4, 1978 Time magazine published an article on black holes. "Hawking was mentioned prominently in the side bar to the article, and referred to as 'one of the premier scientific theorists of the century, perhaps an equal of Einstein. [2.1]'" The discoveries and theories of Stephen Hawking have, dramatically changed the view of the universe in recent years. In a Star Trek® television episode, Data, an android constantly searching to understanding human behavior, assembled what is considered the greatest group of genius in human history. Those seated were facsimiles of Newton and Einstein and the real Stephen Hawking! Some very complementary remarks were made by the Chicago Tribune's review of a book which covers the life and theories of Hawking entitled Stephen Hawking's Universe by John Boslough. Quote, "The story of a remarkable man, destined to rank with Galileo, Newton and Einstein. [2.2]" Stephen Hawking was interested in science from time he was eight years old. His father was a biologist working for the National Institute for Medical Research near London England. Stephen became extremely good at physics and mathematics. He knew this was the career he wanted to take. He is still well known for his phenomenal memory of mathematical field equations. Hawking became fascinated with Astronomy and theories involving the exact conditions under which the universe began. As Hawking perused a career in cosmology and entered his first year of graduate school, the first signs of a debilitating illness occurred. Doctors finally diagnosed the disease as amyotrophic lateral sclerosis, commonly referred to as Lou Gehrig's disease. At this time, Hawking was given only about two more years to live. However, Hawking had enormous determination to survive and live. His condition started to stabilize and after a few months when he meet the person who would change his life forever. Hawking meet his wife- to -be, Jane Wilde, in 1965. With his wife, he soon had a new vigor to live. Stephen Hawking's great contributions to science began after his marriage. He has made great strides in science and become the father of two sons and one daughter, despite his illness.

This chapter will be composed of two parts. Part 1 is a continuation from chapter 1 on the study of universal origin. We will primarily explore the work of Stephan Hawing and Albert Einstein. Much of this chapter is a review of the book Stephen Hawking's Universe by John Boslough. Hawking became famous with his book A brief History of Time. The book Stephen Hawking's Universe generally reviews this publication. John Boslough explains Hawking's work into understanding and expanding General Relativity. Even after nearly a century, many scientists struggle with the complexities of the General Theory of Relativity as presented by Albert Einstein. Hawking is among the elite few scientists that can work with the ideas and equations of General Relativity nearly effortlessly. The second part of this chapter will be exploring the size and age of the universe. These topics have become a source of controversy to many members' of the Christian faith. It would seam that the size and the age of the universe would be two entirely separate issues. However, we will see that many scientists would disagree with this view. The implications are enormous. The evolutionary view needs billions of years to explain the development of a complex order by small changes in structure over time. Although, this view, original ardently supported by followers of Charles Darwin, has given way to the necessity of sudden dramatic genetic mutations to explain various developments by natural forces. This will be explored further in chapters four and five on the principles of genetics. The Christian view, traditionally, is a 6-day creation, a day of rest and approximately 6-10,000 years (varying with interpretation of the historical record from Adam) to the present day. I will attempt to present a fair assessment to the scientific evidence on both sides of this debate. We will summarize some of the various methods and information gathered to address the issues of size and age of the universe. Keeping with the theme of this book, it then comes down to the reader to make a faith decision based on the evidence. You must chose if you believe in a young or old universe. Which ever you decide I hope you will carefully explore the implications of your decision.

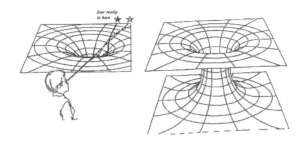

Figure 2.1

Point of Origin in Singularity

There was one disturbing concept developed from the Friedman solution to Einstein's equations most Astronomers didn't want to deal with at the time. Quote, "'One of the features of the Friedman solutions that was not taken too seriously at the time was that these solutions indicated there was a singular epoch in the past in which all the matter of the universe was concentrated into a single point,' Hawking told me. This is the point known as 'singularity [2.3]'" One possible representation of a point of singularity is a black hole shown in figure 1.2 of the last chapter. The point of singularity is where there is an enormous concentration of mass and energy at a single point inside the center of a black hole, i.e. a single point at the end of the funnel like path. Another possible representation of a black hole is found in figure 2.1. In this figure the black hole opens up on the opposite side of the entrance. Some theoretical physicists have speculated that the exit point of a black hole is a quasar. The quasar emits so much energy from such as small amount of space that it can not be explained by normal relativistic physics. It is possible that the structure of the black hole could warp the space-time continuum so greatly that it would explain the power of the quasars. Both theories of black holes are controversial. The possibility that black holes exist came out of the equations of Einstein and Friedman. Physicists wanted to take up the work left by Friedman and Einstein. However, theoreticians meet with failure. It was not until the collaborating efforts of Hawking and Penrose before physicist could prove, mathematically, the existence of black holes. Since that time we appear to have confirmed the existence of black holes, at least in one case, see figure 2.1 on the left side. There is strong evidence that light has been bent to one side due to the gravitational intensity of a black hole. Also, the calculations made by Hawking and Penrose proved, mathematically, the universe indeed had a definite beginning i.e. a beginning to time.

Black Holes

To explore the conditions for the big bang, they began looking for a model to describe the events on a smaller scale. "One logical place for Big Bang theoreticians to look for observable models is at the phenomenon of collapsing stars. These stars, collapsing in on themselves of their own weight, may eventually lead to a black hole at the core of which exists the problematic 'singularity.'... Imagining an endlessly collapsing star, physicists were unable to determine what would happen when a star reaches the point called singularity. Singularity is the end of the road, a place where space and time simply disappear. 'At singularity, normal concepts of space and time break down,' Hawking told me. 'The same thing happened to the equations.' ... It took a brilliant mathematical tour de force from Penrose to show that an endlessly collapsing star was not simply a theoretical plaything, and that it would end as a real, a physical, singularity. Penrose showed that space and time came to a physical, rather than merely metaphorical, end. ... The singularity that Hawking and Penrose uncovered with their calculations ... is mathematically an event in space- time where normal physical behavior breaks down. ... It was not just matter that was created during the Big Bang. It was space and time that were created. So in the sense that time has a beginning, space also has a beginning.' Does he actually believe that time, in fact, did begin with the Big Bang? I asked him. 'When you get back in the very early universe, the ordinary concept of time becomes obscured. You cannot have the normal idea of time carried back indefinitely. There is some point near the Big Bang, when there is simply no way to define time. In that sense time has a beginning. [2.4]'" Hawking used an imaginary time line to attempt to resolve the dilemma. After repeated attempts it was found that there was no resolution to the fact that time had a beginning at the big bang.

The implication of proving mathematically time has a beginning creates enormous theological implications. In the book entitled; "The Case For A Creator" the author outlines a number of excellent points concerning creation. The book outlines the quest for the truth by the author. This and other works by Lee Strobel describes his journey into Atheism and then into a Christian perspective all lead by his understanding of science. The more he understood science, the closer he came to accepting the Biblical viewpoint. In the end, Lee discovered that the evolutionary view, which he easily understood as synonymous to atheism, was not from scientific facts, but ignorance of scientific findings. Concerning the importance of a beginning to the universe, Mr. Strobel describes the views of Aristotle verses the Kalam argument. "Aristotle believed that God isn't the Creator of the universe but that he simply imbues order into it. In his view, both God and the universe are eternal. [2.5]'" This was contradictory to the Christian faith which stated that only God was eternal i.e. never ending or beginning. "There were no scientific arguments against the theory of an eternal universe, so Aristotle's view could be widely accepted. The Christian philosopher Philoponus argued that the universe had a beginning. Since these arguments were centuries before Dr. Hawking, there was no hard evidence to this premise. However the kalam argument went something like this: Whatever begins to exist has a cause. The universe began to exist, Therefore, the universe has a cause. [2.6]'" The kalam argument supposed that the universe came into being and is not eternal. If the universe had a beginning and God as a deity was the only thing eternal then it implies God created the universe. How certain was Hawking concerning his calculations about time having a beginning? "Stephan Hawking has said, 'Almost everyone now believes that the universe, and time itself, had a beginning at the Big Bang. [2.7]'" The implications are summarized by the work of Thomas Aquinas. "In arguing for the existence of God, thirteenth-century Christian philosopher Thomas Aquinas always presupposed Aristotle's view that the universe is eternal. ... Why did he take this approach? Because, Aquinas said, if he were to start with the premise that the universe had a beginning, then his task would be too easy! Obviously, if there was a beginning, something had to bring the universe into existence. But now, modern astrophysics and astronomy have dropped into the lap of Christians precisely the premise that, according to Aquinas, makes God's existence virtually undeniable. [2.8]'"

Given these implications, one can only wonder how Stephan Hawking reacted when he realized he was perhaps proving the existence of God. I have never known what Stephan Hawking's personal beliefs were concerning the existence of God until reading Lee Strobel's work. I own an Errol Morris Film called A Brief History of Time based on Stephan Hawking's best selling book. In the film, Hawking's is said to have liked the Bible stories as a child and has often wondered about the existence of God. His assistant, in the movie, is a devout Christian. I was hoping that Hawking's himself might be a Christian considering his work and its implications. Apparently I was wrong. Quote, "When actress Shirley MacLaine asked Hawking whether he believes God created the universe, he replied simply, 'No.' [2.9]'" It seams that his personal conviction that there is no God has influenced his research into universal origin. It appears Hawking has started unraveling his own work. Instead of proving the universe had a beginning, he now asserts it has no beginning or end. Hawking is a perfect example of how a person can cloud there judgment with a religious zeal. There is a concerted effort to place the faith in Christianity with every other belief system in the world. However, just read over the introduction again and see all the verses that ask the believer to "seek the truth". The Christian faith has no fear in finding "the truth". The absolute single most important "truth" in the universe is that Jesus Christ is the savior of the world and Lord. All scientific and historical evidences point like a arrow to this conclusion. Only carefully selected, misleading statements, can possibly lead a person away from the biblical view. Many people need to "get the facts" and therefore dispel the myth that the Bible is just another "religious" book equal with all others.

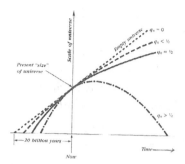

Figure 2.2

Figure 2.2 represents the three theoretical ends to the universe. If the universe is denser than the "critical density" the expansion of the universe will lead to a collapse. If the universe is much less than the critical it will expand forever. If the universe reaches the critical density it may become nearly static and just barely expand indefinitely. "In a chapter called 'The Origin and Fate of the Universe' in the book, A Brief History of Time, Hawking says: 'So long as the universe had a beginning, we could suppose it had a creator. But if the universe is really completely self-contained, having no boundary or edge, it would have neither beginning nor end: it would simply be. What place, then, for a creator? [2.10]'" In chapter 5 of The Case For A Creator, Lee Strobel interviews Dr. William Lane Craig concerning Hawking's other model of the universe. This model states that the universe did not have a beginning as previously stated. "'Hawking's model is like a cone, too, except it doesn't come to a point. ... As you can see there's no sharp edge. ... There is no beginning and no end – no boundaries,' one writer explained. 'The universe always was, always is, and always shall be.' Mr. Strobel summarized this description of the universe: 'Presto!' I exclaimed as I looked at his drawing. 'No beginning, no singularity no Big Bang - no need for God.' [2.11]" See figure 2.1 on the left side where the bottom is round and compare this drawing with figure 1.2 of the previous chapter. Wow, Hawking is finally proven wrong! However, this is disproving his greatest life-long work. Also, it required the brilliance of Hawking to tear down his own achievements. All this to try and hide from the truth that God created the universe. Were Hawking's efforts truly successful? Dr. Craig went on to explain that this was not the case. "'Granted, there isn't any singular point here, but notice this; the universe is still finite in its past. It still has a beginning in the sense that something has a finite past duration. ... And in that sense, Hawking's model has a beginning.' [2.12]" So we arrive at the same point as before. Time has a beginning, which suggests a creator who exists outside the space-time continuum and brought the universe into existence. The Bible supports the concept of space and time having a beginning. "He was in the beginning with God; all things were made through him, and without him was not anything made that was made." -John 1:2-3. All things were made by God through Christ, the Holy trinity of Father, Son and Holly Spirit. "All things" includes the creation of time as well as matter, energy, fundamental laws of physics, fundamental forces and the structure of space. The Bible agrees with Hawking's conclusion that the creation of all things in the universe, time included, was from a single place. The Bible merely refers to this point of singularity, as Hawking calls it, as the place where the first known words of God was spoken. "And God said, 'Let there be light'; and there was light." Gen 1:3.

The Oscillating Universe?

To explain the origin of the universe, scientists describe the current status of the universe and its possible end. There are basically three theories concerning the present state and subsequent end to the universe. Scientists then explore each of the three basic theories and see how each one fits the current scientific information. The three theories describing the current state of the universe are: an open yet bound universe, an open yet unbound universe, and a closed universe (see figure 2.2). All theories support the theory of universal expansion. For many years, the first two theories we considered most correct. They describe a universe in which space is infinite and matter, expanding from the explosion of the big bang, continues to fill more empty space each day. The open unbound universe describes this process continuing forever. Matter is spread through empty space and the relative distance between objects gets larger and larger. Eventually, no gravitational fields will exist between galaxies and the universe will continue to expand, spreading matter ever thinner. One of Newton's principles of physics states that objects in motion will tend to stay in motion unless acting upon by an outside force. Therefore, the power from the big bang explosion will eventually overcome any gravitational fields which currently hold galaxies into clusters. The result: pockets of island galaxies. The open bound universe states that the universe will expand like in the previous theory accept it will eventually stop expanding. This theory states that either there is an end to the universe or that eventually the universe will simply no longer have any power to continue expanding. The universe will reach a point where it doesn't have any more power to expand, and the gravitational fields between galaxies are too weak to affect each other. The universe will eventually become static, according to this theory. The final theory is the one, which has gained considerable acceptance in recent years. A closed universe would exist if there were more gravitational force pulling everything towards a point of origin than momentum expanding the universe forever. If this were true, the universe would eventually collapse in on itself in what some call the "Big Crunch". The Bible states that the universe, as it exists today, is temporary. "Heaven and earth will pass away, but my words will not pass away." Luke 21:33. "Then I saw a new heaven and a new earth, for the first heaven and the first earth had passed away." Revelation 21:1. The only permanent thing in the universe is the word of God. The present world and universe will eventually end.

One of Hawking's greatest achievements is his description of the conditions at the moment of the big bang. Quote, "During the three years after he received his doctorate, Hawking worked as a research associate at Cambridge and began collaborating with Penrose on what was to be his first major piece of research, the mathematical proof of the beginning of time. [2.13]" Roger Penrose is a theoretical physicists and mathematician of Oxford University. The idea of the space time continuum having a beginning is a difficult concept to phantom. "Hawking told Me. 'In fact, most people thought there was no true beginning. We prove them wrong. [2.14]" We tend to consider the passage of time flowing from the present into the future an inevitable part of life. Consequently, we often think of time as something that has always been in the universe and will always continue in the universe. This concept was proven wrong. There was a beginning to time. Now the question remains is there anything independent of time? What existed before time? Was the only thing existing before time began a mysterious collection of unexplainable natural forces, or the Word of God. Hawking's description of time was the result of work done with general relativity. He proposed the concept of a singularity of space, time, energy, matter, and all fundamental forces of nature in the beginning of the universe. The beginnings of the naturalistic ideas concerning the birth of the universe were developed from the work of Alexander Friedman. Friedman explored theoretical solutions to Einstein's theory of General Relativity and found extraordinary results. The idea can be pictured with the graphical representation of a black hole. The only difference is that a black hole is considered the result of gravitational forces of a star collapsing in on itself to a point of singularity. The birth of the universe is described as coming out of a point of singularity and spreading matter throughout the universe.

The theory of General Relativity, released by Einstein in 1917, had been just as successful as Einstein's Special Theory of Relativity in describing the universe. The General Theory explained gravity in terms of the geometry of the space-time continuum. $F_{\mu\nu} = R_{\mu\nu} - \frac{1}{2} g_{\mu\nu}R = -8\pi\,G\,T_{\mu\nu}$ is one of Einstein's equation for general relativity. $F_{\mu\nu}$ = force due to a gravitational field. $R_{\mu\nu}$ = Ricci Tensor, of 23 eq.'s representing curvature of space-time. $g_{\mu\nu}$ = the gravitational tensor. R= Ricci's scalar, a constant of curvature. G= gravitational constant of the universe. $T_{\mu\nu}$ = Energy-stress tensor. The equations had one alarming prediction, however. The basic mathematical interpretations of the theory indicated that the universe was unstable and possibly expanding. The observations of that time did not indicate this to be true and Einstein rejected the concept of an expanding universe despite his own calculations to the contrary. Quote, "Einstein balked. He wanted his equations to show the heavens as portrayed by most astronomers: stable and unchanging, isotopic- the same in all directions- and homogeneous - the same everywhere. … In order to make general relativity fit this model of the universe; he altered his equations, adding a figure he called the cosmological constant, referring to it as a 'slight modification.'… So the 'delta terms,' as they were called, were really unnecessary. Einstein himself was keenly aware of this, and the last sentence of the 1917 paper declared, 'That [delta] term is necessary only for the purpose of making possible a quasi-static distribution of matter as required by the fact of the small velocities of the stars.' In 1922 a Russian mathematician, Alexander Friedman, solved Einstein's equations both with and without the cosmological constant. Like Einstein his solution with the cosmological constant produced a static universe that remained the same forever. Friedman's more daring second solution left out the delta terms and led to the first model of an expanding universe, actually two different models. … The first is one in which the density of matter is less than a certain critical amount, meaning that the universe is infinite and will expand forever. In the second- the one approved by most cosmologists - the density is greater than the critical level. The expansion of the universe will, as a result, one day cease. [2.15]" According to this theory, once the expansion of the universe stops, it will close in on itself, see figure 2.2. Like the collapse of a massive star that forms a black hole, the universe would crash in on itself in "the big crunch". When this occurs, the universe will reach a point of singularity again and possibly begin another universe, with a new big bang. This is how some scientists explain the baffling question of, 'where did all the energy and mass mixture at the beginning of the universe come from?' Supposedly, we exist today as the result of a previous existence in another universe. The universe simply exist in and endless cycle of creating and destroying itself, according to the oscillating universe theory. The fact that the universe seams to expanding at an increasing rate would seam to throw this theory out the window. In Chapter 1 we discussed how the observations of the Hubble telescope indicate the universe indeed is expanding at a faster rate instead of slower. How do we sort through the conflicting ideas and observations? We must have faith in the power of God, not scientific discovery for the answers.

The Oscillating Universe theory remains popular today among scientists. It is believed to explain the existence of the universe without the part of a creator. "This theory eliminates the need for an absolute beginning of the universe by suggesting that the universe expands, then collapses, then expands again, and continues in this cycle indefinitely. [2.16]" There are many serious problems to the theory. "'For one thing, it contradicts the known laws of physics. Theorems by Hawking and Penrose show that as long as the universe is governed by general relativity, the existence of an initial singularity – or beginning – is inevitable, and that it's impossible to pass through a singularity to a subsequent state. … The whole theory was simply a theoretical abstraction. Physics never supported it. [2.17]" Further evidence that the Oscillating Universe theory has little basis in fact is found in calculations for the density of the universe. It is firmly established that the universe has a density far bellow the value needed to contract to a point of singularity. "'Recent tests, run by five different laboratories in 1998, calculate a ninety-five-percent certainty that the universe will not contract, but expand forever. In fact, in a completely unexpected development, the studies indicated that the expansion is not decelerating, but it's actually accelerating. [2.18]" The continued support for this theory is an example of how scientists are not as objectionable as we may think. Some scientists who support such theories act out of rebellion against God and not driven by scientific curiosity. They are guided by an obsessive faith in evolution and in rebellion against God and their own scientific evidence!

Scientists often put their personal faith, sometimes in atheism, into the theories they support. Another example is the Steady State theory proposed in 1948. "It said that the universe was expanding all right but claimed that as galaxies retreat from each other, new matter comes into being out of nothing and fills the void.' [2.19]" This theory was a direct violation of well-known laws of physics and energy conservation. Lee Strobel in his interview with Dr. William Lane Craig asks about the scientific process.

Dr. Craig explains that usually you start with data and create a plausible theory to explain the information. In response to the formation of the Steady State theory, Dr. Craig replies: "'In this case, though, there were no scientific data to support it. It's a good illustration of how scientists are not mere thinking machines but are driven by philosophical and emotional factors as well.'[2.20]" There are a number of examples where scientists take a leap of faith. Often their faith is in the ability of scientific discovery to have absolutely no boundaries. Why do some scientists find it to difficult to accept that there may be some things that will never be understood by science?

Quantum Physics and Cosmology

The road to the mathematical representation of singularity was not easy. Quote, "'Demonstrating that the universe began as a singularity of infinite density, similar to the end product of a star in ultimate collapse, was no easy task. That, of course, was the point all our equations broke down,' Hawking recalled. 'There were solutions to Einstein's equations that most people in those days thought weren't realistic; they represented a universe that was too uniform and isotopic.' [2.21]" The problem is that a uniformed beginning to the universe would not allow for the Galaxies to form. It is assumed that some irregularities at the beginning of the universe were necessary to collect in pockets of matter and form the many galaxies throughout the universe. However, the 3-k background radiation demonstrates that the universe is indeed very uniform. The simplest solution to this puzzle is that God works in a uniform manner and it was the power of God, which created all these things. God created the universe in a mathematically precise manner. What other explanation can be considered reasonable? We will study in Chapter 7 the principles of Mathematics. We can summarize by stating mathematics is a study of relationships. Does not God work with his creation in a personal relationship? That was why Christ came to our world. So we could know him in a personal way. The Bible represents the History of the universe. From man's creation, in the image of God, to the present day God seeks to establish a relationship with His creation. More about the Christian perspective on relationships will be discussed in Chapter 7.

The unlikely alliance of quantum mechanical principles were forged, somewhat, with general relativity to describe the point of singularity. "The uncertainty principle states that certain pairs of quantities, such as the position and momentum of an electron, cannot be measured simultaneously. This means that the electron is not the objective, absolute, and determinate bit of matter classical physics describes, but a sort of objective entity that in a sense is smeared out around the nucleus. The uncertainty principle distinguishes quantum mechanics from all other physics because it declares mathematically that atomic and nuclear particles are distributed in an uncertain and random fashion. The location at any instant of any particle can be described only using a system of probabilities and statistics. It was this element of unpredictability that made quantum mechanics unacceptable to Einstein. [2.22]" Einstein's famous quote on the matter of quantum mechanics was 'God doesn't play dice'. Einstein believed that the universe operated with exact precision from the direction of the mind of God and not in random patterns. The uncertainty was simple due to the lack of ability for physicists to accurately measure events which took place in the subatomic world. The debate continues even today. Is their a fundamental principle of uncertainty in nature or is it the result of particle or wave interactions we do not as yet comprehend? Hawking replies to Einstein's quote with one of his own. Quote, "God not only plays dice, but sometimes he throws them where they cannot be seen. [2.23]" There is a footnote to this quotation by Hawking, which indicates the "hiding place" of the "dice"; i.e. the principles of quantum physics and relativistic physics are inside a black hole. Hawking supports the concept of a "natural" uncertainty necessary for physics to function. "Quantum mechanics seems to suggest that the subatomic world-and even the world beyond the atom -has no independent structure at all until it is defined by the human intellect. ... Physicists have been unable to reconcile this system with the view of the universe posited by general relativity. While general relativity allows for a perfect point like singularity at the beginning of time, quantum mechanics does not, for it prohibits defining at the same time the precise location, velocity, and size of any single particle or singularity. Ultimately, quantum mechanics will have to be brought into play if we are to understand the workings of the infinitesimal universe at its very beginning. [2.24]" The laws of physics for the large scale suggest that quantum mechanics simply does not apply outside the realm of the atom. Experiments seam to verify this conclusion that there is complete uniformity in the universe. The methods of quantum mechanics in using the uncertainty principle can make good approximations to these cause and effect interactions inside the atom. Applying the uncertainty principles to areas it does not belong, simply creates chaos, see figure 2.3 and read the caption. We will discuss some of the theological implications of the uncertainty principle in later chapters. For one thing, you can look at it two ways. One, you can not know anything for certain. Or, two, if there is any certainty it belongs outside the realm of science. In other words, faith in the power of God , controlling the universe, outside of our ability to totally comprehend God's ways, is actually the only thing we can be "certain" exists.

"But you can't go through life applying Heisenberg's Uncertainty   principal to everything."

Figure 2.3

Hawking discovered a simpler approach to solving the irregularities in interpreting the equations which approached the point of singularity in the beginning of the universe. " 'Most people working on the problem believed that to get close to the truth you had to have a complicated solution with numerous irregularities on a large scale,' … 'The thing is that in general relativity, no signal can travel faster than light. So two events cannot be related unless they can be joined and you get from one to the other at a speed equal or less than that of light.' This meant that Hawking and Penrose did not need to explain what would happen to individual particles at the instant of the big bang. … 'We developed a new mathematical technique that was actually an analysis of the way the points in space-time can be causally related to each other. … In fact, we found that you could use large-scale properties to prove that there must have been a singularity at the beginning, a much simpler approach. This meant time has a beginning.' [2.25]" Sometimes the answers are right in from of you. Is it possible that all the answers to your problems are found in one book, the Bible?

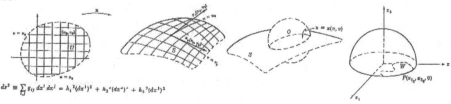

Figure 2.4
Tensor Analysis

Mathematical expressions of such theories of universal structure are in the form of tensors. The universe is believed to be curved, in nature, like a great sphere, see figure 2.4. This belief in the shape of the universe comes from the mathematics of general relativity. Theoreticians take specific events and determine how a piece of matter behaves in the space-time continuum. An orthogonal coordinate system is used to specify placement and movement of objects in the space-time field, figure 2.4. Next we derive the dimensional relationships in this geodesic with deferential equations. When you include the dimensions of time into the position of any material body the dt and c factors come into effect, $ds^2=c^2dt^2-dx^2-dy^2-dz^2=0$. This is where dt is the differential of the dimension of time and c is the speed of light. Of course, x, y, z, are own usual 3-dimensional coordinate system. When you consider that every material body has a variety of properties you include these properties into the equations in tensor form. For example, a change in temperature is related to the increase in energy of the system. In general relativity, Einstein related all the changes taking place in an object traveling through warped space time in a set of field equations. If the speed of the object approaches light, relativistic effects, from the special theory of relativity, must be taken into account. Relating all these factors of the change in the bending of space-time, the magnitude of the gravitational field of a material body as it goes through space, the position of the body as related to a reference position and the changing energy. All content are related in the expression $F_{\mu v} = R_{\mu v}-\frac{1}{2} g_{\mu v}R = -8\pi G T_{\mu v}$, Einstein's equation for general relativity. In other words, expressions such as these are considered short-hand representations of the theories conceived by scientists. If you are a little confused, don't worry! Many professors with advanced degrees become confused by some of the mathematical representations. Scientists often express their ideas in complex form to confuse others. Although, tensor analysis can be an elegant expression of mathematical and physical theories for advanced discussions.

What does it all mean?

All these statements expressing the theory of general relativity may seam very confusing, but most of the basic conclusions are simple. Here are some of the results of the theory of general relativity. 1) Space - Time is curved. Gravity bends light in a curve. 2) Time is the fourth dimension to matter. 3) Matter has properties of heat, energy, electromagnetism, gravity and other properties, which can be considered dimensions to matter. 4) All parts of mater are affected by the speed the object travels, if it approaches the speed of light. 5) The universe is expanding. Sometimes scientists cloud their theories in complex expressions. Because something is presented in a complex manner it doesn't necessarily make the statements truer than expressed in a few simple statements. Basically all the expressions discussed above boils down to the idea that the universe is curved and we can follow particles as they travel in curved paths through space. One very important principle brought out through these ideas is that light bends in the presence of a gravitational field. The bending of light rays was one of the means in which general relativity was proven to be true. This effect is also how astronomers detect possible locations of black holes, see figure 2.1 Again, many scientists believe that understanding black holes will bring us closer to an understanding about our beginnings. "Into a void, so absolute as to mock any human concept of emptiness, appeared a single point of raw potential. And at the very instant of its creation, this point, bearing all dimensions, all energy and all time, burst out, spewing forth its contents. And at the instant of its origin, all matter and all forces were indistinguishable from each other. [2.26]" This is how we are presented with the evidence for the big bang theory. We have already discussed how many of the details could have been precisely correct. However, there are some considerations which are false. We did not originate from darkness but from the light of the power of God. The origin of the universe, according to most physicists, is this explosion creating the universe. "As the universe expanded and cooled, matter and force split apart and then split again. ... All the forces are transmitted by vector bosons-force-carrying particles that exist for a fraction of a second. ... A vector boson called a gluon is responsible for the strong force, and the photon, a massless particle that outside the atom is the constitute of light, is the boson responsible for electromagnetism. ... Three particles - two called W's and one called a Z -transmit the force responsible for radioactive decay. ... An as yet undetected vector boson called the graviton is theorized to cause gravitation, a force that has no meaningful effect inside an atom because it operates only on large mass. [2.27]" This concept of universal beginning is based on our current knowledge of how nuclear forces operate. Scientists attempt to find the source of the unbelievable organization in the universe by speculating on what forces could bring these things together. Particle accelerators are very good at tearing atoms apart to see what they are made out of. However, that doesn't mean that we can make a meaningful explanation of the force that created them at the beginning of the universe. More details on sub-atomic physics are covered in chapter nine.

The Unified Field Theory

A Unified Field Theory is a theorem that will supposedly answer most of the questions about how all the natural forces were first formed. The development of this theory is the subject of worldwide research and intense investigation. "Sheldon Glashow, co-winner of a Nobel Prize for his work with grand unified theories, once told me, 'When the universe was very, very hot, we believe that all the forces may have been one. ...' Hawking agrees. ... 'To unify the four forces in a single mathematical explanation is the greatest quest in science.' ... 'My goal is simple,' he said, suddenly solemn. 'It is a complete understanding of the universe, why it is as it is and why it exists at all.'[2.28]" The beginning of the unified field theory starts with Einstein's theory of relativity. In 1905 Einstein wrote four papers while working at the Swiss Patent Office at Berne. The first paper was on Brownian motion, the second was on the photoelectric effect, the other two on special relativity. A second paper published a short time later summarized his conclusions with his famous matter energy equivalence, $E=mc^2$. In 1907 Einstein left the patent office and began work towards a Generalized Theory of Relativity. In 1916 Einstein concluded the principles of General Relativity and published the results. General relativity makes the following conclusions: 1) gravitational fields affect the frequency of spectral lines. 2) Light rays bend in the presence of a gravitational field. [2.29].From 1917 to Einstein's death in 1955 most of his work was related to developing a unified field theory. Einstein viewed the development of a unified field theory one of the most important endeavors of science. "Today the outer limits of man's knowledge are defined by Relativity, the inner limits buy the Quantum Theory. ... The purpose of a Unified Field Theory is to construct a bridge between them. ... In the same way that Relativity reduced gravitational force to a geometrical property of the space-time continuum, a Unified Field Theory will reduce electromagnetic force – the other great universal force – to equivalent status. ... For the great philosophical triumph of any Unified Field Theory is implicit in the first word of its title. It will carry to fulfillment the long course of science towards the unification of man's concepts of the physical world. ... A complete Unified Field Theory touches the 'grand aim of all science,' which, as Einstein once defined it, is 'to cover the greatest number of empirical facts by logical deduction from the smallest possible number of hypothesis or axioms.' The urge to consolidate premises, to unify concepts, to penetrate the variety and particularity of the manifest world to the undifferentiated unity that lies beyond is not only the leaven of science; it is the loftiest passion of the human intellect. [2.30]"

The recent experiments at the Relativistic Heavy Ion Collider, or RHIC (pronounced "Rick") at Long Island may have taken scientists a giant leap forward in understanding the creation of the universe and completing the unified field theory. First we need to look at some ground breaking theoretical work and then to the experiments that seam to verify the predictions. "It was the summer of 1998, and (Juan) Maldacena had just published a paper that to physicists bordered on the miraculous. He proposed an unexpected link between two ostensibly different theories of fundamental physics: string theory and quantum chromodynamics. String theory purports to describe all the elementary components of mater and energy not as particles but as vanishingly small vibrating strings. ... He proved that his pseudo-QCD and string theory are not in fact different theories at all; mathematically, they are entirely equivalent.[2.31]" The significance to this work is that the string theory was, until then, considered highly skeptical mathematical work. QCD, on the other hand, has successfully explained the workings of subatomic particles for decades. One reason the string theory is not acknowledged by some physicists is that it calls for an almost "supernatural" quality to the universe. String Theory predicts matter has at least five dimensions or more. "According to string theory, the universe may contain as many as 10 dimensions.

[2.32]» The experiments at RHIC seam to confirm Maldacena's theory, which suggests we owe our existence to a "higher power". There are enormous theological implications to the findings at RHIC. First, the plasma energy they created had a viscosity similar to water and then the implication that the universe was sustained, for an instant, by a number of fifth dimensional "black holes". "The quarks and gluons that coursed through the newborn cosmos – and considerably more recently, through RHIC – took the form not of a gas, as physicists expected, but of a liquid. ... The quarks and gluons at RHIC are equivalent to microscopic black holes in a higher-dimensional space. ... To re-create the immediate aftermath of the Big Bang, RHIC reaches higher energies than any other collider in the world. Unlike most accelerators, which smash together simple particles like individual protons, RHIC accelerates clusters of hundreds of gold atoms. ... The initial results, announced in 2005, stunned physicists everywhere. The particles released ... were ... moving smoothly and collectively like a liquid. ... The RHIC physicists describe their creation as a near "perfect" fluid. ... The quarks and gluons make a much better liquid than water. ... (Dam Thanh) Son insists that black holes, quarks, and gluons really do have a big thing in common: They can be described by equations that govern the behavior of liquids. ... They confirmed that the quark-gluon fluid indeed had a low viscosity, at or near the theoretical minimum value predicted by the five-dimensional black-hole model. ... What we think of as atomic nuclei, quarks, and gluons may really be objects that are projections, in a sense, on a screen. ... We are on the screen. It looks to us like there are photons and these other particles, but they might really be manifestations, projections, from a higher-dimensional space, of objects that are more conveniently described in our world by saying, 'There is a photon,' or 'There is a gluon.' So the very hot quarks and gluons at RHIC may really be a hologram of some nasty black hole somewhere. [2.33]» I find it amazing that these scientists describe the plasma energy fluid like "water". "And God said, let there be an expanse between the waters to separate water from water. So God made the expanse and separated the water under the expanse from the water above it." Genesis 1:6-7. Scientists attempt to explain these events occurring as the result of natural forces, apart from God. I have a better assessment: All things are made by the power of God. This seams to be a reasonable assessment considering what particle physics teaches us about matter. More on this subject will be discussed in the last section of Chapter 9. We and every particle in the universe is simply a manifestation of God's power. He has created us, sustains us, and allows us to manipulate these natural forces making technological achievements. "God blessed them and said to them, 'Be fruitful and increase in number; fill the earth and subdue it.'" Genesis 1:28. We have fulfilled God's first commands. We are made in the image of God and have subdued and used the earth God has provided for us to accomplish many wondrous things through science and technology. However, through sin and greed we have misused his gifts in many ways. Now, our planet is threatened by our incompetence and the end of our reign on earth has begun, in my opinion.

It would seam to be an unrealistic goal to unify all knowledge about fundamental forces and scientific discovery into a single equation, but scientists worldwide are attempting to discover the "secret" to everything in existence. It is no secret how the universe came into existence; it was by the power of God. Hawking states at the end of his book, a brief history of time, that the goal of the unified field theory is "to know the mind of God". This is what all scientific learning is discovering. "In the evolution of scientific thought, one fact has become impressively clear: there is no mystery to the physical world, which does not point to a mystery beyond itself. All highroads of the intellect, all byways of theory and conjecture lead ultimately to an abyss that human ingenuity can never span. ... Standing midway between macrocosm and microcosm he finds barriers on every side and can perhaps but marvel, as St. Paul did nineteen hundred years ago, that (By faith we understand that) the world was created by the word of God, so that what is seen was made out of things which do not appear. [2.34]» This is taken from the verses in Hebrews 11:3 RSV. To learn more details about God simply read the Bible. There is a clear explanation of the characteristics of God in the Bible. Science draws us ever closer to the Bible in every encounter. Why deny the obvious? The Bible is the word of God and the source for truth. It is impossible to avoid a discussion of beliefs when you study current scientific theories. Public Schools are running into this axiom on a daily basis! What does a teacher do if the students start asking too many scientific questions? All questions about the origin of life or the origin of the universe lead to a discussion of personal beliefs about your origins. How can anyone with a reasonable amount of intelligent not understand this fact? Faith and science are more bound together that any other time in history. Each new scientific discovery makes the subjects more intertwined.

The Biblical Account

"In the beginning God created the heavens and the earth. The earth was without form and void, and darkness was upon the face of the deep; and the Spirit of God was moving over the face of the waters. And God said, 'Let there be light'; and there was light. And God saw that the light was good; and God separated the light from the darkness. God called the light Day, and the darkness he called Night. And there was evening and there was morning, one day." Gen 1:1-5. Of course the word interpreted as "Earth" is not the planet Earth. That was created on the third day. "God called the dry land Earth, and the waters that were gathered together he called Seas." Gen 1:10. It is possible the event described in verse three is exactly what modern cosmology has proposed? The Big Bang Theory describes the universe coming from unified forces concentrated in a point of singularity. Matter was created out of pure energy according to this theory. The question is where did the energy come from? This could be described in verse three as God saying "Let there be light". Again, during the first few fractions of a second there were forces at work scientists still can not precisely explain. Quote, "'I would like to know exactly what happened between 10^{-33} second and 10^{-43} second,' Hawking said. 'It is there that the ultimate answer to all questions about the universe - life itself included - lies. The classical notion of time would break down somewhere before then -somewhere between 10^{-33} and 10^{-43} second.' [2.35]" The biblical explanation of the events in the creation of the universe is far more in line with the facts than theories which try to omit the presence of God. "The next stopping-off place is over 10 billion years ago, when the universe was a mere 500,000 years old. It was then that elementary particles joined together to form atoms. Before then the universe was still to hot for an electron to fall into a quantum orbit around a nucleus, Physicists can mark this point because they know exactly how much electromagnetic force is required to keep an electron attached to the nucleus of any element. It is only necessary to convert this force into a temperature equivalent and see at what point the cooling universe passed through that stage. ... 'Once atoms had begun to form, then matter could condense into galaxies and stars, and gravity could start playing an important role in the development of the universe.' It also is about the point that light began to be able to travel throughout the universe. [2.36]" This assumes an extremely dense hot beginning to the universe. This is believed to be the conditions at the beginning of the universe because those types of conditions are necessary, on the small scale, to break apart the atom in cyclotron accelerators on Earth. All the theories concerning the conditions of the big bang are based on experiments in particle accelerators. Since the pieces that make up atoms must have been created first, it is assume by breaking apart atoms in laboratory experiments we are re-creating similar conditions of the big bang. The scientists take into account the entire universe broken down and united in a single point of singularity and then they have the basis for the calculations of the temperatures at the beginning of the universe. "Theorists believe that the photons of the microwave background, in fact, were coupled with the protons, neutrons, and electrons that make up matter. As the universe cooled, radiation and matter parted company, this occurring after 100,000 years. The microwave background discovered by Arnold Penzias and Robert Wilson in 1964 is a relic of the instant split off from matter. [2.37]" See figure 1.2 on the right side for a look at the universal background radiation. You can find a color photo of this phenomenon in most Astronomy textbooks.

There is one serious problem with the concept of the universe cooling to the point of separating photons from elementary particles at the age of 100,000 years. One of the biggest mysteries of the twentieth century has been the uniformity of the universal back ground radiation. Scientists did not anticipate such uniformity in the radiation because after 100,000 years, great amounts of space should have developed. This lead to the prediction that the background radiation would be spotty; providing evidence to the creation of galaxies by natural forces. "Another concern is that the microwave background radiation is too uniform. If radiation were actually released when it separated from matter at a cosmic age of around 100,000 years, how is this homogeneity throughout the wholly different parts if the universe explained? At that point in the universe's history, pieces of the sky would already have separated by millions of light-years of space. There would have been no possibility for an exchange of energy over such distance. So why has the same background temperature been detected everywhere? [2.38]" Why is it assumed that matter separated from energy of photons at the 100,000-year mark? Because it would take 100,000 years before the exited stated and intense heat of the universe could be cooled to the point of disconnecting photons from matter. This is due to the limitations placed of heat dissipating by natural laws. But what if the universe was cooled by a supernatural act of God? Or in fact what if the universe was not hot at all at its creation? The background radiation merely indicates a sudden transformation of energy into matter across the entire universe at a single moment in time.

There are a lot of things taking place during each day of creation, according to the Genesis account. Perhaps the background radiation was created during the second day of creation. "And God said, 'Let there be a firmament in the midst of the waters, and let it separate the waters from the waters.' And God made the firmament, and divided the waters which were under the firmament from the waters which were above the firmament: and it was so. And God called the firmament Heaven. And there was evening and morning, the second day." Gen 1:6-7 The background radiation indicating sudden creation of the universe could be evidence that God created the universe as described in these verses. What is the firmament described above? What is this separation of waters? The separation of waters above and bellow may be the separation of matter and energy. The firmament could be all dimensions in the universe. Four for the space- time continuum and a fifth dimension for heaven. This suggests a spiritual dimension where God is always present. This would confirm the concept of an omnipresent God. We have already seen that the unified field theory proposes to simplify all forces to a set of dimensional field equations. This seams completely in agreement with God creating a unified form and then separating the forces on the second day of creation. Heaven is mentioned many times in the Bible as the kingdom of God. But what is heaven? We know that from the scripture it is a place that we can not presently see. It is where the throne of God resides. It is a place where we come before the Lord after death. Could this be another dimensional plane of reality? There are many comparisons made by Christ concerning heaven. All parables indicate a kingdom of perfect organization. The waters in the previous passage could be interpreted as the components of matter and energy. The "quark soup" where photons and elementary particles are united could be the waters which were separated during the second day of creation. This may be an incorrect interpreting of the scriptures, but it deserves to exist as a possible theoretical link between the discovered background radiation and the creation of the universe by God. If this were true, when the microwave radiation was made, it would explain the condition of uniformity because it was created only a short time after the original creation of everything else in the universe.

Even though the events are mere speculations based on knowledge of current physical laws governing the construction of matter, the description of modern astronomy fits nicely into the Genesis account. "Before three minutes, the universe was too hot to allow protons and neutrons to join in a nucleus. ... At three minutes, however, things had cooled sufficiently that the strong force could begin pulling a proton and a neutron or a proton and two neutrons together to form a nucleus of heavy hydrogen. ... It was then that the 75:25 hydrogen-helium ratio that exists to this day was established. ... But it was not until millions of years latter that heavy elements like iron and gold began to be forged in the furnaces of the stars. ... Even medium-sized accelerators can create conditions quite similar to those existing at this time. [2.39]" According to the theories of nuclear physics and theoretical physics of men such as Stephen Hawking, the nuclei of hydrogen and helium were created during the first minutes of creation.

Above we mentioned the possibility of the "waters" in Genesis 1:6 to be some of the parts of matter which existed in the "soup" of matter and energy. What is water? A molecule of two atoms of hydrogen and one atom of oxygen combined. Here we see hydrogen nuclei formed three minutes after creation. Is this just a coincidence that hydrogen is the first nucleus made in the universe and the Bible refers to water among the first of God's creation? Scientists are reasonable sure they have their facts straight about the creation of the universe up to the hundredth -of-a-second mark according to Hawking. "Between one ten-thousandth (10^{-4}) and one millionth (10^{-6}) of the first second is another milestone. The basic constituents of matter in the universe were created as quarks combining in groups of three, forming neutrons and protons. [2.40]" These events are all taking place after God made the universe out of the power in His word. "And God said, Let there be light: and there was light." Genesis1:3. It is not necessary that the forces and power used by God created an intensely hot universe. But, we can be in agreement that the universe was highly energetic in the beginning. The universe followed the second law of thermodynamics and decreased in its energetic nature to atoms and molecules, following principles totally under the control of God.

A Cold Bang?

The theory of a highly dense, hot universe has many problems at this point. "At 10^{-4} second the universe's density is so great that the amount of space between all protons and neutrons is as small as the size of one of the particles themselves. That is a little too close for the comforts of physicists who have been forced to write a new description of the way subatomic particles behave if they are to account for such density. Fortunately for them, one of the properties of the strong force … is that this force increases with distance. The closer the particles, the less the force. [2.41]" The quark soup model proposes that the closer you get to the beginning, time zero, the hotter the universe gets. "If the model is correct, it could mean that the temperature keeps building right on through the Plank wall, the point when the universe is 10^{-43} seconds old, beyond which the calculations of physics do not work. [2.42]" The possibility of cold Big bang has been proposed that exclude the descriptions of high-energy quark interactions in the explanation of the big bang. This theory has been rejected on the basis of thermodynamics. "The universe historically has always cooled down. It is cooling down today. So as we look farther and farther backward in time, the universe should be getting hotter and hotter, right up to the instant of the singularity at the big bang. [2.43]" The universe could have easily been created by a "cold" big bang if God's power created the universe. After all, the principles of physics are not yet even formed, according to the mathematical interpretation of creation according to Steven Hawking. Another problem in theoretical physics, which attempts a natural explanation of creation, is the so-called Plank wall. To speculate on the conditions past this point results in incongruities and discontinuity. "In a sense, theorists have been able to approach but not cross the Plank wall because they have been able to fudge their equations this way or that to carry them backward over crucial points of time in the universe's development. … The Plank wall is the universe's ultimatum: There will be no further hedging of equations, no more jumping over points too complex or obscure to understand. [2.44]" Scientist have attempted every conceivable approach to explain the creation of the universe by natural laws, and they continue to fail. The creation of the universe took place in conditions outside the ability of scientists to explain them physically. By my definition of a miraculous event (any event which must have taken place outside a physically explainable, controlled situation) the creation of the universe was a miraculous event made by God.

The Inflationary or Bubble Theory

When deciding which theoretical explanation of the creation of the universe to believe, consider, once again, the background radiation. The uniformity of this universal radiation is an excellent scientific example of the power of God. The bubble theory attempts to explain this uniformity by natural means. "For one thing, during the universe's inflationary era, the bubbles developed more slowly than in the Big Bang format. This allowed the matter developing inside time to mix evenly, come to the same temperature, and thus produce a uniform radiation throughout the universe. [2.45]" Thus, scientists have developed the bubble theory to explain the creation of the universe by natural forces. This alternative explanation creates addition problems to explain the creation of the universe. These additional problems may create more mysteries than it solves or not, you decide. Hawking believes that the inflammatory theory solves more problems than it creates, I disagree. Quote, "The bubble theory, originated in 1981, eliminates most of the flaws in the Big Bang while, naturally, creating other problems. The basic idea is that not one but several universes arose from bubbles inflating like balloons in a void. At the very beginning there was an uneven mix of energized spots ... Because of their heat, these spots expanded so rapidly that they soon lost their heat. Then they 'super-cooled.' [2.46]" The bubble theory seams to be leading to our previous picture of the creation. The universal background radiation created at an earlier stage in the life of the universe. However, instead of super-cooled, we suggested a supernaturally cooled universe. Which idea is more acceptable? The main difficulty in explaining the origin of the universe by natural laws using either the big bang theory or the inflammatory theory is explaining the combination of universal diversity and universal conformity. "There was a fatal flaw in all the inflationary scenarios. It was that the universe, although homogeneous on a large scale, is not quite uniform on a smaller scale; it contains clumps of matter in the form of galaxies and stars and clusters of galaxies. In other words, it was simply not clear that an inflationary universe could produce the stars and galaxies we observe in our universe today. [2.47]" This was odd, since the inflammatory theory was essentially created to solve this same problem in the big bang theory. Mathematicians began working on the problem and found a way to show how the inflammatory theory of creation could have produced the galaxies and stars we see today. However, problems soon developed in this theoretical explanation of creation. Quote, "Their calculations showed that the inflationary scenario did indeed produce the right number of clumps of matter distributed properly throughout the universe. But if the inflationary scenario were followed to its mathematical conclusion, these clumps of matter would form prematurely and collapse almost instantly into black holes, leaving an utterly black universe. So the simplest model of the new inflationary universe... had to be officially pronounced dead- even though it was but six months old. [2.48]" Hawking and a few other scientists refused to let the theorem die and held a vigil in the belief that they can mathematically re-awaken the theory someday. Quote, "'It appears to be the right approach,' said Hawking. 'It solves more problems than it creates.' [2.49]" It would appear that the bubble theory brings us closer to a view of a younger universe than strictly having a big bang theory. The creation of the universe remains a mystery for scientists today. Again the missing ingredient in all acts of creation is the mind of God. Always in control of the universe and all of it's inner workings.

The Encarta Encyclopedia Standard Edition 2002 explains the inflationary theory in more detail. "The inflationary theory deals with the behavior of the universe for only a tiny fraction of a second at the beginning of the universe. Theorists believe that the events of that fraction of a second, however, determined how the universe came to be the way it is now and how it will change in the future. The inflationary theory states that, starting only about 1×10^{-35} second after the big bang and lasting for only about 1×10^{-32} second, the universe expanded to 1×10^{50} times its previous size. The numbers 1×10^{-35} and 1×10^{-32} are very small–a decimal point followed by 34 zeros and then a 1, and a decimal point followed by 31 zeros and then a 1, respectively. The number 1×10^{50} is incredibly large–a 1 followed by 50 zeros. This extremely rapid inflation would explain why the universe appears so homogeneous: The universe had been compact enough to become uniform, and the expansion was rapid enough to preserve that uniformity. [2.50]" Amazing, a sudden creation followed by rapid expansion. Sounds like the Biblical account doesn't it? The only difference is the size and completeness of the creation. In Genesis the entire universe was made basically in one day with a few details in the other five days. Science continues to bring us to the conclusion the universe was made by the hand of God. A delicate balance of forces, circumstances and events at the instant of creation was necessary to produce the universe we observe today. How can anyone truly believe that this event was not by design? What could have possible caused such a rapid expansion in a short amount of time? Scientists continue their research and new developments occur each day. We could at this juncture discus various so-called string theories on the subject of explaining universal creation. Instead, I believe the point is made clear. Faith and science and inseparably linked together. This re-emphasizes the premise of this book. Which theories you personally accept is a matter of faith. Faith and science are constant companions not enemies as the world would have you believe.

Using Distance to Measure Time

The most common method for measuring the amount of time the universe has existed is found in using the physical principles of light. According to the special theory of relativity, the speed of light is a constant in a vacuum. It is assumed that there is very little substance in space and the universe is essentially a vacuum. Therefore, light traveling from the stars to earth should travel at the constant speed of light. The speed of light is considered the limiting velocity in the universe because nothing can travel faster than light, according to our current knowledge of physical laws. The speed of any object is defined as the change in distance divided by the change in time: $s = dx/dt$. Light travels to earth at the speed of light. If we can determine the distance between the earth and a particular star, we can determine the amount of time it took for the light to reach the earth. Simple algebra yields the equation $dt = dx/s$, where dt is the amount of time the beam of light has been traveling, dx is the distance between the earth and the star and s is the speed of light. The amount of time elapsed from the moment the light was emitted by the star to the moment we observe the light on earth is equal to the distance between the star and the earth divided by the speed of light. However, are we absolutely certain that observations of pulsars, quasars or other distance objects are truly a look backward in time?

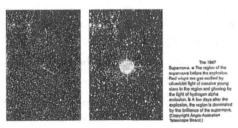

The 1987 Supernova. a The region of the supernova before the explosion. Red wisps are gas excited by ultraviolet light of massive young stars in the region and glowing by the light of hydrogen alpha emission. b A few days after the explosion, the region is dominated by the brilliance of the supernova. (Copyright Anglo-Australian Telescope Board.)

Figure 2.5

We assume the light we receive from a star one light-year away was sent from that star one year ago. For this reason, watching the stars is considered a look back in time. If we see an event taking place in the stars, it is assumed that the event actually took place many years ago. For example, a star in the galaxy called the Large Magellan Cloud went super nova and the event was photographed on Feb. 23, 1987, see figure 2.5. The distance between the star and the earth is estimated at 52,000 parsecs. One parsec is 3.26 light-years. One light-year is the distance light can travel in one year. Therefore, Astronomers believe the supernova event took place approximately 169,520 years ago. [2.51] Could there be another interpretation to the conclusion that astronomical events observed through telescopes have taken place thousands, millions or billions of years ago? This may seam to be more wishful thinking than scientific theory, but what if the time dilation effect is a factor in our observations? In chapter 9 we will explore the physics of special relativity and quantum theory in great detail. For now let's simply state some of the main discoveries in Einstein's theory of special relativity. The following effects take place when any object is accelerated to velocities approaching the speed of light. Mass increases with velocity. The length of an object contracts i.e. gets shorter. Time slows down. The slowing of time is best illustrated by the famous twin paradox. Imagine if you have a pair of twins and one is an Astronaut and the other stays at home on Earth. Take the Astronaut and send him on a space ship that is capable of approaching light speed. Return the twin to earth after a long journey and one twin is still a young man and the other is many years older. Again these principles will be examined in greater detail in later chapters. For this section let's accept that these effects take place without explaining why. The first two effects, mass increase and length decrease, is a part of matter slowly changing to energy as you accelerate to light speed. Thus matter becomes energy when an object travels at the speed of light, $E=mc^2$. Light is considered to be mass-less particles, called photons, traveling through space at the speed of light. All electromagnetic fields travel in packages of energy sometimes called quanta. Thus the study of how energy is created by shifts in matter at the subatomic level is called quantum mechanics. The speed a photon travels through empty space is well documented to be a constant called the speed of light. The speed of light is only a constant in a vacuum, as discovered by the Michelson- Morely experiment. Remember that speed is defined as the change in distance an object travels divided by the time it takes to move that distance. What about the time dilation effect? According to special relativity time slows with increasing speed reach a point where it is mathematically undefined at the speed of light, $T_f = T_i \div \sqrt{[1-(v^2/c^2)]}$. At the speed of light the velocity of the object is at the speed of light. Therefore, v^2 and c^2 are the same value. Anyone who has had grade school math knows, if you have two quantities of the same value divided you get the answer of 1. The value of 1-1 =0. The square root of zero is zero. Any number divided by zero is undefined, $T_f = T_i \div 0 =$ undefined. So how old are the photons of light we observe from astronomical events? There is no way to really know for sure. Matter traveling at the speed of light no longer has a property of time. It is simply a theory but I believe using the constancy of the velocity of light and the distance an object is from our observation is not necessarily proving these events took place thousands, millions, or billions of years ago. [2.52]Again, it is merely a suggestion that the size of the universe has little bearing of the age of the universe. This is more from a "common sense" than from an actual physical property. The age of the universe determined by the measurement of distant objects is easy to accept scientifically. However, considering faith is a factor in any scientific theory, we must consider the possibility that light can somehow instantaneously arrive on earth.

In Genesis Chapter 1 verses 14 and 15, God caused the star's light to shine on the earth. "The God said, Let there be lights in the firmament of the heavens to divide the day from the night; and let them be for signs and seasons, and for days and years; and let them be for lights in the firmament of the heavens to give light on the earth; and it was so." KJV. Therefore, we can not use the distance of the stars from earth and the law of the constancy of the velocity of light to determine the age of the universe. Why? On the fourth day of the account of God's creation the stars were made. Then they were placed in, relatively speaking, their current position. Genesis 1:14 says the stars were signs for the seasons. Ancient Astronomers developed the modern calendar from observations of the stars and the relative position of the sun. First Astronomers notice that certain stars always remained together as they appeared to move across the night sky. They began to identify the constellations. The positions of the constellations in the night sky changed with the seasons. When fall or winter was approaching the constellations were at a certain location. When summer or spring was approaching the constellations were at a different position. Years of observations and calculations and the modern calendar were formed. Also, the light from the stars was sent to earth, and the rest of the universe, instantaneously. Perhaps the limiting velocity to light did not yet exist. Because of this analysis, I believe in a literal 6-day creation, as described in Genesis and the age of the universe to be about 6,000 years old. This age of the universe is obtained by biblical scholar's analysis of the generation of the men of God dating back to Adam. Some Christians at this point are cheering me on while others are disappointed in my seemingly anti-scientific conclusions. The age of the universe is a big issue among some scientists. Dr. Faulkner of the University of South Carolina has this to say. "There are many perplexing problems that we must study within are starting assumptions. The greatest is the light travel time problem. Simply put, the universe appears to be billions of light years in size, so how can we see distant objects if the universe is only a few thousand years old? A number of solutions have been proposed, but I do not find any of them to be entirely satisfactory. [2.53]" Dr. Faulkner is a professor of Astronomy and Physics who believes in a 6,000-year-old universe and a 6-day creation. The belief in a young universe has gained acceptance among many scientists in recent years, mostly because of faith in the Genesis account. As we come to the conclusion that the Bible has an accurate record of scientifically precise truth in every matter, why disregard this one point? There, perhaps, will never be a way to scientifically prove size of the universe has nothing to do with the age of the universe. Considering this is essentially the ONLY scientific principle directly disputed, why should it destroy any further investigation of the evidence which supports the biblical record? Remember, for years scientists considered light traveled in "ether" to explain lights unique properties. Are we absolutely certain something similar doesn't exist throughout the universe?

The age of the universe is paramount to the theory of evolution. Without proving the age of the universe to be 8-13 billion years and the earth 4.5 million years the theory of evolution is completely destroyed. The theory of evolution is man's attempt to re-write history. It takes away from God as the center of the universe and attempts to say that natural forces are responsible for our existence. I believe that the age of the universe has little significance. The important issue is to thank God for our existence because we are His creation. However, the whole subject of evolution can become a tool for promoting the religion of atheism. It attempts to take away recognition of God as creator of the universe. It becomes an issue of forcing students to break the first commandment of God, to worship Him. Is it any wonder why the rest of the laws of God are ignored in school? Could this explain the violence we see all the time in public schools? The first commandment in the laws of God is to worship Him. In the Ten Commandments the first 4 laws are how we are to worship God. The other 6 is on behavior towards one another. "I am the Lord your God, who brought you out of Egypt, out of the land of slavery. 1) You shall have no other gods before me. 2) You shall not make for yourself an idol in the form of anything in heaven above or on earth beneath or in the waters below. You shall not bow down to them or worship them. ... 3) You shall not misuse the name of the Lord your God ... 4) Observe the Sabbath day ... 5) Honor your father and mother ... 6) You shall not murder. 7) You shall not commit adultery. 8) You shall not steal. 9) You shall not give false testimony... 10) You shall not covet ... anything that belongs to your neighbor." Deuteronomy 5:6-21. NIV Jesus summarized the commandments by a few simple words. "Jesus replied: 'love the Lord your God with all your heart and with all your soul and with all your mind. This is the first and greatest commandment. And the second is like it: Love your neighbor as yourself. All the Law and the Prophets hang on these two commandments.'" Matthew 22:37-40 NIV. Jesus was the first to recognize that the Ten Commandments are divided into two sections. One set describing the worship of God the other set dealing with others in a society. The first commandment is to be totally devoted to God and our testimony of faith in Jesus Christ. Isn't our religious freedom constantly under attack today? We must give God the proper respect, recognition, and praise He deserves. By attributing unexplainable forces as the source of all creation, are we not elevating them to a position of an idol? Is there not a fascination over dinosaurs? Why are these creatures nearly worshipped as our distant ancestors? More about the harmful effects of the theory of evolution, and the religion of atheism will be discussed in chapter 4.

Assumptions! Assumptions!

The importance to the size of the universe should be very clear at this point. The bigger the universe, the older the universe is believed to be. Astronomers believe they are receiving signals from quasars that are at least 10,000,000,000 parsecs from the earth. Earth and our solar system are in one of the radial arms of our galaxy called the Milky Way. The next closest star is Alpha Centauri 1.3 parsecs from our sun. Outside our Galaxy, the next closest galaxy is Andromeda 670 k parsecs. Next are clusters of galaxies. We belong to the local cluster of Galaxies which outer edge is 1,000 k parsecs away. Finally the most remote distant objects are quasars 13-16 billion light years from Earth. If these objects exist at these vast distances, according to the principles of physics listed above, the signals must have originated 13-16 billion years ago. Estimates to the age of the universe, based solely on natural laws, require a great deal of faith. Hawking described the situation very clearly when asked about the principles of astronomy as a window to the past. The following conversation is recorded in the book Stephen Hawking's Universe. Quote, " 'But remember that we can always look backward in time by looking out farther into space with our telescopes. The farther into space we look, the closer to the beginning we come.' 'But doesn't that mean making an assumption that everything out there and everything here is the same and operates the same way?' I asked. 'It does.' 'And doesn't it suggest that we believe that the natural laws we have discovered in our time have always been at work in the universe?' 'It does indeed.' 'But are not scientists in making those assumptions taking a leap of faith that is more metaphysical than scientific?' 'One makes some rather strong assumptions in delving into the beginning of the universe.' [2.54]" Faith is an important part of theoretical scientific work. To work on understanding how the universe began, it is understood there are a lot of faith-based assumptions made. Modern Astronomy often dismisses the biblical account as folklore. Instead, I believe it is an accurate description of the events of creation as God revealed to Moses. We can analyze the current state of development of the universe. However, it requires a great deal of faith in the religion of Atheism to dismiss the non-congruent information and believe natural forces created the universe. By the scientists own admission, the physical laws, as there are currently understood, can offer no complete explanation for how the universe began.

The importance of faith in science is clear. Without faith in something, nothing that exists can be explained. You are given simply two choices: a belief that some unexplainable natural force has created the universe or that the universe was created by the power of God. The Bible has a far better explanation for every event than any other religion or set of theoretical work. Can the description of creation from Genesis be reconciled with ideas based on the laws of physics, as we know them today? Absolutely YES! The Bible is consistent with the laws of physics and fills in the gaps that scientists can not currently explain form the naturalistic perspective. "Again, the study of science emphases the handiwork of God.' Pope Pius XII declared in 1951, 'True science to an ever- increasing degree discovers God as though God were waiting behind each door opened by science.' [2.55]" The quest for understanding the creation of the universe by physical forces has brought many individuals to the position of recognizing God as the creator. There is no physical explanation to our origin. We can only accept, by faith in the word of God, that in the beginning God created the entire universe from His unexplainable power. "More than a few scientists think that the facts of the Big Bang, could at the very least suggest the work of a creator or creative force. It may soon become evident that science will never be able to take us to the exact moment of creation- only up to the point where philosophy, metaphysics, and theology begin. [2.56]" Hawking expands on this observation even further. "'The odds against a universe like ours emerging out of something like the Big Bang are enormous. '... Hawking, together with Brandon Carter and other colleagues, discovered that an extremely delicate balance exists in nature. For instance, if the strong force that acts on quarks, neutrons, and protons of the atomic nucleus were just slightly weaker, the only element that would be stable would be hydrogen. No other elements could exist. ... If the constant of gravity were stronger - only 10^{25} times less powerful than the strong nuclear force instead of 10^{38} times weaker -our universe would be small and swift. The average star would have only 10^{-12} times the mass of the sun and could exist for just about a year... 'In fact,' said Hawking, 'a universe like ours with galaxies and stars is actually quite unlikely. ... If one considers the possible constants and laws that could have emerged, the odds against a universe that has produced life like ours are immense.' [2.57]" It all comes down to the fact that it is highly unlikely that we came into existence by anything other than the power of God.

Galactic Clusters: Why Do They Exist?

Another piece of evidence that the universe was made by the power of God and is organized and sustained by the presence of God is the existence of galactic clusters. One mystery to the galactic clusters is the apparent lack of material to provide a gravitational field strong enough to organize the galaxies as they currently exist. Quote, "As early as 1933, Cal Tech astronomer Fritz Zwicky noted that in the coma cluster of galaxies there doesn't appear to be enough mass to hold the galaxies gravitationally in the cluster. Many of the galaxies seam to be moving fast enough to escape from the gravity of the material we can see. Yet the cluster is still there. [2.58]" The leading theories on the subject to explain the presence of galactic clusters are by the existence of 'dark matter'. Dark matter is a theoretical substance that generates a gravitational field, because it has mass, but is otherwise undetectable as matter. Some scientists were convinced that dark matter is large pockets of anti-matter. Recall that when matter is created from the energy of a photon, an equal amount of matter and antimatter is created. So where is all the antimatter created in the beginning of the universe from the big bang? This question is asked almost daily by theoretical physicists. If matter was created from energy, large pockets of antimatter would exist and must remain separate from matter. If the two come into contact they would annihilate each other producing energy once again. How did we come into existence by natural forces in the first place if matter and anti-matter formed in equal amounts in the beginning? With random natural forces supposedly stirring up pockets of matter, what kept matter and antimatter separated so the universe wasn't instantly annihilated as soon as it was made? These are a few of the unanswered questions in theoretical physics. Of course, the Christian solution to all of these problems is faith in the power of God and recognition of all things under His authority. Galactic clusters also provide a strong piece of evidence for a young universe. As we have mentioned, galactic clusters are supposedly organized by gravitational forces. One problem with this concept is the lack of mass for the present organization we see existing today. Observations of galaxies have shown them to moving within the clusters. The whole universe appears to be expanding radically outward. Recall that the speed of the expansion, given by Hubble's constant indicates a universe moving with fantastic speed when considering the size of the universe. Quote, "The relationship is known as Hubble's constant, and its value is 100 kilometers per second for every mega parsec. (A mega-parsec is a million parsecs or about 3.26 million light years) Thus a galaxy that is at a distance of 20 mega-parsecs from our galaxy will recede at a speed of 2,000 kilometers per second from us. [2.59]" Also, the galaxies are apparently rotating with great momentum. The studies of galactic clusters have enabled astronomers to determine the relative speed the galaxies are moving. Astronomers have estimated the relative velocity of galaxy rotation and rough estimates to the total mass of the galaxy. When we apply basic physical principles to this data a conflict occurs. Quote, "There doesn't appear to be enough mass in the clusters to overcome the velocities with which the galaxies are moving. If the measured mass is anywhere near correct, the galactic clusters should have disappeared long ago and should not still exist. ... The huge cluster Virgo cluster, which can be see in the constellation Virgo, contains at least 1,000 galaxies. Yet it lacks 98 percent of the mass needed to hold the galactic cluster together. In other words, if these clusters are indeed billions of years old, why are they still in existence? [2.60]" There are currently two possible solutions that might explain galactic clusters by the force of gravity. One is dark matter, as we previously stated. The second possible solution is a great number of black holes strategically placed throughout the universe. This concept was put forth by Stephen Hawking to explain universal irregularities from a homogeneous universal beginning. Quote, "But if there were irregularities, such as regions far greater density than others, the areas with a certain excess density could have collapsed into little black holes. [2.61]" Either of the two theories concerning the source of organization for galactic clusters can not be proven with current technology. Someday, maybe we will have the solution to what makes the universe have the wonders of spiral galaxies in galactic clusters moving with unexplainable harmony, like a dance in the telescopes trained on the night sky. Not only is it amazing that galactic clusters are able to exist, spiral galaxies should have disappeared long ago. Quote, "It is the spiral structure itself which shows that the galaxies must be young ... As the stars orbit around the galactic center, the stars closer to the center revolve faster than the more-distant stars. ... The effect of these different rotation rates is that the spiral arms soon will wrap themselves around the galactic center until the spiral arms are no longer noticeable. ... By this time in the universe's history (assuming old universe estimates are correct), the spirals should no longer exist. [2.62]" This means that even if we explain why the galactic clusters came into existence by natural forces, if the classical laws of physics hold true for the last 4.5 billion years of the 10-12 billion year history of the universe, the spiral arm of the milky way should not exist. We should only see a ball of stars and live in an almost perfectly round galaxy. This is simple applying the laws of force and circular motion.

The creation of the universe has put the best physicists and theologians to the test. There seams to be no natural explanation to the creation of the universe. This has forced the best minds to face the concept of creation by the power of God. One principle, held by Hawking and others, is a so called "Anthropic principle". Quote, "'Hawking thinks that the only way to explain our universe is by our presence in it.' This principle can be paraphrased as, 'Things are as they are because we are.' [2.63]" This follows the old adage, I think, therefore I am. We do not exist because of anything, it is simply a fact we must accept. This position was expanded by physicist John Wheeler of the University of Texas. "For Wheeler we live in an observer-dependent, participatory universe. All physical laws are dependent upon the presence of an observer to formulate them. [2.64]" These theories have caused a great concern with theologians and scientists. These ideas do not give clear reverence to God as the creator nor do they offer a purely natural explanation to why the universe exists. "Most theologians have found the principle perplexing and unsatisfactory, since it does not clearly call for the work of a creator. [2.65]" It is amazing how some of the greatest men of science run with fear from the truth; the truth that God is the creator of all things. Why do men run in fear of commitment to God as creator and Lord? There are several reasons. One is that they fear the commitment required to become children of God and thereby give up a life of pleasure. Another reason for the seemingly unrealistic denial of God's creation power is the bondage of sin. The reason that these men of science refuse to accept the creation of the universe by God has nothing to do with scientific evidence; the final reasons are concerned with their faith and beliefs.

Does the Universe have an Appearance of Age?

As we have seen, a big controversy between Christians and non-Christians is the age of the universe. Biblical scholars place the estimated age of the earth, and the universe, at around 6,000 years. This estimate is based on the biblical references to men of God and their life spans. The Bible allows us to trace the lineage of man back to Adam and Eve. This places the age of the earth to be approximately 6,000 years old. From the Genesis account, we know that it took God six days to create the universe, and on the seventh day he rested. Since Moses, who wrote the book of Genesis, knew a day as a 24-hour period, some people assume each day in the account was therefore 24 hours. This would make the age of the universe 6,000 years old. This is a considerable discrepancy to the 13-16 billion years estimated by scientists. There is a theoretical possibility that the universe is as young as described in a literal interpretation to the word of God. If we accept that the universe was created by a super natural event i.e. a miracle, then anything is possible. The universe could have an "appearance of age". The concept of the universe having an "appearance of age" is a highly controversial subject and frowned on by scientists. The reason the appearance of age theory is distrusted by scientists is because it places a great deal of emphases on a personal faith in God as the creator. We have seen the importance of faith in science within these first sections. There is still more evidence in other areas of science for the necessity of using a certain amount of faith in science. These subjects will be discussed in subsequent chapters. The appearance of age theory should be treated as any other plausible theory. We need to examine the evidence and then make a personal decision if we accept or reject the theory based on the evidence. Remember, no scientific theory can be proven. When a theory can be used to explain current conditions and be repeated under scientifically approved parameters, then the theory is elevated to the status of a law of physics. A good example is the theory that mass and energy are related by the equation: $E = mc^2$. Since this relationship has been proven in nuclear bombs, reactors and particle accelerator systems it is now called the law of mass and energy equivalence. The principles represented by $E = mc^2$ was once a theory but now is a scientifically proven law.

The appearance of age theory is an important possible solution to resolve the apparent discrepancies between certain geological and radioactive dating evidence and the creation account of Genesis. It would explain a lot of the evidence for the evolutionary perspective and place the evidence in the context of a literal interpretation to the scripture. The theory has not been examined in an appropriate or scientifically justified manner. Instead it has been attacked on the basis of philosophical differences instead of scientific merit. Quote, "The only refuge of the creationist is a device known as 'appearance of age.' He must postulate that a creator, for reasons of his own, made the universe look much older than it actually is, thereby denying us any opportunity to gather actual facts about the age of the planet. This argument allows one to dismiss any scientific evidence as simply an act of deception on the part of the creator. The argument can be used for results in other areas of science as well. The stars in the sky look the way they do not because they are distant galaxies and stars, but because the creator created streams of photons emanating from nonexistent objects. He created an 'apparent' universe. The line of reasoning is, of course, non-disprovable, because a deceptive creator would be capable of nearly anything! ... The 'appearance of age' argument is a complete retreat from scientific argument into the realm of non-testable mysticism. It is the ultimate admission of scientific defeat. [2.66]" What passion, what commitment! This sounds more like a speech from a cult leader on a crusade than a cool headed scientist. We have shown that all scientific theories are based on faith in a set of beliefs of what the physical laws can tell us about the past, present, or future. Evolution is filled with leaps ahead to non-provable conclusions. Yet an acceptance of these "non-testable", "non-disprovable" theories are not referred to as an act of mysticism, but behaving like a "true" scientist. So why is the appearance of age argument considered so objectionable? If you question the age of the universe you attack the theory of evolution and you are faced with an absolute necessity of accepting God as the creator of the universe. Sounds like a purely hypocritical position to me. Let us examine the facts and see if the appearance of age idea is a viable theory.

The appearance of age theorem is used in just two cases. 1) Describing how stars can exist at great distances and still not be billions of years old. 2) The radio-active dating methods used to estimate the age of the earth at 4.5 billion years. We will examine radioactive dating methods and why they are not necessarily accurate. According to the Genesis account, the creation of the stars was made on the fourth day of creation. A supernatural event rather than natural forces made the creation of the stars, like the creation of the universe. If the creation of the stars were by the hand of God, then anything is possible. Was there any deception from God when he made the stars shine from there position to earth? Absolutely not. Our God is the God of truth and light, no deception can be found in Him. There are often things He does that in which we can not comprehend, but God always has a reason for His actions. In the case of the stars, His reasoning is clear. "And God said, 'Let there be lights in the firmament of the heavens to separate the day from the night; and let them be signs for seasons and for days and years, and let them be lights in the firmament of the heavens to give light upon the earth.'" Genesis 1:14-15. The light from the stars were not streams of photons from non-existent points, but the light from the stars was allowed to travel the vast space from their point of origin to earth instantly. God wanted light to shine on the earth, and He wanted man to learn about his position relative to the rest of God's creation in the universe. To have the stars act as signs for the seasons was also necessary, so man would know when to plant seed and harvest his crops. The stars could not have been signs for the seasons if man could not see them. A friend of mine once suggested that the second law of thermodynamics, which states that all natural systems run down, may have been the result of the fall of man. Perhaps many limitations on physical laws occurred after the fall of man, including the limit of the velocity of light. In any case, the stars exist and we can see them. I believe we should not use the great distance that appear to exist in the boundaries of the universe as an indicator to the age of the universe. This is only an opinion; the final judgment is yours.

There is another possible explanation of how the universe could be 6,000 years old and yet the light from distant stars can reach our eyes. "An intriguing creationist theory has been proposed which involves a white hole cosmology, a bound universe, an initial water mass, and Einstein's theory of general relativity. This cosmology allows for a literal six-day creation in the frame of reference of the earth (which is taken to be somewhere in the vicinity of the center of the universe) … It also allows for an expanding universe and red shifts as observed. Other predictions of this theory, such as the temperature of the cosmic background radiation, have yet to be worked out in detail. [2.67]" To the reader wondering about the work towards a plausible theory explaining this problem in the creation, patience please! There is enormous latitude given to skeptical atheistic theories, and we have yet to rise up a Christian genius of the caliber of Stephan Hawking. The solution to the theory is probable a re-working of general relativity. It time, the work might be completed. If not, we are secure in the vast scientific evidence for God's creation of the universe. There is no need to debate the age of the universe as relevant.

We have discussed Hawking's use of the equations to express his personal beliefs. When his research led him to believe in the existence of God he reversed his work. How did he do this? You can manipulate the equations to give you the results you want rather easily. In higher forms of mathematical expressions you can justify any theory, with few limitations. Let us see exactly how Stephan Hawking is able to disprove his previous work and describe the universe beginning without a singularity. "But it's also important to note that he is only able to achieve this rounding-off effect by substituting 'imaginary numbers' for real numbers in his equations.' 'What are imaginary numbers?' 'They are multiples of the square root of negative one,' he said 'In this model, they have the effect of turning time into a dimension of space. The problem is that when imaginary numbers are employed they're just computational devices used to grease the equations and get the result the mathematician wants. That's fine, but when you want to get a real, physical result, you have to convert the imaginary numbers into real ones. But Hawking refuses to convert them. He just keeps everything in the imaginary realm.' … He doesn't pretend to be describing reality, because he says he doesn't know what reality is. So Hawking himself recognizes that it is not a realistic description of the universe or its origin; it's merely a mathematical way of modeling the beginning of the universe in such a manner that the singularity doesn't appear. [2.68]" The reality that God created the universe can not be ignored. No amount of mathematical manipulation can change the truth of God's word.

Is there any Additional Evidence for a Young Universe?

There are many examples in the various fields of science pointing to a young universe with a 6-day creation. In the book In Six Days: Why fifty scientists chose to believe in creation by Dr. John Ashton, many examples are given. One example in Astronomy concerns the orbit of the moon. "Most people assume that the moon has been orbiting the earth since about the time the two bodies formed. To most scientists, the time of formation for either body would have been about 4.5 billion years ago; for recent creationists it was about 6,000 years ago. Over a century ago George Darwin, the astronomer son of the famous Charles Darwin, discovered that the moon is slowly spiraling away from the earth. … Each year the moon moves about 4cm farther from the earth, and the day is increasing at a rate of 0.0016 seconds per century. These are very modest changes, but over time they accumulate. More interesting, the rate of tidal evolution is a very step function of the earth-moon distance, so in the past when the moon was much closer to the earth the rate to change would have been far greater than today. Fixing the modern rate and extrapolating the theory into the past, we find that the moon would have been in contact with the earth as recently as 1.3 billion years ago, about one-third the supposed age of the earth-moon system. About a billion years ago the moon would have been so close to the earth to cause monstrously high tides. No one believes that this was the case. [2.69]" How do the evolutionists response to this apparent non-congruent evidence. "They assert that we live in a time of unusually fast tidal interaction, and that in the past the tidal interaction was far less. This is a possibility, but how does it stand up to scrutiny? Let us assume that the world is billions of years old and that rock layers have been laid down over time pretty much as scientists claim. There have been several studies of fine layers of sedimentary rock that supposedly show daily high and low tides. … These studies span over a half billion years and show that the current rate has been prevalent during this time. This means that by the evolutionists' own data the current rate of tidal evolution is not unusually large. [2.70]" This is a classic example of how simply studying evolutionary theories, very often their own data will conflict with their own theories. Often evolutionists supply large amounts of evidence for creation. You simply need to look more closely at the information presented. Read the articles in periodicals carefully and you will find evidence for God's act of creation.

Another example in Astrophysics suggesting a young universe is the presence of comets. "Comets are extremely fragile things. Comets may be lost by collisions with planets, as witnessed in 1994 when a comet smashed into Jupiter. Another catastrophic loss of comets is by gravitational forces of planets that kick comets out of the solar system. This has been observed a number of times. Perhaps more often comets just wear out. ... As a comet nucleus loses material each orbit, there is less material available in each successive orbit. Since comets gradually wear out, we can estimate an upper limit upon the length of time that comets can orbit our sun. Even with the most generous of assumptions, there should be no comets left after a few tens of millions of years. [2.71]" Do evolutionist have an explanation? Of course, they always have a response in this endless debate between evolution and creationism. "Short period comets are said to originate in the Kuiper belt, a collection of comet nuclei orbiting the sun beyond the orbit of Neptune, while long period comets come from the Oort cloud, a swarm of comet nuclei orbiting much farther out. Gravitational perturbations are suggested to rob comet nuclei of energy and cause them to fall unto the inner solar system to replace older comets as the older comets die. [2.72]" So you have a neat continuous flow of comets wearing out and almost instantly replaced by other comets from the Oort cloud. Is there any empirical data to support this theory? The answer is no. "No Oort cloud object has ever been detected, and given the great distance of the hypothetical Oort cloud, none likely ever will. [2.73]" Both sides of the endless debate over describing the universe start their arguments with assumption about the existence of God. One side presumes God exists, the other that there is no God. Faith is constantly become stretched and evaluated with every scientific theory. Why should we suggest that we should only believe in evolution in our public schools? Why do we allow the promotion of atheism? Atheism is a set of beliefs. Part of those beliefs includes: There is no God. Natural forces are eternal having no end and no beginning. We are the products of random chance. Because our environment controls our development we are expect to return hate for hate. This is a radically different belief system from the brotherly love taught in the gospels.

The creationist view is that the universe began as a supernatural act. God does his day to day work through ordinary natural laws. However, there are specific times God uses supernatural forces to accomplish His tasks. When God acts in a supernaturally way there is a well-planed reason for God's actions. The purpose for super natural events is for God to show His abundant love toward us. All supernatural events have this quality, parting the red sea, the miracles of Jesus, the death and resurrection of Jesus and so on. All the supernatural events described in the Bible were to teach mankind a message or to provide for our well being. We must be willing to accept the limitations of science in order to investigate the universe. Science often is has little to do with historical events. I do not wish to minimize the accomplishments of the scientific field of Archeology. However, scientific investigation often fails in the explanation of historical events. For more information, look at chapter 10 and the works of Josh McDowell. God can not be proven to exist scientifically, but I know He exist because of my faith in the word of God. As I accepted Jesus Christ as savior and Lord, His Holy Spirit filled my life, as was promised by Jesus. The appearance of age theory or any other idea routed in the word of God does not discourage scientific research, but rather encourages scientific study. Why? Consult the Introduction to this book. Probably the best way to verify this truth is to read the book of proverbs. It encourages men to seek all the wisdom they can from the very first verse. "The proverbs of Solomon, son of David, king of Israel: That men may know wisdom and instruction, understand words of insight, ... that prudence may be given to the simple, knowledge and desecration to the youth- the wise man also man hear and increase in learning ... making your ear attentive to wisdom and inclining your heart to understanding; yes, if you cry out for insight and raise your voice for understanding, if you seek it like silver and search for it as hidden treasures; then you will understand the fear of the Lord and find the knowledge of God. For the Lord gives wisdom; from his mouth comes knowledge and understanding; he stores up sound wisdom for the upright; he is a shield to those who walk in integrity, ... for wisdom will come into your heart, and knowledge will watch over you; understanding will guard you; deliver you from the way of evil, ... Get wisdom; get insight. Do not forsake her, and she will keep you; love her, and she will guard you. Prize her highly, and she will exalt you; she will honor you if you embrace her." -Proverbs 1:1-5, 2:2-12, 4:5, 6, 8. These verses, and many more like them, speak of wisdom as a great treasure, a woman to be cherished, a source of strength, and a means to be closer to God and honor Him as Lord. This is why the scientific search for truth and wisdom is very important to the Christian. We welcome any intelligent debate over various ideas interpreting current scientific research. It is consistently the atheists, naturalists and evolutionists that become wildly emotional when responding to tough questions about their theories. "Heaven and earth will pass away, but my words will never pass away." Matthew 24:35. The Bible is complete, perfect and without error. The whole Bible is uniquely connected, from Genesis to Revelation. "I warn every one who hears the words of the prophecy of this book: if any one adds to them, God will add to him the plagues described in this book, and if any one takes away from the words of the book of this prophecy, God will take away his share in the tree of life and in the holy city, which are described in this book." Revelation 22:18-19. This promise can be applied to the entire word of God. There are many warnings of tampering with God's word in scripture. The cult religions should read them over again.

How big is the Universe?

The Trigonometric Parallax Method

Since the distance between the stars is a crucial part of theories concerning the age of the universe, we should examine the procedure used to determine distances between stars. One of the most important techniques used in determining distances is the parallax measurement. The parallax is: quote, "the apparent shift in the position of an object caused by the shift in the observer's position. [2.74]" As the Earth moves around the sun, there is an apparent shift in the position of the stars. The principle can be understood by a simple experiment. "Hold your finger in front of your face and look past it toward some distant objects. Your finger represents a nearby star; the objects, distant stars. Your right represents the view on one side of the sun. Your left eye represents the view 3 months latter... First wink one eye, then the other. Your finger (the nearby star) seams to shift back and forth. Hold your finger only a few centimeters from your eyes; the shift is larger. Hold your finger at arm's length; the shift is smaller. Likewise, the further away the nearby star, the smaller the parallax. [2.75]" This describes how scientists determine the distances between the stars and earth, i.e. by the angle measurements given by the parallax method. This method seams fairly accurate for determine distances between the earth and nearby stars, but is useless when dealing with stars at great distances. "Thus if a star is too distant, its parallax is too small to be measured. Parallaxes smaller than about 1/20 second of arc are difficult to measure accurately. Therefore stars further away than about 20pc are beyond the distant limit for reliable parallaxes, although distances from 20pc to 100 pc can be roughly estimated by the parallax technique. [2.76]" The abbreviation pc stands for parsecs, 3.26 light years. The methods used to determine the distances from the earth to stars beyond the 100-pc mark, becomes highly complex. The distance to the most remote quasar is estimated at 10,000,000,000 pc. There is a great difference between 100 pc and the 10 billion pc. Why do Astronomers believe the universe is so vast? Astronomers use a complex series of equations to estimate that quasars are tiny objects existing at vast distances. Since the discovery of quasars, there has been a great deal of scientific debate to whether they are really tiny objects at great distances or if they exist closer than we currently believe. The reason for the skepticism over the size of quasars is that quasars produce more power from a smaller space than is predicted with the current ideas of nuclear physics. This means if that these objects produce this much power at such a vast distance,

Einstein's special theory of relativity is violated! Objects greater than 100 parsecs or so can not be seen with telescopes on earth. They are "seen" by radio signals received at astronomical tracking stations. The ability to see objects that seam to exist at vast distances from earth has been greatly improved by the Hubble Telescope. The Hubble Telescope has become a widely used instrument in extending and improving our observations from earth. The question still remains, could the universe be smaller than previously believed? Distances of stars in the 100 pc range would be easily acceptable from the Christian perspective. After all, the light reaching earth from a star 100 pc away would have begun only 326 years ago. Stars at this distance would definitely not give an extremely long age to the universe. Apparent brightness has been an important factor in determining the distance of stars. It was found quote, "the brightness of stars have apparent magnitudes about 25 magnitudes fainter than the sun. In 1829, the English scientist William Wollaston used this simple fact to estimate that most typical stars must be at least 100,000 times more distant than the sun, since dimming by 25 magnitudes corresponds to increasing distance 100,000 times. [2.77]" This procedure was one of the first attempts to determine the distance of the stars from earth. Other stellar properties, such as chemical composition, position on the HR star life cycle diagram, nuclear properties of the star, and temperature of the star are used in estimating distances of stars past the 100pc mark.

Methods for calculating the distances of stars beyond 100pc are usually variations of examining apparent brightness of the star. "More than a dozen methods are used to measure distances in the universe. ... Among the various techniques, Cepheid variable stars are the key distant calibrators. The intrinsic brightness of each Cepheid is directly related to its rhythmic oscillations in luminosity. For instance, a Cepheid with a long period of oscillation has a high intrinsic brightness, like a 100-watt light bulb, whereas a short-period Cepheid would be a 40-watt bulb, and so on. Comparing the real luminosity, or wattage, with the apparent brightness reveals the distance. [2.78]" Are these calculations accurate? We will not go into all the methods mentioned. However, I believe we can accept the calculations for the size of the universe. What has this to do with the age of the universe? Again, size is intimately bound with the age of the universe according to modern astronomical theory. There doesn't seam to be a physical principle to resolve this apparent conflict with the biblical record. However, there are many theoretical possibilities. For example, we know that light travels in packages of massless particles called photons. When a light is first turned on, there can be a measured time difference between the time light was first generated and are receiving the image. Scientists have conducted experiments by sending signals back form the moon to verify the speed of light. However, when an image is being sent it travels in a continuous wave pattern. Unless there is someone at the location where the light ray began monitoring the time an event occurred, there is no way of truly knowing when the light left the apparatus. This is also true about light coming from distant astronomical objects. There could be an event; admittedly violating the property that light travels at a definite speed, when an image was sent to earth instantaneously. At that point, we could not distinguish when the event took place because a constant supply of images in the form of waves would continue being sent creating a constant picture. How long ago did this event occur? If God set these principles in place there is no way of knowing when these events took place because distance is no longer a factor in the calculation and the images are effectively timeless.

The Age of the Universe

The most controversial topic between Christians and astronomers, who believe in the theory of evolution, is the amount of time involved in the creation of the universe. An article in the May-92 issue of the magazine Scientific American illustrates the conflict between different estimates to the age of the universe. The article states that Astronomers found globular clusters that appear to be older than the latest estimates of the age of the universe. Objects such as globular cluster M13 appear to be between 13 to 14 billion years old. The accepted age of the universe at the time of this article was 8 to 12 billion years. The article proposes several explanations for the inconsistencies. One suggestion was to re-evaluating

Hubbell's constant. The article speculates that some localized areas of the universe expanded at different rates. Thus, it may be possible that the age of the globular clusters, because of their exceedingly great distance from the center of the universe, might be inaccurate. There is one flaw in the proposal, there doesn't seam to be any evidence to support the theory of parts of the universe expanding at different rates. The Hubbell constant seams to uniformly apply everywhere in the universe. Currently the age of the universe is mostly determined by observing how far the universe has expanded, determined by tracking devices. Radio telescopes receive "pictures" from what is believed to be the edge of the universe. It is assumed that the universe has been steadily expanding since its beginning. Scientists believe that the universe began from a central location. Taking into consideration the rate of currant expansion the distances traveled by the stars an age is given to the universe. Estimates to the age of the universe are constantly being revised. Over the years I have witnessed many different and conflicting estimates to the age of the universe. In newspapers, journals, textbooks and other sources the estimates have changed with new calculations and new discoveries. The encyclopedia Encarta has the following statements concerning the age of the universe. "Current calculations place the age of the universe at 10 billion to 15 billion years." [2.79] Then latter in the section concerning the Hubble's constant the following statement is made. "If cosmologists measure the rate of expansion by examining galactic red shifts and estimate the density of the universe, they can calculate an estimate of the universe's age. Cosmologists calculate the expansion rate of the universe by finding the relationship between the distance of an object from Earth and the rate at which it is moving away from Earth. This relationship is represented by Hubble's constant, H in the formula $v = H \times d$, where v is velocity (or the speed of the object) and d is the distance between the object and Earth." [2.80] And on the rate of expansion of the universe: "The American astronomer Alan Sandage and the Swiss astronomer Gustav Tammann have used a variety of methods to come up with an expansion estimate of 55 km/sec/megaparsec (about 34 mi/sec/megaparsec). A megaparsec is 1 million parsecs, and a parsec is about 3.26 light-years (a light year is the distance that light could travel in a year— 9.5×10^{12} km, or 5.9×10^{12} mi). So far, the cosmologists using the Hubble Space Telescope have found a value of about 70 km/sec/megaparsec (44 mi/sec/megaparsec) for the expansion rate of the universe. These expansion rates correspond to a universe between 8 billion and 13 billion years old. [2.81]" As we discussed in Chapter 1, it is now believed that, due to some unknown force, the rate of expansion is increasing rather than decreasing. Why do scientists become highly emotional when we question their estimates to the age of the universe? Is the range between 10-15 billion years or 8-13 billion? Is there any possibility that there is an "apparent age" and the universe is actually younger than any of these estimates? If we state we believe these estimates are irrelevant, atheists take it as a personal attack. The atheist has great faith in evolution as the source of creation in the universe. When we show inaccuracies in the amount of time that appears to have past in the universe, an atheist can become very insecure and hostile to a Christian's legitimate questions. In schools, many times the students are expected to accept the current estimates as if they are absolute fact instead of the product of a theory. Quote, "The virtually infinite variations of life <u>are</u> the fruit of the evolutionary process. All living creatures <u>are</u> related by decent from common ancestors. Humans and other animals <u>are</u> descended from shrew-like creatures <u>that lived more than 150,000,000 years</u> ago; mammals, birds, reptiles, amphibians, and fishes share as ancestors aquatic <u>worms that lived 6,000,000,000 years ago</u>; all planets and animals <u>are</u> derived from bacteria-like microorganisms that originated <u>more than 3,000,000,000 years ago</u>."[2.82]

The Hubble Telescope

Since the time of my original research many astonishing discoveries in observing the universe has been made by using the Hubble Telescope. Some of the older methods used with earth bound telescopes seam obsolete. "Not since Galileo turned his telescope towards the heavens in 1610 has any event so changed our understanding of the universe as the deployment of the Hubble Space Telescope. Hubble orbits 600 kilometers (375 miles) above Earth, working around the clock to unlock the secrets of the

Universe. It uses excellent pointing precision, powerful optics, and state-of-the-art instruments to provide stunning views of the Universe that cannot be made using ground-based telescopes or other satellites. Hubble was originally designed in the 1970s and launched in 1990. ... Hubble's accomplishments are extraordinary. Before Hubble, distances to far-off galaxies were not well known. Questions such as how rapidly the universe is expanding, and for how long, created great controversy. Hubble data has changed all of that. Every day, Hubble archives 3 to 5 gigabytes of data and delivers between 10 and 15 gigabytes to astronomers all over the world. As of March 2000, Hubble has: Taken more than 330,000 separate observations. Observed more than 25,000 astronomical targets. Created a data archive of over 7.3 terabytes. (That is like completely filling a PC every day for 10 years.) Provided data for more than 2,663 scientific papers, Traveled about 1.489 billion miles nearly the distance from Earth to Uranus. It circles the Earth about every 97 minutes. [2.83]" We have mentioned a few of the unexpected findings of the Hubble Telescope. 1) The universal expansion seams to be faster than previously calculated. 2) The rate of expansion seams to be increasing. 3) There is an amazing uniformity to the universe.

The Hubble is truly a remarkable device. "From detector technology to astronaut tools, the Hubble team is always looking for ways to make performance better. Now over 10 years old (launched in 1990), the telescope is basically a new machine. Upgrades and maintenance keep Hubble operating in top condition to give us the greatest scientific data possible. Since Hubble's modular design allows for these in-orbit instrument and equipment upgrades, the astronauts are also able to bring back the equipment that is being replaced. The ability to refurbish the returned science instruments has proven to be a cost-effective way to enhance the telescope with the latest technology. By installing the new technology in recycled modules, NASA avoids "reinventing the wheel" and reduces the overall cost of science data. From manufacturing to medicine, the creative designs and innovative re-uses are some of the many Hubble improvements which translate into benefits for us all. [2.84]" I believe it was Wednesday March 10 2004 when I read an article about, perhaps, the greatest discovery of the Hubble Telescope. This discovery is described on the NASA web site: "This image from the Hubble Space Telescope provides a glimpse at a tiny sliver of the universe like looking at the sky through a straw. It shows at least 1,500 galaxies at varying distances and at different stages of evolution. Some galaxies are so far away; we see them, as they were billions of years ago, representing what the universe looked like in its earliest stage perhaps less than a billion years after the big bang. To create this image, scientists pointed the Hubble Space Telescope at a single spot for 10 days to capture even the faintest objects. By studying Hubble deep field, scientists hope to answer many questions about the number, evolution, and ultimate fate of galaxies in the universe. If it's hard to grasp the size of the universe, it's equally hard to imagine its age. Astronomers calculate that the universe originated about 13 billion years ago in an explosion of space called the big bang. At that time, all the matter and energy in our observable universe was packed together in a volume smaller than an atom. No one knows what happened before the big bang or what caused the explosion our laws of physics can't explain it but in an instant the energy and matter of our universe poured into existence and expanded with space itself. We still see the evidence of the big bang today, as the superclusters of galaxies continue to fly apart from each other. We also observe the remnant glow of the big bang itself in the form of faint microwave light from all parts of the sky. [2.85]" We have already discussed in great detail the fact that the creation of the universe is still a great mystery that defies the laws of physics. We have also thoroughly discussed the above mentioned background radiation and the uniformity it represents. These images will be studied for years to determine more about the conditions at the beginning of the universe. Does this evidence support the premise of order forming by natural laws out of chaos? The debate has just begun concerning this new discovery. The present evidence shows an unexplainable uniformity in the universe.

More details about this amazing discovery are continued in an article on the NASA web site. "Astronomers at the Space Telescope Science Institute today unveiled the deepest portrait of the visible universe ever achieved by humankind. Called the Hubble Ultra Deep Field (HUDF), the million-second-long exposure reveals the first galaxies to emerge from the so-called "dark ages," the time shortly after the big bang when the first stars reheated the cold, dark universe. The new image should offer new insights into what types of objects reheated the universe long ago. This historic new view is actually two separate images taken by Hubble's Advanced Camera for Surveys (ACS) and the Near Infrared Camera and Multi-object Spectrometer (NICMOS). Both images reveal galaxies that are too faint to be seen by ground-based telescopes, or even in Hubble's previous faraway looks, called the Hubble Deep Fields (HDFs), taken in 1995 and 1998. 'Hubble takes us to within a stone's throw of the big bang itself,' says Massimo Stiavelli of the Space Telescope Science Institute in Baltimore, Md., and the HUDF project lead. The combination of ACS and NICMOS images will be used to search for galaxies that existed between 400 and 800 million years (corresponding to a redshift range of 7 to 12) after the big bang. A key question for HUDF astronomers is whether the universe appears to be the same at this very early time as it did when the cosmos was between 1 and 2 billion years old. The HUDF field contains an estimated 10,000 galaxies. In ground-based images, the patch of sky in which the galaxies reside (just one-tenth the diameter of the full Moon) is largely empty. Located in the constellation Fornax, the region is below the constellation Orion. The final ACS image, assembled by Anton Koekemoer of the Space Telescope Science Institute, is studded with a wide range of galaxies of various sizes, shapes, and colors. In vibrant contrast to the image's rich harvest of classic spiral and elliptical galaxies, there is a zoo of oddball galaxies littering the field. Some look like toothpicks; others like links on a bracelet. A few appear to be interacting. Their strange shapes are a far cry from the majestic spiral and elliptical galaxies we see today. These oddball galaxies chronicle a period when the universe was more chaotic. Order and structure were just beginning to emerge. ... observations began Sept. 24, 2003 and continued through Jan. 16, 2004. The telescope's ACS camera, the size of a phone booth, captured ancient photons of light that began traversing the universe even before Earth existed. Photons of light from the very faintest objects arrived at a trickle of one photon per minute, compared with millions of photons per minute from nearer galaxies. Just like the previous HDFs, the new data are expected to galvanize the astronomical community and lead to dozens of research papers that will offer new insights into the birth and evolution of galaxies. [2.85]" There are many things we could discuss about these discoveries. First, the unexpected result of these observations was the complexity and completeness of the early universe. Also, there was detected the existence of heavier elements, like boron, in the very early universe. This was unexpected because it was always assumed that during the earliest stages of development, the universe would be almost entirely made of hydrogen, helium, and perhaps a few elements from the carbon-cycle of nuclear fusion. More about these observations will be discussed in our next chapter.

The study of Astronomy correlates many disciplines of Physics, biology, chemistry and other scientific fields when applied to theories about the origin of life on this planet. Next we will explore different theories on how all these objects in the universe could be related. The discovery of planets outside our own solar system brings new life to a discussion about evolution. Is there life on other planets? These questions will be discussed in the next chapter. To summarize these last two chapters, if you believe there is a simple natural explanation to the formation of the universe, you do don't understand basic principles of science. The laws of physics summarized in Einstein's General Theory of relativity clearly state that the universe was made by forces beyond our comprehension. There are mathematical limits to natural forces. We will explore these limits in chapter 7 on the principles of mathematics and chapters 8 and 9 on physics. If you think science has a natural explanation to the beginning of the universe, you do not fully understand the fields of mathematics, physics or the formulas of General Relativity already briefly covered. It requires a leap of faith to accept that there could be any possibility of a natural explanation to the origin of the universe. The laws of physics describe limitations on the magnitude of the gravitational and electromagnetic forces. There is also a limit on the range the strong and weak forces can influence objects. Based on these limitations, clearly the universe was made by the "super-natural" power of God and all of creation is beyond a "natural" explanation.

References for Chapter 2

2.1   John Boslough, Stephen Hawking's Universe: The Man and the Theories Behind the Bestseller, A BRIEF HISTORY OF TIME, New York, Avon Books, 1985, p. 49.

2.2   Ibid, Back Cover- quote from Chicago Tribune.

2.3   Ibid, p. 40.

2.4   Ibid, p. 41- 46.

2.5   Lee Strobel, The Case for A Creator, Zondervan, Grand Rapids Michigan. 2004, p 97.

2.6   Ibid, p. 98.

2.7   Ibid, p. 107.

2.8   Ibid p. 107-108.

2.9   Ibid p. 118.

2.10   Ibid p. 118.

2.11   Ibid p. 119.

2.12   Ibid p. 119.

2.13   John Boslough, Stephen Hawking's Universe: The Man and the Theories Behind the Bestseller, A BRIEF HISTORY OF TIME, New York, Avon Books, 1985, p. 17.

2.14   Ibid, p. 40.

2.15   Ibid, p. 36-37.

2.16   Lee Strobel, The Case For A Creator, Zondervan, Grand Rapids Michigan. 2004, p 113.

2.17   Ibid p. 114.

2.18   Ibid p. 114.

2.19   Ibid p. 113.

2.20   Ibid p. 113.

2.21   John Boslough, Stephen Hawking's Universe: The Man and the Theories Behind the Bestseller, A BRIEF HISTORY OF TIME, New York, Avon Books, 1985, p. 43.

2.22   Ibid p. 47.

2.23   Ibid p. 35.

2.24   Ibid p. 48.

2.25   Ibid p. 43-44.

2.26   Ibid p. 75.

2.27   Ibid p. 75-77.

2.28   Ibid p. 77-78.

2.29   Raymond A. Serway, Physics For Scientists & Engineers with Modern Physics Third edition, Philadelphia, Saunders College Publishing, 1990, p.1110.

2.30   Lincoln Barnett, The Universe and Dr. Einstein, Bantam Books, New York, New York, 1957, p. 109-113.

2.31   Tim Folger, The Big Bang Machine, Discover Magazine, February 2007, p. 36-37.

2.32   Ibid p. 38.

2.33   Ibid p. 34-38.

2.34   Lincoln Barnett, The Universe and Dr. Einstein, Bantam Books, New York, New York, 1957, p. 117-118.

2.35   John Boslough, Stephen Hawking's Universe: The Man and the Theories Behind the Bestseller, A Brief History Of Time, New York, Avon Books, 1985, p.78.

2.36   Ibid p.80-81.

2.37   Ibid p.81.

2.38   Ibid p. 88.

2.39   Ibid p. 81-82.

2.40   Ibid p.83.

2.41   Ibid p.83.

2.42   Ibid p.83-84.

2.43   Ibid p.84.

2.44   Ibid p. 88-89.

2.45   Ibid p. 93.

2.46   Ibid p. 91-92.

2.47   Ibid p. 100-101.

2.48   Ibid p. 101.

2.49   Ibid p. 101.

2.50   Microsoft® Encarta® Encyclopedia 2002. © 1993-2001 Microsoft Corporation., Article: Cosmology, Section III, Modern Cosmology, Section E, Inflationary Theory, by Jay M. Pasachoff.

2.51   William K. Hartmann, Astronomy: The Cosmic Journey, Belmont California, Wadsworth Publishing, 1991, P.422.

2.52   Albert Einstein, Relativity: The Special and General Theory, Crown Publishers, New York. MCMLXI, overview of book topics in my own words.

2.53   Lee Strobel, The Case For A Creator, Zondervan, Grand Rapids Michigan. 2004, p. 276.

2.54   John Boslough, Stephen Hawking's Universe: The Man and the Theories Behind the Bestseller, A Brief History Of Time, New York, Avon Books, 1985, p.79-80.

2.55   Ibid p. 109.

2.56   Ibid p. 109.

2.57   Ibid p. 109-110.

2.58   William K. Hartmann, Astronomy: The Cosmic Journey, Belmont California, Wadsworth Publishing, 1991, P.596.

2.59   Meir H. Degani, Astronomy Made Simple, Garden City, New York, Made Simple Books, Doubleday & Company, 1976, p. 112.

2.60   Josh McDowell & Don Stewart, Reasons Skeptics Should Consider Christianity, Wheaton, Illinois, Living Books, Tyndale House Publishers, 1981 p. 126.

2.61   John Boslough, Stephen Hawking's Universe: The Man and the Theories Behind the Bestseller, A Brief History Of Time, New York, Avon Books, 1985, p.67.

2.62   Josh McDowell & Don Stewart, Reasons Skeptics Should Consider Christianity, Wheaton, Illinois, Living Books, Tyndale House Publishers, 1981, p. 127-128.

2.63   John Boslough, Stephen Hawking's Universe: The Man and the Theories Behind the Bestseller, A Brief History Of Time, New York, Avon Books, 1985, p.112.

2.64   Ibid p.113-114.

2.65   Ibid p.112.

2.66   William K. Hartmann, Astronomy: The Cosmic Journey, Belmont California, Wadsworth Publishing, 1991, p. 643.

2.67   John F. Ashton, In Six Days: Why Fifty Scientists choose to believe in Creation, Master Books, 2000- 2003, p. 106.

2.68   Lee Strobel, The Case for A Creator, Zondervan, Grand Rapids Michigan. 2004, p.120.

2.69   John F. Ashton, In Six Days: Why Fifty Scientists choose to believe in Creation, Master Books, 2000-2003, p.272-273.

2.70   Ibid p. 273.

2.71   Ibid p. 275.

2.72   Ibid p. 275.

2.73   Ibid p. 276.

2.74   William K. Hartmann, Astronomy: The Cosmic Journey, Belmont California, Wadsworth Publishing, 1991, p.352.

2.75   Ibid p.352.

2.76   Ibid p.353.

2.77   Ibid p.352.

2.78   Terence Dickinson, The Universe and Beyond third edition, Firefly Books Ltd.,1999, p.100.

2.79   CD-ROM, Microsoft® Encarta® Encyclopedia 2002. © 1993-2001 Microsoft Corporation., Article: Cosmology, Section III, Modern Cosmology, Section A The Big Bang Theory, by Jay M. Pasachoff.

2.80   Ibid, Section IV: Cosmological Evidence.

2.81   Ibid.

2.82   Edited by Ashley Montagu, Science and Creationism, Oxford, Oxford University Press, 1984, L. Beverly Halstead, Evolution- The Fossils Say Yes! p. 100.

2.83   http://hubble.gsfc.nasa.gov/overview/ March 9, 2004, Don Savage NASA Headquarters.

2.84   Ibid.

2.85   Ibid.

2.86   http://www.nasa.gov/vision/universe/starsgalaxies/hubble_UDF.html.

Illustrations for Chapter 2

2.1   William J. Kaufmann, III, Black Holes and Warped Spacetime, W.H. Freeman and Company, San Francisco, 1979, Left side: p. 77. Right side : p.100.

2.2   Ibid. p. 192.

2.3   Raymond A. Serway, Physics For Scientists & Engineers with Modern Physics Third edition, Philadelphia, Saunders College Publishing, 1990, p. 1203.

2.4   Martin M. Lipschutz, Schaum's Outline of Theory and Problems of Differential Geometry, McGraw-Hill Book Company, 1969, p. 151 and p. 155.

2.5   William K. Hartmann, Astronomy: The Cosmic Journey, Belmont California, Wadsworth Publishing, 1991, p.423.

Astronomy Part 3: Star Formation and Development

The Composition and Structure of the Stars

In the last two chapters we discussed the creation of the universe in general. Now we will discuss the composition of the stars, which populate the galaxies. The first scientific concept, which will be explored in this chapter, is the chemical and nuclear changes, which occur in stars. In this chapter, we will discuss current theories about changes in the structure of stars. We will discuss how these ideas can have a profound testimony to the glory of God. Until recently, the structure of the stars was very mysterious. "Twinkle, twinkle little star. How I wonder what you are. Up above the world so high, like a diamond in the sky." This is more than just a child's song. This is an accurate description of our state of knowledge about stars before modern astronomy was born in the early 1900's. Until the development of nuclear physics, we knew very little beyond the fact that stars were shinning points of light in the sky. It was speculated that the stars were similar to our sun, only existing at great distances from the earth. Beyond this concept, we did not know any more about the stars, except that the stars appeared to move as the seasons changed and as time passed over the night sky. The biggest mystery confronting early astronomers was the star's fuel supply. Even with the immense size of the sun, there didn't seam to be enough mass for the sun to produce so much energy. By conventional means of combustion, the sun should have used up it's entire fuel supply long ago and be left in ashes. In 1905, Einstein released his Special Theory of Relativity. This landmark theory reshaped the way we think about the universe. [3.1] It specified that an enormous amount of energy was contained in a small amount of matter. Ordinary chemical means released only a tiny fraction of the total energy contained within the material body. The mysterious fuel supply was becoming clearer. Today we realize that the fuel source for the stars, like our sun, is the fusion of hydrogen nuclei.

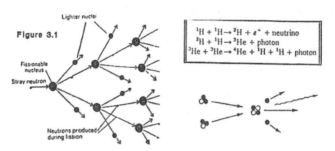

Figure 3.1

$$^1H + {}^1H \rightarrow {}^2H + e^+ + \text{neutrino}$$
$$^2H + {}^1H \rightarrow {}^3He + \text{photon}$$
$$^3He + {}^3He \rightarrow {}^4He + {}^1H + {}^1H + \text{photon}$$

Figure 3.1

Einstein's theory of relativity led to the nuclear power plants and atomic weapons we have today. Nuclear devices use a chain reaction to continue their nuclear processes. There are two types of nuclear reactions: nuclear fission (figure 3.1 on the left) and nuclear fusion (figure 3.1 on the right). Nuclear fission occurs when you split the atom. Atoms that can split and form a chain reaction are sometimes called fissionable material. There are several types of atoms you can split. The most commonly used atomic element in A-bombs is Plutonium. The other type of nuclear reaction is fusion. This is the process used by the stars. Most fusion reactions involve two hydrogen atoms which fuse together to form helium. In both types of nuclear reactions, there is a tremendous amount of energy released with only a small loss in mass. Both types of nuclear processes produce a chain reaction. A chain reaction is the result of the nuclear process that produces by-products, which will serve to continue the reaction. In both fusion and fission, a steady supply of neutrons is required. In A-bombs you have a collection of fissionable material, like plutonium, at the core. Injectors supply the nuclear pile with fast moving neutrons causing the atoms of plutonium to split into two parts. This produces two radioactive by-products and two or more fast moving neutrons. The number of neutrons produced, depends upon the fission fragments produced in the reaction, see fig 3.1. These neutrons quickly interact with another atom of fissionable material, which in turn produces two more new neutrons [3.2]. There is a domino effect, with each nuclear process setting off another nuclear reaction. It can be compared to setting off a string of firecrackers, and will not stop until all of the nuclear material is used up. There is one important difference in comparing nuclear reactions to a domino effect, where a set of dominos is positioned to knock over a set of upright dominos. With dominoes, you just have one domino hitting one other domino. With nuclear reactions, you have one neutron starting the nuclear process and producing two new neutrons, continuing the process with two new reactions. You don't just produce one reaction, but two. Therefore, the nuclear reactions increase exponentially. You can use up the fissionable material in the reaction chamber very quickly with the chain reaction processes. Nuclear reactors control the flow of neutrons and thereby produce a controlled reaction instead of the uncontrolled reaction in a nuclear bomb. The nuclear fusion within the sun is also experiencing a chain reaction, which provides warmth and energy for our world. The chain reactions have continued over many years and the size of the sun is actually shrinking little by little. But don't worry; the sun has enough fuel supply for billions of years to come. [3.3]

There are a number of fusion reactions possible. The nuclear reaction that occurs inside the sun is identical to the chain reaction occurring in an H-bomb. The process takes three steps to complete the reaction. First, two hydrogen atoms are forced together and they produce deuterium (a hydrogen isotope that has two protons), an electron, and a neutrino $^1H + {}^1H \rightarrow {}^2H + e^+ +$ neutrino. The second step takes place when the deuterium produced in the first stage fuses with an ordinary hydrogen element, $^1H + {}^2H \rightarrow {}^3He +$ photon. This produces a helium isotope, having three protons in the nucleus and a photon. Light actually is a mass-less particle traveling through space called a photon. More about the wave-particle duality of light will be discussed in later chapters. In the last stage of hydrogen fusion, the two helium isotopes combine to produce an ordinary helium atom and two ordinary hydrogen atoms plus another photon, $^3He + {}^3He \rightarrow {}^4He + {}^1H + {}^1H +$ photon. The photons produced are the carriers of light, heat, gamma rays and other electromagnetic waves and massless particles. The final reaction leaves the elements needed to start the first stage again, two atoms of hydrogen $^1H + {}^1H$. This series of reactions shows the real value of nuclear fusion. The fusion process is clean, with no harmful radioactive by-products. The only left over "waste" is harmless helium. Much research is continuing in the study of developing controlled nuclear fusion. Deuterium is found naturally on the earth in small quantities. It is found in some water samples and is called heavy water. This is what was most concerning when Nazi Germany began heavy water experiments. Fortunately, the allies defeated Hitler before they could complete their experiments to produce a Hydrogen bomb. Current experiments use deuterium or tritium in solid form. These pellets are placed in chambers where laser beams heat them to millions of degrees. When this process is perfected, the earth will have a nearly inexhaustible supply of clean energy.

The Sun Has a Lot of Power!

The nuclear reactions previously discussed are the types of processes occurring in the sun today. I have found some Christians having reservations about the sun having these kinds of nuclear reactions. One dilemma is the apparent lack of neutrino's coming from the sun. According to the atomic theory previously mentioned, neutrinos are produced in the first stage of nuclear fusion. If the sun undergoes nuclear fusion continually, there should be a tremendously large supply of neutrino's coming from the sun. Quote, "In the sun's fusion sequence, about 0.007 kg (kilograms) of matter is converted into energy for each kilogram of hydrogen processed. This liberates 4×10^{26} J/s inside the sun, and the sun radiates this much every second to maintain its equilibrium (the equilibrium between the power output of the sun and the pull of gravity pulling all matter to the sun's core). This corresponds to 400 trillion watts-, which equals a lot of light bulbs! Every second, the sun converts 4 million tons of hydrogen into energy and radiates it into space. [3.4]" You would expect a large supply of neutrinos with 4 million tons of hydrogen involved in nuclear fusion. However, there doesn't seam to be as many neutrinos coming from the sun as predicted by the nuclear theory. "Even though neutrinos are hard to detect (they pass through huge amounts of material without being adsorbed), detectors to measure neutrino numbers were constructed in the 1970s. To scientists' amazement, the experiments detected only about a third as many solar neutrinos as predicted. Could our understanding of solar processes or atomic physics be flawed? [3.5]" Some people jumped on this discovery to demand that it provided clear evidence for a flaw in the theory that nuclear fusion was occurring in the sun.

Missing Neutrinos

The missing neutrinos were considered a serious dilemma for nuclear physicists. Some Christians have attempted to use the lack of neutrinos as evidence for nuclear fusion not occurring in the sun. These same Christians have also attempted to use this concept to promote the concept of a young solar system. I tend to agree in the concept of a young solar system, although I think the debate over the age of the universe trivial in the overall discussion about Astronomy. Josh McDowell is an author I quote continually in this book. He has a brilliant mind and is a wonderful Christian. However, when he tries to refute the power of nuclear fusion for the source of energy of the sun, I feel he does not have all the facts. He must have researched only Christian books where the writers were out of date or did not have a clear understanding of nuclear physics. In his book, Reasons Skeptics Should Consider Christianity, the following is stated. Quote, "In about 1850, Hermon Von Helmholtz proposed that the energy for the sun's luminescence was caused by its very slow gravitational contraction. In other words, the sun was shrinking under its own weight. George Abell calculated: ... its contraction can have kept it shining at its present rate for a period of the order of 100 million years. ... Lord Kelvin also calculated the age of the sun based upon the contraction hypothesis. But unfortunately for Von Helmholtz and Kelvin, this theory was published at the wrong time. Due to concepts that were then being developed in biology and geology, many scientists did not want to accept the idea of a young earth. ... With the discovery of radioactivity in 1896, geologists quickly began to 'date' the earth. Radioactivity was indicating that the earth was billions of years old. Well, if the earth was that old, then so must the sun. ... They needed some type of energy source, which would allow the sun to shine constantly for around 4.5 billion years. They proposed that hydrogen fusion ... was reasonable for the sun's energy. Neutrinos are difficult to detect but they can be recorded if the detectors are placed in the bottom of mines. The number of neutrinos detected is only about four per month or about one-tenth of the number expected if, in the solar interior, hydrogen fusion was occurring. What this means is that the energy of the sun is not coming from nuclear fusion. What then is it coming from? [3.6]" This is probably the only written statement in all of Josh McDowell's works I have ever had any disagreement with. However, it is a big one.

This portrait of the power of the stars being from a source of energy other than nuclear fusion is not an isolated belief. Donald Young, the author of God's Universe mentioned in chapter 1, also agrees with these conclusions. There are other books from the Creation Science Institute that have taken similar approaches. They have believed that somehow the shrinking of the sun is the primary source of power for the sun. They have believed that somehow going from the higher potential energy to a lower potential energy, as a result of the shrinking sun's diameter, produces this much power. To their credit, the missing neutrinos were a serious puzzle to mainstream scientific research many years ago. However, this discrepancy did not warrant suggesting that we throw out the fusion model for explaining the power of the sun. The shrinking size of the sun is predicted by the hydrogen fusion model. If you lost 4 million tons of weight every second, your waist would get smaller too! The fusion model also requires the sun's diameter to decrease for the equations to balance and remains a clear explanation of the enormous power of the sun. By refuting the fusion model as the power for the sun, you merely exchange the value of 4.5 billion years or more with 100 million years for the age of the sun. This is still far from proving that the universe may actually be 6,000 years old. As we previously discussed there may be an "apparent age" and the universe may actually be very young. If this is true, does it matter how old the sun is predicted to be according to either model? Misconceptions about physical laws like this one are major motivations I had in writing this book. I was sorely disappointed by statements and views against modern scientific research, from books supporting scientific creationism. This work is intended to question scientific theories in precise detail, and be fair about the evidence which is taught in public schools. We need open debates about the conclusions that science presents as facts. We need to know when to fight and when to turn the other cheek. "Be diligent to present yourself approved to God, a worker who does not need to be ashamed, rightly dividing the word of truth." 2 Timothy 2:15- RSV. "But in your hearts reverence Christ as Lord, always be prepared to make a defense to any one who calls you to give an account for the hope that is in you."- 1 Peter 3:15-RSV. Remember we have truth on our side. "But he who does the truth comes to the light, that his deeds may be clearly seen, that they have been done in God." John 3:21-RSV. "And you shall know the truth, and the truth shall make you free." John 8:32- RSV "Jesus said to him, 'I am the way, the truth, and the life. No one comes to the Father except through Me.'" John 14:6. - RSV "For this cause I was born, and for this cause I have come into the world, that I should bear witness to the TRUTH. Everyone who is of the TRUTH hears My voice." John 18:37-RSV. True science is a systematic pursuit of truth and wisdom. We need to embrace every effort, which does not directly violate our faith in Jesus as Lord.

Difficulties in Detecting Neutrinos

The lack of neutrinos detected in the cloud chambers buried in mines is not of great concern to scientists any longer. As stated previously, when two hydrogen nuclei are fused in their first stage of nuclear fusion, a deuterium atom, an electron and a neutrino are produced $^1H + {}^1H \rightarrow {}^2H$ + positron + neutrino (v). The only detectable particles in experiments with nuclear fusion were the deuterium and electron particles. Physicists examined the amount of mass and energy on both sides of the equation. They soon found a discrepancy: there was an unexplained energy loss. After years of research and theoretical work, it was decided that the missing mass was the result of a neutrino produced in their reaction, more about the nature of neutrinos will be discussed later. There is still debate over the production rates of neutrinos in the sun. In laboratory conditions, we can determine the production rate of neutrinos in fusion or fission processes. However, the sun is billions of times hotter than any nuclear reaction produced on earth. Also, the nature of the neutrino is still not fully understood. It may be possible that the energy imbalance of the first stage of nuclear fusion somehow produces a photon instead of a neutrino. Or neutrinos may have the ability to transmute into some other kind of massless particle under the extraordinary conditions at the sun's interior. There were three main theories proposed in the 1980s to explain the lack of detecting the expected number of neutrinos from the sun. A weakly interactive massive particle or WIMP particle could exist in the core of the sun, retarding the neutrinos was one theory. Quote, "WIMPs would transport energy out of the solar core, cool it, and thus retard production rates of neutrinos. A second theory proposes that instead of zero mass, neutrinos have a tiny, unmeasured mass, which would affect the experiments and possibly solve the puzzle. A third theory… suggests that certain types of neutrinos transmute into undetectable particles, thus explaining the deficiency. [3.7]" The last two theories are considered the most plausible. Recent discoveries into the nature of neutrinos indicate that neutrinos may indeed have a certain, small amount of mass. Also, recent experiments indicate that it may be possible for neutrinos to transmute into a package of electromagnetic energy, or photons, which is detectable as radiation. In any case our inability to detect the quantity of neutrinos predicted, in no way diminishes the fact that the energy source of the sun is fusion power.

What are Neutrinos?

To understand how insignificant the lack of detecting neutrinos is, you must first understand the properties of neutrinos. What exactly is a neutrino? Neutrinos were hypothetical particles predicted to occur under certain conditions. The original discovery of the neutrino was from the decay of a neutron into a proton and an electron. This is commonly refereed to as beta decay, n → p + e⁻ + neutrino. Neutrons, when liberated from the nucleus of an atom, decay quickly into an electron, a proton and a neutrino. This theory was put forth by Erico Fermi at the University of Chicago in 1934. Fermi discovered an in-discrepancy in the process of beta decay. By observing "tracks" left behind by these particles emerging from experimental particle accelerator chambers you can calculate the mass of electrons, protons and neutrons. A neutron has a certain amount of mass. When you add the mass of the proton and the mass of the electron produced from the decay of neutrons, there was an imbalance in the equation. There was a certain amount of missing mass. The neutrino was named from the phrase "little neutral one" because the missing particle had no mass and no charge. The first actual neutrino was detected in 1956 almost 20 years after Fermi had predicted it. [3.8] For many years, detection of neutrinos was considered impossible. However, in 1956 the discovery of the neutrino was made by Clyde L. Cowan Jr. and Frederick Reines of Los Alamos. They discovered that the actual particle produced by beta decay was the antineutrino. They theorized that given a steady source of neutrinos or antineutrinos, there is a small chance of the neutrino interacting with a particular atom. Quote, "The fact that the probability of interaction is small can be overcome if the number of neutrinos or antineutrinos is large enough. Nuclear reactors … produce large numbers of antineutrinos-perhaps as many as 10^{18} /second. By placing a large target and counter apparatus near the reactor at Savannah River, South Carolina, Crown and Reines calculated they should be able to get one reaction of the type v_e + p → n + e⁺ every 20 minutes." [3.9] Thus, Crown and Reines set up the experiment to detect neutrinos for the first time in 1956.

There is a complex series of events to occur in order to prove that an antineutrino has been detected. "When one of the rare antineutrino interactions occurs in the water, there are two products - the positron and a neutron. … Thus, the sequence of events that would signal the presence of an antineutrino interaction would be (1) two photons from the electron- positron annihilation, followed in a few millionths of a second by (2) one or more photon characteristic of the cadmium nucleus. When Crown and Reines finally satisfied themselves that they were seeing the events at the expected rate of one every 20 minutes, the physics community had the proof it needed for the existence of the antineutrino. [3.10]" The neutrinos coming from the sun are very difficult to detect and a lack of the expected number is not very alarming. First, instruments are placed in deep mines to avoid interactions with other subatomic particles other than the neutrinos. Neutrinos pass through solid walls effortlessly, without detection. At this very moment millions of them are passing through your body. The ability for the devices in the mines to detect neutrinos is partly determined to its position on the earth. Neutrinos are known to be radiating outward from the sun in random directions. The orientation of the earth to the sun can become a factor in detecting neutrinos. The neutrino is so small that it can normally cruise through atoms. They are so small they pass the empty space between the electron orbit and the nucleus in the atom. However, there are many times when the neutrinos hit the nucleus of a particular atom, such as a water molecule in the atmosphere. Then the neutrinos can be deflected into outer space, the upper atmosphere or somewhere else. The reason detection devices for neutrinos are placed deep within mines, is to increase the chances of detection. Passing through the atmosphere then through miles of solid rock can slow the neutrinos down and allow them to be detected. There is currently strong evidence that neutrinos are not "mass-less" particles but have a small amount of mass. The gravitational field of the sun, the earth, the moon and every other object in the solar system could very well affect the neutrinos. This would throw off their trajectory and allow only a small percentage of the neutrinos produced by the sun to reach the earth. The lack of ability to detect neutrinos is of no great concern to the theory of nuclear fusion as the power source of the stars. There are too many random elements involved. The ability to detect one neutrino is amazing. To have every neutrino detected which is predicted by mathematical calculations would indeed be incredible. It may very well be that we simply need to re-evaluate the probability equations to determining the expected number of neutrinos that should be detected in cloud chambers.

There are several instruments important to the detection of the many particles coming from numerous sources throughout the universe. Cosmic rays and high-energy sub-atomic particles like neutrinos come from many sources, including the sun. Let us look at some of the more significant devices for detecting elementary particles. "A cloud chamber contains a gas that has been super-cooled to just bellow its usual condensation point. An energetic particle passing through ionizes the gas along its path. ... The track can be seen with the naked eye and can be photographed. A magnetic field can be applied to determine the signs of the charges as they are deflected by the field. A device called a bubble chamber ... makes use of a liquid (usually liquid hydrogen) maintained near its boiling point. Ions produced by incoming charged particles leave bubble tracks, which can be photographed. ... A spark chamber is a counting device that consists of an array of conducting parallel plates. Even-numbered plates are grounded, and odd-numbered plates are maintained at a high potential (about 10kV). The spaces between the plates contain a noble gas at atmospheric pressure. When a charged particle passes through the chamber, ionization occurs in the gas, resulting in a large scale surge of current and a visible spark." [3.11] Using these methods, and many variations of these themes, detection devices can determine the type and number of particles passing through these instruments. For example, careful study of the tracks left in cloud chambers allows physicists to determine what particles passed through the device. From the trajectory of the path, scientists can determine the mass of the particle. These devices are used extensively to detect subatomic particles coming from the sun and other sources. The field of particle physics is a large subject and we can not fully cover this field in this book. Is there room for experimental error with these methods of particle detection? The answer, of course, is an absolute yes!

Let us assume for the moment that we can agree that the sun and the stars are powered by nuclear fusion. Is there evidence for a young earth within the nuclear energy model of the solar system? The answer is yes! "If the sun is 4.5 billion years old, then it has exhausted about half of its potential lifetime. ...The conversion of hydrogen into helium in the solar core would have altered the core's composition, which would have resulted in the sun's core slowly shrinking and increasing in temperature. Calculations shows that the sun ought to be about 40 percent brighter today than when it was allegedly formed 4.5 billion years ago and the sun ought to be 30 percent brighter today than when life supposedly appeared on earth 3.5 billion years ago. ...Since the current average earth temperature is 15C, the early earth ought to have had an average temperature below freezing. No one believes that this is the case. Most assume that the average terrestrial temperature has not changed much, if at all, during earth history. How do we explain this early, faint sun paradox? Evolutionists who believe the earth and sun are billions of years old, must assume that the atmosphere of the early earth had much more greenhouse gasses than our current atmosphere. As the sun gradually brightened, the earth's atmosphere gradually evolved so that it had less greenhouse gasses to counter the increase in the sun's luminosity. How two completely unrelated processes could have evolved in exactly compensating ways for billions of years is amazing." [3.12] How convenient, just the right change in atmosphere at the right time. It is amazing how repeatedly the case for a creator at work in the universe is proven again and again. The term "intelligent design" has been coined lately. I applaud the effort to introduce this truth into science classrooms. It merely introduces the student to the fact that all-current, scientific information point to a Supreme Being who has created the universe and all life. "The heavens are telling the glory of God; and the firmament proclaims his handiwork." Psalms 19:1 "For every house is built by some one, but the builder of all things is God." Hebrews 3:4. It is the atheist who has the unreasonable faith in random chance somehow producing all the conditions necessary for the universe to exist, grow and make things seemingly better. Once again, we can turn to the popular book, The Case for a Creator, by Lee Strobel and his interview with Dr. William Lane Craig. "'What's important to understand, Lee, is how reversed the situation is from, say a hundred years ago.' Craig continued. 'Back then, Christians had to maintain by faith in the Bible that despite all appearances to the contrary, the universe was not eternal but was created out of nothing a finite time ago. Now, the situation is exactly the opposite. It is the atheist who has to maintain, by faith, despite all of the evidence to the contrary, that the universe did not have a beginning a finite time ago but is in some inexplicable way eternal after all. So the shoe is on the other foot. The Christian can stand confidently within Biblical truth, knowing it's in line with mainstream astrophysics and cosmology. It is the atheist who feels uncomfortable and marginalized today." [3.13]" Why don't we see these types of statements printed in newspapers? The answer is simple: The world wants to retard these kinds of scientific observations. The world is now desperate to keep the general public ignorant of science that supports the biblical account of creation.

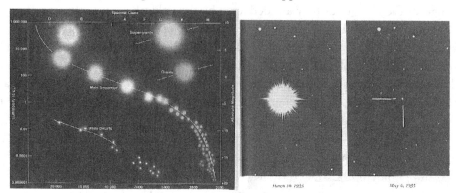

Figure 3.2

The Structure of Stars

The structure of stars is an important part of Astronomy. I was amazed when a Christian friend of mine challenged my acceptance of the categorization of stars according to the Hertzsprung-Russell diagram, or HR Diagram. It is true that this diagram is used to support a theory of stellar evolution, but like so many scientific discoveries the diagram merely supports the Christian perspective that God has given us an orderly universe. Stellar evolution is based on the concept that the universe began with the big bang, and then gravitational forces began shaping the universe. Stars are formed in nebulas; where beginnings of nuclear fusion form first stage stars. As the hydrogen fuel is used up, the composition of the stars changes. The HR Diagram, shown, in figure 3.2, illustrates the changes in the stars. Since the first day of creation, stars have been born, grown old, and died, according to the HR Diagram of the life cycle of stars. Stars are born in nebulas as protostars. Some protostars eventually become yellow stars, like our sun. Stars change, due to gravitational forces and the amount of nuclear material within the star, and finally die. Depending of the stars original mass, stars end their existence as either black holes, or explode as novas and super novas or become white dwarfs. The right side of figure 3.2 shows another picture of a star going supernova, like the one in figure 2.5. This one occurred in 1935. Along their life span, the stars "cough up" star material, which eventually gets collected in nebulas. Much of the description of stellar structure is accurate and proven by observation. Examples of stars changing and exploding, as super novas, have been photographed and documented as shown in the illustrations. What is confusing to some of my Christian friends is that I understand and accept the current structure of stars in their present stages of development. I reject the idea that this is, necessarily, uncontroversial proof that all stars are the result of billions of years of "evolution". Here, the Christian has grounds for an intelligent debate. The simple force of gravity acting over time can not completely explain the complexity of the universe. God works with the natural forces He created, as well as super-natural forces, apart from the fundamental forces. There is clear evidence of both occurring in the creation of the universe.

Stars are considered to exist in different stages of development. All stars are thought to be born in nebulas. Nebulas are collections of inter-stellar gas and dust. According to the theory, gravity unites these elements. When a mass of hydrogen is collected and the pull of gravity is strong enough, hydrogen elements fuse together to begin the nuclear fusion of the star. This is no more mysterious than lightning striking a tree in a forest and a fire starting. Once a star is born, it usually begins as a star similar to our own. Stars begin with different masses. The amount of mass each star has at its birth will determine its fate and its death. Stars generally follow the pattern of Proto-star to Pre-main sequence stars, Main sequence stars, Giants, Variable or unstable stars (supernova, nova, quasars, pulsars etc.), white dwarf or other small stars or black holes. Most of the life of the star is spent in the main sequence. This is the sun's current stage of development. [3.14] "Since stars have a limited supply of hydrogen in their cores, they have a limited lifetime as main sequence stars. This lifetime is proportional to f M / L, where f is the fraction of the total mass of the star, M is available for nuclear burning in the core and L is the average luminosity of the star during its main sequential lifetime. Because of the strong dependence of luminosity on mass, stellar lifetimes depend sensitively on mass. Thus, it is fortunate that our Sun is not more massive than it is since high-mass stars rapidly exhaust their core hydrogen supply. Once a star exhausts its core hydrogen supply, the star becomes redder, larger, and more luminous: it becomes a red giant star." [3.15]

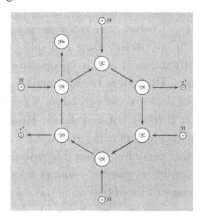

Figure 3.3

Nuclear reactions change as the hydrogen fuel is consumed. The proton-proton chain reaction predominates in smaller main sequence stars, see figure 3.2. Nuclear reactions in other, more massive stars will enter what is called the carbon cycle, see figure 3.3. The different type of nuclear reaction determines the stage of development of the star. [3.16] This is how the stars can produce the abundant lighter elements for the processes of life. Notice that stars can make four of the most important elements in living organisms. These are carbon, hydrogen, nitrogen, and oxygen. Evolutionists will sight these nuclear reactions as scientific proof that we were made from elements produced in the stars. However, there are only 7 different elements produced in the nuclear reactions of the stars shown above. One big question is where did the other 85 naturally occurring elements come from? There are several possible explanations. Some subscribe to the s-process and r-process. "As the core contracts and gets hotter, it initiates reactions involving even heavier elements. Carbon burning may occur. Some of the reactions create floods of neutrons that strike nearby atoms. These initiate the so-called s-process reactions, in which neutrons are slowly added to nuclei to build up still heavier elements, and the r-process reactions, in which rapid neutron addition builds up very heavy elements. The s-process and r-process reactions are very important because of the production of the heavier elements, such as metals. Without such reactions, the universe would still consist of almost pure hydrogen and helium and would lack sufficient heavy elements to make planets such as Earth. [3.17]"

Once again, evolutionists have solved the mystery of creation, or have they? Look at the tremendous forces and flood of rapidly moving neutrons in stars. It is difficult to imagine slow moving neutrons in a star. Yet once again, some scientists expect us to have faith in the power of evolution. They believe there is a smooth transition through the HR-diagram of stellar development. They believe the means to produce all 92 naturally occurring elements are perfectly controlled through random interactions and gravitational forces. Is the evidence that there may have been heavy elements in the early universe? The answer is yes! "Using HST's Goddard High Resolution Spectrograph, the researchers detected traces of boron in a yellow 7th magnitude star called HD 140283, located 100 light-years away in the constellation Libra. At an estimated age of 15 billion years, the star is one of the oldest known. Because it was among the first stars to form in our Milky Way galaxy, HD 140283 should contain elements, which were incorporated into the star long ago. Preserved in the star for billions of years, such material offers clues to conditions of the early universe when the star formed. Predictably, HD 140283 contains mostly primordial elements synthesized in the Big Bang: hydrogen, helium, and traces of lithium. (Heavier elements such as carbon, nitrogen, oxygen, and others which are found in the Sun, the Earth and Solar System planets are thought to have been built up during the lifetime of the galaxy by nuclear reactions in successive generations of stars). The discovery of boron comes as a surprise, however. Previously, another rare element, beryllium, had been detected in the star with ground-based telescopes. The key question is where did the beryllium and boron come from? Scientists know that today, beryllium and boron are produced by cosmic rays. 'Cosmic rays are high-speed and extremely energetic particles, which occasionally collide with atoms in interstellar space and split them apart into lighter elements. ... However, the astronomers found slightly different relative proportions of beryllium and boron than what is expected from cosmic ray production. This offers the alternative possibility that beryllium and boron were synthesized in the first moments of the universe's creation. The currently accepted version of the Big Bang says that the early universe was uniformly hot and dense. However, more recent theories suggest that the Big Bang developed some structure even during the first few minutes. These new theories differ from the traditional one in predicting that small but detectable amounts of beryllium and boron might be created. To confirm these results, astronomers plan to conduct additional HST observations of an even older star later this year. If the boron was produced by cosmic rays within the young Milky Way it should diminish the farther back in time the astronomers look (hence closer the birth of the Galaxy). If, instead, they find the same amount of boron in the older star, rather than less, the finding will support the alternative explanation that boron was produced in the Big Bang. Either way, this will be an exciting test to show which of the possible explanations is correct', concludes Duncan. 'We know that our picture of the beginning of the galaxy and the beginning of the universe is undoubtedly oversimplified, and it is satisfying to be able to add a little more detail.' [3.18]" This quote was taken from the NASA web site.

Could current theories about the beginning of the universe be wrong? We are told that the universe took billions of years to develop. We are taught that it was billions of years after the big bang when older stars developed and began producing the heavier elements perhaps by means of supernovas. There continues to be evidence to a complete universal creation as described in Genesis. The question of which theories to accept keeps returning to the question of which idea you personally have the most faith as the correct explanation. Unable to give a definite answer to this question, some scientists say that the elements were formed sometime during the early universe as the big bang was in a state of making matter from sub-atomic particles. Scientists have suggested that in supernova explosions, somehow the heavier elements are formed. Again, Astronomers describe the changes in a stellar form by the available fuel supply inside the star. "In main sequence stars, one or the other of these reactions consumes hydrogen in the core. Finally, major structural changes happen as hydrogen is used up. [3.19]" Some of these stars are brought into a stage of development whereby they become red giants or super giants. This is described as a funneling effect. The stars contract under the influence of gravity as their hydrogen fuel supply is used up. Quote, "Meanwhile, the star cores contract until they reach temperatures near 200 million Kelvin. This is hot enough to begin to fuse helium nuclei in the center regions of most stars, primarily by the triple-alpha process (named after the alpha particle, another name for the helium-4 nucleus). In this process, three helium-4 nuclei combine to produce a carbon-12 nucleus. [3.20]" Afterwards this process, the carbon cycle begins and the final fate of stars is determined. As stated previously, the end is determined by the mass of the star. "A. If the mass of the star is less than 1.2 times the mass of the sun, the star will become a white dwarf. B. If the star is slightly more than the 1.2 figure, the star will shed part of its mass and become a nova or it will shed parts of its mass several times and become a recurrent nova. Eventually the star will become a white dwarf. C. If the star's mass is a great deal more than 1.2 times the mass of the sun, it will shed a major part of its mass into space, thus producing a supernova nebula as well as either a white dwarf, neutron star, or black hole, depending on the size of the mass being imploded. [3.21]" Changes in the stars are not mysterious. It is simply the result of different stages in the nuclear fusion processes. Each stage of development in a star is currently categorized, depending upon the temperature of the star and the types of elements predominantly located within the star. Information about the type and quantity of any element within a star can be obtained by a simple spectral analysis.

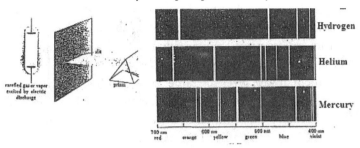

Figure 3.4

Spectroscopy and the HR Diagram

Verification of the types of elements contained inside of stars is achieved through the use of spectroscopy. "Astronomers can determine A. What the temperature is on the surface of any star. B. What chemicals are available on the surface of any star and in what quantities? C. If the star has a magnetic field and if so, how intense is it. D. Whether the star is approaching us or receding from us and how fast. All this information, as well as a great deal of other data about the stars, is derived from careful analysis of the radiation that reaches us from stars. The branch of science that deals with such analysis is called Spectroscopy and its basic instrument is the Spectroscope. The function of a spectroscope is to disperse a ray of light into its constitute colors- a process similar to the one performed by the water droplets in clouds to form a rainbow. [3.22]" I find it fascinating that science can use the same process as found in creating a rainbow to determine a large amount of information about stars. "I have set my rainbow in the clouds, and it will be the sign of the covenant between me and the earth." Genesis 9:13. How is a rainbow formed? "A single ray of ordinary light, say sunlight, will be dispersed upon entering the glass of the prism into a continuous array of colors. ... Such an arrangement of colors is called a Spectrum. ... Light is a form of energy that can be thought as consisting of waves. The experimental evidence is that red light differs from blue light only in wavelength. Red light has the longest wavelength in the visible spectrum; violet, the shortest. Wavelength, as the name indicates, is the horizontal distance between crests of two adjacent waves. ... The refraction suffered by light on entering glass depends on the wavelength: the short wave violet is refracted more than the long wave red light. The several colors originally contained in the ray of white light are thus refracted by different amounts and hence, dispersed. [3.23]" The complete understanding of this is found in a study of quantum physics. The theory describes all electromagnetic radiation, of which light is a part, as having a dual nature. Sometimes the light rays acts like waves of energy. Other times, light acts as a particle. Light is considered to travel in a package called a photon. A photon can be considered a mass-less particle. More about these principles will be discussed in chapter 9.

There are other instruments used in spectral analysis to aid in analyzing materials, see figure 3.4. "In addition to the prism, the other essential elements of a prism spectroscope are a narrow slit, a collimator, and a telescope. ... The narrow slit is placed at the focus of an achromatic lens called a collimator, the function of which is to reroute the rays of light into parallel paths. ... Each parallel ray, on passing through the prism, is dispersed into the various colors. Thus, ray A produces a complete red-to-violet spectrum; similarly, ray B produces a complete red-to-violet spectrum; and so on. ... If some wavelengths are missing in the light entering the spectroscope, the spectrum will not be continuous. The place usually occupied by the missing wavelengths will appear black. Some sources of light, e.g., a neon light, emit only a few definite wavelengths- the spectrum will appear as a series of bright lines separated by wide black bands. [3.24]" It turns out that each element has a characteristic line spectrum associated with it. There are two types of line spectrums: A) The bright-line spectrum and B) the dark-line spectrum. By using one or the other of these methods, we can determine the kind and quantity of any of the 92 naturally occurring elements in a particular sample.

One way the bright line spectrum is produced, is by placing a material in its gaseous state, like hydrogen which is naturally a gas, into a tube. You connect both ends of this tube to a high voltage source. When the light given off is viewed through a spectroscope, it produces a bright line spectrum, see figure 3.4. The bright line spectrum has been used extensively to identify the elements in an unknown sample. Without exception, spectral analysis has identified amazing detail to unknown substances. "It should be carefully noted that each element always gives the same pattern of lines. Each element, so to speak, has its own fingerprints, possessed by no other element. This fact is utilized in chemical analysis and in many other applied fields. [3.25]" Laboratory experiments in high schools and colleges verify the accuracy of this procedure every day. The dark-line spectrum is also used extensively in Astronomy. "Dark-line Spectrum, also know as absorption spectrum, is due to absorption of light of particular wavelength by relatively cool gasses. ... Star spectra are of the 'dark line' kind. The continuous spectrum originates at the surface of the star; the dark lines are caused by the relatively cooler outer atmosphere of the star. ... Some of the dark lines are due to hydrogen, others helium, still others to other elements. ... An analysis of such a spectrum would resolve the lines into several sets, each due to one of the ninety-two natural elements. Thus, spectroscopy aids in determining the chemicals contained in each star and the relative proportions of these elements-determined from the relative brightness of the various sets of lines. [3.26]" The absorption line spectrum is no less accurate than the bright-line spectrum because it rests on the same principles of atomic structure. The absorption spectra looks like the bright-line spectra only reversed. Instead of dark lines on a bright background, they are illustrated as bright lines on a dark background. The bright lines have different sizes and different magnitudes of brightness.

What can we determine about the temperature of the stars? "In some studies (e.g., to find the temperature of a star) it is important to know not only what wavelengths (colors) appear in a spectrum, but also how much energy is available in each wavelength. ... An energy curve of a spectrum is obtained by: A. Producing the spectrum on the screen. B. Changing the light into heat energy for each wavelength by allowing the light to be absorbed by a good absorber .... C. Determine the amount of heat energy for each wavelength. D. Plotting the curve of energy against wavelength. ... When the emitter is at a higher temperature, two changes come about the curve: A. The area under the curve gets larger, i.e., there is more energy emitted at every wavelength. B. The maximum (the peak) has moved toward the shorter wavelength. ... One method used to determine the temperature of a star from its spectrum involves three preliminary steps: (A) to determine the energy distribution of the spectrum; (B) to find the wavelength of maximum energy; and (c) to use Wien's law. ... Wilhelm Wien (1864-1928) derived a simple formula relating λ_{max} to temperature: $T = 289 \times 10^5 \div \lambda_{max}$. [3.27]" By examination of the temperature, composition, and other measurements over time we can conclude that stars appear to fit into the currently held theories of stellar fusion processes and the HR diagram of the stellar life cycle. Does this have any bearing on the Christian position that God created the universe? No, of course not. What keeps all these "natural forces" working together with perfect harmony? Again, we return to a question of faith. I disagree with some of my Christian brothers and sisters who somehow object to modern Astrophysics. We can not emphasize strongly enough that these concepts of nuclear processes in the stars do not conflict with our faith that God created the universe. In fact, these principles demonstrate God's glory of order and harmony which He created for us to study and enjoy the wonderful splendor displayed in the universe.

There seams to be an enormous amount of evidence that the categorization of the stars is correct. There also is a great deal of verifiable evidence that the power of the stars is from nuclear processes beginning with hydrogen fusion and continuing through the carbon cycle. One reference lists 12 basic properties of the stars and methods used to measure these properties; 1) Distance -Trigonometric parallax, 2) Luminosity (absolute magnitude) - Distance combined with apparent brightness, 3) Temperature- color or spectra, 4) Diameter- Luminosity and temperature, 4) Mass- Measures of binary stars and use of Kepler's laws, 5) Composition- Bright Line Spectra, 6) Composition- Dark Line Spectra, 7) Magnetic Field, spectra using Zeeman effect, 8) Rotation- Spectra, using Doppler effect, 9) Atmospheric motions- Spectra, using Doppler effect, 10) Atmospheric structure- spectra, using opacity effects, 11) Circumsteler material, Spectra, using absorption lines and Doppler effect, and 12) Motion- Astrometry or spectra, using Doppler effect. [3.28] Every type of stellar development, from nebulas to black holes, has been located through astronomical observations. You can go to an observatory and see the research for yourself! Figure 2.5 shows two actual photographs. One, before the supernova in 1987 exploded, the other a few days later after the star showered the region with a burst of neutrinos. In the southern hemisphere, the explosion was bright enough to see with the naked eye for several days. Nearly all stages of stellar development have been photographed; all have been identified by radio- telescope tracking stations. Many more pictures are available from orbiting telescopes like the Hubble. Black holes have even been detected by observing the gravitational effect on other stellar forms. There are many sources on the internet or library to see these photographs of stars in various stages of development.

More about the Thermal Properties of the Stars

We have discussed the use of spectroscopy to determine the elements in stars. We have also previously discussed the Trigonometric parallax method for determining distance of stars. We have mentioned a little about determining the temperature of a star. The temperature of a star is determined with infrared detectors. Temperature is simply a measurement of the energy motions of an object. Most scientists use the absolute temperature scale or Kelvin scale when measuring temperature. The Kelvin scale starts at absolute zero and continues to the hottest temperatures. Absolute zero is a theoretical point where there is no thermal radiation given off by matter. In fact, it is the point at which there is no molecular movement at all! To measure the magnitude of temperature in a planet or star we can use Wien's law: The hotter the object, the bluer the thermal radiation emitted. Temperature and the wavelength of the thermal radiation are related by the equation: $W = 2.9 \times 10^{-3} \div T$ (temperature). "The number 0.000290 is a constant of proportionality and remains the same in all applications of the law." [3.29] For example, If the wavelength of strongest solar radiation was 5.1×10^{-7} m, what is the surface temperature of the sun? Using the above formula we obtain: $T = 2.9 \times 10^{-3} \div 5.1 \times 10^{-7} = 5700$ degrees Kelvin. Thus, using this method we can determine the temperature of virtually any star. The diagram in figure 3.2 shows the HR diagram of stars as it is related to temperature and luminosity. Notice the classifications are given at the top of the figure. Type O is hottest, bluest, star with average temperatures around 40,000 degrees Kelvin, consisting of ionized Helium. Type B is bluish with an average temperature at 18,000 degrees Kelvin, with neutral helium atoms. Type A is bluish-white with average temperature at 10,000 degrees Kelvin, with neutral hydrogen. Type F is white at 7,000 degrees Kelvin with neutral hydrogen. Type G is yellowish-white at 5,500 degrees Kelvin with neutral hydrogen and ionized calcium. Our sun is classified type G. Type K is orange at 4,000 degrees Kelvin with neutral metal atoms. Type M is coolest, reddest, at 3,000 degrees Kelvin with Molecules and neutral metals. [3.30]

To take observations of stars, we must use some type of telescope. There are two designs of optical telescopes: refractor, using lenses to bend light rays to a focus, and the reflector, using curved mirrors to reflect light rays to a focus. Many backyard Astronomy enthusiasts use optical telescopes to observe the stars. You can either simply make observations with your telescope, or the images can be focused on a piece of photographical film to make a picture of your observation. There are many good books with spectacular photographs of stars, planets, nebulas and many other exotic objects scattered throughout the universe. Photometry is the study of photographs from telescopes to determine temperature, elemental composition and other properties of remote stellar objects. Radio telescopes operate on principles similar to optical telescopes in that they reflect electromagnetic waves to a focus point. In the case of radio telescopes, radio waves are reflected towards the focus instead of light waves in the case of an optical telescope. Since radio waves are much longer in wavelength than light waves, the reflecting surface (the dish) must be a million times larger than optical telescopes. Interferometry has been developed to enhance the capabilities of radio telescopes. Interferometry is the technique in arranging two or more radio telescopes to act as one. The two telescopes are separated by a distance of approximately one mile. They feed data into a single signal detector. The data is processed by computers and images of incredible distances can be seen. The "Very Large Array", at the National Radio Astronomy Observatory in New Mexico, is a collection of 27 mobile radio telescopes which covers a 35-kilometer area. These telescopes function together to provide images from what is believed to be 10-14 Billion light-years away.

Where did our Solar System Come From?

The solar system is a complex collection of planets and their satellites, comets, asteroids, and a sun perfectly suited for providing needed energy to the earth. What are some of the properties of the solar system, which must be explained, with any theory of planetary origin? One source lists 13 properties of our solar system. Quote "1. All the planets' orbits lie roughly in a single plane. 2. The Sun's rotational equator lies nearly in this plane. 3. Planetary orbits are nearly circular. 4. The planets and the Sun all revolve in the same west-to-east direction, called prograde (or direct) revolution. 5. Planets differ in composition. 6. The composition of Planets varies roughly with the distance from the Sun: Dense metal-rich planets lie in the inner system. Whereas giant, hydrogen rich planets lie in the outer system. 7. Meteorites differ in chemical and geological properties from all known planetary and lunar rocks. 8. The Sun and all the planets except Venus and Uranus rotate on their axis in the same direction (prograde rotation) as well. Obliquity (tilt between equatorial and orbital planes) is generally small. 9. Planets and most asteroids rotate with rather similar periods, about 5 to 10 h, unless obvious tidal forces slow them down (as in the Earth's case). 10. Distances between planets usually obey the simple Bode's rule. 11. Planet- satellite systems resemble the solar system. 12. As a group, comets' orbits define a large, almost spherical cloud around the solar system. 13. The planets have much more angular momentum (a measure relating orbital speed, size and mass) than the Sun. (failure to explain this was a great flaw of the early evolutionary theories.) [3.31]" The current evolutionary theory states that the sun began to form inside a nebulas region of dust and gas approximately 4.6 billion years ago. The first stage of development is called the proto-star stage. Scientists believe that proto-stars are forming today in nebulas regions of dust and gas. The formation of the sun occurred in three fundamental stages, according to the evolutionists. Quote "a. A slowly rotating, interstellar gas cloud begins to contract because of its own gravity. b. A central condensation forms and the cloud rotates faster and flattens. c. The sun forms in the cloud center, surrounded by a rotating disc of gas. [3.32]" Once again, see figure 1.1 to visualize this process. This rotating disc of gas is supposed to condense and form the planets of our solar system. The principle of conservation in angular momentum suggests that the inner parts of the nebula would spin faster than the outer parts. This is why the nebulas region would flatten and the center would form the sun. Scientist believe that a balancing of forces, gravity pulling everything inward, and random gas collisions pushing elements outward, would create the conditions for a gas cloud orbiting the sun. These principles and the rate of contraction in stellar formation are called the Helmholtz contraction after the Astrophysicists Hermann Von Helmholtz. Scientists believe that complex mixtures were formed at various points in the solar nebular, depending on combination of temperature, pressure, and material content of the gas. Scientists support these conclusions by examining the contents of the atmosphere on different planets in our solar system. For example, the Viking explorer on Mars showed a decrease in Argon gas compared to amounts on Venus or the Earth.

The evolutionist explaining the development of our solar system from a swirling mass of gas runs into some serious problems. The nebulas region around the sun was supposedly forming small microscopic grains of matter. These microscopic grains would need to be forced together, in an extremely precise manner, in order for the planets to form. Quote, "But exactly how did microscopic grains aggregate to produce 100-km-sized planetesimals? If they had circled the Sun in paths comparable to present asterodial and cometary orbits, they would have collided with one another at speeds much faster than rifle bullets. They would have shattered and the solar system would still be a nebula of dust and grit. [3.33]" Scientists believe that somehow solar nebulas don't have such high speeds, even though they produce objects in orbit around the sun at such velocities. They believe that low velocity collisions frequently took place and the planets were formed by matter "sticking" together by gravitational forces. Scientists still have major difficulties in explaining how the irregularities in the solar system developed. However, they believe that the regularities in the solar system can be explained by the theory of the solar system forming in a nebulas region.

Scientists believe that the reason the outer planets are more gaseous than the inner planets, is because they obtained more of the gaseous region of the solar nebula. Scientists believe that the reason the outer planets, Jupiter, Saturn and Uranus have such high contents of hydrogen and helium in their atmosphere is because they were formed in the outer reaches of the solar nebula. Earth and the inner planets have comparatively very little hydrogen and helium gases in their atmosphere. The formation of moons about the various planets was supposedly due to the pressure and temperature of the gas nebula and the position of the larger planetary bodies with respect to the center. The hotter inner planets formed metals and silicates, while the colder outer planets kept compositions similar to the solar nebula of mostly hydrogen and helium. One question which puzzled scientists for many years was the "missing" angular momentum. The sun was supposedly spinning fast enough after it's contraction to form a circular disc. It was from this disc that the planets were formed in their respective orbits. Today, however, the overall rotation is slow and spherical instead of fast and circular. To answer this problem, scientists assume that in the past, the sun had a strong magnetic field. To solve other irregularities in their explanation of the solar system, evolutionary scientists depend upon perfectly timed catastrophic events. Quote, "One of the beauties of the modern picture of planet formation is that it requires a few catastrophic events that can explain some of the non regularities of the solar system … a Mars sized planetesimal hit Earth late in its growth and blew off material which the Moon formed. … Uranus was probably hit by a relatively large planetesimal, tipping the rotation axis to lie nearly in the same plane of the solar system instead of perpendicular to it … Other properties of the solar system- such as the different styles of ring systems and the geological differences between hemispheres of some planets such as Mars- may trace back to large impacts. The largest impacts were not enough to randomize the characteristics of planets but they were large enough to give planets individuality of character! [3.34]" Again, there is a lot of faith in random events generating some very precise properties to the solar system. "The mystery is how a batch of radioactive iodine and other isotopes was created just before the first planetary material formed and how it got trapped in the material…. The evidence indicates that a star was located near the pre-solar nebula and exploded, spewing short-lived isotopes and other debris into the cloud that was becoming the solar nebula. Indeed, the blast from the explosion probably helped compress the pre-solar cloud, helping to initiate the collapse that produced the sun! [3.35]" Scientists who believe in evolution place a lot of faith in the right circumstances at the right time, producing conditions far beyond our comprehension to form the solar systems. Wow! They have a lot of faith in chance happenings, of collisions and exploding stars, to form the solar system, as we know it. Hats off to you fellows; who believe we exist because of complex random chance happenings instead of the design of God. It takes more faith than I could ever have to accept such theories. It is far more reasonable and easier to believe in the biblical account than such impossible happenings.

Now, let us consider the development of the heavier elements in the solar system. It has been established that elements can be transformed through the process of nuclear reactions. Where is the source of the heavier elements that exist on the earth and perhaps in the other planets as well? For many years scientists theorized that the only possible source of these heavier elements is either super nova explosions, which produce a few heavier elements, or leftover debris from the beginning of the universe. Is there evidence of super novas routinely occurring? No. Stars ending in a super nova explosion seam to be a rare event. The stars which produce a super nova in the death process must have a mass at least 10 times that of the sun. [3.36]. There is no evidence that super novas contribute massive amounts of heavier elements to nebulas regions. Is there evidence of other solar systems currently developing in nebulas today? There has been some speculation of planetary nebulas where planets are now forming. There are several solar systems with Jupiter sized planets that have recently been discovered. The first discoveries of planets around other stars began in 1995. The smallest planet listed in my research material was 0.42 times the mass of Jupiter. [3.37] Does this discourage our faith in the creation of our solar system by God? Of course not, we continue to come to the inescapable presence of faith in science. The naturalist conceives of increasingly more elaborate theories to explain the miraculous presence of our world. We are asked to accept every new explanation by faith in scientific discovery. The more elaborate the ideas become, the more difficult it is to accept these theories as an accurate representation of natural forces apart from the presence of God. It is extremely hard to believe that anything less than a miracle created our universe or more relevant our solar system.

Again, there are a number of theories to attempt an explanation of our solar system. "Just how our moon was created and came to be orbiting the Earth was a mystery until recently. For more than a century, astronomers had debated the merits of three scenarios: the adopted-cousin theory (the Moon was a small planet gravitationally captured by Earth); the sister theory (Earth and the Moon were born as a double planet); and the daughter theory (the Moon fissioned from a rapidly spinning primordial Earth). Yet studies of the nearly one ton of lunar material returned by the Apollo astronauts failed to support any of these theories. Instead, a fourth hypothesis emerged and is now widely accepted. The new scenario – we'll call it the chip-off-the-old-block theory- is a product of modern computer simulations of the formation of the solar system. The simulations suggest that 10 million years after the solar nebula initially evolved, the material in the region where Mercury, Venus, Earth and Mars were emerging had built up thousands of mountain-sized planetesimals. These, in turn collected into perhaps a dozen bodies in the Mercury-Mars zone. Earth might have had four or five neighbors up to three times the mass of Mars, but all closer than Mars is now. Then: Bang! One of them smashed into the ancient Earth. The heat generated by colliding with something that big would have melted the surface of our young planet. Debris from both Earth and the impacting body vaporized and slashed into nearby space. Some of it fell back to Earth, but a portion lingered in orbit around the Earth, eventually coalescing into the Moon. ... it's the only Moon-origin theory that fits with the Moon samples, which revealed that Moon material is substantially different from Earth rock. [3.38]" So, the reason Moon rocks are different from Earth rocks is that they came from the same nebula soup before they formed planets? Doesn't this seam contradictory? If they both came from the same material source, i.e. the sun's soar nebula, should not all the materials be the same? Of course if this is the result of a 'computer simulation' it must be true, right? I know something about computer generated simulations. Put in the right formulas, with any factors you wish, and you will get what you want as a result. Shrek is a computer-generated character. Does this mean that the Shrek character is real? Once again, we are asked to believe an explanation that is invented in a computer simulation as an absolute truth, when in fact it is simply something created by a highly active imagination. Video games may seam "real" but these "virtual simulations" are not real.

The current state of the universe provides little evidence about the origin of the universe, except it points to the beginning from a creation act of God. The naturalistic approach would base unreasonable theories on only one principle: the expansion of the universe. As we have stated, the Christian perspective would be unaffected by allowing for the possibility that the universe is expanding as described by the astronomical red shift. The evidence remains in favor of the Christian view of the universe, over and above the evolutionary model. The evolutionist relies on the principles of nuclear transformation to explain the development of all material in the universe. Theoretically, nuclear reactions can produce all of the 92 naturally occurring elements. Man has only been able to verify this process for a few elements in laboratories. However, the theory that all substances in the universe were produced in the nuclear reactions of stars is a plausible theory. Accepting this theory still requires a lot of faith in the power of natural forces. There would need to be some extraordinary forces at work to account for the abundance of heavier elements on the earth. Natural forces tend to accomplish tasks in a way that is as direct as possible. For example, forces will always try to take the shortest distance between two points. Anyone with elementary knowledge of electrical circuits knows that electricity always follows the path of least residence. Therefore, natural forces have a tendency toward simple reactions. How can these forces have produced conditions the best scientific minds can not re-create on earth? Some Christians object to the theory that nuclear processes occur in the sun, because it gives the evolutionists a solid foundation for their theory of an immense age to the universe. The development of the stars would have taken a long time, if all stars were born inside nebulas regions and naturally developed to their present stage. However, there is no indication that this was the case. Just as there is no evidence to support the conclusion of solar systems developing in large numbers in the universe, there is no evidence to prove the concept of a purely natural beginning. Perhaps, someday, we will discover planets forming, but there are still many mysteries of how a world like the one we live in could have come into existence. The Hubble space telescope has helped map out several planets outside our solar system. It appears that there are indeed other solar systems in the universe. Does this concern the Christian faith? Not at all. Perhaps if we could find intelligent life on other planets, the Christian faith would be strongly challenged. The search for extraterrestrial life is a serious concern for evolutionists. If there were intelligent life outside the earth; it would raise serious questions about God taking so much interest in this planet. Part of the Christian faith, which will be explored in more depth in chapters 4 and 5, is that God just created one world with life. The existence of other solar systems should not present a challenge to the Christian faith. However, alien life would. I believe that is one reason the search for extraterrestrial life is so important to the evolutionist. Jesus has these words to comfort us. "Do not let your hearts be troubled. Trust in God; trust also in me. In my Father's house are many rooms (often translated mansions); if it were not so, I would have told you. I am going there to prepare a place for you. And if I go and prepare a place for you, I will come back and take you to be with me that you also may be where I am." John 14:1-3. Could these "many rooms" be planets? After all, He teaches us in Revelation that He will establish a new heaven and new earth. For Christ to be with every living and dead person in history who followed the teachings of God could take a lot of room. It may require more than one planet to be occupied in this vast universe. "Then I saw a new heaven and a new earth, for the first heaven and the first earth had passed away." Revelation 21:1. I do realize that His Holy city, as described in the book of Revelation, will be huge. However, God is vast and I believe it may be possible that we will inhabit other worlds with a new Adam and Eve and a new Garden of Eden after the millennial kingdom. Just a little "food for thought".

Appearance of Age for the Stars

God created man out of the dust of the ground, fully developed, on the sixth day of creation. Is it reasonable to assume God created the stars in various stages of development throughout the universe? This leads into one of the most controversial arguments between the purely naturalistic view of science and the Christian view: "the appearance of age" controversy we discussed in the last chapter. Did God create the universe with an "appearance of age"? From the book of Genesis, it seams reasonable to assume that He did. God made the trees, grass, and planets fully mature on the third day of creation: "And God said, Let the earth bring forth grass, the herb yielding seed, and the tree yielding seed, and the fruit after its kind, whose seed was in itself, upon the earth: and it was so. And the earth brought forth grass, and herb yielding seed after its kind, and the tree yielding fruit, whose seed was in itself, after its kind: and God saw that it was good." Genesis. 1:11- 12 God made plant life fully developed and bearing fruit. I have already used the verse in Genesis chapter one, verse 14 in the previous chapter to help explain my belief that the stars were made fully developed. "And God said, let there be lights in the firmament of the heaven to divide the day from the night; and let them be for signs, and for seasons, and for days and years. And let them be for lights in the firmament of the heaven to give light upon the earth: and it was so. And God made two great lights; the greater light to rule the day, and the lesser light to rule the night: He made the stars also. And God set them in the firmament of the heaven to give light upon the earth, and to rule over the day and over the night, and to divide the light from the darkness: and God saw that it was good. And the evening and the morning were the fourth day." Genesis. 1:14- 19 God made the stars fully developed on the fourth day of creation and placed them in their proper positions. The Bible firmly supports the concept of God creating the universe with a certain "appearance of age." After each act of creation, God commanded what He had created to be fruitful and multiply. "And God blessed them, saying, be fruitful and multiply, and fill the waters in the seas, and let fowl multiply in the earth. ... So God created man in his own image, in the image of God created he him; male and female created he them. And God blessed them, and God said unto them, Be fruitful and multiply." Genesis. 1:22, 27, 28 Obviously, God's creation could not have been the parents of children, and the beasts could not have had offspring, if God had not created them fully developed. What really is the firmament mentioned in the word of God? Could this be the binding force of the universe? Could the firmament be the very structure of the four-dimensional space-time continuum? This concept would fall in line with Einstein's description of the universe according to the theory of general relativity. According to the general theory of relativity, the very fabric of space and time follows Riemann geometry, named after German mathematician Bernard Riemann (1826-1866). This means that 4- dimensional space time itself is curved and has a definite geometry, as described in Einstein's theory of general relativity. Recall that there have been problems in understanding what holds galactic clusters together, since there doesn't appear to be enough mass in the individual galaxies to produce a gravitational effect strong enough to hold the system together. Despite the incredibly vast numbers of stars inside of galaxies, their total combined mass can not produce a gravitational field strong enough to overcome the vast distance between two neighboring galaxies. Even gravity itself, is still somewhat of a mystery to theoretical physicists. All we really know is that anything that has mass has a gravitational field. Firmament is something that is permanent, unyielding to change. The firmament could be the four fundamental forces of nature. These forces and concepts were the first things God created. They were the binding principles that brought order to the vast emptiness of space.

The universe, with all the complicated nuclear processes, has been seen as a testimony to the power of God. There is a meaningful order in all the complex structures existing in the universe. This is one of the greatest testimonies to the existence of our creator. God always wants change. Change, in an organized way, shows God's purpose, planning, and control over the universe. The greatest change that takes place in a person's life is the one found by making a commitment to Jesus Christ as Savior and Lord. The Bible refers to this change in the person's life as a new birth. "Jesus answered and said unto him, verily, verily I say unto thee, except a man be born again, he can not see the kingdom of God." John 3: 3 KJV. This is the fulfillment of changing your life into a new creation by allowing the Holy Spirit to enter your life. There is a song which says, "It took Him just a week to make the moon and the stars, the sun and the earth, and Jupiter and Mars. How loving and patient He must be. He's still working on me."

What Does the Bible say About Stars?

There are at least 50 verses in the Bible which refer to the stars, according to Strong's Concordance of the Bible. [3.39] These verses can be divided into four categories in which they describe the stars. 1) The great multitude of the stars. The verses compare the descendants of Abraham and others in the Jewish line, to the number of the stars in heaven. The descendants of Abraham are also compared to sands on the seashore. Both indicate large numbers. The descendants, the stars, the sands of the sea, are all nearly infinite quantities. 2) Verses that speak of the permanence of the stars: these verses refer to the stars as a source of direction and strength. Just as the stars have existed since the foundation of the world, so shall God's love continue forever. Of course, stars are far less dependable than the love of God. 3) The death of the stars. The book of Revelation, in particular, describes a new heaven and a new earth. In the new heaven, apparently the fallen stars previously mentioned in the biblical account are replaced. 4) A special purpose for stars. Some of the objections to modern theories of stellar formation refer to stars having a great multitude, but a definite number. Some Christians mistakenly conclude that these verses exclude the possibility of new stars forming in nebulas clouds. "He determines the number of the stars and calls them each by name. Great is our Lord and mighty in power; his understanding has no limit." Psalms 147:4-5. Does the fact that every star has a name, exclude new stars from being born? By no means! Just as new people are born each day with a new name, so the stars can be forming under the watchful eye of God. "But even the hairs of your head are all numbered." Matthew 10:30. There are relatively few references indicating that stars might continue forever. In fact I could only find one verse which might fit this category. "And those who are wise shall shine like the brightness of the firmament; and those who turn many to righteousness, like the stars forever and ever." Daniel 12:3. Some Christians might refer to this verse as meaning that stars continue forever. This is not true scientifically or biblically. This verse does two things. First, it compares the brightness of stars with the wisdom of men who turn many to righteousness. Second, it compares the ability of wise men to turn men to the glory of God with the testimony of the stars. The stars are referred to many times as a source of inspiration. They are the most permanent physical things created by God. According to the atomic theory of stars, they last for billions of years. The stars we see today may not be that old, but they could last for billions of years. The stars are only temporary just like our bodies. "But in those days, after the tribulation, the sun will be darkened, and the moon will not give its light, and the stars will be falling from heaven, and the powers in the heavens will be shaken." Mark 14:24. Stars actually obey God's will, and God uses them frequently to show his power and control of the universe. "Then Herod summoned the wise men secretly and ascertained from them what time the star appeared; and he sent them to Bethlehem. ... And lo, the star which they had seen in the east went before them, till it came to rest over the place where the child was." Matthew. 2:7-9. Astronomers take great notice of any significant observations of stars, which have occurred in the past. Some Astronomers have attempted to place an exact date for the birth of Christ with knowledge of past super nova explosions which might have provided the brilliant light which led the wise men to Bethlehem. Attempts by Francis Schaeffer and others, to date the day of the crucifixion, were finalized in the study of solar eclipses. Numerous references in Matthew, Mark, Luke, and John placed the crucifixion on a Friday on or just before Passover. Quote, "The scholars restrict the number of possible dates to four Fridays between A.D. 27, and A.D. 34. Additional historical references suggest restricting the date further to April 7, (A.D.) 30 or April 3, (A.D.) 33. At this point the scholars invoke the speech of Peter, reported in Acts, which refers to a blood-red moon, possibly referring to an event at about the time of the crucifixion. Calculating the dates of lunar eclipses, they find that a partially eclipsed moon rose over Jerusalem on the night of Friday, April 3, A.D. 33, which they conclude was the date of the crucifixion. [3.40]" I recently heard the Reverend John McCarthy speak about the birth of Jesus and the Star of Bethlehem. It was an excellent series which I listened on the way to work each night. It opened my eyes to the possibility that the star of Bethlehem may actually be the Glory of God shining forth. Whether it was the presence of God the Astronomers interpreted as a Star or not, has little significance to me. God controls everything in the universe. Can we really know the mind of God? I believe that science in this century is approaching a precise understanding of God, but there are limits. I believe we are living in the "end times". The science of today could be a preparation of everlasting life in the presence of God. We have so many questions about the nature of God. It is in our nature, the nature God gave us, to explore these questions. The Bible gives general outlines for questions on every subject. However, the details are revealed to us through the Holy Spirit. "But I tell you the truth: It is for your good that I am going away.

Unless I go away, the Counselor will not come to you; but if I go, I will send him to you. When he comes, he will convict the world of guilt in regard to sin, and righteousness and judgment; in regard to sin, because men do not believe in me ... I have much more to say to you, more than you can now bear. But when he, the Spirit of truth, comes, he will guide you in all truth." John 16:7-10, 13. Sometimes the communication lines are not exactly clear. Perhaps in the new heaven and new earth we will know all the details. The Holy Spirit will still be present, only we will have no communication barrier. "Jesus did many other things as well. If every one of them were written down, I suppose that even the whole world would not have room for the books that would be written." John 21:25. There is a lot Jesus wants to tell us and explain about the universe He created. How long will it be until the return of our Lord? No one knows, but as the Lord himself said, it will be soon. When we go to live with the Lord forever, we will have the time to get the answers to these questions. I have often wondered what it will be like in the new heaven and new earth. Maybe the Christians of this generation will spend centuries teaching past saints about the science we are now learning. The saints of the past could be our guides to the past. We will learn the true history of the world through these saints. It would be a wonderful experience to learn about the history of the world without the assumptions of present "historians". Wouldn't it be wonderful to study the day to day journey of the exodus from Moses himself?

The Search for Extraterrestrial Intelligent Life (S.E.T.I.)

Most modern Astronomy books end with a section about the search for extraterrestrial life. They portray this as the most important part of studying the universe. If we could ever encounter life outside of the earth, this would be one of the most important discoveries in history. If life existed outside of earth, it would introduce a difficult dilemma for the Christian view of the creation of the universe. It would put theologians to the test to rectify the biblical view of God uniquely dealing with us on this planet with other intelligent life. I submit it would require the discovery of intelligent life, not just microbes, to create a serious challenge to the Christian faith. The plan of salvation is the redemption of man from the original sin of Adam and Eve. Since Christ died "once for all", it is a simple conclusion that any extraterrestrial life could only be angels. After all, a large part of the Old Testament is dedicated to the history of mankind. We are connected with the history of God's dealings with man leading to the sending of His son Jesus Christ for our salvation. Alien worlds with life would suggest they would either be sinless or they would have exactly the same history as our planet. The components for life can be abundant throughout the universe without generating any serious doubt to the Christian faith. We will discuss some of the challenges to the theory and philosophy of Evolution in the next three chapters. Is the search for extraterrestrial life just a scientific endeavor or does it have other motivating factors? I believe the search for extraterrestrial life is strongly motivated by a desperate need to prove the theory of evolution. The search for extraterrestrial life is the ultimate admission of failure for the faith of Atheism. Evolution has failed to explain the origin of life on earth. The evidence for the power of God to be the source of the creation of life is abundant. The atheist can not prove that life came from evolutionary forces on earth so they search the stars for proof that the process exists elsewhere in the universe. If they could find extraterrestrial life they would have a strong case that natural forces, they still do not fully understand, apart from the God of the Bible, began all life. Evidence for the desperation of proving that life came from a natural force instead of God is everywhere. Movies and television shows are abundant with the view that alien life is real. The intensity of the propaganda is enormous. How much evidence is there in the theory that alien life actually exists? Not much, and of course all evidence is circumstantial. If there was really any contact with alien life, it will be well documented and well known.

The search for extraterrestrial life follows the gradual acceptance of the theory of evolution. We will discuss how the theory of evolution became a part of public school curriculum in later chapters. It is not a coincidence that these theories became popular in the turbulent 1960's. "Prior to 1959, there was no dogma on the search for intelligent extraterrestrials. All references to the subject were found only between the covers of science fiction books and magazines, where interstellar spaceships were an integral part of the picture. Then, almost overnight, everything changed. It became scientifically respectable (or, in the view of some, tolerable) to talk about contacting aliens because the prestigious journal, Nature, published an article by physicists Philip Morrison and Giuseppe Cocconi describing the relative ease of transmitting radio signals across the galaxy and how it might be possible, using radio telescopes, to detect such signals from other intelligence. [3.41]" One article published in a periodical and an anxious world rushes to spend million of dollars building radio telescopes. Is this simply a thirst for scientific discovery or a quest to substantiate the misguided theory of evolution? The evolutionary theory proposes that your surrounding environment dictate all responses. If you are being choursed into going to a bar to get drunk, you should do it, according to the evolutionary philosophy. The theory of evolution thereby promotes the concept of "if it feels good do it". This is an ideology of rebellion against God, perfectly promoting sinful acts. It begins with denying the praise that we owe our existence to God for creating life. It continues this rebellious attitude to promote religious relativism, that there are no absolute principles of good and evil. The theory continues to promote the doctrine of survival of the fittest. This leads to justifying theft, bribery, lying to authorities, anything to get the desires of a lustful heart. If the opportunity arises to take something, you go for it. It is only wrong if you are caught. All these are merely signs of a world that is running from submitting themselves to the authority of the Lord Jesus Christ and the words in the Holy Scripture. I am aware that many Christians, guided by the spirit of making peace whenever possible, try to marginalize or avoid the subject of evolution. Many Christians believe there is actually no harm in this theory of science and science and faith are completely separate issues. I must re-state the premise of this book to not cause conflict between dedicated Christians. However, there are certain absolute truths to the Christian faith. I have a few questions for those who have faith in the Bible as the word of God and Jesus Christ as Lord and savior and trivialize the importance of discussing scientific topics and possible believe in many or all the statements in the theory of evolution. Here are a few questions to consider: How important is it to you to compromise and make peace with everyone? Are you sure you understand how un-reliable the theory of evolution has become through scientific study? Is your commitment to Jesus stronger than your desire to get along with everyone? Ask yourself the most important question of all: Where do I "draw the line in the sand"? A person who does not see the significance of the debate over the theory of evolution and it's implications I must question that person's personal faith in Jesus Christ and their commitment to fundamental biblical truths. In the next three chapters I will detail some of the implications to the theory and philosophy of evolution. I can only pray that my efforts to express my commitment to Jesus Christ will over shadow any disagreements with my convictions against the theory of evolution. When I began my research I felt like most Christians that the theory of evolution was really no big deal. However, during the research for this book that opinion drastically changed. This will become clear as I describe the effect this theory had on best selling author Lee Strobel. I feel the same effects experienced by Lee Strobel from the presentation of evolution are widespread. I believe that there are many parts to the ideas expressed in the theory of evolution which have led millions to accept other doctrines, fueled rebellion against God, and have weakened the Christian faith.

The Privileged Planet

It soon became clear that there were enormous obstacles to finding life on other planets by simply listening to the stars. "Even if the galaxy were humming with alien radio communications, we almost certainly would not intercept any of them unless the transmissions were outrageously extravagant in signal power, which goes against the initial argument about the efficiency of radio communication. Signals directed from point A to point B in the galaxy would be undetectable unless we happened to be precisely between two points- an enormous improbability. ... According to a 1978 study conducted by Woodruff T. Sullivan and his colleagues at the University of Washington, existing equipment would be able to pick up electronic "leakage" of television and radio-type emissions from only a few dozen light-years away- a radius that includes fewer than 200 stars. In the decades since that study, the sensitivity of our receivers has advanced to extend the detection radius to include thousands of stars, but this affords us little advantage, because electronic leakage from an Earthlike planet would be swamped within a few light-years by static of natural cosmic radio sources. [3.42]" So, where is the evidence for life on other planets? Again it comes from a faith in the power of evolution. "The most compelling support for the idea that we are not alone is the overwhelming vastness of the cosmos. Our own galaxy, the Milk Way, contains 50 times as many stars as there are humans on Earth. And there are billions of similar galaxies in the known universe. The total stellar cargo in the universe could easily exceed 10 billion trillion stars. Modern theories of star formation predict that at least some stars should have planets, and in the late 1990s, a few other solar systems were finally uncovered. But we are a long way from being able to estimate what fraction of those planets would provide the necessary conditions for the emergence of life. [3.43]"

There have been many attempts to calculate the probability of life on other planets. "The logic is to try to estimate the various fractions- of stars having planets, of those planets that are habitable, of those where conditions remain favorable long enough for life to evolve, of those where life does evolve, of those where intelligence evolves, and of the planet's life during which intelligence lasts. The product of all these fractions is the estimated fraction of all stars harboring intelligence. This statement is sometimes called the Drake Equation, after radio astronomer Frank Drake, who first formulated this scheme for discussing alien intelligence. [3.44]" This estimate to the number of habitable planets with intelligent life has changed with various discoveries. One very important factor in the equation is how easy it is for life to evolve. There are so many unknown factors about how life began on Earth, scientists still debate the conditions required to begin life. There are many other questions that are raised by this analysis as well. What kind of random forces are necessary to create the right conditions for an appropriate atmosphere? Would an alien world require the exact same conditions for life to begin? Can silicon based life, for example, actually exist? Are we extremely lucky to have evolved in a mere 4.5 billion years? These and many other questions are evaluated to produce an estimate of how many civilizations might exist in the universe. Many of these questions will be explored in the next chapter. Scientists have set a lower limit and an upper limit given by the Drake Equation to determine if life can exist on other planets. This reflects what scientists call an optimistic or pessimistic view, based on the assumption that life can easily evolve. Most scientists have resigned to the conclusion that there must be at least some alien life in the universe. Quote, "Nonetheless, there are so many galaxies that it is hard to avoid the conclusion-even with the pessimistic view-that life outside the solar system is likely, with millions or billions of technological civilizations. ... At a 1971 Soviet-American conference on this problem, the favored estimate came out to be one civilization per 100, 000 stars. This would put a million civilizations only a few hundred light-years away. ...So why haven't we heard from aliens? One answer could be that there are no aliens- intelligent life on Earth is some sort of unique accident. [3.45]" The scientific community constantly frowns on this explanation to the question of why we have not been contacted by alien life. They refuse to concede that we could be the only intelligent life in the universe. However, I find this to be the most plausible answer. Why? Evolution has failed in explaining the origin of life. Therefore, there is no scientific basis that life has "evolved" somewhere else. After all, we can not even prove that life came about through evolution on this planet! Why should it have taken place somewhere else? Life is no accident. It is a gift from God.

Let us examine the Drake equation more precisely. "Through the specific numbers that scientists plugged into Drake's equation mostly amounted to rank conjecture fueled by their own biases- one scientist admitted it was 'a way of compressing a large amount of ignorance into a small space' – this did lend an air of scientific certainty to a highly speculative issue. [3.46]" The Drake equation is like any other symbol of evolution we will study in the next few chapters. It is a representation of deception, to influence the general public into accepting the "scientific" evidence for extra-terrestrial life. It is simply the result of scientists committed to a belief in the power of evolution. "If life can emerge from non-life so quickly and efficiently on a planet as undistinguished as ours, they reason, then why not throughout the universe's hundreds of billions of galaxies? To them, life is like a soup mix: just add water!" [3.47] In fact, wherever there is evidence for water, scientists conjecture that there could possibly be life there. For instance, in recent years, there has been renewed discussion about microbes existing on Mars. Why? Scientists have found evidence that water may have flowed on Mars sometime in it's distant past. Again, they believe that where there is water there could be life. So, scientists are searching for possible signs of life frozen in the ground of Mars. How ridiculous can their faith in evolution be? Science repeatedly shows there is no basis for the spontaneous generation of life. And yet, scientists would have us believe that any drop of water could generate life. There have been recent articles in magazines about how microbes could survive inside comets crashing to earth. They even speculate that they could survive the extreme cold of space and the extreme heat of entering Earth's atmosphere to provide the necessary ingredients for life to begin here. Is this possible? We will explore the answer in the next three chapters.

Can just any old planet support life? Research has proven that there is a delicate balance of interacting natural systems that sustain life on this planet. "Earth's location, its size, its composition, its structure, its atmosphere, its temperature, its internal dynamics, and its many intricate cycles that are essential to life- the carbon cycle, the oxygen cycle, the nitrogen cycle, the phosphorous cycle, the sulfur cycle, the calcium cycle, the sodium cycle, and so on – testify to the degree to which our planet is exquisitely and precariously balanced. ... They note how its atmosphere filters out harmful ultraviolet radiation while working with the oceans to moderate the climate through the storing and redistributing of solar energy, and how the Earth is just large enough so that its gravity retains the atmosphere and yet just small enough not to keep too many harmful gases. Then they describe the Earth's interior as ... a gigantic but delicately balanced heat engine fueled by radioactivity ... Were it running more slowly ... the continents might not have evolved to their present form ... Iron may never have melted and sunk to the liquid core, and the magnetic field would never have developed ... If there had been more radioactive fuel, and therefore a faster running engine, volcanic dust would have blotted out the sun, the atmosphere would have been oppressively dense, and the surface would have been racked by daily earthquakes and volcanic explosions. These kind of highly choreographed geological processes - and there are lots of them – leave me shaking my head at the astonishing ways in which our biosphere is precisely tuned for life. [3.48]" We know that all these remarkable conditions are necessary for the life we know on this planet. However, many scientists will argue that there is resilience to life. They site examples of life flourishing in apparently totally hostile conditions. "'But life can also exist in some terribly harsh conditions,' I pointed out. 'For instance, there are life forms that live off deep sea thermal vents. They don't seam to need oxygen or any particular support from the broader environment.' 'On the contrary,' Gonzalez said, 'the only things down there that don't need oxygen are some microorganisms that breathe methane. But larger organisms, which need to regulate their metabolism, are invariably oxygen- breathers. The oxygen comes from surface life and marine algae. The oxygen gets mixed in with the ocean and transported into deep waters. So those organisms are very directly tied to the surface and overall ecosystem of the planet." [3.49]" With continuing research, we become increasingly aware of a delicate balance in our ecosystem. We recognize the necessity of all these systems working harmoniously in order for life to be sustained on earth. As we learn more about the symbiotic relationship all living creatures have with the environment, we can appreciate God as the designer and sustainer of all life. Humans have been given authority over their environment and the life that flourishes over the world. "Then God said, Let us make man in our image, in our likeness, and let them rule over the fish of the sea and the birds of the air, over the livestock, over all the earth, and over all the creatures that move along the ground. ... God blessed them and said to them, be fruitful and increase in number; fill the earth and subdue it. Rule over the fish of the sea and the birds of the air and over every living creature that moves on the ground." Genesis 1:26, 28 NIV. We have learned to do amazing things to change and control our world. Yet, we are helpless when unsuspected forces are suddenly placed in front of us. Look at the recent tsunami in the Indian Ocean. What about hurricane Katrina that hit the southern coast line of the United States? More on the subject of natural disasters will be covered in Chapter 10.

Does this imply that all planets that can support life must be exactly like ours? Scientists are still speculating what types of environment might produce life. Science fiction writers propose elaborate ideas of exotic types of life forms on other planets. "I interrupted to point out that science fiction writers have managed to speculate about extra-terrestrial life that's built in a radically different form – for instance, creatures based on silicon instead of carbon. ... 'That just won't work,' he insisted. 'Chemistry is one of the better understood areas of science. We know that you just can't get certain atoms to stick together in sufficient number and complexity to give you large molecules like carbon can. ... Unfortunately, people see life as being easy to create. They think it's enough merely to have liquid water, because they see life as an epiphenomenon-just a piece of slime mold growing on an inert piece of granite. Actually, the Earth's geology and biology interact very tightly with each other. You can't think of life as being independent of geophysical and meteorological processes of the planet. They interact in a very intimate way. So you need not only the right chemicals for life but also a planetary environment that's tuned to life.'[3.50]" The only known place to support life is the Earth. It becomes increasingly clear that the Earth was made with very precise specifications for supporting life. To suggest that any other type of environment has the possibility to support life is mere speculation. It seams clear to me that any scientist suggesting advanced intelligent life on any other planet must agree that the planet must be an exact duplicate of the Earth. To suggest otherwise would be the result of desperation rather than scientific study. The same size, environment, and located around a similar star. Why the same kind of star, you may ask? The properties of the sun have profound implications on the Earth's environment. The type of star in the center of a planetary system can also limit the possibility of life developing and remaining on a planet, assuming life itself can come from natural forces. Stars like our sun are not as common as was once believed. "If you pick a star at random, you're likely to pick one that's far less massive than the sun, usually red dwarfs, which make up about eighty percent of stars. ... Red dwarfs emit most of their radiation in the red part of the spectrum, which makes photosynthesis less efficient. ... as you decrease the mass of a star, you also decrease the luminosity. A planet would have to orbit this kind of star much closer in order to have sufficient heat to maintain liquid water on its surface. The problem is the tidal forces between the star and the planet gets stronger as you move in, so the planet will spin down and eventually end up in what's called a tidally locked state. ... Red dwarfs have flares ... With a red dwarf, your planet would have to be much closer to the star. ... The luminosity increase would cause temperature spikes on the surface of an orbiting planet. ... Particle radiation has the effect of quickly stripping away the atmosphere, increasing the surface radiation levels, but most importantly, destroying the ozone layer, which we need to protect from radiation. All of this would be deadly for any life on a planet near a red dwarf. [3.51]" The other types of stars don't need to be mentioned. The possibility of life sustaining planets around these stellar forms would not be likely. Therefore you would need a star exactly like ours to sustain life. Next you would need a planetary system exactly like ours to sustain life.

The search for extraterrestrial life has been inspired by recent discoveries of other solar systems. We now know of many other planets outside of our solar system. "In 1995 the first planet orbiting another main-sequence star, 51 Pegasi, was identified. By early 2003 around a hundred planetary systems had been discovered around a wide variety of stars up to 180 light years away. Many of these sub-stellar objects are in very close orbits and are many times the mass of Jupiter. [3.52]" For a more complete listing of these planets and the current discoveries, I suggest the hubblesite.org web site or NASSA.gov web site. So far, only planets close to the size of Jupiter have been detected. This is due to the enormous difficulties of detecting objects smaller than Jupiter sized planets around stars. Several proposed methods and designs for orbiting telescopes are under development to discover smaller planets. There was an article in the National Geographic magazine in late 2004 that listed a general outline for discovering an earth-like world by 2065. I should say a planet the size of the earth. As we saw earlier, it appears our world is far more unique that we are led to believe. This is a time of great excitement for scientific discovery in Astronomy, even without the probability of finding other life forms evolving on other planets. What I find amazing is how passionate some individuals are about finding life on other planets. There are groups with profound faith in the existence of extraterrestrials. Sometimes, I wish we had as many Christians with such profound commitment to their faith in Jesus Christ. However, their passionate faith is based more on philosophy than science. The science we are now discovering is leading in the opposite direction i.e. in the direction of an intelligent design in the universe. "More and more scientists are studying the mind-boggling convergence of scores of extraordinary "coincidences" that make intelligent life possible on Earth and concluding that this can't possibly be an accident. [3.53]" If we take the scientific investigation further, we will conclude that the God of the Bible creating the universe is the only possible explanation for the existence of the universe, our world, and every living thing that resides on earth.

Scientists passionately use probability equations to suggest there must be life on other planets somewhere in the universe. Yet, all the evidence leads to less of a probability of any planet other than earth supporting life. We are in a privileged location in the universe, even in our own galaxy. "You see, the Big Bang produced basically hydrogen and helium. ... The heavier elements were synthesized – cooked, if you will – in the interior of stars. Eventually, when these stars exploded as supernovae, these elements got expelled into the interstellar medium. ... Galaxies have varying degrees of star formation, where interstellar gases coalesce to form stars, star clusters, and massive stars that blow up as supernovae. Places with active star formation are very dangerous, because that's where you have supernovae exploding at a fairly high rate. In our galaxy, those dangerous places are primarily in the spiral arms, where there are hazardous giant molecule clouds. Fortunately, though, we happen to be situated safely between the Sagittarius and Perseus spiral arms. Also, we're very far from the nucleus of the galaxy, which is also a dangerous place. We know that there's a massive black hole at the center of our galaxy. In fact, the Hubble space telescope has found that nearly every large nearby galaxy has a giant black hole at its nucleus. ... Now, put all this together – the inner region of the galaxy is much more dangerous from radiation and other threats; the outer part of the galaxy isn't going to be able to form Earth-like planets because the heavy elements are not abundant enough; and ... the thin disk of our galaxy helps our sun stay in its desirable circular orbit. ... All of this ... works together to create a narrow safe zone where life-sustaining planets are possible. [3.54]" Living within a thin disc on the edge of the galaxy is consistent with scripture. "He wraps himself in light as with a garment; he stretches out the heavens like a tent" Psalms 104:2 Other versions translate the last part of the verse as "stretching out heaven as a curtain." This passage may indicate the stars are "stretched out" in an arm curl like on the cover of this book, and like modern astronomy has shown us with our own galaxy. Also, recall that the lessons of General Relativity Theory teach us that the universe is curved. We know many verses where "heaven" is referred as the place where the stars exist. There are many speculations about the "location" of heaven. Sometimes heaven refers to the outer places of the universe, other times it describes where God resides. Wherever heaven actually exists, in this universe or on in a higher dimensional plane, we will all be called to judgment at God's throne in heaven. More on this subject is covered in Chapter 10.

Increasingly more evidence supports the conclusion that we are a unique creation and there is no other life in the universe, other than those in a place the Bible calls heaven where God and His angels reside. Some will ask, what about other types of galaxies? Could they support life? "Elliptical galaxies look amorphous and are sort of egg-shaped with stars having very random orbits ... The problem for life in these galaxies is that the stars visit every region, which means they'll occasionally visit the dangerous, dense inner regions, where a black hole may be active. ... you're less likely to find Earth-like planets in elliptical galaxies because most of them lack the heavier elements needed to form them. ... Our galaxy is on the top one or two percent of the most massive and luminous. The bigger the galaxy, the more heavy elements it can have, because its stronger gravity can attract more hydrogen and helium and cycle them to build heavy elements. In low-mass galaxies, which make up the vast majority, you can have whole galaxies without a single Earth-like planet. They just don't have enough of the heavy elements to construct Earths.

... Even if you had a few regions in the galaxy where there were sufficient heavy elements to build Earths, they would have been so irradiated (from quasars and supernova occurring rapidly in the distant past) that life wouldn't be possible. ... There are no safe places where there are fewer supernovae exploding, like we have between our spiral arms. ... So the probability for there being civilizations elsewhere actually keeps declining as we learn more about new threats that we didn't know before. [3.55]" As we stated earlier, there has been the discovery of a number of other planets. Most seam to be the size of Jupiter and seams to be gas giants like our Jupiter. So far, no planet outside the solar system seams to have the properties necessary to support life. However, the discovery of other planets opens the possibility of other solar systems with a similar arrangement of planets. How much does the rest of the solar system effect life on earth? It turns out it has a profound effect. So, to have a habitable planet, you may need to have a duplicate of not only the earth, but a similar arrangement of planets and moons in a solar system. "For example, George Wetherill of the Carnegie institute showed in 1994 that Jupiter – which is huge, more than three hundred times the mass of the Earth – acts as a shield to protect us from many comet impacts. It actually deflects comets and keeps many of them from coming into the inner solar system, where they could collide with Earth with life – extinguishing consequences. ... Our first line of defense is Mars, being at the edge of the asteroid belt. It takes a lot of hits for us. Venus does too. If you want to get an idea of the stuff that probably would have hit the Earth, look at the surface of the moon. The moon, unfortunately, has too little surface area to provide much surface protection, but it's a nice record. [3.56]" All these planets, our moon and dozens of other factors act like a protective blanket around the earth. If the solar system was even slightly different the odds of an asteroid or comet crashing into the Earth killing all life dramatically increases.

It is so amazing how all these systems play a role in the protection of our planet. We continue to learn about the critical role of each system. This implies that the earth, and all the planets and moons in the solar system were uniquely created for our benefit. The position of a planet relative to the star is also critical to be able to sustain life, as we discussed earlier. "The main point is that as you go further out from the sun, you have to increase the carbon dioxide content of the planet's atmosphere. This is necessary in order to trap the sun's radiation and keep water liquid. The problem is that there wouldn't be enough oxygen to have mammal-like organisms. ... So if the Earth's distance from the sun were moved by, say, five percent either way, what would happen? ... Disaster ... Animal life would be impossible. The zone for animal life in our solar system is much narrower than most people think. And that's why you need a circular orbit like the one Earth has ... You don't just want to be in the Circumstellar Habitable Zone part of the time; you want it to be continuously. It doesn't do you any good to have melted water for four months and then have a whole planet freeze up again. [3.57]" Once again, it is not enough to simply have another planet exist to spark the interest of life on other planets. There are large numbers of factors that must be synchronized in order for life to exist on a planet. This indicates that the scientist looking for life on other planets, expecting to find other life, is driven more by passion than by reason. Scientific study would put the likelihood of life on other planets very low. Their consuming passionate belief in the power of evolution is the driving force that compels scientists to desperately search for extra-terrestrial life. Once again, the scientific method suggesting that evolution is taking place throughout the universe is a highly skeptical theory. However, it is strongly held to be an absolute fact in science, despite the evidence against the theory. The "true" power of evolution is in the philosophy that surrounds the theory. It is based on an unrealistic faith in forces that can not be proven to exist by science. The theory of evolution is simply an attempt to give a "reasonable" explanation why people have chosen to reject the gospel. The theory of evolution is disproven by science numerous times.

Dr. Jay Wesley Richards and Dr. Guillermo Gonzalez co-authored a book called The Privileged Planet, in which many of the previously mentioned observations are discussed in detail. They also provide one more important observation about the position of the earth relative to the rest of the universe. They suggest that we are uniquely placed in the universe, which helps us discover many important principles of science. " 'For example,' said Gonzalez, 'not only do we inhabit a location in the Milky Way that's fortuitously optimal for life, but our location also happens to provide us with the best overall platform for making a diverse range of discoveries for astronomers and cosmologists. Our location away from the galaxy's center and in a flat plane of the disk provides us with a particular privileged vantage point for observing both nearby and distant stars'. [3.58]" Again, the Bible encourages us to search for the truth. "To the Jews who had believed him, Jesus said, if you hold to my teaching, you are really my disciples. Then you will know the truth and the truth shall set you free." John 8:31-32 "Turn your ear to wisdom and apply your heart to understanding … For the Lord gives wisdom, from his mouth come knowledge and understanding." Proverbs 2:2, 6. You may want to again read the introduction to study many of the verses concerning how God holds scientific pursuits in high regard. It is in the field of Astronomy that we understand the meaning of these verses most clearly. God spoke the universe into existence and through the study of the result; we have gained great knowledge and understanding about God's creation. God purposely placed us in the best possible location in the entire universe for scientific study. This is perfectly understandable when we search the scripture. "This is what God the LORD says – he who created the heavens and stretched them out, who spread out the earth and all that comes out of it, who gives breath to its people, and life to those who walk on it." Isaiah 42:5 Again, God deserves praise for every breath we take as a gift from Him. There are several verses that refer to God "stretching" out His hand and creating the universe. Is it possible that this is demonstrated in the Spiral Arm of our Milk Way Galaxy? We have already discussed a few of the reasons that scientific analysis indicates that a spiral galaxy may be necessary to protect a life-sustaining planet. A Galaxy with a spiral arm might be the only type of Galaxy capable of sustaining life. Moreover, it is extremely likely that we may live in the only habitable Galaxy. Furthermore, this could be the only planet containing life. This is completely opposite to popular belief, but it may be the truth. I would find it wonderful if there was another habitable planet, but the odds are dwindling as we increase our understanding of the requirements necessary for life to exist. Remember, God gives us the stars and the universe to study in order for us to give glory back to Him for his creations power. "It is I who made the earth and created mankind upon it. My own hands stretched out the heavens; I marshaled their starry hosts." Isaiah 45:12. The New International Version intrigues me with the translation of this verse. "I marshaled their starry hosts" presents an image of God setting an order to the many galaxies that exist. Maybe that is why we see so many galactic clusters in the universe. There are many discoveries in Astronomy that uphold our faith in God creating the universe. Also, there is no discovery that conflicts with our faith in any meaningful way. In fact, it is through the field of Astronomy that we learn how God's power has created a place of amazing complexity and wondrous beauty. There are many books with spectacular pictures to inspire your love for the Lord. Every Christian should be inspired by the breath-taking beauty displayed by the pictures we have from the orbiting space telescopes.

Refer back to the Introduction is this book frequently, as I often do, to appreciate God's words instructing us to "seek wisdom". This concludes our section on Astronomy. We will often refer back to these first three chapters as we explore modern physics in chapter nine. As we have stated, the field of modern Astronomy is interwoven with the fields of modern physics and mathematics. However, the constant inclusion of the theory of evolution and the word "evolution" in the field of Astronomy is misleading and totally unnecessary. We will explore the theory of evolution in the next three chapters. We will learn that the theory of evolution is more "science fiction" than "science fact". The theory of evolution is more a philosophy than science. This conclusion is most evident in how the theory of evolution has "spilled over" into other fields of science like the field of Astronomy. In the next three chapters we will explore both the scientific foundations of the theory of evolution and the philosophical implications. While doing research for this book, I became more aware of the dangers of believing the theory of evolution. I hope you will consider the implications I will discuss but in the final analysis realize that I am simply concerned with any idea or philosophy that appears to be a direct attack on both my faith in Jesus Christ and my love for science. The theory of evolution unjustly does both, in my opinion.

References for Chapter 3

3.1   Nigel Calder, Einstein's Universe, Penguin Books, 1981, p. 12.

3.2   Raymond A. Serway, Physics For Scientists & Engineers with Modern Physics Third edition, Philadelphia, Saunders College Publishing, 1990, p. 1388-1395.

3.3   William K. Hartmen, Astronomy: The Cosmic Journey, Belmont California, Wadsworth Publishing, 1991, p. 321-322.

3.4   Ibid. p. 322.

3.5   Ibid. p. 322.

3.6   Josh McDowell & Don Stewart, Reasons Skeptics Should Consider Christianity, Wheaton, Illinois, Living Books, Tyndale House Publishers, 1981, p. 103-105.

3.7   William K. Hartmen, Astronomy: The Cosmic Journey, Belmont California, Wadsworth Publishing, 1991, p.322.

3.8   James S. Trefil, From Atoms To Quarks: An Introduction to the Strange World of Particle Physics, New York, Charles, Scribner's Sons, 1980, p. 30-31.

3.9   Ibid. p. 193.

3.10   Ibid. p. 193-194.

3.11   Raymond A. Serway, Physics For Scientists & Engineers with Modern Physics Third edition, Philadelphia, Saunders College Publishing, 1990, p.1406.

3.12   John F. Ashton, In Six Days: Why Fifty Scientists choose to believe in Creation, Master Books, 2000- 2003, p. 274-275.

3.13   Lee Strobel, The Case for A Creator, Zondervan, Grand Rapids Michigan. 2004, p. 120-121.

3.14   Meir H. Degani, Astronomy Made Simple, Garden City, New York, Made Simple Books, Doubleday & Company, 1976, p.103-106.

3.15   The Life and Death of Stars, Source: http://hubblesite.org/newscenter/newsdesk/archive/releases/ , Don Savage, NASA Headquarters, Washington, Mark Hess, Goddard Space Flight Center, Greenbelt, MD, Ray Villard, Space Telescope Science Institute, Baltimore, MD.

3.16   Arthur Beiser, Concepts of Modern Physics Fourth Edition, McGraw-Hill Book Company, 1987, p. 504-505.

3.17   William K. Hartmen, Astronomy: The Cosmic Journey, Belmont California, Wadsworth Publishing, 1991, p. 408.

3.18   Release Number: STScI-1992-05, http://hubblesite.org Don Savage, NASA Headquarters, Washington, Mark Hess, Goddard Space Flight Center, Greenbelt, MD, Ray Villard, Space Telescope Science Institute, Baltimore, MD.

3.19   William K. Hartmen, Astronomy: The Cosmic Journey, Belmont California, Wadsworth Publishing, 1991, p. 403-404.

3.20   Ibid. p. 407.

3.21   Meir H. Degani, Astronomy Made Simple, Garden City, New York, Made Simple Books, Doubleday & Company, 1976, p.106.

3.22   Ibid. p. 75.

3.23   Ibid. p. 75-76.

3.24   Ibid. p. 76-77.

3.25   Ibid. p. 78.

3.26   Ibid. p. 78-79.

3.27   Ibid. p. 79-81.

3.28   William K. Hartmann, Astronomy: The Cosmic Journey, Belmont California, Wadsworth Publishing, 1991, p 352.

3.29   Ibid. p. 99.

3.30   Ibid. p. 347.

3.31   Ibid. p. 299.

3.32   Ibid. p. 301.

3.33   Ibid. p. 305.

3.34   Ibid. p. 309.

3.35   Ibid. p. 304.

3.36   Terence Dickinson, The Universe and Beyond third edition, Firefly Books Ltd., 1999, p.162.

3.37   Ibid. p. 155 and p.161.

3.38   Ibid. p. 22.

3.39   James Strong, Strong's Exhaustive Concordance of The Bible, Lynchburg, Virginia, The Old-Time Gospel Hour.

3.40   William K. Hartmann, Astronomy: The Cosmic Journey, Belmont California, Wadsworth Publishing, 1991, p. 37.

3.41   Terence Dickinson, The Universe and Beyond third edition, Firefly Books Ltd.,1999, p.130.

3.42   Ibid. p.131.

3.43   Ibid. p. 125.

3.44   William K. Hartmann, Astronomy: The Cosmic Journey, Belmont California, Wadsworth Publishing, 1991, p.629.

3.45   Ibid. p.630-631.

3.46   Lee Strobel, The Case for A Creator, Zondervan, Grand Rapids Michigan. 2004, p. 155.

3.47   Ibid. p. 154.

3.48   Ibid. p. 157.

3.49   Ibid. p. 166.

3.50   Ibid. p. 165.

3.51   Ibid. p. 175-176.

3.52   Firefly Astronomy Dictionary. Firefly Books Inc., Buffalo, New York, 2003, p.74.

3.53   Lee Strobel, The Case for A Creator, Zondervan, Grand Rapids Michigan. 2004, p. 155.

3.54   Ibid. p. 168-170.

3.55   Ibid. p. 170-171.

3.56   Ibid. p. 173-174.

3.57   Ibid. p. 174.

3.58   Ibid. p. 187.

Illustrations for Chapter 3

3.1   Left Side: Arthur Beiser, Concepts of Modern Physics Fourth Edition, McGraw-Hill Book Company, 1987, p. 493. Right side: William K. Hartmann, Astronomy: The Cosmic Journey, Belmont California, Wadsworth Publishing, 1991, p.321.

3.2   Top: William K. Hartmann, Astronomy: The Cosmic Journey, Belmont California, Wadsworth Publishing, 1991, p. 366 Bottom: William J. Kaufmann, III, Black Holes and Warped Spacetime, W.H. Freeman and Company, San Francisco, 1979, p. 37.

3.3   Arthur Beiser, Concepts of Modern Physics Fourth Edition, McGraw-Hill Book Company, 1987, p.505.

3.4   Ibid p. 135.

Chapter 4: Micro-Biology and Evolution
Evolution and Creation: Theories about the origins of life.

The theory of evolution is the most controversial theory of science in history. No other theoretical work has had as much opposition as the theory of evolution, and rightfully so. It is a highly debated subject with lots of opinions. I want to touch on just a few of the main topics of the theory of evolution. To most of the people I have asked about the theory of evolution, they only principle that it teaches they can recognize is that men evolved from apes. It seams that the general public knows very little about the theory of evolution beyond this fact. In public and private schools today, the theory of evolution is taught as if it was an absolute fact, despite recent attempts to modify the standard teaching practices. Students are inundated by implications that the theory of evolution is a proven scientific fact. For example, quote, "The virtually infinite variations of life ARE the fruit of the evolutionary process. All living creatures ARE related by decent from common ancestors. Humans and other animals ARE descended from shrew like creatures that lived more than 150,000,000 years ago; mammals, birds, reptiles, amphibians, and fishes share as ancestors aquatic worms that lived 6,000,000,000 years ago; all planets and animals ARE derived from bacteria-like microorganisms that originated more than 3,000,000,000 years ago. [4.1]" Currently, the theory of evolution is presented as fact, with no room to question the validity of the theory. Descriptions of the theory of evolution strategically place words like "ARE" to represent the evolutionary theory as an absolute truth. Phrases like: according to the theory of evolution, life began with single cell organisms, have been removed from the secular description of evolution in public school textbooks. At one time, the theory of evolution was considered a radical theory, inappropriate to the scientific investigation of the origin of life. This was not just the opinion of the public, but the scientific community as well. So how did this controversial theory become accepted as fact? We will first explore the biological science involved in developing the theory of evolution, and then discuss the history of placing this theory in public classrooms. Both the scientific research and the legal debates occurred over the same period of time. However, we will learn it is not the scientific studies that are the driving force behind placing the theory of evolution in the classroom. Rather, the religious views of politicians and lawyers. The religion that is promoted is Atheism. In essence, when we allow the teaching of evolution in public schools, we are establishing the religion of atheism in public places. Why is it so difficult to remove this religion? The atheist groups refuse to call their belief that there is no God a religion. They insist that it is just the absence of any religion. Yet, atheism is a set of ideas unproven by science and accepted by faith. I would say that makes atheism fall into the category of a religion. I learned from a friend of mine that there are many principles in the Atheism charter. This is the same as a statement of beliefs you will find posted in many churches. In this chapter we will briefly explore the religious aspect of Atheism and its cornerstone, the belief in the theory of evolution.

Much of the theory of evolution started from the categorization of the different animal species into families of animals having similar characteristics. The need to categorize all the different species into separate kinds of animals began with the biblical account of the flood. Theologians realized that not every species was on the ark, but every kind of species was represented. "And of every living thing of all flesh, you shall bring two of every sort into the ark, to keep them alive with you; they shall be male and female. Of the birds according to their kinds, and of the animals according to their kinds, of every creeping thing of the ground according to its kind, two of every sort shall come to you, to keep them alive with you; they shall be male and female. Of the birds according to their kinds, and of the animals according to their kinds, of every creeping thing of the ground according to its kind, two of every sort shall come to you, to keep them alive." - Genesis 6:19, 20. Today there are more than 2,000,000 different species. Early developments towards the theory of evolution were taken from a biblical necessity. Quote, "Their motivation was not biological but rather religious: it would have been impossible to hold representatives of all species in a single vessel such as Noah's ark; hence, some species must have come into existence only after the Noachian flood [4.2]" Of course the Christian has no objection to the process of categorizing the different species into "kinds". After all, this is exactly what is recorded in the Bible. "So God created the great creatures of the sea and every living and moving thing with which the water teems, according to their kinds, and every winged bird according to its kind. And God saw that it was good. ... And God said, 'Let the land produce living creatures according to their kinds: livestock, creatures that move along the ground, and wild animals, each according to its kind.' And it was so." Genesis 1:21, 24. Christians simply maintain there are limitations to the process of changing a species within a particular kind.

There are only a certain number of different kinds of animals and every animal fits into one of these categories. The biggest problem with evolution is the refusal to put any limitations on biological changes. This is a direct violation of biological, chemical and physical laws. Much of the work in the various fields of science is to describe the limitations to physical laws. Hence the millions of different species that exist today came from a parent species of a particular kind of plant or animal. When God originally created all life on earth, there were certain number of different kinds of animals, insects, plants, birds and fish. Actually, the ark might have been large enough to carry every known species, according to recent studies on the dimensions of Noah's ark. The evolutionary theory would have you believe that ultimately there are common ancestors to EVERY kind of animal and at some point in time they diverged into different species. They believe you can trace ALL species back to single cell creatures, which was the first form of life to "evolve" out of organic chemical substances. This process is simply not proven by science and many parts of this process violate bio-chemical and physical laws. Today, the creation of life is still a mystery and the events which caused life to begin from non-living organic substances still can not be duplicated under the most ideal laboratory conditions. This leads to an inescapable fact that "simple" chemistry could not have produced life.

Basic Requirements for Evolution to Work

Charles Darwin is considered the father of the theory of evolution. In his book, 'The Origin of Species', Darwin began to categorize all animals into types having similar physical characteristics. He further extended the categorization and placed man in the same species as apes. Darwin was the first to describe, in detail, how natural selection could be used to cause a new species to develop. Many scientists believed that Darwin's theory of evolution was the cornerstone to scientific research. Scientists began to place the achievements of Copernicus, Galileo, and Newton with the new theory of evolution to present a view of a universe created by natural forces rather than God. Quote, "The significance of these and other discoveries was that they led to a conception of the universe as a system of matter in motion governed by laws of nature. The workings of the universe no longer needed to be attributed to the will of the Creator, but were brought into the realm of science- an explanation of phenomena through natural laws.' [4.3]" We see from the statement a hint of an enthusiastic atheist. Now, it seams, science would be able to explain the universe without any reference to God as the creator. At last, a licensed to sin! The evolutionary theory attributes natural selection as the guiding force behind the development of living organisms. We will discuss the theory of natural selection on three different areas of development. 1) The theory of natural selection due to the environmental factors, such as availability of food supply and competition for survival. 2) The development of change due to the laws of probability and random chance. 3) The theory of natural selection due to subtle changes in DNA structure. We will discuss the errors in the theory of evolution in each of these categories. The naturalistic viewpoint was discussed in the first chapter and the limitations of physics will be discussed further in later chapters. One thing is certain, Darwin is to be commended for his efforts to place different species into separate categories, but man is not an evolved ape. Man is a unique creation of God. Man is a creation which was made with the gift of having the ability to reign over the other creations of God, by virtue of a complex mind. Even most of the general public resent being represented as a "monkey's uncle". The search for interrelationships between species has produced a successful categorization of species in many instances. However, many gaps in the history of a species evolving produce great skepticism in the concept of all species ultimately being related to each other. For example, there are many varieties of cats. There are mountain lions, tigers, cougars, the lions of Africa and household cats. All these different cats have noticeable physical characteristics. It is difficult to imagine that a cat is a distant cousin to a dog or a horse. The relationships between two kinds of species with drastically different physical characteristics have never been proven, at least not in the large animal kingdom. It is true there is evidence that different types of fish are related, but is there evidence of a fish and a dog being related? This is absurd. The evidence for an inter-relationship between a dog and a fish, for example, does not exist. This is where the theory of evolution falls apart.

The Teaching of Evolution

Lee Strobel represents his search for an understanding of science and highlights of his life have been documented in several books. In the book, The Case for a Creator, Lee describes how the teachings of evolution led him to believe in Atheism. Among his most memorable experiences was as a young student in a biology class in the early 1960's. The teacher explained the theory of evolution with a series of images that illustrated the main points to the theory of evolution. The pictures he was shown included: 1.) The set of Chemistry apparatus in the 1953 Stanley Miller experiment. 2) Darwin's Tree of life. 3.) Ernst Haeckel's Drawings of Embryos 4.) Various artist renderings of "missing links". These missing links included drawings of a supposedly half-bird, half- reptile called archaeopteryx. Some other famous "missing links" to man have included the Neanderthal, Lucy, and Hesperopithecus. We will discuss some of these discoveries in detail. One thing that can not be overstated is the power of images. When Lee was in his class, and heard about the principles of evolution, he had come to whole heartedly believe in the theory of evolution as true. While I was reading his book, I kept thinking about my own experiences in science class rooms. I felt a kindred spirit with Lee as he dwelled on these images of evolution. Lee has an inquisitive mind that led him to become an investigative reporter. This same spirit of unquenchable search for the truth is what motivates many young students to pursue careers in science. Let me be clear as we begin our investigation into the principles of evolution and their teaching in public schools. In no way am I suggesting that teachers, who present the theory of evolution, are anything but caring professionals. Yet, there is an undeniable impact the teaching of evolution had on Lee's life, and many other students. I had similar questions about the beginning of life and how it was formed. However, unlike Lee, I was a Christian by the time I entered grade school. I felt as though I was protected from dwelling too intently on these images and somehow, through the Holy Spirit, I was not severely shaken in my belief that life came into existence by the power of God. Lee, on the other hand, found the evidence convincing and became an atheist while he was a high school student. Let us explore these images and why they can have such a profound impact on young minds, and can affect their faith in the existence of God.

The Stanley Miller experiment was one of the first attempts to prove that, given the right circumstances, life could be produced from non-living chemicals. "This was the most powerful picture of all- the laboratory apparatus that Stanley Miller, ..., used in 1953 to artificially produce the building blocks of life. By reproducing the atmosphere of the primitive earth (supposedly) and then shooting electric sparks through it to simulate lightning, Miller managed to produce a red goo containing amino acids. The moment I first learned of Miller's success, my mind flashed to the logical implication: if the origin of life can be explained through natural processes, then God was out of a job! [4.4]" This is the bedrock of the theory of evolution. From the first conception of evolution, it has had as a purpose to explain the existence of life without any references to God. The theory of evolution, from its first inception, was designed more for a natural explanation of life than from the standpoint of a scientific method to search out the truth about life. Evolution has more of a philosophical slant on the investigation that just an objective search for understanding. "Nancy Pearcey, who has written extensively on science and faith, insists that 'you can have God or natural selection, but not both.' She pointed out that Darwin himself recognized that the presence of an omnipotent deity would actually undermine his theory. 'If we admit God into the process', Darwin argued, 'then God would ensure that only the right variations occurred .... and natural selection would be superfluous.' Law professor Philip Johnson, author of the breakthrough critique of evolution Darwin On Trial, agrees that 'the whole point of Darwinism is to show that there is no need for a supernatural creator, because nature can do the creating by itself.'[4.5]" There should be no debate over the fact that there are enormous consequences if evolution is correct. From the beginning, the theory of evolution has focused on approaching science from an atheistic perspective. The difficulty is convincing the public that atheism is not simply the lack of religion, but a belief all its own. When the theory was first introduced in public schools, there was a tremendous outcry for its removal. However, over the years the evolutionist movement has gained ground by bombarding the unprepared public with true or slightly true facts. The evolutionist has done an excellent job of propaganda. At first, Christians were appalled by the obvious implications of the theory of evolution. "If Darwinism is true, ..., then there are five inescapable conclusions: there's no evidence for God, there's no life after death, there's no absolute foundation for right and wrong, there's no ultimate meaning for life, people really don't have free will. [4.6]" Many Christians wholeheartedly challenged the inception of evolution in schools in the early days. However, the evolutionists have used methods of political correctness to promote peace. The Christians know Christ said "blessed are the peacemakers." and "turn the other cheek". Therefore, the widespread demonstrations of the past have become a dim memory. However, scientists and the news media have still supported a propaganda campaign that anyone questioning the theory of evolution is a religious fanatic. Instead, it is the evolutionists that have an overwhelming zeal for "preaching" the virtues of the theory of evolution.

Scientists opposing evolution has been slow to develop. Some of the students and teachers with a background in going to Church believed that you could keep your faith and the theory of evolution separated. This has proven impossible. The theory of evolution is irrevocably connected to attacking Christian principles and doctrine. There are some scientists that have taken a bold stand against the theory of evolution. "There were one hundred of them – biologists, chemists, zoologists, physicists, anthropologists, molecular and cell biologists, bio-engineers, organic chemists, geologists, astrophysicists, and other scientists. Their doctorates came from such prestigious universities as Cambridge, Stanford, Cornell, Yale, Rutgers, Chicago, Princeton, Purdue, Duke, Michigan, Syracuse, Temple, and Berkeley. ... After spokespersons for the Public Broadcasting System's seven-part television series Evolution asserted that ' all known scientific evidence supports [Darwinian] evolution' as does 'virtually every reputable scientist in the world,' these professors, laboratory researchers, and other scientists published a two - page advertisement in a national magazine under the banner: 'A scientific Dissent From Darwinism.' ... [Among those were] Nobel nominee Henry F. Schaefer, the third most - cited chemist in the world; ... In fact, its [the PBS series] one-sided depiction of evolution spurred a backlash from many scientists. A detailed, 151-page critique claimed it 'failed to present accurately and fairly the scientific problems with the evidence for Darwinian evolution' and even systematically ignored 'disagreements among evolutionary biologists themselves.' [4.7]" As more scientific studies are found, the public is slowly becoming more aware of the truth about the scientific findings for and against the theory of evolution. I was astounded by the evidence against the theory of evolution presented in Lee's book. I too, was unaware of the enormous amounts of evidence against the reliability of the theory of evolution. However, there are still millions of casualties in this battle of the opposing philosophical differences between evolution and creation.

It becomes clear that the theory of evolution is directly opposite to faith in God. There are creditable scientists on both sides of the debate between evolution and creation (or intelligent design), despite statements to the contrary from the media. Let us summarize Lee Strobel's work as he decided to pursue and un-biased look at the theories of evolution. "So, I decided to return, in effect , to my days as a student by reexamining those images of evolution – the Miller experiment, Darwin's tree of life, Haeckel's embryos, and the archaeopteryx missing link – which had convinced me that undirected and purposeless evolutionary processes accounted for the origin and complexity of life. Those symbols are hardly outdated. In fact, to this day those very same icons are still featured in many biology textbooks and are being seared into the minds of students around the country. But are they accurate in what they convey? What do they really tell us about the trustworthiness of Darwinism? [4.8]" Instead of building up suspense like a good mystery novel, I'll just skip to the end for a moment. The scientific evidence is consistently pointing away from the truthfulness of the theory of evolution. It is becoming clearer each day that the theory of evolution can not adequately explain the origin of life. We will cover some of the highlights to why this is a true assessment of the direction of scientific research. I suggest reading other books on the subject for further details. This book will merely highlight a few of the basic principles and evidences against evolution and leave many details to further research from the reader. After we cover the scientific points, I want to more closely and passionately examine the long range implications of Lee's search for truth. As Christians, we must be prepared in our **homes and churches** to help our **children and adults** who are searching for answers to their questions. It is inevitable that a debate over the existence of God will begin every time the theory of evolution is mentioned. It is amazing that there is such a stubborn resistance to openly express these ideas in schools. It is not even the Christian who usually opens the door to this discussion; it is the evolutionist who is firmly convinced of his belief in atheism. A religion is taught and promoted in schools. That religion is atheism and it is a lie. When instructors present the theory of evolution inconsistencies soon arise and the debate begins.

Limitations to change

Evolutionists confuse changes within a species with the ability to have transitions between species. The second law of thermodynamics limits the degree of changes allowed in living organisms. As stated in the previous chapter, the first law of thermodynamics is the law of conservation of mass and energy. The second law is the statement that entropy or disorder, tends to increase with time. In other words, physical systems tend to lose energy and increase in random order. The laws of thermodynamics can be applied to the biological processes. Biological processes can and will change throughout a species life. We take in food which causes our physical frame to grow, and our mental processes can increase through time if we exercise our mind as we are exercising our bodies. However, the total energy and entropy of any closed system goes down. All living creatures today have limitations to their growth abilities. All physical forms, all people, age, slow down and eventually die. How could anyone deny this fact? Changes can occur over a period of time with an individual or a species. However, changes within a species family are limited also. Change within a family of species is possible but changing between two families is not. When you have certain change within a species you are not going from a lower ordered life form to a higher life form, in violation of the second law of thermodynamics. Different levels or categories to a species are acceptable scientifically and biblically. "'Before we go any further ... let's get our definitions straight. When some people say 'evolution' they mean merely that there has been change over time. ... If that's all there was to Darwinism, then there wouldn't be any controversy, because we all agree there has been biological change over time. ... Darwinism claims much more than that – it's the theory that all living creatures are modified descendents of a common ancestor that lived long ago.' [4.9]" The Bible describes this theory of variations of a species within a family, but the degree of change is limited to a particular category. Some of these categories include: Plant kingdom, air- breathing land animal kingdom, the fish kingdom and the bird kingdom. "And God said, 'Let the earth put forth vegetations, plants yielding seed ACCORDING TO ITS KIND, upon the earth.' And it was so. The earth brought forth vegetation, plants yielding seed ACCORDING TO THEIR OWN KINDS, and trees bearing fruit in which is their seed, each ACCORDING TO ITS KIND." Genesis 1:11-12. "So God created the great sea monsters and every living creature that moves, with which the waters swarm, ACCORDING TO THEIR KINDS, an every winged bird ACCORDING TO ITS KIND. And God saw that it was good." Genesis 1:21. "And God made the beasts of the earth ACCORDING TO THEIR KINDS and the cattle ACCORDING TO THEIR KINDS, and everything that creeps upon the ground ACCORD TO ITS KIND." Genesis 1:25. After the genesis account separates the animals according to different kinds, it describes the creation of man. Man was created separate from the animals and creatures God had made. He was made with a soul and a wisdom the animals did not have. Man was given dominion over the beasts and was made superior to the animals in many ways. "Then God said, 'Let us make man in our image, after our likeness; and let them have dominion over the fish of the sea, and over the birds of the air, and over the cattle and over all the earth, and over every creeping thing that creeps upon the earth.' So God created man in his own image, in the image of God he created him, male and female he created them." Genesis 1:26-27. One statement that it noticeably missing from the description of the creation of man is, "after its kind" or "according to their kinds". The reason for this is obvious to me. Man was made from the image of God and not through a gradual evolving process. Man has no other "kind" like him. He is unrelated to the animal kingdoms. Man is not made in the "image of the beast", like described in the book of Revelation. The theory of evolution is a total abomination to the word of God. The Bible teaches us to praise God for the works He has done. Evolution attempts to pull us subtly away from this act of worship. The theory implies, God did not create life therefore there is no reason to give God praise for giving us life. Furthermore, are you sure God even exists? We will see how science has failed to remove God from His acts of creation. Furthermore, science is continually giving more evidence for God's presence. "For what can be known about God is plain to them, because God has shown it to them. Ever since the creation of the world His invisible nature, namely, His eternal power and deity, has been clearly perceived in the things that have been made. So they are without excuse; for although they knew God they did not honor him as God or give thanks to Him, but they became futile in their thinking and their senseless minds were darkened. Claiming to be wise, they became fools, and exchanged the glory of the immortal God for images resembling mortal man or birds or animals or reptiles. And since they did not see fit to acknowledge God, God gave them up to a base mind and to improper conduct." Romans 1:19-23, 28 RSV "And beware lest you lift up your eyes to heaven, and when you see the sun and the moon and the stars, all the host of heaven, you be drawn away and worship them and serve them, things which the Lord your God has allotted to all the peoples under the whole heaven." Deuteronomy 4:19.

Methods of Deception

Before we examine the "icons of evolution" more closely, let us consider a central theme in the history of creating a deception. To give us a clear picture of the art of deception we simply turn to the first act of deception from the Father of lies, Satan himself. Just shortly after the creation of the world, described in the first two chapters of Genesis, we come to the famous record of the fall of mankind into sin. First, God created a paradise for Adam. He had, at this time, just one law. Do not eat from the tree of the knowledge of good and evil. "And the Lord God made all kinds of trees grow out of the ground – trees that were pleasing to the eye and good for food. In the middle of the garden were the tree of life and the tree of the knowledge of good and evil. ... and the Lord God commanded the man, 'You are free to eat from any tree in the garden , but you must not eat from the tree of the knowledge of good and evil, for when you eat of it you will surely die." Genesis 2: 9, 16, 17 God provides abundantly for our needs, yet, somehow even before the first act of sin it seams man had a restless nature. God has a timetable for accomplishing the purposes of our life. However, we often become inpatient and want the pace of events to be much faster. Years are not even a blink of an eye with the God of eternity. However, even when we had access to the tree of life, enabling us to live forever, we still had a certain need for instant gratification. Perhaps, Eve, on that fate filled day, was feeling a little restless. Then the serpent, Satan, recognized an opportunity. Satan's first step in his method of deception is to wait for the opportune moment to present his tempting offer. The next step is to make a true statement, and just "sprinkle in" a few lies. "Now the serpent was more cunning than any beast of the field which the Lord God had made. And he said to the women, 'Has God indeed said, 'You shall not eat of every tree of the garden'? And the women said to the serpent: We may eat the fruit of the trees of the garden; but of the fruit of the tree which is in the midst of the garden, God has said, you shall not eat it, nor shall you touch it, lest you die." Genesis 3:1-3. NKJ First the serpent presents the truth, with one important omission. God did say they could eat of every tree, except this one in the center of the garden. This simple omission turned a true statement into a lie. How often do we tell "little white lies"? They can be in form of incomplete truths that lead to some type of misunderstanding. The Laws of God are a test of faith in His guidance and obedience to God's rule. God often tests our faith. This was a test of faith. The laws of God, the Ten Commandments, are rules to show what limits we need to impose on our actions to keep true to God's purpose. One rule to live by in the Bible many people push to the limit is drinking alcohol. "Do not get drunk on wine, which leads to debauchery. Instead, be filled with the Spirit. Ephesians 5:18 "Let us walk properly, as in the day, not in revelry and drunkenness, not in lewdness and lust. Not in strife and envy." Romans 13:13 NKJ Clearly the Bible teaches us that drinking to excess is against God's law. However, what about just a casual drink on a special occasion? "When the wine was gone, Jesus' mother said to him, 'They have no more wine. … Jesus said to the servants, 'Fill the jars with water'; so they filled them to the brim. Then he told them, 'Now draw some out and take it to the master of the banquet.' They did so, and the master of the banquet tasted the water that had been turned into wine. … This, the first of his miraculous signs, Jesus performed in Cana in Galilee. He thus revealed his glory, and his disciples put their faith in him." John 2:3, 7-9, 11 "Stop drinking only water and use a little wine because of your stomach and your frequent illnesses." 1Timothy 5:23 Some Christians have quoted from these verses to support their convictions for and against drinking alcohol. It is clear that the Bible does not condemn all consumption of alcohol. But, it is equally clear it condemns drunkenness. It seams that God teaches us to enjoy life abundantly, but there are limits. As the old saying goes, 'too much of a good thing is bad.' Satan's biggest lie is to offer "something for nothing". He tries to convince you that living without God is to live for yourself. The lie is that without you realizing it, you have handed over leadership of you life to Satan not to some self-driven thought process. Satan promises you freedom and pleasure. In reality, he gives you slavery to sin and a self-destructive nature.

In this first encounter, Satan's first step is to question if you heard or understand God's commandment correctly. The second step in his first act of deception was to call God a liar! "You shall not surely die, the serpent said to the women. For God knows that when you eat of it your eyes will be opened, and you will be like God, knowing good and evil." Genesis 3:4-5 The serpent is not only calling God a liar, but explaining why God has lied to them. He quickly supports his argument with an explanation of God's deception and a true statement. First, it was already known to contain the knowledge of good and evil. Then Satan attempts to convince Eve that the reason God has merely said they would die is to scare them away from the tree. If they ate of the tree, the serpent suggested they would be equal with God and God would be angry. Why didn't they realize that if God was angry with them it would mean death? No one can know for certain. Perhaps Satan had convinced Eve that God was already angry with him and he survived. Perhaps he offered Eve protection from God's wrath. The next step was to convince Eve that the tree was no more dangerous that any other tree in the garden. It was in no way poisons and therefore she shouldn't die if she ate the fruit of the tree. "When the woman saw that the fruit of the tree was good for food and pleasing to the eye, and also desirable for gaining wisdom, she took some and ate it." Genesis 3:6. The deception was complete. She was believing what her eyes were seeing not what God had said. It is because we do not always presently see the work of God that we lose faith. Life is a continuous test of faith. I have often wondered what it would have been like if we had never took the forbidden fruit. I am sure God would have given us all wisdom, only slowly with no need for us to know evil. In the book of Revelation, and other books about heaven and the new Earth, we have a description of paradise restored. What is noticeable restored is the Tree of Life, what is noticeable absent is the Tree of the Knowledge of good and evil. Perhaps, because by the time of the Lord's coming we will have acquired so much knowledge that we will be missing only a "few details" to having all our questions answered. Wisdom from science and the study of scripture has steadily grown since the time of Christ. Perhaps most of the knowledge imparted to the disciples has been re-discovered with the help of the Holy Spirit. Refer to John 21:25 and the Introduction to this book. In any event, obviously God knew the future and the plan of salvation He had in mind for our redemption and His plan to restore all things.

You may be asking yourself, what has all this analysis of mankind's first act of sin to do with science? I want you to keep in mind how Satan uses the truth to twist it into a lie. We will explore how the symbols of evolution influenced Lee Strobel to become an atheist. These symbols represent certain half-truths. The result was to present several lies. 1) Evolution is a well established fact. This is the biggest lie of all. 2) You can not remove evolution from scientific study. They are not as interconnected as you are lead to believe. 3) The lie that anyone believing in the Bible can not be a true scientist. 4) Evolution has nothing to do with religion. The truth is that evolution is the foundation for atheism. The philosophy of atheism is supported by the theory of evolution. Atheism is a belief that there is no God. The continual lie is that Atheism is simply the absence of religion. In fact, atheism has a well defined belief system. And, yes, Evolution and atheism are virtually inseparable. As we discuss Lee's conversion away from the teachings he found in a church setting to atheism we can see the powerful effect of the theory of evolution on young minds. How many more thousands or millions are influenced by the teaching of evolution to become atheists? In our own country, I fear that even as we profess to be Christians, many are simply covering up their acceptance of atheism and their belief that the Bible is simply a bunch of stories. One of the best ways to make people accept a lie as truth is to simply bombard them with half-truths. The same old method Satan has used for centuries, but it works. Just like Satan in the Garden of Eden; tell someone the truth, leaving out one important part and get them to agree with you. Soon, you have the person nodding their head in agreement with everything you say, no matter if it is true or not. This is a powerful sales technique. Just ask anyone in sales about the head nodding technique. I once again must emphasize that I am in no way condemning any group for teaching evolution. Many teachers may simply be unaware of how integrated the theory of evolution is to atheism. Also they could be unaware of the inaccuracies of the theory of evolution. Some of the professors described in Lee's book, had no idea that these images of evolution were faked until they did their graduate work. We will show an example of this very thing occurring in our next chapter. Since most teachers simply have a bachelor degree in their field, they may also be unaware of these discrepancies in the theory of evolution. When Lee is interviewing Dr. Jonathan Wells, he summarized the situation perfectly. "'If these icons are the illustrations most cited as evidence of evolution, then I can see why they're important,' I said. 'What did you find as you examined them one by one? Wells didn't hesitate. 'That they're either false or misleading.' 'False or misleading?' I echoed. 'Wait a second - are you saying my science teacher was lying to me? ... Wells shook his head. 'No, I'm not saying that. He probably believed the icons too. I'm sure he wasn't even aware of the way they misrepresented the evidence. But the end result is the same – much of what science teachers have been telling students is simply wrong.' [4.10]" The Bible says: "Be diligent to present yourself approved to God, a worker who does not need to be ashamed, rightly dividing the Word of Truth." II Timothy 2:15. Let us get to the truth of these images one by one.

The Stanley Miller Experiment

The image of the 1953 Stanley Miller experiment has perhaps the greatest significance in convincing students that evolution is true. The best place to start a discussion is your point of origin. This is extremely important if you are studying geometry, as we will discuss in chapter seven. In Biology, the point of origin is the beginning of life. Stanley Miller took a mixture of methane, ammonia and water vapor to produce amino acids, the building blocks to life. In the 1950's, this type of mixture was thought to be the content of the early atmosphere on Earth. The reason why this was thought to be the atmospheric content is clear. If we start from the assumption we are going to prove that life came from a chemical reaction, you want the right ingredients. Once again, the driving force behind the experiments was starting from a faith in atheism, that there is no God, only natural forces. "Miller chose a hydrogen-rich mixture of methane, ammonia, and water vapor, which was consistent with what many scientists thought back then. But scientists don't believe that anymore. ... And Science magazine said in 1995 that experts now dismiss Miller's experiment because 'the early atmosphere looked nothing like the Miller-Urey simulation.... 'What is the significance of his experiment today?' I asked Wells. 'To me, it has virtually no scientific significance,' he replied. It's historically interesting, because it convinced a lot of people through the years - yourself included - that life could have arisen spontaneously, a point which I believe is false. Does it have a place in a science textbook? Maybe as a footnote. 'But it's more than a footnote in most texts, right? Unfortunately, yes, he said. It's prominently featured in current textbooks, often with pictures. [4.11]" Still used as an image in the indoctrination of children into the lie of evolution.

Today, there are enormous challenges to explain the origin of life on a natural basis. Before we highlight some of these difficulties, I want to comment on the presence of the Stanley Miller experiment further. As stated above, it is commonly portrayed as evidence that science has already discovered how an electrical charge like from a bolt of lightning, and a chemical mixture can produce life. By mentioning the 1953 Miller experiment, you are impressing on the student that the first evidence for life coming from chemicals has been discovered. The teacher is justified to ignore the latest research on how exactly the process works, as too complicated for a high school discussion. The student is therefore left with the impression that, after all these years, they must have an abundant supply of evidence that life began from a simple chemical reaction. The image implies a relatively simple set of events for life to spontaneously generate. This is necessary to make the illusion that the theory of evolution is true. "Would a young person, looking for an excuse to escape the accountability of God, cling to the false conclusion that the origin – of – life problem is only a minor obstacle in the relentless march of evolutionary theory? ... 'It's becoming clearer and clearer to me that this is materialistic philosophy masquerading as empirical science. The attitude is that life had to have developed this way because there is no other materialistic explanation. And if you try to invoke another explanation – for instance, intelligent design – then the evolutionists claim you're not a scientist. [4.12]" The situation is becoming clearer each day. The theory of evolution is more the result of faith in a philosophy than the result of scientific research. As more scientists look at the theory of evolution objectively, more scientists are led to faith in intelligent design.

In order for a person to accept the idea that life began from a chemical reaction in the early earth, implies that there must be a simple way in which life can be formed from simple amino acids. However, researchers continue to discover that the process of generating life from chemicals must require an ever increasing complex set of events taking place. "If you want to create life, on top of the challenge of somehow generating the cellular components out of non-living chemicals, you would have an even bigger problem in trying to put the ingredients together in the right way. ... So even if you could accomplish the thousands of steps between the amino acids in the Miller tar - which probably didn't exist in the real world anyway – and the components you need for a living cell – all the enzymes, the DNA, and so forth – you're still immeasurably far from life. [4.13]" The theory that life began as a chemical reaction in the early earth is becoming increasingly less of a sound scientific hypothesis and more of a faith in mysticism. The more we know about the steps necessary to form a living organism from chemicals the more it seams that the only reasonable conclusion is that life is a miraculous gift from God.

The Miracle of Life

What are some of the problems with the creation of life? We have been taught, from the image of the Miller experiment, that just a little chemical mixture and lightning, and boom! You have life. What are some of the sequence of events to produce a living cell from non-living chemicals? Since life begins with cells, let us look at a few types of cells and see if we can determine their origin. The theory of evolution is based upon the gradual building of material into life. Then, the most primitive forms of life "evolve" gradually into more complex organisms. The problem with this idea is that there are many examples of more primitive life forms requiring more complex life forms to survive. This problem with the theory of evolution was well known by its creator, Charles Darwin. Quote, "If it could be demonstrated that any complex organ existed which could not possibly have been formed by numerous successive, slight modifications, my theory would absolutely break down. [4.14]" Darwin himself knew of many instances his theory broke down. Where Darwin had faith that over time these problems would be resolved, the difficulties have merely increased. "The simplest species of bacteria, Chalamydia and Rickettsia, are the smallest living things known. Only a few hundred atoms across, they are smaller than the largest virus and have half as much DNA as do other species of bacteria. Although they are about as small as it is possible to be and still be living, these two forms of life require millions of atomic parts. Many of the smaller bacteria, such as M. genitalum, which has 256 genes, are parasite-like viruses and can only live with the help of more complex organisms. For this reason, when researching the minimum requirements for life, the example of E. Coli is more realistic. [4.15]" The search for the minimum requirements for life has introduced a new term to science called irreducible complexity. The search for a natural explanation for the origin of life has reached a brick wall. There seams to be several sets of combinations that are required for life to exist. There still seams to be no natural explanation of how these components naturally came into existence through a slow process of evolution. Notice in the above quotation that it is observed that the more simple viruses must have the help of the more complex organisms to exist. If we are to believe that life was the result of evolution, all the components should have an equal level of complexity. Then, they would slowly combine to produce the more complex components of life. Over and over again the opposite has been discovered. There seams to be a natural symbiotic relationship between many life forms. There seams to be no way these relationships could have developed slowly over time. Instead, the conditions for even the simplest form of life to exist require a highly orchestrated set of events to have taken place simultaneously. In other words, instantaneous creation of life seams to be the only reasonable explanation science can give for the beginning of life. There does not seam to be any adequate explanations of why these components come together, in perfect order, without an external intelligence. This leads to another term of science: Intelligent design.

Let us look at the search for the minimum requirements for life. "Oversimplified, life depends on a complex arrangement of three classes of molecules: DNA, which stores the cell's master plans; RNA, which transports a copy of the needed information contained in the DNA to the protein assembly station; and proteins, which make up everything from ribosomes to the enzymes. ... All of these parts are necessary and must exist as a properly assembled and integrated unit. ... Life also requires oxygen, which must be distributed to all tissues, or for single-celled life, oxygen must efficiently and safely be moved around inside the cell membrane where it is needed, without damaging the cell. Without complex mechanisms to achieve these tasks, life cannot exist. ... For this reason, only an instantaneous creation of all necessary parts as a functioning unit can produce life. [4.16]" This leads us to another component to life, how to sustain life once it has begun. Life, like all natural elements and forces, has a tendency to decay. We already discussed the second law of thermodynamics which states all natural forces tend towards disorder. To sustain life is no easy task. Cells require the proper distribution of oxygen to remain alive, and many other functions to continue, grow and reproduce. "Cells require all their millions of necessary parts to remain alive, just as a mammal must have lung, liver, heart, and other organs to live. All of the millions of cell parts are required to carry out the complex biochemical business for life. [4.17]" It is easily shown that it is easier to destroy life than create life. It is common for cells to die, but difficult to sustain life. How can the evolutionists explain these complex systems by slow, gradual, development over millions of years? The truth is they can't and their deception that evolution is a scientific fact is coming apart. The truth that God has created the universe is finally becoming a proven scientific fact.

There are many other examples of "irreducible complex" situations. Some of these examples will be discussed later. Let us return to the Stanley Miller experiment and examine the three basic requirements for life: DNA, RNA and enzymes. The Stanley Miller experiment primarily dealt with the enzyme component. First let us take a closer look at the results of the original experiment. "Take Miller's origin-of-life experiment fifty years ago, when he tried to recreate the early Earth's atmosphere and spark it with electricity. He managed to create two or three of the protein-forming amino acids out of the twenty-two that exist. ... What's also interesting, however, is that Miller's amino acids react very quickly with the other chemicals in the chamber, resulting in a brown sludge that's not life-friendly at all. ... even if amino acids existed in the theoretical prebiotic soup, they would have readily reacted with other chemicals. This would have been another tremendous barrier to the formation of life. The way that origin-of-life scientists have dealt with this in their experiments has been to remove these other chemicals in the hope that further reactions could take the experiment in a life-friendly direction. [4.18]" Do you see this information in textbooks representing the Stanley Miller experiment? Even under the original conditions of the experiment there are enormous problems with explaining the origin of life. This information is purposely left out of the textbooks to represent a lie. Just as we examined the art of Satan to turn truth into a lie, the Stanley Miller experiment is portrayed as a crowning achievement toward the beginning of understanding the origin of life. Instead, it is a dismal failure, even under the original conditions of the experiment. We saw earlier that the Stanley Miller experiment did not reflect an accurate earlier earth atmosphere. Now let us look at a realistic version of the Stanley Miller experiment. Let us look at the result if we perform the experiment under true conditions of the early earth. "I asked the next logical question: 'What happens if you replay the experiment using an accurate atmosphere? 'I'll tell you this: you do not get amino acids, that's for sure.' ... [you get] Formaldehyde! Cyanide! ... 'They may be organic molecules, but in my lab at Berkley you couldn't even have a capped bottle of formaldehyde in the room, because the stuff is so toxic. You open the bottle and it fries proteins all over the place, just from the fumes. It kills embryos. The idea that using a realistic atmosphere gets you the first step in the origin of life is just laughable. ... Do you know what you get? 'He asked. 'Embalming fluid!' [4.19]" I find it interesting that the result of this experiment is embalming fluid. This of course, is used in the preparation of a corpse. Above is also noted that the resulting chemicals actually destroy the proteins you are trying to produce. It is ironic that, to believe the theory of evolution from such conditions is like accepting a false resurrection of life from non-living materials. This is a counterfeit to the supernatural restoration of life like that which took place in the resurrection of Jesus Christ.

Next, let us consider the production of enzymes in the best conditions by random chance. Scientists love to use probability equations to support their arguments. However, when we take a realistic look at evolution, probability equations are on the side of the creationist, not the atheist. "The conclusion of this calculation is that the probability of naturalistic evolution is essentially zero. Sir Fred Hoyle (1982) calculated 'the chance of a random shuffling of amino acids producing a workable set of enzymes' to be less than $10^{40,000}$ ... The probability of the required order in a single basic protein molecule arising purely from chance is estimated at 10^{43} (Overman, 1997). Since thousands of complex protein molecules are required to build a simple cell, probability moves chance arrangements of these molecules outside the realm of possibility. ... The famous illustration 'the probability of life originating from accident is comparable to 'the probability of the unabridged dictionary resulting from an explosion in a print shop' argues that information and complex systems cannot come about by chance, but can only be the product of an intelligent designer. Books likewise do not come about by chance, but are the product of both reasoning and intelligence. [4.20]" To believe that random chance can produce anything but chaos is to ask students to take a huge, blind leap of faith in the power of evolution. The proposal is that by some yet undetermined means, beneficial changes can be accumulated over time naturally. Again, this process is in direct violation of the second law of thermodynamics. Refer back to chapter 1 for further details.

Monkey Typist

A better explanation of this theory that random interaction can produce a meaningful result is the monkey typist scenario. Let us review this scenario more closely than we did in chapter one. The theory has been illustrated by a famous thought experiment. First you place a monkey in a closed room with a typewriter and lots of paper. The theory of natural selection states that out of the random pounding of the keys on the type writer, the monkey supposedly would get around to making distinguishable words appear. If this experiment was given an unlimited time to continue, much longer than the lifetime of one monkey, eventually a classical work, like one of Shakespeare's plays, would appear. This thought experiment assumes a great many things to be true and to occur. The first assumption is that there is the ability for random motion to accumulate beneficial changes and omitting mistakes. We have observed in our discussion of the naturalistic perspective to the creation of the universe in chapter 1 that no such physical force exists. However, the evolutionist claims that this process does occur in the micro-biological level. Is there any scientific evidence for this assertion? The situation of the monkey typist was closely examined in the book The Blind Watchmaker by Richard Dawkins. "Imagine a monkey typist with 27 keys, all the letters in the English alphabet and the space bar. ... Dawkins suggests the sentence spoken by William Shakespeare's Hamlet who, in describing a cloud, pronounces, 'Methinks it is like a weasel.' ... How many attempts at typing this sentence would it take a monkey, which would presumably be hitting keys randomly, to type the sentence? ... The sentence has 28 characters in it, so the probability is $(1/27)^{28}$ or 1.2×10^{-40}. ... To overcome this problem with probability, Dawkins proposed that natural selection could help by fixing each letter in place once it was correct and thus lower the odds massively. ... Proteins can be thought of as sentences like 'Methinks it is like a weasel.', the difference being that proteins are made up of 20 different sub-units called amino acids instead of 27 different characters in our example. .... According to Dawkins' theory, those amino acids in the right location in the protein would be fixed by natural selection, while those that needed to be modified would continue to change until they were correct, and a functional protein was produced in relatively short order. Unfortunately, this ascribes an attribute to natural selection that even its most ardent proponents would question, the ability to select one non-functional protein from a pool of millions of other non-functional proteins. Changing even one amino-acid in a protein can alter its function dramatically. ... As the depth and breadth of human knowledge increases, it washes over us a flood of evidence deep and wide, all pointing to the conclusion that life is the result of design. Only a small subset of evidence, chosen carefully, may be used to construct a story of life evolving from non-living precursors. [4.21]"

The creation of any good work comes from a designer and not from natural forces. All good works ultimately come from God. "Every good endowment and every perfect gift is from above, coming down from the Father of lights with who there is no variation or shadow due to change." James 1:17. The evolutionist has great faith in random motion and time as the ultimate building blocks to the universe. This runs into the age old question of how lucky can you get? Are a set of events taking place precisely the right moment the result of chance or the will of God? I will remind you of the quote I had in Chapter 1. Quote, "One has only to contemplate the magnitude of this task to concede that the spontaneous generation of a living organism is impossible. Yet here we are- as a result, I believe, of spontaneous generation. It will help to disagree for a moment to ask what one means by 'impossible'. ... Time is in fact the hero of the plot. The time with which we have to deal with is of the order of two billion years. What we regard as impossible on the basis of human experience is meaningless here. Given so much time, the 'impossible' becomes possible, the possible probable, and the probable virtually certain. One has only to wait: time itself performs the miracles. [4.22]" The amount of blind faith to accept this proposal is staggering. It is obvious that this is an atheistic belief that assumes, by faith, that there is no God. It further assumes there are no super-natural forces. It is faith on top of faith in the bedrock principles of the atheistic faith. This is not science but a profound religious belief in time and random forces to work harmoniously.

Scientists use a complex set of probability equations to determine how long it would take the monkey in the experiment to complete the specific Shakespearian play, for example. Scientists use a similar procedure to determine the time frame for the developments of life on earth. For instance, the

Cambrian era, when the predominate form of life was to have been fish. All the stages of development for the evolution of different species, from single cell creatures to man, was invented by men working with formulas involving biological growth rates, imaginative mutation estimates and approximating time periods through formulas, mostly made from far fetched guesses. These formulas which help scientists determine time periods for a particularly dominate species, relate currently accepted information about the age of the earth estimated at 4.5 billion years, growth rates of individual species, probable rates of mutations, and fossil evidence. The biological evidence for evolution will be examined in this chapter. In the next chapter we will discuss radio-active dating of rocks and fossils and the sedimentary evidence for the time frames of a particular dominate species. When you are studying the different time periods in a high school or college biology class, learn the information as you would any other required material for the tests. However, realize that this information is more science fiction than science. We shall learn that the evidence for the existence of evolutionary development as described in most textbooks i.e. gradual changes over millions of years, is very shaky. Evolution is far from being proven as a scientific fact and the ideas on which it is based are skeptical at best. Let us examine the experiment with the monkey in a closed room more closely. To suggest that such an experiment would be successful in the real world is ludicrous. According to the laws of thermodynamics, the theory would fail as previously discussed. To develop the Shakespeare play you must have a mechanism that operates much like the human mind. The mechanism must save parts of the monkeys key pounding that makes sense at a particular time. In other words, when a particular word is needed to complete the next logical step in the development of the play, a mechanism must save the right letters to make a word. The next step is to create the word that makes sense for the next part of the Shakespearian play. There is no natural mechanism that can do this, let alone what evolution requires of random motion. Evolution requires the ability to save all combinations that make sense, and reject the ones that don't make sense. Instead of the monkey with a typewriter, it would better to imagine a monkey with a specially designed computer. This computer would accept the next letter necessary to complete the next step in forming the next word in the play and reject any other random key pounding. This mechanism has never been proven to exist in nature. The most recent discoveries of the workings of RNA as the information carrier for the DNA molecule bring us closer to understand the development process. However, does it account for such developments over time? How were the DNA and RNA information 'library' system first formed? Does research into the workings of the DNA and RNA molecules solve the puzzle of how life first formed? We will answer these questions in the remainder of this chapter. We can summarize the results of scientific research by saying that we have become more reliant on faith, now than in any other period of history. Science has helped us understand the complexities of life. From this research, we can confidently say there is now more evidence that ever before in the history of science that life is a miracle from God. Is this observation debated? Of course, it is protested more resoundingly that ever before. The debate is almost never ending. However, the debate continues to be based more on personal convictions than scientific information. "Facts do not speak for themselves – they must be interpreted according to a framework. It is not a case of religion / creation / subjective versus science / evolution / objectivity. Rather, it is the biases of the religions of Christianity and of humanism interpreting the same facts in diametrically opposite ways. [4.23]"

Without a mechanism to intelligently select what information is useful and what is non-sense, the entire theory of evolution falls apart because each random motion cancels any previously made progress. For instance, the monkey's random key pounding may, after years of work and by some "miracle", the monkey may form the word "the". However, the next bunch of letters would be rubbish. Then by another "miracle" the word "play" may appear. Unless there is a mechanism which can put the words, "the" and "play" together, you can not start building a sentence which someday may duplicate the original Shakespeare play. The fact that the words "the" and "play" were made by the monkey's random key pounding are meaningless because the two words are surrounded by useless garbage. The evolutionist teaches that natural selection and trial and error have produced the DNA code that has all the necessary instructions for each life form. First, let us describe the properties of DNA and why it is so important. DNA (deoxyribonucleic acid) is basically an information storage system. Like computer code, DNA provides instructions for a cells activity. "Ever since the 1950s and 1960s, biologists have recognized that the cell's critical functions are usually performed by proteins, and proteins are the product of assembly instructions stored in DNA. ... We know from our experience that we can convey information with a twenty-six-letter alphabet.... – or even just two characters, like the zeros and ones used in the binary code in computers. One of the most extraordinary discoveries of the twentieth century was that DNA actually stores information –the detailed instructions for assembling proteins – in the form of a four-character digital code. The characters happen to be chemicals called adenine, guanine, cytosine, and thymine. ... 'DNA is more like a library,' he said. 'The organism accesses the information that it needs from DNA so it can build some of its critical components.' [4.24] Again, DNA just stores information. How the information got into the DNA molecules is still a great scientific mystery.

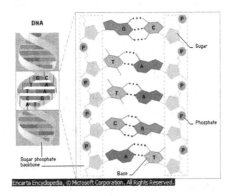

Figure 4.1

DNA on Who's Side?

It is commonly accepted that one of the greatest discoveries of the 20th century is DNA. Is this discovery more evidence that evolution is the blueprint of life, or does it support creation? Let us look at some opinions of two scientists which discovered the DNA molecule in the first place, Dr, James Watson and Dr. Francis Crick. In 1953 they proposed their idea of the DNA molecule and in 1962 won the Nobel Prize in physiology for their work. Dr. Watson is quoted in an interview for the April edition of Scientific American as saying: "Both of us are intellectually opposed to the idea that the truth comes from [divine] revelation ... Every time you understand something, religion becomes less likely. Only with the discovery of the double helix and the ensuing genetic revolution have we had grounds for thinking that the powers held traditionally to be the exclusive property of the gods might one day be ours." In other statements, it is obvious that both Dr. Crick and Dr. Watson approached their discovery as a triumph for their atheistic beliefs. But is it? Also, how can such notarized intellectuals make such ludicrous statements? As we explore science we find increasing evidence for a universe filled with complexity. With each lesson of science, we become more impressed with the power, majesty, and wisdom of God. Later, Dr. Crick began to see that his assumption that the discovery of the DNA molecule leads a person away from religion was illogical. Instead, scientific study leads us to a more profound faith in God and the miracle of our existence. "'Science, you might say, has discovered that our existence is infinitely improbable, and hence a miracle.' Even biochemist and spiritual skeptic, Francis Crick, ... cautiously invoked the Word a few years ago. 'An honest man, armed with all the knowledge available to us now, could only state that in some sense, the origin of life appears at the moment to be almost a miracle, so many are the conditions which would have had to have been satisfied to get it going.' he said. [4.25]" The truth is always revealed. Even when you try every means to deny or skirt around the truth, you are left with only one reasonable conclusion: life began as a miraculous creation act of God. It is amazing how the atheistic scientists are the ones who act childish. Here is a Noble prize winning scientist, trying unsuccessfully, to prove that life is not a miracle. Dr. Crick is showing an unreasonable faith in the power of evolution and a stubborn religious fervor to his convictions towards atheism. Scientists that reject the intelligent design hypothesis must do so not as the result of the evidence, but in denial of the scientific data. The reality is this: there is overwhelming evidence supporting the truth that the universe and all life in the universe is the result of a miraculous creation act from God.

DNA is a perfect example of strong scientific evidence that life was created by God. DNA not only contains vast amounts of information, but the instructions on how to use this information. "In fact, he said the information needed to build the proteins for all the species of organisms that have ever lived – a number estimated to be approximately one thousand million – could be held in a teaspoon and there would still be room left for all the information in every book ever written. DNA serves as the information storehouse for a finely choreographed manufacturing process in which the right amino acids are linked together with the right bonds in the right sequence to produce the right kind of proteins that fold in the right way to build biological systems. [4.26]" The presence of DNA is strong evidence for a creation act. There are mainly two questions which immediately come to mind when faced with the presence of DNA. First, where did the DNA itself come from? Second where did the vast amounts of information in the DNA come from? These two questions are really just one question: How could DNA naturally form? The first attempted explanation we will explore is the evolutionists' favorite 'mysterious' all powerful force: natural selection. "Whether natural selection really works at the level of biological evolution, is open for debate but it most certainly does not work at the level of chemical evolution, which tries to explain the origin of the first life from simpler chemicals. ... Darwinists admit that natural selection requires a self-replicating organism to work. ... However, to have reproduction, there has to be cell division. And that presupposes the existence of information –rich DNA and proteins. But that's the problem – those are the very things they're trying to explain!' [4.27]" We see a constant stream of examples where science has apparently hit a brick wall. Theories are constantly formulated to explain the existence of life, yet no definite solution has been found. It continually goes back to a question of faith. The debate continues as scientists of the naturalist faith battle scientists of the intelligent design faith. Another proposal to explain the development of the DNA information system is the so-called RNA first hypothesis. "For example, some small viruses use RNA as their genetic material. RNA molecules are simpler than DNA, and they can also store information and even replicate. ... [However] the RNA molecule would need information to function, just as DNA would, and so we're right back to the same problem of where the information came from. Also, for a single strand of RNA to replicate, there must be an identical RNA molecule close by. To have a reasonable chance of having two identical RNA molecules of the right length would require a library of ten billion billion billion billion billion billion RNA molecules – and that effectively rules out chance origin of a primitive replicating system. [4.28]" How much faith is required to believe such a set of events taking place? It is the evolutionist that requires enormous faith in atheism to accept some of these highly speculative theories.

Let us take one more look at the possibility of DNA forming from random chemical interaction. How could the DNA sequence form the volumes of information from a self-ordering of chemicals? "The hope was that there would be some forces of attraction between the amino acids that would cause them to line up the way they do and then fold so that the protein can perform the functions that keep a cell alive. ... Consider the genetic information in DNA, which is spelled out by the chemical letters A, C, G, and T. Imagine every time you had an A, it would automatically attract a G. You'd just have a repetitive sequence: A-G-A-G-A-G-A-G. Would that give you a gene that could produce a protein? Absolutely not. Self-organization wouldn't yield a genetic message, only a repetitive mantra. ... Whereas information requires variability, irregularity, and unpredictability – which is what information theorists call complexity – self-organization gives you repetitive, redundant structure, which is known as simple order. ... If you study DNA,... you will find that its structure depends on certain bonds that are caused by chemical attractions. For instance, there are hydrogen bonds and bonds between the sugar and phosphate molecules that form the two twisting backbones of the DNA molecule. However, ... there's one place where there are no chemical bonds, and that's between the nucleotide bases, which are the chemical letters in the DNA's assembly instructions. ... Now, in DNA, each individual base, or letter, is chemically bonded to the sugar-phosphate backbone of the molecule. That's how they're attached to the DNA's structure. But – and here's the key point – there is no attraction or bonding between the individual letters themselves. So there's nothing chemically that forces them into a particular sequence. The sequencing has to come from somewhere else. [4.29]" Again, where did the information come from? We see that there is a chemical system for holding the instructions in place but no such system for creating the information.

DNA and Computer Programming

Let us reflect on this information. There is no current viable theory on how DNA could have formed the necessary information by chemical means. WOW! This is certainly not taught in public schools. Where did the information contained in DNA come from? We know that the DNA acts like a computer program. It contains instruction on how to perform a myriad of tasks, and like a computer program, DNA can access files of stored information. There is an enormous amount of information in its database, or library, as we have already discussed. The similarities to a computer program are enormous. How is a computer program made? First you must have a programmer, in this case it is God who writes a perfect program and has no need for a debugging tool. He designed life to be adaptable. Like a computer program, it can be upgraded. However, there are limitations. When we carry this analogy between DNA and computer programming even farther, we can see even more insights into the complexity of DNA. There are many types of computer programs, let us select just three examples: A word processor, a spread sheet and a game program. All three types of computer programs are adaptable. You are all aware of newer versions of each of these types of programs being introduced practically each year; the newest versions of Microsoft Word, Excel, or Mario Brothers for example. However, like these programs, each type was designed for a specific purpose; the word processor for writing letters and books, the spread sheet for accounting, and the game programs for entertainment. How much fun would it be to use your Excel program for entertainment? Pretty boring game don't you think? Like these computer programs, which are adaptable, DNA can change in a species. But like these programs, DNA also has the limitation of operating within certain kinds. This goes back to the principle theory that evolutionary changes occur within narrow limits, not unlimited as evolutionists believe. Once you have designed a computer program what do you do with it? You save it to a disk. This allows us a clear visualization for the study of the DNA molecule. God designed the DNA instructions and then placed it on the double helix backbone. He created the molecular bonding to loosely hold the instructions in place. There had to be no chemical interactions between the DNA 'letters', otherwise the instructions could be scrambled beyond repair. This would be like running a magnet over the computer disk you just stored your computer program on. Most of us know the result would not be pleasant. The chemical bonding of the instructions also allow minor changes in the sequencing. This allows a species limited adaptation to their environment and natural selection. This explains changes within certain breads of cows, horses and dogs and no transmutation into an entirely different species.

Another problem with believing that DNA is the result of random chemical interactions is the property called "handedness". "Many of life's chemicals come in two forms, "left-handed" and "right-handed." Life requires polymers with all building blocks having the same "handedness" (homochirality) – proteins have only "left-handed" amino acids, while DNA and RNA have only "right-handed" sugars. Living things have special molecular machinery to produce homochirality. But ordinary undirected chemistry, as in the hypothetical primordial soup, would produce equal mixtures of left- and right-handed molecules, called racemates. ... A small fraction of wrong-handed molecules terminates RNA replication. A recent world conference on 'The Origin of Homochirality and Life' made it clear that the origin of this handedness is a complete mystery to evolutionists. [4.30]" There are many other problems in life forming by natural chemical means that are unknown to the general public. However, there is one problem that we all should take note of; water. There is no doubt that water is essential to sustain life, but water is also used frequently for cleaning. Water has the ability to break down food particles as you wash your dishes. The evolutionists teach that if you have any water on a planet, and long periods of time, life will emerge. This is just the opposite of what basic chemistry teaches us. Water breaks down polymers and the longer the exposure, the more polymers are broken down. "By the well-known law of mass action, excess water breaks up polymers. The long ages postulated by evolutionists simply make the problem worse because there is more time for water's destructive effects to occur. While living cells have many ingenious repair mechanisms, DNA cannot last very long in water outside a cell. Condensing agents (water absorbing chemicals) require acidic conditions and they could not accumulate in water. ... Many of the important biochemicals would destroy each other. Living organisms are well-structured to avoid this, but the 'primordial soup' would not be. ... Yet evolution requires these chemicals to form proteins and nucleic acids respectively, rather than destroy each other as per real chemistry. ... Fatty acids are necessary for cell membranes, and phosphate is necessary for DNA, RNA, ATP, and many more important vital molecules of life. But abundant calcium ions in the ocean would precipitate fatty acids and phosphate, making them unavailable for chemical evolution. [4.31]" To suggest that life evolved from a chemical mixture comes from a faith in evolution and an ignorance of chemistry. Which theory, creation or evolution, retards scientific study? Obviously the theory of evolution retards scientific studies.

Dr. John P. Marcus describes in fine detail, the problems involved in believing a chemical origin of life in the book: In Six Days. Why Fifty Scientists choose to believe in Creation. He begins with a comparison of how odds or probability of something occurring effect our beliefs. He quotes Psalm 104:24 "O Lord, how manifold are Your works! In wisdom You have made them all." NKJ There are many other verses that we can quote that show the Bible expressing our belief in the complexities of the universe as strong evidence for a Creator. "The heavens declare the glory of God; and the firmament shows His handiwork." Psalm 19:1. We have already discussed many of these verses. It is one of the best truths that we can share with anyone who has an atheist belief. The point is that everyone has some set of beliefs. As already stated, atheism is a religion, even if those who believe there is no God refuse to accept it as a religion and not just the absence of any belief. Dr. Marcus gives a simple illustration from the field of Archeology of how an individual's belief can cloud the judgment of even the most brilliant men of science. "The orderliness of living things and their mind – boggling complexity are surely unmistakable indications that this creation did not come about by random and disorderly chance processes. There are many ways to illustrate that a simple examination of an object will reveal the presence or absence of design. One can easily appreciate that certain items are extremely unlikely to come about by chance operations acting over time. One can see that even the smallest amount of order exhibited in a simple clay pot is almost completely beyond the reach of random process. That is why archaeologists know that a clay pot is a clear signature of civilization; orderliness is evidence of design. ... Living organisms are so much more complex than is a clay pot that an adequate comparison can not be made. What person would want to believe a clay pot arose by chance processes? Only a person bound and determined to exclude the possibility that civilization might have been responsible for making that pot. One can appreciate that evolutionists are also bound and determined to exclude God from the picture!" [4.32]

Dr. Marcus proceeds to explain in detail, the complexities of living cells. "DNA evidence is often claimed to give support to the evolutionary theory; in reality, DNA illustrates God's handiwork of design in a powerful way. ... Amazing as the DNA molecule may be, there is much, much more to life than DNA alone; life is possible only if the DNA blueprint can be read and put into action by the complex machinery of living cells. But the complex machinery of the living cell requires DNA if it is going to exist in the first place, since DNA is the source of the code of instructions to put together the machinery. Without the cellular machinery, we would have no DNA since it is responsible for synthesizing DNA;

without DNA we would have no cellular machinery. Since DNA and the machinery of the cell are co-dependent, the complete system must be present from the beginning or it will be meaningless bits and pieces. ... The making of RNA from a DNA template is a critical first step in the process of protein formation. For RNA to be synthesized, no fewer than five different protein chains must cooperate. ... This enzyme complex must recognize where to start transcribing DNA into RNA; it must then move along the DNA strand, adding individual building blocks to the growing RNA chain; and lastly, it must know where to finish the transcription process. It is not enough, however, simply to make one kind of RNA; three different types of RNA are required in the process of making proteins, messenger RNA (mRNA), ribosomal RNA (rRNA), and transfer RNA (tRNA). ... Once mRNA, tRNA and rRNA molecules have been synthesized, it is then necessary to translate the information from the mRNA into a protein molecule. ... In a simple bacterium such as E. Coli, ribosomes are composed of some 50 different proteins and three different rRNAs! ... A quick summation will reveal that the process of converting DNA information into proteins requires at least 75 different protein molecules. But each and every one of these 75 proteins must be synthesized in the first place by the process in which they themselves are involved. ... Needless to say, without proteins, life would not exist; it is as simple as that. The same is true of DNA and RNA. It should be clear that DNA, RNA, and proteins must all be present in a living organism. Life must have been created completely functional, or it would be a meaningless mess. To suggest otherwise is plain ignorance (or perhaps desperation). [4.33]" How do evolutionists explain this? They hide the facts, make misleading statements and desperately try to convince the public evolution is true. The theory of evolution is more religion than science.

At this point, I am confident we have covered some of the major obstacles to the theory of life spontaneously generating from a chemical soup. There are many more examples we could give on the subject, but let us limit our discussion. I find it amazing how this lie of evolution is taught even in the news media. The lie that there is conclusive evidence the creation of life from chemicals is an easy process to perform. I recently read an article about the survey missions to Mars. The newspaper reported that the probes have found, amazingly, exactly what they were sent to Mars to find: evidence for water once existing on Mars. They also detected evidence that water may still exist in liquid form bellow the surface of Mars. They then polled, a hand picked group of scientists, to ask the question: Do you believe life ever existed or currently exists on Mars? The results were the best possible for any survey I know to exist. Exactly 75% of those surveyed said that they believed that life once existed on Mars. 25% of the survey said they believed life currently exists below the surface in the form of bacteria or an earlier life form. What is amazing is that there were no scientists undecided or skeptical of life existing, past or present, on Mars. Given that there are thousands or perhaps millions of scientists that would be skeptical; I find it amazing that their opinion was not represented. How is it that even when a murder or robbery is caught on surveillance tape, the news media will refer to the perpetrator as "the suspect"? We have taken "political correctness" to such an extreme as to not want to offend anyone's rights, and yet it seams that murderers are uplifted more than the innocent. How can the news media be so concerned with "innocent until proven guilty" in this example and yet condemn the theory that life is the result of God's creation as religious nonsense? In the news, TV programs, movies, and public schools, evolution is taught as if it was an absolute fact. When was the last time you heard the information listed in this book and others like this one, taught in a public school? The debate is nearly endless. You have professors with long lists of credentials on both sides of the argument, yet the general public usually receives only the evolutionists' theories and information. In the previous paragraph I quoted Dr. Marcus's bold statement that the scientific evidence soundly points to life beginning from God and to suggest otherwise is the result of ignorance or desperation. In the case of high school teachers, I submit that ignorance is present in many cases. The teachers have received the diluted, selected information of college professors while receiving their bachelors to teach their class. We have noted professors who had no idea how religiously slanted towards evolution the information was, given to them in their undergraduate studies, until they went on to do their PhD research. Then you come to the world's renowned professors expressing a commitment to evolution. I believe they have reached their conclusions by a desperate determination to prove their convictions in atheism, their belief there is no God.

This may seam like a conspiracy theory, and you would be correct. If all the facts where to be represented in public schools, the theory of evolution would soon lose all political support. Teachers are kept in the dark about some of the biological principles mentioned in this book to perpetuate the lie that evolution is truth. This operates like a brain-washing mill masquerading as high school biology. It is like a factory with the express intent to produce children with atheistic beliefs. Again, Lee Strobel's testimony is a perfect example of this process. He was taught to respect his teachers and learn from them, rightful so. The teachers began teaching evolution as an absolute scientific truth, because that is what they were wrongfully taught in college. Lee believed his teachers because he accepted that they knew more about science than he did, so they must know what they are talking about. Once he came to evolution, he easily recognized that the underlying theme was to prove God did not exist. Knowing this was a conflict with what he was taught in church, he turned to his pastor for answers. However, his pastor could not explain all the scientific information that he received from his teacher. Lee later explored the subject further and found that his teacher was not given the whole truth, just the parts supporting the theory of evolution. He discovered this as he pursued his investigation to the leading professors in the various fields of science. He concluded that at the professorship level, there was a lot more controversy between equally qualified members of the scientific community. He found that if these professors had come to any conclusions about the origin of life, for example, they usually made their decision based more on their personal beliefs than on the hard scientific evidence. Lee summarizes his decision to reject the theory of evolution at the end of his book The Case for a Creator. "Looking at the doctrine of Darwinism, which undergirded my atheism for so many years, it didn't take me long to conclude that it was simply too far-fetched to be credible. I realized that if I were to embrace Darwinism ... I would have to believe that: Nothing produces everything. Non-life produces life. Randomness produces fine-tuning. Chaos produces information. Unconsciousness produces consciousness. Non-reason produces reason. Based on this, I was forced to conclude that Darwinism would require a blind leap of faith that I was not willing to make. Simply put, the central pillars of evolutionary theory quickly rotted away when exposed to scrutiny. [4.34]" If I am correct and the reliability of the theory of evolution is mainly a conspiracy of lies, then who is behind the plot? We'll I'm not suggesting any person or group of people except one: Satan. Satan, the father of all lies, is desperately keeping a large number of people from hearing the truth about evolution. It is Satan who is responsible for this propaganda being taught by nearly every means of communication possible. The old procedure of saying a lie long enough and loud enough allows you to get a majority to believe the lie. This has even affected dedicated Christians to accept the lie as either true or irrelevant for the study of the scripture. But seeking the truth is at the very heart of the Christian life. "And you will know the truth, and the truth will set you free." John 8:32. Once you have uncovered the truth that the theory of evolution is a lie, you can truly experience the freedom of praising God with all your heart and mind. I respect the belief of Christians who say they believe in evolution and in Christ, although I would question their commitment to the Lord. My curiosity immediately asks, which parts of the theory of evolution do you believe? As previously stated the theory of evolution is a complex mixture of truth, half-truths and lies. If you say you can believe in evolution and in the scriptures, you must be talking about believing in those few evolutionary statements that do not support atheism. I would ask that you re-examine you convictions and the reason you support the theory of evolution. It may be that you need to examine the scientific evidence a little closer as I have done in writing this book.

Again, the word of God is the one absolute truth. "For what can be known about God is plain to them, because God has shown it to them. Ever since the creation of the world his invisible nature, namely his eternal power and deity, has been clearly perceived in the things that have been made. So they are without excuse; for although they knew God they did not honor him as God or give thanks to him, but they became futile in their thinking and their senseless minds were darkened. Claiming to be wise, they became fools, and exchanged the glory of the immortal God for images resembling mortal man or birds or animals or reptiles. And since they did not see fit to acknowledge God, God gave them up to a base mind and to improper conduct." Romans 1:19-23, 28 RSV "And beware lest you lift up your eyes to heaven, and when you see the sun and the moon and the stars, all the host of heaven, you be drawn away and worship them and serve them, things which the Lord your God has allotted to all the peoples under the whole heaven." -Deuteronomy 4:19 When we accept evolution sometimes it can become an object of worship. Isn't there almost a worship in the symbols of evolution in our culture? The ultimate lie from evolution is that escape from God is freedom to "do your own thing" without consequence. This is why it is the perfect example of a lie from Satan. It teaches that you can sin all you want and their will be no consequences because there is no God. No wonder a self-centered society embraces this self-serving philosophy. How much damage has been done to our once Christian culture because of this theory? The idea that life is the result of "survival of the fittest", has nullified the philosophy of "love thy neighbor". No compassion, that is for the weak that gets you left behind in the urban jungle. To this philosophy, violence solves everything. How much school violence could be attributed to this dangerous philosophy?

The next chapter will examine the theory of evolution on the larger scale. Again, we will seek the Lord's help in untangling the complex mix of fact and fiction in current scientific studies. The theme of evolution in the animal kingdom is survival of the fittest. Did this one driving force generate every life form that now exists? One part of the theory of evolution we will closely examine is the concept of every living creature comes from the early oceans. Is every kind of animal ultimately related? Why do evolutionists scoff when we suggest that we did not evolve from an ape? We will return to a few examples of irreducibly complexity. There are many examples of biological systems that indicate they are the result of intelligent design. These systems must have been fully functional at the time of their creation in order to account for their properties. "Evidence for intelligent design is widespread in nature. For example: A. The motorized rotating flagellum of some bacteria. B. Blood clotting and its control. C. The high degree of organization within a typical cell. D. Cell division and its control. E. The system for protein synthesis. F. The human eye. G. The respiratory chain based in the highly organized mitochondria. [4.35]" Not only do we question how these systems first develop, but why we do not see these processes occurring today. Why are none of these complex systems in the process of developing in a species today? Wither you accept by faith that life came from God as described in Genesis Chapter 1 or by some natural means, neither process is at work today. "Neither 'process' is currently observable, testable, or repeatable. Please note that when speaking of evolution, I am talking of the appearance of new (not rearranged) genetic information leading to greater and greater complexity of genetic information. I am also talking about the appearance of life starting from inanimate chemicals. ... Creationists, of course, have not the slightest problem with natural selection. After all, it has been practiced by farmers for centuries in their breeding of plants and animals through selecting preferred offspring and mating or propagating these. ... Evolutionists counter by saying that it is too slow to observe. Even if this were true, it still means that evolution is non-scientific because it is not observable or testable. [4.36]" I must slightly disagree with Dr. Grocott in his definition of science. As previously discussed in chapter one, I would define science as a systematic pursuit of knowledge. The definition he gives for science is actually the definition for scientific laws or concrete scientific knowledge. There is a realm of science called the scientific theory that does not limit our discussion of postulates and ideas. A scientific theory is simply a set of ideas currently believed to be true. A scientific theory, therefore, attempts to reasonably explain a set of events that can not be currently tested for accuracy. The very act of reason is to make decisions about the truth of the situation, based on what facts we personally accept or reject, based on faith in their reliability. In this way, faith and science have always been partners. It is only in the 20th and 21st centuries that we have unsuccessfully attempted to disconnect faith from science. One thing is for certain, the theory of evolution is treated as if it was a proven scientific fact and it is not! This is the greatest lie expressed in books, schools and even the news media today. As more information becomes available, the more reliability we have in the fact God created the universe and all life that exists. Therefore, there should be no question that the scientific complexities that contradict the theory of evolution should in some manner be mentioned in all public and private schools. To do otherwise is to invoke censorship of the scientific facts, to promote the religion of atheism in public schools and to be scientifically inaccurate. These are all in opposition to the calling of science to seek the truth and in opposition of separation of religion from classrooms. As stated, the act of formulating beliefs is a personal experience common to everyone. You can never totally separate religious discussion from any interaction with a group of people as found in public schools. We do need to have guidelines to prevent the inevitable debate from becoming a source of violence. Like any good topic of debate, the discussion should be orderly and respectful of each individual's rights and beliefs. But to remove the debate completely is impossible and the subject will inevitably become a topic of discord in such classrooms as Chemistry, Biology, Astronomy and Particle Physics.

The reliability of the Scripture becomes more a reality each day. You must decide how much faith you have in your facts and the information presented here. Which professors are telling you the truth? Which theory makes the most sense? These types of questions can only be answered individually as you examine each fact for yourself. Our faith is molded by what information we have accepted as true. To test your faith you must continually evaluate the source of your facts. See if the professors who wrote the books I am referring to are accurate. Do your research and make up your own mind about what you should believe. I suggest you carefully examine every source you can to test your convictions. I am amazed at how many people will read all sorts of books and yet seam afraid to examine the one book that contains the most answers to every question in life: the Holy Bible. Read the Bible thoroughly and see if it makes sense to you. Look for good commentaries to help understand the Old Testament. Since we are living in the New Testament days, because of the coming of the Lord Jesus Christ, I suggest that this is the best place to begin a study of the accuracy and principles of the Bible. If you are not familiar with the Bible, begin with the first book of the New Testament and continue to the end. I would highly recommend closely reading the works of John, the books of Romans, Galatians, Philippians, and Ephesians for practical verses that apply to life in today's world. Read these sections of the Bible repeatedly and frequently. Also, I suggest talking with other Christian Pastors about a good translation of the Bible. I pray that my wife I can write more about the Christian Lifestyle in upcoming books.

References for Chapter 4

4.1 The Theory of Evolution, The New Encyclopedia Britannica, Macromedia Knowledge in Depth, Vol. 18, 15th Edition, 1990, Encyclopedia Britannica Inc. p.855.

4.2 Ibid, p. 855.

4.3 Ibid, p. 856.

4.4 Lee Strobel, The Case for A Creator, Zondervan, Grand Rapids Michigan. 2004, p. 19.

4.5 Ibid. p. 23.

4.6 Ibid. p. 16.

4.7 Ibid p. 31-32.

4.8 Ibid. p. 32-33.

4.9 Ibid. p. 35-36.

4.10 Ibid. p. 36.

4.11 Ibid. p. 37 and 40.

4.12 Ibid. p. 41.

4.13 Ibid. p. 39.

4.14 Charles Darwin, The Origin of Species, New York: New American Library, 1958, p.171.

4.15 John F. Ashton, In Six Days: Why Fifty Scientists choose to believe in Creation, Master Books, 2000-2003, p. 25-26.

4.16 Ibid. p. 26-27.

4.17 Ibid p. 29.

4.18 Lee Strobel, The Case for A Creator, Zondervan, Grand Rapids Michigan. 2004, p. 228

4.19 Ibid. p. 38.

4.20 John F. Ashton, In Six Days: Why Fifty Scientists choose to believe in Creation, Master Books, 2000-2003, p. 38-39.

4.21 Ibid. p. 114-117.

4.22 A Scientific American book, The Physics and Chemistry of Life, New York N.Y., Simon And Schuster Inc, 1955, p. 9-12.

4.23 John F. Ashton, In Six Days: Why Fifty Scientists choose to believe in Creation, Master Books, 2000-2003, p. 75.

4.24 Lee Strobel, The Case for A Creator, Zondervan, Grand Rapids Michigan. 2004, p. 223-225.

4.25 Ibid. p. 42.

4.26 Ibid. p. 220.

4.27 Ibid. p. 230-231.

4.28 Ibid. p. 231.

4.29 Ibid p. 232-235.

4.30 John F. Ashton, In Six Days: Why Fifty Scientists choose to believe in Creation, Master Books, 2000-2003, p. 82.

4.31 Ibid. p.82-83.

4.32 Ibid. p.173.

4.33 Ibid. p. 174-177.

4.34 Lee Strobel, The Case for A Creator, Zondervan, Grand Rapids Michigan. 2004, p. 277.

4.35 John F. Ashton, In Six Days: Why Fifty Scientists choose to believe in Creation, Master Books, 2000-2003, p. 140-141.

4.36 Ibid. p.147.

Illustration for Chapter 4

4.1 Dennis Liu, Genetics, Microsoft Encarta Encyclopedia Standard, 2002 edition.

Chapter 5: Biology: Darwin's Tree of Life or Death?

The Debate Continues

In the last chapter, we briefly explored the scientific fields of organic Chemistry and Micro-Biology. There should, at this point, be at least some doubt in your mind concerning the theory of evolution. The fields of biology and chemistry we outlined in the previous chapter are the foundation on which the theory of evolution resides. By now we should recognize that the theory of life evolving from chemicals is shaky at best. There are world renowned scholars and scientists on both sides of the issue. Did life come from an incredible set of "miraculous" events or the purpose driven act of a creator? There is nearly no end to the debate or the number of books on the topic of evolution. This alone should be compelling evidence that we do not have all the facts to settle the matter. Usually, little information is presented in high school textbooks on how life could come from chemicals. The previous chapter outlines a few of reasons why this is NOT true. The theory of life evolving from chemicals, or micro-evolution, is not a proven fact but a skeptical theory. This chapter will deal with macro-evolution and the theories that all large scale life forms came from a common ancestry. The theory that there are many creatures which are related to each other is not an idea that originated with Charles Darwin, as many have been taught. Instead it comes right from the book of Genesis. "And God said, Let the water team with living creatures, and let birds fly above the earth across the expanse of the sky. So God created the great creatures of the sea and every living and moving thing with which the water teems, according to their kind. And God saw that it was good. And God blessed them and said, be fruitful and increase in number and fill the water in the seas, and let the birds increase on the earth. And there was evening and morning – the fifth day. And God said let the land produce living creatures according to their kinds: livestock, creatures that move along the ground, and wild animals, each according to its kind." Genesis 1:20-24 It is obvious from experience, that there is an enormous variety of animals that can be produced by selective breading. However, every variety is within a well-defined limit. The Bible separates living creatures into several distinct types. First, on the fifth day of creation, two types of creatures: sea creatures and birds. Then on the sixth day of creation: livestock, creatures moving on the ground, wild animals and then finally man. These are very distinct categories of life. The theory that **all** creatures are related and came, ultimately, from the sea is not a proven scientific fact. In this chapter we will explore many issues of evolution that are commonly discussed. There is an enormous amount of books on these subjects and we will highlight some of there most important points in this chapter. So, this will in no way exhaust the many scientific findings that are used in the debate over the reliability of the theory of evolution. The one concept I wish to reiterate is this, there are many true statements supporting the theory of evolution. For example the above reference to the biblical support that there are many varieties of life and they are separated by difference kinds. However, the theme of evolution is to twist truth and present statements with some truth and a lot of imaginative ideas based on faith not fact. As we stated in the previous chapter, the theory of evolution is a deliberate attempt to explain how life can exist without the power of God. Many of the explanations are a deliberate one-sided view of the evidence. In the end, each person must examine the evidence and decide if you accept by faith the principles of the evolutionary theory or reject its claims. If you are a Christian and chose to say you "believe in evolution" be careful. There is a dangerous philosophy associated with the theory of evolution. Also, the whole subject becomes immensely complicated as we try to discover the methods and techniques God has used to create the nearly endless varieties of life. Again, some parts of the theory of evolution have helped our understanding of the relationships between different types of species. But, the theory of evolution attributes nearly every step of the process to natural forces and not the designs of the creator of the universe. Be cautious and pray at all times that you are serving the Lord Jesus Christ as an effective witness and testimony to the Lord's word if you support certain parts of the theory of evolution.

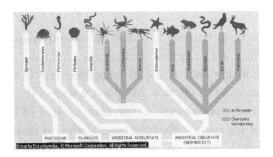

Figure 5.1

Darwin's Tree of Life or Tree of Death

Let us look at the next image described in Lee Strobel's book: The Darwin Tree of Life describing the power of evolution to create all life forms from a single common ancestor. In Darwin's book, The Origin of Species, Darwin produced an illustration of how living creatures are **all** related to each other. Lee questions Dr. Jonathan Wells on the current accuracy of this illustration. "'As an illustration of the fossil record, the Tree of life is a dismal failure. But it is a good representation of Darwin's theory.' ... I didn't want to miss the significance of what Wells was claiming. 'You're saying the tree of life illustrates Darwin's ideas but his theory is not supported by the physical evidence scientists have found in fossils? That' right. .... In fact Darwin knew the fossil record failed to support his tree. He acknowledged that major groups of animals – he called them divisions, now they're called phyla – appear suddenly in the fossil record. ... Darwin believed that future fossil discoveries would vindicate his theory – but that hasn't happened. ... The Cambrian was a geological period that we think began a little more than 540 Million years ago. The Cambrian explosion has been called the 'Biological Big Bang' because it gave rise to the sudden appearance of most of the major animal phyla that are still alive today, as well as some that are now extinct,' Wells said. [5.1]" We see the first major obstacle to the theory of evolution: The fact that there are examples of life resulting from a sudden occurrence not a gradual development over millions of years. The significance of such evidence cannot be over emphasized. Lee was greatly shocked by this discovery. Let us restate the words of Charles Darwin. Quote, "If it could be demonstrated that any complex organ existed which could not possibly have been formed by numerous successive, slight modifications, my theory would absolutely break down. [5.2]" Some have theorized that we just have not discovered all the transitional fossils prior to the Cambrian period or the fossils are too tiny or soft to be preserved. Dr. Wells answers these questions. "(referring to the Cambrian explosion) This is absolutely contrary to Darwin's Tree of Life. These animals, which are so fundamentally different in their body plans, appear fully developed, all of a sudden, in what paleontologists have called the single most spectacular phenomenon of fossil record. ... 'As a scientist,' he conceded, 'I have to leave open the possibility that next year someone will discover a fossil bed in the Congo or somewhere that will suddenly fill in the gaps. ... But I don't think that's likely. ... It hasn't happened after all this time, and millions of fossils have already been dug up. There are certainly enough good sedimentary rocks from before the Cambrian era to have preserved ancestors if there were any. ... As for pre-Cambrian fossils being too tiny or soft to be preserved-well, we have microfossils of bacteria in rocks dating back more than three billion years. ... Based on all this, I think it's reasonable for me, as a scientist, to say that maybe we should question our assumption that this common ancestry exist. ... Of course, descent from a common ancestor is true at some levels. ... Nobody denies that. For example, we can trace generations of fruit flies to a common ancestor. Within a single species, common ancestry has been observed directly. And it's possible that all the cats – tigers, lions, and so on – descended from a common ancestor. ... When you get to the level of phyla, the major animal groups, it's a very, very shaky hypothesis. In fact, I would say it's disconfirmed. The evidence just doesn't support it. ... If you consider all the evidences, Darwin's tree is false as a description of the history of life. I'll go further than that: it's not even a good hypothesis at this point." [5.3]

We are familiar with the term "missing link" and we instantly associate this term to a species that can explain human evolution. There are a number of discoveries and theories concerning the development of man. The most significant "missing link" is the common ancestor to both ape and human. We will explore this research in detail later in this chapter. My point is simply this: There is not one missing link but several or perhaps hundreds or even thousands. The Darwin "tree of life" has a lot of missing pieces, not just one. The Darwin tree of life merely illustrates the hypothesis that **all** forms of life are related by decent. The theory of evolution is based on the premise that random environmental factors affect biological progress. Plants and animals adapt to the environment and alter there natural abilities. The theory of evolution states that there are no limitations to this process and changes not only occur within a particular family of a species but enable the genetic code in the DNA to sufficiently change to produce an entirely new group of animals. The primarily principle of natural selection is based on the idea "the strongest survive". The idea is that the biggest and strongest out-live the smaller ones. The result is that creatures are increasingly more adaptive to their environment. We have associated the term evolution or evolve with growth. If we cross bread a species of animal or plant we use the term; we have evolved a new species. Even in the pursuit of knowledge, we loosely use the term "evolve". When science makes a new discovery in a field, like biology, chemistry, computer programming or any other field of science we say our knowledge has "evolved" to include this new fact. This gives undue credibility to the theory of evolution, without the user realizing he has just reinforced a world view that could be entire opposite to his, or her own personal convictions. Change and adaptation is not necessary evidence for evolution. Dr. Nancy Darrall has brilliantly explained the differences in something adapting and something changing in a fundamentally new way. Let us set the stage for Dr Darrall's research. "Many authors of the scientific papers … referred to the evolution of resistance to pollution. As a biologist involved in research on air pollution, I have had good opportunity to study much of this work … (the research scientists) comment that the most universal occurrence of metal tolerant populations on mine spoils shows the remarkable power of natural selection as a force for evolutionary change in response to environmental factors – evolution in action! Is this true? Can examples like these be used to prove that all life evolved by mutation and natural selection?" [5.4] Dr. Darrall goes on to explain that the theory of evolution does not provide any new techniques for constructing classifications in plants or animals. Most significant scientific theories provide a principle that can be proven or disproved by experimentation. The theory of evolution merely comments on evidence and generates subjective statements considering the facts discovered. In this way, evolution injects an atheistic faith in explaining the observations. This is totally unacceptable to the Christian Scientist who sees God's handiwork in all of creation. In this manner, in the field of biology, faith can not be separated from the scientific investigation. Dr. Darrall put it this way: "As my Christian faith is part of my everyday life, I found that it was impossible to regulate faith to a separate sphere from my observations and understanding of science. Professor Edgar Andrews has discussed the illogical nature of compartmentalizing faith and science in his book Christ and the Cosmos (1986) and I found his arguments helpful in clarifying my own position. … We use our powers of reason to develop an understanding of the natural world. Our five senses enable us to observe the natural world, but faith enables us to observe the spiritual realm of God. … Reason works on faith plus information to give spiritual understanding, just as reason acts on the observations of the five senses to develop our understanding of the way the natural world functions today. Faith is not an alternative pathway to a different form of knowledge unrelated to the material world in which we live. Both routes lead to understanding. However, by the use of reason plus faith plus information, we come to a growing understanding of the way God works in the world, 'the wisdom of God.' [5.5]" In other words: "By wisdom the Lord laid the earth's foundations, by understanding he set the heavens in place; by his knowledge the deeps were divided, and the clouds let drop the dew." Proverbs 3:19-20. And as for the role of faith: "Now faith is being sure of what we hope for and certain of what we do not see. By faith we understand that the universe was formed at God's command, so that what is seen was not made out of what is visible." Hebrews 11:1, 3

In order to understand the faith of the evolutionist we must re-examine the DNA molecule. DNA changes occur when biological life forms adapt to their environment. The evolutionists claim that when this takes place the life form is going from a lower order of life to a higher order. We have extensively explained the workings of DNA in the last chapter. Let us briefly highlight our understanding of DNA with Dr. Darrall's perspective. "The DNA double helix is analogous to the paper and ink of my biology textbooks. Anyone who has sat down in front of a blank piece of paper in an examination will be aware of the need for something more than paper and ink in order to pass. We need ideas, concepts, plans, purpose, memory of lecture notes, mathematical equations – in other words information. ... Where does the information come from? Is it the property of the materials, the paper and ink? ... The information is not a product of the paper or ink, but the thinking mind that has so organized these two things. ... There is nothing special about DNA; it is just a collection of molecules as is paper and ink. DNA molecules can be strung out in line, copied, and still not contain information. It needs a thinking mind to design the cells of living things and then to commit that design in code form to the DNA, so that each organism can function and reproduce itself. [5.6]" Dr. Darrall reminds us of the fact that there is no scientific explanation to where the information came from. By reason and by faith we can accept the fact that the information came from God. There are various other theories concerning the origin of this information, some of which we discussed in the last chapter. All natural explanations for the presence of the DNA information have thus far failed. This is a crucial point to the theory of life evolving from a primordial soup. This will become clear when we discuss the process of mutations. Dr. Darrall reviews the attempt by Dawkins in his book The Blind Watchmaker, and in his lecture presentations, to explain the source of DNA information by natural means. One example by Dawkins is where a computer program randomly selects letters and eventually generates the famous line in Hamlet's play, "To be or not to be." Dr. Darrall points out some of the flaws in his example and that this is NOT a true example of something newly created by random forces. "He omits just one thing from his discussion: the information was already in hand. ... In the first, the target phrase "tobeornottobe" was in the memory of the computer and all that was necessary was a matching exercise. In the second, the design was already present in his own intelligent mind and he was controlling the process. In sharp contrast to his intention, he has provided a powerful demonstration of an intelligent designer at work. [5.7]"

Now let us go back to the assertion that a plant growing in a highly polluted area producing metal tolerant offspring is strong evidence for evolution. The evolutionists suggest that this an example of new information generated in the DNA and a new species forming. They claim this is clear evidence that all life forms are the result of beneficial mutations. Is this true? Or is it manipulating information that is already present and therefore not generating anything new? Are there limitations to this process or are there no limits as the evolutionists claim? Dr. Darrall explains her observations. "Planting a mixed bag of seed at a polluted site would mean that the more tolerant individuals would survive and the less tolerant would die, or at best survive to grow less as healthy individuals and produce less seed. This is a clear example of natural selection acting on a pre-existing gene pool, in response to change in environment. ... It is equivalent to the selection of red Smarties from a bag of mixed sweets; nothing new has appeared in the genes, no new information. Many other examples of such variation are known ... Here we simply have a reworking of what is already present. ... Spetner (1997), in his book Not by Chance, discusses details of changes leading to antibiotic resistance in bacteria. ... One example of resistance to antibiotics that involves changes in genes is that of the antibiotic streptomycin. The molecule works by interfering with the facture of protein within the bacterial cell. This happens when the streptomycin molecule attaches itself to the specific part of the cell where the reaction to form a protein is taking place. ... The bacterium is now unable to put the right amino acid in the chain at this point; the wrong amino acid is included, and so the wrong protein is made. This wrong product cannot fulfill its task in the bacterium; the cell cannot grow, divide, and multiply, and the infection disappears. ... Similar changes have occurred in the example of sickle-celled anemia. ... The mutation alters the composition of hemoglobin that caries the oxygen in red blood cells and, as a consequence, the red blood cells change to become sickle-shaped. This means that the malarial parasite is no longer able to live and grow inside the red blood cells, and the individual with this altered gene does not suffer from the malaria. Again this change has also occurred by a loss of information. ... In a recorded interview, Dawkins was asked to give examples of changes in organisms that have occurred by the addition of new information. He was unable to do so (Keziah, 1997). As Spetner points out, 'The failure to observe even one mutation that adds information is more than just a failure to find support for the theory. It is evidence against the theory.' [5.8]" What does all this mean? Simply put, every example of a genetic change or mutation, that I am aware of, can be explained by the loss or re-arrangement of information. If no new information is observed to be created, evolution can not work. This goes back to a fundamental law of physics which is applied to bio-chemistry. The second law of thermodynamics, as we have previously discussed, states that all quantities tend to go from a higher order to a lower order. Applied to cells, it implies that cells tend to lose information, not gain new information. Once again, the laws of science coincide with the Christian prospective and not the evolutionists. We know that the principle of life wearing out, and running down of all physical and living things is consistent with the biblical account of the fall of man. "To Adam he said, 'Because you listened to your wife and ate from the tree about which I commanded you, 'You must not eat of it,' Cursed is the ground because of you; through painful toil you will eat of it all the days of your life." Genesis 3:17. It is the evolutionists that ask you to take a blind leap of faith and accept their theory of evolution. They ask that you simply believe on the power of natural selection to create all life in an increasing complex order, in spite of physical and chemical laws that prevent the possibility of this to naturally occur. To believe in evolution is to reject fundamental laws of physics, chemistry, and biology and accept by faith, the power of mutations to do the impossible. Why is this religion taught in public schools? Why are we not receiving a balanced amount of information about the subject of evolution? Why do we continually see examples of evidence supporting evolution in schools and none of the hard scientific data that dispute the theory? There are hundreds of excellent books on the subject. I will only attempt to highlight a few in this chapter. The theory of evolution is worthy of a scientific debate. Why are we receiving only one side in the public classrooms? Darwin's tree is not the tree of life, (the tree of life is mentioned several places in scripture) instead, Darwin's tree is an illustration of intellectual suicide and rejection of the scientific principle to seek the truth. Continually, more scientific data is giving more scientists reasons to reject the theory of evolution. This is evident in the growing number of scientists who believe in the literal account of Genesis. "Many of the world's greatest scientists have been convinced, Bible- believing Christians. In my own discipline of electrical engineering, one has only to think of names like Michael Faraday, James Joule, Lord Kelvin, and James Clark Maxwell (who wrote against evolution) that this is true. The Creation Research Society currently has a membership of 650 scientists, each one holding a master's degree or above in a recognized field of science. Dr. Russell Humphreys estimates there are around 10,000 practicing professional scientists in the USA alone who openly believe in a six-day recent creation. [5.9]" I deeply applaud these men and women of science for their stand for the truth of the gospel. There are many more scientists, perhaps millions, which concede in the scientific need for the presence of a creator God to make life and the universe. Most of them have caved under the pressure of popularity to dismiss or avoid the evidences against evolution. The scientists of the Creation Institute have taken an admirable stand for a literal interpretation of the Bible. There have been times I have struggled with my faith on this subject. I too, considered incorporating evolution into my Christian faith. However, during my research for this book I have rejected this idea and have been convinced that the evolutionary theory and the Christian faith are, generally speaking, wholly incompatible. We will continue to outline a few of the thousands of scientific facts concerning the debate over the age of the universe and the development of the world's life forms. For more information, I suggest a personal research of all available books on the subject. The endless continuation of this debate among world renowned scientists should be sufficient evidence that the subject is far from closed on a scientific basis. Only a personal conviction can settle the questions about the theory of evolution, and its implications. You must individually decide how much faith you place on your research and the scientists presenting the information. Then, by faith, you must conclude if you reject some or all the principles of evolution. My opinion should be clear, to believe in evolution is to reject the worship of God as creator of all life. Truly, Darwin's tree is a tree of death, showing a path towards destruction and the wrath of God.

Examples of Irreducibly Complex Systems

The real death blow for evolution is found in the increasing number of biological systems that fit into the category irreducibly complex. What do we mean by the term irreducibly complex? Scientists are finding more information every day about the intricate workings of biological systems. As a result, they find that all the parts must have been created simultaneously in order for these biological systems to exist. The possibility of organs, biological systems, and many life forms resulting from "gradual slight modifications" as evolutionists claim are becoming slim and none. "Behe then goes on to demonstrate design in the natural world using several examples of irreducible complexity taken from biochemical process and structures within cells. These examples include the cilium, a sub-cellular structure 'which looks like hair and beats like a whip'; the process of blood clotting, and intra-cellular transport. He also discusses the human eye, making the point that here there are a number of irreducibly complex systems, for example, the retina, the tear ducts, and eyelids. I would agree with Darwin when he wrote of his difficulty in understanding how the eye could have evolved, because he was aware that such a complex organ could not have originated in a few steps. In his words, the idea was 'absurd in the highest possible degree' (Darwin, 1859, edited 1959). Nevertheless, Darwin proposed that beneficial changes leading to the development of the eye accumulated over many generations. [5.10]" Blood clotting is an even more significant evidence for creation than you might first realize. "As it turns out, the system of blood clotting involves a highly choreographed cascade of ten steps that use about twenty different molecular components. Without the whole system in place, it doesn't work. ... The real trick with blood clotting isn't so much the clot itself–it's just a blob that blocks the flow of blood- but it's the regulation of the system. ... If you make a clot in the wrong place – say, the brain or lung – you'll die. If you make a clot twenty minutes after all the blood has drained from your body, you'll die. If the blood clot isn't confined to the cut, your entire blood system might solidify, and you'll die. If you make a clot that doesn't cover the entire length of the cut, you'll die. To create a perfectly balanced blood-clotting system, clusters of protein components have to be inserted all at once. [5.11]" Darwin and the followers of evolution should not be considered logic driven scientists but cultists that promote a false religion. Even when confronted with the truth that God created life, they insist on teaching and believing in a lie. They insist that it is more scientifically accurate to blindly believe in the power of natural selection to overcome any difficulty of explanation to produce the systems life requires.

An example of adaptive behavior improving a physical condition, according to the theory of evolution, is an amphibian animal. The theory of evolution states that this was once a creature with gills that only "breathed" water. One day a few of these fish like creatures ventured onto dry land, probably looking for food. When successive generations of these creatures continued to explore the land for food, a species developed that could live both in water and on dry land. Once again, the theory of evolution makes the following claims: All modifications to a species are developed by subtle small changes developing over several generations. All of these physical and biological changes are due to environment conditions. This must always be proven true or the theory of evolution falls apart. One creature that is difficult to explain by evolution is the Surinam toad. Quote, "The female toad lays her eggs on her back by means of a long oviduct. After the eggs are laid, the skin on her back grows around the eggs and forms a nursery for the young. One would have great difficulty explaining how such a toad evolved. ... First, the long oviduct must have evolved; secondly, the skin on the back must have become capable of surrounding the eggs, or they would have dried out rapidly on the toad's back. Finally, the two physiological structures would have been useless, unless the toad had used them properly. There is absolutely no reason for either of these structures to have evolved by themselves. ... This is an example of a structure which can't be evolved by small modifications. It must appear all at once or it is useless. [5.12]" There are numerous other examples of creatures which defy the evolutionary description of their origin. One bird with amazing attributes is the woodpecker. Rather than list all their physiological characteristics in this text I suggest consulting books by other Christian authors.

The evidence for the creation of God is everywhere in biological systems. Evolutions do not like to be reminded of obvious evidence for design in the complexity of life. It is a simple point everyone can understand and represents the true failure in the theory of evolution. "The presence of complexity – interdependent parts that do not function unless other parts are also present – poses another major problem for evolution. For instance, a muscle is useless without a nerve going to the muscle to direct its contracting activity. But both the muscle and the nerve are useless without a complicated control mechanism in the brain to direct the contracting activity of the muscle and correlate its activity with that of other muscles. ... If evolution is a real ongoing process, why don't we find new developing complex organs in organisms that lack them? We would expect to find developing legs, eyes, livers, and new unknown kinds of organs, providing for evolutionary advancement in organisms that lacked desirable advantages. ... The simple example of a muscle, mentioned above, pales into insignificance when we consider more complicated organs such as the eye or the brain. ... Then there are the 100,000,000 light-sensitive cells in the human eye that send information to the brain through some 1,000,000 nerve fibers of the optic nerve. In the brain this information is sorted into various components such as color, movement, form, and depth. It is then analyzed and combined into an intelligible picture. This involves an extremely complex array of interdependent parts. ... How did evolution from simple to complex counter the tendency towards randomness that is so prevalent in nature? For two centuries evolutionists have been searching for a mechanism that would explain the origin of complexity, but so far this has been a virtually futile search. [5.13]" The evolutionists teach us that it doesn't matter that science has not solved the mystery of complexity. According to them, we simply need *to believe* in some undiscovered force that has accomplished this for us. No thanks, I will believe that the God of the Bible created all these things, not make some undiscovered "natural" force the "god" of my life.

Does Violence Solve Anything?

The people who support the theory of natural selection from Darwin's original theory of evolution must have watched a lot of boxing matches. Either that or they fully believe that bullies always win. They probably had some unfortunate encounter with a well endowed football player while they were freshmen, (I am not stereotyping muscular men. I deeply enjoy bodybuilding myself.) In either case, they apparently haven't watched many P.B.S broadcasts about the nature of wild life. In nature, seldom does the strongest survive. Usually when two predators battle to the death, there is a third party standing by. When the winner is finished, the third party is waiting to move in for the kill. The victor, usually the larger animal, is too weak from the struggle to defend itself and becomes victim to the watchful predator. This occurs frequently in the wild when there is the rare encounter for territorial survival. The weaker species adapt their behavior to win over the larger predators, maintaining a consistence in size and abilities of the species. Another example of this wildlife principle at work is with a pack of wolves. The strength of the pack is sufficient to overcome the largest enemies. Vultures attack their prey in groups and few creatures can withstand their assault. The balances of strong and weak and those traveling alone and in groups make the steady flow of evolutionary development impossible. This is one of many reasons we do not see any clear evidence of evolutionary principles occurring in the wild today. Once again, there are exceptions and adaptive behavior sometimes shows up as a range of changes within a family of animals but transforming from a dog to a cat, for example, does not exist.

The similarities in different phyla of animals are not, necessarily, any evidence for the theory of evolution. It is reasonable to assume that God created all life forms with similar characteristics because that shows consistency in His nature. "Was there any reason why God should not have created all forms of life as 'variations on themes' and so have provided the observed orderly degrees of genetic and phenotypic resemblance as evidence in taxonomic classification? Relatives tend to resemble one another in physical, functional, and behavioral characteristics. This is a phenomenon which is basic to the science of genetics. … The theory of evolution assumes a common origin for all forms of life and, therefore, infers that species, genera, families, orders, etc. are genetically related. They all do carry some genes with similar structure and function, yes, but did this imply genetic relationship in the normal, within-species sense, and was one at liberty to assume a common origin for all forms of life? Was there any reason why God should have created different species, genera, etc. in completely different ways and with completely different genes? [5.14]" The theory of evolution is merely a philosophy of rebellion against God. It teaches that if you have enough faith in the power of evolution, through natural selection, anything is possible. The same old promise by Satan: If you believe in me I will show you a party with no end. Satan promises that if you rid yourself of obedience to God you can get drunk and have a really good time. I don't know about you, but when I was in my rebel years and got drunk, I had no fun at all. I just had a hangover the next day. I always had a much better time when I simply drank a little and danced with a lot of pretty girls. When I got drunk I simply acted like a fool and alienated everyone around me. Throwing away the rules does not give you more freedom, but makes you more a prisoner of sin. The theory of evolution is in line with Satan's lies. The theory states that if you follow these teachings we can go beyond the physical laws of biology, chemistry, genetics, etc, and anything is possible. It is God's nature to establish order in the universe through limits expressed in laws. From science we have the physical laws, for the human spirit, we have the laws listed in the Bible. The Ten Commandments, and others, show us how we can live an abundant life when we observe these laws.

Competition: Good or Bad?

There are two types of competition: competition between two different species and competition between members of the same species. Competition between members of the same species is a significant part of developing a new species according to Darwin's theory of evolution. Darwin's theory depends heavily upon competition between two members of the same species for evolutionary development. Quote, "But the struggle will almost invariably be most severe between individuals of the same species, for they frequent the same districts, require the same food, and are exposed to the same dangers. [5.15]" Through these struggles, mutations are formed according to Darwin's theory. The stronger members of each species dominate, as the weak ones of the same species are killed off, and over time a new species emerges, according to the evolutionary theory. The primary reasoning for these struggles is over territory, according to the evolutionary theory. Quote, "Territoriality is defined as the tendency of an animal to hold and defend a territory against all undesirable intruders of the same species. … The effects of territoriality in relation to evolution are two-fold. First, territoriality spreads the population out so that there is generally an over-abundance of food in relation to the population. The second effect of territoriality is that when direct battles between two individuals occur, there are rules. Lethal fighting between two individuals of a territorial species is exceptionally rare. When two enraged animals face each across their mutual border, they generally will not fight but will engage in displacement activity, an activity totally unrelated to fighting. … (Robert) Ardrey points out that this displacement activity is widespread in territorial animals and acts as an outlet for their energy so neither party gets hurt. [5.16]" These field observations show that there is a lack of evidence for the theory of evolution on the basis of competition between members of the same species. Another effect of territory is to spread out the population of the other species. One example cited in Josh McDowell's book of Reasons Skeptics Should

Consider Christianity is the arctic wolf which has territories of approximately 100 square miles. This provides an abundance of food supply for the animals and little room for the struggle for survival which Darwin mentions. Darwin also believed that the struggle for survival, which is the driving force behind evolution, was due to over-crowding in the animal population. Many field observations of the animal kingdom have shown this conclusion to be false.

The other form of competition was described as a territorial struggle between different species. In Josh McDowell's book Reasons Skeptics should consider Christianity, Josh asks the question: Competition or mutual aid? In this chapter, Josh points out examples where animals of the same species come to each others aid. There are many examples of animals helping each other. In times of conflict, with intruders from a different species, often packs will aid each other for survival. Petre Kropotkin, in his book Mutual Aid, shows numerous examples of animals of the same species giving mutual aid instead of the fierce competition as Darwin suggested. Again, Darwin proposed this conflict was the result of over population and a lack of food supply. "Paucity of life, under-population – not over-population- being the distinctive feature of that immense part of the globe which we name Northern Asia, I conceived since then serious doubts – which subsequent study has only confirmed – as to the reality of that fearful competition for food and life within each species, which was an article of faith with most Darwinists, and consequently, as to the dominant part which this competition was supposed to play in the evolution of new species. ... that when animals have to struggle against scarcity of food, ..., the whole of that portion of the species, which is affected by the calamity, comes out of the ordeal so much impoverished in vigor and health that no progressive evolution of the species can be based upon such periods of keen competition. [5.17]" This observation is made commonly today. In areas where man has encroached on the natural habitat of the animal kingdom, starvation often depletes a population. Is there a new species about to form in these areas? Of course not! The animal rights activists will point out that the population of that natural habitat is in danger of extinction. Starvation does not encourage competition within a species. Instead, the commonly observed effect is the whole species will die off altogether. This point of mutual aid was even made by Charles Darwin himself. Quote, "Animals also render more important service to one another: thus wolves and some other beasts of prey hunt in packs and aid one another in attacking their victims. Pelicans fish in concert. ... Social animals mutually defend each other. Bull bison in North America, when there is danger, drive the cows and calves into the middle of the herd, whilst they defend the outside. [5.18]" Darwin continues to list examples of the same species aiding one other. So where is the struggle needed to produce drastic changes within a species? Answer: It doesn't exist in the animal kingdom and the evolutionary theory falls apart at every instance without a shred of scientific evidence to support it! Most "struggles for survival" occurred when animals try to find food or shelter from the natural elements. This search for food and the construction of shelters usually involves animals helping each other. There are a great number of examples of symbiotic and family relationships in wildlife that aid in the search for food and shelter. Among many wildlife groups, the concept of community is ever present. Just as we observed in earlier chapters with Stephan Hawking, Darwin contradicts himself while gathering evidence for evolution. First he proposes that there is wide spread struggle for survival within a species and then sites examples of mutual aide. This reoccurring internal conflict is present in many of the cases to present the theory of evolution. When a person lies or attempts to cover up the truth, usually sooner or later the liar is trapped in his own web of lies. "He will turn their own tongues against them and bring them to ruin; all who see them will shake their heads in scorn." Psalms 65:8 "Let their lying lips be silenced, for with pride and contempt they speak arrogantly against the righteous." Psalms 31:18 "Not a word from their mouth can be trusted; their heart is filled with destruction. ... with their tongue they speak deceit." Psalm 5:9. The bible warns that anyone who loves to fight will love evil. "He who loves a quarrel loves sin." Proverbs 17:19 "Everyone who does evil hates the light, and will not come into the light for fear that his deeds will be exposed. But whoever lives by the truth comes into the light, so that it may be seen plainly that what he has done has been done through God." John 3:20-21 NIV. Where is the concept of struggle for individual superiority, which is vital to the theory of evolution? It only exists in the unique dilemma of man and not the animal kingdom. The real "struggle for survival" exists when mankind tries to accomplish works apart from the will of God. Opposing the will of God is a fatal mistake and all plans contrary to the will of God will fail. There is a great separation between man and God because of sin. This fact will be carefully explained in the last chapter. When man tries to provide material things, like clothes, shelter and food, without first seeking a relationship with God, he discovers a life of increasing difficulty. Depression, despair, and a sense of a desperate, difficult struggle for survival permeate the person's thoughts. Also, a sense of loneliness develops as the person believes that there is no one to help in their struggle to survive. This is the natural condition of a man born in sin. God wants to change this natural condition of man brought by the inheritance of the sin of Adam. God wants to help you with every day necessity of life. "Therefore I tell you, do not be anxious about your life, what you shall eat or drink, nor about your body, what you shall put on. ... Look at the birds of the air; they neither sow nor reap nor gather into barns, and yet your heavenly Father feeds them. ... Consider the lilies of the field, how they grow; they neither toil nor spin; yet I tell you, even Solomon in all his glory was not arrayed like one of these. But if God so clothes the grass of the field, which today is alive and tomorrow is thrown into the oven, will He not much more clothe you? ... Therefore do not be anxious, saying, What shall we eat? or What shall we drink? or What shall we wear? ... these things shall be yours as well." Mathew 6:25-33. The point is that the struggle for survival is a concept unique to the human condition of disobedience and is not shown to exist abundantly in the animal kingdom. The animal kingdom is well provided for. Human beings could equally be well cared for, if they seek the kingdom of God and put their minds and hearts on serving God.

Are Mutations Beneficial to a Species?

The next fundamental principle of evolution is the concept of mutations. "A mutation is a change in the structure of the DNA molecule. Since it is a chemical change, it is subject to the laws of physics and chemistry like any other chemical change. Harold F. Blum observes: Whatever the nature of mutation, it will have to follow certain lines that are determined by molecular pattern and energetic relationships. Mutation, then, is not random, but may occur within certain restricting limits and according to certain pathways determined by thermodynamic properties of the system. Thus, to state the case in a somewhat animistic fashion, the organism cannot fit itself to the environment by varying unrestricted in any direction. [5.19]" This supports the conclusions we made previously i.e., that the laws of thermodynamics limit the degree of change allowed within a species. This allows changes within a species to occur, according to chemical and physical limiting conditions, but unrestricted changing from a lower order species to a higher order species is physically impossible! Genetic changes are limited to stay within the same level of genetic organization. This is why there are varieties of cows, horses, dogs, cats etc. but the variations are limited to a species. The DNA molecule is not flexible enough to allow for the possibility of evolution from single-celled creatures to modern man. Again, the theory of man and all forms of life evolving from chemicals is not science but science fiction in the worst sense. There are many examples of the DNA molecules of a particular species that remain unchanged for long periods of time. Quote, "The nautilus, a deep sea creature, comes to the surface of the ocean only during the night. The nautilus is found in the strata as far back as the Early Cambrian period nearly 600 million years ago. Matthews states, 'The nautilus has remained unchanged since the Early Cambrian period. Thus the DNA of the nautilus has not changed in the last 600 million years. If the dates are to be believed, the horseshoe crab has remained unchanged for the last 500 million years. The king crab is found, unchanged from today, in strata believed to be over 225 million years old. Tripos cancriformis, a crustacean, has remained unchanged for 75 million years. The Ginkgo tree of Chinese temples has remained unchanged for 200 million years.' [5.20]" These examples and many more, show the extreme stability of the DNA molecule. So where is the evidence for the rapid changes in the DNA molecule necessary for the theory of evolution to work? One of the arguments against evolution is the lack of evidence for the evolutionary process continuing today.

We should see the entire evolutionary process continuing today, if evolution is true. Remember evolutionary theory states that life began as a random mixing of chemical elements. Therefore, we should be able to see life forming today, if we could recreate the necessary conditions. We should also be able to see a great number of "transitional" elements and species existing today. These "missing links" are creatures with similar characteristics of two entirely different species. Like a creature having the characteristics of both a dog and a cat. There are very few animals, especially in the large animal groups, which provide any evidence for any rapid changes in the DNA molecule necessary for the theory of evolution to work. The evolutionists state that the reason we do not see the process of life forming from simple chemical substances today is that the circumstances that took place to first bring life to the earth do not exist today. The Christian will agree that the first creation of life was a special one time event. "In the beginning God created the heavens and the earth." -Genesis 1:1. Many years of research have been spent in searching for the origin of life through chemical evolution. All efforts have failed to show that there is a natural mechanism to transform organic chemicals to life. Some of the probable circumstances are found each year through research, but all that is known about the creation of life is that it is highly complex. In fact, life is so complex; particularly the DNA and RNA molecules necessary for life's systems, that it is unreasonable to assume life came from random mixing of chemicals. Believing in Evolution to explain the origin of life requires a large amount of unrealistic faith.

Some scientists have explored the process of genetic duplication and drift to try to explain how seemingly irreducible complex systems could have formed by natural means. Barry Hall of the University of Rochester conducted experiments with the bacterial E. Coli in an attempt to prove that random motion of "spare" genes could explain the construction of complex systems. "Gene duplication can happen during the process of cell division when DNA is being copied from the original cell for use in the new cell. Occasionally, the process goes awry and a piece of DNA, perhaps a gene, is copied twice. This creates an extra gene. While the original gene can go about its pre-assigned role, the extra gene can drift and perhaps create a new function. ... I faced Behe squarely, 'Tell me, has Hall proved through his experiment your theory (that complex inter-working systems could not be formed by evolution) is incorrect? Unflustered, Behe replied: 'No, not really. ... He didn't knock out a complex system and then show how evolution can replace it. Instead, he knocked out one component of a system that has five or six components. And replacing one component in a complex system is a lot easier than building one from scratch. ... There was a complex system with a number of different parts, he knocked out one of them, and after a while he showed that random processes came up with a fix for that one part. ... But there's something equally important: Hall made it clear that he had intervened to keep the system going while evolution was trying to come up with a replacement for the missing part. In other words, he added a chemical to the mixture that gave it time to come up with the mutation that fixed the glitch. ... Hall made it clear that he intervened so that he would get the results that would never have actually happened in the natural world. And that is injecting intelligence into the system. When you analyze the entire experiment, the result is exactly what you would expect of irreducibly complexity requiring intelligent intervention. Unintentionally, he has shown the limits of Darwinism and the need for design. [5.21]" Case after case, the debate continues between Creationists and Evolutionists. The major issues continue to be a debate of faith in a particular view point, not hard scientific facts. The truth inevitably comes to light under scrutiny. It is the theory of evolution that does not stand the test of scientific investigation. Repeatedly, within the theory of evolution, we see contradicting statements that do not withstand the test of time.

Ernst Haeckel's Sketches of Embryos

The next subject we will explore is the visual image that has had a profound impact on the minds of millions of high school and college students. The Ernst Haeckel drawings are considered by many to be conclusive evidence for evolution. "Haeckel's most renowned images depict the embryos of a fish, salamander, tortoise, chicken, hog, calf, rabbit, and human side-by-side at three stages of development.

The illustrations support Darwin's assertion that the striking similarities between early embryos is 'by far the strongest single class of facts' in favor of his theory that all organisms share a universal ancestor. I was mesmerized by the nineteenth-century drawings when I first encountered them as a student. ... 'It wasn't until I was doing my graduate work that I began to compare actual photographs of embryos to what Haeckel had drawn.' 'And what did you find?' 'I was stunned!' he said, his eyes widening. 'They didn't fit. There was a big discrepancy. It was really hard to believe. ... Apparently in some cases Haeckel actually used the same woodcut to print embryos from different classes because he was so confident of his theory that he figured he didn't have to draw them separately'. ... They were first exposed in the late 1860s, when his colleagues accused him of fraud. ... When some biologists exposed this in an article a few years ago, the evolutionist Stephan Jay Gould of Harvard complained that this was nothing new. He had known about it for twenty years! It was no secret to the experts. ... 'There are two other kinds of mammals that he didn't show, which are different. The remaining four classes he showed – reptiles, birds, amphibians, and fish – happened to be more similar than the ones he omitted. He used a salamander to represent amphibians instead of a frog, which looks very different. So he stacked the deck by picking representatives that came closest to fitting his idea – and that he went further by faking the similarities. ... If you go back to the earlier stages, the embryos look far more different from each other. But he deliberately omits the earlier stages altogether.' ... Why is that important? Remember Darwin claimed that because the embryos are most similar in their early stages, this is evidence of common ancestry. ... You see, vertebrate embryos start out looking very different in the early cell division stages. The cell divisions in a mammal, for example, are radically different from those in any of the other classes. There's no possible way you could mix them up. In fact, it's extremely different within classes. ... Then at the midpoint – which is what Haeckel claimed in his drawings was the early stage – the embryos become more similar, though nowhere near as much as Haeckel claimed. Then they become very different again. ... One explanation that's often given... is that although the drawings are false, they teach a concept that's basically true. Well, that is not true. Biologists know that embryos are not most similar in their earliest stages. ... What was supposed to be primary evidence for Darwin's theory- the fossil or embryo – turns out to be false, so they immediately say, well, we known the theory's true, so let's use the theory to explain why the evidence doesn't fit. [5.22]" In other words, we believe that the theory is correct, so lets fake the evidence. Evolutionists are often so desperate for evidence for their theories they resort to lies and deception.

At the conclusion of this explanation Lee Strobel felt like the victim of a con game. And this is precisely what happened. How do these scientists know that their theory is true? Not due to the scientific evidence, but rather due to their faith in the theory of evolution. We see this occurring over and over again. We have been manipulated, lied to, and given false or misleading information to convince the general public that evolution is a scientific fact. Some involved in this plot are merely innocent pawns in this struggle to reveal the truth about the evidence for and against evolution. Others are more directly involved in the conspiracy by a commitment of faith that natural forces have the power to create life, in spite of hard evidence to the contrary. Many times, it is these same scientists that persecute the efforts of qualified scientists who oppose their views. Again, evolutionists do not argue with scientific facts but rather conjecture based on faith. There is an endless supply of evidence that can fall into the category of support for the theory of intelligent design and a lesser volume of evidence that can support evolution. The general public is usually exposed to only one side of the argument, the evidence for evolution. As more scientists rally to the truth of creation, the debate over evolution will widen. Hopefully, more books will find their way into the hands of people earnestly seeking the truth. Then the lie of evolution will be even more exposed. "Everyone on the side of truth listens to me." (Jesus speaking) John 18:37.

The next evidence we will explore concerning evolutionary development is the so-called gill-like structures that we have been told exist in early stages of development. "The encyclopedia I consulted as a youngster declared unequivocally that 'the fetus of mammals at one stage have gill slits which resemble those of fish,' which to me was dramatic confirmation of our aquatic ancestry. In 1996, Life magazine descried how human embryos grow 'something very much like gills,' which is 'some of the most compelling evidence for evolution.' ...Now, feel your neck, he said. There are ridges in the skin, right? I nodded. Well, if you look at an embryo, it's doubled over. It has ridges in the neck. I'm not saying they're only skin folds; they're more complicated than that. ... Let me be clear: they're not gills! ... Even fish don't have gills at this stage. In humans, the ridges become one thing; in fish, they become gills. They're not even gill slits. To call them gill-like structures is merely reading evolutionary theory back into the evidence. [5.23]" The evolutionists take every opportunity to promote their religion of atheism and their faith in evolution. It is almost endless the amount of distortion of the truth the evolutionists will resort to. How long will the world remain in the dark concerning these practices of deception?

Once again, let us turn to the fossil evidence to see if there is or is not a strong case for evolution. As we stated earlier, when Darwin published The Origin of Species in 1859, scientists confronted Darwin with the lack of physical evidence that his theories were correct. "As if on cue, two years later unearthed the archaeopteryx (pronounced ar-key-OPT-er-icks) in a German quarry. Darwin's supporters were thrilled — surely the missing link between reptiles and modern birds, unveiled so promptly after the appearance of Darwin's book, would just be the first of many future fossil discoveries that would validate Darwin's claims. ... The question is, do you get from a reptile to a bird — which is an astonishing huge step — by some totally natural process or does this require the intervention of a designer? An archaeopteryx, as beautiful as it is, doesn't show us one way or the other. Besides, we see strange animals around today, like the duck-billed platypus, which nobody considers transitional but which has characteristics of different classes. 'But the archaeopteryx is a half-bird half-reptile, right?' 'No, not even close,' he insisted. 'It's a bird with modern feathers, and birds are very different from reptiles in many important ways- their breeding system, their bone structure, their lungs, their distribution of weight and muscles. It's a bird, that's clear — not part bird and part reptile.' [5.24]" Again, evolutionists have used imagery to build a case for evolution. They point to the external features of the archaeopteryx and say, 'look at this, evolution is true'. But when you examine the evidence more closely and study its inner structure, an entirely different picture is presented. There is some evidence of similarities in different classes, but this by itself does not support the theory of evolution. "'But,' I protested, 'the similarities are there — you can't deny that.' 'Yes, but the explanation can go either way: design or descent with modification. How do we determine which is true? Listen- similarity alone doesn't tell us.' ... A designer might very well decide to use common building materials to create different organisms, just as builders use the same materials — steel girders, rivets, and so forth — to build different bridges that end up looking very dissimilar from one another. ... It sounds ridiculous to suggest a golf path could evolve into a sidewalk and street, but it's not any more outlandish than some of the claims for biological evolution. The important point is that similarity by itself doesn't distinguish between design and Darwinism. [5.25]" We are victims of radical preaching of the theory of evolution. The theory of evolution has numerous "missing links" and in some cases the theory of evolution is completely contrary to many fields of science such as bio-chemistry. Join with me and proclaiming the gospel. "The heart of the discerning acquires knowledge; the ears of the wise seek it out." Proverbs 18:15 "Apply your heart to instruction and your ears to words of knowledge." Proverbs 23:12. Turn towards wisdom and away from the lies and deception of the evolutionary theory.

Is the Fossil Record Complete?

The fossil record is presented by evolutionists to be strong evidence for evolution. We have already mentioned the fact that the fossil record is incomplete. There is a lack of evidence for the transitional animals needed to make the theory of evolution work. This lack of physical evidence for evolution is no different today as it was in Darwin's time. "We see in the last chapter that whole groups of species sometimes falsely appear to have abruptly developed; and I have attempted to give an explanation of this fact, which if true would be fatal to my views. [5.26]" This statement is from Darwin himself from his book, the Origin of Species! Darwin knew that the evidence did not support his theories, but he still had great faith that he was correct in assuming natural selection caused all the varieties of life to form. Darwin believed that with future excavations and advances in paleontology, his theories would be supported. Over the years, the lack of evidence for evolution has become more profound. Yet, Darwin and his followers knew that the alternative was to accept that life was created by God. This was something he, and those who followed his teachings, wholeheartedly rejected. The people, who followed his teachings, were like religious fanatics pursuing a cult leader, and continued to believe Darwin's theories were true. Over the years, Darwin's original tree of life has been filled with highly imaginary "transitional" species that have never been proven to exist. "In truth, it doesn't matter whether the fossil record is complete or not. If it is complete, meaning a large percentage of fossil life has been preserved, the fossil record does not support evolution. If, however, the fossil record is very incomplete, meaning a small percentage of past life forms have been preserved, what right does science have to fill these gaps with imaginary animals for which there is not the slightest evidence of their existence? [5.27]" Evolutionists believe that the fossil record is very incomplete. The evolutionists proceed to fill in huge gaps in the fossil record with fictitious species and justify their dishonesty by using unscientific principles of genetic mutation theory. Evolutionists are following principles of atheistic philosophy instead of principles of scientific investigation as they have filled in the gaps left in the fossil record. They are not attempting to seek the truth, as science was intended to do, but seek to justify a belief in natural forces creating life instead of God creating life. They cloud their judgment with preconceived ideas, which they accept as axioms i.e. undeniable truths. The theme of this book is re-emphasized. If you judge all the facts without bias; you will be faced with the fact that the Bible is intellectually acceptable. Furthermore, you will be led to make a decision to accept or reject the gospel based on the facts. It is the atheist and evolutionist that take blind leaps of faith to justify their denying the gospel. No wonder the atheist and evolutionist act with such passion over the mere mention of the term Creation Science. Instead of having an intelligent debate, the evolutionists are the ones who wildly accuse any evidence for creation as un-scientific. "Watch out for false prophets. They come to you in sheep's clothing, but inwardly they are ferocious wolves. By their fruit you will recognize them." Mathew 7:15-16. These "false prophets" come in white lab coats and "preach" (or lecture) that they know the secrets of life. There is only one person, Jesus Christ that has the answers to the questions of life. "In him was life, and that life was the light of men." John 1:4

Are all Fossils Alike?

Do you always believe what you see? I hope not. I hope you are a person who takes the time to investigate evidence to see if it is real or faked in some way. Why then accept every sentence that is in a scientific journal as truth? So often people will accept anything if you lead the statement with, "scientists say." There are many examples of fossils that have been supposedly discovered to support the theory of evolution. Instead, many of these fossils are falsified to line someone's pocket with a lot of money and prestige. "A few years ago the National Geographic Society announced that a fossil had been purchased at an Arizona mineral show that turned out to be 'the missing link between terrestrial dinosaurs and birds that could actually fly.' ... They called it the archaeraptor, and it had the tail of a dinosaur and the forelimbs of a bird. ... 'Well, the problem was that it was a fake!' Wells said. 'A Chinese paleontologist proved that someone had glued a dinosaur tail to a primitive bird. He created it to resemble what the scientists had been looking for.' ... 'Fakes are coming out of these fossil beds all the time,' he said, 'because the fossil dealers know there's big money in it.' ... The Chinese fossil trade has become a big business. These fossil forgeries have been sold on the black market for years now, for huge sums of money. Anyone who can produce a good fake stands to profit. ... Then a group of molecular biologists at the conference reported finding bird DNA in dinosaur bones that were sixty-five million years old. ... They suggested that this was genetic evidence that birds are closely related to dinosaurs. The problem is that the bones from which the DNA was supposedly extracted are from a branch of dinosaurs that had nothing to do with bird ancestry. Furthermore, the DNA they found was not ninety or ninety-nine percent similar to birds – it was one-hundred percent similar to turkey DNA! Even chickens don't have DNA that's one hundred percent similar to turkey DNA. Only turkeys have one hundred percent turkey DNA. [5.28]" The evolutionists have become desperate to supply evidence for their theories. The lack of true fossil evidence is a major embracement to scientists teaching evolution as a proven fact. The examples listed here are not isolated incidents. There are many more examples of forgeries produced by zealot evolutionists. We will list a few of the more well- documented examples.

The Development of Man

There are many other examples of mistakes made by evolutionists concerning the fossil record. The one field of study many Christians and Evolutionists find to be a center of the debate is the development of man. Darwin proposed that we came from apes. Ever since this announcement, the theological debate has become a personal passionate debate based as much, or probably more, on faith than fossil records. There have been many attempts to trace the evolution of man. Just as we discussed in the previous sections, evolutionists have little support for their theory of human evolution from the fossil record. You can call this group of scientists; evolutionists, atheists, Darwinists, or humanists. Each of these designations describes a group of people driven by philosophical ideas they believe based on faith. The Evolutionists and other groups mentioned have a similar view about the universe, i.e. natural forces created or developed all life forms. These groups are sometimes extremely zealous for their beliefs. The greatest lie they have managed to convince the public of, is that they are dispassionate scientists seeking the truth. They have convinced many people that atheism, for example, is not a religion but the absence of religion. This is in spite of their own organizations, debating over how to describe their ideas without mentioning the word "belief". All of the above mentioned groups have a set of philosophical ideas they believe with a radical fervor. They continually make false announcements that they have discovered fossils validating skeptical theories. When this occurs they validate the biblical account in Romans. "Although they claimed to be wise, they became fools and exchanged the glory of the immortal God for images made to look like mortal man and birds and animals and reptiles." Romans 1:22-23 Again, in the Old Testament: "Therefore once more I will astound these people with wonder upon wonder; the wisdom of the wise will perish, the intelligent of the intelligent will vanish." Isaiah 29:14 In each association who believe in evolutionary principles, there is a certain measure of ignorance about the scientific method and their discoveries. Nearly every person, in my opinion, has a lack of understanding of science, me included. It is this lack of wisdom that leads to the formation of various beliefs based on evidences you have only partially learned. As I have personally evaluated my own convictions, my faith on various convictions has changed. The various groups who accept the theory of evolution can compare with various forms of religion. Even within the general outline of people confessing to be Christian there are an enormous variety of beliefs. Baptist, Christian, Assembly of God, United Church of Christ, Methodist, Wesleyan, and the Catholic faiths are only a few examples of denominations who believe in Jesus Christ. Each of these groups generally believes in the teachings of Jesus Christ as described in the Bible. Although each church has variations in theology, there are many similarities in their beliefs. Some are very committed to their beliefs, others are not. It is possible that some true Christians believe in evolution as the means in which God used to bring out his purpose of creating life. It is not any individual's place to judge the convictions of others. All these ideas will be examined by God in heaven on the Day of Judgment. "Do not judge, or you too will be judged. For in the same way you judge others, you will be judged, and with the measure you use, it will be measured to you. Why do you look at the speck of sawdust in your brother's eye and pay no attention to the plank in your own eye? How can you say to your brother, 'Let me take the speck out of your eye,' when all the time there is a plank in your own eye? You hypocrite, first take the plank out of your own eye, and then you will see clearly to remove the speck from your brother's eye." Mathew 7:1-5 "Not everyone who says to me, 'Lord, Lord,' will enter the kingdom of heaven, but only he who does the will of my Father who is in heaven. Many will say to me on that day, 'Lord, Lord, did we not prophesy in your name, and in your name drive out demons and perform many miracles?' Then I will tell them plainly, 'I never knew you. Away from me, you evildoers!'" Mathew 7:21-23

There are many examples of people who claim to be scientists, who radically believe in evolution, and are over-zealous to prove their theories. This presents convincing evidence that we are dealing with a religion not just debating scientific discoveries. One instance involves a discovery by Harold Cook, a field geologist. Cook found a tooth of unknown origin. He sent the tooth to Henry Osborn, director of the American Museum of Natural History. Osborn suspected the tooth to belong to an ancient ape-like man. Osborn confirmed his suspicions of the tooth with two experts in the study of teeth, Dr. Hellman and Dr. Gregory. Cook was sited as having made the first discovery of an ape-man in the western hemisphere. Quote, "They named him Hesperopithecus, ape of the west. ... Professor Wilder published a book claiming that Nebraska Man, Hesperopithecus was halfway between Java Man and Neanderthal Man. Elliott Smith wrote an article on Mr. and Mrs. Hesperopithecus, including a reconstruction of what they looked like. In all, the discovery created quite a sensation for a period of four-and-one-half-years. [5.29]" It seams amazing how one tooth can be the cause of tremendous scientific intrigue. Also, this shows how eager scientists who support evolution are in proving their theories. An entire skeletal structure, a book published in regards to their life-style, and various other scientific reports in journals, all over one tooth! The great excitement was finally put to an end after four and a half years. The mysterious origin of the tooth was finally solved by a scientific expedition to the neighbor's property close to where the tooth was discovered. "The expedition went to a neighbor's property where they found further evidence of this amazing creature. Hesperopithecus was a pig. Not in manner, but literally. Hesperopithecus, it turned out, was a peccary- a wild pig! [5.30]" It is amazing how much accurate "scientific" support of evolution exists? Why are Christians considered radical for there support of creation? Scientists, who follow the teachings of evolution, seem extremely eager to support their ill-conceived theories. When the evidence is closely examined, the picture is clear. Evolution is a hoax!

One other example of discoveries made by scientists looking to support evolution was the discovery of the Piltdown man. "In 1912, William Dawson and A.S. Woodward reported the discovery of an ape-like man in the gravels of the Kent Plateau in England. The fossil skull was broken but was nearly complete and essentially human. The jaw, on the other hand, was very ape-like. ... In 1953, Kenneth Oakley completed some chemical tests on the material. They proved that the skull and jaw did not belong together and that neither belongs with the animal bones. The Piltdown man turned out to be nothing more than a modern skull with the jaw bone of an ape. The material had been chemically treated to make it look old, and the teeth had been filled down to make them look worn. No one knows for sure who the forger was, but he was able to fool modern scientists for more than forty years. One must wonder why these facts were overlooked for forty years. [5.31]" The evolutionists have a very strong "religious" zeal for the theories and beliefs. They are like people on a crusade, determined to prove that their theories are correct, but continue to fail miserably. It took a great deal of effort by someone with a lot of chemistry and archaeological background to pull off the hoax of the Piltdown man. He was probably a layman and not a professor or he probably would have realized that the hoax could be discovered through chemical analysis. Still, this incident is merely one of many that show the commitment level of evolutionists. This incident is one in a long list of deceptions used to "prove" evolution so they can promote atheistic, false views of man's origins.

There is still much debate over how man evolved from apes. After over 145 years since Darwin's Origin of Species was published, there is still little conclusive evidence for the theory of evolution. Scientists are still searching for a clear cut idea of how man supposedly evolved from apes. One of the most noteworthy examples is the Neanderthal Man. "In 1848, at the Forbes quarry at Gibraltar, workmen recovered a fairly complete fossil skull. This skull, as it turned out, was the first Neanderthal skull ever discovered. ... In 1856, in a quarry in Germany near the village of Neander, workman recovered another partial skeleton from the soil in a cave. The skullcap and fifteen skeletal features were given to a Professor Schlaaffhausen who reported on the find in early 1857. ... Within a few years, the evolutionists would seize upon Neanderthal as their missing link between apes and humans. Neanderthal man was reconstructed to show how he walked with a stooped gait with his head set far forward. This appearance gave this man the characteristic ape-ish look. ... Rudolf Virchow, a pathologist, studied the fossil material and concluded that the man had rickets. ... In 1888, the Galley Hill skull, a very modern-looking skull, was found in strata believed older than Neanderthal. His authenticity was rejected at the time. More modern-appearing discoveries in 1855 at Ipswich, and in 1863 at Abbeville, also were rejected. In 1932 in Kenya, a modern human jaw was discovered in deposits "older" than Neanderthal. Any time a modern creature was found, his authenticity was questioned. In 1939, the first serious attack was made on the view of Neanderthal as an intermediate between ape and man. Professor Sergio Sergi, after studying the skulls of two Neanderthals, proved that they walked erect like we do and not with the ape-like crouch so often depicted. Then in 1947, a Neanderthal was discovered to have lived in a cave after a modern man had inhabited the cave. Thus it was finally proven that Neanderthal was not our ancestor. [5.32]" Why are there not more published facts against the theory of evolution? Here is your answer. It took 100 years and a mountain of evidence to overcome the prejudice and religious zeal of the evolutionists and scientific establishment. Over 100 years to expose this fraud. It will take time and talent as more of the truth is revealed. As more about the truth of evolution is exposed, the case for evolution deteriorates.

Another attempt at establishing a link between man and ape was the so called "Java man." Let us review the impact the artist renderings had on a young, impressionable Lee Strobel, and millions of grade school and high school students worldwide. "With his sloping forehead, heavy brow, jutting jaw, receding chin and bemused expression, he was exactly what a blend of ape and man should look like. For me, studying his face and looking into his eyes helped cement the reality of human evolution. ... What is not well known is that Java man consist of nothing more than a skullcap, a femur (thigh bone), three teeth, and a great deal of imagination. ... As a youngster beginning to form my opinions about human evolution, I wasn't aware of what I more recently have discovered: that Dubois' shoddy excavation would have disqualified the fossil from consideration by today's standards. Or that the femur apparently didn't really belong with the skullcap. Or that the skull cap, according to prominent Cambridge University anatomist Sir Arthur Keith, was distinctly human and reflected a brain capacity well within the range of humans living today. ... In short, Java man was not an ape-man as I had been led to believe, but he was 'a true member of the human family.' ... One of the major problems with paleo-anthropology is that compared to all fossils we have, only a minuscule number are believed to be of creatures ancestral to humans, Wells said. Often, it's just skull fragments or teeth. So this gives a lot of elasticity in reconstructing the specimens to fit evolutionary theory. For example, when National Geographic hired four artists to reconstruct a female figure from seven fossil bones found in Kenya, they came up with quite different interpretations. One looked like a modern African-American women; another like a were-wolf; another had a heavy, gorilla-like brow; another had a missing forehead and jaws that looked a bit like a beaked dinosaur. ... As one anthropologist said, the process is 'both political and subjective' to the point where he suggested that paleo-anthropology has the form but not the substance of a science. ... In the end, Darwinism has remained a philosophy still in search of convincing empirical data to back it up. [5.33]" We need to reflect on the tremendous impact these pictures had on Lee as a teenager. How much have these artist renderings illustrating evolution had on countless millions? Exactly how much harm has these "images of the beast" done to the world and what is yet to come?

Evolutionists claim they have strong scientific evidence to support their theories. I would like to know one thing: Where is it? Let us, for a moment, return to micro-biology and the more technical differences between apes and humans. "Cytochrome-c is a protein and is a gene product. It functions as a key enzyme in oxidation reactions and seems to occur in practically every living organism. ... The amino-acid constitution of human cytochrome-c differs from that of many but not all other species. There are no differences in the cytochrome-c taken from humans and from chimpanzees, and only one difference between human cytochrome-c (the amino-acid isoleucine in position 66) and that from the Rhesus monkey (threonine in that position). The numbers of differences in the cytochrome-c of various species compared with that of human are cow, pig, and sheep (10), horse (12), hen and turkey (13), rattlesnake (14), dogfish (23), fly (25), wheat (35), yeast (44), etc. ... The fact that cytochrome-c has a fixed number of 112 amino-acids is an indication of the importance of the three-dimensional structure of the molecule. ... only 19 of the 112 are identical in all organisms tested. ... The remaining 93 amino-acids differ among organisms. ... Apart from the single gene controlling the constitution of cytochrome-c, humans and chimpanzees differ in many thousands of other genes. As a conservative estimate, let us say 5,000. What the theory of evolution is saying is that while humans and chimpanzees have evolved independently from a common ancestor so as to now differ in these 5,000 genes, there has been no change in the 93 amino-acids specified by the cytochrome-c gene. ... According to Weaver and Hedrick, however, the lack of differentiation in the cytochrome-c between humans and chimpanzees is due to the very slow (0.3×10^{-9}) estimated rate of amino-acid substitution in cytochrome-c. How is this rate determined? It is estimated on the basis of the assumed time since the species diverged. .... Haldane ... came to the conclusion that the number of genetic deaths needed to secure the substitution of one gene for another by natural selection is in the region of 30 times the number of individuals in a generation. ... The cost of substituting 5,000 successive, independent mutant genes ... can be calculated. On the basis of an average mutation rate of 10^{-6}, the size of the population must be at least in the order of one million. This implies some 150,000,000,000 forerunners of 'modern man,' ... belonging to small groups of cave-dwelling hunters called australopithecines who roamed the African savannah. Why is there such a shortage of evidence in the form of fossils, tools, or whatever, for the existence of such vast numbers of australopithecine-like pre-humans? [5.34]" What does all this mean? Evolutionists are always over emphasizing the similarities among different forms of life. The presence of cytochrome-c in nearly all forms of life and organic material is presented in modern Biology classes as conclusive evidence for evolution. Often the numbers of cytochrome-c is used to determine how close any two animals are related to a common ancestry. The evolutionists then attempt to fill in the gaps of Darwin's tree of life. However, you are not usually given the details of the differences between species, only their similarities which present a one-sided view of the evidence. When you analyze the results carefully, you will find over and over again, flaws in the evolutionary theory. As we stated earlier, similarities in construction of life does not necessarily support life from evolution, but can support creation by one God using the same basic materials. The debate over evolution has no end. Experts on both side of the debate will generate point and counter-point. Why does this continue? Simple, God wants us to explore the universe and test our personal faith. "But the just shall live by faith." Habakkuk 2:4 NKJ The continuation of the debate is perhaps the strongest evidence that the subject of evolution is far from settled. You must examine the evidence and decided for yourself, as Lee Strobel did. You must individually decide to accept or reject the principles of Evolution based on your personal "investigative report".

References for Chapter 5

5.1   Lee Strobel, The Case for A Creator, Zondervan, Grand Rapids Michigan. 2004, p. 43.

5.2   Charles Darwin, The Origin of Species, New York: New American Library, 1958, p.171.

5.3   Lee Strobel, The Case for A Creator, Zondervan, Grand Rapids Michigan. 2004, p. 44-47.

5.4   John F. Ashton, In Six Days: Why Fifty Scientists choose to believe in Creation, Master Books, 2000-2003, p 182-183.

5.5   Ibid, p. 186-187

5.6   Ibid, p. 188-189.

5.7   Ibid, p. 190.

5.8   Ibid, p. 191-193.

5.9   Ibid, p. 304.

5.10   Ibid, p. 196.

5.11   Lee Strobel, The Case for A Creator, Zondervan, Grand Rapids Michigan. 2004, p. 209-210.

5.12   Josh McDowell & Don Stewart, Reasons Skeptics Should Consider Christianity, Wheaton, Illinois, Living Books, Tyndale House Publishers, 1981, p. 165.

5.13   John F. Ashton, In Six Days: Why Fifty Scientists choose to believe in Creation, Master Books, 2000-2003, p. 87-89.

5.14   Ibid, p. 128-129.

5.15   Charles Darwin, The Origin of Species, New York: New American Library, 1958, p.83.

5.16   Josh McDowell & Don Stewart, Reasons Skeptics Should Consider Christianity, Wheaton, Illinois, Living Books, Tyndale House Publishers, 1981, p. 158-159.

5.17   Petre Kropotkin, Mutual Aid, New York: Doubleday Page and Co., 1909, p. viii and p. ix.

5.18   Charles Darwin, The Origin of Species, New York: New American Library, 1958, p.474-475.

5.19   Josh McDowell & Don Stewart, Reasons Skeptics Should Consider Christianity, Wheaton, Illinois, Living Books, Tyndale House Publishers, 1981, p. 154-155.

5.20   Ibid, p. 151.

5.21   Lee Strobel, The Case for A Creator, Zondervan, Grand Rapids Michigan. 2004, p. 210-213.

5.22   Ibid, p. 47-50.

5.23   Ibid, p. 51.

5.24   Ibid, p. 55-57.

5.25   Ibid, p. 52-55.

5.26   Charles Darwin, The Origin of Species, New York: New American Library, 1958, p. 316.

5.27   Josh McDowell & Don Stewart, Reasons Skeptics Should Consider Christianity, Wheaton, Illinois, Living Books, Tyndale House Publishers, 1981, p. 173.

5.28   Lee Strobel, The Case for A Creator, Zondervan, Grand Rapids Michigan. 2004, p. 58-60.

5.29   Josh McDowell & Don Stewart, Reasons Skeptics Should Consider Christianity, Wheaton, Illinois, Living Books, Tyndale House Publishers, 1981, p. 194-195.

5.30   Ibid, p. 195.

5.31   Ibid, p. 195-196.

5.32   Ibid, p. 197-198.

5.33   Lee Strobel, The Case for A Creator, Zondervan, Grand Rapids Michigan. 2004, p. 61-65.

5.34   John F. Ashton, In Six Days: Why Fifty Scientists choose to believe in Creation, Master Books, 2000-2003, p. 129-131.

Illustration for Chapter 5

5.1   Evolution, Microsoft Encarta Encyclopedia Standard, 2002 edition, Contributed By: Christopher King, Reviewed By: Eugenie C. Scott.

Chapter 6: Fossils: How are they formed?
And how old are they really?
World History

There is one opinion that both evolutionists and creationists can agree on, there has been at least one cataclysmic event during earth's history. The evolutionists believe that the fossil records indicate several major shifts in climate during the 4.5 billion year history of the world. There are many books and movies based on these ideas. The movie Armageddon starts out in the introduction by explaining that the "great dying period", where nearly all dinosaurs were suddenly killed, was caused by a meteorite crashing into the earth and creating an ice age. The animated movie Ice Age depicted the adventures of pre-historic animals during the last ice age. Most evolutionists believe that there was some sort of cataclysmic event that dramatically shifted the earth's environment into an "ice age" and that this explains the great deposits of fossils in a single geological period. There are still some debates as to the cause of this "ice age". Some hold to the meteorite theory mentioned above. Others, faced with no conclusive evidence of such a large scale impact, hold to the theory that wide spread volcanic activity blanketed the earth with dust and gas which blocked out the sun for a least 1000 years. There is a complete lack of conclusive evidence that there was a large meteorite striking the earth, or wide spread volcanic activity millions of years ago. The only thing that is known for certain is that there was a major world wide event killing off a large number of plants and animals sometime in the past. This chapter will briefly explore the possibility that the world wide flood described in Genesis can explain the fossil and sedimentary evidence even more thoroughly than these other theories. Of course, when someone mentions the flood they are immediately dismissed by the majority of the scientific community. Why? Is there more evidence for these other theories? The answer is no. This book will not detail the case for evolution but rather for the flood as a historic event. As it has been shown throughout this book, the final decision of which theory is acceptable is placed in the hands of the reader. You must individually weigh all the arguments and personally decide which theory you are willing to accept.

There is absolutely no unique historical event that can be proven or disproven scientifically. The scientific method of investigation only applies to events and principles that can be repeated in the presence of anyone who wishes to challenge the experimental conclusions. To decide the validity of any historical event, you must use the Legal-Historical method outline in Josh McDowell's book, Evidence That Demands a Verdict. Science can have some bearing on revealing facts and information entered into evidence. However, we must consider the source of the information and any written or eyewitness testimony. One might ask what kind of written testimony do we have concerning the event of a worldwide flood? That is easy of course, it is the Holy Scriptures. You must take into consideration how much faith you place in the reliability of the Holy Bible in accurately reporting historical events. You might have been taught that the Bible is just a bunch of good principles and fair tales. However, you need to remind yourself of the many "fairy tales" evolution has presented without a shred of evidence to support their conclusions. One final note before we move on: There is very little disagreement that the Bible teaches us to tell the truth. "You shall not give false testimony." Exodus 20:16. Then how can you justify the Bible lying about these historical accounts? They are not referred to as "parables", stories to explain a certain truth, but actual historical events. "For the word of God is living and active. Sharper than any double-edged sword, it penetrates even dividing soul and spirit, joints and marrow; it judges the thoughts and attitudes of the heart. Nothing in all creation is hidden from God's sight. Everything is uncovered and laid bare before the eyes of him to whom we must give account." Hebrews 4:12-13. The point is this, you must consider the faith you have in the scriptures and in the testimony of Jesus that the word of God is true. "In the beginning was the Word, and the Word was with God, and the Word was God. He was with God in the beginning. Through him all things were made that has been made. ... The Word became flesh and made his dwelling among us. We have seen his glory, the glory of the one and only, who came from the father, full of grace and truth." John 1:1-3, 14. "Heaven and earth will pass away, but my words will never pass away." Luke 21:33. Why should we simply accept the evolutionary "story" of how the fossils came into existence and dismiss the most trustworthy testimony any event could possibly have, the Word of God?

How to Make a Fossil

The theory that the flood is the source of this period of large scaled fossilizing is far more reasonable that the evolutionary model. For one thing, the large amounts of time required for the evolutionary model is not supported by the fossil record. Fossilization requires two things to take place, nearly simultaneously. First, the body of an animal or plant must be removed from the oxygen of the atmosphere which causes the bones to decay to dust. Also, the bones must be protected form micro-organisms, bacteria and other animals which may destroy the remains of the plant or animal. The remains of a plant or animal, especial a plant specimen, must be removed from these sources of decomposition as quickly as possible to preserve the remains in the form of a fossil. Quote, "This means that for an animal to be preserved, it must be buried deep enough so scavengers can't get to it and deep enough so oxygen, which bacteria need, is excluded. This implies, however, that the animal must be buried shortly after its death or there will be nothing left to preserve. As Beerbower states: In general, the more rapidly an organism is buried and the tighter the seal of its sedimentary tomb, the better the chance of preservation.... It is very difficult to find creatures currently in the process of being fossilized. Robert J. Cordell notes: Modern sediments average only about one percent organic matter. ... Most of that organic mater is composed of chemicals, not recognizable proto-fossils. [6.1]" Fossilization is a difficult process. It is truly amazing that we have as many discovered fossils as we do. Fossilized bones are somewhat of a wonderment, but fossilized plants and footprints are almost miraculous! Fossilization requires such unique conditions, that it is amazing that we have any fossils at all.

How Were The Fossils Buried?

It is difficult to imagine the process of fossilization through natural weather conditions. Soil deposits from average amounts of wind and rain could not account for the process of fossilization. Quote, "J.B. Birshell estimates that during the last geological epoch (the Pleistocene), the average rate of deposition was only 0.024 inches per year. If deposition rates like this had prevailed throughout geological history, and Birshell contends that they did, then how can there be any fossils at all? As we saw earlier, to preserve an organism, one must bury it deeply – 0.024 inch cannot be classified as deep. [6.2]" Some evolutionists contend that fossilization takes place over thousands, or even millions of years. If soil erosion were the only source of covering an animal remains, it would take thousands and millions of years to bury the animal far enough to allow fossilization to occur. One problem: In only a few short years the bones would have decayed to dust. With only 0.024 inches of sediment per year, bacteria would have destroyed the bones. Also, when making conditions right for fossilization we must consider occurrences such as worms tunneling down providing oxygen for bacterial to decompose the bone fragments. These factors make it nearly impossible to accept the concept of natural, average, sedimentation rates to account for fossilization. Evolutionists would have us believe that "magically" bones are preserved while they are covered with normal deposits of soil. We will discuss the various methods of dating fossils by how deeply they are buried later in this chapter. Once again, the bones must have been fossilized suddenly and then left for millions of years for normal soil deposits to cover the fossilized remains, according to their illogical theory. Therefore, evolutionists return to the theory that geological periods produced conditions conducive to fossilization of a large number of plants and animals during each era of the earth's 4.5 billion-year-old history. However, the evidence does not support this conclusion.

Some scientists account for large scale fossilization with volcanic activity. There are a number of large deposits of fossils in pits. But, what is the source of these deposits. Do these formations show evidence of past volcanic activity or from the worldwide flood? "Robert Broom, the South African paleontologist, estimates that there are eight hundred million skeletons of Vertebrate animals in the Karoo formation. ... Other places with fossils like the Karoo formation are easily found. The Monterrey shale contains more than a billion fossil fish over four square miles. The Mission Canyon formation of the northwestern states and the Willistone Basin are estimated to represent 10,000 cubic miles of broken crinoid plates. A crinoid is a deep sea creature. ... With these and other examples, is it really reasonable to believe slow deposition preserved these fossils? How much more reasonable to assume they were deposited rapidly in a worldwide flood such as described by the Bible. [6.3]" Many more examples of large scale fossil deposits are available. The fossil deposits appear to be at random locations around the world. The limited effect of volcanic activity could not explain such large scale fossil formations. Some scientists propose that millions of years ago the earth was consumed with volcanic activity. This is one possible theory, but not conclusively proven through geological surveys. The majority of the evidence seams to conclude that the earth did suffer the worldwide destruction of the flood.

Evidence for the Flood in Fossils

Another evidence for the earth suffering the destructive forces of the flood is found in the types of fossils in each rock layer. "If the geological record is indeed, the result of slow deposition and erosive forces acting over millions of years, then one should NOT expect to find animals and plants from widely different environmental zones buried together in one rock stratum. If the fossil record were the result of a world-wide flood, then tropical animals should be expected to be buried with temperate and arctic animals as well as with life from other environments. This would be a good test as to which viewpoint, creation or evolution, was true. [6.4]" Josh McDowell proceeds to list and describe seven major sites of fossilized deposits which were environmentally mixed. The mixture of fossilized specimens is what would be expected if the fossils were the result of a worldwide flood. "The Pleistocene marine faunas of California have long attracted attention. Many of them are large: 100 to 350 species of mollusks in one formation. ... These fauna show different associations. Some associations included cool-water and warm-water species. ... The London Clay flora, of early Eocene age, includes 314 species of seeds and fruits. ... The present-day distribution of the families which make up the London Clay flora are: 5 are entirely tropical ... 14 are almost exclusively tropical ... 21 families are equally tropical and extra-tropical and five are chiefly temperate. ... A similar conclusion is drawn from the evidence of the fossil-bearing layers of Geiseltal in Germany. Here also is a complete mixture of plant, insects and animals from all climate zones of the earth capable of supporting life. ... on top of the artic freshwater plants and shells in a marine bed. Astarte Borealis and other mollusk shells are found in the position of life, with both valves united. These species are artic. But the bed seams in other places to contain Ostrea edulis (a mollusk), which requires a temperate sea; the evidence is conflicting as to the climate. ... One final example of mixed environmental fossils ... is found ... in the Amber beds of East Prussia (Poland). ... Some insects are found encased in the amber, and it is speculated that they got there when the insects, walking on the tree, got stuck and encased in the resin. ... Within the lumps of amber are found insects, snails, coral and small portions of plant life. ... Coral? Obviously, the coral was not walking on a tree or in the forest. Coral grows only in the ocean. [6.5]" There are numerous other evidences for the majority of all fossils coming from the Biblical flood. As scientific investigations continue, the evidence continues to support a relatively young age for our world and fossils formed almost exclusively by the flood. Again, the belief in geological time periods lasting millions of years seams more science fiction that science fact. Many of the theories of evolution border on an intense, un-reasoning, desperate faith in attempting to discredit the Bible and confuse people into doubting their faith in God. There are a mired of conflicting reports about geological evidences for long geological time periods. If a paleontologist and geologist is willing to concede the possibility of a worldwide flood early in Earth's history, they must concede that it is the best possible explanation for the fossil formations.

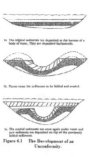

1a. The original sediments are deposited at the bottom of a body of water. They are deposited horizontally.

1b. Forces cause the sediments to be folded and eroded.

1c. The eroded sediments are once again under water and new sediments are deposited on top of the previously folded sediments.
Figure 6.1   The Development of an Unconformity.

Figure 6.1

A third evidence for the flood may be found in the unconformities in rock strata. "One of the most interesting features of the earth's geological record is an unconformity, a break in time, between the deposition of two rock strata. During a time of no deposition of sand, clay or limestone, the underlying rocks are eroded, folded, or both (see figure 6.1), then more rock is deposited on top of them. [6.6]" The evolutionists, of course, believe in natural forces over millions of years for the explanation of the rock strata. "What do you see in the geology of the world? Massive sedimentary deposits. ... Belief that these formed through gradual erosion over millions of years does not fit with common sense or good science. The lateral extent of identical deposits (i.e., hundreds of kilometers of exactly the same rocks) implies catastrophism. So do features like the Grand Canyon. ... The belief that it was a little bit of water over a long time (verses a lot of water over a little bit of time) is a faith-based position that is not supported by science, since it lies outside science. ... On the contrary, modern-day catastrophes have been observed to cause massive local sedimentary deposits and other geological features. The Bible ... (describes) a worldwide flood with massive volcanism and tectonic activity. This fits very well within what we see. [6.7]" Again, the theory of evolution is at odds with the science of geology. The field of geology may contain some of the strongest evidence against the dating of fossils over millions of years. As more discoveries are made, the case for the biblical flood grows stronger.

The significance of this unconformity of the earth's geological strata is tremendous. "The phenomena in question are those related to the Cambrian-Precambrian unconformity. This is the most striking and universal break in the secession of rocks covering the earth. The event which they represent has been used to divide the history of our planet into two equal and contrasting parts. The continental nuclei at that time were largely stripped down to the crystalline basement. Ancient mountains were worn down to their roots, reducing the continents more nearly to a plain than they ever been before or since, leaving a clean slate on which the record came to be written which is, usually, called historical geology. [6.8]" Once again, the formation in the earth's rock layers indicates a pattern of events as indicated in figure 6.1. The question which must be answered is whether these events took place in a short span of time as the result of the great flood or over millions of years from normal amounts of sedimentation and rain fall. There are two possible explanations for the development of the rock strata formation. One is that this formation was created by the worldwide flood described in the Bible. The smooth horizontal rock strata represent conditions prior to the flood. The segments of rock strata, which have been folded or eroded, were done rapidly by the forces occurring in the turbulent depths below the surface of the flood. The smooth top layer was created by the subsiding forces from the worldwide cataclysm of the flood. The other view is that the world was slowly covered by water, the water subsided and wind and rain eroded the land in a manner to produce the sedimentation between the layers of rock, and then the world was again covered by water or ice. "Since the time of erosion between the Cambrian and Precambrian is worldwide, the famous American geologist Charles D Walcott named this period, which was supposed to have lasted millions of years, the Lipalian Interval. During those millions of years of erosion, no permanent deposition occurred anywhere in the world. That in and of itself appears highly illogical and unlikely. [6.9]"

There are at least two problems with the theory that this event took millions of years. One is in the deposition of the sedimentation. The necessity for no erosion over millions of years is to allow the "fold", shown in figure 6.1, to develop and not be smoothed out by additional erosion. If this took millions of years to form, how could you suspend erosion for millions of years to allow the fold that is sandwich between the two smooth layers to form? Obviously the evidence supports a worldwide cataclysm. But, scientists are in disagreement as to the source, there is no evidence of an ice age and scientists refuse to accept the possibility of a worldwide flood. Another problem with the evolutionary model is the lack of clay in the formation. If the erosion was done largely by normal amounts of wind and rain over long periods of time, as the evolutionary theory believes, there should be approximately equal amounts of clay and quartz in the rock formation and the clay should be on top with quartz underneath. "Upper Cambrian sandstones, the dominate cratonic sediment, rank among the most mature in the world. They are unrivaled for perfection of rounding and sorting of grains and contain 90 to 99 percent quartz. … When the original granite rocks, the source rocks, are weathered, they produce two minerals: clay and quartz. [6.10]" In the Cambrian formation you should not be seeing such a large concentration of quartz. Instead, you should be seeing approximately equal proportions of clay and quartz if this formation were the result of a slow process over millions of years. Samples have consistently shown large quantities of quartz on the surface, but the clay is missing. The rocks observed, support the conclusion that the deposits were formed by the flood instead of the slow process of erosion from climatic conditions. The lack of clay is evidence for the flood, since erosion without the clay deposits is what you would expect in the sifting process of the flood instead of the theory of natural erosion, which leaves the clay deposits. Also, the quartz at the top of the formation is what you would expect if the formation was due to the flood. Quote, "Quartz is the heavier mineral so it *always* is deposited before the clay. … Where is all the clay that must have formed by decay of the immense volumes of igneous and metamorphic rocks indicated by the pure quartz sand concentrate? … Remembering that clay requires still waters to be deposited, one can construct a picture of what could have happened geologically from the Cambrian-Precambrian unconformity on. … If the erosional period that the unconformity represents lasted only a short catastrophic period, rather than millions of years currently believed, then the lack of sediments, worldwide, would be reasonable. As the waters calmed, the heavier sand would be deposited, but not the clay since it requires still waters to deposit it. Later, the clay would be deposited. A flood of worldwide proportions would explain these facts well, since all would have occurred over a very short time span. However, if one desires to believe that the geologic events outlined above took millions of years, then it is up to him to explain why there could be worldwide erosion over millions of years with no deposition. He must also explain how the waters could be kept turbulent enough over millions of years for clay not to be deposited but yet still allow sand to be deposited. [6.11]" Again and again it takes more unscientific, unrealistic faith to believe the evolutionary model over the literally accepted biblical view.

Footprints

Fossilized footprints could be an additional evidence for the flood taking place and creating the majority of the fossils we have today. Fossilized footprints are phenomena which is difficult to explain with the evolutionary approach. First, fossilization of footprints involves a process similar to the fossilization of skeletons, but special considerations must be made for the tendency of footprints to disappear by weather conditions after a short time span. "Because of the fragility of the original tracks, it is obvious that they must be covered quickly or their existence will cease. The only way to keep the tracks long enough for them to be preserved in stone is to cover them with a different kind of material until the sand or mud they are in turns to stone. One does not preserve a footprint in sand by covering the footprint with sand. [6.12]" The fossilization of footprints involves two distinctly different kinds of materials. This seams to imply a sudden cataclysmic event, since the footprint would have to be preserved in a short time or the footprint would disappear. Also, an entirely different substance must suddenly cover the footprint to protect the imprint and allow for fossilization. How does the evolutionary approach explain the fossilization of footprints? "Normal explanations of the fossil record suppose that the whole area sank gradually into the ocean where more sediment was then piled on top of the footprints which turned to stone. However, it is unlikely the footprints could be preserved while sinking because the waves of the ocean would erode them. ... Whatever the precise means by which these fossils are preserved, one thing is certain. They must be quickly protected from the erosive forces of the earth or they would not exist. [6.13]" Again, the evolutionary model maintains that fossilization occurs over long periods of time. The evidence seams to disagree with this conclusion. A footprint does not stay around for millions of years or even several years. If you make a print in the mud, the impression is generally destroyed by the next rainstorm. Fossilized footprints from sandy seashores are impossible to explain from the evolutionists' perspective of material that can form a fossil, covering an area over a long period of time. If you walk along the beach, the next tide usually washes away any impression you just made.

Are there any other evidences of rapid fossilization? Yes. A fossil deposit in Germany supports the flood with two evidences. It describes fossilization of environmental mixed sources in a single location. This would be expected if the flood occurred, since all animals over the entire earth were destroyed and could have been swept by under water currents to a single location. Second, it describes a process of fossilization over an extremely short period of time. Quote, "A similar conclusion is drawn from the evidence of the fossil-bearing layers of the lignite of Geiseltal Germany. Here also is a complete mixture of plants, insects, and animals from all climatic zones of the earth that are capable of supporting life. In some cases leaves have been deposited still green, so that the "green layer" is used as a marker during excavations. Among the insects presented are beautifully-colored tropical beetles, with soft parts of the body including the contents of the intestines, preserved intact. Normally such materials decay or change color within a few hours of death, so that preservation by inclusion in an aseptic medium must have been sudden and complete. [6.14]" There are many more examples of fossil evidence for rapid fossilization and the flood. "Lea in 1849 collected a most interesting slab, a little over 5 feet long, with six successive series of foot impressions made by an amphibian (Paleosauropus) with a 13 inch stride. This slab is ripple-marked and has rain imprints indicating a mud flat of land origin, over which the animal walked when the deposit was yet wet. ... The Permian Coconino sandstone covers parts of northern Arizona. ... An intriguing feature of the Coconino footprints is that they almost always run uphill on the steeply inclined bedding planes of this dune sandstone. Why are the animals all running uphill? Why do they not go down? They certainly weren't running from a forest fire in the middle of a desert. Could they have been trying to escape rising flood waters? [6.15]" What more proof do you need for a catastrophic event, taking place, causing mass fossilization?

What a Mixture!

Another evidence for the flood may be found in coal formation. Coal is formed by intense compression exerted on large quantities of plant material. One question about the process of coal formation is: where did the plant material come from? There are two theories of how coal is formed. The most widely accepted theory of coal formation is called the autochthonous formation theory. This is based on the evolutionary perspective of formation over long periods of time. "This view of coal formation ... sees coal as the result of uniform forces acting over millions of years. The plant would have had to grown, died, and been turned into coal all in the same location. [6.16]" The theory makes several assumptions about the process of producing coal by compressing plant material. Among those assumptions is that all the plant material came from huge swamps which existed through out the early history of the earth. This is an important part of the evolutionist theory of coal formation. Quote, "All of the plants found in the coal would have to be swamp plants. It would hardly do to have non-swamp plant or animal life found in the swamp. [6.17]" If there were found any non-swamp plants in coal, the swamp theory of coal formation would fall apart. Is there any indication of this occurring in coal deposits? Yes. There is evidence of non-swamp plants in coal deposits. "Wilfred Francis, in Coal: Its Formation and Composition, tells of many non-swamp plants found in coal. These include: pine, sequoia, and spruce. Rehwrinkle cites palm, magnolia, poplar, willow, laurel, maple, and birch. Among other non-swap plants found in coal. [6.18]"

The second theory of coal formation is called the Allochthonous Theory. The theory describes coal formation by a different process. In this process, the source of plant material in coal formation comes from various plant life remains washed in from a variety of locations. This process of coal formation is described in Josh McDowell's book Reasons Skeptics Should Consider Christianity. Many scientists are skeptical of this method of coal formation. However, the evolutionary theory fails to explain the evidence of non-swamp plants contained in coal deposits. The Allochthonous theory is one of the possible explanations. The theory describes plant life from all over the world as the source of material for coal formation. The forces necessary to produce coal from the plant material could come from several sources, as the theory describes. The most obvious source for large scale production of coal is the force exerted by the flood as the water pressure compressed material in the depths of ancient oceans. Again, we are reminded that scientific theories are based on faith. The Christian faith is rooted in the word of God. Scientific theories constantly change based on new evidences and new scientific developments. The Christian faith, however, is something more lasting. It is based on a spiritual relationship with God through the Holy Spirit. There are many mysteries we can not explain using the scientific method. For example, the origin of life is a mystery. The Christian doesn't have any more scientific answers to this mystery than the non-Christian, but the Christian knows that the answer to every important question can be found in the Holy Bible. By trusting the Word of God we have a source of strength, courage, wisdom, and assurances in the things of yesterday, today and tomorrow, all being under the control of God. This is how all things are made possible. "I can do all things in him who strengthens me." Philippians 4:13.

Lots of Fossils in a Short Amount of Time

The flood also answers a number of questions about fossilization. We have already mentioned the great number of fossil occurring in a relatively short span of time called the Cambrian explosion. If the unconformity was caused by the great flood and the great flood destroyed all the animals of the earth, except those in the Ark, we would expect nearly all the fossils occurring on top of the unconformity. The evidence supports this prediction. "There are practically no fossils below this unconformity, and almost all fossils of the world are in rocks deposited after this time. [6.19]" The rock strata could have been formed by the 40 days and 40 nights of violent rain and forces from the wrath of God's vengeance on the earth. Animals killed by the flood would have been washed on shores or deposited in ocean depths after the rock formation was made, as the flood was drying up. As more of the flood evaporated, large deposits of dead bodies would have been left covered with large clay deposits. These conditions were ideal for encasing dead plants and animals in a tomb, preserving the remains to allow for fossilization to occur, as we have already discussed. If nearly all fossils were made during the period of the great flood, this would explain the discovery of large concentrations of fossils in the same "evolutionary" development found in different levels of rock strata. The theory that all fossils are largely the result of the flood is far more in line with the facts than the evolutionary theories. One reason this explanation is refuted so passionately by evolutionists is that it would destroy the little remaining evidence for the theory of evolution. The evolutionary theory depends on these fossils being created millions of years ago. Otherwise, there would be no evidence for a gradual development of life over a period of millions of years. "Some consider the fossil record that we find in the rock layers of the earth to be the strongest evidence for evolution, because there is an increase from the simple to complex, as one ascends through the rock layers. ... On our present earth, we have simple life in the deep rocks, more complex life in the oceans and the most complex on land. Destruction of these realms by rising flood activity would result in a general increase in complexity. ... The problem for evolution is that it is between the major groups of plants and animals (phyla and divisions) that we would expect the greatest number of intermediates... Any gradual process would be expected to leave all kinds of fossils between major groups as major changes evolve. ... Animals require plants for food in order to survive. Yet in several of our important geological formations we find good evidence for the animals, but little or no evidence for the plants necessary to support the animals. ... A more plausible scenario for these deposits is that they represent layers laid down rapidly during the biblical flood, with the waters of the flood sorting the organisms into various deposits, the plants forming some of our huge coal deposits. [6.20]"

There are many instances where dating fossils according to its position in the earth's geological strata have failed. In fact, the number of examples is too extensive to mention all the instances in this book. There has been a large amount of controversy over the fossil record in the past few decades. In the book, Evolution-The Fossils Say Yes! , by Beverly Halstead, the author disputes the observations of Dr. Gish. Dr. Gish is a part of the Creation Institute and has written several good books on the subject of evolution. One of these books is called Evolution: The Fossils Say No! Which viewpoint is correct? I have some problems agreeing with all the findings of Dr. Gish, however I think he is right more often than he is wrong. One of Dr. Gish's main proposals concerns the lack of evidence for a smooth transition in the evolution of different species. We have already stated that there is a number of missing links between species in the fossil record. Halstead's main argument for the fossil record as evidence for evolution was made with examples of small fossilized organisms and insects. Many evolutionists sight examples of mutations formed in bacteria and small insects as evidence for evolution. The wide variety of changes and developments in the very small insects and bacteria is acceptable in the framework of the creationists view. Certain changes can occur in the tiny kingdom of insects which evolutionists misinterpret as evidence for the theory of evolution. It returns to the concepts of limits. Once again, the evolutionists tend to ignore the natural biological limitations which exist. Changes within a species are possible and constantly occurring. Changing from one species to another, however, is not possible. Changing structure, which could be considered mutations, is possible in the small scaled bacteria kingdom, but it does not occur in the large scaled kingdom. There are too many limiting factors for evolution to have taken place. Halstead could only sight evidences in the small scaled animal kingdom to dispute Dr. Gish's claims. This in itself is evidence for creation. If evolution actually took place, there would be no adequate explanation for the lack of fossil evidence in massive amounts of mutations in the large animal kingdom.

Dinosaurs: For Evolution or Creation?

What about the dinosaurs? Some Christians have had great difficulties over their existence since they are not directly mentioned in the Bible. They were great creatures of God. "So God created the great creatures of the sea and every living and moving thing with which the waters teems, according to their kinds, and every winged bird according to its kind. And God saw that it was good." Genesis. 1:21. This would indicate that man and dinosaurs lived together. One evidence for the existence of dinosaurs in the same era as man is in a fossil found a few years ago. It clearly shows a human footprint inside a footprint of a dinosaur presumed to have died millions of years prior to the existence of man. Quote, "Additional evidence for their existence, at the same time as man, is in the pictographs left in Africa and North America, and from fossil evidences of human and dinosaur footprints in the sane formation. [6.21]" This fossil was a tremendous blow to the evolutionists which put man and dinosaurs millions of years apart. The final decision of which to believe, Evolution or Creation can not be decided on a scientific basis. The foundation for an intelligent decision remains to be based on faith. Science can say little about historical one time events. The scales of evidence for and against evolution, in the field of zoology, seams relatively balanced with an increasing number of discoveries leaning towards creation instead of evolution. The theory of evolution was created from a fundamental principle of life created without God, by natural forces alone. It takes a lot of faith to believe this theory because of the numerous physical and bio-chemical laws evolution violates. Much of the "proof" of evolution occurring in the past, lies in missing links yet undiscovered. There doesn't seam to be a solid body of evidence for evolution existing in the past. Perhaps more importantly, there is no available evidence for these events currently taking place. The biological change of one species transforming into an entirely new species doesn't occur today. When you take into account **all** the evidence of science, the Christian perspective has far more support than the naturalist. Some Christians have fallen into the pit of compromise. They believe that God somehow used evolution and that the "days" mentioned in the Bible are actually time periods. I do not believe this is true. God does not lie! If the world was formed over an extended period of time I believe God would have instructed Moses to write it down. Instead God had him state that he created the universe in 6 days and on the 7th day He rested. The numbers 6 & 7 are extremely important throughout the Bible. It is exactly the number of days God used to create the universe. Each day may or may not be as we know them today, in my opinion. "The Hebrew word for day, Yom, is used elsewhere in the Bible to indicate longer periods of time than twenty-four hours, such as Psalm 90:4 and 2 Peter 3:8; also Zechariah 12-14. Those who oppose the age-day view, point out that the Genesis account doesn't need to harmonize with the Scriptures. ... The geological and fossil evidence do not conclusively prove an earth age of millions of years, and can, in part, be explained by the apparent age theory. This is the theory that God created everything at full maturity, with the appearance of having gone through the normal developmental states. Examples of this would be Adam and Eve, created fully grown, and the wine Jesus created in Cana, fully fermented in an instant of time. ...Those who oppose the age-day theory point out that when Yom is used with a specific number, in this case six days; it always means a twenty-four hour day. ... More than 700 times in the Old Testament, the plural of Yom is used and always has twenty-four hour days in view. ... As for the argument that the first three days could not be solar days, God could have caused things to operate on the kind of plan He later used in the solar days, in preparation for the sun's creation on day four. The Genesis account clearly reports 'there was evening and there was morning, one day.' [6.22]" When discussing a 6 day creation theory, you get a diverse response among Christians theologians. I am currently undecided if each "day" in Genesis was 24 hours long. The main events in the first two days of creation did not require 24 hours, but micro-seconds according to our understanding of quantum physics. Of course, God could have suspended time during these events. The question remains are the "days" in the Genesis account symbolic or literal or a combination of the two. You decide.

The biblical account is far more consistent with the physical laws. According to the Bible, all life forms on earth were made by God. The first law of thermodynamics remains established in God's Word. The infinite power of God made the substances of the earth. Then God created man by re-organizing the matter He created. "Then the Lord God formed man out of the dust of the ground, and breathed into his nostrils the breath of life; and man became a living being." Genesis 2:7. Truly, each of us has a part of the spirit of God in his or her own life. Praise God with every breath you take, because it is a miracle given each day by God. "I appeal to you therefore, brethren, by the mercies of God, to present your bodies as a living sacrifice, holy and acceptable to God, which is your spiritual worship." Romans 12:1. Some people believe the world or God owes us something. Actually, they are correct. God owes us the penalty of death for our crimes against God and the penalty of sin we have inherited through Adam and more importantly through our own rebellion against God. Mankind has broken God's laws through disobedience ever since Adam and Eve first sinned. The penalty for these crimes is death, according to the justice of God. Some are confused with the apparent cold justice of the Old Testament with the loving mercies of the New Testament. The whole Bible speaks of a relationship with God. God desires to have a personal relationship with each individual. The apparent change in the relationship under the law in the Old Testament, to living under grace in the New Testament is due to the coming of Christ. Through the power of Jesus Christ, his life, his teachings, and his sacrifice on the cross, we have redemption. He paid the price for our sin. We will explore ore about this subject in chapter 10.

The Two Methods of Dating Fossils

One of the main concerns for the apparent conflict between science and the creationist's perspective is concerning radio-active dating methods. Like many of the topics that we have discussed, the general public has been misled towards the accuracy and methods used to obtained the ages of fossils with radio-active dating methods. Do not fear! We will only discuss the basics of nuclear principles. These principles are now being taught at the grade school level. Parents should be familiar with there principles to answer their children's questions if the subject arises. Christians need to support each other and help our Children understand that we are not just "stupid parents". We need to share our faith and why we believe what we do. If we believe in a young earth, we need to share with our family why we have this faith and others may have a different faith. The dating of fossils can be broadly placed into two categories. One is radioactive dating methods, such as carbon-14. The other method is through sedimentary evidence. Evolutionists believe that the deeper a fossil is buried in the soil, the greater the age of the fossil. The theory is based upon the idea that slow amounts of soil erosion have covered some fossil or artifact that once existed on the surface of the earth. The more sedimentation above the fossil, the longer the fossil had been dead and swept over by the dust of the ground. This seams reasonable, however this method has produced inconsistent results in several instances. "The present rate of erosion of our continents by rain and consequent rivers into the ocean is so rapid that we would expect the continents to be eroded down to sea level in about 10 million years. Why are the continents still here if they are thousands of millions of years old? … Renewal of the continents from below is sometimes proposed to resolve the dilemma. This does not seam to be a solution … we don't seam to have completed even one full cycle of continent erosion and uplift. You are probably familiar with the usually flat-like sedimentary layers (strata) that are widespread over the surface of the earth. … Between major sedimentary units there are gaps where, according to the standard geological time, often scores to hundreds of millions of years of deposits are missing. … If these millions of years really took place, why don't we see the abundant irregular erosion of the lower layer that is expected over such long periods of time? The contracts between the layers at these gaps are usually flat with little evidence of erosion. This suggests little time. [6.23]"

Observations like these inconsistencies have caused evolutionists to change their ideas about the Neanderthal man. Once it was shown that modern man was found in strata "much older" than Neanderthal, scientists had to give up the notion that they had discovered man's ancestor. When evolutionists encountered these kinds of inconsistencies, it was much easier to give up their premise that they have discovered a "missing link" than to admit to a totally inaccurate time scale. To throw out the strata method of dating fossils would be a devastating blow to the theory of evolution. Yet, the evidence seams clear that the strata is not evidence for millions of years in time, but the result of a world wide flood. "That the catastrophe was global in extent is clear from the extreme horizontal extent and continuity of the continental sedimentary deposits. That there was a single large catastrophe and not many smaller ones with long gaps in between is implied by the lack of erosional channel, soil horizons, and dissolution structures at the interfaces between successive strata. The excellent exposures of the Paleozoic record in the Grand Canyon provide superb examples of this vertical continuity with little or no physical evidence of time gaps between strata. … The ubiquitous presence of crossbeds in sandstones, and even limestones, in Paleozoic, Mesozoic, and even Cenozoic rocks is strong testimony for high energy water transport of these sediments. Studies of sandstones exposed in the Grand Canyon reveal crossbeds produced by high velocity water currents that generated sand waves tens of meters in height. The crossbedded Coconino sandstone exposed in the Grand Canyon continues across Arizona and New Mexico into Texas, Oklahoma, Colorado, and Kansas. It covers more than 200,000 square miles and has an estimated volume of 10,000 cubic miles. [6.24]"

It should be clear that dating a fossil according to its positions in the earth's strata, i.e. how deeply it is buried, should be treated with skepticism. The next method for dating a fossil or artifact is radioactive dating. Radioactive dating methods are commonly used to determine the ages of geological and biological artifacts. With objects having a biological origin, radiocarbon, commonly referred to as carbon-14, is used to determine age. The earth is constantly being bombarded by highly energetic cosmic rays. After the cosmic rays strike the upper atmosphere, they produce an enormous variety of particles. Among these particles are neutrons. Some of the neutrons can react with nitrogen atoms high in the atmosphere. The resulting reaction forms a radioactive carbon-14 atom, $^{14}N_7 + {}^1n_0 \rightarrow {}^{14}C_6 + {}^1H_1$ and a standard hydrogen atom with 1 neutron and 1 proton. "The reaction provides a small but reasonably constant source of carbon-14. The carbon-14 is radioactive, undergoing beta decay with a half-life of 5700 yr: $^{14}C_6 \rightarrow {}^{14}N_7 + {}^1e_{-1}$. In using radiocarbon dating, it is generally assumed that the ratio of carbon-14 to carbon-12 in the atmosphere has been constant for at least 50,000 years. The carbon-14 is incorporated into carbon dioxide, which is in turn incorporated, through photosynthesis, into more complex carbon-containing molecules within plants. The plants are eaten by animals and the carbon-14 thereby becomes incorporated within them as well. Because a living plant or animal has a constant intake of carbon compounds, it is able to maintain a ratio of carbon-14 to carbon-12 that is identical with that of the atmosphere. [6.25]" Carbon-14 dating has been proven fairly reliable, but it has a limited time frame in dating archeological findings. "When an organism dies, however, it no longer absorbs ^{14}C from the atmosphere, and so the ratio of ^{14}C to ^{12}C decreases as the result of beta decay of ^{14}C. It is therefore possible to measure the age of a material by measuring its activity per unit mass due to the decay of ^{14}C. Using carbon dating, samples of wood, charcoal, bone, and shell have been identified as having lived from 1000 to 25,000 years ago. This knowledge has helped us to reconstruct the history of living organisms – including humans – during this time span. A particular interesting example is the dating of the Dead Sea Scrolls. ... Carbon dating applied to fragments of the scrolls and to the material in which they were wrapped established their age at about 1950 years. [6.26]" Wait just one minute. The half-life of carbon-14 is 5700 years. This mean in a given sample approximately half should be gone after 5700 years. This means in approximately 12,000 years all the carbon-14 should be gone, doesn't it? Actually, a sample of carbon-14 can undergo as many as 4 "half-life cycles" reducing the amount in each remaining sample by ½. This process is proven true with other radioactive isotopes. This could mean accurate readings to 50,000 years, or does it?

There is great number of assumptions made by scientists in using this information to estimate the age of fossils. This dating method assumes that every plant on earth has approximately the same level of radiocarbon. This supply of radiocarbon is assumed to have always existed at this same level throughout history, since the supply of cosmic rays is assumed to been at the same level for at lest 50,000 years. This would seam reasonable if you believe in evolution, since there should be no atmospheric differences for the last 50,000 years. Of course, according to evolutionary theory the atmosphere of the earth prior to 50,000 years ago was different. After all, the atmosphere of the earth must have had different properties in its early history to be more conducive to chemical evolution, as we have discussed. Again, there is a lack of evidence that this hypothesis is true as the theory of evolution is constantly contradicting its own assumptions. Remember, there was no evidence that the early atmosphere was significantly different than it is today. The next assumption is that roughly the same ratios of carbon-14 to carbon-12, which exist in the atmosphere today, exist in all plants and animals. There are a few variations which have been discovered by experiments, but the carbon-14 to carbon-12 ratio seams to get into the plants and animals as the result of different methods. Disintegrations per minute from beta decay of carbon-14 to carbon-12 are different in different plants and animals due to their body chemistry. Carbon-14 dating assumes these ratios have never changed, since plants and animal body chemistry has supposedly remained unchanged in the last 50,000 years.

Let us examine the carbon-14 dating process a little more closely and then determine the likelihood of it's accuracy given the biblical accounts. The first step in carbon-14 dating was in establishing the ratio of carbon-14 to carbon-12 in the upper atmosphere. The next step in radioactive dating is to compare the levels of carbon-14 in a dead animal as compared to a living one. To evaluate how old an artifact is, a sample is converted into a gas. Some of these gases include carbon dioxide. The gas is passed through a special beta-sensitive detector. The amount of radiocarbon within a plant or animal which has recently been alive is similarly determined. Then the two values are compared, taking into account the rate in which carbon-14 decays. For example, we have an ancient piece of wood which is found to have 13 disintegrations per second. The radio-activity in living wood is 16 disintegrations per second. We use the equation $R = R_0 e^{-\lambda t}$, to find the age of the ancient piece of wood. In the formula, t is the amount of time the artifact has been dead. In our case of the wood, it represents the time between the day the tree was cut to provide lumber for the ancient structure, to the present day. R_o is the original reaction rate; in the case of the ancient wood it equals 16. R is the activity of a similar type of wood at the present time, in this case 13. (e) Stands for the natural logarithm, found on most calculators. It is the log to the base e. Refer to mathematical textbooks for more information. The Greek letter lambda represents the decay rate for radiocarbon, which has the value of .693/ 5760 years, or 1.203125E-3. Put these values into any scientific calculator and you determine that the wood is 1726 years old. Radiocarbon dating is limited to 50,000 years, according to some scientific textbooks. Beyond this time limit, scientists rely on other dating methods such as Potassium-Argon, Rubidium-Strontium and Uranium-Lead dating.

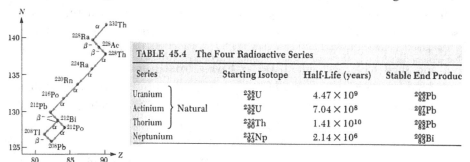

TABLE 45.4 The Four Radioactive Series

Series		Starting Isotope	Half-Life (years)	Stable End Produc
Uranium	⎫	$^{238}_{92}U$	4.47×10^9	$^{206}_{82}Pb$
Actinium	⎬ Natural	$^{235}_{92}U$	7.04×10^8	$^{207}_{82}Pb$
Thorium	⎭	$^{232}_{90}Th$	1.41×10^{10}	$^{208}_{82}Pb$
Neptunium		$^{237}_{93}Np$	2.14×10^6	$^{209}_{83}Bi$

Figure 6.2

Always Assuming On and On and On …

Carbon-14 has been shown to be accurate for most artifacts within a 50,000 year range. The biblical account places the age of the earth and the universe, given a 6-day creation, at around 6,000 to 10,000 years given the genealogical account. This places little discrepancy with carbon-14 dating since it generally verifies artifacts such as the Dead Sea Scrolls within this 10,000 year time frame. The other dating methods are used primarily in established the age of rocks. With these methods, you make even greater assumptions about the original elemental contents of the rocks. For example, in uranium-lead dating, you assume that the original content of the rocks were radio-active substances. Have you ever wondered how scientists have established the age of the earth at 4.5 billion years? This Chemistry textbook is a good example of what is taught in public schools. "The age of rocks containing uranium can be determined by measuring the ratio of lead-206 to uranium-238. If the lead-206 had somehow been incorporated into the rock by normal chemical process instead of by radioactive decay, the rock would contain large amounts of the more abundant isotope, lead-208. In the absence of large amounts of this "geonormal" isotope of lead, it is assumed that all the lead-206 was at one time uranium-238. The oldest rocks found on earth are approximately 3×10^9 yr old. This age indicates that the crust of the earth has been solid for at least this length of time. Prior to crystallization of rock, lead-206 and uranium-238 could separate. It is estimated that it required $1-1.5 \times 10^9$ yr for the earth to cool and its surface to become solid. This places the age of the earth at 4.0-4.5 billion yr. [6.27]" Notice the number of faith based assumptions in the calculations. First, you assume that if a particular rock is deficient in large amounts of lead-208, and the isotope lead-206 must be the result of natural radioactive decay. Next you assume that you have obtained an accurate reading of the oldest known rocks. Then you assume that the rock was entirely uramium-238 at the moment of its creation, apparently from the star nebula that formed the sun. Next you assume the uranium-238 solidified from molten rock to a crystallized form, remaining pure uranium-238. All these steps are believed to take place without any contamination of the original sample.

Radio-active dating is a somewhat complex subject. However, it is a subject introduced at even the grade school level. The basics are simple enough; you merely need to understand the basic nature of the elements on a periodic table. The different elements are separated by the number of protons and neutrons in the nucleus. There is usually a balance of neutrons and protons in the nucleus and the atom is stable. However, if an atom has "captured" enough "free" neutrons, the element can become radioactive. Over time, the excessive neutrons in radioactive material will naturally decay to protons and electrons. "In the language of particle physics, a neutron outside of a nucleus 'decays,' and the products of this decay include a proton and an electron. ... There are, however, nuclei where the neutron can and does decay. Such nuclei are unstable. When this happens, the nucleus emits an electron and acquires a unit of positive charge. ... We are left with an atom that has one more proton in its nucleus than it did before the decay. ... Usually such an atom will pick up a stray electron from the surroundings, becoming electrically neutral in the process. The net result of all this is a new atom, one which has one more electron than its predecessor. [6.28]" The radioactive materials continue the process of decay until they have become a stable atom, see figure 6.2. How long does this process take? The length of time for a particular radioactive element to decay varies depending on the number of neutrons that are needed to be released to stabilize the atom. It turns out that the decay of individual neutrons themselves does not decay during a set amount of time. "If we watched a large number of free neutrons, we would notice that they do not all decay at the same time. Rather, we would see one decay, then another, and so on at irregular intervals until all had completed the transformation into the decay products. ... One common way of describing decay times is to talk about the half-life of the sample. This is the time it takes for one-half of the original number of particles to decay. [6.29]" The decay rate of various radioactive elements has been determined by experimentation and mathematical calculations. See figure 6.2. Usually the end product of radioactive decay is one of the most stable, dense, elements in nature, lead.

Material	Location	AGE IN MILLIONS OF YEARS				
		Dating Technique			Reference	
		U^{235}	U^{238}	Th^{233}	Lead-Lead	
Monazite		1360	1640	1180	2010	2
Granite	South Africa	330	356	238	530	3
Granite	Ontario	1030	1050	390	1090	3
Granite	Colorado	624	707	313	980	3
Granite	Arizona	630	770	271	1210	3
Granite	Colorado	925	1130	530	1540	3
Monazite		2170	2380	2100	2570	4
Monazite		1590	1420	995	1170	4
Monazite		950	930	690	880	4
Monazite		930	915	900	880	4
Monazite		390	410	440	540	4
Zircon	Ontario	1030	1050	390	1090	5
Beolite	Colorado	3180	2065	1100	1640	5

Figure 6.3

In summary, let us consider the step-by-step procedure for using radioactive dating methods. "First, to date an event, one must know how rapidly the original isotope decays into the final isotope. ... Second, you must be able to measure how much uranium of a given type a rock contains and how much of the daughter product (lead 206, in the case of uranium 238) the rock has. This information also can be measured in a lab. Third, you must know the original ratio of parent to daughter isotopes. This is hard to verify. For instance, it takes 4.5 billion years for half of the uranium 238 to change into lead 206. If you find a rock that has 50% uranium 238 and 50 percent lead 206, you could tell how old it is only if you assumed that all of the lead was originally uranium. ... However, if I had manufactured that rock last week, by mixing equal portions of lead 206 and uranium 238, the rock would be one week old, not 4.5 billion years old. ... The fourth assumption in these dating methods is that the rock has not been altered in such a manner as to remove the lead or uranium. ... If chemical reactions occurred which removed uranium or added lead, then the rock would date older. [6.30]" Evolutionists assume that no mixing of elements has occurred using chemical reactions. This is a faith based assumption. This gives their estimates to the age of the earth, the oldest possible readings. Are there conflicting reports found when using different radioactive dating methods? Yes. Figure 6.3 shows the various reading indicating the age of several samples using different dating methods. As you can see, a single rock can be dated with an enormous range of possible ages depending upon the method of radioactive dating used. These estimates are hundreds, thousands and sometimes millions of years off. This is a clear indication that radioactive dating methods are more guess work than science, and the whole radioactive dating process for rocks should be scrapped as useless.

Obvious failures to Radioactive Dating

There are many examples where the radioactive dating methods fail. "C.S. Noble and J.J. Naughton used potassium-argon to date an underwater lava flow. Judging by the unweathered appearance of the flow, they judged that it was less than 200 years old. However, when they dated the rock using potassium-argon, the rock dated from 12 to 21 million years old. ... Lovering and Richards extracted different minerals from the same volcanic structure and dated them. For the Kimberlite pipe in South Africa, two different minerals yielded ages from 68 million years and 142 million years. That's a large variation when they should have yielded approximately the same age. ... The 1800-1801 Kaupulehu lava flow in Hawaii, a flow *which man watched coming out of the ground,* yielded potassium-argon ages of 1 to 2.4 billion years. This lava flow was less than 200 years old! The same flow, when dated by helium dating yielded ages of 140 million years to 670 million years. ... In the Auckland volcanic field of New Zealand, the lava flows have buried the forests at the base of the volcanoes. As in Pompeii, the trees, being encased in lava, were not destroyed, but were preserved. This presents a tremendous opportunity to test two dating methods against each other. By dating the wood with carbon-14 and the lava with potassium-argon one can compare the results. McDougall, Polach and Stripp note: ... For the volcanic island of Rangitoto, the radiocarbon, geological and botanical evidence unequivocally shows that it was active and was probably build during the last 1000 years. The (potassium-argon) dates on basalts from this volcano range from 145,000 to 465,000 years. [6.31]" These observations would indicate that radioactive dating methods are very unreliable. Of course, evolutionists take the opposite belief. "Time magazine chides the creationists' position by stating: other radioactive methods have been used to date earlier epochs ... and in a variety of trials have produced a consistent pattern. The creationist's argument is a bit like claiming that because some trains are cancelled and others run way off schedule, the basic timetable is totally inaccurate. [6.32]" Considering the enormous number of examples where radioactive dating methods have been proven to be inaccurate, I must disagree with this assessment of the situation. Radioactive dating by any means other than carbon-14 should be taken with extreme skepticism. The argument against the creationists' point of view again is based on faith. It is the evolutionists that passionately, religiously express unrealistic faith in their view of geological history. They continually refuse to listen to the arguments against their point of view. Our debate is not about scientific methods but rather about the passions of those who intend to impose their atheistic religion on public schools. How much faith do you place in the accuracy of the dating methods given the cited examples of inaccuracies? One of the examples of inaccurate readings I find most interesting, is when we have records of personal observations of these rocks forming from lava eruptions. One example is the 1800-1801 Kaupulehu lava flow mentioned previously. Another excellent example is the more recent eruption of Mt. St. Helens. "We have numerous examples in which radiometric dating gives the wrong answers, such as 1/3 to 3 million years for Mount St. Helens' lava, historically dated at about 20 years old. Potassium-argon dating, upon which most of the geological column and especially hominid fossils are dated, is particularly prone to 'excessive argon' which gives inflated ages.[6.33]" What is amazing, is the evolutionists failure to accept that there can be a great mixing of chemicals when these rocks or fossils are formed. There are many of us who remember when Mt. St. Helens erupted. This was not millions of years ago!

The evidence from these reports leads to the conclusion that carbon-14 dating is the only radioactive dating method which has any degree of reliability. This method is very limited in range. As we have already stated, the carbon-14 dating method only has a range of up to 50,000 years. This places measurements of artifacts close to the range where biblical scholars place the age of the earth by a literal interpretation of the Scriptures. Where is the reliable scientific basis of a 4.5 billion year old earth? We return to the basic conclusion that many scientific theories about conditions of the past, rely on faith. Do you believe the earth is 4.5 billion years old or not? Which takes more faith: believing in the Scripture as truth or believing unsubstantiated theories which do not prove reliable under observed conditions? If you believe that science has established that the earth is 4.5 billion years old, I suggest you may not know much about nuclear physics. If you have a Ph.D. in nuclear physics, and believe these methods are true, I submit you should not impose a lot of faith based assumption on the accuracy of the dating methods. If you are honest, you will admit that there is a very real possibility that all the radioactive dating methods can give false estimates to the age of a sample.

Have We Had a Constant Supply of Cosmic Rays?

How accurate is carbon-14 dating? As we have seen, the reliability of carbon-14 dating is dependent upon the steady and unchanging supply of cosmic rays to form radiocarbon in the upper atmosphere. Let us take a look at the physical conditions of the earth, assuming that a worldwide flood did actually occur. Most biblical scholars agree that the Genesis accounts indicate that the flood was a surprise to the inhabitants of the earth. Many believe that there was a great canopy existing over the earth prior to the flood. This held back the flood waters until it was time for God to bring his judgment upon the earth. This canopy could have affected the supply of cosmic rays to the earth. The Bible speaks about men of God living for hundreds of years. The longevity of these men can be partially attributed to better environmental conditions in the early history of the world. God made a perfect world for Adam. After Adam and Eve's sin, they were cast out of the Garden of Eden which contained the tree of life. If they were to stay in the garden and eat of the tree of life, they would have never died, according to the Scriptures. However, God's punishment of death was on Adam for his sin. Instead of immediate death, Adam would repent of his sin and live a long life before eventually dying. His longevity, and all men of God in the early history of the world, could have been the result of two things: 1) A good relationship with God. 2) A nearly perfect environment to live in. Today, research is conducted on the effects of cosmic rays on the aging process. There appears to be strong evidence that many of the features of cosmic rays interacting inside our bodies cause our bodies to degenerate. Obviously, cosmic rays and other forms of radiation cause skin disease and sometimes skin cancer. What other possible effects could cosmic rays have on our bodies? We can speculate that there were both natural and supernatural forces at work in the lives of the people God had chosen to work through.

As we said earlier, scholars believe that the flood was the first large scale rain the earth had seen. Prior to this time, the plants, animals, and people had an abundance of moisture from dew and other sources of water. We know that the flood took place a relatively short time after the creation of man. Is it possible that the early atmosphere gathered a large collection of moisture in preparation for the coming flood? This could have provided a barrier surrounding the earth, effectively screening out the cosmic rays. If the supply of neutrinos to the atmosphere were somehow reduced, the supply of radioactive carbon dioxide molecules would be reduced. The number of disintegrations per second per second would be reduced in a living plant or animal. Therefore, the plant or animal would date much older that it actually was, using the carbon-14 method. Recall that, to predict the age of the sample, we compare the number of carbon-14 atoms in the body with the number of carbon-14 atoms currently in a living organism. If the supply of neutrons were reduced or cut off, the normal number of carbon-14 atoms in a living creature would be reduced. Instead of the number of carbon-14 atoms becoming reduced because of great amounts of time, the number of carbon-14 atoms would have been reduced in the body as a result of a lack of available radiocarbon atoms in the early atmosphere. There is no way to sample the atmosphere that existed 50,000 years ago to verify this hypothesis. We can only examine the evidence and decide which theory we are led to accept, by faith, as the evidence is presented. In any case, if we accept the biblical account of the flood and the creation of the world by God, radiocarbon dating should be considered unreliable prior to the time of Noah, about 6-10,000 years ago.

A close look at the biblical record after the flood indicates a slow process of men of God living shorter lives. Look at the life spans of the people before the flood. Adam lived 930 years, Seth 912 years, Enosh 905 years, Kenan 910 years, Mahalel 895 years, Jared 962 years, Enoch lived 365 years and did not die. "Enoch walked with God; and he was not, for God took him." Genesis. 5:24. Methuselah 969 years, Lamech 777 years, Noah 955 years. All the men of God mentioned in the Genesis accounts prior to the flood were living lives in the 895-969 range. The only two exceptions was Lamech who lived a relatively short life of 777 years and Enoch who found favor with God and went to heaven instead of receiving death. Look at the ages after the flood. Nahor 148 years, Terah 205 years, Abraham 175. There is a noticeable drop in the life span of the men of God. From an 800-900 year range to about a 150-200 year range. To me, this provides strong evidence that environmental conditions before the flood were different from conditions after the flood. Again, the Bible can explain all apparent inconsistencies of scientific investigations in a clear and precise manor.

Radio-halos: Strong Evidence for God's Sudden Creation

At this time there should be at least some doubt in your mind about radioactive dating methods. We have discussed some of the evidences which discredit the ideas of the earth being billions of years old. Now, let us look at evidences of God creating the earth instantaneously, or at least, in a very short period of time. The evidence which most indicates an instantaneous creation by God is in radio-halos. "The radio-halo, found throughout various minerals, is a discoloration of the rock, caused by the radioactive decay of a small speck of a radioactive element contained in the rock. When a small speck or inclusion of a substance, such as uranium 238, is trapped in the rock, the uranium emits alpha particles which destroy the crystal structure of the radioactive mineral. Since alpha particles are emitted from uranium with a particular speed, the alpha particles can travel only a certain distance through the rock before they stop. Since the alpha particles are emitted in all directions, a spherical shell of discoloration is produced. While uranium is decaying to lead, it passes through fifteen steps. During this process alpha particles with five distinct velocities are given off. Because of this, when uranium is trapped in a rock a set of five concentric discolorations of the rock will occur. ... Two factors are required before a halo can form. 1. a small speck of a radioactive substance must be included in the molten rock before it cools. 2. The rock must solidify and form a crystal before all of the radioactivity is ended. ... It was surprising when two and three-ring halos were discovered in a size which indicated they had been formed by three isotopes of polonium. ... The situation gets more interesting with polonium 214 halos. ... The half live of polonium 214 is 0.000164 second. This means that the rock would have had to cool in less than one-thousandth of a second after the polonium 214 was created. [6.34]" Since no natural force or process can account for the formation of solid rocks at this rate of speed, these radio-halos represent strong evidence for instantaneous creation.

We have reviewed many evidences for the creation account. There are many more books, written by scientists who believe in the creation account, which have recently been published that have more details on the subjects than we have covered. Why are these books which have scientific evidences for intelligent design, as it is sometimes called today, excluded from the discussion of ideas presented in public schools? What makes the evolutionists so convincing in asserting their view of the creation of life as more scientific? The perception that the natural or evolutionary view is more scientific comes from the history of the theory of evolution introduced into public schools in America. There continues to be an attempt to "re-write" American history from a naturalistic perspective. They have misinterpreted the separation of Church and State mentioned in the first amendment to the Constitution. This nation was founded as a Christian nation. Our founding fathers established such things as the posting of the Ten Commandments in as many public places. Congress has always opened with a Christian prayer asking for our Lord Jesus to guide our nation. The Bible is in every court room and was in every school room, until the later part of the twentieth century. People quickly recognized that the theory of evolution was more a philosophy than a science. The view of evolution is based on an atheistic faith with its purpose of removing God from our country. When it was first proposed to introduce evolution in the class room, it was understandable that much of the public reacted violently. Even dedicated Christians who believed in "love thy neighbor" were outraged by the thought of evolution, and the underlying religion of atheism, being taught in their public schools.

One of the first attempts to introduce the theory of evolution into public educational systems was in 1925. The concepts of evolution had been around since many of the original concepts were first introduced by Charles Darwin in 1859. The theory was heavily ridiculed for many years by both scientists and the general public. The conflict between public opinion and the obscure group of scientists supporting the theory of evolution came to a high point on January 28, 1925. The Tennessee state legislature passed the Butler Bill forbidding the teaching of evolution in public schools. This was the beginning of the entrance of a scientific debate into the court systems. On March 13, 1925 Tennessee State senate pass the Butler Bill 24 to 6. On March 21 Governor Peay signed the bill into law. On May 5, 1925, after repeated warnings, John Thomas Scopes, a high school science teacher and football coach, refused to stop teaching evolution in his biology classroom. A warrant for his arrest was issued. May 10, preliminary hearing was conducted. Counsel for the defense was Clearance Darrow. Scopes was bound over for the Grand Jury. July 10, the trial began. July 21 the trial ended, and Scopes was found guilty and charged with a $100 fine. He was granted a right to appeal on January 14, 1927. Quote, "Tennessee Supreme Court upholds the constitutionality of the Butler Act but reverses judgment against Scopes because the trial judge had violated the State Constitution in imposing a $100 fine. [6.35]" The referenced text was published in 1960. According to the publication, a hearing in 1951 was the last attempt to repeal the Butler Act. The appeal failed and the constitutionality of the Butler act was upheld to the date of the publication. This is typical of court cases across the nation until the 1960's. The theory of evolution was widely recognized as an atheistic philosophy and not supported by the scientific evidence of the time. One point which we have mentioned is the lack of fossil evidence for the theory of natural selection as the driving force for **all** life forms. This was sufficient evidence to rule that the theory was un-scientific. Also, the theory of evolution was obviously introducing into the schools, a religion that was incompatible with our Christian heritage.

The debate over the acceptance of the theory of evolution continues today at the state level. Many of the decisions concerning the controversy over evolution today concern a legal position that the theory of creation is more a statement of faith than science. How did a theory which has so many flaws and was banned from teaching for 100 years become so widely accepted today? The answer lies in a long process which involves legal battles, social changes, and scientific discoveries. It seams as if the shift in acceptable behavior and radical social changes in the sixties are more responsible for the acceptance of evolution than the scientific discoveries. The evolutionists were appalled by the court decision of 1925. The evolutionists sighted the superiority of William Jennings Bryan, prosecutor, over Clarence Darrow, defendant, as a trial lawyer. Some people still accuse the "Monkey trial" as having been a part of a "kangaroo" court. Evolutionists also site the fact that the trial was more concerned with the constitutionality of the Butler Act than getting to the "facts" about evolution verses the creation theory. Evolutionists began to push the position that the entire motivation for the rejection of evolution was religious. They began to push for the total acceptance of evolution in public classrooms. From 1925-1960 there were a number of changes and compromises to the state laws, which following the Butler Act, banned the teaching of evolution. From 1961-1970 the process of nationally accepting and teaching evolution occurred with sweeping changes across the nation. [6.36]

During the period of time which began the integration of evolution into the school system, 1960-1970's, new discoveries in science were made which seemed to support the theory of evolution. We have discussed a number of these discoveries in this book, there are a great many more. The general public was unprepared to challenge many of the conclusions of the theory of evolution because college professors were endorsing the ideas as fact. As stated earlier, one sure way to get people confused and to blindly accept any statement you want to make is to simply start your sentence with: 'Scientists say'. This book was intended to help students, and people in general, understand the basis of most of the scientific discoveries, which are often misused to support evolution. The ideas of evolution were slowly incorporated into the school curriculum, until the theory of evolution was influencing every class. The acceptance of the theory of evolution was a long process. The teaching of evolution in high school classrooms is still a controversial subject. First, the basis for the teaching of evolution was that it was not religiously biased. Conversely, it was taught that the Bible was culturally and religiously biased and should not be taught as an alternative to the evolutionary model of the origin of life. Most of the early Americans learned to read using the Bible. Bible teaching was an important part of this country's history. This is the same country, which ratified the constitution, in which the first amendment effectively separates church and state. Based on the provision that the United States will not have a specific state endorsed religion, the teaching of creation has been replaced by the teachings of evolution. There is a serious problem with the current interpretation of this protection of civil rights in the constitution and its original meaning. The founding fathers came to this country for a number of reasons. One of these reasons was to escape the religious persecution of England. The early Americans generally did not believe in the views established by the Church of England, which were derived from an English version of the Roman Catholic Church. The first amendment was to ensure that this country would not become like England, imposing the religious views of the King upon the population of the country. Again, the early Americans were seeking religious freedom. The founding fathers were concerned with the government passing laws, like the ones in England, which could punish people with opposing political or religious views. The laws could impose fines, jail terms, religious persecution or excommunication. The first amendment separating church and state was added to ensure the government would not interfere with our religious freedom. Most of the founding fathers rejoiced in preachers' and religious leaders' suggestions in forming our "one nation under God." As we stated earlier, the Christian view of the universe was still taught up until the early 1960's. The school system was intended for learning. The open and free discussion of beliefs anywhere any time is a fundamental right given to every citizen by the first amendment guaranteeing free speech. This fact seams to have been forgotten in recent years. There have been recent cases in California where young Christians, 5-12 years old, were expelled from school simply for reciting John 3:16 during recess. This is persecution in the purest and most terrible form. This is a direct violation to the first amendment guaranteeing freedom of speech. We should not misuse the "no establishment of religion" clause to destroy our fundamental right of free speech. It is time to stop the religious persecution in this country. It is radical fundamentalist who believe in atheism that have made every effort to outlaw expressions of the Christian faith. The effort to eradicate our Christian heritage must be halted. Let us remember that the first amendment is to allow the free expression of any religious view.

We need to return to the perspective that the first amendment guarantees us the right to allow the full and open debate of evolution and creationism in all levels of the school system, from kindergarten through Doctorates in college universities. The recognition that the U.S. Supreme Court has changed their interpretation of the first amendment in recent years was observed by Edward J. Larson. Quote, "The establishment clause has undergone a reinterpretation by the Supreme Court in the past forty years. [6.37]" He continues to describe how the changed interpretation of the first amendment has unjustly excluded the teaching of creationism in public schools. There have been several recent attempts to return the teaching of creationism to the classroom. On May 19, 1981, Arkansas Governor Frank White signed into law Act 590. This was the bill for "The Balanced Treatment for Creation-Science and Evolution Science Act." It established a law which required that equal time be given for the teaching of evolution and creation. The act was overturned in 1982. On January 5, 1982 a Supreme Court case, Rev. Bill McLean vs. Arkansas Board of Education, decided that act 590 was unconstitutional on the following basis. Quote,

"(1) It had been passed with the specific purpose of advancing religion, (2) It had as a major effect the advancement of particular religious beliefs, (3) it created for the state of Arkansas an excessive and prohibited entanglement with religion. [6.38]" This is absurd. Act 590 was about freedom of speech not imposing religious views. It is a recent concept that religion discussions should have many limitations. The founding fathers supported the uninhibited expression of the Christian faith. Allowing evolution to be taught in public classrooms is just as much a violation of the separation of church and state clause as the theory of creationism. Evolution is a direct representation of the religious beliefs of atheism and humanism. By supporting the teaching of evolution, we are breaking the first amendment! We are sponsoring a concept of atheism as a religious view of the universe sponsored by the United States government. The constitution was designed to be amended, changed based on the will of the people. To put the issue to rest we need a constitutional amendment to, once and for all, settle the matter. I suggest an amendment that will take into account the majority of the citizens' view in a particular area. For example if a particular courthouse wants to display the Ten Commandments, it should be allowed if the majority of the citizens in the area vote to display such a monument. Let us return to our governmental principle: Majority rules and minorities have rights; not minorities rule and the majority should suffer.

It seams unreasonable to assume that it was simply a coincidence that evolution became popular and finally accepted in the public school system during the 1960's. This was a time of a great cultural revolution towards sexual freedom, rebellion against God, against religion and other symbols of authority. The theory of evolution provided a description of the universe perfectly consistent with the rebellion against God expressed on college campuses across the nation. The theory of evolution was based on belief in natural forces creating the universe and not God. This provided the basis to support the religious belief of atheism. The theory of evolution also supported the belief that the only person you can trust is yourself. This is the basic view of humanism. Humanism teaches that, since there is no God, the only thing to worship is you. Evolution teaches that you can only depend on yourself. You must remain selfish in this great "struggle for survival". Evolution teaches that we are evolving into ever greater life forms. Self awareness and self actualization concepts are supported by the philosophy of humanism. Many well educated people began looking towards other religions to support their quest for freedom from the authority of the Bible and God. In the last chapter, we will discuss some of the different religious views and conclude that these beliefs simply reduce to a question of a personal belief about Jesus Christ. Do you accept or reject Jesus Christ as savior and Lord? I believe the weight of evidence makes Christianity the only doctrine worthy of a lengthy discussion. To reemphasize, the theory of evolution supports the philosophy and beliefs of humanism and atheism. In this sense, evolutionary theory is as much a religious doctrine as creationism.

The Christian parents were extremely agitated by the atheistic view taught to their children. They knew that evolution was obviously contradicting with the biblical account. From the 1930's when these court cases began through much of the 1960's and beyond, even Pastors and Christian leaders became violent protestors for introducing evolution into the school system. Even book burning events became common. Lee Strobel shares an experience which cemented his faith in atheism and convinced him that Christians were merely radical fanatics with no knowledge of science. Lee was sent on one of his first assignment as a journalist. "The year was 1974. I was a rookie, just three months out of the University of Missouri's school of journalism. ... Crazy stuff in West Virginia. ... People getting shot at, schools getting bombed- all because some hillbillies are mad about the textbooks being used in the schools.... To me, the controversy in West Virginia was a symbolic last grasp of an archaic belief system hurtling toward oblivion. [6.39]" Throughout this book, we have referenced a number of scientific evidences that reversed Lee's beliefs that Christianity was a fraud. It was by an increased understanding of the basic principles of science that Lee Strobel became a Christian. As a Christian, I can understand the reaction of the protestors in West Virginia. Evolution was an attack against the instructions parents were giving their children. They were essentially telling their children their parents were ignorant about science, religion and everything in life. Therefore, the children were lead to believe their parents did not know what was true and what was false. Consequently, children were fueled with rebellion. Sure, children have always rebelled, but evolution was pouring gas on the fire. Besides creating dissention in the family, more importantly, evolution was a direct attack on the Christian faith. To the Christian, Jesus is Lord, Savior and best friend. Surly everyone can understand their reaction, even if you are not a Christian. How would you feel if a government program was telling you that you are not teaching your children properly and your beliefs are non-sense? How would you feel if the government was saying your best friend was nothing but a liar? Even from a world view it is understandable that the Christians reacted the way they did in the 1950's and 1960's. However, by in large, the dedicated Christian knew they were not handling the situation properly. They were not acting according to their Christian principles of "love thy neighbor". Through prayer, there has been an emotional "calming period." These days are like the original days of Christian persecution. Just as the Apostles and early followers of Christ were persecuted, so society is ridiculing our ideas and values. After looking to the scripture, Christians have sought after the Holy Spirit's guidance. Christian groups recently have realized that, in the book burning days they were not advancing their cause, they were hurting it. They were not displaying the fruits of the Holy Spirit in their life. "But the fruit of the spirit is love, joy, peace, patience, kindness, goodness, faithfulness, gentleness and self-control." Galatians 5:22 Now Christians are taking a peaceful but firm stand against the teachings of evolution based on scientific information.

Since the 1970's to the present day Christians have produced a great number of books describing the hard core scientific evidences for an intelligent design. The good news for us is that Christian perspective is winning the scientific battle. In the early days in the debate of evolution verses creation, the debate was more simply a shouting match. However, the evolutionists very often remained cool and collective as they knowingly omitted evidence for creation and taught evidence for evolution. This book explains only a handful of the many evidences for creation. The situation in the last 20 years or so has been reversed in scientific circles. However, creation scientists are still in a minority, but growing. Dr. Jonathan Wells has been an outspoken critic of evolution, which the world believes is absolutely true. In a recent newspaper article he was asked if he preferred to be in the minority or to be right. He replied that he prefers to be right, if he was in the minority, so be it. There are other scientists who are less bold. They want to avoid the outcast status in the scientific community and avoid discussing the areas of their research which can support intelligent design over evolution. Evolutionists are now showing their true colors. "Watch out for false prophets. They come to you in sheep's clothing, but inwardly are ferocious wolves. By their fruit you will recognize them." Matthew 7:15-16. This portion of scripture is referring to those professing to be follows of Christ but who preach contrary to God's Word. But this scripture also applies to the evolutionists who are becoming increasingly more violent when they are challenged in their beliefs with new scientific findings. It is sometimes very difficult for the Christian to determine which teachers are right with God's Word and which have skewed the teachings. It is far less difficult to detect obvious enemies of the Christian faith. The evolutionists are the ones that are becoming emotionally driven radical activists. As their evidence for evolution erodes, they can only bring up some moment in time a Christian, or group of professing Christians, made an error in evaluating some kind of scientific information. When all else fails, watch them bring up the unfortunate incident that religious leaders persecuted Copernicus for his view of the earth revolving around the Sun. There is strong evidence that support the creation view in science. The evidence will continue to grow as our scientific studies continue. The theory of evolution is a lie. It is slowly being exposed by the truth found in scientific study.

Racism is Supported by Evolution

If you want to know the true colors of evolution, just look at racism. The theory of evolution has been used repeatedly to support racism. Just look at the title of Darwin's 1859 publication: The Origin of Species By Means of Natural Selection; or, The Preservation of Favored Races in the Struggle for Life.

Charles Darwin portrayed that "the struggle for survival" was the ultimate creative force. Also, Darwin described the principles of selective breading that was later pursued by Hitler. "Both sexes ought to refrain from marriage if they are in any marked degree inferior in body or mind." [6.40] The Bible continually tells us we are "made in the image of God" and therefore all races are ultimately equal. "The Scripture says, 'No one who believes in him will be put to shame. 'For there is no distinction between Jew and Greek; the same Lord is Lord of all and bestows His riches upon all who call upon Him. For, 'every one who calls upon the name of the Lord will be saved.'" Romans 10:11-13 "There is neither Jew nor Greek, there is neither slave nor free, there is neither male nor female; for you are all one in Christ Jesus." Galatians 3:28 "Here there cannot be Greek and Jew, circumcised and uncircumcised, barbarian, Scythian, slave, free man, but Christ is all, and in all." Colossians 3:11. In America, it might be appropriate to substitute the names White and Black for the words Jew and Greek. However, the hatred and violence between blacks and whites have never escalated near to the level of conflict between the Greek and Jew of ancient times. Therefore, these verses truly apply to the racial and religious violence we are facing today. The evolutionists say that the color of a person's skin is the result of prolonged exposure to environmental conditions i.e. longer exposure to the sun over many generations has made the skin darker. This is obviously true, and the evolutionists say there is no harm in this. Well if you accept the Christian view that we all came from Adam and Noah, and therefore are all equal, then there is no harm in explaining race as merely different exposures to the sun. However, evolution implies even more. It implies that we all evolved from apes. This opens the door to cultural and anthropological theories about the "evolution" of society. "The astonishment which I felt on first seeing a party of Fuegians on a wild and broken shore will never be forgotten by me, for the reflection at once rushed into my mind – such were our ancestors. These men were absolutely naked and bedaubed with paint, their long hair was tangled, their mouths frothed with excitement, and their expression was wild, startled, and distrustful. They possessed hardly any arts, and like wild animals lived on what they could catch; they had no government, and were merciless to every one not of their own small tribe." [6.41] This is the type of image we receive concerning all past civilizations, primitive and violent towards anyone outside their tribe. Consider the fact that there is always "more than meets the eye" in these observations. The evolutionists believe that society has developed over time with some tribes remaining more primitive than others. This has opened the door to theories that those who stayed more tribal, and had darker skin, were less "evolved" than other groups that developed more modern societies. This led many groups to associated physical characteristics of race to intelligence and the belief that certain groups were more closely related to apes.

Some of the beliefs derived from the theory of evolution include Nazism. Hitler believed that the Aryan race was superior to all others. Blacks and Jews were believed to be from an inferior race more closely related to their ape ancestors than the Aryan race, predominately German. According to Hitler the blonde hair, blue eyed group was supposedly superior physically and mentally. The dark skin of blacks was considered a throwback to primitive man due to excessive exposure to the elements, whereas the Aryan race was developed from advancing an already superior intellect. Hitler was pushing for the development of a supreme race; supreme physically, mentally, and having the authority to rule the world. Hitler's views were supported by a belief in Evolution. Think of the story of Hitler for a moment. In 1914, Adolph Hitler joined the Germany Army and fought in World War I. In 1918, Hitler was lying in a hospital and he contemplated his war experiences. He concluded that the struggle between races was like trench warfare. This fit well into the survival of the fittest mentality of evolution. He started to believe that the ills of his country were caused by other races influencing the Germany nation. In particular he blamed the Jew for the downfall of the war. After the war he entered politics and, by July 1921, became the leader of the newly formed Nazi party. On November 28, 1923 Hitler attempted to take over the Bavarian government in the so- called "Beer Hall revolt". It was unsuccessful and Hitler was sent to prison. Hitler gained popularity through a number of means. Perhaps his greatest achievement was writing Mein Kampf while in prison. In his book Hitler specified his views of race and politics. On January 30,

1933 Hitler became chancellor of Germany. How did one desperate, jailed, defeated man take over an entire country, over-turning an existing government in just 10 years? There were many political and economic factors, but basically it was the power of convincing lies through his book Mein Kampf. This is how propaganda works; tell a lie long enough and often enough and they will believe it is the truth. You also must have some elements of truth in what you say to convince the public that everything you say is true. One of the most predominant themes of Hitler's Nazi party was the idea that the German people were superior to all other races and therefore, destined to rule the world. Hitler sited examples of German ingenuity, and then sited the theory of evolution which convinced the general public that the German race was superior to all other races. *Many people around the world were not alarmed at Hitler's movement when it first began.* For example, when Hitler was first coming to power, industrialist Henry Ford was applauding the economic growth of Germany under Hitler's leadership. Ford was also proud of his German heritage and supported Hitler's early views. There was nothing that alarmed the nations when he spoke in public. Only when his military machinery was growing at a fantastic rate were there the first signs of concern. Immediately, Hitler began to enact ant-Jewish laws. From 1933 to 1938 Hitler began separating the German people according to race. This was not alarming to world leaders and the continued economic growth of Germany, many believed, would help stabilize the world economy. The world applauded Hitler for his economic success. His views of racism were only mildly alarming to a few groups. Why? Simple, many accepted the theory of evolution and agreed with Hitler's ideas of racism. Some leaders began to become concerned when, in 1938, Germany seamed to be threatening Czechoslovakia. In September 29, 1938 the Munich Pact was signed by Germany, Italy, France, and Britain, giving part of Czechoslovakia to Germany. This was in hopes of establishing a long lasting peaceful relationship with Germany. (Arthur) Neville Chamberlain called the Munich Pact a political triumph declaring "peace in our time." Chamberlain was convinced that the Munich Pact would stabilize the world wide economy and establish peace around the world by uniting Europe. The rest is history. We know that a lasting peace was never a part of Hitler's plan but rather, world domination. This is only one extreme case of one man's faith in evolution and the principle of "survival of the fittest". It is also a demonstration of what lengths a man will reach for to become the "fittest" in the world.

Who knows how much damage the theory of evolution has caused society? The theory of evolution teaches survival of the fittest. This encourages the idea to win at any cost. The philosophy states that it's not how you play the game that matters, only if you win or lose, and you must do anything to win. This encourages violence and cheating. There is no doubt that the theory of evolution is based on a religious conviction of winning at all costs, fighting, and rebellion against God. Is it any wonder we have so much violence in our schools today? The theory allows people a "reasonable" excuse for any action a person wants to take. Since the theory states that we came from animals, a person can do or say anything and reply that it is his nature to do these things. Phrases like "the animal in me made me do it" takes a whole new meaning when defended by the theory of evolution. "For although they knew God, they neither glorified him as God nor gave thanks to him, but their thinking became futile and there foolish hearts were darkened. Although they claimed to be wise, they became fools and exchanged the glory of the immortal God for images made to look like mortal man and birds and animals and reptiles. Therefore God gave them over in the sinful desires of their hearts to sexual impurity for the degrading of their bodies with one another. They exchanged the truth of God for a lie, and worshiped and served created things rather than the Creator who is forever praised. Amen. Because of this, God gave them over to shameful lusts. Even their women exchanged natural relations for unnatural ones. In the same way the men also abandoned natural relations with women and were inflamed with lust for one another. Men committed indecent acts with other men, and received in themselves the due penalty for their perversion. Furthermore, since they did not think it worthwhile to retain the knowledge of God, he gave them over to a depraved mind; to do what ought not to be done. They have become filled with every kind of wickedness, evil, greed and depravity. They are full of envy, murder, strife, deceit and malice. They are gossips, slanderers, God-haters, insolent, arrogant and boastful; they invent ways of doing evil; they disobey their parents; they are senseless, faithless, heartless, and ruthless." Romans 1:21-31. It seams clear that these verses in Romans are clearly describing the theory of evolution and the results of accepting such a belief in natural forces creating everything over the super-natural power of God. In this passage of scripture, is an extensive list of the fate of any person or society that believes in evolution. Doesn't this list reflect the state of the world today? Despite the terrible consequences of believing in evolution, I do not support its total abandonment of teaching some of the principles of evolution in public schools. One reason is that I do not believe it is currently possible to totally remove the theory of evolution from the public school system. Second, the law which must be upheld is freedom of speech. This would encourage the free and continuous discussion of ideas explored by science. The debate between evolution and creationism will not be ended until Christ returns. However, the freedom to discuss the issue should always be encouraged. There are far too many scientific facts that are purposely left out of High School and College Biology textbooks that discredit the theory of evolution. We can be assured that if a person looks at *all* the evidence rationally, there can be only one conclusion: The Bible is the one and only infallible Word of God and our best source for learning.

Why is there so much racism in this century? Many atheist scientists have tried to convince the world, that without a belief in God we would have enormous benefits. This opinion is fully demonstrated in the movie The DaVinci Code. In the movie one of the charters, Sir Ian McKellen, concludes his point by saying that "the Church" has held back mankind from achieving success on every level. I am concerned that a number of people are convinced of this lie. What I found almost equally disturbing is that the hero of the movie, Dr. Langdon, proposes that Sir Isaac Newton and the church were life long enemies. Many people believe this lie that science and religion are exact opposites. We will explore more information about Newton's views in the next chapter. People like the DaVinci Code character Sir Ian McKellen, have tried to convince us that through intellectual achievement we can solve any problem. If we only educate the world enough, racism would disappear. With enough education, they teach us that we would realize the logic in "love thy neighbor". Has this happened? No. Just the opposite has occurred. The reason why is simple, their attempt to write God out of the history of creation has had disastrous side effects. One obvious problem is racism. According to evolution, we began as apes and lived as cave men for a time. They point to tribes in Africa, Asia, or on islands like Australia as examples of ancient cultures. The theory states that, as man's physical form changed from apes to present humans, our mental abilities also developed. Skin color is also a factor in determining racial development. Some tribes developed agricultural cultures instead of tribal hunting parties. After centuries, of "evolving" these skills, some tribes were more capable of intellectual pursuits. As these groups spent less time in the sun, their skin color became lighter. Some evolutionists do not speak about the development of race too often, because they realize the violent response they would receive, although some followers of evolution, such as Hitler, spoke their views loud and clear. His arguments were supported by evolutionists who taught that skin color and physical features determined the magnitude of evolutionary development. For example, skull size has been considered an indication of mental growth. This would mean any man of small stature was considered mentally inferior as well as physically inferior. Tell this to some of our world renowned men of science with an average size skull. Skull size is still used, to some extent, by evolutionists to determine brain development. Many archaeological finds have encountered a great many skull fragments indicating skeletal size to be on average, smaller than modern man. This is considered conclusive proof of intellectual inferiority. This is an absurd idea, but is one of the pillars of the beliefs from scientists who support the theory of evolution. It seams to me that intelligence has little or nothing to do with skull size. A child who grew up 1,000 years ago, lets say from birth to age 15, could develop small skeletal size because of a lack of calcium in his diet, or other factors. Exposure to few teachers and little knowledge would make his I.Q. small compared to a similar average child of the twentieth century. However, let us perform a simple thought experiment. Lets us take and average 3 month old baby from the twentieth century and place him in a tribe living 1,000 years ago. Similarly, let's take a baby from that same tribe and transport him to an average American household in the twentieth century. Let us say they both grow normally both physically and mentally with no unusual diseases. The child living 1,000 years ago grows up to be an average adolescent for that time. The primitive child growing up in the twentieth century develops normally. With proper resources, teachers and tutors it is possible that this "primitive" child at age 15 could enter college with a 4.0 high school record! The child could develop exceptional skills in the twentieth century. The 15 year old in the tribe, accomplishes great things and becomes a warrior. Compare I.Q.'s at this time and you will find the child of the tribe sorely lacking in knowledge because of unavailability of information. It would appear, on the surface, that I have just proven a fundamental principle of evolution. The principle that environment shapes the development of a species. This is not true. Evolution states that environment controls not only emotional and intellectual development but physical development as well. The evolutionary theories also state that there are no limits to this development. Many theories of evolution state that physical development necessary go hand in hand with mental development. This is not always true. If it were, it would mean that every great athlete would always be a genius and everyone physically deprived would be little more than mental vegetables. This is obviously untrue. I believe that it is important to grow spiritually, physically, and mentally as much as possible. However, evolutionary theory states that this process makes some superior to others. Evolutionist would have you believe that we are somehow more "evolved" or better than those primitive tribes. In some ways we have made progress, but in the basic aptitudes we are all the same. In the theory of evolution, knowledge somehow makes us have a conciseness. This is how we supposedly developed from apes. Apes learned new things, explored their surroundings and eventually developed the human characteristics. Time, and exploration of their environment, was supposed to allow the physical characteristics of man and the spiritual, emotional, and intellectual characteristics to be developed. This is contrary to the biblical concept of man made in the image of God. The theory of evolution gives abilities that do not exist to animals, and degrades man in every sense. Man is not made in the "image of the beast".

This brings us to the question of human thought. Are we simply just a bunch of chemicals, or something more? Many renowned scientists have been convinced that there is more to the human mind than just chemicals. "One scientist whose opinions were reversed on the issue is Wilder Penfield, the renowned father of modern neurosurgery. ... Penfield ended up agreeing with the Bible's assertion that human beings are both body and spirit. ... Penfield electrically stimulated the brains of epilepsy patients and found he could cause them to move their arms or legs, turn their heads or eyes, talk, or swallow. ... Invariably the patient would respond by saying, 'I didn't do that. You did. ... No matter how much Penfield probed the cerebral cortex, he said, 'There is no place ... where electrical stimulation will cause a patient to believe or decide. That's because those functions originate in the conscious self, not the brain. [6.42]" This is one of the most difficult subjects to explore. There seams to be an unexplainable dual nature to the mind. There is a physical property to the mind that controls the body, yet no one can grasp the nature of thought. "(Nobel prize winner) physicist and atheist Steven Weinberg said scientists may have to 'bypass the problem of human consciousness' altogether, because 'it may just be too hard for us.'[6.43]"

Understanding the inner workings of the human mind is extremely difficult. Sure, we know that different regions of the brain control different physical behavior, but what causes the formation of thoughts in our minds. There have long existed two approaches to understanding brain activity. One is to emphasize the importance of individual neurons. The other is to show the interaction of neurons collectively to form a vast communication network. The answer to approaching an understanding of brain activity may indeed lie in a combination of both approaches. "The two prevailing models, which have been at odds since their founders were jointly awarded the Nobel Prize 100 years ago, are both relevant. Indeed, by joining the models and adding a third, yet unanswered piece to the puzzle raised by recent research – how brain cells give rise to brain waves – we can finally explain not only how the human brain works but also what makes it unique in the animal world. ... Why are the capabilities of the human brain so superior to those of all other animals? The neurons in animals' brains are not all that different; even the fly exploits the same neurotransmitters. ... (Theodore H.) Bullock had begun to explore brain waves in a variety of animals. ... He determined that patterns of brain waves in humans differed markedly from those of simpler animals. Brain waves arise from the collective activity of thousands of neurons working together. ... Work by Bullock and others also showed that the electrical activity in different groups is often coupled, even though the neurons are not physically connected. ... Perhaps, Bullock suggested, the unparalleled abilities of the human mind arise not as a unique property of our neurons or brain circuitry but as an emergent property of the way its billions of neurons operate cooperatively. But how is activity in different neurons coordinated?" [6.44]" The article goes own to suggest some form of convergence in brain wave frequencies to explain this coordination of neurons and the thought process. One thing this research makes clear: the reason we are different from animals is found in our brain waves. Brain waves are electromagnetic signals i.e. a form of light. Again, proof that we are made in the image of God. Roger Penrose, whose brilliant work with Stephan Hawking we mentioned earlier, proposes a radical explanation to understanding the human mind. "If the fundamental levels of reality are more informational than material, as quantum physics suggests, then consciousness may be the interface between the fundamental quantum world of information and the 'classical' physical world that is more accessible to our senses. ... Penrose proposed that consciousness was a quantum computation within the brain, an infinitesimal collapse of quantum information into classical information that takes place at the level of the neurons. [6.45]" These theories offer further evidence of the Christian perspective. In chapter 9 we will explore more about the field of quantum physics. In chapter 2 we explored how recent experiments merge quantum physics with string theory. Combined with the above observations we may conclude that science has essentially told us: 1) We have an eternal soul. Brain waves are timeless in nature as they may be propagated electromagnetic waves freed from the constraints of physical dimensions. 2) We are made in the image of God and not from animals. We have brain waves, a form of light or spirit, in our minds that is similar to God yet He is infinite we are finite. Again, Man is not made in the "image of the beast", but made in the image of God. 3) Heaven is a real place where God and His Son Jesus Christ reside. Heaven may be the 5th dimension to the universe. 4) God hears our prayers. Our brain waves, our thoughts are received by God through the 5th dimensional quantum-flux gateway, possibly. 5) He can answer our prayers through the Holy Spirit. God can answer prayer in various ways including in the form of visions as described in scripture. 6) Every verse in the Holy Bible concerning prayer is absolutely true! "Do not be anxious about anything, but in everything, by prayer and petition, with thanksgiving, present your requests to God. And the peace of God, which transcends all understanding, will guard your hearts and your minds in Christ Jesus." Philippians 4:6,7. "For the eyes of the Lord are on the righteous and his ears are attentive to their prayer, but the face of the Lord is against those who do evil." 1 Peter 3:12. We are coming ever closer to explaining God's word through science. We are learning How God has created the universe, the human mind and all life. This does not somehow eliminate God but in fact gives us an endless number of reasons to praise His Holy name and share our faith in the author and finisher of all things – Jesus Christ.

The process of forming ideas is largely based on information you believe is accurate. This is where faith is such an integral part of life that you can never eliminate your personal beliefs totally from any discussion, especially discussions concerning science. What scientific information do you believe is true? Do you trust the source? Do you believe the conclusions presented are logical? You must ask yourself these questions. How can we summarize the situation? The proponents of intelligent design merely want to accomplish two tasks. First and foremost, we need to update current textbooks to include the evidence for intelligent design. Many opponents to this proposal react violently and emotionally. Some newspaper articles assert that, to introduce this idea into the public school system is to take a step backward in science. Tell me this, how is adding new scientific information taking a step backward in science? We have cited many examples where the theory of evolution has failed on a purely scientific basis. Why is scientific information that may conflict with the evolutionary theory purposely excluded from science textbooks? For example, there is currently no known method of producing a living cell from a vat of organic chemicals. The Stanley Miller experiment is mentioned predominantly in science textbooks, where the proteins as organic building blocks are produced. But, as we have seen, this is far from showing a proven connection with the formation of life. Yet, the student is left with the impression that life has been proven to have begun by chemical means. What happens if a student decides to pursue a career in biochemistry and finds their instructions severely lacking in this area of study? Imagine a student who advances to become a graduate student at a prominent university. He is assigned to help a professor work on the problem of what conditions existed in earth's early atmosphere to produce life. How embarrassing! For years he believed that this problem was solved by the Stanley Miller experiment. Now, who is behind in scientific knowledge? By ignoring these scientific discoveries which question the validity of evolution, students are falling behind in their education. The atheists who support evolution, only cares about the perpetuation of their beliefs. This makes us once again return to the effect these images had on Lee Strobel. The student is "brainwashed" into believing that evolution is a proven fact. The technique is classic. Just like Hitler and his associates developed brainwashing into almost an art form. The indoctrination process begins with showing only one side of an argument. Then, bombard the listener with images and words that present a clear picture of the falsehood you wish to represent. It was very effective for Hitler, and it has been very effective by evolutionists worldwide today. What intelligent design is proposing is to remove the religious indoctrination already present in our schools. There is an established religion of atheism already being taught. Atheism, again, is a faith that there is no God. Lee Strobel is a perfect example of how science taught in schools brought him to a belief in atheism. His books also allow us to see how it is the lack of scientific information in schools that has caused the false assumption that science has proven evolution. Why is there so much censorship in public schools? The student is prompted to ask questions, but not too many. If a student were to ask how exactly cells developed from chemicals, the teacher would simply reply, we don't know. If a cleaver student asked if we could see the fossils representing all the transitional creatures in Darwin's tree of life, that field trip could not take place. Not because the school could not afford the trip or the pictures, but because the fossils do not exist! The teacher is left with the dilemma that these scientific questions can not be answered. The real conflict is when the teacher is a Christian and knows the answers to these questions from the Bible. However, he or she can not answer the student because it is a "religious" discussion that can not take place in public schools.

We need to remove or minimize the influence of the religion of atheism in the public school system. What is amazing is how blinded the world seams to be from seeing atheism as a religion. Is there a conspiracy? Are there forces at work to keep most parents, students and teachers blind to the doctrine of this belief? The answer is YES! The source of this conspiracy is not from a correlated effort of the scientific community. They are just pawns in the struggle between God and Satan that is as old as the beginning of universe. My wife and I intend to write a book on the spiritual war we are all involved in. We plan to describe details of how we can understand this war and what we can do about it. We will detail the effects, the weapons at our disposal and what the Bible tells us of what our enemy can and can not do. There are many victims of the spiritual war. Some include well meaning scientists who believe they are supporting scientific pursuit, when in reality they retard information from the school system to protect their theory of evolution. "For though we walk in the flesh, we do not war after the flesh: (For the weapons of our warfare are not carnal, but mighty through God to the pulling down of the strong holds;) Casting down imaginations, and every high thing that exalteth itself against the knowledge of God, and bringing into captive every thought to the obedience of Christ." 2 Corinthians 10:3-5. KJV.

The conflict between evolution and creationism is not about science verses religion but rather censorship verses freedom of speech. Freedom of speech has been eroding within all public places in recent decades. It seams that if you do not conform to the religion of the day, i.e. atheism or agnosticism, you are considered a radical. This is evident in Pastors who have been fined or arrested for expressing political views in Church. There is no way to totally avoid a religious discussion, nor should you. Christians today are often persecuted for expressing their faith because it opposes the established religion of agnosticism. There are certain points in science where there can be no avoidance of a religious discussion. The scientific pursuit is to seek answers to all questions and inevitably that endeavor introduces questions that can only be discussed on a religious basis. The most common source for these discussions is found in the search for origins. The origin of life or the origin of the universe can not be approached without some in depth study of religion. The only question is how do you handle the situation? Do you calmly examine the evidences or become offended if someone disagrees with your personal convictions? To accept the theory of evolution would require an unbelievable amount of faith. The theory of evolution requires a total disregard to time honored laws of physics. The next set of chapters on mathematics and physics will give the reader a better understanding of the ideas discussed in earlier chapters on Astronomy. The theory of evolution is more of a religious concept than a scientific theory. There is no reason to accept the fundamental principles of evolution on the basis of scientific evidence. The facts simply do not give the theory of evolution enough support to conclude that the concepts are true. These facts should be openly and freely discussed in public schools. We should not tolerate the current display of censorship in scientific information that opposes evolution.

References for Chapter 6

6.1   Josh McDowell & Don Stewart, Reasons Skeptics Should Consider Christianity, Wheaton, Illinois, Living Books, Tyndale House Publishers, 1981, p. 202.

6.2   Ibid, p. 202-203.

6.3   Ibid, p. 203-204.

6.4   Ibid, p. 205.

6.5   Ibid, p. 205-208.

6.6   Ibid, p. 219.

6.7   John F. Ashton, In Six Days: Why Fifty Scientists choose to believe in Creation, Master Books, 2000-2003, p. 150-151.

6.8   Josh McDowell & Don Stewart, Reasons Skeptics Should Consider Christianity, Wheaton, Illinois, Living Books, Tyndale House Publishers, 1981, p. 220.

6.9   Ibid, p. 222.

6.10   Ibid, p. 222.

6.11   Ibid, p. 222-224.

6.12   Ibid, p. 216.

6.13   Ibid, p. 216-218.

6.14   Ibid, p. 211-212.

6.15   Ibid, p. 218-219.

6.16   Ibid, p. 209.

6.17   Ibid, p. 209.

6.18   Ibid, p. 211.

6.19   Ibid, p. 220.

6.20   John F. Ashton, In Six Days: Why Fifty Scientists choose to believe in Creation, Master Books, 2000-2003, p. 92-96.

6.21   Josh McDowell & Don Stewart, Answers To Tough Questions skeptics ask about the Christian faith, San Bernardino, California, Here's Life Publishers, Inc., 1980, p. 198.

6.22   Ibid, p. 199-201.

6.23   John F. Ashton, In Six Days: Why Fifty Scientists choose to believe in Creation, Master Books, 2000-2003, p. 96-97.

6.24   Ibid, p. 232-233.

6.25   Theodore L. Brown and H. Eugene LeMay, Chemistry: The Central Science, Prentice-Hall Inc, 1977, p. 597.

6.26   Raymond A. Serway, Physics For Scientists & Engineers with Modern Physics Third edition, Philadelphia, Saunders College Publishing, 1990, p. 1363.

6.27   Theodore L. Brown and H. Eugene LeMay, Chemistry: The Central of Science, Prentice-Hall Inc, 1977, p. 598-599.

6.28   James S. Trefil, From Atoms To Quarks: An Introduction to the Strange World of Particle Physics, New York, Charles Scribner's Sons, 1980, p. 26, 28-29.

6.29   Ibid, p. 26-27.

6.30   Josh McDowell & Don Stewart, Reasons Skeptics Should Consider Christianity, Wheaton, Illinois, Living Books, Tyndale House Publishers, 1981, p. 106-107.

6.31   Ibid, p. 111- 113.

6.32   Ibid, p. 108.

6.33   John F. Ashton, In Six Days: Why Fifty Scientists choose to believe in Creation, Master Books, 2000-2003, p. 281.

6.34   Josh McDowell & Don Stewart, Reasons Skeptics Should Consider Christianity, Wheaton, Illinois, Living Books, Tyndale House Publishers, 1981, p. 117-119.

6.35   Edited by Sheldon Grebstein, Monkey Trial, Houghton-Mifflin Research Series No. 4. Cambridge, Mass., The Riverside Press, 1960, p.1-2.

6.36   Edward J. Larson, Trial & Error: The American Controversy Over Creation And Evolution, Oxfords University Press, 1989, summary of p. 90.

6.37   Ibid, p. 93.

6.38   Marcel Chatkowski La Falletle, Creationism, Science, and the Law: The Arkansas Case., The Mass. Institute of Technology, The President & Fellows of Harvard College, 1984, p.1-2.

6.39   Lee Strobel, The Case for A Creator, Zondervan, Grand Rapids Michigan. 2004, p. 8, 16.

6.40   Charles Darwin, The Descent of Man, and Selection in Relation to Sex, 1871, New edition, revised and augmented. Published by D. Appleton and Company, New York, 1896, p. 617.

6.41   Ibid, p.618-619.

6.42   Lee Strobel, The Case for A Creator, Zondervan, Grand Rapids Michigan. 2004, p. 249, 258.

6.43   Ibid, p. 269.

6.44   R. Douglas Fields, Beyond The Neuron Doctrine, Scientific American Mind, June/July 2006. p. 22-27.

6.45   Jay Tolson, Is There Room for the Soul?, U.S. News & World Report, October 23,2006, p. 63.

Illustrations for Chapter 6

6.1   Josh McDowell & Don Stewart, Reasons Skeptics Should Consider Christianity, Wheaton, Illinois, Living Books, Tyndale House Publishers, 1981, p. 221.

6.2   Raymond A. Serway, Physics For Scientists & Engineers with Modern Physics Third edition, Philadelphia, Saunders College Publishing, 1990, both sides: p. 1365.

6.3   Josh McDowell & Don Stewart, Reasons Skeptics Should Consider Christianity, Wheaton, Illinois, Living Books, Tyndale House Publishers, 1981, p. 109.

Chapter 7: Calculus and Modern Mathematics
It's all about Relationships
A Study of Limits

Mathematics is the language of science. Through mathematics, the physical relationships are related. For example, in the study of Newton's laws of force, the definition and principles of a force is defined mathematically. A force is defined as a push or pull on something which has the magnitude of the mass of an object multiplied by the acceleration of the object in a vacuum, F=ma. The importance of mathematics will be discussed throughout the next three chapters. This will include numerous examples of mathematics used in the fields of science such as classical principles of physics, modern physics, and the use of mathematical expressions to describe geometric shapes. Geometry is considered a field in mathematics dealing with standardized shapes, such as the circle or a triangle. Mathematics is needed to describe physical relationships, which are needed to give practical uses for mathematic principles. The interconnecting of mathematics and the physical sciences is a natural part of the two fields. In particular the connection between mathematics and physics is virtually inseparable. Consequently, most books on mathematics include practical, physical problems solved by mathematical calculations. These are usually the same kinds of questions that can be found in a textbook introducing the subject of physics. Most physics textbooks assume a working knowledge of mathematics. It is necessary to introduce a few basic principles of mathematics before describing physical principles. It is the intention of this section of the book to prepare you for discussions about mathematical principles and relationships in the high school or higher science classes. Therefore, I have decided to follow the traditional approach of providing a basic understanding of mathematics before discussing physical principles.

Relationships and Geometry

Mathematics is the study of relationships. It is necessarily to have a firm grasp of mathematical concepts to explore other fields of science. Many people don't realize the importance of understanding mathematical concepts beyond simple addition, subtraction, multiplication and division. They feel that after they have had the required mathematical courses, particularly courses such as algebra and geometry, many students believe they will never use the information again. They are very much mistaken! We use geometry every day whether we realize it or not. Besides engineering fields such as electrical engineering, mechanical engineering and other fields, people use geometry every day. The direction you take with your car as you come home from work is an example of using geometry and directional vector analysis. When you decide whether or not you have enough time to stop at the grocery store on the way home from work, you are using geometry principles unconsciously. Any time we make calculations, like how long it takes you to go from point A to point B we are using both algebra and geometry. We roughly know the distance between the two points, for instance the distance from home to work. Also, we know the approximate average speed we travel between the two points. Through repetitious experience we have a good approximation of how long it takes to drive between home and work. Taking into account variable factors such as traffic conditions and light signals, we can determine approximately the amount of time required to journey home. With this knowledge, we can determine if we have sufficient time to stop for coffee or gas. This is one example in which we make mathematical calculations each day subconsciously. Mathematics affects our lives every day in ways we don't even realize. Our minds are constantly working calculations to make decisions. This is basic principles of mathematics, i.e. to take known information and use it in calculations to determine new information. For instance, you have $10. You wish to buy an item which costs $4. Now you want to know how much money you will have left over after you buy the item. This can be expressed as $10-$4= X. Completing the subtraction makes X have the value of $6. As you can see we use algebra all the time without realizing it. This is simply one of many possible examples we could use to show how we use mathematical equations in our daily lives.

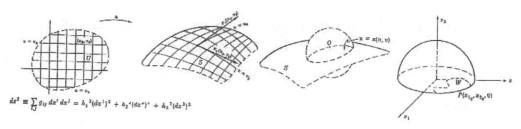

$$ds^2 \equiv \sum_{i,j} g_{ij}\, dx^i\, dx^j = h_1^{\,2}(dx^1)^2 + h_2^{\,2}(dx^2)^2 + h_3^{\,2}(dx^3)^2$$

Figure 7.1

Introduction to Geometry

Geometry is a study of shapes and measurements. Geometry is the picture representation of mathematical expressions. Standard geometric shapes represent the first step in categorizing the physical world. We stated previously that one definition of science is the systematic pursuit of knowledge. The next step is to categorize this information and specify the conditions the principles hold true. Geometry allows us to analyze the world in an idealized frame of reference. For example, we study different types of 4 sided objects and place these objects in categories. These objects can be given one of the following classifications: a square, rectangle, parallelogram, rhombus or trapezoid. If you wish to find a particular property of one of these objects, say the area, you must use the appropriate mathematical formula. The study often begins by imagining one side of the object and therefore, works in only 2-dimensions. When we extend this analysis to three dimensions, we must adjust the formula. A classic example is with a cylinder. The top of a cylinder rod can be considered a circle and the area of the top is given by the equation: area $= \pi r^2$. However, to calculate the lateral surface area over the entire length of the rod we must take into account the length of the object: Area $= 2\pi rh$ and the volume in the sphere $= \pi r^2 h$. We must remember that when we are calculating actual physical objects, seldom are these objects perfect illustrations of these examples. In other words, seldom do you find a perfect square or cylinder. This brings us back to some of the limitations in any scientific study. When we examine an object, we are assuming that it perfectly fits into one of our previously designated categories. Since this is never truly the case, we must admit to some amount of experimental error. We can approximate our calculations to estimate values of the properties we are analyzing, but there is always a limit to our accuracy. Second, we must exactly specify what we are analyzing and keep the experiment as free as possible from unknown outside influences. This is what is meant by laboratory conditions. In the real world, not the imagination of the scientists, there is no truly isolated system. There is always external forces that will effect our experimental results. Even in the best laboratory conditions, some experimental error is accepted.

Through geometry, science becomes practically an art form. When we briefly reviewed the strange higher mathematical concept of tensor analysis in General Relativity in previous chapters, we saw just how far mathematics can be pushed to represent ideas in a complex from, see figure 7.1 and review the section on tensor analysis in chapter 2. In the laws of physics we will study in the next two chapters, we will demonstrate the use of mathematics to express relationships. Geometry displays functions on graphs. A function simply describes the dependence of one or more quantities to another quantity or set of quantities in terms of variables. A function is usually represented as: f(x), pronounced the function f of x. The function is represented by a combination of independent variables and dependent variables. In the case of f(x) the dependent variable is the x. For example, f(x) = x+y is the equation for a straight line. If you draw a straight horizontal line on an x-y plane, you represent this function. Points along the line are determined by placing numerical values in the equation for the function. The graph of a function is a mathematically precise picture representing a physical relationship. Figure 7.1 shows a few more complex functions than your standard triangle. Figure 7.1 shows (a) a flattened surface part of a sphere, (b) another section of the surface of a sphere, (c) a sphere with a 2-dimensional plane slicing the center and (d) the top half of the sphere. The equations below the caption show a representation of the 3-dimensions of space. These equations were mentioned in the first three chapters on Astronomy. Einstein showed that the overall structure of space was like a sphere, indicating the universe is expanding in all directions like a balloon getting bigger and bigger. Figure 7.2 is a graphic representation of the gravitational field, and lines of force due to a black hole, as previously discussed. Figure 7.1 represents a non-Euclidian, or curved, coordinate system. More about curvilinear or non-Euclidian reference systems will be discussed later in our discussion of tensors. Einstein showed that the overall geometry of the universe was curved due to the pull of all the gravitational forces generated by all material bodies. The stars, the planets, and all other objects in the universe are supposedly responsible for this effect. There is one other piece to the puzzle; dark matter. We mentioned this in previous chapters briefly. It is still a scientific mystery to what "dark matter" actually may be. All that is known is that something is acting like a gravitational force and holding the universe together as the universe gradually expands and spreads out material.

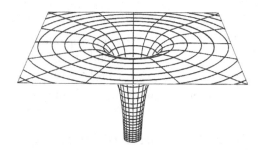

Figure 7.2

Common and Uncommon Coordinate Systems

In this section, I simply want you to be aware of the fact that there are a virtually endless number of geometric shapes and a multitude of ways to express the same shape in different forms. When expressing a geometric form, you can use any number of coordinate systems. The coordinate systems most often used in science courses are rectilinear (the x-y line system). This is used when you are talking about analyzing the system by use of a flat surface, like a sheet of paper, called a two-dimensional plane. In these situations you draw a horizontal line representing the x-axis and a vertical line to represent the y-axis. Any point on this paper is represented by co-ordinates x and y. The point P (4,3) for example, represents a point four units to the right and three units up from the point of origin. If you are talking about all three dimensions the line going into and out of the paper is usually called the z- axis. There are many other coordinate systems which can be used when you are talking about three dimensional objects. Sometimes they simplify calculations because the objects are related by an angle, or the objects are spherical in nature. Some other examples of coordinate systems include the polar and the spherical coordinate systems. Different coordinate systems are used because they make it easier to express certain theoretical concepts. The coordinates in one system can determine the coordinates in any other system through coordinate transformation equations. These equations can become very complex in advanced mathematics such as the coordinate transformations from rectilinear coordinates and the non-Euclidean coordinates used in tensor analysis like those shown in figure 7.1.

There are many uses to these graphic representations. They can help us visualize many theoretical concepts. For example, imagine a tree in the center of figure 7.2. This picture makes a good graphic representation of our relationship with God through Christ as described in the scriptures. Christ said, "I am the true vine, and my Father is the vinedresser. Each branch of mine that bears no fruit, he takes away, and every branch that does bear fruit he prunes, that it may bear more fruit. Abide in me, and I in you. As the branch cannot bear fruit by itself, unless it abides in the vine, neither can you, unless you abide in me. I am the vine, you are the branches. He who abides in me, and I in him, he it is that bears much fruit, for apart from me you can do nothing." John 15:1, 2, 4-5. We can see in the illustration, figure 7.2, the bond between man and God, through Jesus Christ and the power of the Holy Spirit. When we become

Christians and are saved from our sins, we are yoked with Jesus through the Holy Spirit. "Come to me, all who labor and are heavy laden, and I will give you rest. Take my yoke upon you, and learn from me; for I am gentle and lowly in heart, and you will find rest for your souls. For my yoke is easy, and my burden is light." Mathew 11:28-30. When you accept Christ into your life, he promises to be with you through your daily lives. Christ and the saved sinner are bonded forever. Again, refer to figure 7.2. We are represented by a point somewhere on one of the lines of force. Following the tunnel down, imagine it reaches a single point. The point where the tunnel would end is where the Lord Jesus resides, in His heavenly kingdom. The lines of force in the illustration represent the Holy Spirit which influences our lives, pulling our will towards the kingdom of God. Our spiritual position changes during our lives. When we first accept Christ as Savior, we are on the outer edges of the diagram. We have accepted by faith, Christ as Savior and Lord. We have been changed, born again. However, we are spiritually babies and do not know how to live the new life we have begun in the Lord. As we learn more about the principles of living the Christian life, we grow towards Christ. We receive guidance from the Holy Spirit as we read God's word. We also receive help from pastors and friends that strengthen our faith. We continue to grow in wisdom until we have a continuing close personal relationship with Jesus Christ. To be a Christian requires a certain lifestyle. We plan to explain some of the guidelines to a "typical" Christian lifestyle in an upcoming book.

Jesus the Center of all Things

Some Christians reach a point where they just spin in circles. They go around and around, following one of the circles in figure 7.2. This illustrates a point in a Christian's life where they go to church, go through the motions of a Christian, but have lost their desire to learn and grow towards a closer relationship with Christ. The Lord does not approve of this condition of the spirit. We are commanded to seek wisdom, and learn to serve God more each day. We are asked by God to become a more effective witness of the presence of Christ in our lives. We are commanded to bring others the knowledge of the saving grace of Jesus Christ. "He said to them, 'Go into all the world and preach the good news to all creation.'" Mark 16:5. We are also to become teachers of the word of God. "For though by this time you ought to be teachers, you need some one to teach you again the first principles of God's word. You need milk not solid food; for every one who lives on milk is unskilled in the Word of Righteousness, for he is a child. But solid food is for the mature, for those who have their faculties trained by practice to distinguish good from evil." Hebrews 5:12-14. Some other Christians move backwards. Some call this backsliding. However, the relationship began by faith in Christ is not broken, just strained. Christians who re-evaluate their commitment to God may go to the outer edges of God's influence of the Holy Spirit, but the Holy Spirit is still in their lives. Most Christians can recall struggles they have had where their faith was weakened by tragic events. However, if you earnestly seek the Lord in prayer, God will bring about the circumstances in your life to be brought back to a path towards a close relationship with Jesus Christ. Look at figure 7.2 and imagine that different points on the intersection of two lines are different times in your life when you were far from Christ and times you were filled with the Spirit and therefore close to the Lord. The intersecting lines can also represent the intersection of friends and family that have encouraged you to "walk on the narrow road" while continuing on there own journey of faith.

Using illustrations helps us focus our minds on biblical principles. Science can be a means for appreciating and visualizing the power of God. Remember, "The heavens are telling the glory of God; and the firmament proclaims his handiwork." Psalms 19:1. Jesus used parables to relate physical situations to spiritual realities, see Matthew chapters 20, 21, 22, and 25. There are many more biblical references demonstrating the usage of parables to help others understand the principles of Biblical doctrine. I am using a similar procedure by using geometry to illustrate certain biblical principles. The purpose of these illustrations is to recognize your spiritual position relative to the ideal position of becoming in complete harmony with the will of Christ. Once you recognize your relative position, you need to take steps to constantly improve that position. This is the path which leads your life toward a truly abundant life, in Christ Jesus. Jesus said, "I came that they might have life, and have it abundantly." John 10:10. The Holy Spirit gives us guidance in times of making educated decisions. Through the Holy Spirit tugging at your heart, you are directed to follow the actions which are pleasing to God. Remember, in our illustration; see figure 7.2, the lines of force is pulling you towards the center of the tunnel. This represents the Holy Spirit pulling your heart down the long and narrow path towards a perfect relationship with God. God requires perfection. "You, therefore, must be perfect, as your heavenly Father is perfect." Mathew 5:48. To help keep our minds and hearts in perfect harmony with the will of God, read the Bible, pray continuously and seek wisdom from the Holy Spirit. The verses in John 14, written previously, describe God as a vinedresser pruning our lives to become better servants. The "pruning shears" God uses to change our lives is the Holy Spirit acting on our hearts. Sometimes God "prunes" us with difficult struggles that help our faith stretch and grow.

Lesson 1: Line Intervals

Now, let us turn our attention to some basic principles of mathematics you will encounter in high school curriculum. In the beginning of most textbooks on mathematics, even calculus textbooks, we learn about numerical sequences. Also, the simple mathematical operations like addition, subtraction, multiplication and division are discussed. These two topics, line intervals and numerical operators have numerous applications. There are many companies that use math skills on tests to verify that the applicants have basic problem solving abilities. They are especially useful when applying for a management position and test the ability of applicants to think logically. A line interval is a representation of a sequence of numbers. The numbers usually begin with zero as a point of origin and the numbers continue in both the positive and negative directions to infinity. Most line intervals show a sequence of numbers in increments of one unit. However, some show a sequence of numbers in other intervals. For example, the numerical sequence from zero to 30 counting by threes, 0, 3, 6, 9 ... etc. Some tests include out- of- order number sequences, 0, 3, 21, 4, 28, etc. Then the question will ask: what number comes next? These types of questions are designed to test our abilities to logically evaluated a set of circumstances and conclude what is true and what is false. In this way, principles of mathematics become the basis of principles of logic and philosophy. Some theologians contend that religion and logic do not have anything in common. This is ridiculous. As we have seen, faith is the result of facts you believe to be true. You start with the axioms you accept as true, then you base other assumptions on these accepted facts. This is where faith extends our accepted truth. What ideas or principles do you accept as true? This is your point of origin on which you form a basis for you religious belief system. Next, you build on that foundation ideas and opinions you accept by faith as true. "If you hold to my teaching, you are really my disciples. Then you will know the truth and the truth will set you free." John 8: 31-32. In all mathematical operations you must begin with a point of origin. Our preoccupation with our beginning is expressed in the fields of science we have already discussed. Starting with the origin of the universe in the study of astronomy and continuing through biology and the search for the origin of life. A person, who by faith, believes that only presently "provable" events are acceptable tends to dismiss the possibility of super-natural events. People with this type of faith are sometimes called a naturalist or atheist. They believe that only things you can prove in laboratory conditions are to be accepted as true. According to their belief, anything else is to be treated with skepticism. Therefore, some call these groups who believe in atheism, skeptics. The difficulty in accepting this philosophy is that there are a number of events that can not be explained by science, but obviously have occurred. Most of these events are dealing with our scientific investigation into our point of origin. The decision that is made by faith is, does a person believe in God or an unknown natural force creating our point of origin? We can not express enough how ridiculous the atheistic faith is. Atheists believe that random forces beyond scientific explanation created the universe and life. In other words, they believe a random force similar to forces we can understand but totally beyond any present day description, performed the same actions as the Bible has declared the Lord God has done. Why not just accept that the God described in the Bible supernaturally performed these acts? The answer lies in a faith in random forces, to attempt to give a reasonable explanation to their stubborn refusal to accept the truth. They have unknowingly given their lives to Satan. Satan promises that freedom from God means freedom to do whatever you want to do. Is this a good thing? We know of rebellious children who refuse to obey their parents. What happens when you refuse to obey the rules? How about society's rules? What happens when you do drugs? You will get sick and possibly die. What happens when you steal? You usually get caught and go to jail. What happens if you commit murder? You are a danger to society and are locked away for the rest of your life or you may receive the death penalty. Rules are in place to help us live an abundant life. There is a reason some of the Ten Commandments includes: do not to steal, do not kill, do not commit adultery, do not lie. Satan is the ultimate rebellious child who is trying to lead as many astray as possible. His only offering is the ultimate party and the lie is that there will be no consequences. Just like a drug dealer, he offers something claiming to be good and lies about the effects. To the evolutionist, he offers a belief in undefined, un-real forces to explain away God. This explanation does not work.

The beginning of most geometry books starts with a study of number lines. Number lines show distances between two points. These distances are called intervals. There are two types: open and closed intervals. A closed interval has a definite beginning and ending. An open interval has definite limits, but no definite beginning point or a definite ending point. The closed interval is a segment of the number line which includes the beginning and ending points as well as all the points in between the two end points < •--------------• >. An open interval includes all the points between the two end points, like the closed interval, but not the end points themselves, <o--------------o >. This leads us into the concept of a limit. A limit is something that approaches a certain value, but never reaches that value. The open interval includes all whole number points along the line segment and when it approaches the end points it includes all fractional values approaching the limiting value but never reaches it. To determine the increments you use to move closer to the limiting value, you divided the previous number in half. So, your fractional values could be: ½, ¼, 1/8, and 1/16 ... etc. The limiting value is never reached because you are moving increasingly smaller intervals forward. Since each movement forward is halved, the increments get to a point where they are approximately zero. The graphic representation of this process is given by an asymptote, see figure 1.5 in Chapter one.

The open and closed intervals can be used as a comparison of the Christian prospective verses the philosophy of the naturalistic or atheist position. The Christian view of the universe is a view of life without time limits. The Christian view is that all life comes from God and when you die your soul returns to God. You have a definite physical birth, but you were thought of before you were born by God who has a special plan and purpose for your life. "Then the King will say to those at his right hand, Come, O blessed of my Father, inherit the kingdom prepared for you from the foundation of the world." Matthew 25:34. "Blessed be the God and Father of our Lord Jesus Christ, who has blessed us in Christ with every spiritual blessing in heavenly places, even as He chose us in Him before the foundation of the world, that we should be holy and blameless before Him. He destined us in love to be His sons through Jesus Christ, according to the purpose of His will." Ephesians 1:3-5. I do not want to enter a prolonged discussion about pre-destination, however, the Bible clearly shows we were planned to come into existence and be born. This is our beginning which took place in the mind of God at some point before our birth. The Bible tells us we, as Christians, will be given access to the kingdom of God which was prepared for us before the foundation of the world. I believe that everyone was intended for this kingdom. God has given us free will. We can accept or reject the gospel of Jesus depending on our judgment of the evidence and having faith in the Word of God. If we reject the offer with our free will, we will lose the kingdom we were intended to have.

To return to the concepts of line intervals, we see that the Christian life is one with a previous beginning in the mind of God, as he planned our existence to take place in our birth and a life having no ending. "Jesus said to her, 'I am the resurrection and the life, he who believes in me, though he die, yet shall he live, and whosoever lives and believes in me shall never die." John 11:25,26 Therefore, our lives are expressed as both an "open interval" having no ending and a "closed interval" having a beginning before the foundation of the world at some unknown but definite point. The atheistic view is that of life as a "closed interval" only. We are born, made from chemicals, and eventually die, meaning the chemical reactions in our bodies simply cease to function and life does not continue. Not only is this a closed interval concept of life it is also a narrow minded view of the universe. The Bible describes this philosophy in Romans: "For although they knew God they did not honor him as God or give thanks to him, but they became futile in their thinking and their senseless minds were darkened. Claiming to be wise, they became fools. And since they did not see fit to acknowledge God, God gave them up to a base mind and to improper conduct." Romans 1:21-22, 28.

Closed Minds of Naturalists

The naturalistic perspective is a belief that the universe was created by natural forces and everything in the universe can be explained by scientific laws. They believe that science holds all the answers and nothing beyond a scientific explanation can exist. If we do not currently know how a particular event took place, someday we will find the answer through scientific means. With this view of the universe, no supernatural event could have ever taken place. This belief is unsubstantiated by the evidence available. We have already discussed many reasons for rejecting this belief. The exclusion of God from the universe and the occurrence of God performing supernatural events could only remotely be acceptable if science could currently explain every event. In other words, all scientific research would be complete if we had an answer for every question ever asked. Obviously, science can not answer every question we have about life and the universe. There are still a great number of mysteries to the universe. How can people elevate the power of science to exceed its own limitations? Science has "evolved" over the centuries through rigorous exploration of the universe. The process is nowhere near complete. Naturalists chose to believe that science can find solutions to every mystery. I believe it is not so much a decision by these people to elevate science beyond reason, as the naturalist is desperately searching for a basis to support their unreasonable fear of accepting God as the maker of the universe. Science is very limited. We will discuss the fundamental principles of limits in this chapter and describe the mathematical uses of limits. These limiting conditions represent the boundaries which guide science into ways of expressing relationships which work under certain specified conditions. If the circumstances change, the law of science no longer applies. The most noteworthy example of this, as truth, is found in Einstein's theories of relativity. We will discuss the significance of this theory and how the whole world of science was changed by the introduction of the theory of relativity. The most astonishing fact that the theory exposed was that all the laws of physics had to be modified when they were describing events in objects traveling at speeds close to that of light. In other words, there are special cases where the laws of physics do exist in the same mathematical expressions we use to describe these principles in every day life.

Graphs and Geometrical Forms

When a particular function follows a specific pattern, it sometimes defines a geometrical shape. Functions do not needed to be precisely determined but can be arbitrary. All functions have one thing in common: They are related to a point of reference i.e. the point of origin, and they change depending upon changing values of the coordinate variables. The route you take to work can be considered a function. It probably is a wavy line of some irregular or erratic shape. You take your home as the point of origin. The path you travel with your car is a shape defined by distance and directions you travel, relative to your home (point of origin). The Bible says that God is the origin of all things. "In the beginning was the Word, and the Word was with God and the Word was God. He was in the beginning with God; all things were made through Him, and without Him was not anything made that has been made. In Him was life, and the life was the light of men." -John 1:1-4. Who is the person with God? It is Christ. "The true light that enlightens every man was coming into the world. He was in the world, and the world was made through him, yet the world knew him not. ... But to all who receive Him, who believe in His name, He gave power to become children of God; who were born, not of blood nor of the will of the flesh, nor of the will of man, but of God. And the Word became flesh and dwelt among us, full of grace and truth; we have beheld His glory, glory as of the only Son from the Father." -John 1:9-14. These verses describe the Holy Trinity of the Father, the Son, and the Holy Spirit. The Holy Spirit is not directly mentioned here, but its part in a relationship to the Father and the Son is described in the book of Acts. For the Christian, God is the center of everything. Every action, every person, every event is relative to the power, presence and purpose of the will of God and his Son Jesus Christ.

Your belief of origins determines your spiritual condition. In geometry, the shape of the object is determined by the set of all points represented by the function. All points are a function of the direction and distance from the point of origin. A function merely describes the dependence of the magnitude and direction of one position, or quantity, relative to the point of origin. Likewise, whatever you believe about life is dependant on what you accept as the source from which your life came into existence. There are a multitude of philosophies; all have a particular view based on a central accepted truth i.e. a point of origin. Each person should constantly test their faith in their beliefs. You should examine your life and the evidence of changed lives from each viewpoint you are considering. There are many skeptics that have taken the challenge to test Christianity. Josh McDowell and Lee Strobel are two authors mentioned throughout this book. They, like many other theologians, began their journey by attempting to refute Christianity. Josh attempted to destroy what he once considered an irrational belief through a study of the historical reliability of the scriptures. His result was a conversion to Christianity and his first best selling book: Evidence That Demands a verdict. Likewise, Lee Strobel tackled the problem through getting clear and precise answers to his questions about science. The result was several books on the evidences supporting the Christian faith. Take up the challenge! Test and see if your basic, accepted foundational truth to your belief system is true or false.

Limits Defined

Calculus is an extension of geometry based on a concept of limits, which we briefly examined. A limit is a very simple concept to understand. In fact, we deal with limits every day! For instance, a child tries to get a cookie out of a cookie jar. If the jar is on a high shelf, it is out of the child's reach. It is, therefore, said to be beyond the child's limit of reach. This doesn't stop the child from trying to reach the jar, see figure 1.5 of chapter one. This graph shows a function which is a vertical asymptote. The line extends upwards towards a point on a vertical line. The graph displays the equation: the limit of the function of x as x approaches infinity. As you can see, for each increased increment of x, the line gets closer to the vertical line. This diagram is also a good pictorial representation of how our lives are related to God. We try to reach the perfection of God with an active prayer life and moral behavior. However, we can never reach this point of perfection because of our sinful nature. This should not discourage the pursuit of perfection. When we keep the word of God in our heart and have an active prayer life, we grow closer to God daily. The non- Christian spends his life in search of perfection and wisdom, and never achieves "any peace of mind". The person may receive some limited peace of mind through philosophies or positive thinking methods. These methods may make a temporary solution to understanding universal mysteries, but the only permanent solution is to accept the Word of God by faith in Christ. The Christian never reaches the perfection of God either, but we have the spirit of God living each day in our lives by way of the Holy Spirit. The more active the prayer life, the faster the rate we move along the asymptote towards unity with God and the purpose He has for our lives. This brings us an increasingly abundant life filled with joy and contentment, because we trust in God's guidance. What is amazing is when some people think that they can do a better job of managing their life than God can.

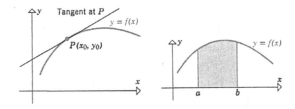

Figure 7.3

Two Principles of Calculus: Derivative and Integral

There are two basic principles introduced by calculus. These ideas have significant value to the laws of physics and to the principles of philosophy. In fact, Sir Isaac Newton is believed to have invented calculus to solve problems he was having in explaining his theory of gravity. Later, Newton's theories were proven to be true and we rely on calculus for many things other than proving Newton's laws of gravitational fields. The two new mathematical methods introduced by the field of calculus are the derivative and the integral. Once you understand these two mathematical operators, most of the work in calculus problems is just applying these principles to different situations. First the derivative can be considered the slope of a line tangent to a curve at a particular point, see figure 7.3 (a). The slope of a line is simple the rate at which a function changes. This is somewhat a simplistic explanation of the derivative and a more accurate explanation is necessary. A more accurate explanation is that the derivative is the *instantaneous rate of change* of y with respect to x. To understand the concept of instantaneous change, we need to review a physics problem. "While average velocity is useful for some purposes, it is not always significant in physical problems. For example, if a moving car strikes a tree, the damaged sustained is not determined by the average velocity up to the time of impact, but rather the instantaneous velocity at the precise moment of impact. ... In order to really understand the concept of instantaneous velocity and work with it mathematically we must think small! Suppose we are interested in the instantaneous velocity of a car at a certain instant of time, say exactly 5 seconds after it starts to move along a straight road. Although the car may be moving with varying velocity it is evident that over a short interval of time, say 0.1 second, the velocity does not vary much. Thus we make only a small error if we approximate the instantaneous velocity after 5 seconds by the average velocity over the interval from 5 seconds and 5.1 seconds. This average velocity can be calculated by measuring the distance traveled during the time interval between 5 and 5.1 seconds and then dividing by the time elapsed, which is 0.1 second. Thus, even though the instantaneous velocity after 5 seconds cannot be calculated directly, it can be approximated by an average velocity that can be determined from physical measurements. [7.1]" Here is an excellent example of how the scientific fields of physics and mathematics are virtually inseparable. This also shows that the foundations of higher mathematics, starting with the basic principles of calculus are approximations. To say that science is always accurate is only true in perfect laboratory conditions. To assume that science has the answer to everything is ridiculous. Science can only generally explain everyday events, not any event which is not common to everyday life. There are various limits of a scientific explanation to any physical reality. Science can approach a reasonable explanation, but the actual acceptance of these facts comes from the faith that you have in all the information explaining the event. When you go into higher mathematics, beyond basic calculus to tensor algebra, things become a lot stranger. Tensors equations are, by definition, a shorthand method for expressing ideas.

Let us look a little closer at the first mathematical operation in calculus, differentiation. "The process of finding a derivative is called differentiation. It is often useful to think of differentiation as an operation which, when applied to a function f, produces a new function f'. ... Up to now we have interpreted the derivative dy/dx as the slope of a tangent line to the curve y= f (x). [7.2]" There are basically two ways to describe the result of doing the process differentiation. One, we can think of it as a method to produce a new function that is different from the original. There are a number of rules that apply to the process that determine the value of the new function. Secondly, when we differentiate a function we can say that we get as a result a function of a line tangent to the curve represented by the original function, see figure 7.3(a) or figure 1.5 of chapter one. The derivative is more accurately defined by the expression: the $\lim_{\Delta x \to 0} \Delta y / \Delta x = dy/dx$. Where, Δy is the change in y values or y_2-y_1. Likewise, Δx is the change in x values or x_2-x_1. This is the standard definition of a derivative i.e. the limit of the change in y values divided by the change in x values as the change in x values approaches 0. If x were 0, then the quantity would be infinite. The change in y gets increasingly larger and the change in x gets increasingly smaller. By definition, any quantity divided by zero is undefined or infinite. Therefore the derivative would be the instantaneous rate of change of a function. This is used in technical physics classes where students solve, e.g., problems for the acceleration of a body under a uniform force.

The Christian knows the meaning of instantaneous change from God's word. "Therefore, if any one is in Christ, he is a new creation; the old has passed away, behold, the new has come. I have been crucified with Christ; it is no longer I who live, but Christ who lives in me; and the life I now live in the flesh I live by faith in the Son of God. Lo I tell you a mystery. We shall not all sleep, but we shall all be changed, in a moment, in the twinkling of an eye." 2 Corinthians. 5:17, Galatians 2:20, 1 Corinthians. 15:51-52. When we accepted Christ as Savior, there was an instantaneous change in our lives. We were no longer sinners, but saved Christians with our names in the Lamb's Book of Life. When the Lord returns we will be again changed. The twinkling of the eye is the reflection of light from the cornea within the eye. This means the change will take place at the speed of light. According to Einstein's equations, nothing can travel faster than the speed of light. Therefore, we can say that the change is essentially instantaneous. More about the unique qualities of light will be discussed in chapter 9 on modern physics.

The Derivative

Let us re-examine the definition of the derivative. The derivative, if you recall, is defined as a measure of an instantaneous change in a function. One thing the derivative determines is the slope of any given line. If you are given the equation of a line, the derivative will provide you with the slope of the line. If the equation you are differentiating is a curve, the derivative of the function will provide the equation of a line which is tangent to the curve. These facts have great significance in courses of differential geometry. The next fundamental topic introduced by calculus is the integral. There are two types of integrals: the definite integral and the indefinite integral. The definite integral is the summation of all differentials performed on a function within certain limiting points 'a' and 'b'. Therefore it performs the opposite mathematical operation on an equation representing a function as the derivative. All of Calculus depends upon the two basic concepts of the deferential and the integral. And Calculus is essential for a complete understanding of science. You can use the derivative to express a person's spiritual condition. Look at figure 1.5 of chapter one and take the horizontal line to be the x-axis and the vertical line to be the y-axis. Let us consider that the change in Δ Y (delta y) is the increase in our dedication to God in prayer and other deeds expressing our dedication to the Lord. Let the change in Δ x (delta x), be the change or divergence, in our lives away from the discipline of the Christian lifestyle. As the amount of sin in our lives (Δ x) gets smaller and the devotional time spent in worship of God, (Δ y) gets bigger, the function representing our lives moves closer to a harmonious relationship with God. Follow the line as we get closer and closer to some point, a, on the vertical axis. The point A represents a point where our lives are completely sinless and in perfect harmony with the will of God. This is a point we will never reach, but a position we strive for. When the divergence from God is kept less than our growth towards God, the function representing our lives in relationship to the Spirit of the Lord gets closer with each increment. Therefore, we become closer to the infinite power and glory of God during each day of our lives and in every action we make in serving God. Our righteous acts increase and our sinful desires decrease as the Holy Spirit works in our lives and fills us with the presence of our Lord and Savior. This process continues towards infinity as we develop sensitivity to the presence of sin in our lives.

The Integral

The mathematical principle of integration is exactly opposite of the derivative. The integral is used to sum up all the instantaneous changes within the function, represented by the derivative. When you work calculus problems, you can differentiate a function and then integrate the new function and the result will be the original function. The integration function is represented by an elongated 's', $\int dy = f(y)$, $\int dx = f(x)$. There are two types of integrals: the definite integral and the indefinite integral. The definite integral specifies a segment of the curved function in which the integration takes place, see fig 7.3(b). The indefinite integral sums the differentials over the entire length of the function instead of just a short segment. Sometimes the indefinite integral must be approximated since the functions can not extend from a positive infinity to a negative infinity. The algebra equivalent to the calculus summation is represented by the sigma notation, Σ. Both methods of summing up data are useful in mathematics. The sigma notation is used primarily in statistics and probability equations. The integral is used extensively in higher mathematics, engineering, and physics. For example, the distance an object is displaced is found by a summation of the instantaneous velocity vectors of an object during a specific time interval. Another example is found in the calculation of the work performed by a varying force in a single dimension. The total work done by the force is found by the area under a curve graphically representing the work function. This is expressed in several laws of physics e.g. Gauss' Law. We will discuss Gauss' Law in the next chapter in physics. This physical principle makes use of a special type of integral. This is represented by $\int$ with a circle in the middle. This symbolizes an integral over a closed surface.

One last method for summarizing physical laws, spatial orientation and other information is called the tensor analysis or tensor algebra. For an example, $F_{\mu v} = R_{\mu v} - \frac{1}{2} g_{\mu v} R = -8\pi\, G\, T_{\mu v}$ represents some of the basic relationships in Einstein's theory of general relativity. Tensor analysis is used extensively in many theoretical physics research papers. Some of these methods of representation will be examined at the end of the chapter. As we stated earlier, the integral is used to sum up the changes in a particular function. The integral is also used in calculus problems to determine the "area under the curve". Much of the second and third semester calculus classes involve using the integral to determine the area of a function, a circle, cone, box, rectangle, etc. You are given an equation of a particular function, such as the equation for a circle of a specific radius and circumference. You can use integration to determine the area of the circle. You can imagine the applications to these two functions of differentiation and integration in the fields of engineering. When a mechanical engineer, for example, is designing a new structure these mathematical principles allow the person to make quick an accurate calculations to the structural integrity of the new design. There are many applications of calculus to the various engineering fields.

We can apply the integral concept to spiritual concepts like we did with the deferential. Taking the function we discussed earlier, the differentials represented the changes we make in our daily lives. In the Christian heart, the summation of all the changes in life is to come closer to the Lord Jesus Christ. The integration of our life function determines the area, or total amount, of our heart consumed in dedication to the Lord. Jesus Christ is the reason for all the changes we make in our lives and our purpose for living is to give glory to our Father in heaven. "Let your light so shine before men, that they may see your good works and give glory to your Father who is in heaven." Matthew 5:16. "But sanctify the Lord God in your hearts and be ready always to give an answer to every man that asketh you a reason for the hope that is in you." 1 Peter 3:15- RSV. In Christ is the answer to every prayer and every question. He is the center of all things and all things are made through Him. We must guard ourselves at all times to hold tight to the word of God. In this way, we develop our life to function according to the plan of God.

Let us examine some of the ideas of the man who, among other things, invented calculus and discovered the workings of gravity; Sir Isaac Newton (1642-1727). "Newton was born in the village of Woolsthorpe, England. His father died before Newton was born and his mother raised the boy on the family farm. ... In 1661 he entered Trinity College in Cambridge with a deficiency in geometry. ...

Because the plague was spreading through London, Newton returned to his home in Woolsthorpe and stayed there during the years of 1665 and 1666. In those two momentous years the entire framework of modern science was miraculously created in Newton's mind - he discovered calculus, recognized the underlying principles of planetary motion and gravity, and determined that "white" sunlight was composed of all colors, red to violet. For some reason he kept his discoveries to himself. ... Then in 1669 Newton succeeded his teacher, Isaac Barrow, to the Lucasian chair of mathematics at Trinity. ... Thereafter, brilliant discoveries flowed from Newton steadily. He formulated the law of gravitation and used it to explain the motion of the moon, the planets, and the tides; he formulated basic theories of light, thermodynamics, and hydrodynamics; and he devised and constructed the first modern reflecting telescope. ... In 1687, only after intense coaxing by the astronomer, Edmond Halley (Halley's Comet), did Newton publish his masterpiece, Philosophae Naturalis Principia Mathematica (The Mathematical Principles of Natural Philosophy). This work is generally considered to be the most important and influential scientific book ever written. In it Newton explained the workings of the solar system and formulated the basic laws of motion that to this day are fundamental in engineering and physics. However, not even pleas of his friends could convince Newton to publish his discovery of calculus. Only after Leibniz published his results did Newton relent and publish his own work on calculus. [7.3]" It is a true curiosity why Newton was so reluctant to publish his work on calculus, and many of his other discoveries. This passage represents Newton as a somewhat shy person with a deep sense of humility and reverence for God. I find it amazing that Newton credits his main discoveries in science to the two years (1665-1666) he was back on the family farm. I imagine Newton was doing what I and many other Christians have done throughout history. We often go for long walks to ask God for guidance and pray that the secrets of the universe be revealed to us. "But the Counselor, the Holy Spirit, whom the Father will send in my name, will teach you all things." John 14:26. "But there is a God in heaven who reveals mysteries." Daniel 2:28. "If any of you lacks wisdom, he should ask God, who gives generously to all without finding fault, and it will be given to him." James 1:5. It would seam that God actually helped Isaac Newton to discover some of the most profound inner workings of the universe. After this "revelation", Newton returned to Cambridge with new ideas in science and mathematics. Newton's reluctance to publish his work was probably the result of humility. He knew that publishing his work would bring even more prestige to his name. Therefore, he seamed content to simply discuss his findings with friends, colleagues and students at Cambridge. His reluctance to publish his work may have had a noble reason but it has diminished the proper recognition of Newton's accomplishments. Even in Newton's day, there was controversy over who invented calculus first, Newton or Leibniz. Some suggest this has diminished the recognition of the accomplishments of Leibniz. "Gottfried Wilhelm Leibniz (1646-1716) ... was an expert in law, religion, philosophy, literature, politics, geology, metaphysics, alchemy, history, and mathematics. Leibniz was born in Leipzig, Germany. His father, professor of moral philosophy at the University of Leipzig, died when Leibniz was six years old. ... In mathematics Leibniz was self-taught; he learned the subject by reading papers and journals. ... Leibniz often duplicated the results of others. This ultimately led to a raging conflict over who invented calculus, Leibniz or Newton? The argument over this question engulfed the scientific circles of England and Europe. ... The fact is that both men invented calculus independently. Leibniz invented it 10 years after Newton, in 1685, but he published the results 20 years before Newton published his own work on the subject. [7.4]"

Newton believed that the study of science leads us to appreciate the great works of God. "It is interesting to note that Newton was a learned theologian. He viewed the primary value of his work to be its support of the existence of God. Throughout his life he worked passionately to date biblical events by relating them to astronomical phenomena. [7.5]" There are atheists who would like to take away from the accomplishments of any scientist, past or present, which believes in God. Some critics have gone as far as to make the absurd statement that no one that is classified as a "Christian Scientist", has contributed anything to the development of science. What about Newton's paper on The Mathematical Principles of

Natural Philosophy? As we have already stated, this is still considered **the** most important work in science ever published! Newton's view on the subject of science is clear. He believed that science was to discover a greater appreciation of the way God has constructed the universe. Towards the end of this paper he explicitly refers to the God of eternity, the God of Israel as the creator of the universe. Quote: "This most beautiful system of the sun, planets, and comets, could only proceed from the counsel and dominion of an intelligent and powerful Being. ... This Being governs all things, not as the soul of the world, but as Lord over all; and on account of his dominion he is wont to be called Lord God pantokrator, or Universal Ruler. .... The Supreme God is a Being eternal, infinite, absolutely perfect; ... for we say, my God, your God, the God of Israel, the God of Gods, and Lord of Lords. ... The word God' usually signifies Lord; but every lord is not a God. ... The true God is a living, intelligent, and powerful Being. ... He is eternal and infinite, omnipotent and omniscient; that is, his duration reaches from eternity to eternity; his presence from infinity to infinity; he governs all things, and knows all things that are or can be done." Source: The Mathematical Principles of Natural Philosophy (1687) How can any reasonable person not appreciate the many scientific achievements of Sir Isaac Newton? How can anyone question Newton's convictions to biblical study? Newton is obviously specifying that there is only one true God and he is known as the Alpha and Omega, the beginning and the end. "I am the Alpha and the Omega, the first and the last, the beginning and the end." Revelation 22:13. Once again, we have strong evidence of the religious fervor some atheists attack men of science who are devout Christians, including Sir Isaac Newton by distorting his convictions. We mentioned the movie The DaVinci Code and how there is a commonly held belief among a large portion of the world population, that you can have faith or you can study science but you can not do both. I found it refreshing to discover that Sir Isaac Newton had the same convictions I have described in this book. As the title states; and as we have explored this theme many times in this book, I believe that faith and science or faith and reason are inseparable. When we reach the "outer limits" of scientific discovery we instinctively call upon a faith in an almighty God to make sense out of our observations. "Who can explain what is the essence of the attraction of gravity? No one now objects to following out the results consequent on this unknown element of attraction; notwithstanding that Leibnitz formerly accused Newton of introducing 'occult qualities and miracles into philosophy.' [7.6]" Newton realized that we can not entirely separate our work from our personal convictions. In the Introduction, we explored the role of "seeking wisdom" and how all paths towards truth and understanding eventually lead back to Jesus Christ as savior and Lord. The world continually points out that "religious leaders" persecuted Sir Isaac Newton. So what? "Religious leaders" executed Jesus Christ and insisted on him dying on a cross at Calvary. Many "religious leaders" may object to my similar stand of science supporting our Christian faith. The fact remains: All historical evidences say Sir Isaac Newton was a Christian.

In this chapter let's look at other mathematicians who contributed monumentally to the development of calculus. There is a common theme with most of these men of science: a profound faith in the existence of God. "Leonhard Euler (1707-1783). Euler was probably the most prolific mathematician who ever lived. It has been said that, 'Euler wrote mathematics as effortlessly as most men breathe.' He was born in Basel, Switzerland, and was the son of a Protestant minister who had himself studied mathematics. Euler's genius developed early. He attended the University of Basel, where by age 16 he obtained both a Bachelor of Arts degree and a Master's degree in philosophy. ... At the urging of his father, Euler then began to study theology. The lure of mathematics was too great, however, and by age 18 Euler had begun to do mathematical research. Nevertheless, the influence of his father and his theological studies remained, and throughout his life Euler was a deeply religious, unaffected person. ... What is particularly astonishing is that Euler was blind for the last 17 years of his life, and this was one of his most productive periods! ... His ability to solve problems in his head was beyond belief. He worked out in his head major problems of lunar motion that baffled Isaac Newton and once did a complicated calculation in his head to settle an argument between two students whose computations differed in the fiftieth decimal place. ... He was the first mathematician to bring the full power of calculus to bear on problems from physics. He made major contributions to virtually every branch of mathematics as well as to the theory of optics, planetary motion, electricity, magnetism, and general mechanics. [7.7]" How can anyone deny that this was a brilliant man who had a love for God? We have many accomplishments built on the brilliant work of Leonhard Euler.

Next, let us rapidly go through a list of accomplished mathematicians who expressed faith in God, starting with Bernhard Bolzano. "The relationship between continuity and differentiability was of great historical significance in the development of calculus. In the early nineteenth century mathematicians believed that the graph of a continuous function could not have too many points of non-differentiability bunched up. ... This misconception was shattered by a series of discoveries beginning in 1834. In that year a Bohemian priest, philosopher, and mathematician named Bernhard Bolzano (1781-1848) discovered a procedure for constructing a continuous function that is not differentiable at any point. ... Bolzano became an ordained Roman Catholic priest, and in 1805 he was appointed to a chair of Philosophy at the University of Prague. ... Bolzano's main contribution to mathematics was philosophical. His work helped convince mathematicians that sound mathematics must ultimately rest on rigorous proof rather that intuition. In addition to his work in mathematics, Bolzano investigated problems concerning space, force, and wave propagation. ... George Friedrich Bernhard Riemann (1826-1866) German mathematician. Bernard Riemann, as he is commonly known, was the son of a Protestant minister. ... He studied physics under W.E. Weber and mathematics under Karl Friedrich Gauss, whom some people consider to be the greatest mathematician who ever lived. ... For his introductory lecture prior to becoming an associate professor, Riemann submitted three possible topics to Gauss. Gauss surprised Riemann by choosing the topic Riemann liked the least, the foundations of geometry. .. The results presented by Riemann that day eventually evolved into a fundamental tool that Einstein used some 50 years later to develop relativity theory. ... Blaise Pascal (1623-1662) ... Pascal published a highly respected essay on conic sections by the time he was sixteen years old. Descartes, who read the essay, thought it was brilliant. ... Pascal's contributions to physics include the discovery that air pressure decreases with altitude and the principle of fluid pressure that bears his name. ... Pascal made major contributions to a branch of mathematics called 'projective geometry,' and he helped develop the probability theory through a series of letters with Fermat. ... In 1646, Pascal's health ... led him to become increasingly concerned with religious matters. ... (He) spent most of his final years writing on religion and philosophy. ... Augustin Louis Cauchy (1789-1857) French mathematician. ... In 1814 he wrote a treatise on integrals that was to become the basis for modern complex variable theory; in 1816 there followed a classic paper on wave propagation in liquids that won a prize from the French Academy; and in 1822 he wrote a paper that formed the basis of modern elastic theory. Cauchy's mathematical contributions for the next 35 years were brilliant and staggering in quantity, over 700 papers filling 26 modern volumes. ... It is difficult to get a clear picture of the man. Devoutly Catholic, he sponsored charitable work for unwed mothers, criminals, and relief for Ireland. Yet other aspects of his life cast him in an unfavorable light. ... In any event, Cauchy is undeniably one of the greatest minds in the history of science. ... Colin Maclaurin (1698-1746) Maclaurin entered Glasgow University as a divinity student, but transferred to mathematics after one year. He received his Master's degree at age 17 and, in spite of his youth, began teaching at Marischal College in Aberdeen, Scotland. Maclaurin met Isaac Newton during a visit to London in 1719 and from that time on became Newton's disciple. During that era, some of Newton's analytic methods were bitterly attacked by major mathematicians and much of Maclaurin's important mathematical work resulted from his efforts to defend Newton's ideas geometrically. ... Brook Taylor (1685-1731) ... Taylor's most productive period was from 1714-1719, during which time he wrote on a wide variety of subjects- magnetism, capillary action, thermometers, perspective, and calculus. In his final years, Taylor devoted his writing efforts to religion and philosophy. ... Bernoulli (family), An amazing Swiss family that included several generations of outstanding mathematicians and scientists. The family fled from Antwerp to escape religious persecution. ... Following Newton and

Leibniz, the Bernoulli brothers, Jakob I (1654-1705) and Johann I (1667-1748), are considered by some to be the two most important founders of calculus. ... Among the other members of the Bernoulli family, Daniel (1700-1782), son of Johann I, is the most famous. ... He did work in calculus and probability, but is best known for his work in physics. A basic law of fluid flow, called Bernoulli's principle, is named in his honor. He won the annual prize of the French Academy 10 times for work on vibrating strings, tides of the sea, and kinetic theory of gases. ... George Gabriel Stokes (1819-1903), Irish mathematician and physicist. Born in Skreen, Ireland, Strokes came from a family deeply rooted in the Church of Ireland. ... Stokes was one of several outstanding nineteenth century scientists who helped turn the physical sciences in a more empirical direction. He systematically studied hydrodynamics, elasticity of solids, behavior of waves in elastic solids, and diffraction of light. For Stokes, mathematics was a tool for his physical studies. He wrote classic papers on the motion of viscous fluids that laid the foundation for modern hydrodynamics; he helped elaborate the wave theory of light; and he wrote papers on gravitational variation that established him as a founder of the modern science of geodesy. ... He was deeply religious and vitally concerned with the relation between science and religion. [7.8]" Even this college textbook used in major secular colleges will recognize the significance of religion on the scientific pursuit. As we have seen throughout this book, to seek an understanding of the universe brings us to a better appreciation of the wonders of God's creation power. The atheist has unsuccessfully attempted to re-write history leaving out the influence of faith on science. Science was based on an honest pursuit of the nature of the universe. These men of faith were inspired by Bible verses encouraging them toward the pursuit of wisdom. "Blessed is the man who finds wisdom, the man who gains understanding, for she is more profitable than silver and yields better returns than gold. ... By wisdom the Lord laid the earth's foundations, by understanding he set the heavens in place; by his knowledge the depths were divided, and the clouds let drop the dew. " Proverbs 3:13-14, 19-20. "The heavens declare the glory of God; the skies proclaim the work of his hands." Psalm 19:1 "For since the creation of the world God's invisible qualities - his eternal power and divine nature - have been clearly seen, being understood from what has been made, so that men are without excuse. ... Although they claimed to be wise, they became fools." Romans 1:20, 22. The atheist is trapped by his own lies. They are like so many people that pick through the Bible for a few verses that are "non-controversial"; like the pursuit of wisdom is good or that we should "love thy neighbor." However, they refuse to examine other passages referring to the power of God. We can stand amazed that there is virtually an inexhaustible supply of wisdom found in the Bible. There is essentially no end to the commentaries we can discuss from the Bible passages.

Many of the founders of the scientific fields we have today, not only believed in God but were Bible believing Christians. "At least we creationist scientists can take comfort in the fact that many of the greatest scientists of the past were creationists and for that matter, were also Bible-believing Christians, men who believed in the inspiration and authority of the Bible, as well as in the deity and saving work of Jesus Christ. They believed that God had supernaturally created all things, each with its own complex structure for its own unique purpose. They believed that, as scientists, they were 'thinking God's thoughts after Him,' learning to understand and control the laws and processes of nature for God's glory and man's good. They believed and practiced science in exactly the same way that modern creationist scientists do. And somehow this attitude did not hinder them in their commitment to the 'scientific method.' In fact one of them, Sir Francis Bacon, is credited with formulating and establishing the scientific method! They seem also to have been able to maintain a proper 'scientific attitude,' for it was these men (Newton, Pasteur, Linnaeus, Faraday, Pascal, Lord Kelvin, Maxwell, Kepler, etc.) whose researches and analysis led to the very laws and concepts of science which brought about our modern scientific age. The mechanistic scientists of the present are dwarfed in comparison to these intellectual giants of the past. Even the achievements of Einstein (not to mention Darwin!) are trivial in comparison. The real breakthroughs, the new fields, the most beneficial discoveries of science were certainly not delayed (in fact probably were hastened) by the creationist motivations of these great founders of modern science. [7.9]" We will study some of the achievements of these scientists in our next two chapters on physics. As previously reviewed, Albert Einstein was not a Christian as far as we know, but a devout Jew. Let us reiterate Einstein's view of science. "But science can only be created by those who are thoroughly imbued with the aspiration toward truth and understanding. This source of feeling, however, springs from the sphere of religion. To this there also belongs the faith in the possibility that the regulations valid for the world of existence are rational, that is, comprehensible to reason. I can not conceive of a genuine scientist without that profound faith. The situation can be expressed by an image: science without religion is lame, religion without science is blind. ... I have asserted above that in truth a legitimate conflict between religion and science cannot exist." [7.10] We will explore the meaning of this statement in greater detail in the next chapter.

In recent years many atheists are determined to dismiss the convictions that science teaches us about God. This elevation of natural science (or the study of nature) to a religion is not an entirely new concept. There have always been those who are determined to take reverence away from God. It is interesting that these groups have a common "faith" in natural forces and believe that these "natural forces" are to be worshiped. This is no different than the worship of beasts or man- made objects in ancient religions. In fact, the faith of the evolutionists bears a striking resemblance to the Baal worship discussed in the Old Testament. "The basic idea of Baal worship was this. The most mysterious force in life is growth. What makes the corn grow, and the grape swell, and the olive ripen? That, said the other nations, is Baal or the Baals at work. Baal is the power of growth behind all living and growing things. [7.11]" Isn't this the belief of the evolutionists today? They worship an unknown power that began life, sustains it and by the power of natural selection produced the nearly endless varieties of life on the earth? This faith is very similar to those who worshiped Baal. They displace reverence for the God revealed in the Bible with a false god. They worship the creature instead of the creator. Discover more about Baal in the Bible.

Our Function in Life and the Meaning of Life

Let us return to our previous discussion of functions as illustrated in figure 7.2. I'm not intending the ideas of functions, derivatives, and integrals to be just a play on words. Life is a function. We are all connected, in some way, to the will of God. Our exact position, within the plan of God, is governed by our free will response to the gospel of Jesus Christ as presented in the Holy Bible. We should constantly seek to become closer to God. This is our function in life and the "mysterious" meaning of life that so many philosophers attempt to find. There is a prayer which is very useful in our daily lives. It has been called the serenity prayer. It goes something like this: Lord God grant me the serenity to accept the things I cannot change, the courage to change the things I can, and to have the wisdom to know the difference between the two. We need to ask God for wisdom in every situation. "Trust in the Lord with all your heart, and lean not on your own understanding; in all your ways acknowledge him, and he will make your paths straight." Proverbs 3:5-6. It is not difficult to remember to say a short prayer before we try any new situation. Simply pray, "Lord, give me direction by your Holy Spirit." The Lord has promised you will receive an answer, sometimes in the form of a thought entering your mind. Other times it may be a feeling, leading you to a sense of purpose. God has promised to give a sense of direction in our lives if we call on His name. "Ask and it will be given you; seek, and you will find; knock and it will be opened to you. For every one who asks receives, and he who seeks finds, and to him who knocks it will be opened." Mathew 7:7-8. "If any of you lacks wisdom, let him ask God, who gives to all generously and without reproaching, and it will be given him." James 1:5. When we integrate our lives into the plan of God, we become closer to our fellow man as well. The integration of the endless diversity of talent is called the body of Christ. "For as in one body we have many members, and all the members do not have the same function, so we, though many, are one body in Christ, and individually members one of another. Having gifts that differ according to the grace given to us, let us use them." Romans 12:4-6. The "body" is the church of God. No particular name is needed. As Christians we are united in spirit, the only name which is needed is the name of Christ written in our hearts. Sometimes it seams we become too divided over a name on a particular church building and do not come together as Christians united in faith. I feel that everyone needs a good church to support their spiritual lives. It is important to find a good church that is a place in which Christians can help each other in serving the Lord. No particular name on the door should be of interest as long as the gospel of Jesus Christ is taught. The condition of the hearts of the members inside the church is all that matters.

Functions

Calculus describes various processes you can perform on a function, primarily taking the derivative or integral of a function. A function is a description of changes between variables. There are two types of variables; independent variable and dependent variables. In the non-Christian perspective, there are many independent variables. Weather conditions and other circumstances of nature are all random environmental factors which influence their judgment. There are many independent variables in the non-Christian life. A naturalist believes that most things are the result of luck or random chance. According to the naturalistic perspective, most things occur as a result of a random forces and non-related variables. The Christian believes in a relationship between God and man which involves God's control of all events on a daily basis. God is continuously providing miracles through the power of His will. Circumstances don't just happen at the right time as the result of "good luck". God is providing these things. The more difficult circumstances are a challenge to us, the more God provides for our needs through Christian helpers. We must endure the ravages of Satan, our source of trouble, which God allows to continue until the Day of Judgment. God always supplies you a way to overcome the difficulties this world produces to test your faith. "My grace is sufficient for you, for my power is made perfect in weakness." 2 Corinthians 12:19. In our weakness, we have the strength of the Lord by the presence of the Holy Spirit in our life. The more the difficulty remains, the more we recognize our dependence on God. Everything in life is a dependent variable, according to the Scripture. We are directly affected by the circumstances we must endure, and the circumstances are directly related to the plan of God. How well do we follow the plan of God? To evaluate our position to the will of the Lord, we need to be aware of some of the variables which determine our position relative to the will of God.

Return to figure 7.2. We can again visualize our spiritual position as one of the points of intersections of two lines. Some of the variables which determine our position and how fast we are moving in the direction of the plan of God are: 1) the amount of time we spend in prayer and reading the word of God, 2) the frequency of Christian fellowship and worship of God in church, and 3) the relationship with our fellow men, Christian and non-Christian friends and acquaintances. Our relationship to other members of our human community is expressed by a relationship to our "neighbor". "You shall love the Lord your God with all your heart, and with all you soul, and with all your mind. This is the great and first commandment. And a second is like it. You shall love your neighbor as yourself. On these two commandments depend all the law and the prophets." Mathew 22:37-40. Sometimes I wonder how church members can claim they are serving God when the first commandment commands to love God with all their heart, mind, and soul. Often, they refuse to defend their faith against some of the intellectual challenges presented to them outside of church! I pray this work will aid in the preparation of defending the faith and in the worship of the Lord with your entire mind. Also, how we treat our fellow members of society, our neighbors, is a critical concern of God. "For I was hungry and you gave me food, I was thirsty and you gave me drink, I was a stranger and you welcomed me, I was in prison and you came to me. Then the righteous will answer him, Lord, when did we see thee hungry and feed thee, or thirsty and give thee drink? ... And the King will answer them, Truly, I say to you, as you did it to one of the least of these my brethren, you did it to me." Mathew 25:35-40. How closely we follow these Christian principles of sharing and caring for our fellow man, helps determine how well you are serving God. This allows us to check ourselves on how close our spiritual position is to the plan God has for our lives. If we are concerned with our own pleasure more than serving others, we should re-evaluate our priorities.

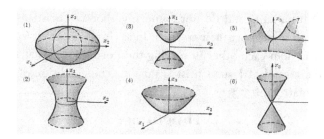

Figure 7.4

Levels of Mathematics: High School through College

Let us review the courses required to have the highest level of understanding of mathematics. In high school, an advanced mathematics curriculum includes: 1st year: Algebra 1 & Algebra 2. 2nd year: Trigonometry & Geometry. 3rd year: Pre-calculus and first semester calculus. At this point we have covered some of the main principles leading to the end of pre-calculus, which concludes with the definition of the derivative and the integral. In the first semester college level calculus, a typical college text will cover the concepts of pre-calculus in the first five chapters. After we define the derivative and integral, several chapters of a college text are dedicated to application of the derivative. Next, typically, are techniques of integration for both definite and indefinite integrals. In the first semester calculus class you are dealing with differentiation and integration in just one dimension. For example, integrating and differentiating lines in the x-y plane. The line is two dimensional, but you only differentiate or integrate with respect to one direction. In the second college semester calculus class you deal with conic sections and using calculus techniques on these forms of geometry. Conic sections include the parabola, the ellipse, and the hyperbola, figure 7.4. The second semester calculus classes usually discuses infinite series calculation and a host of other uses of calculus with geometric figures. Also, second semester calculus classes usually teach students about polar coordinate and spherical coordinate transformations. These techniques will become essential in the understanding of more advanced mathematical concepts. In the third and last college calculus course you will learn about vectors and vector addition. There are two types of vector multiplication called the dot product and cross product. Then you will cover calculus extended to more than one dimension. To differentiate in more than one dimension you need to use partial derivatives, $dz/dt = {\partial z}/{\partial x}\, dx/dt + {\partial z}/{\partial y}\, dy/dt$ is one definition of the partial derivative.

The electromagnetic wave equation is another example of an equation containing partial derivatives. To integrate in two dimension requires a double integral, in three dimensions requires the triple integral. After, three semesters of calculus, a course of deferential equations is required to continue your education in mathematics. Sometimes, a student in deferential equations can wonder about the purpose of the course. In this course you learn to use more complex methods of derivatives and partial derivatives to deal with incredibly complex equations. The main purpose of the course is to take complex problems and break them down to equations which are more manageable. After deferential equations, you have completed all the basic requirements for a career in science or mathematics. After differential equations, the classes diverge depending upon the scientific career of your choice. If you chose a career in Mathematics, Physics, Medicine, Biology, the classes in mathematics will be different. Engineering or medicine you take various classes which teach specific applications to the level of mathematics you have achieved. In the more advanced scientific careers: Mathematics, Physics, and Engineering, you will continue to more advanced levels of mathematics through a course in differential geometry and finally tensor analysis. Tensors analysis is the final plateau of higher mathematical concepts. When scientists present work in physics and mathematics to be considered for a PhD or work on a Nobel Prize winning thesis, the paper is generally expressed in the mathematical language of tensors.

Tensors algebra, as it is called, is a collection of methods and techniques used to summarize physical principles in a few sets of symbols representing almost anything. Tensors can represent a coordinate plane, the position and movement of a particular particle, the change in electromagnetic charge due to movement through a particular area of space, and any physical or geometrical principle which affects any kind of material body from quarks, electrons and subatomic particles to stars, black holes, and galaxies. Tensors are the ultimate expression of scientific principles, laws, and theories. Tensors are powerful tools for expressing scientific theories. One of the primary examples of tensors used to express physical concepts is in Einstein's theory of general relativity. $F_{\mu v} = R_{\mu v} - \frac{1}{2} g_{\mu v} R = -8\pi\, G\, T_{\mu v}$ Einstein's equation for general relativity. $F_{\mu v}$ = force due to a gravitational field. $R_{\mu v}$ = Ricci Tensor, of 23 eq.'s representing curvature of space time. $g_{\mu v}$ = gravitational tensor. R= Ricci's scalar, a constant of curvature. G= gravitational constant of the universe. $T_{\mu v}$ = Energy-stress tensor. All this is to merely express the fact that the universe has a geometric form that is generally spherical. This is due to the collective force of gravity in all the material bodies throughout the universe. In addition to this statement from examining classical physics, general relativity theory also includes the influence of mass increasing with velocity. Einstein's first theory of relativity, the special theory, Einstein specified the relationship with matter and energy by $E=mc^2$. One of the results of this relationship is that mass actually gets larger when an object approaches the speed of light. As the speed of the object increases, the amount of mass contained in the object increases. These principles will be discussed in detail in the upcoming chapters. The point we need to specify is that expressing ideas in tensor form does not mean that the theorem is absolutely true! Sometimes scientists use this "razzle dazzle" to confuse the general public. Do not be overly swayed if someone uses these advanced concepts of mathematics in an attempt to support a theoretical concept. These mathematical forms are just a complex way of expressing ideas. These ideas expressed in words instead of equations can be easily understood and their validity can be debated.

There are over twenty equations represented in the field equation $F_{\mu v} = R_{\mu v} - \frac{1}{2} g_{\mu v} R = -8\pi\, G\, T_{\mu v}$. These equations inter-relate position to properties of energy, mass and other physical properties of particles. This equation is a good example of how tensor analysis can summarize a great number of concepts in a few simple symbols. The thing to remember is that the same principles discussed in earlier chapters apply here. Theories, even ones expressed in tensor form, are subject to limitations. The first step in establishing any law or theory in scientific form is to begin with describing an isolated system. In many texts describing the theory of relativity in tensor form, you notice many of the field equations set equal to zero, for example the expression $R_{\mu v} = 0$. This is simply to specify that you begin with an isolated system and then add information as it becomes available through observation and experiment. For example, you attempt to explain a particle set in motion. You then isolate the cause of the motion, since the "natural" state of any particle is static equilibrium or at rest. You describe all the forces acting on the object, and determine their magnitude and direction. If there is the presence of a gravitational field, does this influencing the particle? Is there another force present as well? You proceed to describe the magnitude and direction of each force in mathematical form. You then describe as many properties about the object in motion as you can. For example, a ball is drooped from a certain high position. You can mathematically describe the event as gravity influencing the ball and drawing the ball towards the center of the earth. You can also describe the event in terms of energy relationships. The ball has a certain potential energy or so called stored energy, before it is released because it is at a point above the surface of the earth and there is an influence of gravity on the object. When the ball is released, some of the potential energy is converted into kinetic energy i.e. energy of motion.

The transformations of energy, position in a coordinate system, or from mass to energy in relativistic transformations, sometimes involve complex equations. However, we need to remember that scientific analysis operates in a narrow limited region in which circumstances must be mathematical specified. The same principles of science apply in every form it takes. You need to specify the limitations of science and specify if you are discussing a scientific theory or a scientific law. People who believe that everything has a mathematically precise scientific solution, solely involving natural forces are greatly mistaken. Some events have occurred as the result of the supernatural involvement of our creator and Lord Jesus Christ. Science works only in certain limitations which must be recognized. There is a simple "scientific" approach to determining if an event has a natural or supernatural cause. Any historical event needs to start with an isolated system approach. We take all the available evidence to describe what event accurately occurred. We examine the possible influences of the physical laws, which are the laws which operate on a daily basis. Then we ask the question: Could the known physical laws have caused this particular event to occur? If the answer is no, then we must decide if the event did actually occurred, despite the lack of ability for science to explain the event. Recall that science does not have all the answers and there are a number of events, like the origin of life, we can not scientifically explain. We must use the legal-historical method of examining the evidence and then make a personal decision if the event took place, as discussed in the book Evidence That Demands a Verdict by Josh McDowell. If we accept that it did occur, by a decision based on faith and the evidence presented, and no natural scientific explanation is available, the event was a miracle. There is one criterion to base a faith decision to accept or reject the presence of a miracle. The event must take place during the presence of a holy man of God like Moses or the apostle Peter. If Christ is present, of course, you accept the record of a miracle taking place. It is important to examine the person God is using to perform the "miracle". Otherwise, our faith is miss-directed. Does the existence of miracles conflict with science in any way? No. If the event can not be explained by our daily physical laws there must be some yet unknown force which could have caused the event to occur. Every scientist should accept this statement. The next question is what is the nature of this unexplainable force? Since we can not explain such things as the origin of the universe by natural laws, the force must be "super"-natural. There is no way to avoid this opening. Even if we discover a force to explain these events in the future, there are still mysteries we can not explain by natural means. Every scientist must come to the conclusion to identify this unseen force as "super-natural" no matter how hard they try to avoid the term. Then there must be an explanation for the source of this force. By definition of the term force, it must have a cause. A force is the result of a push or pull from some source. It takes little effort to say that the Christian faith explains the source as from the supreme Lord God. Other explanations are equally based on faith. Another example of a miraculous event is Christ's walking on the water. There was apparently nothing for Christ to walk on, but Christ walked across the sea. How? Simple, there was some kind of supernatural force supporting Christ above the water allowing Christ to walk across the sea. The force of gravity pulling down on the body of Christ was counteracted by a supernatural force supporting Him. The force of gravity was canceled by a force from God. Therefore, supernatural events generally involve a supernatural force which counteracts a natural force creating conditions where natural forces do not apply.

The argument over the existence of miracles and how certain unexplainable events take place revolves around questions about faith. We need to decide, by faith, the source of the forces which cause unexplainable events to take place. The decision comes back to a question of faith in the existence of God and the characteristics of God. The decision is based on an individual's beliefs and understanding of spiritual matters. As I have stated throughout this book, my opinion is that the Bible is the one and only complete record of God. Through the Bible, God has revealed himself to men. The Bible was not written solely by men seeking God, but was written by the moving of the Holy Spirit in the lives of men. The talent to use words to express ideas given by God was a part of the individual author's abilities. However, the union of man and God in writing the Bible has produced a work which is infallible. Some critics have challenged the view that the Bible is the infallible word of God because it was written by men. It is true that the Bible had human authors. It is also true that people make mistakes. However, not everything everyone does all the time is a mistake. We can present strong evidence that God worked with the writers to produce a perfect written history of the relationship of God and man. One of the books we intend to write will address the Christian lifestyle. The ones who ridicule the Christian perspective do not understand the tremendous freedom and happiness we have in living for Christ. Some Christians over criticize their life. They act as if everything they do all day long is a sin. The truth of the Gospel shows us we can have a fun filled Christian day with no sin involved. By not celebrating the joy we can experience with the Christian lifestyle, we unwittingly damage the witness we could have to non-believers. This is not to suggest that you will be forever perfect in this world, but as you grow in Christ you can live without sin for a prolonged period of time. This is not to be abused and have a "holier that thou" attitude. We need to simply humbly obey the commandment to perfectly follow the teachings of Christ. We need to follow the teachings of Christ with mathematical precision, always presenting a witness to others of the presence of Christ in our lives. "Be perfect, therefore, as your heavenly Father is perfect." Matthew 5:48. "Therefore, I urge you, brothers, in view of God's mercy, to offer your bodies as living sacrifices, holy and pleasing to God." Romans 12:1.

The Theory of Probability

The last subject we will cover in this chapter is on probability. The idea of probability is somewhat difficult to explain precisely. The subject usually falls into the category of intuition. "In everyday language we call something 'probable' if we believe it likely to happen, 'improbable'; if we believe it unlikely to happen, or 'certain' if we believe it sure to happen. In the mathematical theory of probability we try to define such concepts more precisely so as to assign them measures, or numerical indices, which can be computed, and therefore compared, arithmetically. [7.12]." We see that from the very inception of probability theory, it is another scientific field that is influenced by faith and assumptions. This introduces an element or possible error into the calculations. There are actually very few situations that there is little or no error in the mathematical results. There are some areas where it seams that statistics and probability equations are absolutely necessary. However, there are other cases where you receive extremely diverse results because not all the parameters are taken into account. The field of statistics has numerous applications in dealing with analyzing data concerning opinion polls, longevity studies for insurance companies and many other ways to generalize your given data. "The most important applications of probability theory which you are likely to encounter later are in economics, genetics, thermodynamics, nuclear physics, information theory, and other highly technical sciences which require special backgrounds for an adequate understanding of their problems. However, most essential principles of the probability theory involved in such applications can be more simply illustrated in elementary experiments like tossing coins, or in common games of chance. [7.13]." These methods are used to formulate theories in these more technical fields. The next step in the scientific process is to test these theories in actual experiments. In chapter nine we will discuss the use of probability equations in modern physics. It has been shown that probability equations are a necessary part of analyzing information about the nature of the atom and sub-atomic physics. The need for probability equations to estimate the apparent random nature of the atom was unsettling for Dr. Albert Einstein. "Albert Einstein never liked quantum mechanics, even though he played an important role in the foundation of the subject. The unpredictability and uncertainty of quantum physics was repugnant to him. He expressed his feelings of revulsion by saying 'God does not play dice.' Although this book is a testament to his genius, on this one point Einstein was wrong. Quantum mechanics works. There is an inherent uncertainty in the quantum world. But in view of Hawking's discoveries, there may be a level of randomicity that extends even across the universe. As Stephen Hawking put it: 'God not only plays dice but also sometimes throws them where they cannot be seen.' [7.14]" Was Einstein wrong? Do you see atoms as stable or randomly unstable in nature? Einstein proposed this simple question to explain his view of quantum mechanics. Is the random nature of the sub-atomic particles due to their nature or due to our methods of examining these tiny particles? We will discuss quantum mechanics in more detail in chapter nine.

There are areas like biology and the theoretical origin of life from natural forces and chemicals where different scientists get radically different results to their probability calculations. Why is there such a wide variety of values expressing the probability of life developing from chemicals or the universe coming into existence? To follow how this "calculated error" becomes a part of the results let us examine a few simple illustrations of using probability calculations. One of the most basic calculations is in finding the probability of a coin landing on heads or tails as it is tossed in the air and allowed to land on a flat surface. Another situation where there is apparent exactness to the calculations is in rolling a pair of dice. On the surface, these seam to be relatively simple calculations with little room for error. However, there are some "unseen" assumptions present in making these calculations. These include that the coin or dice are of a standard size. Is there any wind to affect the results? You assume that there are no external forces like the wind to effect your experiment. You are also making assumptions that the dice are rolled on a smooth surface and they are not "fixed" dice so the result of the toss remains the same with each roll. If these conditions are met, you can make some reasonable analysis of the chances of a certain combination of events taking place. "If the probability of events E_1 and E_2 are p_1 and p_2 respectively, then by definition event E_1 is p_1 / p_2 times as probable (likely to happen) as event E_2. ... To illustrate the relative likelihood of all the possible outcomes of a game, it is sometimes convenient to prepare a table of all its basic events and their consequent probabilities. In the game of dice, for instance, each of 2 (cubical) dice has its faces numbered from 1 to 6 by a corresponding number of spots, and when the dice come to rest after being rolled, the player adds the 2 of these numbers faced upward. We have already seen that the total number of possible combinations of the faces of 2 dice is $6^2 = 36$. [7.15]"

Is this always an accurate estimate of the probability of a certain number coming face up? If, for example, you had an unusually large set of dice, the likelihood for the dice to roll over is less than a smaller pair of dice. Just imagine rolling a pair of large "fussy" dice like the ones you have seen hanging from a rear view mirror. When you roll these dice they do not roll as easily which can affect the results of the experiment. You are therefore assuming that you have a pair of standard dice when making these calculations. There is always a certain amount of assumptions in probability equations and their results. You must ask, for example, is the person performing the test an honest person? There is often a certain amount of bias when making the probability equations. "The uncertainties of chance, which is the subject matter of probability theory, is also the subject of many hopes and fears. Understandably, therefore, the field is one in which wishful thinking often leads to misconceptions, or to superstitions based on misconceptions. [7.16]" We observe that the field of probability and statistics leaves open the influence of a researcher's faith, perhaps more than any other scientific field. It is actually part of the mathematical calculations. "When no two outcomes of an experiment can occur at the same time, the outcomes are said to be mutually exclusive. If no outcome is any more likely to occur than any other is, the outcomes are said to be equally likely. The usual way of determining whether the outcomes of an experiment are mutually exclusive and equally likely is by reason alone. One simply thinks about the experiment prior to performing it, and decides, on the basis of his reason alone, whether the outcomes are mutually exclusive and equally likely. ... 'The probability of Event A equals the number of outcomes favorable to A divided by the total number of outcomes.' ... P (A) = Favorable outcomes ÷ Total outcomes ... Note that in order to use the above definition we must be dealing with equally likely, mutually exclusive events. ... The only way one can determine whether the outcomes of an experiment are equally likely and mutually exclusive is by reasoning through the situation a priori. [7.17]." This is why we get radically different probabilities about situations occurring in biology. The evolutionist will assume that as soon as you have basic amino acids, as in the Stanley Miller experiment previously discussed, we will shortly have a living cell. They therefore assume, by some undiscovered process, life can easily form from chemicals. In each case they assume that events leading to a natural explanation of every event are likely to occur. In fact they assume that nothing apart from a natural explanation can occur. The evolutionists' position is less scientific than the creation scientist. Why? Simple, when it comes to natural phenomena, the creation scientists give natural forces only the ability that we can prove in the laboratory. Therefore, the list of acceptable capabilities of natural phenomena is in perfect agreement with experiment. The evolutionists, on the other hand, give physical forces an almost god-like ability to overcome the most difficult circumstances. They justify their view by saying that these forces act in combination in a way we simply do not understand as yet. They appear to have been influenced by a supernatural mind of God, but we accept as a prior knowledge that this can not exist. In other words, they are committed to an atheistic belief in the universe. The creationists explain the probability of the universe forming, or life developing, in terms of only what has been proven experimentally. There are no experimental evidence that chemicals can "spontaneously generate" life. On this basis, the likelihood of life forming without the presence of God is zero. Why do evolutionists quote probability estimates so much? Using statistics and probability estimates is one of the easiest ways to confuse someone. They quote so many estimates without specifying the bias nature of their estimates that the general public is fooled into believing the lie of evolution.

References for Chapter 7

7.1   Howard Anton, Calculus with analytical geometry, John Wiley and Sons, Inc., New York, 1980, p.78-79.

7.2   Ibid, p. 126-127, p. 156-157.

7.3   Ibid, Introduction p. xxiii.

7.4   Ibid, Introduction p. xxi- xxii.

7.5   Ibid, Introduction p. xxiv.

7.6   Charles Darwin, The Origin of Species By Means of Natural Selection (1859), Sixth London Edition, A.L. Burt. New York, 1900, p. 496

7.7   Howard Anton, Calculus with analytical geometry, John Wiley and Sons, Inc., New York, 1980, p. 52.

7.8   Ibid pages. 181,327,389,549,634,637-638,741-742,1094 .

7.9   BIBLE-BELIEVING SCIENTISTS OF THE PAST- IMPACT No. 103 January 1982 by Henry M. Morris, Ph.D. © Copyright 2004 Institute for Creation Research. Web site: ICR.org.

7.10   Albert Einstein, Ideas and Opinions, New York, Dell Publishing Co., Crown Publishers MCMLIV, p. 54-55.

7.11   William Barclay, The Ten Commandments Pocket Guide, Westminster John Knox Press, Louisville, Kentucky, 2001, p. 8.

7.12   Abraham Sperling and Monroe Stuart, Mathematics Made Simple, Made Simple Books, Doubleday & Company INC. Garden City, New York, 1962, p. 158.

7.13   Ibid p. 160.

7.14   William J. Kaufmann, III, Black Holes and Warped Spacetime, W.H. Freeman and Company, 1979, p. 215-126.

7.15   Abraham Sperling and Monroe Stuart, Mathematics Made Simple, Made Simple Books, Doubleday & Company INC. Garden City, New York, 1962, p. 161.

7.16   Ibid. p. 165.

7.17   H.T. Hayslett, Jr., Statistics Made Simple, Made Simple Books, Doubleday & Company INC. Garden City, New York, 1968, p. 36.

Illustrations for Chapter 7

7.1   Martin M. Lipschutz, Schaum's Outline Series Theory and Problems of Differential Geometry, McGraw-Hill Book Company, New York, 1969, p. 151, p.155.

7.2   William J. Kaufmann, III, Black Holes and Warped Spacetime, W.H. Freeman and Company, San Francisco, 1979, p. 196.

7.3   Howard Anton, Calculus with analytical geometry, John Wiley and Sons, Inc., New York, 1980, p. 75.

7.4   Ibid p. 164.

Chapter 8: Classical Physics and the Applied Sciences.

Introduction to Classical Physics

The field of science known as physics is the study of all the fundamental physical relationships. Through physics, we learn the basic relationships between quantities and the parameters in which physical laws work. The basic principles of physics are usually taught in a two semester course in high schools and universities. The first semester is primarily dedicated to mechanical principles, projectile motion, co-ordinate systems, and movements within a particular reference frame. After the study of physics, you can apply the principles to a number of different areas. For instance, the principles of mechanics learned in a first semester physics class is applied to specific examples to acquire a Mechanical Engineering degree which requires several more courses. To receive a degree in Electrical Engineering, you expand the elementary principles of energy and electricity taught in the second semester physics class. Modern technological achievements all come from specific applications of basic physical principles, almost all of which are introduced in a basic college or high school course. We have previously discussed some of the beliefs in science. With science, we are supposed to be able to explain every type of phenomena. Some scientists go as far as to say that with science there is no need to turn to God for an explanation of any event. This view point is not reasonable. Science, in particular physics, can only show inter-relationships of one property to another. When describing an event in scientific terms, we must accompany the scientific principles with the conditions in which the principles hold true. We shall learn in the next chapter that Einstein's theory of Relativity revolutionized physics. It showed us that there are no absolutes in the physical realm, but all things are relative to one another. Einstein's theory also showed how every principle of physics is subject to change. The primary example of this profound statement is found in the unique conditions discovered when you accelerate a system of particles to velocities near the speed of light. When any material system is subjected to such high velocities a great number of changes occur and all the laws of classical physics must be modified. The philosophical point to be made is that, if there is any absolute in the universe, it must exist outside the physical laws. We, as Christians, believe in a supernatural realm in which God lives today. God is the only truly absolute constant in the universe. All other principles are relative to the plan, presence, and power of God. In physics, you will use many of the physical constants. Just remember that these physical constants have limitations and God has no limits, except the ones He imposes on Himself. Physical constants are limited in accuracy of measurement because the device determining the value of each constant has a limited accuracy. Also, physical constants are subject to where they are used. Remember all equations using physical constants are modified in systems traveling at speeds approaching light.

As we mentioned earlier, science is the study of relationships between fundamental quantities. There are just three fundamental physical quantities. These are time, length, and mass. "In mechanics, the three fundamental quantities are length (L), time (T), and mass (M). All other physical quantities in mechanics can be expressed in terms of these. ... In 1960, an international committee established rules to decide on a set of standards for these fundamental quantities. The system that was established is an adaptation of the metric system, and it is called the International System (SI) of units. ... In this system, the units of mass, length and time are the kilogram, meter, and second, respectively. Other standard SI units established by the committee are those for temperature (the Kelvin), electric current (the ampere), luminous intensity (the candela) and for the amount of substance (the mole) ... Definitions of units are under constant review and are changed from time to time. The SI unit of mass, the kilogram, is defined as the mass of a specific platinum-iridium alloy cylinder kept at the International Bureau of Weights and Measures at Severes, France. ... Before 1960, the standard of time was defined in terms of the mean solar day for the year 1900. ... In 1967 the SI unit of time, the second, was redefined using the characteristic frequency of a particular kind of cesium atom as the "reference clock": One second- the time required for a cesium-133 atom to undergo 9,192,631,770 vibrations. ... Until 1960, the standard for length, the meter, was defined as the distance between two lines on a specific platinum-iridium bar stored under controlled conditions. ... However, in October 1983, the meter was redefined as follows: One meter- the distance traveled by light in vacuum during a time of 1/299,792,458 second. In effect, this latest definition establishes that the speed of light in vacuum is 299,792,458 meters per second. [8.1]" The study of physics is all about referencing the quantities of an object to a point of reference. Again, the study of physics is inseparable with the field of mathematics as both fields are primarily concerned with relationships. We try to analyze the effects of a force on an object and describe the changes in a precise manner. Sometimes the property of something we are examining is derived from a combination of two or more known fundamental properties. For example, there are many cases when it is useful to know the density of an object. Density (Greek letter rho) can be defined as the mass per unit volume ($\rho = m/v$). Here we derive the density of the object in terms of our fundamental property of mass and length. What is volume? It is the measure of what the object can hold based on its physical dimensions. The volume of an object goes back to the geometry skills we discussed in the last chapter. So, we must measure the length of the object in all three dimensions to determine its volume. The result is we now can know something about the material property of density in terms of more fundamental units of length and mass. It is important to known the density of an object if you are working in a particular field like ship building. After all, you would not want a multi-million dollar ship to sink because it was too heavy to float.

In previous chapters on Astronomy we referred to the fundamental forces in the universe. Actually, there are three fundamental forces. "In 1979, physicists predicted that the electromagnetic force and the weak force are manifestations of one and the same force called the electro-weak force. This prediction was confirmed experimentally in 1984. Thus the current view is that there are only three fundamental forces in nature. [8.2]" Even though this work has combined the electromagnetic force with the weak force in an effort to bring us one step closed to a unified field theory; it is useful to think of these two forces as separate. The electromagnetic force is used extensively in understanding the macroscopic world of electronics. The weak nuclear force has only a short range and only operates inside the atom's nuclei. Therefore we can see that in spite of the similarities, there are some distinct differences to the two forces. For this reason, this book will continue to refer to the number of fundamental forces as four. These are gravity and the electromagnetic force for the macroscopic world, the strong force (the "mysterious" force holding the atom together), and the weak nuclear force for explaining the instability of certain sub-atomic particles. Most physical principles involve the use of one or more of these fundamental forces. For example, all matter, by the definition of a material body, has a gravitational field. The larger the mass the stronger the gravitational field. The force of gravity is what holds the atmosphere to the earth and allows us to live on the earth. The inter-relationship of one property to another is described by mathematical formulas. Science endeavors to do two things. Describe **how** something works, and **why** it works or why it was designed to function a certain way. [8.3] Just because there is a method to describe **how** something works, it doesn't mean we understand **why** it works. These are two separate questions concerning the internal workings of a system. For example, you may be a good automobile driver, but know little about the internal design of a car. You know **how** to operate a car but do not know **why** it works, and a good Mechanical Engineer is not necessarily a good driver. The theory of evolution states that random motion created order through the progression of time. This makes as much sense as suggesting that the car we are driving was made by a gust of wind blowing dust into the air and forming our car. The forces of nature were not made by their own random motion but by the wisdom and power of God. This is the ultimate answer to the question of **why** the universe works the way it does. Science is simply the endeavor to explain **how** God has designed the universe. Physics is the field of science that provides the laws and principles for the foundation of all our technological achievements. Cars, refrigerators, microwaves, computers, are just a few of the practical applications of the principles of physics. We will list and discuss a few of the formulas used in college and high school textbooks. The formulas represent relationships between two or more physical properties or forces. The combined total amount of physical formulas and theories describes a universe of inter-relationships and inter-dependencies. The laws of physics describe what can and must happen under certain conditions. The laws of physics can be compared with the laws we have been given by God, through the laws of Moses and the commandments of Christ. Just as the laws of physics set the boundary conditions for physical phenomena, the spiritual laws set the boundaries for the relationships between man and God. I will mention a few of the theories of physics relevant to our discussion of biblical principles. From these principles, I want to draw a parable to the human condition and our relationship with God.

Tools for Learning

Science was once considered a vehicle used to learn more about the power of God. This is how Sir Isaac Newton perceived the goal of science. However, science is a "neutral" tool for learning. It is neither good nor bad; it is simply a tool for learning about the universe. In recent years it seams as through this tool has been turned from a device used to give glory to God as the creator of all these physical principles, to an attempt to disprove the existence of God. The attempt to disprove the existence of God has failed miserably in every instance. The possibility of a 6 day creation of the universe by the supernatural power of God has become a real, plausible theory. All of the theories describing the universe as the result of merely natural forces acting randomly over long periods of time, has been exposed as being filled with inconsistencies and contradictions. A simple paradox can be derived from the first law of thermodynamics. If nothing can be created or destroyed in the physical universe, how did the universe ever come into existence? You are given two choices by science. One: A point of singularity which has no beginning but simply always existed or some oscillating system, ambiguous and well beyond our scientific understanding. Or two: The God of the Bible always existing, "the Alpha and Omega", by a supernatural power created everything. The choice is completely dependent on faith in the evidence presented. I hope that I have made the case clear in the chapters on Astronomy that God has created the universe. Is there enough evidence to cause you to take a leap of faith and accept the Bible as the word of God? The center of the entire Bible is Christ. Who is he, really? Many secular documentaries attempt to explain his teachings without recognizing His deity, and fail every time. We can answer these questions and numerous other questions about life in general and the history of mankind by a close study of the Bible. Many of the theories in science rely heavily on faith. The theory of evolution is an unproven theory which relies on an individual's faith to accept or reject the theory on the basis of faith in the quantity and quality of the evidence. So far the evidence in favor of evolution is far from conclusive.

Einstein often spoke of the role of faith in the scientific pursuit. One of his most famous quotes explains the relationship between science and faith in a fashion typical of Einstein's style. "The situation can be expressed by an image: science without religion is lame, religion without science is blind. ... I have asserted above that in truth a legitimate conflict between religion and science cannot exist. [8.4]" We reviewed this quote in the last chapter. To translate this quote into language used by ordinary people, Einstein believed that science requires a faith in an ordered universe to direct the scientists on their quest for answers. Religion, on the other hand, has a need for the knowledge obtained by science to complete a long list of things we praise God for creating. Science provides a look into the specific acts of God's creation. There are other quotes where Einstein describes his belief in a "cosmological god." This is different than the personal God we find in the New Testament. Einstein had a sense that there is a God in the universe, because science requires the presence of God. Take this quote from Einstein: "You will hardly find one among the profounder sort of scientific minds without a religious feeling of his own. ... His religious feeling takes the form of a rapturous amazement at the harmony of natural law, which reveals an intelligence of such superiority that, compared with it, all the systematic thinking and acting of human beings is an utterly insignificant reflection. [8.5]" Again, Einstein saw the need for religion in science from the history of the development of science. "The interpretation of religion, as here advanced, implies a dependence of science on the religious attitude. ... Those individuals to whom we owe the great creative achievements of science were all of them imbued with the truly religious conviction that this universe of ours is something perfect and susceptible to the rational striving for knowledge. [8.6]" We covered a brief list of scientists who believed in God and made extraordinary contributions to the field of physics and mathematics in our last chapter. Einstein goes on to explain the necessity of a "religious drive" that is necessary if anyone claims to be a scientist. "The individual feels the futility of human desires and aims and the sublimity and marvelous order which reveal themselves both in nature and in the world of thought. Individual existence impresses him as a sort of prison and he wants to experience the universe as a single significant whole. The beginnings of cosmic religious feeling already appear at an early stage of development, e.g., in many of the Psalms of David and in some of the Prophets. ... The highest principles for our aspirations and judgments are given to us in the Jewish-Christian religious tradition. ... Accordingly, a religious person is devout in the sense that he has no doubt of the significance and loftiness of those super-personal objects and goals which neither require nor are capable of rational formation. They exist with the same necessity and matter-of-factness as he himself. In this sense religion is the age-old endeavor of mankind to become clearly and completely conscious of these values and goals and constantly to strengthen and extend their effect. If one conceives of religion and science according to these definitions then a conflict between them appears impossible. [8.7]" Einstein had a way of explaining difficult subjects like religion and science in a long draw out way. He was deeply a man of peace and tried to "negotiate" conflicts as peaceably as possible. However, you can see that Einstein had convictions concerning the necessity of religion in scientific pursuits, even if we may disagree with his particular definition of religion. "For the scientific method can teach us nothing else beyond how facts are related to, and conditioned by, each other. ... Yet it *is* equally clear that knowledge of what is does not open the door directly to what *should be*. One can have the clearest and most complete knowledge of what *is*, and yet not be able to deduct from that what should be the *goal* of our human aspirations. ... Here we face, therefore, the limits of the purely rational conception of our existence. ... Intelligence makes clear to us the interrelation of means and ends. But mere thinking cannot give us a sense of the ultimate and fundamental ends. To make clear these fundamental ends ... seems to me precisely the most important function which religion has to perform in the social life of man. [8.8]" Again, Einstein was deeply concerned with the attempts of some scientists to disregard religion in there studies and see religion as a hindrance to the pursuits of science.

This introduces an interesting question to briefly explore. What is the consciousness? This topic has becoming widely debated in the scientific community. We already stated in chapter six how the renowned father of modern neurosurgery, Dr. Wilder Penfield, became convinced that scientific experiments lead him to the conclusion that there is something that operates in the mind that goes beyond the bio-chemistry of the brain. This is understandable from the standpoint of physics. Once again, we are reminded of the laws of conservation. "'Darwinian evolution will never be able to explain the origin of consciousness,' he told me. 'Perhaps Darwinists can explain how consciousness was shaped in a certain way over time, because the behavior that consciousness caused had survival value. But it can't explain the *origin* of consciousness, because it can't explain how you get something from nothing.' ... If the universe began with dead matter having no consciousness, 'how, then, do you get something totally different – consciousness, living, thinking, feeling, believing creatures – from materials that don't have that?' But if everything started with the mind of God, he said, 'we don't have a problem with explaining the origin of our mind.' ... Nobel Prize winning neurophysiologist John C. Eccles concluded from the evidence 'that there is what we might call a supernatural origin of my unique self-conscious mind or my unique selfhood or soul.' [8.9]" There are many other evidences that the brain has a supernatural origin and a "dual nature". One such support of this nature is found in certain amnesia patients. In some cases, there is a large amount of memory loss. They can forget their husbands and children which once occupied a great deal of their life. However, their basic talents and personalities remain unaltered from the injury. This re-opens the classic debate between what controls your personality and abilities more, genetics or environment. If the amnesia patient retains a great deal of their personality while losing large portions of their memory, is this not strong evidence that what you do with your life is partially pre-destined? Doesn't this show that God has a plan for your life? Some of us as Christians would like to think so. But, once again it depends upon how each person's individual faith interprets the evidence.

The founders of modern science who believed in a deity have a long list of names. There are also a select group of scientists with a devoutly Christian faith. "The founders of modern science were all bunched into a particular geographical location dominated by a Judeo-Christian world view. I'm thinking of men like Louis Aggasiz (founder of glacial science and perhaps paleontology); Charles Babbage (often said to be the creator of the computer); Francis Bacon (father of the scientific method); Sir Charles Bell (first to extensively map the brain and nervous system); Robert Boyle (father of modern chemistry); Georges Cuvier (founder of comparative anatomy and perhaps paleontology); John Dalton (father of modern atomic theory); Jean Henri Fabre (chief founder of modern entomology); John Ambrose Fleming (some call him the founder of modern electronics/inventor of the diode); James Joule (discoverer of the first law of thermodynamics); William Thomson Kelvin (perhaps the first to clearly state the second law of thermodynamics); Johannes Kepler (discoverer of the laws of planetary motion); Carolus Linnaeus (father of modern taxonomy); James Clerk Maxwell (formulator of the electromagnetic theory of light); Gregor Mendel (father of genetics); Isaac Newton (discoverer of the universal laws of gravitation); Blaise Pascal (major contributor to probability studies and hydrostatics); Louis Pasteur (formulator of the germ theory)." [8.10]

Vectors and scalars

Among the first chapters in most physics textbooks is a description of vectors and scalars. Basically, a vector is any quantity which has both a magnitude and a direction. A scalar is a unit which has only a magnitude and no direction. Examples of vector quantities are displacement, velocity, acceleration, and all fundamental forces. All of these quantities have both a magnitude and a direction. For instance, torque is a familiar term to car mechanics. Torque is the amount of twisting force applied to a particular object. When working on the engine, torque describes how tight you turn certain bolts. It has a magnitude i.e. the amount of force applied to turn a bolt and a direction, the direction of the twisting motion of the bolt, clockwise or counter- clockwise. Examples of scalars are quantities like speed, weight, and density. These quantities describe amounts, like how much you weigh. Vectors and scalars are two terms of paramount importance to physics. All the physical quantities can be divided into these two categories. There are various methods for adding vector quantities. When two vectors are added we say the result is the resultant vector. The various methods of vector addition follow the various rules of geometry. For example, you can use the triangle method of vector addition or in other cases the parallelogram rule of vector addition.

Ideas about vectors are important to philosophical ideas developed from scientists studying physical laws. The extension of physical theorems is sometimes called metaphysics. The prefix Meta is defined in Webster's dictionary as referring to a change in place or form, to transcend or modify. When it is placed in front of the word physics it means to transcend physics. In other words, to go beyond the concrete information gathered from the physical laws describing the universe, to describing something else. I only want to describe a few of the conclusions which have been made. The first observation is about vector quantities. As stated, a vector is anything having a magnitude and a direction. To go beyond purely scientific laws we must have faith. The scientific laws fail to completely describe the universe. There are a lot of mysteries to understanding the universe. Physical laws alone can not solve these mysteries. Thereby, it becomes necessary to make some sort of sense out of these mysteries to give an individual a sense of purpose and order. Without some sort of belief that is used as a moral center, life is dull, boring and extremely difficult to live. If we have no faith in a supernatural God and no faith in things beyond our ability to explain in scientific terms, we have no direction in our life. Direction is necessary if we are to be complete as an individual. The theory of evolution is based on a faith of survival of the fittest principles. The "direction" you take is random depending on what environmental forces affect your life. You simply "go where the wind blows" This faith leads to degeneration into chaos. Violence, selfishness and other "animal-like" characteristics are promoted in this imagined struggle for survival. The Christian perspective is the exact opposite. Christianity teaches us the value of loving one another and the security of God's grace in providing our physical and spiritual needs now and for eternity. "Jesus answered, 'I am the way, and the truth, and the life; no one comes to the Father (the creator God), but by me.'" John 14:6 Christ teaches us that the only way to put direction into your life, at least a positive direction, is to put faith in Him as savior and Lord. According to the Bible all people are lost without accepting Jesus Christ as Lord of their life. Applying the concepts of physics to these statements, the situation becomes increasingly clear. If you are without faith in Christ you have no direction in your life. If you have no direction, you have just quantity. In other words, you simply exist and your life has no meaning or universal significance. Even our most basic "instincts" tell us we are more than just a collection of chemical elements.

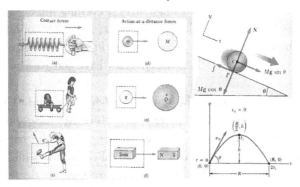

Figure 8.1

Sir Isaac Newton's Principles

Most of classical physics are derived from the theories and principles of Sir Isaac Newton. One of his most significant achievements was his three principles of force, mass and motion. We can understand, somewhat, from experience the concept of a force. Simply speaking, a force is defined as a push or pull on an object. All forces fall into one of two categories, a contact force or a force that acts on an object from a distance, see figure 8.1. "Everyone has a basic understanding of the concept of force from everyday experiences. When you push or pull an object, you exert a force on it. You exert a force when you throw or kick a ball. [8.11]" You can cause an object to move if you exert a powerful enough force to overcome the other forces acting on the object. In the case of kicking the football, you must overcome the force of gravity pulling the football to the ground. You will notice when you are successful the football travels in basically an arc due to the two forces acting on the object. This is an example of rectilinear or projectile motion. Other forces affect objects from a distance. The force of gravity, for example, is due to the mass of each object and can affect objects over a great distance. The strength of this force is related to the mass of each object affected, and the distance between them. The gravitational force of the sun keeps the earth in orbit around the sun. Another force that can influence objects at a distance is electricity. If you have a negatively charged particle, like an electron, it will be attracted to an object with a positive charge. This forms the basis of all our various electrical circuits which operate inside our technological devices.

We have already discussed the fundamental forces of the universe. But how can we define them? Isaac Newton attempted to define these forces, in his time there were just gravity and electricity, by their characteristics. Newton's first principle states that any object in an isolated system will remain in the state in which it is found. Or stated more simply, an object in motion will stay in motion and an object at rest will stay at rest until acted upon by an outside force. According to this first law of motion, if an object is in motion, it will tend to stay in motion with a constant velocity. Newton's first law of motion is often referred to the law of inertia. The law of inertia is profoundly important in our understanding of the universe. The concept of inertia is strongly associated with the amount of mass an object will posses. We often think of mass and weight as the same thing, because we measure them as the same on earth. However, these two quantities are vastly different. "Inertia is the property of matter that relates to the tendency of an object to remain at rest or in uniform motion. ... Mass is a term used to measure inertia, and the SI unit of mass is the kilogram. ... It is important to point out that mass should not be confused with weight. Mass and weight are two different quantities. The weight of a body is equal to the force of gravity acting on the body and varies with location. For example a person who weights 180 lb on earth weights only about 30 lb on the moon. [8.12]" Newton's law of inertia can be considered part of the many laws of conservation. We will examine this more closely when we cover the principles of energy and the law of conservation of mass and energy. The law of inertia is another obstacle for scientists who chose to believe in the creation of the universe by natural forces alone. If the universe tends to stay in the state it is found in, why was it formed in the first place? This is no trivial matter. There are many elaborate theories on what factors could have caused the proposed singularity preceding the big bang to become unstable and bring forth the entire universe from this singular point. So far, the exact conditions at the beginning of the universe are a mystery to those who believe there is no God. In the next chapter, we will discuss the principles of sub-atomic physics and how these discoveries have led to a proposed picture of how the universe began.

Inertia is the tendency to remain in the state in which it is found. This could be considered the degree in which we resist change. We all have the tendency to resist change, to one degree or another. In the spiritual realm, what is usually the cause? In a word, sin. Sin is the natural tendency to rebel that makes people reject the gospel. "For when we were controlled by the sinful nature, the sinful passions aroused by the law were at work in our bodies, so that we bore fruit for death." Romans 7:5 "I know that nothing good lives in me, that is, in my sinful nature. For I have the desire to do what is good, but I cannot carry it out. For what I do is not the good I want to do; no, the evil I do not want to do–this I keep on doing." Romans 7:18-19. As Christians, we still struggle with a lack of desire to serve the Lord, but through the strength of Christ we can overcome our sinful nature. "The mind of sinful man is death, but the mind controlled by the Spirit is life and peace; the sinful mind is hostile to God. It does not submit to God's law, nor can it do so. Those controlled by the sinful nature cannot please God. You, however, are controlled not by the sinful nature but by the Spirit, if the Spirit of God lives in you. And if anyone does not have the Spirit of Christ, he does not belong to Christ. But if Christ is in you, your body is dead because of sin, yet your spirit is alive because of righteousness. And if the Spirit of him who raised Jesus from the dead is living in you, he who raised Christ from the dead will also give life to your mortal bodies through his Spirit, who lives in you." Romans 8:6-11. It is only by the power of Christ that we can overcome our sinful nature and be "good". No amount of physiological treatment, philosophies or other religions can establish inner peace and fulfillment like the love of Christ.

Newton's second law is his famous equation defining any given force. It states that the resultant force placed on an object is equivalent to the mass of the object multiplied by the acceleration of the object, F=ma. Newton's third law is the famous principle of applied force and counter force. Simply stated, for every force there is an equal and opposite force accompanied. Or for every action there is an equal and opposite reaction. In every situation involving a force we must consider two forces, not just one. "This law ... is equivalent to stating that forces always occur in pairs, or that a single isolated force cannot exist. [8.13]" The majority of mechanical principles depend on these fundamental properties of force. When a truck pulls a load, a crane lifts a crate, or an automobile moves down the road, these principles are always at work. There are many examples of using these simple principles in complex ways. Even though we understand these characteristics of all natural forces, it is amazing that we can not define the term force, any more precisely than a push or pull on something. In the next chapter we will discuss the attempt to go beyond this simple explanation of force, by concepts introduced in the study of sub-atomic physics. We will see some of the same difficulties in explaining how the atom was created that we discovered in explaining how the universe began.

In my opinion, these simple principles of physics have paramount significance to the spiritual principles of Christianity. We have already discussed one aspect of Newton's first law applied to our spiritual conditions. Another way physics can be applied to the spiritual realm is in the fact that there is an order to the universe. The Bible puts it this way: "And I am sure that he who began a good work in you will bring it to completion at the day of Jesus Christ." Philippians 1:6. Everything works together with God's plan for mankind. The scripture indicates that all events in the universe follow a logical pattern taking place according to the will of the Lord, ultimately. However we, with our limited intellect, can not always see the logic in every event. According to physical laws, Newton's first law is an idealization because there is no particle which is truly isolated. The Bible supports this conclusion. We have already seen how the natural forces could not have created life on earth. It took the outside power of God's word to make life exist. Nothing is beyond the influence of God's Word, and all events are part of God's plan. In every day life, the one lie accepted by many people is that you can be totally "independent" of other people and even the presence of God. In reality, no man is an island, as the saying goes. My father in law has lived a long life in search of being independent from every person he can. In his youth he sought to be independent of his parents. In his youth, he thought a job could help him find independence and freedom. He discovered that the "farming business" was as close as he could come to freedom. As he planted and harvested crops he felt that, at last, he was far removed from other people. However, he still was dependent on people in stores to supply parts for the tractors occasionally and fuel for the daily operation. Again, there is no place on earth where we are not influenced, to some extent, by other people. Likewise, we can never truly remove ourselves from spiritual influences at work. We are either pulled toward God in the things we know to be right or pulled in the direction of rebellion with God. One of the forces will become the dominant spiritual influence on each person's life, depending on what thoughts most occupy your mind. "See to it that no one takes you captive through hollow and deceptive philosophy, which depends on human tradition and the basic principles of this world rather than on Christ." Colossians 2:8 "The mind of sinful man is death, but the mind controlled by the Spirit is life and peace; the sinful mind is hostile to God. It does not submit to God's law, nor can it do so. Those controlled by the sinful nature cannot please God. You, however, are controlled not by the sinful nature but by the Spirit, if the Spirit of God lives in you. And if anyone does not have the Spirit of Christ, he does not belong to Christ. But if Christ is in you, your body is dead because of sin, yet your spirit is alive because of righteousness. ... For if you live according to the sinful nature, you will die; but if by the Spirit you put to death the misdeeds of the body, you will live, because those who are led by the Spirit of God are sons of God. For you did not receive a spirit that makes you a slave again to fear, but you received the Spirit of sonship. And by him we cry, 'Abba, Father.' The Spirit himself testifies with our spirit that we are God's children." Romans 8:6-10, 13-16.

Newton's second law demonstrates how the magnitude of any force is dependant upon the amount of mass and the amount of acceleration of the object. The Bible is filled with relationships of how our lives are affected on the amount of faith we have in the Word of God and the amount of time we spend in prayer. The amount of time we devote to serving others can be repaid a thousand fold both now and in heaven. These things, and many more aspects of a Christian lifestyle, are part of a treasure that can be cherished both now and in the future. "Each man should give what he has decided in his heart to give, not reluctantly or under compulsion, for God loves a cheerful giver." 2Corinthians 9:7. "Whatever you do, work at it with all your heart, as working for the Lord, not for men, since you know that you will receive an inheritance from the Lord as a reward. It is the Lord Christ you are serving." Colossians 3:23-24. "Do not lay up for yourself treasures on earth, where moth and rust consume and where thieves break in and steal, but lay up for yourself treasures in heaven. For where your treasure is, there will your heart be also. Truly, I say to you, whatever you bind on earth shall be bound in heaven and whatever you lose on earth shall be loosed in heaven." Mathew 6:19-21, 18:18. There are many equations in the Christian view of man's relationship with God through Christ. This principle teaches us to dwell on reading the Word of God daily and doing what we are instructed to do through the Scriptures. The more you talk to God in prayer, the more answers to prayer you will receive. The more praise you give unto God, the more the joy of the Lord, through the Holy Spirit will fill your life. These are just a few of the biblical principles that demonstrate how events in our lives depend upon our relationship with God. Newton's third law of force is a principle of a cause and effect relationship. For each force applied to an object, there is an equal and opposite force opposing the motion caused by the first force. The counter force in most physical circumstances is usually either friction or gravity. There are basically two spiritual forces at work in each of our lives each day. There is the pulling of the Holy Spirit towards the straight and narrow path of righteous living. There is an opposing force of temptation from Satan pulling us towards sinful acts. "Be self-controlled and alert. Your enemy the devil prowls around like a roaring lion looking for someone to devour." 1 Peter 5:8. As stated earlier, these two opposing spiritual forces are constantly at work. The force of rebellion and sin against God is strongest when we struggle for independence. The obsession with the "me" generation to be independent causes us to be susceptible to the influence of Satan. We can not worship God if we think we have accomplished everything by ourselves. We can not know the ways of righteousness when we think we already have all of life's answers. And we can not be saved when we believe we are already saved by our own "good works". Why do you need a savior when you, who is the closest thing to God that exists (in your mind), has judged yourself "okay"?

Sometimes the opposing spiritual forces merely create friction between fellow believers which tend to stifle our effectiveness in teaching and spreading the Gospel. "If you forgive anyone, I also forgive him. And what I have forgiven–if there was anything to forgive–I have forgiven in the sight of Christ for your sake, in order that Satan might not outwit us. For we are not unaware of his schemes." 2 Corinthians 2:10-11 Satan's greatest weapon against believers is to create dissention among us over usually minor issues. We see this battle taking place each day as it seams that for every step we take forward, we make two steps backward. There are many principles of this Spiritual Battlefield which my wife and I intend to cover in a future book. As we also learned earlier, no force is ever isolated. There are always two forces at work according to the laws of physics. The Spiritual law is that there is a continual battle of God against Satan at work until the final battle described in detail within the book of Revelation. The answer to winning the war in the here and now is simple: if you allow the Lord to control your life, the victory is already won. "Thanks be to God! He gives us the victory through our Lord Jesus Christ." 1Corinthians 15:57 "I have told you these things, so that in me you may have peace. In this world you will have trouble. But take heart! I have overcome the world." John 16:33. You can live in a relationship with Christ where your spiritual, financial, and material needs are met with gracious abundance. If you have a problem, ask God for a solution. You may be astonished with how God can place circumstances into your life to help you overcome your difficulties.

The cause and effect principle of Newton's third law also applies to the spiritual principle of judgment. There is payment due for a lifetime of partying and living on a continual "valley high". The punishment is eternal separation from God; the same fate awaits Satan and his angels. "For all have sinned and fall short of the glory of God." Romans 3:23. "For the wages of sin is death." Romans 6:23. The relationship between man and God prior to the birth of Christ in Bethlehem has much like a contract relationship. Sin was brought into the world through Adam. "Nevertheless, death reigned from the time of Adam to the time of Moses, even over those who did not sin by breaking a command, as did Adam, who was a pattern of the one to come. But the gift is not like the trespass. For if the many died by the trespass of the one man, how much more did God's grace and the gift that came by the grace of the one man, Jesus Christ, overflow to the many! Again, the gift of God is not like the result of the one man's sin: The judgment followed one sin and brought condemnation, but the gift followed many trespasses and brought justification. For if, by the trespass of the one man, death reigned through that one man, how much more will those who receive God's abundant provision of grace and of the gift of righteousness reign in life through the one man, Jesus Christ. Consequently, just as the result of one trespass was condemnation for all men, so also the result of one act of righteousness was justification that brings life for all men." Romans 5:14-18. The result is that all the judgments of God against you as a sinner can be passed by. Jesus offers to take your punishment. What could motivate someone else to take another's punishment of death? Jesus offers to be your substitute if you make Him your best friend and follow all the teachings of scripture. The most important one is to follow the commandments of loving God first and others second.

All people where deserving of death. God in his great mercy reached down to man and offered a way for God to hold back his anger. The only way to appease the Lord in the Old Testament was to make sacrifices to the Lord. Adam and his children, Cain and Abel, made sacrifices to the Lord to ask for mercy and forgiveness. Abel received mercy but forgiveness came later with Christ's death on the cross. The sacrifices of lambs led to God's relationship to man through a covenant made with Abraham. In the Old Testament, there was no forgiveness of sin, only the laws of God and penalties for breaking the laws. Man made sacrifices to compensate for his disobedience and sin. In this manner, the Old Testament gave ways for people to outwardly show they had a commitment to love God. In this chapter we will explain the difference in the relationship God had with mankind in the Old Testament and in the New Testament. The relationship between man and God in the Old Testament was developed from Adam and continued through the prophets. It started with general guidelines for a good relationship with the Lord and then culminated in Moses bringing specific laws to his people. The Ten Commandments were the first and most important of these laws. Other laws followed which specifically described how we should live and the sacrifices man needed to make to the Lord. One element in the acceptance of the sacrifices was the condition of the heart making the sacrifice. The importance of this condition was not fully realized until the coming of Christ. "In the course of time Cain brought to the Lord an offering of the fruit of the ground, and Abel brought of the firstlings of his flock and of their fat portions. And the Lord had regard for Abel and his offering, but for Cain and his offering he had no regard." Genesis 4:3-5. The reason Cain's offerings was not acceptable is explained in the verses which follow. Cain had a problem with sin in his life. His heart needed to be right with God before any sacrifice of any amount would be acceptable. The point to be remembered here is that no amount of good deeds will be acceptable to God unless you first give the Lord total control of you life. That is to say, give your heart to God.

Differences between the Old and New Testaments

The relationship between the Old Testament and the New Testament is a lot like the relationship between classical physics and modern physics. Classical physics was largely developed from general principles which became specific laws. These are the limits placed upon certain physical phenomena. In modern physics we are able to generalize and expand on these physical laws. The laws are no longer universally true, but true under certain initial conditions. In the next chapter we will explore the concepts of modern physics and show how relativity and quantum mechanics have reshaped the scientific view of the universe. Similarly, the laws of the Old Testament occupy a special place in the New Testament. There are some instances where they don't even apply! Just like Newton's laws depend upon a frame of reference, all laws of physics had to be modified for conditions of high velocities; velocities approaching the speed of light, the principles of the Old Testament had to be modified if you accept Jesus Christ as Lord. "But now the righteousness of God has been manifested apart from the law, although, the law and the prophets bear witness to it." Romans 3:21. "Christ said, 'Think not that I have come to abolish the law and the prophets; I have come not to abolish them but to fulfilled them.'" Mathew 5:17. "But now, by dying to what once bound us, we have been released from the law so that we serve in the new way of the Spirit, and not in the old way of the written code." Romans 7:6. "There is therefore now no condemnation for those who are in Christ Jesus." Romans 8:1. "For Christ is the end of the law, that every one who has faith may be justified." Romans 10:4. "But if you are led by the spirit you are not under the law." Galatians 5:18. "For I through the law died to the law that I might live to God. I have been crucified with Christ; it is no longer I who live, but Christ who lives in me; and the life I now live in the flesh I live by faith in the Son of God." Galatians 2:19-20. "The entire law is summed up in a single command: Love you neighbor as yourself." Galatians 5:14.

In the New Testament we are under the sanctification of grace. We are no longer under the contract condition we had in the Old Testament. Grace means that we are now given the opportunity to be pardoned, totally forgiven, for our sins. As we stated earlier, the Old Testament is basically a contract type of relationship. Laws and punishment, actually just appeasing the anger of the Lord for our sin, was all we had. The penalty of our sins was eternal death, separation from God. With Christ we have complete forgiveness of our sins by the mercies of his grace. Forgiveness by grace means we are forgiven even though we didn't deserve it. "But God shows his love for us in that while we were yet sinners Christ died for us. Since, therefore, we are now justified by his blood, much more shall we be saved by him from the wrath of God." Romans 5:8-9. Salvation is free gift. Some are confused by salvation and what happens after salvation. When you accept Jesus Christ as Lord you are saved, born again and that will never change. The actions you take as a Christian to serve God is the natural result of your commitment. Salvation is complete when you accept Christ. "For the wages of sin is death, but the free gift of God is eternal life in Christ Jesus our Lord." Romans 6:23. "For by grace you have been saved through faith; and this is not of your own doing, it is the gift of God- not because of works, least any man should boast. For we are his workmanship, created in Christ Jesus for good works, which God prepared beforehand, that we should walk in them." Ephesians 2:8-10. The first step is accepting the gift of salvation. It is free! Ask for it! This means to ask Jesus Christ to be Lord of your life. At that moment you are joined with God and your name is written in the Lamb's book of life. You are sealed with Christ. "Therefore, if any man is in Christ he is a new creation, the old has passed away, behold, the new has come." 2 Corinthians 4:17. There are several steps toward a close walking with Jesus which follow this transformation in your life. The works and other requirements for living and receiving the abundant life God has waiting for you, come after your prayer dedicating you life to God. Only a prayer of dedication turning control of your life to Christ will save you from the Day of Judgment.

The Changed Relationship with God

The changed relationship we have with God, due to the coming of Christ, can again be compared with the transition between classical and modern physics. Again, classical physics develops from general ideas about nature to specific laws and principles. In modern physics there is a new attempt to simplify all the laws of physics. The general theory of relativity gave us concepts of gravitational fields and concepts of the space-time continuum. It gives a generalized view of the universe. The concepts of quantum mechanics have brought us closer to an understanding of the subatomic structure of the atom. There is a renewed attempt at a grand unified field theory to describe all fundamental forces as some combination of a single force. To accomplish this goal requires the almost unimaginable attempt at relating quantum mechanics and relativity, two theories which seam completely incompatible. Similar to this type of simplifying the view of the universe to a single equation with GUT theories, the changed relationship in the New Testament involves a simplification of all the laws of the prophets. "You shall love the Lord your God with all your heart and with all your soul and with all your mind. This is the great and first commandment. And a second is like it. You shall love your neighbor as yourself. On these two commandments depend all the law and the prophets." Mathew 22:37-40. If you love God then you won't want to do sinful acts like blasphemy. Also, you will want to gather to worship God i.e. go to church and will dedicate time for prayer everyday. If you love your neighbor you will not steal from them, lie to them or break any of the other commandments. All of the laws of the prophets are fulfilled in these two commandments. We went from the specific to the general case. With this in mind, when we study the

Old Testament and we can find applications in New Testament living. This is why we don't disregard the Old Testament teachings, but look at the passages as fulfilled in Christ. This is why it is important that someone reading the Bible for the first time read passages that related to the age in which we live. A good suggestion would be the Gospels of John then Mathew and the rest of the New Testament. The book of Romans gives a lot of clear directions to a new Christian. Then, the book of Ephesians give good guidelines on how to "love thy neighbor" in a specific way. The general outline of love is specified in other works by the disciple John. Next you may want to read Psalms and Proverbs. Then once these books are read, you can examine the Old Testament more clearly. This is why many places, like the Gideon's, hand out just the New Testament with the Old Testament books of Psalms and Proverbs copied in the back. These are the books of the Bible essential for new believers to read first, in my opinion. In physics it is just the opposite approach, we must study the old physics for basic engineering principles. Then, on the basis of the old principles, we begin to understand the workings of the inventions of our atomic age.

The Study of Forces

Again, we turn our attention to the study of classical physics. The study of physics begins with the concept of force. As we have stated, an applied force is defined as a push or pull placed on an object. We define the nature of forces with Newton's three laws. Applying Newton's three laws allows us to work many problems in the fields of physics. Statics is the field of physics where the net forces equal zero and the object is at rest. Dynamics is the study of physics where the objects move as the result of a resultant net force. The ultimate source of a force is linked to the energy in a system. As we stated earlier there are only four fundamental forces; Electromagnetic force, the weak nuclear force, the strong force, and gravity. The only two forces we commonly view are gravitational forces and electromagnetic forces. By our definition of a force, we exert kinetic energy upon a certain mass and we say that a force is applied. When we exert a force to cause a push or pull to be applied to an object we are using some type of energy to generate an applied force. If the force is created by a person, the force is caused by the electrochemical stimulation of muscles in the body. If the force is created as a result of a combustion engine, it is due to the energy released as a result of a chemical explosion. All forces we describe in every day life require an exchange of energy and it usually involves the electromagnetic force. Gravity is still a relatively undefined quantity. We know the magnitude of gravity from Newton's law: The amount of force exerted on an object by using gravity, is the amount of weight for the object given by: W=mg, as you may recall from chapter one. However, the source of gravity is unknown. Current theories suggest that gravity is the result of the interaction of gravitons at the subatomic level. All we really know is that any object that occupies space and has mass possesses a gravitational field. The magnitude of a gravitational field between two masses, like the earth and your body, is determined by the size of each mass, the distance between the two masses and the gravitational constant. We can summarize this effect with two different formulas both described in chapter one. The formula: W=mg is easier to use in making computations about the pull of gravity. All you need to know is the amount of mass of the object and the value of the acceleration due to gravity, g. This value can change depending on several factors. Newton proposed the theory of gravity, mentioned above, to explain why objects fall toward the center of the earth. Newton's theory was that there are a number of natural forces are present in every material object, now known to be four. We call the force pulling two objects together, due to their mass, gravity. Through repeated laboratory experiments, under controlled conditions, precise measurements are taken. In the case of gravity, it is found that the amount of force due to gravity is proportional to the mass of the two objects attracted by gravity and the distance between the bodies. This is represented by the expression $F_g=G(m_1m_2/D)$ where F_g is the magnitude of the force of gravity, G is the universal gravitational constant, m_1 is the mass of object one, m_2 is the mass of object two and D is the distance between the two objects. Relationships such as these are the heart of physics. Most of classical physics is derived from the concepts of Sir Isaac Newton. Most work deals with the magnitude and direction of forces. This represents the limiting conditions upon the structure of the universe. Equations, such as the one describing gravity, represent the boundaries of how strong a force can be and how far away it can influence an object. The boundaries are very apparent when you compare forces at the "normal" level and at the sub-atomic level. For example, in everyday experience nearly every object on earth is affected by the earth's pull of gravity. However, when working with subatomic physics the effect of gravity is practically non-existent. Scientist must be more concerned with the strong nuclear force or the other fundamental forces in their experiments. Likewise, if you travel a great deal into space, the pull of gravity is greatly reduced. These types of limitations to the expressions must be taken into account when we study the universe. There are times when these scientific laws simply do not apply to the current situation.

Statics and Dynamics

The study of forces in the field of physics can be divided into two categories: Statics and Dynamics, as we mentioned earlier. Statics is the study of forces in equilibrium. We are affected by forces every minute of every day. When an object is not moving the forces are balanced. For example, as you sit on your chair you have equilibrium of at least two forces acting on your body. You are experiencing the force of gravity pulling your body toward the earth. This force is countered by a force applied by the springs in the chair, or other supporting mechanism, to keep your body off the floor. Since you have a balance of forces you do not fall to the floor unless someone pulls the chair from under you, you are at a state of rest. The other type of study of forces is called dynamics. This is the study of forces in motion. Some examples include projectile motion, motion of free falling bodies, circular or orbital motion, and pendulum motion. All these types of situations can be described in terms of vectors. We can describe the velocity, acceleration and magnitude of applied force acting on these objects in motion. Such studies usually begin with motion in one dimension, then with two dimensions, and finally three dimensions. Some of the calculations can become highly complicated.

Most of the principles and uses of classical physics are found in describing the quantity, magnitude and direction of forces, but the true nature of these forces is left to the field of modern physics. As we have discussed earlier, there are four fundamental forces: gravitational force, electromagnetic force, weak nuclear force, and the strong nuclear force. All motions and all conditions of equilibrium are the result of some combination of these forces. We will discuss many aspects of these forces in the next chapter, but for now the only principle to remember is that these forces were made by God, in my opinion. These four basic forces are the foundation for all organized nuclear and chemical structures in the universe. The God of the Bible works in organized ways and created these forces on the first or second day of creation. The god of chaos is Satan, not the God of creation which we worship through Jesus Christ our savoir and Lord. Therefore, it is not by a mysterious random force the universe was formed but by the power of God. The Bible tells us of many spiritual truths which allow the "force" of the Holy Spirit to control a person's life and allow the will of our Father in heaven to be done on earth. The individual interpretation of the words of God, as to discover a specific meaning for our own lives, is guided by the Holly Spirit and allows us to grow and maintain a spiritual equilibrium. Part of this equilibrium of forces, good and evil, is in the daily decisions we make. We sometimes take the wrong path, but God in his infinite wisdom and grace is always present to pull us toward the straight and narrow path as we give our lives to Him in prayer. Just as we are constantly influenced by the force of gravity, we are constantly impressed upon by two spiritual forces each day. One force is the Holy Spirit pulling us to the ways of righteousness the other is Satan pulling us towards destruction. In this way we are in a constant spiritual war and we must be prepared for the attacks that come into our life.

There is another way to look at the "Statics and Dynamics" of the human spirit. God is always encouraging us to keep improving ourselves and grow to a better understanding of what He has planned for our life. God sternly warns us against being in a spiritual state of equilibrium, or stagnant. "I know your deeds, that you are neither cold nor hot. I wish you were either one or the other! So then, because you are lukewarm -neither hot nor cold- I am about to spit you out of my mouth. ... Those who I love I rebuke and discipline. So be earnest, and repent. ... To him that overcomes, I will give the right to sit with me on the throne, just as I overcame and sat down with my Father of his throne." Revelation 3:15-16, 19, 21. God gives us strong warnings against becoming idle and not fulfilling His plan for our lives. We are commanded to actively spread the Gospel and to be constantly doing God's work. Hence the phrase "idle hands are the devil's workshop". However with each warning, God gives us an opportunity to have a closer relationship with Him. He gives us help and a multitude of instructions on how to live out a Christian life. "I am the true vine, and My Father is the gardener. He cuts off every branch in me that bears no fruit, while every branch that does bears fruit He prunes, so that it will be even more fruitful. You are already clean because of the word I have spoken to you. Remain in Me, and I in you. No branch can bear fruit by itself; it must remain in the vine. Neither can you bear fruit unless you abide in me. I am the vine; you are the branches. If a man remains in me and I in him, he will bear much fruit; apart from me you can do nothing. If anyone does not remain in me, he is like a branch that is thrown away and withers; such branches are picked up, thrown into the fire, and burned. If you remain in me, and my words remain in you, ask whatever you wish, and it shall be given you. This is to My Father's glory, that you bear much fruit, showing yourselves to be my disciples." John 15:1-8. We are made to increase in learning and teach others about the principles of salvation. This is how we show ourselves to be disciples of Jesus. We are not to sit around thinking about ourselves, but doing God's work of helping others in need.

Energy and Work

The next subjects we will study are the concepts of energy and work. Work is a quantity defined by the magnitude of an applied force in a given direction times the distance traveled, $W=F*d=F\cos(\phi)d$ in the example given in figure 8.1 (b). In other words, work is the magnitude of force, in the direction the object moves, multiplied by the distance traveled by this same object. Work is the result of using an applied force to move an object, like a box of merchandise onto a shelf if you are working at a grocery store. You are applying a force under the box, which is opposing the force due to gravity, and causes the box to move a certain distance upward. The net force times the distance you moved the box to put it on the shelf is the amount of work you preformed. Again, work is the result of using an applied force in specific direction. It should be noted that if the object does not move, you are not considered to have done any work. You know this to be true if you have ever had a warehouse job. You can exert all the force you want on a box and exert a lot of energy, but if the box doesn't move up, no work is considered to have been accomplished. If you don't get the required help or equipment to cause the box to move, you job security will diminish and your paycheck could become quite small. Performing work expends energy. Everyone who has done much physical labor understands this principle. During the process of moving the box, your body will expend energy and sometimes you will perspire. Here is an instance when we can combine the concepts of force and energy. Kinetic energy is defined as the energy of motion. The change in kinetic energy is defined by the magnitude of the work done, $W= \Delta K.E.$ Kinetic energy is also determined by the amount of mass you are moving and the speed in which you are moving, $K.E.= \frac{1}{2}mv^2 .=$ Force x Distance.

Work is actually done by an exchange of energy. Let us take the example of the person lifting the box onto the shelf in reverse. Let's say the person is lifting the box from the shelf and putting it onto the floor. Since the object starts at rest, there is no initial kinetic energy. However, there is a certain amount of potential energy associated with the box: $P=mgh$ The potential energy is due to gravity puling on the object which sits at a height (h) and the weight of the box (mg). In the process of lifting the box from the shelf to the floor you are again doing work, but not as much. We start with the kinetic energy of the box as zero, because it is not moving. We say that all the energy in the box is stored in the form of potential energy, $P=F\ dx$. As the object begins to move, the potential energy becomes kinetic energy. The work to lift the box to the floor is less than the work it took to put the box onto the shelf. Everyone is aware that it is easier to lift something off of a shelf than to put something onto a high shelf. As the box moves down, the pull of gravity aids your work and you do not expend as much energy. When the object returns to a state of rest, all the potential energy of this system has been used to help you do the work of lifting the box to the ground. In this process the exact same amount of work takes place as occurred when the box was originally put on the shelf. The amount of work is equal to applied force times the distance moved ($W = Fd$). The total amount of work is considered to "conserved", meaning the amount of energy before lifting the box and after is exactly the same. There are numerous times in this process the energy of the box and the energy of the person lifting the box exchanges form. We can see that when we analyze almost any process by means of physics principles we find an exchange of energy has taken place. In the case of the work done by lifting this box, we realize that work is a function of a change in energy. Also, since work is related to the magnitude of the force and force is given by mass multiplied by acceleration ($F = ma$), the faster you work the more energy you use up. Anyone who has worked in a warehouse or retail setting understands this principle easily. You can work up a good sweat the faster you move those boxes. We take the vector sum of all the forces which resulted in moving the box up to the self and back down then back up to its original position, the net work done is zero. This can be summarized by the observation that you did not accomplish anything new by simply putting a box onto a shelf and then back down to the ground again. It is easy to understand this principle. If you stood at a shelf and simply moved a box up and down you would never accomplish your task of filling the proper merchandise in the proper position. The condition of the non-Christian is like this, always spinning your wheels, never fully understanding the meaning of life. When we realize that we are in a condition of wondering aimlessly through life, we must return to the Bible for answers.

Return to your point of origin

Repeatedly, science teaches that we are faced with the reality that the origin of the universe is from an all powerful God. Since God is the source of all life, it makes no sense to suggest that we can have any kind of life without a spiritual relationship with the creator and sustainer of all life, our Father God. Only a personal relationship with the creator of the universe can save our soul from total destruction. Another example of how we are pulled back to our point of origin is found in the study of springs, see fig 8.1 (a). When you pull on a spring there is a force of elasticity pulling you back to your original position. There is a potential energy stored in a coiled spring, figure 8.1(a). The amount of force is directly proportional to the potential energy of the spring; $F = -kx = ma$. This is directly proportional to the material of the spring, (the k factor), and the distance from your point of origin (x). Likewise, the further away from the straight and narrow path God wishes us to live, the more the Holy Spirit will pull you towards the word of God. There are two factors determining how much tugging the Holy Spirit will do to bring the "lost sheep" back into the fold. 1) The distance you are from the life you should be living i.e. how far you are into your sin i.e. drugs, alcohol violence etc. 2) The kind of stuff you are made of. This is determined by the nature of your personality and from the teachings of your parents, teachers, relatives and friends. What are you made of? What personality traits do you have? Do you have the courage to investigate God's word and promises? Are you somehow scared to read the Bible? It is amazing how many people have an opinion of what is right or wrong but never have read the entire Bible or study it continually. There are those with various opinions about Jesus Christ that have never read or at least carefully studied the New Testament. Why? If you want to know about Jesus, go to the source. If you have questions, just ask someone with knowledge about the Bible. Do not ask just anyone but someone you can trust to be honest and can help you in your Bible study.

What is Power?

Power is defined in the study of physics as a change in the amount of work done over a period of time: P= ΔW/Δt. Recall the definition of work (W= F*d=Fcos(ø)). To change the amount of work done you can adjust one of the determining variables, the force, the distance or the angle between the applied force and the direction the object moves. One option is that you can increase the magnitude of the force applied or apply the same force over a longer distance. Another possibility is to adjust the angle the force is applied to the object. If the amount of work would increase per a unit of time, the amount of power is increased. This definition of power can apply to the amount of "horsepower" inside a car engine or the electrical power delivered to your home. The main difference between mechanical power and electrical power is the force used to perform the work. In the form of mechanical power in an automobile, we are usually referring to the force generated by the combustion of gasoline. In electrical power we are considering the force of an electrical charge as it travels through the conducting medium. It is simply customary to refer to power from combustion in terms of horsepower and electrical power in Watts, named after James Watt. "Power is defined as the time rate of energy transfer. ... The unit for power in the SI system is J/s, which is also called a watt. ... The unit of power in the British engineering system is the horsepower (hp), where 1hp=550 ft* lb/s= 746 W. ... Although the W and the kWh (kilowatt-hour) are commonly used only in electrical applications, they can be used in other scientific areas. For example, an automobile engine can be rated in kW (kilowatt) as well as in hp. [8.14]" The relationship of work to power and energy exchange is best understood by the expression J/s, referring to joules per second. The unit of joule is named after James Prescott Joule (1818-1889). "Joule's most active research period, from 1837 through 1847, led to the establishment of the principles of conservation of energy and the equivalence of heat and other forms of energy. His study of the quantitative relationship between electrical, mechanical, and chemical effects of heat culminated in his announcement in 1843 of the amount of work required to produce a unit of heat: First: that the quantity of heat produced by the friction of bodies, whether solid or liquid, is always proportional to the quantity of energy expended. And second: that the quantity of heat capable of increasing the temperature of water ... by 1° Fahr requires ... the expenditure of a mechanical energy represented by the fall of 772lb through the distance of one-foot. This is called the mechanical equivalent of heat (the current accepted value is equal to 4.186 J/cal). ... One calorie is now defined to be *exactly* 4.186 J without reference to the heating of a substance: 1 cal ≡ 4.186 J. [8.15]" Again, we must understand that power is a transfer of energy. There are more technical specifications and equations to represent how this occurs. Are you beginning to see a pattern? Nearly every relationship in classical physics involves the transfer of energy in one form or another.

Is there a spiritual analog to these principles? Yes. The work of the Holy Spirit in a person's life is discussed throughout the New Testament. The force applied to your spiritual "heart" is the Holy Spirit wanting to lead in your life. God is constantly pulling on your heart to let Him control your life and bring you to a saving knowledge of the power of Christ. Recall the definition of a force; a push or pull on something. The force is a constant, unchanging love God has for you. The distance is the amount of room you allow the Holy Spirit to work in your life. The more spiritual "distance" you give the Holy Spirit to penetrate your life, the more "work" God can accomplish in your life. Another way you can look at this situation is that the further you live life away from sin, the more work the Holly Spirit can do on your life. This is not just a play on words. The Lord wants you to grow in your faith by having the Holy Spirit at work in your heart. By this, God can have a powerful impact on your life. "I pray that out of His glorious riches He may strengthen you with power through his Spirit in your inner being, so that Christ may dwell in your hearts through faith. And I pray that you, being rooted and established in love, may have power, together with all the saints, to grasp how wide and long and high and deep is the love of Christ, and to know this love that surpasses knowledge - that you may be filled to the measure of all the fullness of God. Now to him who is able to do immeasurably more than all we ask or imagine, according to His power that is at work within us, to Him be glory in the church and in Christ Jesus throughout all generations, for ever and ever! Amen" Ephesians 3:16-21 "But you will receive power when the Holy Spirit comes on you; and you will be my witnesses in Jerusalem, and in all Judea and Samaria, and to the ends of the earth." Acts

1:8 "I am not ashamed of the Gospel, because it is the power of God for the salvation of everyone who believes: first for the Jew, then for the Gentile." Romans 1:6 "I pray also that the eyes of your heart may be enlightened in order that you may know the hope to which He has called you, the riches of His glorious inheritance in the saints, and His incomparably great power for us who believe. That power is like the working of His mighty strength, which He exerted in Christ when He raised Him from the dead and seated Him at His right hand in the heavenly realms, far above all rule and authority, power and dominion, and every title that can be given, not only in the present age but also in the one to come." Ephesians 1:18-21 The spiritual truth is that if you want to experience the most abundant power of God in your life, you will give your life totally to Him. God wants to work on your life daily to fulfill your potential. God has a plan for your life and wants you to fulfill it. The only thing standing in the way is your self-directed will. When you accept the Lord Jesus as Savior, the work on you life to be a disciple of His begins. If you have a totally yielded heart, the Holy Spirit can do the most work in your life. The Power for abundant living comes through the work of the Holy Spirit and the passage of time. Again, in the principles of classical physics, power is the amount of work done over a period of time. As time goes by, the "spiritual power" in your life for love and joy can increase tremendously.

Laws of Energy Conservation

We learned previously that work is defined by a change in energy. Now we can explore the law of conservation of mechanical energy. This fundamental law states that the total amount of energy in any mechanical system remains constant. In other words, energy is neither created nor destroyed, but only changes from one form to another. "The principle of conservation of energy is one of the most far-reaching general laws of physics. It states that energy is neither created nor destroyed but can only be transformed from one form to another in an isolated system. Because the total energy of the system always remains constant, the law of conservation is a useful tool for analyzing a physical situation where energy is changing form. [8.16]" One example of using this law is in pendulum motion. The motion back and forth demonstrates the conversion of potential energy to kinetic energy and vise versa. When the pendulum is toward the top, most of the energy of the system is in the form of potential energy. As the force of gravity pulls the pendulum down, the energy of the system is transformed into kinetic energy. The total energy is the sum of the potential and kinetic energy at any given time, $E = K + U$, where E is total energy, K is the kinetic energy and U is the potential energy. We already looked at another example of this conservation principle. Remember the work done by placing a box on a shelf and then taking it down again? Here is another example of the conservation of energy in a closed system. By this physical law, we know the universe can not be a "closed" system. If it were, by all the laws of physics, the universe would never exist! Instead, the laws and principles of physics imply that the universe was, any maybe remains to this day, an "open" system. This is to say that the universe came into existence by receiving power from a source outside the known universe. This obviously leads to the conclusion that it was the power of God, existing outside the physical realm, which created the universe. Also, we discussed some of the results of the experiments at RHIC that connects our existence to a "higher dimension". We will explore this in greater detail in the next chapter and show how these experiments indicate that we may still be dependant on God sustaining the universe. Once again, to deny the presence of God and His hand in creating all things is a complete denial of science!

"The first law of thermodynamics is the restatement of conservation of energy. Mathematically, it reads $\Delta Q = \Delta U + \Delta W$, where ΔQ is the heat energy supplied to the system, ΔU is the change in the internal energy, and ΔW is the work done by the system against external forces. [8.17]" The second law of thermodynamics simply states that in the "real world" there is no such thing as a perfect system. There is a tendency to lose energy over time, usually due to radiation in the form of heat. This leads to the observation that there is a tendency to disorder in the universe. "Isolated systems tend toward disorder and entropy is a measure of this disorder. ... The entropy of the universe increases in all natural process.

This statement is yet another way of stating the second law of thermodynamics. [8.18]" We have covered many of the problems this law of science generates in explaining the creation of the universe by natural forces in previous chapters. Another way to look at this situation is to imagine the universe as a tightly wound watch. It has great potential energy which is often converted to kinetic energy. Yet every natural process loses some of the energy in the exchange. One difficult question to answer is this: If the universe is like a tightly wound spring slowly unwinding, how did the universe get wound up in the first place? This was the question Hawking explored and we discussed in earlier chapters. We are reminded once more that only the power of God, operating outside the known laws of physics, can explain the universe's existence. Every law of science leads us to this inescapable conclusion. We can never emphasize enough that the position that there is no God has no basis in science. The philosophy and beliefs of atheism is completely against all laws of physics and the principles of science. Science can explain a lot of details about how God has created the universe. However, science always confirms that God did indeed create all things throughout the universe. A person can only deny the existence of God through a profound, unyielding, stubborn faith in fields of science that person is only vaguely aware of. This person would rather have faith in unknown "natural" forces than accept the "truth" that all things are created and sustained by God. If you have questions about the nature of God, turn to God's Holly Bible for the answers to life's questions.

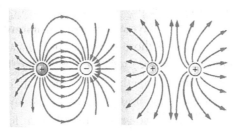

Figure 8.2

Electro-Static Fields

Next, let us discuss the world of electrical forces. We can divide the field into two separate categories. One is the study of stationary charged objects called electrostatics (we will learn in the next chapter that actually charged particles are never stationary). The second field is the study of charged particles in motion called electrodynamics. First, every charged particle has a force associated with it due to the presence of a charge, see figure 8.2. It was the Christian inventor, philosopher, statesman Benjamin Franklin (1706-1790) who discovered there are two types of charges which he named positive and negative. The basic principle of electrical charge that nearly everyone understands is that like charges repel each other and opposite charges attract each other. Another basic property of charge is that, like matter, charges can not be created nor destroyed, only displaced. Once again, we have another law of conservation to explain the properties of matter. "Another important aspect of Franklin's model of electricity is the implication that electrical charge is always conserved. That is, when one body is rubbed against another, charge is not created in the process. The electrified state is due to a transfer of charge from one body to the other. ... For example, when a glass rod is rubbed with silk, the silk obtains a negative charge ... We now know from our understanding of atomic structure that it is the negatively charged electrons that are transferred from the glass to the silk in the rubbing process. ... In 1909, Robert Millikan (1886-1953) discovered that electric charge always occurs as some integral multiple of some fundamental unit of charge, e. In modern terms, the charge q is said to be quantized. That is, electric charge exists as discrete 'packets'. Thus we can write q=Ne, where N is some integer. [8.19]" N represents the number of free electrons or protons in the charged sample. Therefore, the total charge of an object, q, is equivalent to the number of charged particles times the elemental unit of charge e= 1.602 177 33(49) x 10^{-19}C.

Here we discover another universal constant, the magnitude of charge of an electron, e. We have already discussed the universal Gravitational constant, G. There are actually a number of these universal constants with specific values. It should be noted that scientists have discovered these fundamental universal constants through experimentation, calculation, and observation. These physical constants represent the harmony in the universe. Einstein often referred to these "regularities", as Einstein called them, as conclusive proof of a universal God. The values of these physical constants are exactly what we need for the universe to operate properly. Here is a short, but not all- inclusive, list of these constants and their values. The Gravitational constant $G= 6.67 \times 10^{-11}$ Nm^2/kg^2. Electron and proton charge $e=1.6 \times 10^{-19}$ C, Planck's constant $h=6.63 \times 10^{-34}$ J*s. Boltzmann's constant$= 1.38 \times 10^{-23}$ J/K. Bohr radius $a_0=0.529177 \times 10^{-10}$ m. Compton wavelength $\lambda_c = 2.426\ 31058 \times 10^{-12}$ m. Hydrogen ground state $E_0=13.605698$ eV. The Permeability of free space $4\pi \times 10^{-7}$ N/A^2. The speed of light in a vacuum $c= 2.99792458 \times 10^8$ m/s. As you may be aware, they are still trying to find the last digit to the value of pi. $\pi \approx 3.14159$. Some of these constants, we will discuss in the next chapter on nuclear physics. We will examine the vital role of some of the above universal physical constants in the construction of the atom. In any case, these universal constants provide a pivotal role in the construction of the universe. There is no reason for these universal constants to be the way they are except because it is part of the magnificent design made by God. "The principle (Anthropic principle), as Glynn learned, essentially says that 'all the seemingly arbitrary and unrelated constants in physics have one strange thing in common – these are precisely the values you need if you want to have a universe capable of producing life,' ... 'Let's talk about gravity' ... 'Imagine a ruler, or one of those old-fashioned linear radio dials. ... The entire dial represents the range of force strengths in nature, with gravity being the weakest force and the strong nuclear force that binds protons and neutrons together in the nuclei being the strongest. ... Even if you were to move it (the dial) by only one inch, the impact of life in the universe would be catastrophic. ... 'That small adjustment of the dial would increase gravity by a billion-fold.' ... 'Animals anywhere near the size of human beings would be crushed.' ... In fact, a planet with a gravitational pull of a thousand times that of the Earth would have a diameter of only forty feet.' ... 'As you can see, compared with the total range of force strengths in nature, gravity has an incomprehensibly narrow range for life to exist. ... And gravity is just one parameter that scientists have studied. One expert said there are more than thirty separate physical or cosmological parameters that require precise calibration in order to produce a life-sustaining universe.' [8.20]" Here we can stand amazed at the fact that gravity is so vital for life and yet it is the weakest of the four fundamental forces. Recall that we discussed some of the properties and limitations of gravity in our chapters on Astronomy. We can reflect once more on the verse that summarizes the situation: "The heavens declare the glory of God; the skies proclaim the work of his hands." Psalms 19:1. These physical constants are not independent of God but were made by God. Science clearly shows God's presence in His creation.

The force between charges is sometimes called Coulomb's force, named after Charles Coulomb (1736-1806). The magnitude of this force is given by Coulomb's law: $F= k\ (q_1 q_2) / r^2$ where, k is called the Coulomb constant. $k= 8.9875 \times 10^9$ $N*m^2/C^2$. The amount of charge of each object is designated by q1 and q2 respectively. The value of k is a constant in a vacuum. When we conduct experiments, this fact must be taken into account. The k factor must be adjusted if we are taking our measurements outside of a vacuum. We have already discussed how all physics principles assume an isolated system. The calculation of electrostatic force strength is a prime example of how physics calculations are often estimates and actual values will vary with experiments. There are many similarities between the attractive force between two opposite electrical charges and a gravitational field. Notice the similarity between the formulas for calculating the force between two electrical charges and the gravitational force between two masses. Like the force of gravity, an electrical charge has a field associated with the charged particles. "The gravitational field g at a point in space was defined in Chapter 14 to be equal to the gravitational force F acting on a test mass m_0 divided by the test mass. That is $g=F/m_0$. In a similar manner, an electric field at a point in space can be defined in terms of the electric force acting on a test charge q_0 placed at that point. ... $E \equiv F/q_0$. ... Note that E is the field external to the test charge – not the field produced by the test charge. [8.21]" Therefore the electric field vector is defined as the force per unit of charge. We can re-write the above equation to give the magnitude of the electrical force as the product of the electrostatic field and the test charge, $F = E*q_0$. Recall that work is defined as the magnitude of a force multiplied by the distance the object moves. Also, recall the work done in a closed system can be the explained as deference in potential energy. This introduces the concept of electric potential, or volt, which determines the energy in an electrical system. "Since potential difference is a measure of energy per unit charge, the SI unit of potential is joules per coulomb, defined to be a unit called the volt (V): $1 V \equiv 1 J/C$. That is, I J of work must be done to take a 1-C charge through a potential difference of 1 V. [8.22]" This is the basic definition of voltage. Remember, the definition of work is force times distance. Moving a small test charge q_0 a short distance creates an electrical field E. Voltage is a measure of the number of charged particles available in any electrical circuit. Basic circuits are studied in all levels of science classes using batteries and electrical outlets as voltage sources. In advanced electrical engineering classes, the circuits become quite advanced.

Moving Charged Particles

Voltage is measured in volts after Alessandro Volta (1745-1827), who invented the electric battery. The next property to discuss in electrostatics is capacitance. "The capacitance, C, of a capacitor is defined as the ratio of the magnitude of the charge on either conductor to the magnitude of the potential difference between them: $C \equiv Q/V$. .... The capacitance of a device is a measure of its ability to store charge and electrical potential energy. [8.23]" A car battery consists of parallel plates which store energy due to the capacitance between the plates. The measure of capacitance is given in Farads, after Michael Faraday (1791-1867), a Christian scientist. This is the beginning of electrical circuits that is vital to our modern world. We find that there are two types of circuits. Parallel Circuits, where the voltages are added together, and series circuits, where the charge must be distributed the same for all components. The first property in the study of electrodynamics is current. Current is defined as the amount of change in charge per unit of time: $I \equiv dq\backslash dt$. This describes the speed of an electron through a medium. Current is measured in amps, named after Andre Ampere (1775-1836) Resistance is defined as the opposition to current flow. We can relate resistance to voltage and current flow by the famous Ohm's law: $V=IR$, where V is voltage, I is current, and R is resistance. Resistance is measured in Ohms after George Simon Ohm (1787-1854). Electrical power can then be given by: $P=IV$ where P is power, I is current, and V is voltage. Power, in the electrical field as well as in classical physics of motion, is given in kilo-Watts (kW) or 1,000 watts. The watt is named after James Watt (1736-1819) who is most remembered for producing the first commercial steam engine. Note that 1 watt is the equivalent of the amount of work required to move a 1 kilogram object from a stationary point with the acceleration 1 meter per second in the time of one second. As we shall see, the relationship between force, energy, and power become exceedingly clear in the study of electricity. The same principles and laws of physics apply in electrodynamics as in larger bodies in motion.

Recall that the definition of power is the change in work divided by the change in time, $P = \Delta W /\Delta t$. Also, work=force x distance. Therefore, Power= Force x (distance/time). Distance divide by time is equivalent to velocity. Therefore Power is also equivalent to a force times the velocity of the object which is moving, $P=F*v$. This definition of power is extremely significant when we study moving electrical charges. The power produced by a moving charge is thus related to the speed in which the charge is moving, current (I) and the electromotive force (Voltage). So in electrical systems we say that Power= the amount of voltage times amount of current in the circuit ($P=IV$). There are only a few types of devices that are needed in an electric circuit. First, a source of voltage potential is needed. This can be in the form of a battery, a capacitor or an electrical outlet. Next to control the speed at which the electricity flows, i.e. current, resistors are placed in the circuit. Sometimes you will want to switch off the flow of electricity completely or partially. This is done through a switch called a transistor. Transistors have the ability to change the direction of current flow, or change the amount of current flowing through a circuit like a dimmer switch. These three simple components: resistor, capacitor, and transistor, have changed form over the years. However, their basic functions are still employed in every electrical device. In electronic circuits, these devices are miniaturized and placed on an "integrated circuit" chip. These are the basic principles of electrical circuits used to create all the wonderful devices we use today. Radios, TV's, video games, cell phones and a nearly endless list of technological achievements are based on these scientific principles and the laws of physics.

You can see how the principles Newton discovered for material bodies i.e. F=ma, can be applied to charged particles. Physics has many principles that are inter-related. Physics relates many quantities together with several mathematical formulas. This allows physicists to determine a lot of information about a situation given only a few pieces of data. The old principle follows that if you have the same number of equations as unknown values, you can solve all unknown values, if the quantities are inter-related. Many physics problems will ask questions like: how much work is done on a particular charge to move a certain distance? Next, you may need to calculate the power used to perform this task. In this case, you will need one more piece of information to determine electrical power. You could be given the current of the circuit or the resistance and calculate the current from the known values, (Volts=Current x resistance). In physics classes you are often asked to answer many questions by applying the appropriate formula. It should be noted that nearly every physics problem can be related to an exchange of energy. One system of components loses energy; another system gains energy. Usually, the situation involves the "loss" of energy. This does not mean energy is destroyed, just dissipated into space. For example, most mechanical systems lose energy in the form of heat from friction. The energy is radiated out and becomes unusable. In this sense, the energy is "lost" because it can not be recovered back into a useful system. Once the heat energy is radiated into space, there is currently non technique to recover this loss of energy as it travels into space becoming increasingly more separated from its source. Again, the laws of physics depend on the fact that matter and energy can not be created or destroyed, they just change form. What science does not understand is where all the mater and energy of the universe originated from; unless you accept the inevitable conclusion it was an act of God. All scientific fields give us reasons to praise God for His divine nature. To say that we have discovered through science God doesn't exist is a demonstration of complete ignorance of science, or simply an act of stubborn rebellion against God's truth.

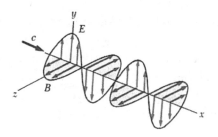

Figure 8.3

The next subject we will discuss is the magnetic field. Magnetic fields can be naturally occurring magnets or be man made. "The phenomenon of magnetism was known to the Greeks as early as around 800 B.C. They discovered that certain stones, now called magnetite (Fe_3O_4), attract pieces or iron. Legend ascribes the name magnetite to the Shepard Magnes, 'the nails of whose shoes and the tip of whose staff stuck fast in a magnetic field while he pastured his flocks.' In 1269 Pierre de Maricourt, using a spherical natural magnet, mapped the directions taken by a needle when placed at various points on the surface of the sphere. He found that the directions formed lines that encircle the sphere ... which he called the poles of the magnet. Subsequent experiments showed that every magnet, regardless of its shape, has two poles, called the north and south poles, which exhibit forces on each other in a manner analogous to electric charges. ... Although the force between two magnetic poles is similar to the force between two electric charges, there is an important difference. Electric charges can be isolated (witness the electron or proton), whereas magnetic poles cannot be isolated. ... All attempts thus far to detect an isolated magnetic monopole have been unsuccessful. No matter how many times a permanent magnet is cut, each piece will always have a north and south pole. [8.24]" As previously stated, natural magnets are only one source of a magnetic field. A magnetic force is also generated when a charged particle is moving through a current carrying wire. "The magnetic field of naturally occurring magnetite is too weak to be used in devices such as modern motors and generators; these magnetic fields must come from electric currents. Magnetic fields affect moving charges, and moving charges produce magnetic fields; therefore the concepts of magnetism and electricity are closely intertwined. [8.25]" We can see that these concepts are leading toward the conceptualization of the combined electric and magnetic force called the electromagnetic force. This has great significance in the field of science and there are enormous implications to our faith in Jesus Christ, as we will learn.

The magnetic field is always perpendicular, at a right angle, to the electrostatic force, see figure 8.3. "If a charge moves through a magnetic field at an angle, it will experience a force. The equation is given by $F= qvB$ or $F=qvB \sin(\emptyset)$, where q is the charge, B is the magnetic field, v is the velocity, and ø is the angle between the directions of the magnetic field and the velocity; thus ... the definition for the magnetic field is $B= F \div qv \sin(\emptyset)$. Magnetic field is expressed in SI units as a tesla (T), which is also called a weber per square meter: $T= Wb/m^2 = N/ Cm/s = N/ Am$. [8.26]" The study of magnetic fields and the properties of moving charges lead the way to the production of electrical generators. The AC (alternating current) generator converts mechanical energy into electrical energy, by an induced electrical potential. The type of current traveling from power plants to business, schools, and homes is AC. This type of current is not useful in most electronic devices. For household items like television sets and DVD players, you must convert the AC current to DC (direct current) through a set of diodes , called a transformer, inside the electronic unit. The basic principle of a magnetic field generated by a moving charge is called Faraday's law of induction, named after a Bible- believing Christian Scientist named Michael Faraday. Michael Faraday (1791-1867) discovered that when a conducting rod moved through a magnetic field, a certain voltage was induced into the conducting rod. This discovery of electromagnetic induction led Faraday to invent the electric motor and the electric generator. "Michael Faraday was a British physicist and chemist who is often regarded as the greatest experimental scientist of the 1800s. His many contributories to the study of electricity include the invention of the electric motor, electric generator, and transformer, as well as the discovery of electromagnetic induction, the laws of electrolysis, the discovery of benzene, and the theory that the plane of polarization of light is rotated in an electric field. [8.27]" Most of our modern world depends on these accomplishments by Michael Faraday. Not bad for a mere Christian Scientist.

What a difference these inventions and discoveries have made to the world! It is nearly impossible to imagine life before electricity. It is amazing, to me that there are so many uses for electricity. It is also fascinating how many of the discoveries of electricity and the various usages for electricity are the result of scientists who have been recognized by some historians as Christians. There seams to be a considerable effort to re-write history, omitting the fact that these great men of science believed in God. We can begin with the discoveries of Benjamin Franklin, as we previously mentioned. Some have called Benjamin Franklin a person who believed in deism. What does that mean? "Deism: The belief that there is a God who created all else, but who stands apart and does not ... interfere in any way with that creation." [8.28] Benjamin Franklin made many statements that suggest he might have this disposition in his early years, however there is strong evidence that he was a devoted Christian in his later years. In fact, some historians have used Benjamin Franklin as evidence that our country was in fact not founded as a Christian nation. Dr James Kennedy presents convincing evidence that the above statement is a lie. In fact, Dr, Kennedy gives many examples of long prayers, sometimes three hours in length, beginning the United States opening sessions of Congress in the early years. Some of these prayers were led by Benjamin Franklin, addressed to our savior and Lord Jesus Christ. Dr. Kennedy has written many books on the subject and I encourage you to investigate the evidence for our Christian heritage as a nation. It seams that the same so-called historians are attempting to re-write the history of the development of science as well as our national heritage. They consistently try to exclude or minimize the fact that most scientists, past and present, believe in God. Also, most of the greatest scientists have been, and are, Bible believing Christians.

In recent years, there has been a considerable effort to re-write all historical events with an atheistic slant. The historical truth is clear; some of the most profound discoveries leading to a scientific description of the electromagnetic force, and the description of light come from a long list of scientists with a biblical faith. Isaac Newton, Benjamin Franklin, Michael Faraday, and James Clerk Maxwell all had Christian convictions. The world may not understand the significance, but someone who believes in the Christian faith might. It makes "biblical sense" that those who sought to have a closer understanding of the properties of light might be Christian. Jesus calls those who follow His teachings "the light of the world." Mathew 5:14. Jesus also commands us to share this light of wisdom to the world. "Neither do people light a lamp and put it under a bowl. Instead they put it on its stand, and it gives light to everyone in the house. In the same way, let your light shine before men, that they may see your good deeds and praise your Father in heaven." Mathew 5:15-16. "For my eyes have seen your salvation, which you have prepared in the sight of all people, a light for revelation to the Gentiles and for glory to your people Israel." Luke 2:30-32 "When Jesus spoke again to the people, he said, "I am the light of the world. Whoever follows me will never walk in darkness, but will have the light of life." John 8:12 "The precepts of the LORD are right, giving joy to the heart. The commands of the LORD are radiant, giving light to the eyes." Psalms 19:8 "Your word is a lamp to my feet and a light for my path." Psalms 119:105 "God is light; in him there is no darkness at all." 1John 1:5 "The unfolding of your words gives light; it gives understanding to the simple." Psalms 119:130 Again, it is a lack of knowledge and understanding that is the reason for lack of faith in the Gospel. It is time to set the facts straight! It was Christian scientists throughout history, seeking to get a better understanding of God's works that created most of the great scientific discoveries we have today. Christians should be aware of these facts as they share there faith.

The Work of James Clerk Maxwell

The theoretical union of the concepts of electrical and magnetic fields belongs to one outstanding scientist of Christian faith, James Clerk Maxwell (1831-1879). Many of the principles of electrodynamics are found in Maxwell's equations, see figure 8.4(b). The equations of Gauss's law of electrical fields and of magnetism show how electrical and magnetic fields are conserved. We return to a cornerstone of physics: the laws of conservation of energy. It is on the basis of the laws of conservation we have the law of conservation of charge and correspondingly conservation of fields on any closed surface. This is why the four formulas in Maxwell's equations are shown by a closed integral, $\int$, with a circle. "We conclude this chapter by presenting four equations that can be regarded as the basis of all electrical and magnetic phenomena. These equations, known as Maxwell's equations, after James Clerk Maxwell, are as fundamental to electromagnetic phenomena as Newton's laws are to the study of mechanical phenomena. [8.29]" We find that the theoretical work of James Clerk Maxwell laid the ground work for the beginning of "modern physics". Modern physics is the study of the atom and its properties. The study of the atom reveals the beginning of understanding the many properties and attributes to light. How is light produced? Can we understand the true source and nature of light? The properties of light have been studied for centuries. However, with the study of electromagnetism, we begin the first major step in uncovering the true nature of light. Light is a part of the electromagnetic spectrum or we could say the electromagnetic spectrum is different manifestations of light. We will explore many more details to the nature of light in our next chapter on modern physics.

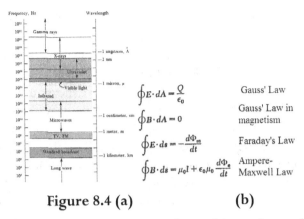

$$\oint E \cdot dA = \frac{Q}{\epsilon_0}$$ Gauss' Law

$$\oint B \cdot dA = 0$$ Gauss' Law in magnetism

$$\oint E \cdot ds = -\frac{d\Phi_m}{dt}$$ Faraday's Law

$$\oint B \cdot ds = \mu_0 I + \epsilon_0 \mu_0 \frac{d\Phi_e}{dt}$$ Ampere-Maxwell Law

Figure 8.4 (a)   **(b)**

"The consequences of Maxwell's equations are far-reaching and very dramatic for the history of physics. One of Maxwell's equations, the Ampere-Maxwell law, predicts that a time - varying electric field produces a magnetic field just as a time – varying magnetic field produces an electric field (Faraday's law). From this generalization, Maxwell introduced the concept of displacement current, a new source of a magnetic field. Thus, Maxwell's theory provided the final important link between electric and magnetic fields. Astonishingly, Maxwell's formalism also predicts the existence of electromagnetic waves that propagate through space with the speed of light. ... Electromagnetic waves were first generated and detected in 1887 by (Heinrich Rudolf) Hertz (1857-1894), using electrical sources. ... In a series of experiments, Hertz also showed that the radiation generated by his spark-gap device exhibited the wave properties of interference, diffraction, reflection, and polarization, all of which are properties exhibited by light. Thus, it became evident that the radio- frequency waves had properties similar to light waves and different only in frequency and wave- length. [8.30]" Maxwell's equations had many profound implications. One consequence of his theories is the concept of electromagnetic waves that travel through space at a constant speed i.e. the speed of light. "In Chapter 34, we shall show that these equations predict the existence of electromagnetic waves (traveling patterns of electric and magnetic fields), which travel with a speed $c = 1/\sqrt{\mu_0 \epsilon_0} \approx 3 \times 10^8$ m/s, the speed of light. [8.31]" In this relationship μ_0 is the permeability of free space, $\mu_0 = 4\pi \times 10^{-7}$ N/A^2. And ϵ_0 is the permittivity of free space, $\epsilon_0 = 1/\mu_0 c^2 = 8.8542 \times 10^{-12}$ C^2/N*m^2. The value of c, the speed of light in a vacuum, is a measured value found to be a constant in a vacuum. This again reminds us that all physical principles approximate the "ideal" conditions in an isolated system. In reality, there are never "ideal" conditions. In fact, the principles of physics imply that THE UNIVERSE IS NOT AN ISOLATED SYSTEM! It was created by God and is sustained by God. "For by Him all things were created: things in heaven and on earth, visible and invisible, whether thrones or powers or rulers or authorities; all things were created by Him and for Him. He is before all things, and in him all things hold together." Colossians 1:16-17. The book that I have extensively referenced for this chapter is one of my college textbooks in engineering physics. You may be pleased to know that I will not cover all the subjects mentioned in this college textbook, in this chapter. The referenced book, Physics for Scientists and Engineers, has 47 chapters and 1321 pages. I have essentially summarized over 950 pages in this chapter. Let me explain what I mean. There are a few principles found in first semester physics I have skipped until the next chapter. Also, the principles I have mentioned can be expressed in many different forms. For example, the textbook I am referring to also expresses some of the equations in this chapter in "calculus form". The textbook I am referencing also has numerous pictures and examples applying these basic physics principles to everyday life. It is a typical physics book and I will continue to periodically reference the subjects covered in the remainder of this chapter and in the next chapter on modern physics. Just a reminder that you may disagree with my philosophical conclusions in this book, but the works of science that this book summarizes are accurate with all textbooks on science found in public high schools and colleges. Again, science and faith absolutely have no conflict with each other, as Einstein has stated.

To describe the nature of light in a scientific manner has been a source of controversy over the centuries. "The nature and properties of light have been a subject of great interest and speculation since ancient times. The Greeks believed that light consisted of tiny particles (corpuscles) that were emitted by a light source and then stimulated the perception of vision upon striking the observer's eye. Newton used this corpuscular theory to explain the reflection and refraction of light. ... In 1678, a Dutch physicist and astronomer, Christian Huygens (1629-1695), showed that a wave theory of light could explain the laws of reflection and refraction. ... The first clear demonstration of the wave nature of light was provided in 1801 by Thomas Young (1773-1829), who showed that, under appropriate conditions, light exhibits interference behavior. [8.32]" The Thomas Young experiment is illustrated in figure 3.4 of chapter 3 and in figure 9.2 of the next chapter where we present more details about this important discovery. We see that throughout history there has been a controversy about the nature of light. Is light a particle or a wave? The answer is that light is both particle and wave. "The modern view is that light has a dual nature. To debate whether light is a particle or a wave is inappropriate because in some experiments light acts like a wave and in others it acts like a particle. Perhaps it is most accurate to say that both waves and particles are simplified models of reality and that light is such a complicated phenomena that no one model from our common experience can be devised to explain its nature. [8.33]" As we can see, even modern science has some difficulties explaining all the properties of light. The properties of light will lead us to another area of scientific research and discovery that is difficult to explain, quantum physics. The dual nature of light again reminds us of our dual nature: spirit and body.

As we have already seen, Hertz provided confirmation of Maxwell's assertion that light was a high-frequency electromagnetic wave. This led most scientists to accept the wave theory of light. However there is another phenomenon, discovered by Hertz, called the photoelectric effect that seams to indicate there are times light behaves as a particle. "The photoelectric effect is the ejections of electrons from a metal whose surface is exposed to light. ... Experiments showed that the kinetic energy of the ejected electron is independent of the light intensity. This was in contradiction of the wave theory, which held that a more intense beam of light should add more energy to the electron. [8.34]" From these discoveries in 1887, scientists had to wait to 1905 for a satisfactory explanation for the property of light known as the photoelectric effect. Scientists are simply people exploring the universe in a more detailed way than most of us. They still have the same feelings, apprehensions and frailties as we all do. Faced with this problem of a dual nature to light, the problem was simply put aside awaiting an explanation. "At the end of the 19th century, scientists believed that they had learned most of what was to be known about physics. Newton's law of motion and his universal theory of gravitation, Maxwell's theoretical work in unifying electricity and magnetism, and the laws of thermodynamics and kinetic theory were highly successful in explaining a wide variety of phenomena. However, at the turn of the 20th century, a major revolution shook the world of physics. In 1900 Plank provided the basic ideas that led to the formation of the quantum theory, and in 1905 Einstein formulated his brilliant special theory of relativity. [8.35]" In that same year Einstein released his paper on the photoelectric effect.

The beginning of the field of modern physics ironically starts at the very first year of the 20th century with the work of Max Plank (1858-1947) in 1900. Then in 1905 we have the work of Albert Einstein (1879-1955) on the photoelectric effect and the far-reaching theory of relativity. From their foundations a whole new era in physics begins. "A successful explanation of the photoelectric effect was given by Einstein in 1905, the same year he published his special theory of relativity. As a part of a general paper on electromagnetic radiation, for which he received the Nobel Prize in 1921, Einstein extended Planck's concept of quantization to electromagnetic waves. [8.36]" We will discuss more details about Plank's theory of quantization of energy in the next chapter. In addition, we will explore how the study of the structure of the atom led to a more accurate explanation for where light comes from. All these subjects are inter-related and come from both theoretical and experimental science. We have a great deal of thanks to give Heinrich Hertz for his experiments with electromagnetic fields. His discovery of methods to produce electromagnetic waves led to the development of creating a "carrier wave". This is an electromagnetic wave, like radio waves, that can carry your voice over long distances. The great invention of radio was born from this discovery and years later, television was first invented. His work exposing the photoelectric effect offered science a new puzzle to solve. This led the way to the birth of modern physics. This provided a clear separation between "classical physics" and "modern physics". Classical physics is the developments in science prior to the 20th century. Modern physics is primarily based on the development and applications of two theories: Quantum theory by Max Plank and the theories of Relativity by Albert Einstein. Classical physics deals with the events, which take place that we can experience by our senses. Modern Physics works with the structures of the atom, which lie underneath our perception and yet is the foundation for all of our experiences. Light is the bridge between both areas of science. We can see light with our eyes yet it has unseen properties that are produced inside the atom. In the next chapter we will explore both the physical explanation of the atom and philosophical conclusions some scientists make. The theory of relativity is a vital truth about the nature of the universe. However, some people with only a marginal understanding of science has misused the principles of relativity. They have constructed support for a philosophical point of view called moral relativism. "The philosophy of relativism claims that all so-called truth is relative, there really is no absolute truth, but that different things may be true for me and you. [8.37]"

In the next chapter we pick up on these philosophical discussions and dive deep into the atom itself. We will explore the structure of the atom from electrons, protons and neutrons to the quark model. The quark model explains the structure of nearly all sub-atomic particles including protons and neutrons. We will discover that electrons are totally indivisible particles and are not made from quarks. We will show how experiments in atomic research facilities have given exact measurements to the life span of "unstable" particles. We will explain, in more detail, how subatomic physics has helped construct a theory about the conditions at the beginning of the universe. This will explain in more depth, the subjects discussed in the first three chapters on Astronomy. How do scientists know that certain events occurred in 10^{-23} second after the big bang? The answer lies in how the atom is presently constructed. Also, we can construct the building blocks of the atom in particle accelerator chambers. Through the theories and discoveries of modern science, we can have a more precise understanding of the conditions at the beginning of the universe and we can reflect on how God's wisdom has created all things. Both modern and classical physics lead us to the same conclusion: God is the creator of the universe. The more we study modern physics, in particular, the more we understand how true the previous statement has become. There is an inner world in the atom, more complex than most people realize. Most people have no problem believing in the presence of atoms inside everything. Some may believe it is a relatively simple place of electrons, protons and neutrons. That is not true! There are still unsolved mysteries inside the atom. We are continuing to learn more about the origin and structure of the atom. Each year billions of dollars are spent building and developing new more powerful particle accelerator machines and sophisticated detection devices. Just look at current and back issues of numerous scientific magazines and you can see a long list of articles on the progress of science to understand the mysteries inside the atom. As we learn more, we are given more reasons to recognize that all things are created and sustained by God's power and nothing is beyond the power of God. We have every reason, as Christians, to accept Jesus Christ as Lord and worship Him for His gift of creation. Every breath we take is a gift from God. Give the Lord praise for every minute we are allowed to live in the wondrous world God has made. Every moment the universe is allowed to exist, is a gift from God. Continually praise His Holy name. We can also look to the future home He has prepared for us by His infinite grace and mercy. A home that he has been preparing for a long time where there is no more death and decay. More about the future of the world and some of the history of the Christian faith will be explore in chapter 10. To God, be the glory forever and ever. Amen.

References for Chapter 8

8.1	Raymond A. Serway, Physics For Scientists & Engineers with Modern Physics Third edition, Saunders College Publishing, Fort Worth, TX., 1990, p. 4-6.

8.2	Ibid p. 142.

8.3	Dudley Williams & John Spangler, Physics for Science and Engineering, D.VAN NORSTRAND COMPANY, New York, 1981, summary of concepts on p. 4.

8.4	Albert Einstein, Ideas and Opinions, New York, Dell Publishing Co., Crown Publishers MCMLIV, P. 54-55.

8.5	Ibid p. 49-50.

8.6	Ibid p. 61.

8.7	Ibid p. 47-48, 52, 54.

8.8	Ibid p. 51.

8.9	Lee Strobel, The Case for A Creator, Zondervan, Grand Rapids Michigan. 2004, p. 269, p. 283.

8.10	Michael Bumbulis, Ph. D, Christianity and the Birth of Science, http://www.ldolphin.org /bumbulis/#anchor5332524.

8.11	Raymond A. Serway, Physics For Scientists & Engineers with Modern Physics Third edition, Saunders College Publishing, Fort Worth, TX., 1990, p. 96.

8.12	Ibid p. 100.

8.13	Ibid p. 104.

8.14	Ibid p. 166-167

8.15	Ibid p. 528-529.

8.16	Linda Huetinck, Cliffs Quick Review Physics, Wiley Publishing, New York, New York, 2001, p. 34.

8.17	Ibid p. 69.

8.18	Raymond A. Serway, Physics For Scientists & Engineers with Modern Physics Third edition, Saunders College Publishing, Fort Worth, TX., 1990, p. 600.

8.19	Ibid p. 628.

8.20	Lee Strobel, The Case for A Creator, Zondervan, Grand Rapids Michigan. 2004, p. 126, p.131-132.

8.21	Raymond A. Serway, Physics For Scientists & Engineers with Modern Physics Third edition, Saunders College Publishing, Fort Worth, TX., 1990, p. 634.

8.22	Ibid p. 681.

8.23	Ibid p. 711.

8.24	Ibid p. 805.

8.25	Linda Huetinck, Cliffs Quick Review Physics, Wiley Publishing, New York, New York, 2001, p. 97.

8.26	Ibid p. 98.

8.27	Raymond A. Serway, Physics For Scientists & Engineers with Modern Physics Third edition, Saunders College Publishing, Fort Worth, TX., 1990, p. 878.

8.28	Tom Morris, Philosophy For Dummies, Hungry Minds Inc., New York, N.Y., 1999, p. 238.

8.29	Raymond A. Serway, Physics For Scientists & Engineers with Modern Physics Third edition, Saunders College Publishing, Fort Worth, TX., 1990, p. 890.

8.30	Ibid p. 955, 957, 958.

8.31	Ibid p. 890.

8.32	Ibid p. 983-985.

8.33	Linda Huetinck, Cliffs Quick Review Physics, Wiley Publishing, New York, New York, 2001, p.114.

8.34   Raymond A. Serway, Physics For Scientists & Engineers with Modern Physics Third edition, Saunders College Publishing, Fort Worth, TX., 1990, p. 985.

8.35   Ibid p. 1101.

8.36   Ibid p. 1151.

8.37   Tom Morris, Philosophy For Dummies, Hungry Minds Inc., New York, N.Y., 1999, p. 46.

Illustrations for Chapter 8

8.1   Raymond A. Serway, Physics For Scientists & Engineers with Modern Physics Third edition, Saunders College Publishing, Fort Worth, TX., 1990, p. 97.

8.2   Ibid p. 643.

8.3   Ibid p. 960.

8.4   Ibid left side: p. 973, right side: p. 890 (edited).

Chapter 9: Modern Physics
Relativity and Quantum Physics
The Many Properties of Light

In the previous chapter on Classical Physics, we skipped some important subjects. In particular, there are two concepts that are necessary to cover in order to understand the principles of modern physics. These two subjects are: the study of mechanical waves and the study of the forces on an object traveling in a circle. The study of mechanical waves helps us understand the wave properties of light, and other forms of electromagnetic radiation. The properties in orbital motion are necessary to explain the problems of explaining the orbit of electrons around the nucleus of an atom. Therefore, we will review these concepts in this chapter. First, let us look at the wave properties of light. In the last chapter we began an investigation into the nature of light. We found in the last chapter that Maxwell's equations, and the experimental work of Hertz, show that light is part of the electromagnetic spectrum. Electromagnetic waves are combined electrical and magnetic fields which move at the speed of light. There are a few important concepts that are used in the study of any type of wave motion, electromagnetic, or mechanical waves. Examples of mechanical waves can include ripples in a pond, waves from a string attached to a wall, and numerous other examples. In any case, all wave motion carries energy. We are once again back to the fact that nearly all examples in the study of physics are related to an exchange of energy. What are the common characteristics of all waves? "Three physical characteristics are important in characterizing waves: the wavelength (λ), the frequency (f), and the wave velocity (v). One wavelength is the minimum distance between any two points on a wave that behave identically. ... Most waves are periodic in nature. The frequency of such periodic waves is the rate at which the disturbance repeats itself. Waves travel, or propagate, with a specific velocity, which depends on the medium being disturbed. ... A special class of waves that do not require a medium in order to propagate is electromagnetic waves. [9.1]" One other property of a wave is the amplitude. This property is important in radio signals, and represents the maximum displacement, distance from the imaginary x-axis, and the top of the wave crest. Therefore, you can have frequency modulated, FM, or amplitude modulated, AM, signals in radio waves.

The frequency, wavelength and velocity of any wave can easily be related mathematically. "The period (T) is the time for one wave to pass a given point. Period is measured in seconds. Frequency of waves is measured in cycles per second or in the SI unit of hertz (Hz). ... Frequency is the reciprocal of the period: $f = 1/T$. From the definition of velocity as distance/time (distance divided by time) – for all types of waves- the velocity is given by $v = \lambda/T$. ... Because frequency is the reciprocal of period, velocity is also $v = f\lambda$. [9.2]" All waves' velocities are given by multiplying the frequency and wavelength, ($v = f\lambda$). All electromagnetic waves travel through space at a constant velocity, c, the speed of light. Thus the formula becomes $c = f\lambda$. There are many types of electromagnetic waves. They are distinguished by their differences in wavelength and frequency. There have been many types of electromagnetic waves discovered through the years since the experiments of Heinrich Hertz. "At this time (1887), the only electromagnetic waves recognized were radio waves and visible light. It is now known that other forms of electromagnetic waves exist which are distinguished by their frequency and wavelength. ... Visible light, the most familiar form of electromagnetic waves, may be defined as that part of the spectrum that the human eye can detect. ... The various wavelengths of visible light are classified with colors ranging from violet ($\lambda \approx 4 \times 10^{-7}$m) to red ($\lambda \approx 7 \times 10^{-7}$m). The eye's sensitivity is a function of wavelength. [9.3]" Isn't the gift of sight an amazing blessing from God? It is amazing how we can distinguish between different wavelengths and thus are able to see colors coming from electromagnetic radiation traveling through space at the speed of light. The range of wavelengths for light is such a narrow band in the electromagnetic spectrum it is amazing how our eyes are sensitive to the different colors.

Refer to the illustration 8.4 (a) in the last chapter. This is a standard drawing representing the various ranges in electromagnetic waves, called the electromagnetic spectrum. We can generally divide the electromagnetic spectrum along the narrow line where we have visible light. The waves below visible light are relatively harmless long waves that are useful in communications. Television, radio, and short wave communications are in this area of the spectrum. Electromagnetic waves above the range of visible light include "energetic" waves that, in some cases, can be extremely harmful to human life after prolonged exposure. Ultraviolet, X-rays, Gamma-rays and beyond fall into this category of radiation and can come from a wide variety of sources. We will discuss some of the principles of radioactivity in this chapter. All forms of electromagnetic waves are ultimately due to an exchange of energy within the atom. We return to our re-occurring theme that all of the laws of physics are related to an energy exchange. In the case of electromagnetic waves, the amount of energy each wave has depends of its frequency. "The quantization model assumes that the energy of a light wave is present in bundles of energy called photons; hence the energy is said to be quantized. (Any quantity that appears in discrete bundles is said to be quantized. For example, electrical charge is quantized because it always appears in bundles equal to the elementary charge of 1.6×10^{-19} C.) According to Einstein's theory, the energy of a photon is proportional to the frequency of the electromagnetic wave: $E = hf$ where $h = 6.63 \times 10^{-34}$ J*s. is Planck's constant. [9.4]" This demonstrates that waves of higher frequency transfer more energy to objects than electromagnetic waves of lower frequencies. Again, naturally occurring high frequency electromagnetic waves can damage a person's body because they transmit an excessive amount of random energy. However, modern technologies can control the harmful effects of x-rays, for example, and x-rays are now useful in examining the internal parts of a person's body. There are many other useful applications to controlling high frequency radiation through the development of modern technologies. One common example is microwave ovens used to cook or re-heat our food.

To be "energized" as a Christian is to be filled with the Holy Spirit. One way to do this is to frequently read the Scripture, listen to sound doctrine, and dwell continually on the Word of God. "So I will always remind you of these things, even though you know them and are firmly established in the truth you now have." 2Peter 1:12 It is often easy for Christians to be caught up with distractions in this modern world. But, we must guard our hearts from sin by constantly listening to God's Holy word. "What you heard from me, keep as the pattern of sound teaching, with faith and love in Christ Jesus. Guard the good deposit that was entrusted to you—guard it with the help of the Holy Spirit who lives in us." 2Timothy 1:13-14 We learned in the previous paragraph, the physical principle, that the amount of energy and correspondingly power is effected by frequency. So, the magnitude of the power of the Holy Spirit indwelling a Christian's life is affected by the frequency we turn to God in prayer and read his Word. "May the God of hope fill you with all joy and peace as you trust in him, so that you may overflow with hope by the power of the Holy Spirit." Romans 15:13. Incidentally, the reverse is true for both Christians and non-Christians. In a Christian's life, a person is more vulnerable to sin when there is a lack of frequency in studying God's word. In the non-Christian, this lack of power is manifested in the lack of self-control. Even non-Christians know some basic, logical rules of living that is from parts of the Bible. Principles like "Thou shall not steal." "Love thy neighbor." and so on, are understandable to nearly everyone. When a non-Christian reflects on these timeless truths they have some self-restraint. When they do not dwell on these things they become more available to the power of Satan instead of the power of the Holy Spirit. This is manifested when things get "out of control" and the non-Christian is puzzled as to why this is happening in their life. The non-Christian seams extremely confused when a "good" marriage ended in a messy divorce. They often wonder why personal relationships are hard to maintain, especially in dating or marriage. The fact is that they are unknowingly in a spiritual battle and they do not have the "power" to defend themselves against their enemy, Satan. More on this subject will be explored in an upcoming series of books my wife and I intend to write soon.

In Chapter eight we discussed the debate over whether light was particles or waves. There are some phenomena of light that can be explained by a wave theory others can only be explained by a particle theory. One property of light that has been known since ancient times is the reflection of light. The most obvious example of reflection can be found by looking into a clear pool of water or a mirror. "Most visible objects are seen by reflected light. ... For an object to be visible, light from a source is reflected off the object into our eyes. ... The original ray is called the incident ray, and after reflection, it is called the reflected ray. ... The law of reflection states that the angle of incidence equals the angle of reflection. This law applies to all reflecting surfaces. ... Diffuse reflection occurs when light is from a rough surface. Regular reflection is reflection from a smooth surface, such as a mirror. ... The eye extends back the diverging reflected rays to see an image behind the mirror. An image formed in this manner by extending back the reflected diverging rays is called a virtual image. [9.5]" The concept of a virtual image is useful in understanding the properties of light. We will study the concept of "virtual particles" in quantum physics. The whole stability of the atom is dependant on the strong nuclear force. We will look at the important role of so called "virtual particles" in the understanding of this elementary force. The idea of light as particles seams to be supported by the properties of reflection. This would appear to be particles just bouncing off a smooth surface. The law of refraction, however, tends to be better understood by the behavior of light as a wave. "Refraction is the bending of light when the beam passes from one transparent medium into another. ... When Willebrod Snell (1580-1626) observed light traveling from air into another transparent material, he found a constant ratio (index of refraction) of the sines of the angles measured from normal to the light ray in the material. ... For the more general case of light traveling from medium 1 to medium 2, Snell's law can be written $n_1 \sin \lambda_1 = n_2 \sin \lambda_2$. ... The index of refraction is also the ratio of the speed of light in a vacuum (c) and the speed of light in that medium (v); thus, $n = c/v$. [9.6]" From this we see refraction refers to bending a light wave as it travels through a medium. Refraction of light thus demonstrates the wave nature to light. However, the slowing of the speed of a light wave suggests a particle nature as the photons drag through the medium. Both properties are therefore present as we study the refraction of light.

The subject of image can be very important to a person's esteem. Some people think that your appearance, or image, is greatly important. We are told that we were created in the image of God. "So God created man in His own image, in the image of God He created him; male and female He created them." Genesis 1:27 However, shortly after God created man, rebellion began. Mankind had tarnished his image with the stain of sin. He was no longer worthy to be called "the image of God." The only person who could have that distinct honor was our Lord Jesus Christ. "He is the image of the invisible God, the firstborn over all creation." Colossians 1:15 If we are truly concerned about our image, we need to reflect on how closely we follow the teachings and actions of Jesus Christ. Christ taught us to love one another and be kind to one another. "Be kind and compassionate to one another, forgiving each other, just as in Christ, God forgave you. Be imitators of God, therefore, as dearly loved children and live a life of love, just as Christ loved us and gave himself up for us as a fragrant offering and sacrifice to God." Ephesians 4:32-5:2 In this way, we regain our precious gift of becoming like the image of God. "Do not lie to each other, since you have taken off your old self with its practices and have put on the new self, which is being renewed in knowledge in the image of its Creator." Colossians 3:9-10 You could even extend this verse to say we must daily walk in the new life Christ has given us and put aside our sinful nature. When we do, we display an image of Christ to the rest of the world. This produces a strong testimony to the saving power of God in displaying the new life you have by being born again. "We were therefore buried with him through baptism into death in order that, just as Christ was raised from the dead through the glory of the Father, we too may live a new life." Romans 6:4 2 "Therefore, if anyone is in Christ, he is a new creation; the old has gone, the new has come! All this is from God, who reconciled us to himself through Christ and gave us the ministry of reconciliation: that God was reconciling the world to himself in Christ, not counting men's sins against them. And he has committed to us the message of reconciliation. We are therefore Christ's ambassadors, as though God were making his appeal through us. We implore you on Christ's behalf: Be reconciled to God" Corinthians 5:17-20.

Figure 9.1

The bending of light waves generates a wide range of colors in this wonderful world. How dull life would be without all the many colors of the rainbow. "An important property of the index of refraction is that it is different for different wavelengths of light. ... Since n is a function of wavelength, Snell's law indicates that light of different wavelengths will be bent at different angles when incident on a refracting material. ... Now suppose a beam of white light (a combination of all visible wavelengths) is incident on a prism. ... The rays that emerge from the second face spread out in a series of colors know as a spectrum. These colors, in order of decreasing wavelength, are red, orange, yellow, green, blue, indigo, and violet. [9.7]" This is how a rainbow is formed after a rain storm, see figure 9.1. "Rainbows are formed by dispersion and total reflection of sunlight in raindrops. [9.8]" The first creation of a rainbow is recorded in Scripture. "And God said, 'This is the sign of the covenant I am making between me and you and every living creature with you, a covenant for all generations to come: I have set my rainbow in the clouds, and it will be the sign of the covenant between me and the earth.'" Genesis 9:12-13. We discussed some of the various implications of this verse in previous chapters. We discussed the possibility that the reason the first rainbow appears after the flood was that the upper atmosphere had changed. Indeed, God's promise is that He would not destroy the world by means of a flood again. "I establish my covenant with you: Never again will all life be cut off by the waters of a flood; never again will there be a flood to destroy the earth." Genesis 9:11. The rainbow has become a symbol of peace, harmony and unity for many years. It is with the modern understanding of the properties of light and realizing that all the various colors that exist are contained within a single ray of white light, that the rainbow has had the greatest impact on our culture. Many have pointed to the rainbow as a representation of unity in all races. It is ironic that the study of light and its' dual nature has given scientists such a great appreciation of this covenant sign. By realizing the dual nature to light, we recognize our dual nature. All human beings have both a physical and spiritual part to our essence. We will explore more attributes to the properties of light in the next section. Light has numerous and amazing properties we are only now beginning to comprehend. Studying these properties may help us understand why the Bible refers to the followers of Jesus as "children of light". In the book of revelation we see a description of our heavenly home decorated by light from precious stones (Rev 21:18-31).

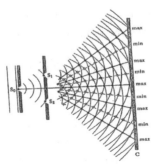

Figure 9.2

As stated previously, strong support for the wave theory of light was given by Thomas Young in

1803. Young's double-split experiment, see figure 9.2, consists simply of a monochrome light source, a pair of barriers with slits in them and a screen. As a light beam is shown through the apparatus, a series of dark and bright lines appear on the screen. The reason for this pattern is from the wave nature of light. There are points in which constructive and destructive interference occurs between two waves. "If the path difference is either zero or some integral multiple of wavelength, the two waves are in phase at P and constructive interference results. Therefore, the condition for bright fringes, or constructive interference, at P is given by $\lambda = d \sin (\emptyset) = m \lambda$ (m = 0, $\pm$ 1, $\pm$ 2, ...) The number m is called the order number. ... Similarly, when the path difference is an odd multiple of $\lambda /2$, the two waves arriving at P will be 180° out of phase and will give rise to destructive interference. Therefore, the condition for dark fringes, or destructive interference, at P is give by $\lambda = d \sin (\emptyset) = (m + \frac{1}{2}) \lambda$ (m = 0, $\pm$ 1, $\pm$ 2, ...). [9.9]"

In figure 3.4 of chapter 3 you can see another use for a prism is to identify the substances in a sample of material. We discussed how this process is used to verify the atomic reactions in stars. This is using the fact that different elements have a different atomic configuration. "All substances at some temperature emit thermal radiation. ... The shape of the distribution depends on the temperature and properties of the substance. In sharp contrast to this continuous distribution spectrum is the discrete line spectrum emitted by a low-pressure gas subject to electrical discharge. When the light from such a low-pressure discharge is examined with a spectroscope. ... The wavelengths contained in a given line spectrum are characteristic of the particular element emitting the light. ... In early studies of the solar spectrum, some lines were found that did not correspond to any known element. A new element had been discovered! The new element was named helium, after the Greek word for sun, Helios. [9.10]" We see that spectral analysis has a long history of detecting elements in the stars. As we discussed in earlier chapters, this is in complete agreement with our current understanding of nuclear fusion. How does this work? Where does light come from? These questions were puzzling to the scientists at the beginning of the twentieth century. The current model of the atom took years to develop. Finally, the atomic theory was developed which put all the pieces of the puzzle together explaining the periodic table of elements.

The Early View of the Atom

There have been many theories about the structure of the atom. "The model of the atom in the days of Newton was that a tiny, hard, indestructible sphere. This model provided a good basis for the kinetic theory of gases. However, new models had to be devised when later experiments revealed the electrical nature of atoms. J.J. Thomson (1856-1940) suggested a model that described the atom as a volume of positive charge with electrons embedded throughout the volume, much like the seeds in a watermelon. Thomson referred to this model as the 'plum-pudding' atom. [9.11]" Sir Joseph Thomson is recognized as discovering the elementary particle, the electron. However, his ideas explaining the inner workings of the atom were, of course, inaccurate. "In the early 1900s, a rather extraordinary figure appeared on the stage of world science. ... Ernest Rutherford became the leading figure in the exploration of atomic structure. ... Almost as an afterthought, he suggested to some co-workers in 1911 that it might be interesting to see if any particles were ever bounced back when they hit a nucleus. According to the ideas current at the time, the atom was a large, diffuse, positively charged material in which electrons were embedded like raisins in a bun. ... A surprisingly large number of alphas were scattered through angels close to 180°. This could only be understood if it was assumed that the atom ... actually had virtually all of its mass concentrated in a small spot in the center. This concentration of mass Rutherford called the nucleus of the atom. ... In 1919, using techniques similar to those ... Rutherford was able to show that a certain particle emitted from nuclear collisions of alphas with nuclei was itself the nucleus of hydrogen. ...The new particle the proton (the first one). ... In passing we should note that in 1920 Rutherford suggested that there was probably another constituent to heavier nuclei; that is, an electrically neutral particle about as massive as the proton. He called this hypothetical particle the neutron. [9.12]" The neutron was finally discovered in 1932 by British physicist James Chadwick for which he was given the

Nobel Prize in 1935. It took years to discover all the elemental parts to the atom. But how does the atom work? There is a myth that the atom is identical to planets in a solar system with electrons going around the nucleus. This makes an easy picture to visualize, but we will see that the atom is not quite that simple. In fact, we are still searching to uncover all the secrets to the atom. This is a strong testimony to the wisdom of God in creating the universe. The atom is the ultimate building block of all things, but scientists have discovered that the atom is anything but simple.

In order to approach the subject, let us step back and take a traditional approach of explaining Einstein's theories of relativity before explaining quantum mechanics, and the inner workings of the atom. Einstein's theories of relativity were a fundamental shift in thinking for everyone. In many ways, his theories were revolutionary. Many scientists disregarded his conclusions for years until they realized there was really no conflict between his ideas and classical physics. In fact, his ideas were necessary for a more complete explanation of the atom. "Relativity does not therefore contradict classical physics. It simply regards old concepts as limiting cases that apply solely to the familiar experiences of man. ... The present-day scientists, coping with the tremendous velocities that prevail in the fast universe of the atom ... finds the old Newtonian laws inadequate. But relativity provides him in every instance with a complete and accurate description of nature. [9.13]" We can compare the coming of the theories of relativity to complete the laws of physics, with the coming of Christ. Christ came into our world to fulfill the law requirements of the Old Testament. The Lord Jesus, by His sacrifice, made a new covenant with all people who chose by faith to follow Him. "God presented him as a sacrifice of atonement, through faith in his blood. He did this to demonstrate his justice, because in his forbearance he had left the sins committed beforehand unpunished - he did it to demonstrate his justice at the present time, so as to be just and the one who justifies those who have faith in Jesus." Romans 3:25-26 "You see, at just the right time, when we were still powerless, Christ died for the ungodly." Romans 5:6 "But when the time had fully come, God sent his Son, born of a woman, born under law, to redeem those under law, that we might receive the full rights of sons." Galatians 4:4-5 "For there is one God and one mediator between God and men, the man Christ Jesus, who gave himself as a ransom for all men -the testimony given in its proper time." 1Timothy 2:5-6. We discussed some of the principles of our changed relationship to God through Christ in the last chapter. This is an enormous subject and will be discussed in upcoming books my wife and I will write. Additionally, there are a number of authors who have explored the Christian experience. Please continue to read about the universal impact found in the first coming of our Lord Jesus Christ.

Relationships: Before Christ and After His Coming

We have already discussed some of the principles of modern physics in previous chapters. Modern physics and classical physics have developed during the 20th century and combined in an eloquent form of science. Just as it is now impossible to separate the Old Testament from the New Testament, it is hard to separate modern physics from classical physics. There was a long period of time where leading scientists refused to accept the postulates of Einstein. There was an even larger debate over the acceptance of quantum mechanics. We will explore how science was incomplete without the laws and principle of modern physics and the extraordinary value modern physics has on our daily lives. Many of Einstein's ideas are now proven daily in modern laboratories. Science must use these principles in the research of cosmological origin, sub-atomic structure, and energy production, among many of the thousands of applications of modern physics. Similarly, we can not separate the New Testament which tells the story of the coming of Christ with the Old Testament, which describes the preparations for the coming of Christ. Each part of the Bible is incomplete without the other. The Old Testament described the relationship between man and God similar to a contract agreement. You were given laws to live by and if you broke those laws you must make a sacrifice to pay for your crimes against God. These payments were nowhere near the just compensation for your sins. The only payment for sin is death- Ours! It is all or nothing with God. Since we could not pay the full price, God showed great love and mercy by accepting the sacrifice of lambs, if the heart of the person was sincere about repentance from their sin. In Genesis we have the accounts of Cain and Abel. Abel's sacrifice of sheep given to God was accepted. On the other hand, Cain was unwilling to sacrifice what the law required and his offering was rejected. This contractual relationship between God and man was incomplete until the coming of Jesus Christ. Jesus was brought into the world at the proper time to pay the full penalty for our sins. We were freed from the bondage of sin and the power of the law. We are no longer held accountable under the law but are sanctified by grace and made pure by the shed blood of Jesus. The law is still a crucial instrument of guidance along the path of righteousness, but the relationship with God has changed to a personal level. The old laws have been modified and new laws have been added since the coming of Christ. This changed relationship between man and God is due to the love of God expressed in Christ.

Changing the Laws of Physics

Einstein published three papers in 1905. First was a paper concerning the photoelectric effect, as we previously mentioned. Einstein showed that light had both particle and wave properties. The second paper published by Einstein in 1905 was on the so called Brownian motion. His third and most famous paper was on special relativity. At first the theories were examined with much skepticism. However, his predictions from his first two papers were soon confirmed and modern physics began. Two years later, in 1907, Einstein published his first principles of General Relativity. Einstein later finished his work on General Relativity in 1915. General Relativity was an attempt at describing gravitational fields with the incorporation of special relativity and the principle of mass and energy equivalence. The principles of relativity dealt with some of the same things as Newton's theories of gravity, like the motion of free falling bodies. The principles led to the conclusion that space-time was curved in the presence of a gravitational field. The curved space-time geometry is call Reimann space. Einstein related the shape of the space-time continuum with a mathematical expression in tensor form, $F_{\mu\nu} = R_{\mu\nu} - \frac{1}{2} g_{\mu\nu} R = -8\pi\, G\, T_{\mu\nu}$. which we have discussed in previous chapters. This is a fundamental expression describing the principles of General Relativity. With the concepts of relativity, Einstein proposed three tests to confirm his theoretical work. "One of these tests was an immediate success- the explanation of the anomalous advance in the perihelion of Mercury of 43 arcseconds per century, a problem that had bedeviled celestial mechanics of the later part of the 19th century. The next test, the deflection of light by the Sun, was such a success that it produced what today would be called a "media event." The measurement of the deflection, amounting to 1.75 arcseconds for a ray that grazes the Sun, by two teams of British astronomers in 1919, made Einstein an instant international celebrity. [9.14]" At last, Einstein's most skeptical theories were accepted, the theories of Relativity. In 1917 Einstein published a paper on new formulations of Plank's blackbody radiation, which was the foundation for the laser, 40 years later. Einstein left his home in Germany under the persecution of Hitler's Nazi party. He came to America to work at the Institute for Advanced Study in Princeton, N.J. Einstein spent the rest of his life in an unsuccessful search of a unified field theory to unite all the fundamental forces as merely different forms of the same force. The recent theoretical and experimental developments we mentioned in Chapter 2 may led the way to completing a unified field theory. Refer back to the section on the Unified field theory in chapter 2 beginning on page 52 for further details. The significance of these developments can not be over emphasized. If these developments are correct, theoretical physics may now have established once and for all that the universe came into existence and is sustained by the supernatural power of God!

Figure 9.3

Special Relativity

The special theory of relativity is the most significant development for particle and nuclear physics research. Thorough the special theory of relativity we receive the most famous equation of Einstein's career, $E=mc^2$. Scientists realized that there was an enormous amount of power contained in a small amount of mass. Soon German scientists realized than an atomic bomb was possible and the race to produce an atomic device began. Most of us are aware that the Manhattan project was formed in the U.S. to win the race towards developing an atomic bomb. On July 16th 1945, the first successful test was made of an atomic bomb at the trinity test site and the nuclear age was born. We now have nuclear energy in power plants as a direct result of Einstein's theories. There are two basic principles in the special theory of relativity. "The laws of physics are the same in all inertial reference frames. The speed of light is the same regardless of the frame of reference of the observer. [9.15]" The second principle had long range ramifications; one included disproving the existence of ether. Ether was an imagined substance that scientists believed existed and gave light its unique properties. "Light is now understood to be an electromagnetic wave, which requires no medium for its propagation. As a result, the idea of having an ether in which these waves could travel became unnecessary. [9.16]" Why is this significant? There are two reasons the concept of ether is an important footnote in the development of physics, in my opinion. One, the concept of ether can be considered indirect evidence that many past scientists were Christians. Ether was supposed to be an invisible "fluid" which was to allow light to appear to travel at the same velocity. It was a way of explaining the particle-wave duality problem with a theoretical substance. "Praise the LORD, O my soul. O LORD my God, you are very great; you are clothed with splendor and majesty. He wraps himself in light as with a garment; He stretches out the heavens like a tent and lays the beams of His upper chambers on their waters. He makes the clouds His chariot and rides on the wings of the wind. He makes winds His messengers, flames of fire His servants." Psalms 104:1-4 Often theologians look to the Bible for insights and understanding. It is possible that the reference that God "wraps himself in light as with a garment" and "lays beams of his upper chambers on their waters" is an origin to the concept of ether. Perhaps there is an ether-like substance that explains the observations of stars over vast distances and yet the "light" is not originating billions of years ago. In any event, the second reason we should not ignore the idea of ether, is that science is a continuing process of learning. When we look back, we wonder what these scientists were thinking for so long, to accept the concept of ether to explain the phenomena of light. It seams almost as ridiculous, in hindsight, as Thompson's plum pudding idea.

The second postulate of Einstein's theory of relativity was that the speed of light in a vacuum is a constant. The speed of light does not change and is the same for all observers. The two postulates of relativity seam simple on the surface and very similar to principles of relative motion developed by Isaac Newton. However, both postulates put limitations on all physical laws. Some of these limitations were never perceived before Einstein's theory of relativity was introduced. The first postulate specifies that all physical laws are only valid in reference systems moving with a constant velocity with respect to each other. This implies that the laws of physics do not apply, or must be modified, when you have two systems moving at different speeds. The principles of relativity state that the Lorentz factor must be used when you have two systems moving at substantially different velocities. The theory of relativity states that the differences in speeds usually must be above 0.5 times the speed of light to become noticeable. The principle of the speed of light as a constant had profound implications. The Newtonian view placed no limits on how fast an object could travel. Einstein's theory, however, proved this to be incorrect and there was indeed a limiting velocity to the universe. Newton also believed that such quantities as time, length, and mass were absolute constants, never changing. Einstein's work also proved this to be untrue. All these properties: length, mass, and time, is affected by the speed in which an object travels.

Relativistic Mass and Length

There are three main physical properties to all matter. These include length, mass, and time. All three properties are affected by relativistic speeds. To describe the principles of relativity, it is often helpful to have an illustration, see figure 9.3. You are standing at a position we call your reference point. The relativistic effects are determined by comparing physical properties at your reference point with the properties inside a fast moving imaginary means of transportation, in this case it is a railway car. The railway car needs to be moving at relativistic speeds, velocities between 0.5c and 0.999...c, to have noticeable relativistic effects. Length, mass, and time all seam to be affected by the relativistic speed of the railway car, according to the observations of an outside observer. First, mass increases with increasing velocity, $M_f = M_i \div \sqrt{[1-(v^2/c^2)]}$. The mass of an object we would have at rest, with zero velocity, is called the rest mass, M_i. It is the amount of mass we had before entering our imaginary railway car. The relativistic mass, M_f, is the amount of mass your object has as it journeys inside the imaginary railway car. The result is that mass increases with a corresponding increase in speed of the object. The situation in which this effect actually takes place is inside a cyclotron, a type of particle accelerator. Relativistic mass effects must be taken into account when conducting research with particle accelerators, because the trajectory of the particles is affected by the changing mass. The trajectory is affected by the centripetal force. Why did the mass increase? Einstein discovered that at a certain point, relativistic effects start to occur and mass increases with velocity. For example, the equation for kinetic energy, $K.E. = \frac{1}{2}mv^2$, becomes: $K.E. = \frac{1}{2}m_0v^2 + \frac{3}{8}m_0v^2(v^2/c^2) + \dots$.

The next relativistic effect to discuss is length. Length is contracted, or becomes shorter, with increasing velocity according to the relationship: $L_f = L_i \div \sqrt{[1-(v^2/c^2)]}$. This means, as an object accelerates towards the speed of light, its physical dimensions get smaller. This is the scientific version of 'Honey I shrunk the kids'. However, when we put the first two relativistic conditions together, we see matter becoming exceedingly dense as it is accelerated. Since mass increases and the physical dimensions decrease, we can say the density of matter increases towards infinity. This principle has led scientists to conclude that there could have existed a point in universal history where mass was infinitely dense and was initially formed in a point of singularity. We have discussed this possibility in the first three chapters of this book. This may be a theoretical possibility, but it would lead to the conclusion that light is matter of infinite density instead of the current definition of light as mass-less particles called photons.

Time Dilation and the Twin Paradox

The third effect is that time seams to move more slowly with increasing speed, $T_f = T_i \div \sqrt{[1-(v^2/c^2)]}$. Many science fiction authors have imagined time travel through applying Einstein's relativistic principles. Traveling backward in time is not theoretically possible because it would require traveling faster that light; which is impossible as far as current science knows. However, there are many imagined paradoxes to near light travel. One famous thought experiment which illustrates the time dilation effect of relativity is called the twin paradox. In our example we will take a pair of twins, who are 20 years old named Speedo and Goslow. "Speedo … sets out on a journey toward a star located 30 light-years from earth. His spaceship is able to accelerate to a speed close to the speed of light. After reaching the star, Speedo … returns to earth at the same high speed. … Speedo's twin brother, Goslow, has aged to about 80 years old. …. Speedo, on the other hand, has aged only about ten years. …. In order to resolve this paradox, it should be pointed out that the trip is not as symmetrical as we may have led you to believe. Speedo, the space traveler, had to experience a series of accelerations and decelerations during his journey. [9.17]" Remember that Einstein's theory states that all the laws of physics are the same in all inertial reference systems. Since we are comparing two different frames of references, both twins think that time is moving normally. However, when we compare their clocks, it seams that the space traveler has a slower running clock. Another example of the time dilation effect is found in particle accelerator units that produce high energy muons. "In 1976, experiments with muons were conducted at the laboratory of the European Council for Nuclear Research (CERN) in Geneva. Muons were injected into a large storage ring, reaching speeds of about 0.9994c. Electrons produced by the decaying muons were detected by counters around the ring, enabling scientists to measure the decay rate, and hence the lifetime of the muons. The lifetime of the moving muons was measured to be about 30 times as long as that of the stationary muon, in agreement with the prediction of relativity to within two parts in a thousand. [9.18]" How is this possible? The time dilation effect is often the most misunderstood of all relativistic principles. To properly understand the principle of time dilation, we must remember that time passed at the same rate for the space traveler and the person on earth. By this, I mean the watches on earth and in the spacecraft appear to run at the same rate to the two respective observers. However, comparing watches before and after makes the appearance that the watches in the space craft were running slow. You don't need relativistic speeds to notice this effect. Experiments with aircrafts at high altitudes show this effect to be true, by comparing synchronous watches before and after their trips. "The experiment involved the use of very stable cesium beam atomic clocks. Time intervals measured with four such clocks in jet flight were compared with time intervals measured by reference atomic clocks located at the U.S. Naval Observatory. ... Their results were in good agreement with the predictions of the special theory of relativity."[9.19]

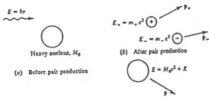

Figure 9.4

When discussing the principles of relativity, in particular the time dilation effect, we must remember the limiting factor of the speed of light. Due to numerous physical properties, largely covered in the theory of special relativity, we can not exceed the velocity of light in free space. Notice in all three relativistic equations, determining the change in mass, length and time, is the Lorentz factor, $\sqrt{[1-(v^2/c^2)]}$. This factor has the term of the square of the speed of the object, divided by the square of the speed of light. Mass, for example, increases with increasing velocity asymptotically, never reaching the velocity of light, see figure 9.3. At the speed of light, time, mass, and length are no longer part of the parameters. At the speed of light it would seam that mass is infinite, time slows to zero, and length is contracted to a single point with zero length. Just put the velocity of the object as the speed of light and work the equation. What is the result? The square root of zero. Which can be considered zero or an undefined quantity. Scientists interpret the equations as; mass is zero at the speed of light and matter accelerated to the speed of light becomes completely energy. Energy has both properties of wave motion and particle collision properties simultaneously. This is called the wave-particle duality of electromagnetic fields. Mass-less "particles" such as photons, is the result of converting ordinary matter into pure energy. It has been found that, due to the laws of relativistic motion, nothing can be accelerated to the speed of light artificially. The conversion of matter to energy usually occurs when two particles traveling at high velocities collide. In essence you must cause a high speed particle to collide with a slower moving or stationary particle and "kick" the high velocity particle to the speed of light. At that same time it is converted to pure energy. In making matter from energy, the opposite must take place. The high energy photon must be "slowed down" to form matter, see figure 9.4.

What Does God Look Like?

It is fascinating to look at what occurs when you attempt to reach the speed of light. Mass increase towards infinity, length contracts toward zero, and time slows to a stop. This presents an interesting question. How old is light? We now know that light is produced by an energy shift within the atom. We also know that light can (presently) only travel at the speed of light. Therefore, as we discussed in earlier chapters in Astronomy, scientists assume that light from a star is a look back in time. They also assume that the further out into space, the longer you estimate the age of the universe. On the surface this theory seams reasonable. However, we also discussed the "appearance of age" argument. We also need to understand that photons travel in packages of light. To view an event, we are seeing a group of images all traveling together. Could the speed of light not have been limited at one time? There is no external way to determine the age of a photon like the age of a rock. We examined these ideas in our Astronomy chapters. Just to remind the reader, there is nothing in our current understanding of the nature of light that can rule out the possibility that we live in a "young" universe. You must believe that the universal laws have never changed in order to use the distance from here to the edge of the universe as a measurement of time. However any scientist that accepts the idea that the laws of physics have always been the same, must accept that there can be no explanation for the beginning of the universe. The laws of conservation of energy, for one, would prevent the emerging of the universe. As Hawking explained to us, all the physical laws break down at some point near the beginning of the universe. As we have stated many times, any assumptions about the past are done entirely on faith and has nothing to do with experimental science. If you believe in a 13-20 billion year age of the universe, or whatever the current estimate is today, you do so almost entirely based on faith, not science.

There are many references to God as a person of pure light. If God had some of the attributes of light, He would exist outside of time, or at least time would have no real meaning to Him. Indeed God is the Alpha and Omega, the beginning and the end. God would, perhaps, live in another dimension. The only connection with man is through the fullness of God manifested in human form, Jesus Christ. The coming of Jesus would be exactly what the Trinity doctrine teaches i.e. the fullness of God putting on the limitations of human flesh. "Jesus answered 'I am the way the truth and the life. No man comes to the father except by me.'" John 14:6 "In the beginning was the Word and the Word was with God and the Word was God; all things were made through Him and without Him was not anything made that has been made. In Him was life, and the life was the light of men. ... The true light that enlightens every man was coming into the world. He was in the world, and the world was made through Him, yet the world knew Him not. ... And the Word became flesh and dwelt among us, full of grace and truth; we have beheld His glory, glory as of the only Son from the Father." John 1:1-4, 9-10, 14 God would have infinite mass. God would indeed be creator of all things and exist through all things. His presence, His glory would be in everything in the universe. And indeed, these attributes of an all powerful, just, and loving creator is exactly how the Bible describes God. The many physical constants exist throughout the universe as a testimony to a perfect designer. The strong nuclear force, which "mysteriously" binds the atom and keeps it from flying apart (which will be discussed later), is a testimony to God's power and design. God could exist in the threshold between matter and energy, in another dimension. Indeed, to solve many of the problems of explaining the beginning of the universe there are a variety of theories on this subject. Many scientists have turned to concepts of dimensions to the universe on a higher plane than the four dimensions of length, width, height, and time. They also explore various "string" theories to connect this higher plane to our perceptions of reality. God is all powerful, full of justice and grace, all loving, and all knowing. Notice, as stated above, nothing can be converted from matter to energy without a collision of some kind. Is it possible that from this physical principle we can see the spiritual law that nothing enters the kingdom of God with out the direct touch of the creator's hand? "No one can come to me unless the Father who sent me draws him, and I will raise him up at the last day." John 6:44. How are we touched by God? We are touched by the Holy Spirit, sent from God, when we have turned our lives over to God by faith in Jesus Christ.

There are many interesting hypothesis about the nature of God, from various other religions. We will not have all the answers to our questions about God until we meet Jesus face to face. And even then, there may remain some secrets of God we can never comprehend. To understand the Lord God, we simply examine all biblical references to Jesus. "Philip said, 'Lord show us the Father and that will be enough for us.' Jesus answered: 'Don't you know me, Philip, even after I have been among you such a long time? Anyone who has seen me has seen the Father. How can you say, 'Show us the Father?' 'Don't you believe that I am in the Father, and that the Father is in me?" John 14:8-9. "I and the Father are one." John 10:30. I believe we need to save our questions about the nature of God and just accept by faith that He is all the things the Scripture describes, even if we can not fully comprehend this truth.

Moral Relativism

We began a discussion on moral relativism in the last chapter. Support for this philosophy is from an interpretation of the theory of relativity. The supporters of moral relativism often have some knowledge of science, enough to be aware of some of the basics of relativity. Recall that moral relativism is a view based on the idea there is no absolute truth. The popularity has grown, since they claim to be supporters of tolerance of all beliefs. They often accept that any belief is equally valid, and if it works for you, fine for you. We have seen that one of the principles of relativity is that the laws of physics only apply to inertial frames of reference. "Everything is relative", is the battle cry. Some have interpreted this principle of relativity to support the philosophy that the laws in a particular religion are only valid for the person who has faith in that doctrine. In other words, the Ten Commandments, for example, are not valid for everybody, but only for Jews and Christians. In other words, there is no absolute God who will judge you by an absolute standard. This is a misunderstanding of philosophy and physics. First, it is true that relativity states that everything is compared with a reference frame. In physics, this reference point can shift from place to place. However, there is an absolute frame of reference in all matters of religious discussion. This is the Word of God given to us through the Holy Bible. No other book explains the principles and character of God as the Holy Bible does. Next, all frames of reference do have a single standard that is unchanging no matter what the reference frame. The second postulate of special relativity states that the speed of light remains the same no matter which reference frame you are in. In fact it is by this "standard" that all changes in our reference frames are modified by the Lorentz factor. So, the philosophy supported by relativity is that there is an absolute standard. All things in any person's "frame of reference" are affected by a relationship to this standard. In the Christian faith, the joy in our lives is directly related to our faith in the saving power of Christ. Chapter 7 discussed a great deal about relationships and the Christian faith. We will discuss these principles in more depth at a later time.

Moral relativism is not valid on a purely logical basis. "But notice a problem with mere statement of relativism. There really is no such (thing) as absolute truth. Is relativism suggesting that this is the ultimate, absolute truth about truth? In that case, it actually asserts what it denies, and so it's self-defeating, simply logically incoherent as a philosophical position. Why then are so many college students relativists? Why has relativism been so attractive to a number of intellectuals in the 20th century? I think the answers here are quite simple. ... A little philosophy is a dangerous thing. Too many undergraduates are exposed to relativism in a way that they tend to misunderstand. [9.20]" By suggesting that the ultimate truth about the universe is that there is no absolute truth contradicts the assertion that the previous statement is a universal absolute. Any attempt to claim you are seeking the truth at the same time you are running away from the truth leads to continual confusion. It is an intellectual trap from the "father of lies"- John 8:44, the Devil. The ultimate downfall of relativism is that, it is a desperate running from the absolute truth, which is the Bible. Many people on college campuses have been exposed to evangelists, and they struggle to hide from the truth of the Bible. Also, they sometimes struggle with having a tolerance for other religions. They misunderstand the Christian perspective of loving even your enemies who passionately disagree with your beliefs. A Christian can be firm in his faith that Christ is the only way to know God and yet approach someone who believes in another religion with kindness. Another point to consider is the need for a clear understanding of the Gospel and science. There are often Christians who do not fully understand science and the support it gives the Christian faith. If you think you know science and are not led to a closer relationship with Christ, you either do not understand science or have never studied the Bible in depth. Even if you have a PhD in some field of science, the evidence remains the same. Each day science produces more evidence for the Christian faith. Once again, the truth of the Bible is validated. "For although they knew God, they neither glorified him as God nor gave thanks to him, but their thinking became futile and their foolish hearts were darkened. Although they claimed to be wise, they became fools." Romans 1:21-22. Any scientist, who does not believe the Bible, believes a false doctrine. "For the time will come when men will not put up with sound doctrine. Instead, to suit their own desires, they will gather around them a great number of teachers to say what their itching ears want to hear. They will turn their ears away from the truth and turn aside to myths." 2Timothy 4:3-4 It is a myth to believe that science and Christianity are incompatible. Those who agree with this concept believe a lie by faith. Again, any true scientist who rejects the Bible either does not know enough about science or is desperately running from the truth of the Bible. Why do this? The Bible convicts the heart of our sin nature and demands a Christian life style. Some people, even award winning scientists, would rather live in sin than conform to the truth of the gospel teaching. The decision to accept or reject the Bible is based on each person's knowledge and experience which produces their set of beliefs. As all the prophets have warned, your everlasting soul will depend on the decision you make to accept or reject the gospel of Christ. Each person should test their convictions to see if they are reasonable every day.

Light Behavior, Colors and the Compton Effect

"Much of the work on describing photon interactions was done by Arthur H. Compton (1892-1962) who original coined the term "photon". The result of a photon striking a particle is a change in the wavelength of the photon and a change in position for the electron. In 1923, Arthur Holly Compton and Peter Debye ... realized that the scattering of x-ray photons from electrons could be explained by treating photons as point-like particles with energy hf and momentum hf/c, and by conserving energy and momentum of the photon-electron pair in a collision. [9.21]" When light strikes an electron, the photon will change wavelengths and thus produce different colors. Sometimes the change is unnoticeable, but other times a definite change is not seen. For example, when coherent white light passes through a prism, a rainbow of colors will bee seen from the diffracted light on the other side. Photons are packages of energy, which means they would also have a certain mass if they were somehow converted to matter. The relationship between matter and energy is again Einstein's famous equation $E=mc^2$. Photons are material bodies which have been converted into energy. Photons can be converted to matter in pair production, as we have already discussed, see figure 9.4. From laboratory experiments, we can produce an electron-positron pair of particles from a single photon. Another behavior of light, or photons, is their reaction to a gravitational field. It was assumed that light would be unaffected by gravitational attraction since light has no mass. However, one of the principles of general relativity states that beams of light will be bent from gravitational attraction. One of the reasons Einstein proposed that this rather radical idea was that photons sometimes behaved as particles, as the above mentioned Compton Effect illustrates. The bending of light by a gravitational field has been proven through many observations. The phenomenon known as gravitational red shift can occur in light leaving objects such as white dwarfs. It is only in white dwarfs and black holes that the gravitational pull is strong enough to affect the frequency of light and cause a slight red shift. Be cautioned not to confuse gravitational red shift with the general red shift of the expanding universe. According to the calculations, the gravitational fields of ordinary stars do not produce enough force to cause a gravitational red shift. However, ordinary stars can bend light waves. This fact was used to prove Einstein's theory of General Relativity. Universal red shift is therefore the result of the Doppler Effect and the moving of the universe in a general expansion, as we have discussed in previous chapters.

Particles and Properties of the Atom

Most of modern physics has a goal of making sense of the sub-atomic universe. However, the structure of the atom has become more mysterious with each new discovery. "Until 1932, physicists viewed all matter as consisting of only three constituent particles: electrons, protons, and neutrons. With the exception of the free neutron, these particles are very stable. Beginning in 1945, many new particles were discovered in experiments involving high energy collisions between known particles. These new particles are characteristically very unstable and have short half-lives, ranging between 10^{-6} and 10^{-23} s. So far more than 300 of these unstable, temporary particles have been cataloged. [9.22]" These unstable particles eventually form one or more of the stable particles, such as electrons and protons, by a decay reaction. It is therefore assumed that a similar method was used to form the stable components of the atom at the beginning of the universe. This explains the theoretical events taking place in 10^{-23} s after the beginning of the "big bang". This has lead scientists to announce they have uncovered more about the events at the beginning of the universe. This makes sensational announcements for T.V. News broadcasts and articles in magazines and news papers. These types of announcements sell a lot of newspapers and magazines. But, the only thing we can know for sure is that modern science confirms a set of sudden spectacular events on the first day of creation. A sudden event exactly as described in the Genesis account.

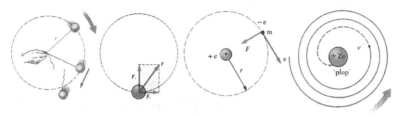

Figure 9.5

The first modern picture of the atom was made by Niels Bohr in 1913, see figure 9.5. This is a diagram of the hydrogen atom. For heavier atoms, such as lead, the electrons follow more complicated orbital paths. The picture leads one to believe that the atom is similar in design to a planetary system orbiting the sun. This is, however, not exactly the case. In the orbital paths of a planetary or satellite system, the motion of the object is determined by the counter-balancing of two forces acting on the object. One force is the force due to gravity pulling the satellite or planet toward the center of the sun or other object. This force is countered by the centripetal force, caused by the acceleration of the satellite around the mass it is circling, which opposes the pull of gravity. The result of these two forces counter-balancing each other is a circular, or an elliptical path of orbital motion. This is how the earth continues to circle around the sun, and the moon around the earth. Likewise, inside the atom, there are primarily two forces acting on the electron which causes orbital motion. There is the electromotive force, due to the mutual attraction of the positively charged nucleus, to the negatively charged electron. This tends to pull the electron towards the center of the nucleus. The other force is again, the centripetal force due to the motion of the electron around the nucleus. However, physicists had known that moving charges emit light, generate a magnetic field and lose energy. This leads to the conclusion that the electrons should spiral to the center of the nucleus, see figure 9.5 "According to the laws that govern charged particles, an orbiting electron should emit light, loose energy, and eventually fall into the nucleus. Calculations indicated that for the hydrogen atom, this process would take less than a second. Since hydrogen has been around since the beginning of the universe, there was clearly something wrong with these arguments. In 1913 ... Niels Bohr suggested a way out of this dilemma. .... Bohr's picture of the atom is that electrons circle the nucleus only at certain well-defined distances ... known as allowed orbits. Why the atom should arrange itself in this way did not become clear until the advent of quantum mechanics in the next decade. ... If an electron happens to be in the orbit at radius r_1, the only way it can move to a lower orbit is to make an instantaneous jump, called a quantum jump. .... These two orbits have different energies. ... The lost energy must be radiated away from the atom. [9.23]" This is how radiation is created in the atom: An instantaneous jump from one energy level to another. This is how all electromagnetic radiation is created, including light. There are four basic ideas proposed by Bohr. "1. The electron moves in circular orbits about the proton. ... 2. Only certain orbits are stable. These stable orbits are ones in which the electron does not radiate. ... 3. Radiation is emitted by the atom when the electron 'jumps' from a more energetic initial stationary state to a lower state. ... The frequency f of the photon emitted in the jump is independent of the frequency of the electron's orbital motion. The frequency of the light emitted ... is give by the Plank-Einstein formula $E_i-E_f=hf$, where E_i is the energy of the initial state, E_f is the energy of the final state. ... The size of the allowed electron orbits is determined by ... $mvr=n\hbar$ [9.24]" Where h stands for the previously mentioned universal physical constant known as Plank's constant. And $\hbar = h/2\pi$. By these equations, you can calculate the allowed orbits in the atom. We should note that this calculation is based on energy conservation laws and the amount of kinetic and potential energy in the orbital system. Again, the second law of thermodynamics is critical to understanding the atom.

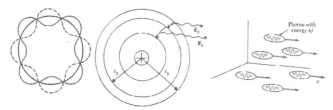

Figure 9.6

Wave Properties of Material Bodies

Niels Bohr made great progress in understanding the structure of the atom. Bohr determined that the total energy of the atom is simply the addition of the kinetic and potential energy, $E=K + U = \frac{1}{2}mv^2 - k\,e^2/r$. The kinetic energy is due to the electron moving around the nucleus and the potential energy is in the form of Coulomb's attractive force. If we generalize the orbit as similar to orbital motion, we get the Coulomb force as equivalent to the centripetal force, due to the electron's acceleration, $k\,e^2/r^2 = mv^2/r$. After some mathematical substitutions, we can find the smallest radius that an electron can exist in, without crashing into the nucleus. Any other stable orbits are given in multiples of this "ground state" so that, we say n=1 is the lowest orbit, n=2 for the next higher orbit and so on. "The orbit for which n=1 has the smallest radius; it is called the Bohr radius, a_0, and has the value $a_0 = ... = 0.529$ Å ... The lowest stationary or non- radiating state is called the ground state, has n=1, and has an energy $E_1=$ -13.6eV. The next state or first excited state has n=2, and an energy $E_2 = E_1/2^2 = $ -3.4eV. ... The minimum energy required to ionize the atom (that is, to completely remove an electron in the ground state from the proton's influence) is called the ionization energy. [9.25]" Ionization of atoms is a familiar term to anyone who has taken a class in Chemistry. "A familiar example of an ionically bonded molecule is sodium chloride, NaCl, which forms common table salt. Sodium ... is relatively easy to ionize, giving up its 3s valence electron to form a Na^+ ion. .... When the two ions (Na^+, Cl^-) are brought closer than 0.24 nm, the electrons in the closed shell overlap, which results in a repulsion between the closed shells. ... As they are brought closer together, the core-electron wave function begins to overlap. Because of the exclusion principle, some electrons must occupy a higher – energy state. [9.26]" Ionic bonding should not be confused with covalent bonding, which is sharing electrons. In the above mentioned salt molecule the ionic bond is due to the overlapping of the wave functions. What is this? This brings us to the next subject in this chapter. The wave function, used to explain mechanical waves like the motion of a rope attached to a wall, is also used to explain the stability of the atom.

There were many questions left un-answered by Bohr's proposals. "Bohr's model of the atom has many shortcomings and problems. For example, as the electrons revolve around the nucleus, how does one visualize the fact that only certain electronic energies are allowed? Why do all atoms of a given element have precisely the same physical properties regardless of the infinite variety of starting velocities and positions of the electrons in each atom? De Broglie's great insight was to recognize that wave theories of matter handle these problems neatly by means of interference. ... All of the possible states of the electron are standing waves states, each with its own wavelength, speed, and energy. The residual standing wave patterns thus account for the identical nature of all atoms of a given element and show that atoms are more like vibrating drum heads with discrete modes of vibration than like miniature solar systems. [9.27]" Electrons orbit the atom in a wave like manner, see figure 9.6. This gives a picture of the electron "skipping rope" until its properties are needed. In other words, the electrons orbiting the nucleus have wave properties that hold them in their allowed orbits without the electrons giving off radiation. When something upsets this delicate balance, the electrons move into a higher or lower orbit without going past the "ground state". This change in energy state will produce electromagnetic radiation.

There are even more far reaching implications with De Broglie's hypothesis. "Lois De Broglie (1892-1987) postulated that because photons have both wave and particle characteristics, perhaps particles also have wave characteristics. ... De Broglie hypothesized that material particles with momentum p should have a wave nature and a corresponding wavelength given by his equation: $\lambda = h/p = h/mv$. Notice that the De Broglie wavelength is directly proportional to h (Plank's constant), which is a constant to the -34 power. With the relatively large masses and velocities of ordinary life, the De Broglie wavelengths are so small they are virtually undetectable. [9.28]" ***Thus all moving objects have a "wave nature"*** with a wavelength given by the De Broglie equation. This nature is not noticeable until you have particles traveling at high speeds, like approaching the speed of light, or with very small particles like the electron. We are once again reminded of the dual nature of matter and light. Einstein showed that matter and energy are related by $E=mc^2$. The De Broglie equation again tells us that matter has wave properties. Why should we doubt the idea of all people having a dual nature? We have a spiritual side and a physical side to our lives. How can anyone doubt this? "There are also heavenly bodies and there are earthly bodies; but the splendor of the heavenly bodies is one kind, and the splendor of the earthly bodies is another." 1 Corinthians 15:40. Again, science proves biblical principles!

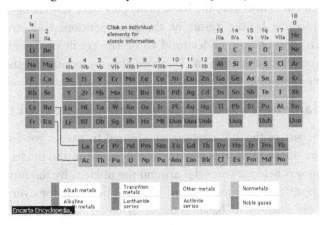

Figure 9.7

Basic Chemistry

We have thus far only described the theories about the simplest atom, hydrogen. The hydrogen atom consists simply of one electron circling a nucleus containing one proton. However, there are 92 naturally occurring elements and a number of man-made elements, see figure 9.7. Each atom has unique chemical properties and electron configurations. The electron configuration simply refers to the arrangement of electrons in the allowed orbits around the nucleus of a particular element. The development of the modern theory of atomic structure has had numerous contributions from many well known scientists. The debate over the ultimate building blocks of all things, living and non living, has covered many centuries of ideas from philosophers and scientists. "The main line of Greek thought, following the views of Aristotle and Plato, was that matter was continuous. However, some Greek philosophers, notably Democritus, disagreed with this view and argued that matter was composed of small indivisible particles that Democritus called *atomos*, meaning indivisible. [9.29] The atomic view grew in popularity, but there were many questions about the nature of the atom. One of the first milestones was the atomic theory developed by teacher and Quaker (Christian), John Dalton (1766-1844). "Dalton's atomic theory, published in the period 1803-1807, was strongly tied to experimental observation. His efforts were so successful that his theory has dominated our thinking since his time and has had to undergo little revision. The basic postulates of Dalton's theory were as follows: 1. Each element is composed of extremely small particles called atoms. 2. All atoms of a given element are identical. 3. Atoms of different elements have different properties (including different masses). 4. Atoms of an element are not changed into different types of atoms by chemical reactions; atoms are neither created nor destroyed in chemical reactions. 5. Compounds are formed when atoms of more than one element combine. 6. In a given compound, the relative number and kind of atoms are constant. ... We visualize an element as being composed of tiny particles called atoms. Atoms are the basic building block of matter; they are the smallest units of an element that can combine with other elements. Compounds involve atoms of two or more elements combined in definite arrangements. [9.30]" Here is the foundation of modern chemistry and the modern periodic table of elements, see figure 9.7. The periodic table began with Demitri Mendeleev and Lothar Meyer. "In 1869, Dmitri Mendeleev in Russia and Lothar Meyer in Germany, working quite independently of each other, published very similar schemes for classification of the elements. .... Mendeleev arranged the elements in order of increasing atomic weight and observed that when this is done, similar chemical and physical properties recur periodically. By arranging the elements so that those with similar characteristics are in vertical groupings, Mendeleev constructed the periodic table. [9.31]" This grouping specifies the elements natural form and how it can be used. For example, is the element naturally a solid, liquid or gas? The periodic table has been updated repeatedly over the years with more information about each element. However, the basic principles have not changed. The properties of each element are now understood to be the result of the fore-mentioned electron configuration of each element. The mass of each atom is now understood to be the result of three fundamental parts to the atom: the electron, the proton and the neutron. We have already mentioned the role of the electron and proton in the atomic theory explaining the hydrogen atom. However, what about the neutron?

The Fundamental Parts of the Atom: The Rest of the Story

Again, in the early part of the 20th century we seemed to have a good idea of how the hydrogen atom works. However, one of the mysteries was the composition of the nuclei of heavier elements. We explained how the electron was held into an orbit around the nucleus by the force between the negatively charged electron and the positively charged proton. This implied that for every electron in orbit, there must be a proton inside the nucleus to balance the total electrical charge. This created a theoretical problem that is still a subject of research today. "One of the basic laws of electricity tells us that while opposite charges must attract each other, similar electrical charges are repelled. This means that in any nucleus other than hydrogen (i.e., in any nucleus containing more than one proton), there will be a force that tends to push the protons apart. If this repulsive force were not countered by some other force, the nucleus of every atom would fly apart. ... The simple fact that the nucleus does exist leads us to the conclusion there must be some process in nature that is capable of overcoming this repulsion between protons. ... Physicists have named this process the strong interaction, and refer to the force generated by this interaction as the strong force. ... The existence of stable nuclei poses a major problem in our understanding of the atom. [9.32]" Does the Bible have anything to say on this topic? After this problem was discovered, theologians searched the scripture and were reminded of verses describing our Lord Jesus Christ which seams to correlate with this problem in advanced scientific research. "He is the image of the invisible God, the firstborn over all creation. For by Him all things were created: things in heaven and on earth, visible and invisible, whether thrones or powers or rulers or authorities; all things were created by

Him and for Him. He is before all things, and in him all things hold together." Colossians 1:15-17 More about current theories on the strong nuclear force will be briefly discussed later. For now, Christians can see that these verses declare that Jesus is responsible for holding the atom together. This should come as no surprise to the person of faith in God's Holy word. As we have said, "The heavens declare the glory of God; the skies proclaim the work of His hands." Psalms 19:1 All areas of science lead us to praise God for His wonderful creation.

The neutron was discovered by physicist James Chadwick. "The next most complicated atom – helium has two electrons circling its nucleus. If helium is to be electrically neutral, then it must have a nucleus that contains two positive charges. ... Since virtually all of the mass of an atom is in the nucleus, we would expect helium to weigh twice as much as hydrogen. In point of fact it does not. The helium atom weighs four times as much as hydrogen. ... One of several hypothesis that were put forth was that there ought to be another, hitherto unknown particle that had about the same mass as the proton but which carried no electrical charge. ... In 1932 the British physicist James Chadwick, working at Cambridge, England, was studying something called the radiation of beryllium. ... Chadwick found that the unknown radiation consisted of particles whose mass was essentially the same as the proton. ... Thus, the radiation of beryllium could only be the missing piece of the nucleus – the neutron. For this discovery, Chadwick was awarded the Nobel Prize in 1935. [9.33]" This discovery was the true beginning to the atomic era. The neutron plays many important roles in the atomic structure. The ability to have a controlled supply of neutrons is of vital importance in nuclear research. A short time later, nuclear fission was observed by Otto Hahn and Fritz Strassman in 1938 after bombarding uranium with neutrons. In 1942 the first controlled nuclear self-sustained chained reaction was produced by Enrico Fermi at the University of Chicago. All these processes were the result of understanding the nature of the neutron and producing a steady supply. We now realize that the stability of the atom is due to the presence of neutrons and the strong force generated by the exchange of pi-mesons.

The neutron has some unusual properties. Inside the nucleus, the neutron is generally stable. However, if you have a supply of neutrons outside the nucleus they would "decay" in a matter of minutes. "In the language of particle physics, a neutron outside the nucleus 'decays,' and the products of this decay include the proton and an electron. ... If we watched a large number of free neutrons, we would notice that they do not all decay at the same time. ... It would be something like watching popcorn being made. Not all of the kernels 'pop' at the same time. ... One common way of describing decay times is to talk about the half-life of the sample. This is the time it takes for one-half of the original number of particles to decay. [9.34]" We have already discussed radioactive decay in our section on radioactive dating methods. Radiation from radio-active materials is from the break- down of neutrons in the nucleus. Essentially, the nucleus has "too many" neutrons and begins to decay. We need to examine a few more details about the decay of a neutron before moving on to our next subject. "When the decay occurs, two charged particles are created – a proton and an electron. Thus, the total electrical charge of the final decay products is zero, which is exactly the charge of the neutron. ... This is called the Law of Conservation of Electrical Charge. [9.35]" Once again, a conservation law comes into play i.e. the conservation of electrical charge. The conservation of energy law was applied to the decay process of the neutron and another particle was discovered. The decay of the neutron is sometimes referred to as beta decay. "If E_0 is the total energy of the neutron before it decays, and if the beta decay is really described by the reaction n → p + e, then it follows that, if energy is conserved, the final energies of the proton and electron must add up to E_0. ... It turns out that they are not! ... In 1934 the Italian physicist Enrico Fermi ... supposed that beta decay is actually described by the reaction n → p + e + ν, with the Greek letter ν (nu) standing for the new hypothetical particle. ... It was given the name neutrino (little neutral one). [9.36]" We discussed what neutrinos are, and the difficulty in detecting them, in our chapters on Astronomy.

The discovery of the neutron led scientists to believe they were on the road to discovering one of the most difficult puzzles in science, the origin of the strong force. There were many ideas on how the neutron might somehow mediate the strong force enabling the atom to become stable. Also, with the discovery of the neutron, it was thought that we have all the basic building blocks to the atom. However, this was found to be untrue. The neutrons and protons that make up the nucleus were themselves, made up of something called quarks, see figure 9.9. This leads us to another question: Are quarks composed of anything smaller? Are we back to the view of Aristotle and is there no end in the search for the smallest building block to the universe? Some of these questions have been answered; others have not and are the subject of current sub-atomic research. Current theories describe the strong force as the result of interactions with the quarks inside the neutron as well as gluon interactions. To understand the strong force, we must have some background in the principles of quantum mechanics.

A Quick Review of Quantum Mechanics

The particle-wave duality, previously discussed, leads to another physical principle: the Heisenberg Uncertainty principle, formulated in 1927. "The Heisenberg uncertainty principle, formulated by Werner Heisenberg (1901-1976), states that it is impossible to simultaneously measure a particle's position and velocity exactly. Specifically, the uncertainty in the measurements are given by (Δx) $(\Delta p) \geq$ h/2 π. Another form of the expression refers to the uncertainty in measurements of energy and time (ΔE) $(\Delta t) \geq$ h/2 π. .... In other words, the very act of the measurement procedure in quantum mechanics introduces uncertainty into the data collected. [9.37]" The uncertainty principle is based on the fact that our ability to measure momentum and position is limited. For example, if we attempt to measure the momentum of a moving electron with a beam of light, we would change the original momentum of the electron. The very act of measuring position or momentum would alter the results. The uncertainty principle has more far reaching consequences than just accuracy of measurements. It is a cornerstone to how science evaluates many situations inside the atom. Because we are incapable of knowing exact measurements, in some cases, the laws of probability are introduced. "There is a striking similarity between the behavior of light and the behavior of matter. Both have dualistic character in that they behave both as waves and as particles. ... In the case of light waves, we describe how a wave theory gives only the probability of finding a photon at a given point within a given time interval. Likewise, matter waves are described by a complex-valued wave function (usually denoted by Ψ, the Greek letter psi) whose absolute square $| \Psi |^2 = \Psi^0 \Psi$ gives the probability of finding the particle at a given point at some instant. ... The wave function contains within it all the information that can be known about the particle. .... This interpretation of matter waves was first suggested by Max Born (1882-1970) in 1928. In that same year, Erwin Schrodinger (1887-1961) proposed a wave equation that described the manner in which matter waves change in space and time. The Schrodinger wave equation represents a key element in the theory of quantum mechanics. [9.38]" The Schrodinger equation helps us to mathematically describe the wave function. Again, the wave function describes all the information we can know about a particle. Also, recall that one of the special limitations within the atom is that momentum and position can never be known simultaneously, according to the Heinsburg uncertainty principle. This leads us to some principles that apply only within the world of the atom, as far as we know. To explain how an electron moves in orbit around the nucleus, we can apply the ideas of classical physics concerning wave motion. In classical physics the study of standing waves lead us to an understanding of how the electron moves. "In figure 2-4, (figure 9.8), a pulse generated by a flip of the string on the left travels to the right end, which is fixed to a wall. ... Now, suppose that pulses are sent along the string at regular time intervals. The reflected pulse traveling to the left side adds to the original pulse traveling to the right toward the wall. Standing waves are produced by the superposition of these similar but inverted pulses that are traveling in opposite directions. [9.39]" When you generate a wave by flipping a string, you can produce a harmonic wave or a so-called sin wave. "A harmonic wave has a sinusoidal shape. ... The displacement of the curve can be written y = A sin $((2 \pi / \lambda)x)$.[9.40]" This helps us understand a small portion of the wave function describing the motion of the electron around the nucleus. The electron does not simply go around in an orbit like a planet around the sun, the electron's orbit also follows a wave pattern, see figure 9.6

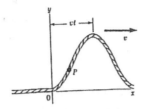

Figure 9.8

"As we mentioned earlier the wave function is generally a function of both position and time. Equation 41.7 ($\Psi(x) = A \sin((2\pi/\lambda)x)$) represents that part of the wave function dependent on position only. For this reason, one can view as a 'snapshot' of the wave at a given instant. ... Although Ψ itself is not a quantity that one can measure, the quantity $|\Psi|^2$ can be measured. ... If Ψ represents a single particle, then $|\Psi|^2$ is the probability per unit volume that the particle will be found at a given point. [9.41]" In classical physics, you can know both the position and momentum of a particle, in quantum mechanics you can not. The above mentioned formula represents the behavior of the electron at one specific moment. In other words when it is theoretically "stationary", and the momentum is zero at a given position. This can not happen in reality, but the concept gives us a more detailed explanation of why the electron remains in only allowed energy states. To explain this phenomenon further, we must look at the so-called particle - in- a- box phenomena. The "particle in a box" scenario in quantum mechanics explains the allowed energy states of the electron. The electron moving around the nucleus moves in the form of a sin wave function, see figure 9.6. We can think of the situation as a particle (ball) bouncing around in an enclosed space. "From a classical viewpoint, if a particle is confined to moving along the x axis and to bouncing back and forth between two impenetrable walls, its motion is easy to describe. ... The wave mechanics approach to this problem is quite different and requires that we find the appropriate wave function consistent with the conditions of the situation. ... $|\Psi|^2$ is always zero at the boundaries, indicating that it is impossible to find the particle at these points. In addition $|\Psi|^2$ is zero at other points, depending on the values of n. ... As we see from this expression ($E_n = (h^2/8mL^2)\,n^2$), the energy of the particle is quantized, as we would expect. ... Note that the state n = 0 is not allowed. This means that according to wave mechanics, the particle can never be at rest. ... This result is clearly contradictory to the classical viewpoint, in which E=0 is an acceptable state, as are all positive values of E. [9.42]" This means you can never have a "stationary" electron, for example. In fact, it seems that all subatomic particles are moving in some manner. These particles can change form or give off energy, but never stop moving. There are a set of formulas which leads to the conclusion that "the energy of the particle is quantized", as Max Born predicted. We will not follow all the formula substitutions, which lead to these formulas in this book. You can find more details in any college, and some high school physics textbooks. The important point to recognize is that this explanation is based on the wave-particle duality of matter and the uncertainty principle. Applying the appropriate formulas we can predict the allowed orbits in the atom.

Science endeavors to explain how and why things work. The situation is best explained as a child asking his parents, "Why does this thing work Daddy?" You give an answer and what comes next? Of course, the next thing the child does is ask a never ending set of questions. "But why Daddy? ..." The dutiful dad tries to give a complete answer to the child's questions. In frustration, the dad finally throws up his arms and says, "It is just that way because it is that way!" A scientist asks questions like, "Why is the electron in a stable orbit?" We have described several theories, which led to an explanation of this phenomenon. However, the "final answer" given by the "parent" is that this is simply the way of the universe. Why is there a wave-particle duality? The answer is, that is just the way it is designed. The next obvious question is: Designed by whom? Some scientists portray these laws of physics as just "natural laws". We have explored these barriers to our understanding several times, especially in the previous chapter. The ultimate question is what do you revere as your point of origin? Have you, by faith, elevated "natural forces" from a mysterious "power of nature" to the status as your point of origin, your God? It is far more reasonable to give praise and thankfulness to the one true God, the God of the Holly Bible. Science is best illustrated by the quest of mankind to understand the nature of the universe by asking God for direction. The most complete image is us with our child- like minds sitting of the lap of Jesus asking, "Why does this work?" The Lord reveals the answer slowly through revelation by the Holy Spirit. Some people are simply misled when they do not give credit to God for the creation of their mind and the thoughts that we can formulate. If we were given any more information we would be unable to comprehend the answer. With each new discovery in science our list of things to give honor to God increases. Each new bit of knowledge gives us one more reason to lift our eyes to God and praise Him for the wonderful works of His creation. Scientific discovery should not be seen as an opportunity to become boastful and arrogant of our accomplishments, but revere the Lord for His gifts.

The particle wave duality, combined with the uncertainty principle is used extensively to explain the inner-workings of the atom. This brings us to some of the "outer limits" in the scientific explanation of the design of the atom. There is always an element of uncertainty in our calculations. "They found that electrons, which normally exhibit the kind of localization associated with particles, could also behave like waves under certain conditions. Similarly, light, which normally displays the behavior of waves, would start to look like particles. ... They coined the term wave-particle duality to express this feature of the objects they were studying, and philosophers picked up this term and used it to 'prove' that there are inherent limits to what the scientific method can uncover. [9.43]" There seams no way to avoid the philosophical conclusion that there are inherent limitations to scientific discovery. Quantum mechanics leads us inch by inch to a more complete understanding of the wisdom of God. However, I believe, we will never have all the answers to our questions until we see Christ face to face. In this sense it seams to me, that we are approaching a limit to what science can discover about the nature of the atom and the rest of the universe. All we can do is give glory to God for his wisdom. The great barrier to our understanding is found in the uncertainty principal and the wave-particle duality of matter. These two principles lead us to some very strange conclusions about the working of the atom. However, there is irrefutable evidence that these events do indeed take place in the sub-atomic world.

Tunneling Through a Barrier

One of the strangest events inside the atom is the so-called tunneling through a barrier. This occurs when a particle passes through a barrier that should block its path. "A very interesting and peculiar phenomenon occurs when a particle strikes a barrier of finite height and width. ... Classically, the particle is reflected by the barrier since it does not have sufficient energy to cross, or even penetrate it. ... The possibility of finding the particle on the far side of the barrier is called tunneling or barrier penetration. Although the particle *can never be observed inside the barrier* (because it would violate conservation of energy), it is able to tunnel through that region and be observed in region III. How can the particle penetrate the barrier? The answer is that it can't if we describe it as a classical particle. Only the de Broglie wave associated with the particle can penetrate the barrier. Thus, we must invoke the wave-particle duality to explain this unusual phenomenon. ... There are many examples in nature on the atomic and nuclear scales for which tunneling is very important. ... The tunnel diode, ... alpha decay. [9.44]" The tunneling through a barrier phenomenon has many theoretical implications. First, we should take note that this not just a skeptical theory but a phenomenon which has been demonstrated to take place in numerous examples. This is not just an obscure theory, but a physical reality that takes place in many applications. The tunneling through a barrier is another proof of the wave-particle duality of all material bodies. We have examined that according to de Broglie's theories all objects have a wave nature. Again, it is accepted that we do not notice the wave nature of large objects because the wavelength of the object depends on its momentum. It would take a great deal of momentum, like if the object traveled at near light speed, to see noticeable effects. However, let us imagine for a moment that a large object had a lot of potential energy and thus the wave nature was noticeable. A person could indeed pass straight through a solid wall! Sounds like a comic book fantasy like the Flash® who can move his molecules so fast he could pass through walls. But, this is exactly what would happen. If for a moment quantum physics applied to large objects instead of only atomic sized parts, a person could travel through solid objects at will! Energy could be formed into all sorts of matter at will. In short, a person could perform miracles if the principles of quantum physics were applied to large scaled objects for a short period of time.

"Now Thomas (called Didymus), one of the Twelve, was not with the disciples when Jesus came. So the other disciples told him, 'We have seen the Lord!' But he said to them, 'Unless I see the nail marks in his hands and put my finger where the nails were, and put my hand into his side, I will not believe it.' A week later his disciples were in the house again, and Thomas was with them. Though the doors were locked, Jesus came and stood among them and said, 'Peace be with you!' Then he said to Thomas, 'Put your finger here; see my hands. Reach out your hand and put it into my side. Stop doubting and believe.' Thomas said to him, 'My Lord and my God!' Then Jesus told him, 'Because you have seen me, you have believed; blessed are those who have not seen and yet have believed.' Jesus did many other miraculous signs in the presence of his disciples, which are not recorded in this book." John 20:24-30 There are many principles found in this encounter between Jesus and Thomas. First, since the door was locked, it is assumed that Jesus merely past through the walls to be with His disciples. Luke's gospel has many more details about the encounter from a physician's perspective. As a physician, Luke's gospel has numerous references to the fact that Jesus Christ was a real person, sometimes debated in historical circles. From the beginning of his gospel, Luke has the most detailed account of the lineage and birth of Jesus. Luke's gospel also describes Jesus growing up as a boy, a detail left out of the other Gospels. So, it should come as no surprise that Luke's account of the encounter of Jesus and the disciples would be more concerned with the physical characteristics of the resurrected Christ. "While they were still talking about this, Jesus himself stood among them and said to them, 'Peace be with you.' They were startled and frightened, thinking they saw a ghost. He said to them, 'Why are you troubled, and why do doubts rise in your minds? Look at my hands and my feet. It is I myself! Touch me and see; a ghost does not have flesh and bones, as you see I have.' When he had said this, he showed them his hands and feet. And while they still did not believe it because of joy and amazement, he asked them, 'Do you have anything here to eat?' They gave him a piece of broiled fish, and he took it and ate it in their presence." Luke 24:36-43.

Remember that the wave nature of a material body is also determined by the amount of energy in the object, $E = f\lambda$. So the wavelength depends on the amount of energy in an object. What would happen if a body suddenly had a tremendous increase in energy? The quantum mechanical principle of "walking through walls" would be manifested. In short, we now have a "scientific" explanation of miracles, somewhat. If God were to give a person a sudden increase in energy or "power", that particular person would be able to perform miracles. There are several books written around the premise that quantum physics might explain miracles. Please realize that there is no laboratory evidence for this supposition, but there are many things that science has not uncovered. Somehow, God has worked miracles; so we must simply praise His holy name for the miracles that demonstrate His power. It is through the power of His miracles that Moses led the Israelites out of bondage. I merely ask the question, is it possible a resurrected body or glorified body has the ability to control its own energy level? Could a resurrected body control the wave nature of material objects? This could explain how the glorified, resurrected Christ walked through walls effortlessly. Because of this ability, the disciples first reasoned that Jesus was a ghost. Christ then made great efforts, over the next forty days before His ascension, to prove he had physically risen from the dead. Perhaps a resurrected body has the best of both the physical attributes and the energy properties of materials. No one will know until the day of the resurrection what a resurrected body will be like. However, we can make a few speculations from the references in scripture. "Jesus said to her,

'Your brother will rise again.' Martha answered, 'I know he will rise again in the resurrection at the last day.' Jesus said to her, 'I am the resurrection and the life. He who believes in me will live, even though he dies; and whoever lives and believes in me will never die. Do you believe this?' John 11:23-26 "So will it be with the resurrection of the dead. The body that is sown is perishable, it is raised imperishable; it is sown in dishonor, it is raised in glory; it is sown in weakness, it is raised in power; it is sown a natural body, it is raised a spiritual body. If there is a natural body, there is also a spiritual body. ... And just as we have borne the likeness of the earthly man, so shall we bear the likeness of the Man from heaven. I declare to you, brothers, that flesh and blood cannot inherit the kingdom of God, nor does the perishable inherit the imperishable. Listen, I tell you a mystery: We will not all sleep, but we will all be changed - in a flash, in the twinkling of an eye, at the last trumpet. For the trumpet will sound, the dead will be raised imperishable, and we will be changed. For the perishable must clothe itself with the imperishable, and the mortal with immortality. When the perishable has been clothed with the imperishable, and the mortal with immortality, then the saying that is written will come true: 'Death has been swallowed up in victory" 1 Corinthians 15:42-44,49-54 More on this subject has been written by other authors who have explored several ways quantum physics applied to large bodies could describe how God performs miracles.

Virtual Particles and the Beginning of the Universe

At this point, we see some concepts in quantum mechanics can be difficult to understand because they are so far removed from our every day experiences. "The concepts of quantum mechanics, strange as they sometimes may seam, developed from older ideas in classical physics. In fact, if the techniques of quantum mechanics are applied to macroscopic systems rather than atomic systems, the results are essentially identical with those of classical physics. This blending of the two theories occurs when the De Broglie wavelength is small compared with the dimensions of the system. The situation is similar to the agreement between relativistic mechanics and classical mechanics when v<<<c. [9.45]" In other words, the principles of quantum mechanics have built into the equations, a limitation that they apply only to small objects like those inside the atom. The same is true in the theory of relativity. The effects of relativity are only noticeable when objects travel at speeds approaching light. As we previously mentioned, the time dilation effect, for example, is not noticeable until an object is traveling at velocities approaching 0.5c. One of the discoveries that can be most difficult to comprehend is the so-called "virtual particle". There is an entirely new set of particles that are temporarily created for a specific purpose. Modern nuclear physics has determined that these particles, some which are the result of virtual particle creation, are absolutely necessary to explain the stability of the atom. These "short-lived" particles are considered the fore-runners for the stable particles that comprise the basic building blocks of the atom. Which particles were created first in the beginning of the universe? Modern theories explain the creation of all matter in the universe from a complex set of events taking place in microseconds. Recall the diagram of the beginning of the universe in Chapter 1, figure 1.4. In nearly every textbook on Astronomy you can find a similar diagram. The diagram includes a time where quarks and leptons were formed, then hadrons. This represents the theory that matter was first formed by energy creating these temporary, unstable particles which decayed into protons, neutrons, and electrons. Scientists create these same particles, some found in nature, in particle accelerators. You will probably be relieved to discover we will not cover all the transformations from the decay of these "unstable" particles into the neutrons and protons of the atom's nucleus and into electrons that orbit the nucleus. Just remember, virtual particles are created both naturally, and in man-made particle accelerators.

Let us consider how "virtual particles" are made within the atom. "The energy-time uncertainty relation leads to a very interesting concept in physics- the concept of the virtual particle. ... If Δt is small enough, it is even possible that the uncertainty in the mass may be large enough so that during the time Δt we cannot tell whether there is a single particle of mass M or a set of particles M + ΔM sitting at a particular point in space. ... We call the extra object a virtual particle. ... One way of visualizing the appearance of a virtual particle is to think of it as 'sneaking out' while no one is looking. So long as it gets back 'home' before a time Δt has elapsed, the uncertainty principle guarantees that no one will know the difference. … We could then have a situation in which one particle fluctuates into itself plus a virtual particle, and, provided that the mass of the virtual particle is such that it can travel a distance d, during its life-span, the virtual particle could be absorbed by the second of the original two particles. This is called the exchange of a virtual particle, and, again, the uncertainty principle tells us that such a process can go on without our being able to detect any violation of the law of conservation of energy. … In 1934, the Japanese physicist Hideki Yukawa …wrote a landmark paper that showed that if two protons exchanged virtual particles, the result of the exchange would be an attractive force between the protons. Furthermore, he showed that if the virtual particles had a mass something like 1/9 of the proton mass, then the result would be a force strong enough to overcome the electromagnetic repulsion between the protons and would, in fact, tend to hold them together. … His hypothetical particle was later termed meson (intermediate one) because of its mass. [9.46]" It is now known that particles like the ones Yukawa predicted do exist and are routinely formed in experiments. Scientists avoid the term "virtual particles" anymore because these particles actually exist for a short time and some have a significant amount of mass, relative to the size of atomic particles. As we stated earlier, scientists have discovered over 300 of these "unstable" particles.

The particles that Yukawa was searching for have been discovered and we have a fairly complete explanation of the strong force. "In 1948 a group of physicists headed by Cecil F. Powell at the University of Bristol in England began publishing the results of their examination of emulsions. … They saw tracks of mu-mesons, of course, but, in addition, they saw collisions of energetic particles with nuclei that produced another kind of meson that was heavier than the muon. … The new particle was christened with the Greek letter π (pi) and called the pi-meson, or pion. … It turned out that the meson come in three varieties – there are pions with a positive electrical charge, pions with a negative electric charge, and pions that are electrically neutral. … By 1948, therefore, the riddle of the mesons had been solved. Not one, but two groups of particles with a mass between that of the electron and the proton had been found. The pions are the particles predicted by Yukawa, and all three of them are routinely exchanged within the nucleus to generate the strong interaction. [9.47]" There are pastors and theologians who have a "distaste" for a scientific explanation of the strong interaction. They would prefer for us to simply say that God holds the atom together and we should not investigate how God performs this miracle. This attitude is unnecessary and has severely harmed the cause of spreading the Gospel. This is the same "attitude" that the church used to persecute Nicolaus Copernicus for his model of the solar system. It is sad to see some professing Christians continue to persecute the endeavors of Christian scientists today. When will the "religious leaders" ever learn to listen to the word of God? "Do not judge, or you too will be judged. For in the same way you judge others, you will be judged, and with the measure you use, it will be measured to you." Mathew 7:1-2. Again, refer to the introduction for many verses asking us to "seek wisdom".

Unknowingly, pastors and theologians who preach against the study of science have done considerable harm to the spreading of the Gospel. They have aided the world's view portraying Christians as unknowledgeable and that it makes no sense to listen to the Gospel message. The result is a group of people who profess Christ to avoid a fight, but are not committed to Christ in their hearts. How many evangelistic messages have fallen on deaf ears because they have not addressed their doubts of God? It is possible that many people are "caught up in the moment" of emotion and "come forward" during an invitation call but the next day believe that it was not "real" because science tell them God is not real. How many have been lost that an evangelist thought had been saved because all the person's concerns were never addressed, and the heart was never truly turned over to God? We must respect and applaud the calling of evangelists to their ministries, but all messengers of the gospel should be well equipped to answer any concerns about believing in Jesus Christ, including questions about science. We have already mentioned many verses that contradict the tendency of pastors to avoid scientific study. "The heavens declare the glory of God." Psalms 19:1 In fact, the scripture encourages a scientific study of the universe. "Lift your eyes and look to the heavens: Who created all these?" Isaiah 40:26 This sounds like God's command to "look to the heavens." It is through science that we stand in awe of His power and glory. "When I consider Your heavens, the work of Your fingers, the moon and the stars, which you have set in place, what is man that You are mindful of him?" Psalms 8:3-4 The person who avoids scientific explanation is the person who doubts the gospel. This person is scared that some obscure fact will someday prove that the scripture is just a bunch of stories and not truly the word of God. There is absolutely no reason to fear science! The fact remains that all roads that search for the "truth" in the universe leads to only one conclusion: Jesus Christ is Lord of All!

The ideas presented to explain the strong nuclear force, leads us to some rather remarkable observations. It is fascinating to discover that everything we know to physically exist is dependent on these "tiny miracles" occurring within the atom at a constant rate. The strong force is generated by a constant supply of these "virtual" particles exchanged between neutrons and protons. Think of it. Without this constantly taking place the atom would simply fly apart! The creation of these particles even seams to violate the conservation laws of energy! But, as we said in the earlier reference, it does it so quickly scientists state that we will simply ignore this fact. We simply chalk up the explanation to the uncertainty principle. Following this logic, anything is possible. What is the most likely conclusion? All these things operate inside the atom by the direction of God's will. As I have often said, "The more scientists rely on the uncertainty principle, the more certain I am in the presence of our Lord watching over us." Think of it, these particles are the result of uncertainty in position and energy due to someone observing them. Who is watching every atom in the universe? It must be God the Father. As a popular song says, "God is watching us." Later in this chapter and in the next chapter we will explore more about the theological implications to this discovery. In the next chapter, we will primarily look at historical events that seam to be leading to the last days of the planet earth as prophesied in many of the books of the Bible. However, when discussing the nature of God and the fore-told "wrath of God" that is to come, we need to be careful not to point to every natural disaster and accident as a judgment from God. God is ultimately in control of all things, but there are still times that bad things happen and it is not a punishment from God!

The atom is a complex world that speaks volumes about the wonder of God's ingenious design. "The nucleus is now seen not as a static collection of protons and neutrons ... but as a dynamic system in which mesons are whizzing around from particle to particle. They are continuously being created at one spot and absorbed at another and this process is what holds the nucleus together. ... Since both protons and neutrons emit and absorb mesons, it is easy to see the role the neutrons play in the nucleus. ... Although we have discussed this idea only for the strong interaction, it should not be too hard to accept that modern physicists think of all forces as being due, ultimately, to the exchange of particles. The electrical force, for example, is thought to arise because of the exchange of virtual photons. [9.48]" Wow! All forces, anything that exerts a push or pull depends on the exchange of "virtual" particles. Any motion, any movement is ultimately from an exchange of "virtual particles". It is as if the universe is dependent on the "heart beat" of God expressed in the pulsating exchange of virtual particles. How can anyone doubt that God controls the universe? The more we learn, the more we discover our dependence on the power of God. "For by him all things were created: things in heaven and on earth, visible and invisible, whether thrones or powers or rulers or authorities; all things were created by him and for him. He is before all things, and in him all things hold together." Colossians 1:16-17 How can anyone doubt this verse? Science clearly indicates that the hand of God has made us. Science clearly shows that Christ deserves to be worshiped for sustaining our life. To deny this fact, is to deny numerous principles of science, particularly the principles of quantum physics. More discoveries are made every day in the field of sub-atomic physics. With each new discovery, we again have more reasons to praise the wisdom of God. The entire concept of "virtual" particles is difficult to comprehend. Why should the skeptics of Christianity scoff at a service if the pastor is preaching about the invisible power of God? Quantum mechanics seam to prove that we owe are very existence to these "virtual" particles. But where do these particles really come from?

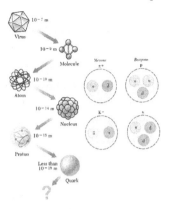

Figure 9.9

Early studies in subatomic physics depended on detecting elementary particles created by the sun and other stars. It soon became apparent that scientists needed a more reliable supply of specific particles to conduct experiments. The idea of producing accelerated particles for experimental study is credited to Ernest Lawrence. "Lawrence commandeered an old shack on the Berkley campus for his laboratory. ... An improved version of the 4-inch machine yielded protons with energies of 80 keV in 1931, and in February 1932 an 11-inch version achieved Lawrence's original goal of 1 million volts (1 Mev). ... The cyclotron beam had produced new chemical elements that were now decaying like any other radioactive material. ... In 1939 he received the Nobel Prize. The cyclotron quickly developed into the principle instrument for the study of nuclear physics, and it also became one of the prime sources for exotic radioactive materials, which were used in medicine as diagnostic tracers and for the treatment of cancer. ... This is still a field in which beams of accelerated particles are used, and there are treatment facilities in the United States where beams of protons, neutrons, and even pi-mesons are used in cancer treatment. [9.49]" The impact of the particle accelerators is enormous. Particle accelerator experiments have provided many answers to questions about the nature of the atom and the universe which is made from these atoms. Particle accelerators are not only tools for pure scientific research, but they have greatly advanced medical research. One of the many applications from this research is the Magnetic Resonance Imaging Device or MRI. The MRI uses many principles of quantum physics to produce a highly useful tool in medical diagnosis. "MRI is a diagnostic technique that is considered to be noninvasive. Photons associated with the rf signals have energies of about 10^{-7} ev. Since molecular bond strengths are much larger, the rf photons cause little cellular damage. In comparison, x-rays and Υ-rays have energies ranging from 10^4 to 10^6 eV and have the potential of causing considerable damage. [9.50]"

The last subject to briefly cover is the subject of quarks. The concept of quarks came as the result of an effort to organize the many particles that were being discovered in particle accelerator experiments. In 1961, Murray Gell-Mann and George Zweig independently proposed a connection between different particles in different families. The development of the so-called "eight-fold way" is compared with the development of the periodic table. "The periodic table worked, but until the advent of quantum mechanics in the twentieth century no one understood why. This same spirit of order-without-explanation led to the development of the periodic table of the elementary particles, which has been called the eight-fold way (because it predicts that many hadrons will be grouped in sets of eight) ... In 1964, Murray Gell-Mann ... and George Zweig ... independently suggested a simple physical explanation for the success of the eightfold way. ... In the original picture ... there were three constitutes making up all hadrons. These were called quarks (from a line in James Joyce's Finnegan's Wake – 'Three quarks for Muster Mark'). In order to produce the known elementary particles, the quarks must have unusual properties. For example, they have to have electrical charges that are fractions of the charge on the electron and proton. [9.51]" It turns out there are a number of unusual properties to quarks. This makes many scientists wonder if we will ever uncover all the properties of the atom or if it will be an endless search for answers, see figure 9.9. On the right side of figure 9.9 we see how the Baryons of a proton (top) and a neutron (below the proton) is believed to be made up of three quarks, while mesons are made up of two quarks and are therefore unstable. There are many more observations we could explore, but this becomes a seemingly never ending topic. The amount of scientific discoveries made in laboratories today is increasing at an incredible rate. "At this point, you are probably wondering whether or not such discoveries will ever end. How many 'building blocks' of matter really exist? At the present, physicists believe that the fundamental particles in nature include six quarks and six leptons (together with their antiparticles). ... It should be noted that in spite of many extensive experimental efforts, no isolated quark has ever been observed. Physicists now believe that quarks are permanently confined inside ordinary particles because of an exceptionally strong force that prevents them from escaping. ... The strong force between quarks is often called the color force. As mentioned earlier, the strong interaction between hadrons is mentioned by massless particles called gluons (analogous to photons for the electromagnetic force). [9.52]" Since this referenced text was written, there have been many more efforts to produce the energy level in a particle accelerator to separate quarks. In spite of reaching the theoretical limit to this strong force, an individual quark has never been detected. Recent experiments offer an explanation for why no individual quarks can be detected. As you add more energy to the particles, you exceed pair production levels. The so-called bag theory states that as you approach the energy level to pull quarks apart, 1Gev or so, you exceed pair production energy levels. Thus you create mesons as the quark and anti-quark pairs combine. [9.53] The subject of quark confinement was explained further in the 2004 Nobel Prize for Physics. The latest theory for explaining the strong force is quantum chromodynamics (QCD). The theory states that the quarks are permanently confined inside hadrons but can move around. When the quarks interact they can produce a "strong interaction" due to the "color" charges.

So what makes up quarks? It turns out that both theory and experiment agrees that there are six known quarks that make up all mater. These are called constituent quarks and are differentiated by a property known as flavor. The six flavors are up, down, charm, strange, top, and bottom. A constituent quark is a so called current or bare quark surrounded by virtual particles called gluons. Bare quarks and the electron are both point-like objects, meaning they are like points in space with nothing more elemental "below the surface". [9.54] We discussed how the experiments at the RHIC particle accelerator on Long Island, has fundamentally changed our view of the universe in our section on the unified field theory of chapter 2. The results of the experiments also give us a new perspective in the way all mater is constructed. "Every proton and neutron is made of three quarks. But all three quarks together account for less than 2 percent of the total mass of any proton or neutron. So where does the rest of the mass come from? Physicists theorize that each quark in every nucleus is surrounded by countless "virtual particles" that constantly emerge from the vacuum and then almost instantaneously subside into nothingness again. It is these evanescent particles that are thought to give heft to all we see and feel. ... 'So what that really means, 'says (RHIC researcher Bill) Zajc, 'is that 98 percent of the mass of protons and neutrons ... doesn't come from quarks. It comes somehow from these balls of stuff. ... The way I think of it is, it's really frozen Big Bang energy. ... So yeah, lurking inside every proton and neutron in your body is the residual energy of the Big Bang. It's a weird idea.' [9.55]" That statement doesn't sound weird to me. "So God created man in his own image, in the image of God he created him; male and female he created them." Genesis 1:27 "This is the message we have heard from him and declare to you: God is light; in him there is no darkness at all." 1John 1:5. "You are the light of the world." Mathew 5:14. We are made in the image of God, God is light, and we are the light of the world. In chapter 2 we discussed how the researchers described all objects as "projections on a screen". It is as if our reality was only just a "hollow-novel". In the Star Trek® Next Generation and Star Trek® Voyager television series and books there are numerous examples of stories played out on "the hollow-deck". In one episode, they accidentally give life to a fictional charter. The line between reality and fiction, life and random elements of a computer program is explored in this episode. They end the episode with the question of wither or not we are just acting out events from an elaborate computer program. The implication was that a Supreme Being was orchestrating our lives from an elaborate script. It would seam that science leads us to the conclusion that this is absolutely true! Almighty God, the God of Israel, is ultimately in control of all things. Remember where these gluons are coming from? The theorized source to all this is a fifth dimensional portal in space, a higher dimension, possible the very throne of God in heaven! We are being supplied with a seemingly endless supply of "virtual particles" called gluons that hold every atom in place and gives substance (i.e. mass) to everything we touch and believe is physically real. Why is it so hard for some to believe in the power of God? People seam to have no problem believing all mater is made up of atoms. Also, these atoms are anything but stationary objects. Electrons circling around the nucleus and now we know that quarks, mesons, and gluons are moving inside the nucleus. Yet, people say they must "see it to believe it" and refuse to have faith in God. Why? They claim they believe in all these "miraculous" events inside the atom are possible because of all the evidence, but not in the Bible because of lack of evidence. Is this really true? Or is the real reason they do not believe is because of a stubborn refusal to look at the truth? There is more than enough evidence for the historical reliability of the Bible than any other work, if a person chooses to look for it. In any event, the same evidence for the creator is present in the atom as in the rest of the universe. The complexity of the universe is undeniably the result of the wisdom of God. Yet, there seams to be no end to the debate to the philosophical opinions on the subject. Each person is committed to his or her beliefs. It takes a lot of proof to change a person's beliefs. It takes both reason and the Holy Spirit to change someone's accepted view of "truth". Both preaching and the power of the Holy Spirit can save a person's soul, and nothing else can.

Final Remarks

In this chapter we have studied the physical principles of the atom and modern physics. Einstein's principles teach us that everything is relative to absolute laws of physics which are constant and unchanging. The Christian believes our absolute center to life is the Lord Jesus Christ. All other factors in our life should be judged relative to the relationship we have with Christ. Einstein's second postulate is about another constant to the universe, i.e. the speed of light. In 1905 it was a profound statement that the speed of light is a constant. Newtonian physics taught us that by the principles of motion, velocity had no limits. Einstein's postulate showed a new limitation to the universe. Likewise, we can recognize that our Lord Jesus Christ is the author and creator of the universe. There is a limit to life, both in duration and quality. There is no other way to have a truly abundant life without a personal relationship to God through Jesus Christ. Our time in this life is limited, in the next life we will come before God's judgment. The only way to pass through the judgment to eternal life is by committing your life to Jesus **NOW** and making Him Lord of your life. In quantum mechanics we have learned about the uncertainty principle. The uncertainty principle teaches us there are limitations to how "certain" we are of "truth" and events taking place. This emphasizes the need for faith in a person's life. Only when we accept Christ as Lord, by faith, can we be certain of a present and future life. How much longer will we live? When will Christ return? What will I do if I'm present during the tribulation period? Ask yourself these questions and remember that the answers to every question are in the Holy Word of God, the Bible. Turn to God's Holly Word daily and pray for the Holy Spirit to guide you in your studies.

In quantum mechanics we learned how to deal with uncertainty by using probability equations. The next chapter applies these principles to analyzing historical information. An historical event, as we have stated earlier, can not be analyzed exclusively by the scientific method. Again, the scientific method is used to analyze a phenomenon by observing the event repeated under controlled laboratory conditions. To accept or reject that an historical event has taken place, you must analyze all available information and personally decide if the event did indeed occur. If there were a scientific principle or theorem, like the properties of light discovered by Thomas Young, you didn't believe was true, you could decide to test your belief by going to a laboratory and seeing the results of the experiment for yourself. There is always a certain degree of uncertainty in the process of deciding to accept or reject a belief in an historical event taking place. Similarly, there are "experimental errors" in repeating any laboratory experiment. All experiments have experimental ranges that give the limits to what results is considered to verify or disprove the theory you are testing. We studied in quantum physics, that there are certain situations that can only be analyzed by probability equations. Events in history must be handled in the same manner. How much quantity and quality of historical facts does it require for a person to accept an historical event has taken place? Most of this book has dealt with historical events. The origin of the universe and the origin of life are one time historical events. We have discussed in precise detail the inevitable element of faith in approaching these subjects and deciding what scientific principles can be applied to these situations. In this last chapter we will discuss principles of the Christian faith, the fulfillment of prophecies, and evidence for the Christian faith. Although I summarize several parts of Evidence that Demands a Verdict Volumes 1 & 2 by Josh McDowell, I strongly encourage you to read the complete texts for yourself and other books by Josh McDowell. Josh provides extraordinary evidences for the Christian faith in his many published works. There are many great Christian authors with many wonderful books to explore. Josh McDowell holds a special place in my heart for words of encouragement many years ago at one of his seminars. Research the evidence carefully. If you examine the evidence honesty and carefully, the truth of the Gospel will be revealed. The scientific method is to explore ideas, expressed as theorems, and then test those ideas through mathematical calculations and experimentation. Why are there so many so-called scientists with doctorates in various scientific disciplines refusing to explore all the alternatives? Why do they refuse to follow the scientific method to its ultimate conclusion? The scripture always encourages the pursuit of wisdom and invites each person to test the reliability of the scripture, as we explained in the introduction. With testimonies like those of Lee Strobel and Josh McDowell, we have seen how an honest pursuit of the truth always confirms the gospel. It is atheists and other so-called scientists with pre-conceived ideas and personal convictions that attempt to hide or distort the evidence for the Christian faith. The Bible has endured persecution, ridicule and testing for thousands of years and continues to pass every test from every critic. If these so-called scientists would simply be honest to the pursuit of wisdom, they would see the undeniable reliability of the Gospel of Jesus Christ. The Gospel of Jesus Christ is the only gospel of salvation which can change a person's life in a meaningful way. It is the only way to come to a saving relationship with God. The particle in a box experiment in quantum theory shows us how to deal with unknown values by confining certain particles. Likewise, we can see how the Bible fits all the facts within the bounds of good intellectual reasoning, and other philosophies fall miserably short. We see in modern physics an explanation of the world, so remarkable that it is totally beyond the bounds of good reason to accept the idea that we came from an explosion of natural forces. Even if we came from natural forces, we have shown that "natural forces" are not independent of God but merely manifestations of His power as proven by our understanding of virtual particles. The intricate design in the atom is a continual testimony to the craftsmanship and wisdom of God.

References for Chapter 9

9.1 Raymond A. Serway, Physics For Scientists & Engineers with Modern Physics Third edition, Saunders College Publishing, Fort Worth, TX., 1990, p.431.

9.2 Linda Huetinck, Cliffs Quick Review Physics, Wiley Publishing, New York, New York, 2001, p. 51.

9.3 Raymond A. Serway, Physics For Scientists & Engineers with Modern Physics Third edition, Saunders College Publishing, Fort Worth, TX., 1990, p. 973, 974.

9.4 Ibid p.985-986.

9.5 Linda Huetinck, Cliffs Quick Review Physics, Wiley Publishing, New York, New York, 2001, p. 118-120.

9.6   Ibid p. 126-127.

9.7   Raymond A. Serway, Physics For Scientists & Engineers with Modern Physics Third edition, Saunders College Publishing, Fort Worth, TX., 1990, p.994-995.

9.8   Linda Huetinck, Cliffs Quick Review Physics, Wiley Publishing, New York, New York, 2001, p. 133.

9.9   Raymond A. Serway, Physics For Scientists & Engineers with Modern Physics Third edition, Saunders College Publishing, Fort Worth, TX., 1990, p. 1051

9.10   Ibid p.1157-1158.

9.11   Ibid p. 1213.

9.12   James S. Trefil, From Atoms To Quarks: An Introduction to the Strange World of Particle Physics, New York, Charles Scribner's Sons, 1980, p.11-14.

9.13   Lincoln Barnett, The Universe and Dr. Einstein, Bantam Books, New York, New York, 1957, p.58-59.

9.14   Raymond A. Serway, Physics For Scientists & Engineers with Modern Physics Third edition, Saunders College Publishing, Fort Worth, TX., 1990, p. 1136.

9.15   Linda Huetinck, Cliffs Quick Review Physics, Wiley Publishing, New York, New York, 2001, p. 142.

9.16   Raymond A. Serway, Physics For Scientists & Engineers with Modern Physics Third edition, Saunders College Publishing, Fort Worth, TX., 1990, p. 1107.

9.17   Ibid p.1116-1117.

9.18   Ibid p. 1115.

9.19   Ibid p.1116.

9.20   Tom Morris, Philosophy For Dummies, Hungry Minds Inc., New York, N.Y., 1999, p. 46.

9.21   Raymond A. Serway, Physics For Scientists & Engineers with Modern Physics Third edition, Saunders College Publishing, Fort Worth, TX., 1990, p. 1153.

9.22   Ibid p. 1414.

9.23   James S. Trefil, From Atoms To Quarks: An Introduction to the Strange World of Particle Physics, New York, Charles Scribner's Sons, 1980, p. 14-15.

9.24   Raymond A. Serway, Physics For Scientists & Engineers with Modern Physics Third edition, Saunders College Publishing, Fort Worth, TX., 1990, p. 1159.

9.25   Ibid p.1161.

9.26   Ibid p.1254.

9.27   Ibid p.1173-1174.

9.28   Lincoln Barnett, The Universe and Dr. Einstein, Bantam Books, New York, New York, 1957, p. 149-150.

9.29   Theodore L. Brown, H. Eugene LeMay, Jr., Chemistry the central science, Prentice-Hall, Inc., Englewood Cliffs, New Jersey, 1977, p. 33.

9.30   Ibid p.33-34.

9.31   Ibid p. 177-178.

9.32   James S. Trefil, From Atoms To Quarks: An Introduction to the Strange World of Particle Physics, New York, Charles Scribner's Sons, 1980, p. 22-23.

9.33   Ibid p. 23-25.

9.34   Ibid p. 26-27.

9.35   Ibid p. 29.

9.36   Ibid p. 29-31.

9.37   Linda Huetinck, Cliffs Quick Review Physics, Wiley Publishing, New York, New York, 2001, p. 150.

9.38   Raymond A. Serway, Physics For Scientists & Engineers with Modern Physics Third edition,

Saunders College Publishing, Fort Worth, TX., 1990, p. 1181.

9.39   Linda Huetinck, Cliffs Quick Review Physics, Wiley Publishing, New York, New York, 2001, p. 52-53.

9.40   Raymond A. Serway, Physics For Scientists & Engineers with Modern Physics Third edition, Saunders College Publishing, Fort Worth, TX., 1990, p. 441.

9.41   Ibid p. 1182-1183.

9.42   Ibid p. 1184, 1186.

9.43   James S. Trefil, From Atoms To Quarks: An Introduction to the Strange World of Particle Physics, New York, Charles Scribner's Sons, 1980, p.37.

9.44   Raymond A. Serway, Physics For Scientists & Engineers with Modern Physics Third edition, Saunders College Publishing, Fort Worth, TX., 1990, p. 1192-1193.

9.45   Ibid p.1182.

9.46   James S. Trefil, From Atoms To Quarks: An Introduction to the Strange World of Particle Physics, New York, Charles Scribner's Sons, 1980, p.49-51.

9.47   Ibid p.72-73,75.

9.48   Ibid p.51-52.

9.49   Ibid p. 86-88.

9.50   Raymond A. Serway, Physics For Scientists & Engineers with Modern Physics Third edition, Saunders College Publishing, Fort Worth, TX., 1990, p.1384.

9.51   James S. Trefil, From Atoms To Quarks: An Introduction to the Strange World of Particle Physics, New York, Charles Scribner's Sons, 1980, p.134, 137-138.

9.52   Raymond A. Serway, Physics For Scientists & Engineers with Modern Physics Third edition, Saunders College Publishing, Fort Worth, TX., 1990, p. 1430-1431.

9.53   http://hyperphysics.phy-astr.gsu.edu/hbase/particles/qbag.html.

9.54   Timothy Paul Smith, Hidden Worlds: Hunting For Quarks In Ordinary Matter, Princeton University Press, Princeton N.J.,2003, p. 6.

9.55   Tim Folger, The Big Bang Within You, Discover Magazine, February 2007, p. 36. sub-article of The Big Bang Machine.

Illustrations for Chapter 9

9.1   Microsoft Encarta Encyclopedia Standard, 2002 edition, David Parker/Photo Researchers, Inc.

9.2   Raymond A. Serway, Physics For Scientists & Engineers with Modern Physics Third edition, Saunders College Publishing, Fort Worth, TX., 1990, p. 1050.

9.3   Left side: Dudley Williams, John Spangler, Physics for Science and Engineering, D. Van Nostrand Company, New York, 1981, p. 922. Right Side: Raymond A. Serway, Physics For Scientists & Engineers with Modern Physics Third edition, Saunders College Publishing, Fort Worth, TX., 1990, p. 1105.

9.4   Ronald Gautreau and William Savin, Schaum's Outline Series of Theory and Problems of Modern Physics McGraw-Hill Book Company, New York, 1978, p. 68.

9.5   Raymond A. Serway, Physics For Scientists & Engineers with Modern Physics Third edition, Saunders College Publishing, Fort Worth, TX., 1990, p. 129, 133, 1159, 1214.

9.6   Ibid Far left: p. 1174, Far right 1152. Middle: James S. Trefil, From Atoms To Quarks: An Introduction to the Strange World of Particle Physics, New York, Charles Scribner's Sons, 1980, p. 15.

9.7   Microsoft Encarta Encyclopedia Standard, 2002 edition

9.8   Raymond A. Serway, Physics For Scientists & Engineers with Modern Physics Third edition, Saunders College Publishing, Fort Worth, TX., 1990, p.433.

9.9   Ibid p. 1434.

Chapter 10: History, Theology, and Prophecy:
Are we living in the end times?

Religion and Science are Inseparable.

This book has covered many principles of science. There have been many examples of faith and science merging together. We have shown the indication of an "intelligent design", which of course implies a creator God. What are the exact characteristics of the God of all creation? How was the universe made? Did the power of God or some set of natural forces, somehow independent of any god, make the universe? Exactly how did God make the universe, if God made it as Einstein believed? There seams to be nearly endless controversy in answering these questions. It seams that just about every person has a particular set of views on the subject of universal origin and the character of God. It also seams that these questions receive the most passionate responses. To describe a person's origin affects a person's outlook to the future. Also, some of the most personal thoughts and feelings are expressed in a person's beliefs in the character of God. If a person considers them self an atheist you will get an even more passionate response about why they believe God does not exist at all, because the case against God's existence is so weak. One of the most significant scientific theories discussed in this book has been the theory of evolution. Overall, the theory of evolution promotes a specific set of religious views. First, I would like re-emphasizing the importance of faith in science. Throughout this book, I have repeatedly shown the necessity of exercising faith in any discussion about scientific theories. Scientific laws are only valid under certain precise circumstances and represent the day-to-day operation of the universe, as we know it. However, scientific theories, based on the scientific laws, are not provable. They seam to fit our present understanding of the universe, but theories are not laws and often change through time as our understanding of the universe changes. Theories, therefore, can not be uncontroversial or proven as fact, since they simply present a set of scientific beliefs explaining a physical phenomenon. We discussed the religious convictions of scientists who accept the theory of evolution and "worship" the power of natural forces. The faith in evolution as an uncontroversial truth is misplaced and unjustified. The theory of evolution should be "dissected" carefully to separate fact from fiction. Secular, public and private, schools support the religions of Secular Humanism and usually some form of Atheism, Agnosticism or Skepticism when they teach that all parts of the theory of evolution is an undeniable truth. We have examined some of the regularities of science and how the presence of universal structure indicates the existence of a design made by God. The evidence presented from the fields of science, physics and mathematics has lead scientists, like Einstein, to have a profound faith in God. We discussed the necessity of understanding faith to understand quantum mechanics. If you can't understand how a person makes a "leap of faith" you can not understand quantum mechanics. The reverse can also be true. If you are a teacher or a scientist that believes you understand basic quantum physics, you must also understand faith and its importance in the scientific study of the universe. Quantum mechanics deals with isolating a particle as much as possible by the "particle in the box" method. Then we attempt to ascertain the location and momentum of a particle through experimental means. However, the Heinsberg uncertainty principle is a constant deterrence to an absolutely precise reading. Therefore, we must estimate the location and momentum of a particle and give a percentage of error. We then specify our "belief" in the position of a certain subatomic particle at a certain time, with a certain degree of inaccuracy. Similarly, we examine all evidence concerning an event in history, like the death and resurrection of Jesus Christ. Next, based on the evidence, we determine if we believe the event actually took place. We still have a certain amount of uncertainty, because the conclusion that Jesus died and was resurrected is basically a theory because it can never be repeated to be proven as a scientific fact. To bridge the gap between uncertainty of an event taking place and an absolute certainty in the belief that it did actually take place requires faith. There are a multitude of skeptics that have tried to dismantle the Christian faith through science. Each and every time they have failed. Now that we have discussed many of the uses of faith in science, it is time to define faith.

What is faith?

"Now faith is the assurance of things hoped for, the conviction of things not seen. For by it the men of old received divine approval. By faith we understand that the world was created by the word of God, so that what is seen was made out of things which do not appear." -Hebrews 11:1-3 RSV. Some have misinterpreted this verse to assume that faith comes out of nothing, "things unseen". The King James Version expresses this verse as; "Now faith is the substance of things hoped for, the evidence of things not seen." Some have described faith as merely the product of uneducated people 'hoping for an existence after death', perhaps because their existence in this life is miserable. This portrays all religions, including Christianity, as merely wishful thinking. This is not true. Faith allows you to go beyond the here and now to accept something that is not universally proven as truth. Do you use faith to accept the scripture or do you use faith to accept something else? Everyone has a faith in something beyond "proven" scientific fact. Faith is necessary to have a reasonable assessment to the origin of life. You may have a "religious conviction" that all that really matters is pleasure. Just have a good time, live in the moment is your religion and you do not want to take a close look at any religion. Each and every individual constantly evaluates their experiences and knowledge to evaluate there convictions of faith, no matter what faith or current religious convictions that person may have. In this manner, your religious convictions are constantly being stretched and tested like a rubber band. And like a rubber band, your convictions can break. When this happens, your convictions are given to a new faith in a new religion. This is what some call a "religious experience". An awakening of both your mind and spirit makes the person have a new excitement in their life and clarity of thought. What religion has impacted the world the most, obviously Christianity. As stated earlier, *every serious critic* of Christianity has become a Christian after they have completed their investigation. Not only is it the overwhelming evidence for the Christian faith in the study of science and history, but they experience a transformation into a new life. This is beyond the experience found in those converting to Islam, New Age philosophy, or some other supposed "reasonable alternative". There are numerous examples of "born again Christians" with incredible testimonies of faith. This is one of the greatest evidences for the Christian faith: The millions of testimonies of a fundamental change in mind and spirit when they are "born again".

In the past, God demonstrated His power by miracles that are recorded in the Bible. Now, the really big miracles do not seam as common, but there is a long history of God's work recorded in scripture. Additionally, we have many "modern miracles" through both technological achievements and reports of miraculous events taking place that give testimony to God for His grace and provisions. Again, the best example of a miracle is the salvation we receive in accepting Jesus Christ as our Lord. There are millions of Christians that give testimony to the blessings of God. If you seek a reason to having faith in Christ, you will find plenty of evidence. You simply need to look for it. There are limitless testimonies to the great things God has done in the lives of those who follow Him and dedicate their lives to serving the Lord Jesus Christ. The pseudo-scientists that make statements describing faith in God as a lack of knowledge believe they have insights into the universe that the average person simply can not understand. They are filled with a confidence in their superiority because of their "highly evolved" mind and often have delusions of grandeur. These scientists are skeptical about an "after" life. They see only atoms and molecules in the body and do not recognize the presence of any "spirit". But how do they explain life? To them it simply exists and the creation of the mind is simply the result of natural forces acting on chemical substances. Once you are dead, you simply do not exist any more. These scientists believe that natural forces create us and when your "machine" body finally malfunctions beyond repair, you simply return to the natural elements, which created you. To them the Bible is a mystery. The Bible has the most perfect explanations to any question of any great importance. It is the only book that can boast this claim and back it up. As proof, there are hundreds of examples of people who have had their lives totally changed by the Bible. For example, C.S. Lewis who changed from a critic and skeptic to a Christian merely by stopping his criticism of the Bible long enough to actually read the word of God. Faith in God and the Bible as the

Holy word of God is reasonable based on the internal and external evidences. Based on the evidence, it is more reasonable to place your faith in Jesus Christ as Lord and the Bible as God's word than in any other religion or philosophy. How can you believe in the existence of "natural forces" which lack the ability to create life? Having "faith" in science as the only answer to why life exists is a "blind faith." Only science combined with the Christian faith can give a complete view of the beginning of life.

Figure 10.1

Faith is how we can accept the things that are unseen, but faith comes through reason. By faith, men of God were justified in their actions according to the book of Hebrews verse 3, previously quoted. Some times the Lord led the people of Israel to attack and destroy their enemies. For instance, the story of David and Goliath is an example of following the Lord's guidance. David was lead by faith that his God would protect him and allow him to defeat the enemy of his people. Sometimes faith leads men, such as Moses, to perform miracles. By faith in God, men, lead by the Holy Spirit, wrote the Holy word of God with perfection. Faith, also, allows us to bridge the gap between the facts we know as true and the things we need to know. Verse three shows a prime example of faith settling the question about how the universe was made. "By faith we understand that the universe was formed at God's command, so that what is seen was not made out of what was visible." Hebrews 11:3 We can learn from science more about what the probable conditions which took place during the original formation of the universe, but many of the exact circumstances remains a mystery. What have we learned out of the overall study of science? We have learned about atoms and how they are constructed. We have learned many things about how different atoms have different properties, depending upon the numbers of electrons and protons they have. We have learned how these properties form the basis of predictable chemical reactions. We have learned all these things and hundreds more facts that allow us to appreciate the fact that the world was made by the word of God. There are still many unanswered questions, but to bridge the gap between an uncertainty of how the universe began, the existence of "things not seen", to the absolute certainty that the universe does exist from God's power, requires faith. However God made the world, He did make it by His word. We can be assured of this fact through faith.

Faith is a very important part of living, according to the Bible. In a search of the New International Version of the Bible, Faith is mentioned 142 times. The word faithful is mentioned 82 times, faithfulness 18 times and there are numerous references to the consequences of becoming faithless. How do we receive faith? "So faith cometh by hearing, and hearing by the word of God." Romans 10:17 KJV. What does this mean? It means that we receive faith in the word of God by hearing the word of God. To "hear" the word of God, we must comprehend the words. The facts are presented to us, and then we accept the things we can not see, or can not understand, by faith. First comes the facts or principles in which you believe. For example, the fact that Christ is the Son of God and he was resurrected from the dead. Then comes by faith in the facts, even though you might not completely understand how these facts or principles could be true. Then comes the felling of assurance that you have made the correct decision in believing the facts, see figure 10.1. This is how we can accept the Christian faith. First there is an over abundance of evidence to support the principles of the Christian faith. Next the ability to believe in these principles is given to every person. This ability is through a combination of faith and reason. Evidence presented to a person in the form of miracles or scientific information can only take you to the edge of changing your belief. The next step in this transformation is in the condition of the spirit. Are you willing to take a step of faith and go in a difference direction? Some psychiatrists try to explain a "religious experience" by simply saying it is a "state of mind" brought on by people who have influenced you life. There is a bit of truth in this assessment. But if you recall our discussions about the human mind, there is strong evidence that the mind is made in the image of God. The mind is not just chemical reactions but something spiritual as well. The "regeneration" of a person who "realizes the truth of the Gospel" and become a Christian is from both the influenced of the Bible, books and people stating their evidences and the Holy Spirit. It is from having a spirit open to the gospel message and allowing the Holy Spirit to enter your life through prayer. "Then he said to Thomas, 'Put your finger here, and see my hands; and put out your hand, and place it in my side; do not be faithless, but believing.' Thomas answered him, 'My Lord and my God!' Jesus said to him, 'Have you believed because you have seen me? Blessed are those who have not seen and yet believe." John 20:27-29. Throughout the Old Testament the Bible refers to God defining himself by his actions. "I am the LORD your God, who brought you out of Egypt, out of the land of slavery. "You shall have no other gods before me" Exodus 20:2-3. "I am the LORD your God, who brought you out of Egypt to be your God. I am the LORD your God.' " Numbers 15:41. One of the most important facts to accept, by faith, is that Christ was raised from the dead. "For if the dead are not raised, then Christ has not been raised. If Christ has not been raised, your faith is futile and you are still in your sins. Then those also who have fallen asleep in Christ have perished. ... But in fact Christ has been raised from the dead, the first fruits of those who have fallen asleep. For as by a man came death, by a man has come also the resurrection of the dead. For as in Adam all die, so also in Christ shall all be made alive." -1 Corinthians. 15:16-18, 20-22. Without the resurrection of Christ, we have no hope of salvation from death. The New Testament writings thoroughly describe the interdependence of the whole Bible on the fact of the resurrection of Jesus Christ.

Josh McDowell has written several good books that describe many of the evidences for the resurrection and the deity of Jesus Christ. In McDowell's first book, Evidence that demands a verdict, he describes Christ as the fulfillment of prophecy. The verses describing Old Testament prophecies in the coming of the Messiah is presented with the fulfillment of prophecy described in the New Testament. First, the signs for Jesus as the Son of God from the lineage of Joseph and Mary and the conditions of the birth of Jesus. Jesus was born of a virgin. "Therefore the Lord Himself will give you a sign: Behold, a virgin will be with child and bear a son, and she will call His name Emmanuel." Isaiah 7:14. The virgin birth foretold. Jesus was the Son of God. "I will surely tell of the decree of the Lord: He said to me, 'Thou art My son, Today I have begotten Thee.'" Psalms 2:7. "...And behold, a voice out of the heavens, saying, 'This is my beloved son, in whom I am well-pleased.'" Mathew 3:17. Jesus was of the seed of Abraham. "And in your descendents, all the nations of the earth shall be blessed, because you have obeyed my voice." Genesis 22:18. "The book of the genealogy of Jesus Christ, the son of David, the son of Abraham." Matthew 1:1 Jesus was the son of Jacob. "I see him, but not now; I behold him, but not near; A star shall come forth from Jacob, and a scepter shall rise from Israel, and shall crush through the forehead of Moab, and tear down the sons of Seth." Numbers 24:17. Seth was a son of Noah who rebelled against God. "Jesus ... the son of Jacob..." Luke 3:23,34. We also see in the verse in Numbers foretold the star which lead the wise men to find Jesus. Jesus was of the house of Judah. "The scepter shall not depart from Judah, nor the ruler's staff from between his feet, until Shiloh comes, and to him shall be the obedience of the peoples." Genesis 49:10. "Jesus ... the son of Judah..." Luke 3:23,33. Jesus was of the tree of Jesse. Jesus was descended from David. "Behold, the days are coming, declares the Lord, 'When I shall raise up for David a righteous branch; and he will reign as king and act wisely and do justice and righteousness in the land.'" Jeremiah 23:5. "Jesus ... the son of David..." Luke 3:23,31. Jesus was born in Bethlehem. "But as for you, Bethlehem Ephrathah, too little to be among the claims of Judah, from you one will go forth for Me to be ruler in Israel. His going forth are from long ago, from the days of eternity." Micah 5:2. The wise men bringing gifts to Jesus was foretold. "Let the kings of Trashish and the islands bring presents; the kings of Sheba and Seba offer gifts." Psalms 72:10. The killing of the children of Bethlehem is foretold. (See Jeremiah 31:15 and Matthew 2:16). A messenger preceded the ministry of

Jesus. "A voice is calling, 'Clear the way for the Lord in the wilderness; Make smooth in the desert a highway for our God.'" Isaiah 40:3. "John the Baptist came, preaching in the wilderness of Judea, saying 'Repent, for the kingdom of heaven is at hand.' " Mathew 3:1,2. There are many more prophecies about the Messiah in the Old Testament that are perfectly fulfilled in the coming of Jesus Christ.

Blind Faith and Intelligent Faith

In this book, there are many verses to show the correlation between the Bible and principles of science. We have in no way exhausted either the subject of science or of biblical study. There are many more volumes of books on scientific theories and principles that we could cover. Nearly every one should be aware that new discoveries occur every day in various scientific fields. In addition, there are many more verses that could have been included to support the correlation between biblical principles and scientific principles. There is no end to the resources that can be explored from the Bible. There is literally no end to the number of sermons which can be given based on one or more verses from the Holy Bible. You should regularly attend church and bible studies to explore this fact further. There are many religions throughout the world, but none can compare to Christianity in content, clarity and completeness. The Bible is unique in history, message, content, reliability and many more attributes we can never completely understand. Many other religions have "borrowed" from the Bible to create their beliefs, ideas and philosophies. We will not explore very many of these other religions in this book. The Bible begins with what is called the Pentateuch, which contains the first five books of the Bible. The credit for authorship of these books is given to Moses. The first book of Moses, Genesis, is the book of origins and explains the history of the universe from God's acts of creation to the time of Moses. Until the time of Moses, these events were handed down mostly in the form of stories. I believe God inspired Moses to write the history of the world in the book of Genesis to "get the facts straight". Genesis describes the beginning of man and the "fall of man" i.e. the beginning of man's rebellion against God. The next four books of Moses deals with the events of God's work in the life of Moses and the Israelite people. They include the Ten Commandments and many other guidelines and laws for the people of Israel to live by. The worldwide view is that all religions are the same, an attempt by man to understand God. This is not true in one and only one religion. The nature of God has been revealed to the writers of the Bible. The men who wrote the scripture were guided by the Holy Spirit to write God's perfect word. The Bible is based on a promise: "Seek and you shall find." The promise is that if we seek God with an "open mind" he will reveal himself to us through his Spirit. This spirit of revelation is available to every person on earth if they are seeking to know the truth about God. The Bible clearly describes a situation entirely reversed from all other religions. In the Christian - Jewish faith, it is God reaching down eagerly trying to reach our mind in revelation. This is the one true God, the Father of Jesus Christ. His method for reaching us is through His Spirit guiding men to write the Holy Bible.

What is an "open mind"? The world teaches society that if you believe the Bible you have "lost your mind". The worldview is that intelligence and faith is complete opposites. I found that this premise was the most offensive statement mentioned in the movie The DaVinci Code. This is true with every religion but one, Christianity. Throughout this book we have covered a few scientific principles that support the Christian faith. Christianity is the ultimate "reasonable faith". The concept of having an "open mind" is taught to suggest that to "open" you mind to a "religious faith" in something, you must "empty your head" of thought or reason. You certainly run into this situation if you try to believe many other religions. To believe in Hinduism, Islam, Fascism, Nazism, Atheism, Darwinism, Communism or any other "ism" you must have a desire to put your "brain on hold". In all faiths, except Christianity, you will find flaws in their ideologies and theories. You simply need to examine the evidence close enough or long enough to see the truth of the Gospel. The world teaches that there is no absolute right or wrong but everything is "shades of gray". The Bible teaches us there IS an absolute right and wrong. The Bible is true every other religion is false. Anything leading you away from the Bible can be deadly, anything leading you to the study and practice of God's word found exclusively in the Bible is good. This is the definition of "good" and "bad", there is no other! The Bible teaches us a clear message about God and His many attributes. Without the revealed word of God contained in the Bible there is no hope of salvation, in this life or the life to come. All religions that in any way deviate from the gospel of the Bible are not worthy of close study. Any faith that leads anyone to explore the pages of the Bible has either some or has great benefit. Any belief that leads you to examining more closely the Bible helps a person on a journey of discovery that should end with the acceptance of Jesus Christ as savior. The simple truth is that all paths of wisdom lead to the Bible as the ultimate truth and Jesus Christ is the embodiment of that truth. The Bible teaches us clearly to be kind to all people but also to stand firm concerning your convictions to share the Christian faith. There have always been people who have embraced the word of God and those who have rebelled against God's authority. Those who rebel formed philosophies or religions that would strive to explain the world without the God of the Bible. The tendency continues today with a failed attempt to explain the universe by some other means than what is described in the Bible. There are many questions people have about the Bible. The first, best source is to read the book for your self! Cover to cover and repeatedly read the New Testament, Psalms and Proverbs, since they have more direct implications today. I know it's a big book, but there are many commentaries and study guides to help you through a Bible study. Don't forget God has many friends to help you step by step read through the Bible. It is so amazing that there is a diverse opinion on the Bible from people who have never read it! If you are going to review a novel of equal length you read it thoroughly. Why do people who read volumes of other books run in terror when asked to read the Bible? Simple, the Bible convicts us of our sin and we have a rebellious nature wanting to do whatever we want without consequence. Even those who do not read the Bible are aware of this truth, so the run and hide rather than read what the Bible has to say.

There are two types of faith, intelligent faith and blind faith. An example of intelligent faith is to close your eyes, and respond to someone asking you to sit down on the chair which is directly behind you. First, you feel for a chair behind you. If your hands can provide evidence to confirm that there is a chair behind you, you accept, by faith, that there is a sturdy chair is behind you. With intelligent faith, you do not relay on only one source of information, but rather explore all the facts and make a decision if it is reasonable to accept information another person is telling you. If someone asks you to sit down, you can act on that faith and sit down confident that there is a chair under you, even though you haven't seen the chair with your eyes. An example of blind faith is for some one to tell you to sit down and tells you that there is a chair under you, when in fact there isn't. You do not follow the same tests you used in applying intelligent faith. So, to your surprise you fall flat on your buns! It is like the old question of: If some group you believed in, ask you to follow them and they were about to jump off a cliff, would you join them? The tragic answer is that many people do follow cult leaders off a "cliff". Sometimes they follow what others tell them with out checking the source. Haven't you heard yet, not everything said or done on television is true? Many people are their own "cult leader" who blindly follow a faith in ultimately nothing. They believe a philosophy based on a handful of facts that has no completeness or cohesion. The Bible is the one source of truth you can depend upon 100%. If you have questions, turn to a pastor or teacher who has your respect as dedicated to God's word as absolute truth. Remember, ask as many questions as you can. If one person or group does not have the answers, keep exploring other Christian sources. All other sources are often diluted, un-educated and deceptive concerning the study of the Bible. It finally comes down to this: If you are following any one but Jesus Christ as your final source of authority you are heading for destruction.

The key to salvation is faith. "And behold, a women who had suffered from a hemorrhage for twelve years came up behind him and touched the fringe of his garment; for she said to herself, 'If only I touch his garment, I shall be made well' Jesus, turned, and seeing her said, 'Take heart, daughter; you faith has made you well.'" Mathew 9:20-22. "And he said to her, 'Your sins are forgiven.' Then those who were at the table with him began to say among themselves, 'Who is this, who even forgives sins?' And he said to the women. 'Your faith has saved you; go in peace," - Luke 7:48-50. Other references include Romans. 3:28,5:1, Galatians 2:20, Ephesians 2:8, Hebrews 10:38, Romans 4:12 , 14:23 ,1Timothy 4:1, and others. "For by grace you have been saved through faith; and this is not your own doing it is the gift of God-not because of works, least any man should boast. For we are his workmanship, created in Christ Jesus for good works, which God prepared beforehand, that we should walk in them." Ephesians 2:8-10." The worldview is that religion as a product of society or a collective work "evolved" within a particular culture. This binds all religions together, including Biblical Christianity. The Bible does not allow the option for someone to believe it is one of many possible ways to please God or know about God. To the evolutionist, all religions are a product of man reaching out to God and carrying their culture with them in their pursuit of understanding God. I believe that this is true with every religion except one, Christianity. Why do I believe this? Simply because Christianity is the only religion in the world which is not man made. The Bible is the holy inspired word of God as God revealed himself to men. God reached down from heaven, and with the Holy Spirit, the Bible was written. "All scripture is inspired by God and profitable for teaching, for reproof, for correction, and for training in righteousness, that the man of God may be complete, equipped for every good work."- 2 Timothy 3:16-17. It is through the study of the Holy Scriptures that we are corrected, trained in the ways of the Lord and fulfilled by the joy of the Lord. There are many faiths and religions in the world, but only one true faith according to the word of God. But when the Bible speaks of faith and the good things it brings, it is taking about the intelligent faith of the gospel of Jesus Christ. This is the one and only true faith. "Beloved, do not believe every spirit, but test the spirits to see whether they are of God." 1John 4:1 Take the time to compare a few other religious books against Christianity. You will soon discover errors and inconsistencies with every other religion in the world. There are an enormous number of worldwide religious beliefs. Some are currently practiced in our public schools! Atheism, Agnosticism, Skepticism, and Secular Humanism are commonly promoted in public high schools and grade schools. Some of these religious beliefs are described as the simple natural extension of scientific research. What do you find in the dictionary? "Atheism- The belief that there is no God." [10.1]. Atheism is a belief with many assumptions accepted by faith, as this book has discussed. The greatest deception of all has been to convince the public that the anti-Christian religions currently taught in schools in not religion but science. This is a blatant lie!

There are religious doctrines taught in schools with zeal and a passionate plea for students to disregard Christianity as anything to do with reason. Naturalism, a bi-product of atheistic faith, is taught in nearly every class. Not only in the purely scientific classes, but in History, political science, anthropology, current affairs, health and all other classes. This constant bombardment with this philosophy has had a profound effect on students. "Naturalism is ultimately a pessimistic world view. ... On the naturalistic world view, you are an almost unimaginably small and unimportant part of a huge, and mostly alien physical universe. You're just a temporary blip on the screen of a totally impersonal reality, ruled by mindless forces. But, hey, have a nice day anyway. [10.2]" Is there any wonder why teen suicide is so high in America? Why does the abundance of violent behavior surprise a society that teaches evolution and the naturalistic philosophy every day? There is a sharp contrast in believing in God and believing we are created from random natural forces. "On the theist, or supernaturalistic world view, you are an eternally intended and welcomed addition to a spiritually rich and ultimately fulfilling reality, meant to flourish forever. ... On the theistic picture, God has created us for a specific and everlasting purpose. On the naturalistic world view, blind chance has given us a brief opportunity to exist on the earth, with no meaning or purpose intended. [10.3]" Why is there such a problem with stress and depression? With the philosophy of naturalism taught everywhere there can be no doubt of the source of these problems.

There are many religions that have attacked traditional Christian principles throughout the centuries. Also, Biblical principles have had attacks from within the Christian faith. These groups of people are referred to as cults because they claim to be following biblical principles and yet contradict many basic Christian truths. "I am astonished that you are so quickly deserting him who called you to the grace of Christ and turning to a different gospel- not that there is another gospel, but there are some who trouble you and want to pervert the gospel of Christ. But even if we, or and angel from heaven, should preach to you a gospel contrary to that which we preached to you, let him be accursed. As we have said before, so now I say again. If any one is preaching to you a gospel contrary to that which you received, let him be accursed." -Galatians. 1:6-9. "For such men are false apostles, deceitful workmen, disguising themselves as apostles of Christ. And no wonder, for even Satan disguises himself as an angel of light." -2 Corinthians 11:13-14. I felt it necessary to review some of the characteristics of a cult. First, what is a Christian cult? It is a group that claims to be Christian in nature but has rejected one or more of the teachings in Orthodox Christianity as described in 2 Corinthians 11:13-15. Orthodox Christianity believes that the Bible is literally the word of God. The "Trinity" and other doctrines of traditional Orthodox Christianity are foundational principles clearly described in the Bible. I strongly encourage you to read 'Understanding the Cults' by Josh McDowell & Don Stewart for more details on the subject. The faith of "born again" Christians has survived for centuries. The Bible has survived attacks from outside the Christian faith and attempts of perversion from members within the various churches. Each question about religious beliefs comes back to the individual. Only you, as an individual person can decide what road you whish to travel and what views you chose to accept or reject by faith. The decision is yours but the Bible also warns us that we will be held accountable for our beliefs and actions at the Day of Judgment. "I tell you, on the Day of Judgment men will render account for every careless word they utter; for by your words you will be justified, and by your words you will be condemned." Matthew 12:36. Also, you must be sure you are following the right doctrine. "Not everyone who says to me, 'Lord, Lord,' will enter the kingdom of heaven, but only he who does the will of my Father who is in heaven. Many will say to me on that day, 'Lord, Lord, did we not prophesy in your name, and in your name drive out demons and perform many miracles?' Then I will tell them plainly, 'I never knew you. Away from me, you evildoers!'" Mathew 7:21-23.

The Jewish-Christian beliefs are unique in the entire world. They do not teach that the characteristics of God were discovered by man, but rather God revealed himself to men earnestly seeking Him. God had a special convenient with the Jewish nation because of Abraham's faith in God. Because Abraham's belief in God's power and Abraham's faithfulness to the word of God, his people was given a special place in the heart of God. With the coming of Christ, there is no distinction between race, color, or creed. We are all equal in God's sight. "There is neither Jew nor Greek, there is neither slave nor free, there is neither male nor female; for you are all one in Christ Jesus." -Galatians 3:28. How does the Bible explain the actions of men? The Bible describes men who do not believe in the Bible as ones that use any means to accomplish a certain agenda. They live a life in sin. Many are unaware of the fact that they are in sin and controlled by Satan. Many refuse to believe that Satan is real and has power to control individuals. Many people believe fervently that they are in control of their own lives. This is simply not the case. The evolutionary perspective describes decisions people make as either evolving towards a higher plane through positive actions or regressing towards animal passions. However, there is no consistency in the theory of evolution. When things "evolve" they describe the process as the natural result of biological response to environmental conditions. As we have described in detail, there is no natural force of evolution. There is no natural tendency towards an improved species, only a natural tendency towards regression and destruction, according to the laws of thermodynamics. The evolutionists "worship" the so called "power of growth". This is seen in trees that bear fruit and so on. This is Satan's greatest weapon, because there is a small bit of truth found in the fact that God intends all things in nature to grow. However, natural forces are not entirely separate from the control of God. Life was created by God but it is also sustained by God. Even Satan has deluded himself into thinking he can become "equal with God" and totally independent of God. Someday, as prophesied in Revelation, he will inherit eternal death in the lake of fire. We have seen how natural forces are created and sustained by God. This is similar to the fact that we have a freedom to make decisions for ourselves. However, there are consequences if we chose to rebel against the will of God, instead of following His direction and leadership.

The Bible agrees with the fundamental physical laws of thermodynamics as we have frequently discussed. Since the first man and woman, Adam and Eve committed the first sin; man has had a natural tendency towards committing sin. In other words, man tends to be both rebellious and self-destructive. For example, how many marriages are lost to irrational fears and self-centered destructive behavior? The Bible views marriage as sacred. The Christian perspective encourages a loving partnership relationship rather than the male dominant relationship described by the evolutionary perspective. "Have you not read that he who made them from the beginning made them male and female, and said, 'For this reason a man shall leave his father and mother and be joined to his wife, and the two shall become one flesh?' So they are no longer two but one. What therefore God has joined together, let not man put asunder. ... and I say to you; whosoever divorces his wife, except for un-chastity, and marries another, commits adultery." - Matthew 19: 3-6,9. Josh McDowell has an excellent lecture series on love, sex and dating. One of his points is that it seams all too often teenagers want to cleave one another before they leave mom instead of leave and then cleave. Josh also describes how the Christian marriage relationship involves becoming 'one flesh' spiritually, psychologically and physically. The Bible does not promote male domination, as some radical groups' claim, but a mutual loving relationship design for an eternity. The evolutionary philosophies are the ones that promote "survival of the fittest" and male dominance, not the word of God. The Evolutionary perspective surely has sought to promote evil and corruption in every facet of society. You can witness in the unbridled passion of a person fully committed to the theory of evolution and its philosophical implications, a wide range of destructive behaviors. From stealing, hate crimes and sexual perversion the theory of evolution is the sinful person's "rational" explanation of why these kinds of things occur. These behaviors are explained as simply people acting out their "survival of the fittest" natural instincts. This is exactly what Hitler and other leaders of the Nazi movement believed, and why it was so widely accepted as making sense at the time of its origin.

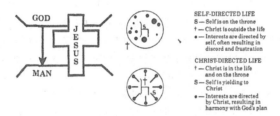

Figure 10.2

The Bible states that the natural condition of every living man and women since the fall of Adam and Eve is in the depths of sin. "For all have sinned and fall short of the glory of God" Romans 3:23. The situation is summarized in a booklet by Bill Bright and distributed by Campus Crusade for Christ. It is again placed in the back of Josh McDowell's book, Evidence That Demands a Verdict. "Man was created to have fellowship with God; but, because of his stubborn self-will, he chose to go his own independent way, and fellowship with God was broken. This self-will, characterized by an attitude of active rebellion or passive indifference, is an evidence of what the Bible calls sin. 'For the wages of sin is death" (spiritual separation from God) (Romans 6:23). This diagram (see fig. 10.2) illustrates that God is holy and man is sinful. A great gulf separates the two. The arrows illustrate that man is continually trying to reach God and the abundant life through his own efforts, such as a good life, philosophy or religion. [10.4]" My apologies, I have a missing illustration I am unable to included because of computer difficulties. Figure 10.2 illustrates the only bridge between God and man is Jesus Christ. As we previously stated, all other religions are failed attempts of man reaching out towards God. This can be illustrated with a multitude of arrows going towards God. This represents man's attempt to understand God on a purely intellectual basis through various philosophies and religions of the world. This attempt has failed because man is incapable of understanding the true nature of God through philosophy or religion. To bridge the gap between God and man, God sent to us His only son to clarify what God is like. As one of my favorite songs states: "If you want to know what God is like, just take a look at His son". The top right side of figure 10.2 illustrates that a person is in chaos without Christ as the center of their life. This illustrates the initial condition of a person's life without the spirit of God. The Bible teaches that you are either a Child of God or a child of evil. If you live a "self" directed life; you are merely putty in the hands of Satan. "No man can serve two masters: for either he will hate the one, and love the other; or else he will hold to the one, and despise the other. You can not serve both God and mammon." -Matthew 6:24. The Bible teaches us that there is a spiritual war for control of your soul. The battle between doing good and evil is described as the battle over the "flesh". "We know that the law is spiritual; but I am carnal, sold under sin. I do not understand my own actions. For I do not do what I want, but I do the very thing I hate. So then it is no longer I that do it, but sin which dwells within me. For I know that nothing good dwells within me, that is, my flesh. I can will what is right, but I cannot do it. For I do not do the good I want, but the evil I do not want is what I do. Now if I do what I do not want, it is no longer I that do it, but sin which dwells within me. ... For those live according to the flesh set their minds on the things of the flesh, but those who live according to the Spirit set their minds on the things of the Spirit. To set the mind on the flesh is death, but to set the mind on the Spirit is life and peace. For the mind that is set on the flesh is hostile to God; it does not submit to God's law, indeed it can not; and those who are in the flesh can not please God." -Romans 7:14-15,17-20, 8:5-8. The person Paul is so critical of in these passages is himself. There are other verses that Paul writes to help us understand how the mercies of God can overcome sin in our life. The Spiritual war continues, but there are seasons of victory. In the end, the final physical and spiritual battle for our souls and the control of the world is fought at Armageddon. I am eternally grateful that we know that this battle is won by Jesus. More details on these subjects will be covered in upcoming books on spiritual warfare, if God allows us to continue serving Him in this manner.

On of the things that confuse both adults and children is the source to influences of "good" behavior and "bad" behavior. Does it merely come from inside our selves? Are their external factors, which affect our behavior? Are these factors merely physical or physiological effects brought about from friends introducing "peer pressure"? Or, are some of these influences spiritual? Does fear play an important role in these influences? These are some of the questions we plan to explore in upcoming books about fear and spiritual warfare. One thing which has been taken too far in our society is the concept that bad is good and good is boring. It seams everyone likes the rebel "bad" boy. The ideas of heroes and villains have been smeared. There are fewer clear-cut ideas of the characteristics of "good" and "evil". What is most distressing is cartoons that have inappropriate language and improper moral values. Children are conditioned to be attracted to any cartoon show or character, so their improper influence is especially distressing. So, what is "good"? "Why do you ask me about what is good?" Jesus replied. "There is only One who is good. If you want to enter life, obey the commandments." Mathew 19:17 Everyone must deal with these ideas daily. There are often times it is hard to know the right thing to do. This is the times we need to turn to God the most. Just say a simple silent prayer asking for wisdom in that particular situation. God has a plan to solve man's problem with sin. Like imperfect children, the mischievous, naive, unknowing, careless kids of the world get into trouble, and our Father in Heaven offers a way to bail us out. All we need to do is accept His great gift of His plan of salvation. "For God so loved the world that He gave His only begotten Son, that whoever believes in Him should not perish, but have eternal life. For God did not send his Son into the world to condemn the world, but to save the world through him. Whoever believes in him is not condemned, but whoever does not believe stands condemned already because he has not believed in the name of God's one and only Son." John 3:16-18. Jesus said, "I came that they might have life, and might have it abundantly" John 10:10. "But God demonstrates His own love toward us, in that while we were yet sinners Christ died for us" -Romans. 5:8 Christ sacrificed His life as a substitute for the penalty of sin. There are some aspects of salvation we might never fully understand or appreciate. However, the basic condition is that we are under the judgment of God for our sins. The penalty of committing sin is death. Christ took our place and died for us. Like when you get a speeding ticket and your dad goes down to the municipal court to pay the fine, Christ took our place for our sins when He died on the cross. What does God ask in return? Simply to pray giving thanks to God for His blessings and then follow the commandments of God to the best of our ability, with the aid of the Holy Spirit. Let God be your guide. Too often, we think that we must "take charge" of the situation. Trust in the Bible first and foremost for salvation, giving God control of your life. "For I delivered to you as of first importance what I also received, that Christ died for our sins in accordance with the scriptures, that he was buried that he was raised on the third day in accordance with the scriptures, and that he appeared to Cephas, then to the twelve. Then he appeared to more than five hundred brethren at one time, most of them are still alive." 1 Corinthians. 15:3-6. By Christ's sacrifice, we have salvation to eternal life. (See fig. 10.2) Jesus said, "I am the way, and the truth, and the life; no one comes to the Father, except through Me." John 14:6. Now, the final step in entering the Christian life is accepting God's promise of salvation. "But as many as receive Him, to them He gave the right to become children of God, even to those who believed in His name." John 1:12. Our salvation is based on faith in the grace of God through the sacrifice in the life of Christ. "For by grace you have been saved through faith; and that not of yourselves, it is the gift of God; not as the result of works, that no one should boast" -Ephesians. 2:8,9. Christ said, "Behold, I stand at the door and knock; if any one hears My voice and opens the door. I will come in to him." Revelation 3:20. Answer the call of the Lord by surrendering your life to Christ. Another upcoming book will explore the Christian lifestyle. In this book, we intend to present the Christian lifestyle as a way to live life to the fullest. God wants you to have a life of abundant joy and happiness. You never need to commit any sin to have a good time. Because of our society, many children are confused on this issue. They do not understand what sin is and what it is not. We will attempt to explore this difficult and complex subject in an upcoming book on the Lifestyles of the Born again believer.

The Uniqueness of the Bible

The nature of God is to use our talents and gifts for His purposes is apparent in the writing of the Holy Bible. Many different kinds of people, led by the Holly Spirit, were used to bring the Holy word of God to us. The Bible is unique in many ways, totally different from any other book. Quote, "Here is a book: 1. Written over a 1,500-year span. 2. Written over 40 generations. 3. Written by over 40 authors from every walk of life including kings, peasants, philosophers, fisherman, poets, statesmen, scholars, etc.: Moses, a political leader, trained in the universities of Egypt. Peter, a fisherman. Amos, a herdsman. Joshua, a military general. Nehemiah, a cupbearer. Daniel, a prime minister. Luke, a doctor. Solomon, a king. Matthew, a tax collector. Paul, a rabbi. 4. Written in different places: Moses in the wilderness. Jeremiah in a dungeon. Daniel on a hillside and in a palace. Paul inside prison walls Luke while traveling. John on the isle of Patmos. Others in the rigors of a military. 5. Written at different times: David in times of war. Solomon in times of peace. 6. Written in different moods: Some writing from heights of joy and others writing from the depths of sorrow and despair. 7. Written on three continents: Asia, Africa and Europe. 8. Written in three languages: Hebrew: Was the language of the Old Testament. In II Kings 18:26-28 called "the language of Judah." In Isaiah 19:18 called "the language of Canaan." Aramaic: was the 'common language' of the near east until the time of Alexander the Great (6th century B.C.- 4th century B.C.) Greek: New Testament language. Was the international language at the time of Christ. 9. Its subject matter includes hundreds of controversial subjects. A controversial subject is one, which would create opposing opinions when mentioned or discussed. Biblical authors spoke on hundreds of controversial subjects with harmony and continuity from Genesis to Revelation. There is one unfolding store: 'God's redemption of man.' Geisler and Nix put it this way: "The 'Paradise Lost' of the Genesis becomes the 'Paradise Regained' of Revelation. Whereas the gate to the tree of life is closed in Genesis, it is opened forevermore in Revelation. [10.5]"

The establishment of uniqueness is not absolute proof that the Bible is the word of God.

However, it is important evidence towards the conclusion that the Bible is the work of God, not just men and women creating a philosophy. Too make the point more clear, we can look to the now famous challenge of Josh McDowell to a salesman for 'Great Books of the Western World.' Quote, "I challenged him to take just 10 of the authors, all from one walk of life, one generation, one place, one time, one mood, one continent, one language, and just one controversial subject (the Bible speaks on hundreds with harmony and agreement). Then I asked him: "Would they (the authors) agree?" He paused and then replied, "No!" "What would you have?" I retorted. Immediately he said, "A conglomeration. [10.6]" The Bible represents a conglomeration of opinions and views spanning 1,500 years, written over 40 generations, with over 40 authors in different occupations, in many different places, during many different moods, on three continents, in three languages. All this diversity and yet the Bible has perfect uniformity in the message of Jesus Christ. How can anyone not believe this is the work of God? It does take faith that it is the accurate word of God, but there is every reason to make this small leap of faith. It seams to take an unreasonable amount of faith to believe that the Bible is entirely man made. It is not just one of many "religious" works, as the world attempts to teach us. Again, the world does not appreciate the uniqueness of the Bible. If you consider the impact the Bible has had on the lives of those who seriously study it, you can not help but conclude that the Bible is the one and only true word of God.

AUTHOR	When Written	Earliest Copy	Time Span	No. of Copies
Caesar	100-44 B.C.	900 A.D.	1,000 yrs.	10
Livy	59 B.C.-A.D. 17			20
Plato (Tetralogies)	427-347 B.C.	900 A.D.	1,200 yrs.	7
Tacitus (Annals)	100 A.D.	1100 A.D.	1,000 yrs.	20 (-)
also minor works	100 A.D.	1000 A.D.	900 yrs.	1
Pliny the Younger (History)	61-113 A.D.	850 A.D.	750 yrs.	7
Thucydides (History)	460-400 B.C.	900 A.D.	1,300 yrs.	8
Suetonius (De Vita Caesarum)	75-160 A.D.	950 A.D.	800 yrs.	8
Herodotus (History)	480-425 B.C.	900 A.D.	1,300 yrs.	8
Horace			900 yrs.	
Sophocles	496-406 B.C.	1000 A.D.	1,400 yrs.	193
Lucretius	Died 55 or 53 B.C.		1,100 yrs.	2
Catullus	54 B.C.	1550 A.D.	1,600 yrs.	3
Euripides	480-406 B.C.	1100 A.D.	1,500 yrs.	9
Demosthenes	383-322 B.C.	1100 A.D.	1,300 yrs.	200 *
Aristotle	384-322 B.C.	1100 A.D.	1,400 yrs.	49 †
Aristophanes	450-385 B.C.	900 A.D.	1,200 yrs.	10

*All from one copy.
†Of any one work.

Figure 10.3

The Bible is unique in many other ways. Unique in its circulation, no other work has been as widely copied and distributed as the Bible. Quote, "Hy Pickering says that about 30 years ago (about 1927), for the British and Foreign Bible society to meet its demands, it had to publish 'one copy every three seconds day and night; 22 copies every minute day and night; 1,369 copies every hour day and night; 32,876 copies every day in the year. And it is deeply interesting to know that this amazing number of Bibles were dispatched to various parts of the world in 4,583 cases weighing 490 tons. [10.7]" Of course, since that time duplication and translations of the Bible have only increased. The Bible is unique in its translation. In 1979 it had been translated into over 1,280 languages around the world. This sets the Bible apart from all other ancient texts. The chart in figure 10.3 shows a few of the classic works of antiquity. Listed is the name and author who wrote the original manuscript, the approximate time when the manuscript was originally written, the time of the earliest known copy of the work, the time span between the original and the first known copy, and the number of copies which remain today of a portion or all of the original work. The data has a number of important factors in determining the accuracy of the copies as compared to the original manuscript. One statement many non-Christians and cult leaders use to support lies about the gospel is that the Bible has been corrupted through time. Many religious leaders convince their followers that the Bible has been subtly altered over the years. This gives these false teachers the power to manipulate the gospel for their own warped purpose. Through Josh McDowell's books, Evidence that Demands a verdict volumes 1 & 2, Josh provides evidences for the reliability of the biblical translations we have today. Translations of the Old and New Testament come from copies of the original writings of the authors. Before the printing press and modern technology, the only way to preserve an important document and keep it from being destroyed was to copy it by hand. Many important classical works received a great deal of attention and are considered undeniably the work of the original author. But nothing can compare to the painstaking efforts to preserve the Jewish-Christian documents. In making Old Testament copies, first special paper was used, called papyos. Second, a copy was made one letter at a time. If there were more than three errors, which included punctuation marks, which we would consider insignificant were made, the entire book was thrown away and the process was started all over again. There was a process of preparing the mind and the spirit to handle the sacred writings before a person would attempt to copy the manuscripts. Modern men can hardly grasp the perceived sacredness of these ancient writings to the Jewish people. Josh McDowell outlines conclusive proof that the Bible we have in our hands today is an accurate translation of the original writings of the ancient authors. There are several good English translations that are accurate in every detail. Among some of the best translations include: The New International Version, The New King James version, and the Revised Standard Version. I recommend these versions and a few other translations to compare and study.

WORK	WHEN WRITTEN	EARLIEST COPY	TIME SPAN	NO. OF COPIES
Homer (*Iliad*)	900 B.C.	400 B.C.	500 yrs.	643
New Testament	40-100 A.D.	125 A.D.	25 yrs.	over 24,000

Figure 10.4

To get any Bible in English form, we must translate the manuscripts from the one of the three languages in which the Document was written: Hebrew, Aramaic, or Greek. Greek, of course, was the New Testament language. McDowell proposed a system of testing the accuracy of any translated manuscript from ancient times. The results are found in figures 10.3 and 10.4. First, the shorter the space of time from the original manuscript to the earliest known copy the more likely you have an accurate copy of the original manuscript. Notice that of all the notable classical works around this time the shortest time span is the New Testament, which is only 25 years. The next shortest is Iliad by Homer which has a 500 year time span, see figure 10.4. The next important evidence of reliability is the number of copies you can examine. The more manuscripts surviving to the present day that can be examined and studied, the more likely you could find any errors or discrepancies between the copies. As you can see in the chart, again the two closest in accuracy is the Iliad and the New Testament. The Iliad has 643 surviving manuscripts and the New Testament has over 24,000. Again, the reliability of the Bible far out distances any other classical work. Another factor in the accuracy of the Bible we have today is the delicate process used in copying the writings, which was always considered sacred works. This is far more apparent in the Old Testament than in the New Testament as far as I know. But I can't help wondering, how many of the Jewish practices carried over into the process of copying the New Testament documents? The number of original manuscripts surviving is amazing when compared to other works of antiquity. The final result is that the Bible is the most unique book ever written. When you take any part of the Bible, and examine it in context, you will find it is a series of statements and concepts without any error what so ever. In context, simply means to read each verse in context on the time it was written, culture, and relationship to the whole Bible. F.F. Bruce put it this way, Quote "Any part of the human body can only be properly explained in reference to the whole body. And any part of the Bible can only be properly explained in reference to the whole Bible. [10.8]" As long as your remember to take the word of God in the context in which it was written, the Holy Spirit will give you clarity of thought in interpreting it and applying it to your daily life. We have every reason to accept the modern day Bible as the word of God. God uses every type of man and women from every walk of life to accomplish His goals. The Bible teaches us that every man and every woman is a unique creation of God and that God has a personal plan for each individual's life. Evolutionary theory teaches you that you are in a great struggle for survival and that is all that matters. You are left in the pit of despair, with no one to trust but yourself. The Bible teaches us that this condition is not simply "the natural order of things" but the result of the original sin of man. God's plan is to liberate you from the struggle for survival by giving you a life free from the dominance of sin. "So if the Son sets you free, you will be free indeed." John 8: 36. By accepting Christ as savior and Lord you have an eternal friend in Jesus. And Jesus is a friend you can always trust and a friend that will never fail you. We have his promise. "God has said, 'Never will I leave you; never will I forsake you.' So we say with confidence, "The Lord is my helper; I will not be afraid. What can man do to me?" Hebrews 13:5-6. Jesus said: "I will not leave you as orphans; I will come to you. Before long, the world will not see me anymore, but you will see me. Because I live, you also will live." John 14:18-19

The Bible is not just "stories" but an accurate account of History. "William F. Albright, known for his reputation as one of the great archaeologists, states: 'There can be no doubt that archaeology has confirmed the substantial historicity of Old Testament tradition.' Albright adds: '... Discovery after discovery has established the accuracy of innumerable details, and has brought increased recognition to the value of the Bible as a source of history.' [10.9]" There are numerous examples of the Bible accurately describing events in history. One example is given by the Ebla tablets. "Since 1974 17,000 tablets have been unearthed from the era of the Ebla Kingdom. ... The proponents of the 'Documentary Hypothesis' have taught in the past that the period described in the Mosaic narrative (1400 BC., a thousand years after the Ebla Kingdom) was a time prior to all knowledge of writing. ... However, the tablets containing the law codes of Ebla have demonstrated elaborate judicial proceedings and case law. Many are very similar to the Deuteronomy law code (example: Deuteronomy 22:22-30). ... The five Cities of the Plain (Sodom, Gomorrah, Admah, Zeboiim and Zoar) (were described as) legendary. Yet the Ebla archives refer to all five Cities of the Plain and on one tablet the Cities are listed in the exact same sequence as Genesis 14. [10.10]" This would seam to confirm that the Old Testament writings are from the authors who we claim to have written the books. The historical accounts specified in the Old Testament are continually confirmed by the study of archeology. All too often this fact has not been properly revealed to the public.

One of the most established historical events is the life of Christ and the accuracy of the New Testament. "The life of Jesus was written by eyewitnesses or people who recorded firsthand testimony. The writers were all living at the same time these events transpired, and they had personal contact with the events or with the people who witness the events. ... The Book of Acts ends with the Apostle Paul being alive in Rome, his death not being recorded. ... We have some reason to believe that Paul was put to death in the Neronian persecution of A.D. 64. ... If the Book of Acts was written before A.D. 64, then the Gospel of Luke, to which Acts was a sequel, had to have been composed some time before that. ... The death of Christ took place around A.D. 30. ... The early church generally taught that the first Gospel composed was that of Matthew. [10.11]" This indicates that a good portion of the New Testament, the gospels, the letters of Paul, all were written within 34 years of Christ's crucifixion. There are volumes of books written about the reliability of the Bible and the testimonies written inside. The Bible is not a "fairy tale" as the world would have you believe. Instead it is a diary based on eyewitness testimony. The DaVinci Code was about the possibility that certain books about Jesus were purposely left out of the Bible to portray Jesus as more divine. Again this is a half-truth. There was a great deal of concern about which books to be included in the New Testament. This is understandable since the scholars wanted only the best and most accurate accounts of Jesus to be included in what is considered "holy" documents. The four gospels clearly quote Jesus as saying he was the "son of man". His human nature is clearly portrayed as well as His divine nature. Some of the reasons the other so called "gospels" were excluded from the early Bible was a doubt of the origin of these writings as well as their content. Jesus was truly the son of God and the son of Man and this fact is clearly shown in the four Gospels.

Present and Future Events

One aspect of the Bible that has great interest in society is Prophecy. There is an enormous supply of books on the subject of biblical prophecy. "Another research result that amazed me was the abundance of material written on the subject of prophecy. It is overwhelming. Several thousand books cover the timing of Christ's Second Coming, the rapture, the tribulation, the millennium and related subjects. Many of these writings are very reliable and well researched about the "signs of the times" and the chronology of God's prophetic schedule. [10.12]" The Left Behind Series is an excellent example of taking Biblical prophecies and adapting a plausible interpretation to a story-like format. The popularity of the book series is strong evidence of the public's interest in the subject. There are, however, many wild interpretations of prophecy that have been used to attack the reliability of the Bible. The checkout counter is filled with magazines that have some wild interpretation of prophecy. We can look at these articles two ways: to give the general public reason for concern about the approaching judgment of God. Some people will have their curiosities raised and read the actual books of the Bible concerned with prophecy. It is wonderful when a person's curiosity has led them to read the Bible, and come closer to the truth revealed in God's word. Others dismiss the entire subject of prophecy as nonsense and just laugh about all biblical matters. Since many of the magazines create outlandish interpretations of biblical prophecy, some readers dismiss anyone reading the bible as "religious fanatics". Obviously, many of the articles in these magazines are just wild, sensational, stories created for the express purpose of increase sales. What is sometimes frightening is that it works! It is hard to believe that the majority of the public would actually believe most of the articles. The popularity of these magazines makes us wonder if people enjoy fantasy to the point of a sincere desire to remain in a state of constant confusion over what is real and what is not. Maybe some of the readers need continual reassurance that the bible is non-sense. Maybe they believe that instead of picking up a Bible, the article will tell them the same thing. This goes back to our discussion of the irrational fear some people have in reading the bible. On thing should be made clear, biblical prophecy is very real. But like so many other topics, the Bible has been attacked on every possible front. Our only hope is that people will be challenged enough to simply go to Church, attend a Bible study, or read the Bible carefully to get the answers to their questions from "the source" instead of comical articles.

Many people are once again looking to the Bible for answers to their fears. Scientists are among those most concerned about the inevitable end to the world. "Dr. Harold Urey, a Nobel prize-winning scientist, said, 'I write this to frighten you. I am a frightened man myself. All the scientists I know are frightened. Frightened for their lives and frightened for your life.' Dr. George Wald, another Nobel prize-winning scientist and professor at Harvard University, said, 'I think human life is threatened as never before in the history of this planet. Not just by one peril, but by many.' [10.13]" Most theologians and scientists agree that the time for the destruction of our world is close, but no one knows exactly how close. This is also referenced in the Bible, "But of that day and hour no one knows, not even the angels of heaven, nor the Son, but the Father only." Mathew 24:36. There are many other references in scripture about the "last days". The recent work of Al Gore to make the public aware of the pending disaster is commendable, however somewhat naive and misguided. Sure, industrial pollution can cause global warming. Global warming can cause a wide variety of natural disasters as the film The Day After Tomorrow graphically illustrates. This includes a new ice age brought on by global warming. It is amazing that there is still a large segment of society that ignores these warnings or believes that somehow scientists and political leaders will solve these problems for us. How ridiculous is it placing your hope for a solution to global warming in the hands of industrialists that caused it in the first place? Sure, people are motivated to "save the world" but can they? Can all the problems we face with the environment be fixed by technological innovation or the political process? How can citizens trust congress to fix the social security system with politicians most people believe is dishonest? The only solution is to trust in the Lord Jesus Christ to save us as the predictions of the Biblical prophecies are unfolding in front of our very eyes each day. There are many books, which cover the prophecies Jesus Christ has already fulfilled. Jesus himself appealed to prophecy as evidence for his claim to be the Christ. "And beginning with Moses and all the Prophets, he explained to them what was said in all the Scriptures concerning himself. ... He said to them, 'This is what I told you while I was still with you: Everything must be fulfilled that is written about me in the Law of Moses, the Prophets and the Psalms.' Then he opened their minds so they could understand the Scriptures." Luke 24:27,44-45.

Now let us turn our attention to modern day events that seam to fit within the context of prophecy. One of the most recognized fulfillments of prophecy and evidence that God keeps his promises concerns the nation of Israel. In the book of Genesis we read God's promise to Abraham concerning his decedents, who became the nation of Israel. "The LORD said to Abram after Lot had parted from him, 'Lift up your eyes from where you are and look north and south, east and west. All the land that you see I will give to you and your offspring forever.'" Genesis 13:14,15. There are many other verses that show how God sent his people, the Jewish nation, into exile for disobedience. Once their chastening has ended God brings His people back to the Palestine area. "In 606 B.C. King Nebuchadnezzar took the people captive to Babylon. ... However, as God promised, He allowed those who desired to return to the land in 537-536 B.C. or after seventy years. ... The removal from their homeland occurred a second time in A.D. 70 when Titus the Roman destroyed the city of Jerusalem and scattered the people. For almost 1,900 years, the Jews wandered about the earth as strangers who were persecuted from every side. This culminated in the holocaust of World War II. ... Yet, against all odds, the state of Israel was reborn on May 14, 1948. ... Since 1948 they have survived some terrible conflicts, including the 1967 Six-Day War and the 1973 Holy Day War. [10.14]" Every day in the existence of Israel is a testimony to the fulfillment of God's promise. There are a number of books, which point out that there is a clear explanation why Israel is in the news so much. It is as if the Lord is taking the attention of the whole world to the Middle East. The message is clear. It is the same message which preceded the first coming of Christ. The message of John the Baptist is as relevant today as it was prior to Christ's first appearance into human history. "Repent, for the kingdom of God is at hand" Mathew 3:2. Most theologians believe the beginning of then end times will start with a pre-millennium rapture. In other words, the beginning of the "end times" or tribulation period will begin with the disappearance of every Christian on Earth! Astonishingly, it seams that it will be a complete surprise to the world. How can the disappearance of millions of Christians and the fulfillment of prophecy be surprising to a world that has had the gospel preached for over 2,000 years? Simple, there is a philosophy that blinds the world to the impending danger and what can be done about it. The philosophy and ideas of evolution has already caused millions to reject the gospel and seek any explanation other than fulfilled biblical prophecy. Evolution has so indoctrinated the world that any other explanation of an event is considered totally unreasonable. Therefore, people are told to simply stay away from the Bible and all its teachings. Fortunately, we have Christian leaders who have taken the charge to preach the word of God. In spite of the efforts of Christian teachers, preachers, and theologians there are many people of the world who are blinded by the philosophy found in the theory of evolution. One of the best ways to understand the philosophy of evolution is by watching the television series Star Trek®.

The "Star Trek®" Philosophy

First, let me be clear, I am a big fan of Star Trek. I have been a huge fan since the original episodes first appeared on T.V. One of my favorite attributes of the television series is the promotion of science. No other science fiction movie or television series in history has had as accurate and detailed scientific facts as Star Trek. The stories in each of the television "spin-offs" challenge the mind in many areas. It seams that there is a philosophical or moral challenge to nearly every episode. Most of the episodes written by Gene Rodenberry challenged philosophical and social issues. Many of these episodes had Christian principles as their guiding theme. I applaud the work of the writers on the vast majority of Star Trek movies, books and television series episodes. One episode called "Bread and Circuses", promoted the Christian faith, to a degree. In one of the scenes the communications officer, Lt. Uhura, made reference to the strength of the Christian faith and the Roman Empire of the planet. Both she and Spock agreed that the "Son Worship" on the planet represented a philosophy of "total love" and "total brotherhood". It was not the worship of "the sun up in the sky" but "the Son of God". Kirk replied "Caesar and Christ, they had them both", indicating that Christianity was professed on this planet. One last minute comment alluded to the fact that the leaders of the planet were unable to discredit their faith and that this faith would eventually conquer the Roman Empire as it did here on Earth. In the fifth movie: Star Trek IV: The Final Frontier®, the Enterprise and her crew go in search of God. Star Trek has promoted the questioning of religious beliefs and different philosophies through many episodes. Some episodes have been done very well, others have been sorely disappointing. Throughout the various Star Trek television series spin-offs there is a dangerous philosophy, which is generally promoted by scientists. Most of these ideas are an extension of the philosophy of evolution and the abundance of alien life. These same ideas are also widely accepted by the public sector. The "Star Trek mentality", as I call it, is a set of beliefs based on the acceptance of the theory of evolution as an absolute truth. There seams to be an enormous amount of faith in the existence of life on other planets. The search for extraterrestrials has reached a new height in recent years. Billions of government dollars have been allocated for the search of extraterrestrial life, as we previously mentioned. A part of the motivation to search for advanced intelligent life is the result of a desire to find help for this troubled planet. It seams that people are searching for any solution to maintain their pleasures and still not pay the price. Instead of looking for solutions that already exist, there is a belief that continual scientific development will solve all of mankind's problems. If it seams we are running low on oil and other natural resources, the world's response is don't worry just have faith that science will solve these problems before it is too late. What if there are serious shortages suddenly? One way to get new abilities to solve our problems suddenly is to find advanced extraterrestrial life that will solve our problems through corporation. I believe this is one of the driving forces behind the popular belief that alien life, does indeed exist. There is a realization that the world is running out of time and we will need a sudden intervention from an outside source to restore the planet to full health. The concept of life developing on other planets is promoted in public high schools and colleges. This is part of a desperate search to look for anything, except turning toward God's word, to find a solution to our mounting problems. However, we have already discussed that the assertion of abundant alien life is a faith unsubstantiated by science.

There is a sense of a growing anticipation for alien visits. Such a belief in alien life has not been so high since the days when H.G. Well's first aired the War of the Worlds on radio. Back then, alien visitation was synonymous with alien invasion. Back in the 1950's, there were serious concerns of "men from mars" invading earth. This time, however, there is a sense of mutual benefit upon the encounter with alien life. The current popular belief is based on the Star Trek® concept that most intelligent life prefers peace to war. The Star Trek philosophy states that most alien life forms want peace, because it is the intelligent thing to do. This allows the alliance of two or more worlds to solve problems they could not have achieved separately. This led to the formation of the United Federation of Planets, according to the Star Trek series. This apparent Christian concept of "love thy neighbor" is not as beeline as it seams on the surface. In the Star Trek philosophy there exists a principle called the prime directive. The prime directive simply states that all civilizations are evolving and that nothing should interfere with the natural evolution of a society or life form. The level of advancement in technology determines the level of evolution of the society. In other words, as technology increases the general population is more intelligent. When the general intelligence is high, then the society is more peaceful. War and violence becomes a thing of the past because it is not "intelligent" to engage in such destructive behaviors. The amount of technology a particular society possesses determines if that planet should be approached by the United Federation of Planets, represented by the U.S.S. Enterprise in the television series. For example, according to the future in the Star Trek series, we evolved beyond violence in society by the early 22nd century. Much of the problems experienced on Earth were due to the lack of food supply or available land. In the ancient history of planet Earth, according to episodes in Star Trek the next generation, hunger was eliminated in the early 22nd century. This was probably due to the early developments of the food replicators. These devices could reproduce food from energy patterns stored on information storage devices. According to Star Trek, by the 22nd century the ability to convert matter to energy and back to matter had been relatively perfected. The transporter was invented, and the food replicator was a similar device, which converted food into energy, stored the pattern and then you duplicated the food as many times as you want, provided you had enough energy. With warp drive and the use of a matter -anti-matter reaction chambers for a power source, people were traveling to distant habitable planets and colonizing them. With unlimited food supply and unlimited land area through these technological achievements war was a thing of the past, according to Star Trek history. Is this realistic? No. The United States of America is the most abundant country in the world. It is abundant in resources, food supply, jobs (if some people would get off their buns and look for work) in land, and has the greatest amount of freedom and personal liberties of any nation in the world. However, America also has one of the highest crime rates of any industrialized country. Why? Simple, people who live in sin will abuse their freedoms and take advantage of any situation to conduct sinful acts, as predicted by the Bible. Technology is wonderful, but only God can solve the problems of the evil men will do. Only by accepting Jesus Christ as Lord can a man truly change and violence end on Earth. Only the saving grace of God will cleanse the soul and prevent men and women from reenacting their previous crimes. As for the jobless rate, the voice of experience tells me that nearly any healthy American can find a job, with a few notable exceptions. It might not be the ideal job, but there is an abundance of opportunities. "For even when we were with you, we gave you this command: If any one will not work, let him not eat. For we hear that some of you are living in idleness, mere busybodies, not doing any work. Now such persons we command and exhort in the Lord Jesus Christ to do their work in quietness and to earn their own living. Brethren, do not be weary in doing well." - 2 Thessalonians. 3:10-13. Doesn't this sound like modern America? We are generally people who are idle, more concerned with entertainment than work. Everyone seams to enjoy the latest gossip above all else. Instead, we need to be about the business of discussing the gospel and doing "good deeds". There are some people in America who do go hungry, on occasion, even though they are working at a job. We need to "love thy neighbor" and constantly help others fulfill their physical and spiritual needs. Is all this entertainment in movies and video games giving us a truly wiser and "good" society?

Technology: Good or Bad?

There can be little argument that technology has dramatically changed the way of life in most parts of the world. Some groups have rejected technology, like the Amish, others have embraced technology wholeheartedly. As you might imagine from the subject manner of this book, I believe technology is generally something to be admired. Technological developments have increased the quality and length of life for many individuals. Medical advances have saved many lives. There can be little argument that medical research is a powerful tool in helping those with disabilities to live better lives. We have cured many of the diseases that have plagued mankind over the years. Television and recording devices gives us programs not only for entertainment but educational aides. History, Mathematics, Astronomy, Physics and many more fields come "alive" in documentaries. Videos can provide extremely effective learning tools. Technology falls into the same category as all areas of science, wisdom, or any other subject. If technology is used to help people give glory to God it is valuable. If these subjects or developments take away from the glory of God, they have no value. Like we discussed in the introduction, wisdom that gives glory to God is "true" wisdom. Wisdom in the form of "craftiness" that diverts glory from God is an abomination to God and will be destroyed by God. "The Lord says: 'These people come near to me with their mouth and honor me with their lips, but their hearts are far from me. Their worship of me is made up only of rules taught by men. Therefore once more I will astound these people with wonder upon wonder; the wisdom of the wise will perish, the intelligence of the intelligent will vanish.' Woe to those who go to great depths to hide their plans from the LORD, who do their work in darkness and think, "Who sees us? Who will know?" Isaiah 29:13-15 The people working with technology that give glory to God and improve the quality of life should be commended. If the technological advances divert praise from the Lord and only reverences the overall achievements of man, it is has no value. There are many examples of both "kinds" of technological achievements. Popular Science is one of several excellent sources that list the newest technological achievements. An article entitled, 'Better ... Stronger ... Faster ... Popular Science Introduces the Engineered Human' lists several technological achievements that are presently available and others in the process of development. Some of these achievements are undeniably wonderful accomplishments; others raise enormous doubts of their value and direction of human progress. One example of an achievement that should have little controversy is the "C-leg". "The C-leg, now being used in the military, allows amputees to tackle hills and walk down stairs with a natural stride. A sensor sends data from the joint to hydraulic actuators in the leg, fine-tuning the amount of resistance needed for almost any terrain. [10.15]" How can we question the benefit to amputees by this wonderful gift of increased mobility? Again, there are many technological achievements that should provide no controversy in their usefulness. I believe God is pleased with these achievements. There are other developments on the horizon that are very disturbing. One article that raises many moral questions is entitled, 'Will We Grow Babies Outside Their Mothers' Bodies?' by Gretchen Reynolds. This article describes the possibility that we could create an "artificial womb" in the not to distant future. The article refers too many of the beneficial applications to this controversial development, if the problems in its construction will ever be overcome. "An artificial womb would vastly extend the period of fetal viability. In theory, an embryo could survive outside its mother's body from the moment of its conception. Some anti-abortion activists have said that women should therefore be required to incubate aborted fetuses in artificial wombs. [10.16]" This idea may indeed be based on a desire to save the lives of un-born fetuses but this may not be as "humane" as requiring the mother to take the baby to full term. There are so many properties of the human womb we still do not comprehend. It is hard to accept that we will ever truly be able to create an artificial womb. If successful, there are some grounds for debating its usefulness.

The idea of an artificial womb brings into question the increased research into tampering with God's design of our individual human attributes, in other words genetic engineering. The term genetic engineering is sometimes avoided in research projects, because of the alarming images we generate based on science fiction movies. But, laboratories around the world are investigating procedures of genetic manipulation. "We're working on an entire suite of biological enhancements: smart drugs to improve memory beyond normal doping methods that promote muscle growth by inhibiting certain proteins, gene therapy to stimulate the birth of neurons in the brain to above-normal levels. ... In my lab at Stanford University, we're developing gene-therapy approaches to, among other things, transfer genes into the hippocampus – an area of the brain involved in learning and memory – with the goal of making a rat learn better under stress, a state that typically impairs cognition. ... Still, with an imagination stepped in science-fiction literature- and a deep-routed trust in our ability to solve humanity's problems – it's not hard to dream up fanciful ways in which science will make us better than well. But I think it's a good idea to consider whether this sort of tinkering is a good idea. [10.17]" It should be clear that the Bible encourages the search for wisdom and growth in all aspects of human development. If you doubt that this is the view of the Holy Scriptures, re-read the introduction and continue into the rest of the book. However, this scientist, who is on the cutting edge of research into the advancement of human abilities, admits that we need to proceed cautiously. There is a spiritual question that the world has labeled as a question of morality. How far do we push genetic enhancements and what are the limits of scientific research? Medical research to help someone to lead a better life is commendable. However, when we are acting in rebellion against God, God's wrath is provoked. When we, as a people in various parts of the world, make a claim unto God that "we can do anything you can do, even better", the wrath of God and His judgment is kindled. Some scientific advancements are for the sole purpose of attempting to take God entirely out of the picture. In this manner, I believe the advancement of technology is pushing us ever closer to the end of the world, because of the pride and arrogance expressed in some of these achievements. It is inevitable. The end of the world will come. We are running out of natural resources and the Bible clearly describes how God's wrath will be poured out on "all flesh". Additionally, the book of Revelation provides many details about the end to the world, the sun, the moon, the stars, and even the present heaven will be destroyed. Revelation describes the replacement of these old places with a new heaven and new earth. Man is incapable of creating a utopia, only God can make everything work perfectly. "The great promise of technology in Western civilization is that it will make all our lives better. It's a nice sentiment, but it rarely works this way. ... Technological innovations have done precisely the opposite of leveling the playing field, concentrating more power into the hands of the few. ... It is those high on the socioeconomic ladder who are most likely to hear about a medical innovations, to understand its implications, to have a cousin whose friend's sister can get them at the top of the list to receive it, and be able to afford it. [10.18]" Where is the evidence that technological achievement has made society better off than before? We still have the same old sin problems of greed, envy, hatred, bigotry, violence, and a long list of other problems. "In the last days, people will be lovers of themselves, lovers of money, boastful, proud, abusive, disobedient to their parents, ungrateful, unholy, without love (for one another), unforgiving, slanderous, without self-control, brutal, not lovers of good, treacherous, rash, conceited, lovers of pleasure rather than lovers of God, having a form of godliness but denying its power. ... They are the kind who worm their way into homes and gain control over weak-willed women, who are loaded down with sins and are swayed by all kinds of evil desires, always learning but never able to acknowledge the truth." 2nd Timothy 3:1-7. Sound familiar? Jesus said, "I am the way, and the truth, and the life."

In the television series Star Trek the decision to approach a planet and reveal to the inhabitants that you were a space traveler was sometimes determined by the Captain of the starship exploring the universe. Someone like Captain Kirk or Captain Picard would approach a planet on the basis of their estimation of the planet's evolutionary development, which depended upon their level of technological achievement. Usually they would consult with Starfleet Command on wither or not to approach a planet considering all available information about the planet. The amount of social development was considered harmonious with the level of technology the planet had achieved. As a result, planets with warp drive technology were approached to join the United Federation of Planets and share in an exchange of information. Once a member of the Federation, you received protection from foreign attack, medical support, and technical support for research and development on scientific pursuits. However, if you were designated as a primitive planet, like the Earth would be considered today, according to the Star Trek prime directive, you would be ignored. If there were people hurt or injured and you could help them, you are prevented from rendering any assistance because of the Prime Directive. If you tried to save even one life with the advanced technology of the Enterprise, you would be considered to be interfering with the natural evolution of the planet. There are many episodes on Star Trek that demonstrates how the evolutionary prospective causes a person to become barbaric, self centered, filled with greed and calloused towards others. You become greedy by sharing information and assistance with only members of technologically advanced worlds. This promotes the attitude of associating yourself only with people similar to you. This returns to the concept of racism that is promoted by evolution. According to several theories of evolution, race developed through people evolving under different climactic conditions. As stated earlier, some have used these ideas to promote the concept of white superiority. The prime directive principle of Star Trek promotes a sense of separating yourself to people of like intelligence and gifts. Although Star Trek is notorious for promoting cooperation between different people, despite color race or creed, the prime directive seams to contradict these high principles originally intended by Gene Rodenberry. Instead of sharing equally with everyone, knowledge and assistance in solving problems, Star Trek promotes the concept of selective association according to the wealth of knowledge a person possesses. This definitely is opposite the "love thy neighbor" principle of the Bible. A Christian is commanded to love even his enemies and do good things toward all people, no matter what their level of intelligence. What can you expect? The entire concept of life on other planets is contrary to many principles of the Bible. This is one more example of attempting a philosophy to do better than the principles of the Bible, and falling into a pit of contradictions.

Many episodes in the Star Trek series show the insistence of allowing a person to die because of the prime directive. Imagine the cruelty of forcing a doctor to stand over a dying man with the antidote of the disease and unable to give the medicine to the person because the patient came from a technologically backward society. This is cruelty at its worst. In the Star Trek series what is the penalty for violating the prime directive, without a reasonable explanation? The answer is death. Many episodes show how the prime directive can inspire great evil. Be aware that the principles of the Prime Directive in the Star Trek series were derived from the theory of evolution. The theory of evolution is taught as fact in all public schools and many of the principles of the prime directive are promoted which lead towards greed, violence, prejudice and neglect. I still have great respect and admiration for the Star Trek series because it generally promotes peace and quality entertainment. However, there are episodes involving the prime directive which are morally confusing and in many cases opposite the principles of Christianity. The Star Trek series promotes the concept of abundant life developing throughout the universe as the result of evolution. This is of course false. Life defiantly did not come from a random mixture of chemical elements, as we have discussed in previous chapters. However, the star trek television and movie series makes one of the best shows for entertainment purposes today. Just do not take the idea of alien life or the "logic" of the prime directive too seriously; they are based on non- Christian principles.

The Rapture

One of the most significant events in the history of the Earth will take place during the "last days" predicted in the book of first Thessalonians and other prophetic books of the Bible. "For this we declare to you by the Word of the Lord, that we who are alive, who are left until the coming of the Lord, shall not precede those who have fallen asleep. For the Lord himself will descend from heaven with a cry of command, with the archangel's call, and with the sound of the trumpet of God. And the dead in Christ will rise first; then we who are alive, who are left, shall be caught up together with them in the clouds to meet the Lord in the air; and so we shall be with the Lord." 1 Thessalonians. 4:15-17 This event is the called the rapture. The word translated as "caught up " in the verse above is rap ere, which is also the root word for rapture. The rapture will be at a time when it is somewhat unexpected by a sin-filled world. "But of that day and hour no one knows, not even the angels of heaven, nor the Son, but the Father only. As were the days of Noah, so will be the coming of the Son of man. For as in those days before the flood they were eating and drinking, marrying and giving in marriage, until the day when Noah entered the ark, and they did not know until the flood came and swept them all away, so will be the coming of the son of man. Then two men will be in the field; one is taken and one is left. Two women will be grinding at the mill; one is taken and one is left. Watch, therefore, for you do not know on what day your Lord is coming." Mathew 24:36-42 I believe that unique insights concerning events of the last days can be found by studying the events which took place in the days of Noah, as recorded in the book of Genesis.

The days of Noah are described in Genesis chapters 6 through 10. God's wrath was on the entire Earth. "The Lord saw the wickedness of man was great in the earth, and that every imagination of the thoughts of his heart was only evil continually. And the Lord was sorry that he had made man on the earth, and it grieved him in his heart. So the Lord said, 'I will blot out man whom I have created from the face of the ground, man and beast and creeping things and birds of the air, for I am sorry that I have made them.' But Noah found favor in the eyes of the Lord." Genesis 6:5-8 Similarly, we are leading up to the time when God can no longer tolerate the sins of man. God will not destroy the world by flood, as he has promised, but He will destroy the world by fire and other judgments from God, purifying the world for

Christ's reign on earth. Those who have been cleansed by the blood of Jesus will be saved from the wrath of tribulation, just as Noah found favor in the eyes of the Lord. Instead of getting into an ark, we will be raptured. In Mathew we have a good record of the words of Jesus concerning His return. The mentioning of eating and drinking, marrying and giving in marriage has a dual meaning. One, it will be a time when the world is just going about their daily routine, oblivious to the warning signs. There are other verses that indicated that people will have heard the warnings so many times by then that they will think the end will never come. Another way of looking at the passage is that it could be describing men and women doing evil deeds in eating, drinking and giving in marriage. What is wrong with these things? If you do these things according to the scriptures, with reverence to God, these things are pleasing to God. However, for eating we are practicing the sin of gluttony, for drinking we are practicing the sin of drunkenness and the use of other drugs, and as for marriage we are divorcing and remarrying many times, in contrast to the will of God. Another example of the perversion in the sanctity of marriage is the rise of gay and lesbian marriages. The world is fulfilling the prophecies of doing evil continually. Noah was commanded by God to build an ark. There is no record of what others were thinking about Noah, only the obedience of Noah unto the Lord is recorded. However, it kindles the imagination to think of large numbers of people laughing at this 'crazy' man who was building this huge boat on dry land. Similarly, Christians today are often ridiculed for their faith in Christ. The signs are presented for the coming of the Lord, but are rejected by the majority of the population of the world. The rapture will be a big surprise to those who have refused to believe the warnings for so many years.

In the 1970's there was a series of movies describing some of the events occurring in the last days before the judgment of God. In one of the movies, A Thief in the Night, the coming of the rapture was preached. Despite the warnings, many were stunned by the sudden disappearance of thousands of Christians worldwide. The movie interprets the previously mentioned verses in Matthew by Christians going about their normal daily lives, and then suddenly disappearing. This type of movie was re-made in an excellent version called 'Left Behind'. The effect might be compared to the transporter beam described in Star Trek. Finally, we are beamed up to heaven because there are only sinful people on this planet. Actually, the transporter beam analogy might not be too far from the truth. "Lo! I tell you a mystery. We shall not all sleep, but we shall all be changed, in a moment, in the twinkling of an eye, at the last trumpet. For the trumpet will sound, and the dead will be raised imperishable, and we shall be changed. For this perishable nature must put on the imperishable, and this mortal nature must put on immortality." 1Corinthians 15:51-53 How fast is a twinkling of an eye? The twinkling of an eye is the effect of light reflected off the surface of the eye. So the speed of the transformation from mortality to immortality would be at the speed of light. Refer back to chapter nine about the qualities of the speed of light. If any material object is accelerated close to the speed of light, time slows down. At the point matter reaches the speed of light, by a collision, it becomes pure energy and time is no longer a factor. This implies that we have a quality of immortality as we a clothed in the power of God, which is pure inexhaustible energy. Another interesting event in the previously mentioned movie is that the rapture was explained as the result of an attack from alien life forms. I wonder if this is truly how the event will be explained after it occurs. After all, you are faced with the sudden disappearance of thousands or millions of individuals from every walk of life and every country on earth. Also, perhaps only moments before, every grave with the remains of a Christian is overturned. How can this event be described by any other explanation than the rapture predicted in the Holy Scripture? Satan, the ruler of the world at that time, will attempt this or another explanation for the rapture. Perhaps Satan will toy with the popular belief in extraterrestrials to explain the rapture. Or maybe he will invoke fears of "neutron bombs" that have selectively killed millions. In any event he will still have many followers and only a part of the remaining individuals will turn to the Bible and become Christians. Again, this series of events is assuming what theologians call a pre-millennium rapture. There are respected theologians that argue the case for a mid-millennium and post-millennium rapture. All three views can be supported by references to scriptures.

The Reason for Judgment

Jesus continually teaches us that this life is temporary and that there in another life to come. From birth to death our faith is constantly being tested. Following this life there is judgment and eternal life or punishment for our transgressions. The key event for which all people will be judged is their acceptance or rejection of the Word of God. Accepting Christ washes the person from all ungodliness and allows that person to stand before God's judgment blameless. Rejecting Christ seals the fate of the individual to the punishment of eternal death. This is no elaborate fable or the result of just one of many primitive religions, as some scientists and theologians will tell you. These events will take place someday, and the day is fast approaching. "The Lord is not slow about his promise as some count slowness, but is forbearing toward you, not wishing that any should perish, but that all should reach repentance" 1Peter 2:9. This portion of scripture was written about the Second Coming of Jesus Christ. Some believe that this event is slow in coming, and some believe that he is not coming at all. "In the last days scoffers will come, scoffing and following their own evil desires. They will say, 'Where is this coming he promised? Ever since our fathers died, everything goes on as it has since the beginning of creation.' But they deliberately forgot that long ago by God's word the heavens existed and the earth was formed out of water and by water. By these waters also the world was deluged and destroyed. By the same word the present heavens and earth are reserved for fire, being kept for the Day of Judgment and destruction of ungodly men." 2Peter 3:3-7. This book has dealt with how some scientists scoff at the Bible. They constantly ridicule the idea of God creating the universe. They "deliberately forgot" that science essentially proves a supernatural origin to the universe as we have discussed. They "deliberately forgot" that science clearly shows the universe created by the "waters" made by God. Recall our review of the particle physics experiments at R.H.I.C. The scoffers are deliberately becoming entrenched in their anti-Christian views.

In 1st and 2nd Peter, previously quoted, the verses do two things: The verses assures us that Christ is indeed coming and God is making every available effort for every man, women and child to hear the Gospel and have every chance to escape the wrath of God's judgment. God is unwilling for any to perish. Therefore, God is holding out as long as possible the judgment of all nations. This gives every person many opportunities to repent and be passed over from judgment. Just as God provided for the Jewish people during the first Passover, the angel of death will pass over your house if you have accepted the blood of the Lamb of God, Jesus Christ. God doesn't want anyone to perish because of their foolish disobedience. "The Lord is not slow in keeping his promise, as some understand slowness. He is patient with you, not wanting anyone to perish, but everyone to come to repentance." 1Peter 3:9. He loves us all so much, "But God shows his love for us in that while we were yet sinners Christ died for us." Romans 5:9 However, our God is just and in the name of justice, judgment on the earth will come down from heaven. The Holy Spirit is urging you to commit yourself to Christ as savior and Lord. Through the guidance of the Holy Spirit, the Christian has a dynamic and abundant life. Christ said, "I came that they may have life, and have it abundantly." John 10:10 Our life has a direction, although it can be difficult to follow. "For the gate is narrow and the way is hard that leads to life and those who find it are few." Mathew 7:14 But the Lord is always there waiting for any person to call upon the tremendous resources available to help that person accomplish the difficult tasks facing the Christian life. "Behold, I stand at the door and knock; if any one hears my voice and opens the door, I will come in to him and eat with him, and he with Me." Revelation 3:20 In the days of our Lord it was a special time of fellowship when someone shared a meal together. Even today it is considered a great honor to sit down and share the intimacy of a meal with a distinguished guest, like the President of the United States or some other important person. How much more should we feel honored by the presence of Jesus, the one through which the entire universe was created? Jesus wants to have an intimate relationship with you. "Ask and it will be given to you; seek and you will find; knock and the door will be opened to you." Luke 11:9 "But God, who is rich in mercy, out of the great love with which he loved us, even when we were dead through our trespasses, made us alive together with Christ (by grace you have been saved), and raised us up with him, and made us sit with him in heavenly places in Christ Jesus, that in the coming ages he might show the immeasurable riches of his grace in kindness toward us in Christ Jesus." Ephesians .2:6-7. This condition of free access to the presence of God and the richness of His glory is available to everyone until the moment of death or the day of judgment when the door will be shut. "When once the householder has risen up and shut the door, you will begin to stand outside and to knock at the door, saying, 'Lord, open to us.' He will answer you, I do not know where you come from.' ... There you will weep and gnash your teeth, when you see Abraham and Isaac and Jacob and all the prophets in the Kingdom of God and you yourself thrust out. And all men will come from east and west, and from north and south, and sit at the table in the kingdom of God." Luke 13:25,28,29 The image is clear. If you have rejected Christ as savior during you lifetime, you will see on the other side of the "pearly gates" the saints who reign with Christ. Meanwhile you will be cast out to suffer horribly. Why risk it? Just turn your heart over to the Lord. It is our decision to accept or reject the gospel through our gift of free will given to us by God. Learn from the Bible how to live the Christian lifestyle and you will realize it is peaceful, secure, and a lot of fun! We are planning an upcoming book on this very subject of having a fun Christian lifestyle.

There is strong evidence that we are indeed living in the "last generation". I personally believe that anywhere from now to 70 years into the future, Christ will return to earth. This statement has been made many times and many times it has been wrong. In every generation since the death and resurrection of Jesus Christ there have been indications that some of the signs of the "last days" have come upon the world. Hitler seamed to be the perfect candidate for the antichrist at one time. However, there are more prophecies being fulfilled today than during any other period of history. The present conditions appear to indicate that we are indeed living in the last days. One popular book written and published in 1991 is a book entitled, 'The Rise of Babylon: Sign of the End Times' by Charles H. Dyer. In this book, the author makes the observation that quote "Descriptions of Iraq's rise to power today parallel descriptions of Nebuchadnezzar's rise to power in 605 B.C. Once again the eyes of the world are riveted on the Middle East. [10.19]" Iraq is where the capital city of the Babylonian Empire once existed. This city plays an important role in "end times" prophecy. Some have merely dismissed the rise of power in the old Babylonian Empire as figuratively the rise of evil. This is a reoccurring debate over how much of the imagery of the book of Revelation should be taken literally and how much is merely symbolic. The Babylonian Empire was extremely large in the days of Nebuchadnezzar. Quote, "In his day, the lands of what are now Iraq, Saudi Arabia, Syria, Lebanon, Jordan, Israel, and Kuwait were all under Babylonian control. [10.20]" The Babylonian Empire has at its roots the first organized rebellion against God. "Wickedness would be deposited in the land where man first rebelled against God, where a rebel named Nimrod led mankind to build a tower whose top would reach God. Babylon was the city that had threatened God's land of promise and sacked and burned Jerusalem. [10.21]" Nimrod represented a person devoted to a life of rebellion against God. He is another historical figure that can give us insights into what the coming antichrist might be like. "Nimrod was the architect of man's union against God, and Genesis 11:1-9 records the catastrophic consequences of his actions. [10.22]" Nimrod is a grandson of Noah. The Bible documents many times men of God have rebellious sons and daughters, to their grief. "Cush became the father of Nimrod; he was the first on earth to be a mighty man. ...The beginning of his kingdom was Babel. ... Then they said, 'Come, let us build ourselves a city, and a tower with its top in the heavens, and let us make a name for ourselves, least we be scattered abroad upon the face of the whole earth.... And the Lord said,' Behold they are one people, and they have all one language; and this is only the beginning of what they will do; nothing that they purpose to do will now be impossible for them. Come, let us go down, and there confuse their language, that they may not understand one another's speech.' So the Lord scattered them abroad from there over the face of all the earth, and they left off building the city." Genesis 10:8, 11:4, 6-8 This was not to be the end of man's organized rebellion against God or the importance to the city of Babel and the Babylonian Empire. The city of Babylon is a center of evil throughout the Bible from Genesis to Revelation. "The Bible mentions Babylon over two hundred and eighty times, and many of those references are to the future city of Babylon that is rising from the fine sands of the desert today. [10.23]" We are seeing the rise of a "New World Order" endorsed by the United Nations. Through education and translators we are establishing lines of communication like never before in the history of the world. We are becoming a world with a single language and a single voice once again. With the aid of sophisticated modern technology, it does indeed seam that there is nothing we can not accomplish. However, the problems of crime and evil acts are everywhere, showing how mankind makes a mess of things when he rebels against God. The only solution to the problems of the world is for each person to individually surrender control of their lives to the Lord Jesus Christ. No technological achievement can solve the problem of sin. Only by the Holy Spirit entering a person's life can the problem of sin be destroyed, or minimized. "Jesus answered him, 'Truly, truly I say to you unless one is born anew, he cannot see the kingdom of God.'... 'How can a man be born when he is old? Can he enter a second time into his mother's womb...? Jesus answered, 'Truly, truly, I say to you unless one is born of water and the Spirit, he cannot enter the kingdom of God. That which is born of the flesh is flesh, and that which is born of the spirit is spirit.'" Mathew 3:3-6 To be born again requires the acceptance of the Holy Spirit into your life through faith and prayer. To be born of water requires baptism of water and the Holy Spirit. Accepting the will of the Lord will cause your life to change dramatically. First an inner peace will start forming and then the outward actions will become more in line with the principles of the Holy Scriptures. A person who has just been born again will start to show noticeable changes shortly after the person has committed their lives to God. The outward expression of the inner joy will continually grow as each day passes and you give more reverence to the power of God. "Therefore, if any one is in Christ, he is a new creation; the old has passed away, behold, the new has come." 2Corinthians 5:17.

Current Events

Sadam Hussein is no longer in power or a threat to anyone. He has in fact been put to death for his crimes. However, we must wonder how events will unfold in the coming years of reconstructing Iraq. Will the United States and other countries around the world be used as gigantic pawns in Satan's chess game? Considering the enormous resources committed to restoring the country of Iraq we must wonder about the result. We can assume the countries of the world will not only rebuild the basic necessities of water and electricity, but the cultural developments started by Sadam Hussein. Perhaps they will fulfill Sadam's plans of building an economic, cultural and political center of the world. "But as of February 1990, over sixty million bricks had been laid in reconstruction of Nebuchadnezzar's fabled city. Saddam Hussein has ignored the objections of archaeologists who consider it a crime to build over ancient ruins. He has scraped a plan to rebuild Babylon on a nearby site across the Euphrates River. On the exact site of ancient Babylon, he has reconstructed the Southern Palace of Nebuchadnezzar, including the Procession Street, a Greek theater, many temples, what was once Nebuchadnezzar's throne room, and a half-scale model of the Ishtar Gate. [10.24]" Nimrod, the originator of the city of Babel, which began the city of Babylon, was a descendent of Ham; refer to Genesis 10:8-10. "Some of the nations and peoples that developed from Ham's line included Egypt, the Babylonians, the Assyrians, the Philistines, and the various groups of the Canaanites. Virtually all of Israel's major enemies in biblical history came from the line of Ham. Genesis 10 lists Ham's descendants, and tucked in the midst of the list of names is Nimrod. [10.25]" It is not a coincidence that Israel's major enemies are in this area; it has a relationship to a linage of conflict over this region since the time of Noah. These countries are a part of the history of this region and they continually fight over this land. The Middle East is a land rich in many natural resources and the world has been fighting for the land God promised to Israel for many centuries.

The rebuilding of Iraq seams to fit perfectly into the picture of a new Babylonian Empire reminiscent of the old one. The real significance to the city of Babylon is found in the book of Revelation. The scripture places great importance on its destruction. "Another angel, a second, followed, saying 'Fallen, fallen is Babylon the great, she who made all nations drink the wine of her impure passions. And another angel, a third, followed them saying with a loud voice, 'If any one worships the beast and its image, and receives a mark on his forehead or on his hand, he also shall drink the wine of God's wrath." Revelation 14:8-10. Here we can associate Babylon with the Throne City of the beast, the anti-Christ. Further clues to Babylon as a great seat of power for the beast, is found throughout the text. "Come, I will show the judgment of the great harlot who is seated upon many waters, with whom the kings of the earth have committed fornication, and with the wine of whose fornication the dwellers on earth have become drunk.' And ... I saw a woman sitting on a scarlet beast which was full of blasphemous names, and it had seven heads and ten horns. The woman was arrayed in purple and scarlet, and bedecked with gold and jewels and pearls, holding in her hand a golden cup full of abominations and impurities of her fornication; and on her forehead was written a name of mystery: 'Babylon the great mother of harlots and of earth's abominations." Revelation 17:1-5. "Fallen, fallen is Babylon the great! It has become a dwelling place of demons, a haunt of every foul spirit, ... for all nations have drunk the wine of her impure passion, and the kings of the earth have committed fornication with her, and the merchants of the earth have grown rich with the wealth of her wantonness." Revelation 18:2-3. "'Alas! alas! thou great city, thou mighty city, Babylon! In one hour has thy judgment come.' And the merchants of the earth weep and mourn for her, since no one buys their cargo any more, ... The merchants of these wares, who gained wealth from her, will stand far off, in fear of her torment, weeping and mourning aloud, ... In one hour all this wealth has been laid waste. ... 'Then a mighty angel took up a stone like a great millstone and threw it into the sea, saying, 'So shall Babylon the great city be thrown down with violence, and shall be found no more; ... for thy merchants were the great men of the earth, and all nations were deceived by thy sorcery." Revelation 18:10,11 15, 17, 21, 23.

One of the most puzzling things about the book of Revelation a few years ago was that the events described in Revelation seam far from becoming an actual reality. However, events in recent years have lead more and more prophecies to be fulfilled or to the verge of fulfillment. One example is the rise of Babylon. A hundred years ago it was inconceivable that the long lost Babylonian Empire would rise again or that Israel would be established as a nation once more. However, these events, and many more events of prophecy, are taking place today. "The Middle East is the world's deadliest neighborhood. It has 17 Arab countries and a Persian republic populated by 231 million Muslims as well as small Christian minorities and one Jewish State with a population of 5 million. It has known few days of true peace in this century, none since Israel was born to a rattle of gunfire 42 years ago. Lurching from crisis to moments of ill-conceived optimism and back into crisis, it has spent more on weapons, fought more wars and suffered more casualties than any other part of the third world. ... Arabs took the formation of Israel as an insult and declared war against the new state. Israel courageously fought off the combined armies of seven Arab states, and after the war ended, Israel had more land than it had been granted under the original United Nations plan! ... In the 1950's, General Gamal Abdel Nasser rose in Egypt and called for Arabs to unite against western powers and Israel. He nationalized the Suez Canal in 1956 and closed the Gulf... In 1967 Naser and the Syrians threatened once more to invade Israel, but Israel struck first and humiliated the Arab nations on all sides in the Six Day War. [10.26]" The rise of Israel is predicted in the Bible. "The Lord will have compassion on Jacob; once again he will choose Israel and will settle them in their own land. Aliens will join them and unite with the house of Jacob. Nations will take them and bring them to their own place. And the house of Israel will possess the nations as menservants and maidservants in the Lord's land. They will make captives of their captors and rule over their oppressors." Isaiah 14:1-2. This event did not occur in 539 B.C. when a few Jews returned to the land of Israel after the fall of Babylon to Cyrus. However, the creation of Israel as a nation in 1948 seams to fit the prophecy. "Aliens", the United Nations headed by the United States, did join with Jews to bring them to "their own place", which is the Holy land. This seams an undeniable fulfillment of prophecy.

The nation of Israel will have a profound place in world events during the last days before the Second Coming of Christ. Quote, "The Bible predicts a seven-year period of prophetic history before the

Second Coming of Christ to the earth. God's prophetic clock will begin ticking when a world ruler, called in various places the prince, the Antichrist, or the beast, makes a seven year treaty with the nation of Israel (Daniel 9:27). … This leader will arise from the remnants of the Roman Empire, probably Europe or the area of the Mediterranean basin. He will control an empire of ten nations and will dominate the world through military power. But peace with Israel will be shattered midway through the seven years. The leader will arrive in Israel, enter the temple (which will have been rebuilt by the Jews), and declare himself to be God. A statue of this man will be erected in the temple, and everyone will be ordered to bow down to the image. [10.27]» It has been speculated that the European Union, with its thirteen member nations, will become the ten nations headed by the Antichrist. "And I saw a beast rising out of the sea, with ten horns and seven heads, with ten diadems upon its horns and a blasphemous name upon its heads. One of its heads seemed to have a mortal wound, but its mortal wound was healed, and the whole earth followed the beast with wonder." -Revelation. 13:1,3. The apparent mortal wound and amazing healing will be a false resurrection of an important world leader. Then one of the followers of the beast who will give this leader praise for power over life and death, even though it is only God who can truly conquer death. The beast merely gives death, not life. "And the ten horns that you saw are ten kings who have not yet received royal power, but they are to receive authority as kings for one hour, together with the beast These are of one mind and give over their power and authority to the beast; they will make war on the Lamb, and the Lamb will conquer them, for he is Lord of lords and King of kings… and he said to me, 'The waters that you saw, where the harlot is seated, are peoples and multitudes and nations and tongues. And the ten horns that you saw, they and the beast will hate the harlot; the will make her desolate and naked, and devour her flesh and burn her up with fire, for God has put it into their hearts to carry out his purpose by being of one mind and giving over their royal power to the beast, until the words of God shall be fulfilled. And the women that you saw is the great city which has dominion over the kings of the earth.'… 'Fallen, fallen is Babylon the great! It has become a dwelling place of demons, a haunt of every foul spirit." Revelation 17:12-14, 15-18, 18:2. These verses present a picture of some of the events in the end times. It seams that there is a rise of power in Europe headed by an alliance of ten nations, the leader of this alliance will at some point be the beast, the Antichrist. The ten leaders had risen to power and once they were the leaders of these ten providences, or countries, they had their own wisdom and power for only one hour. After this hour, the beast took possession of their souls. Apparently each of them received the mark of the beast and gave their souls to the beast to become united in one mind. These events are taking place after the rapture when the beast is gathering the powers of the world until he is the absolute monarch of the entire earth. There is one last pocket of rebellion. Apparently, at this time, Babylon has become a great economic power totally independent of this European alliance. There is a refusal to bow to the beast as lord. So, the beast conquers and destroys Babylon. After, he establishes the city as symbol of iniquity, "a haunt for every foul spirit". This establishes his position for the final assault against God's people. Even though the Jews were not raptured, they stand as a symbol of God's people. When the beast claims to be God and enters the temple of God and makes the people of Israel bow before a golden image of the beast, the people of Israel at last realize the truth. Here is the Antichrist prophesied by the Bible and the New Testament of the word of God is true. They realize that they had indeed crucified the Son of God on the cross and that Jesus Christ was and is Lord. This sets the stage for the battle of Armageddon. This is when the beast will attempt to eradicate all the Jew's people, which are a constant testimony to the power of God, just by remaining alive.

One thing, which troubles Americans, is the fact that there seams to be no mentioning of the United States in all the prophecies concerning the last days. This is really is not too unreasonable. There is alliance of nations in Europe called the European Union designed to pool the resources of the European nations. Already the United States has been impacted by this alliance and exports have suffered. The rise of a European power is on the way. Perhaps the EU will have economically superior to the United States very soon. The other factor in America's downfall could be the rapture. "It is possible that the United

States is not mentioned in prophecy because we will become a second-class international power overnight when God removes Christians from the earth, an event scheduled to occur just before the beginning of this seven-year period. True believers who placed their faith in Jesus Christ will be taken to heaven before the Antichrist is revealed. Today as many as half of all Americans claim to be "born again," or believers in Jesus Christ. If only one-fourth of that number have genuinely made a personal commitment to Christ, then over 28 million Americans will suddenly "disappear" when God removes the church from the earth! Can you imagine the effects on our country if over 28 million people- people in industry, government, the military, business, agriculture, education, medicine and communications- disappear? [10.28]" There are many Christians in key positions throughout the United States. Also, there is much speculation of the effects of extreme weather conditions on the worldwide population. Combining these two factors, it is easy to see how the United States could be devastated overnight.

Changes in the Weather

There are references to strange changes in weather conditions as a "sign" of the end times approaching. There is certainly evidence for many unusually strong natural events taking place around the world. One of the most significant natural disasters in modern times was from the recent Tsunami. "Humans are fleeting visitors on this roiling rock in the universe. On December 26, 2004, at 58 minutes and 49 seconds past midnight GMT, Mother Earth reacquainted us with this immutable fact. ... The ensuing force - equal to 25,000 Nagasaki - size atomic bombs detonated in tandem – jolted the Earth from its axis, permanently shortened the length of the day, and hurled walls of seawater onto thousands of miles of coastline - ... sweeping away at least 200,000 in an instant. [10.29]" There have been many natural disasters during the 20th century. There are strong indications that the trend towards large scale natural disasters will continue to increase in frequency and magnitude. "Humans are also relentlessly altering or destroying the planet's natural protection mechanisms. 'If you remove mangroves, damage coral reefs, and take away wetlands ... you are much more exposed to storm impact or tsunami damage.' The bad news is that the danger is only growing, because wherever population densities soar, the landscape must be transformed to sustain more and more people. ... Since A.D. 79, when Vesurvius exploded with little warning and entombed Pompeii and its 3,000 townsfolk under 15 feet of scalding ash, the volcano has erupted at least 30 times. ... If that eruption happened today, it would probably kill 90 percent of the population of the country. [10.30]" Volcanoes, hurricanes, landslides, tsunamis, and earthquakes all show signs of causing more damage to property and human life than any other time in history. Look at the devastation of hurricane Katrina. The Bible refers to changes in the weather during the last days. "Nation will rise against nation, and kingdom against kingdom. There will be famines and earthquakes in various places. All these are the beginning of birth pains." Mathew 24:7-8. Some theologians interpreted this passage to suggest that the earthquakes, wars and famine will be exceptionally great in the "last days". These "birth pains" could be interpreted as great natural disasters that increase in frequency and severity leading to the destruction of the world as recorded in Revelation. There are many signs of the end times listed by our Lord in the twenty-fourth chapter of Mathew. Many of these signs could be attributed to any generation since the Lord ascended into heaven. Like previously stated, the time of World War II seamed to fit some of these verses. Hitler was an excellent candidate for the anti-Christ and the "nation shall rise up against nation" certainly fit into the events of World War II. Add to these facts, Hitler's obsession with wiping out the Jews and this historical period provided a good pre-view of the end times. There were still many prophecies mentioned in this same section of scripture, Mathew Chapter 24, that were not fulfilled during those years. But like so many other events in history, God uses cataclysmic events to get our attention. No one can live forever in this world, so why question God's presence or sovereignty in spectacular events? Why should cataclysmic events be so shocking? Everyone dies sometime. This may seam cold, but it is a reminder that God does care for us but allows catastrophic events to "shake" our faith sometimes. But we have the promises of God to comfort us and help us through these great tragedies.

"'Do not let your hearts be troubled. Trust in God; trust also in me. ... If you love me, you will obey what I command. And I will ask the Father, and he will give you another Counselor to be with you forever – the Spirit of truth. The world cannot accept him, because it neither sees him nor knows him. But you know him, for he lives with you and will be in you. I will not leave you as orphans; I will come to you. Before long, the world will not see me anymore, but you will see me. Because I live, you also will live. On that day you will realize that I am in my Father, and you are in me, and I am in you.'" John 14:1, 15-20 Cataclysmic events are primarily for the non-Christian to "wake up" and realize that death could be around any corner. So, evaluate your convictions and your relationship with the Lord who has the power of life and death. "For whoever wants to save his life will lose it, but whoever loses his life for me will find it. What good will it be for a man if he gains the whole world, yet forfeits his soul?" Matthew 16:25-26 "I tell you the truth, whoever hears my word and believes him who sent me has eternal life and will not be condemned; he has crossed over from death to life ... Jesus said to her, 'I am the resurrection and the life. He who believes in me will live, even though he dies; and whoever lives and believes in me will never die.'" John 5:24, 11:25-26.

Again, let me be clear about the reason for God's judgment. It is simply a "wake up" call. Look through out the Bible and you will find that God's wrath is pour out when there is a prolonged and severe disobedience to God's laws by a large segment of the total population. Look at the Old Testament; it is filled with God pouring out His righteous judgment when His children are continually disobeying Him. It is similar to when parents run out of patience with their children. The parents might try a variety of parenting techniques, but nothing seams to work. There are some problems that are not solved simply, despite what certain television shows indicate. When all else fails, some children won't respond to anything but some "ultimate punishment" such as "spanking" or even prison when they become adults. Sometimes it takes dramatic events for children to realize they are doing wrong. God has some characteristics similar to ours. It is not that we have extended our attributes to form a concept of God, but rather we are made in the image of God and therefore we have similar attributes. The only way we can visualize this is through what we can understand about the Lord Jesus through scripture. There is a profound mystery in the trinity as we have mentioned in the introduction. Similarly, there are aspects about the nature of God we can never fully understand. For example, we must be careful in interpreting natural disasters as a sign of God's judgment. When tragic events occur, many theologians turn to words of comfort from the Bible. Jesus was asked about His view concerning certain tragic events which occurred during the time Jesus walked on the earth. "Now there were some present at that time who told Jesus about the Galileans whose blood Pilate had mixed with their sacrifices. Jesus answered, 'Do you think that these Galileans were worse sinners than all the other Galileans because they suffered this way? I tell you no! But unless you repent, you too will all perish. Or those eighteen who died when the tower in Siloam fell on them – do you think they were more guilty than all the others living in Jerusalem? I tell you, no! But unless you repent, you too will perish'" Luke 13:1-5. From these verses we are reminded of the Lord's warning against judging others found earlier in this same book. "Do not judge and you will not be judged. Do not condemn, and you will not be condemned. Forgive and you will be forgiven." Luke 6:37. The passages in Luke 13 remind us not to come to the conclusion that anything bad that happens to someone is a sign of judgment from God. If we do, we are judging people instead of letting God perform the righteous judgments. Therefore, when natural disasters, wars and other bad things happen we must treat the event as a tragedy. In the early history of the United States, the judges took very seriously this point of view to consult scripture before making their decisions. This is why there is a Bible in every courtroom. Judges in early America often made sure the Ten Commandments were prominently displayed to remind everyone of God's most important laws, some of which is also used to guide society. Judges often prayed for God's guidance in judging court cases. To have an orderly society there must be laws and judges to decide if a person is guilty of a crime or not. In the Old Testament, the Bible explains the role of judges and gives specific penalties for breaking certain laws. The first judges in history were appointed by Moses to aid in the task of deciding small matters of conflict. "Choose some wise, understanding and respected men from each of your tribes, and I will set them over you. ... And I charged your judges at that time: Hear the disputes between your brothers and judge fairly. ... Do not be afraid of any man, for judgment belongs to God. Bring me any case too hard for you, and I will hear it." Deuteronomy 1:13, 16-17. So, when a bridge collapses, a tornado destroys a town or terrorists attack, like on 9-11-2001, we must not think that the people who died were somehow evil and God judged them. Jesus knew that this is what some of them were thinking and plainly responded "I tell you no!" This passage opens many deep theological questions. For one, many people look for a reason why God would allow something like these tragedies to happen. As with all inquires, scripture hold clues to answering these questions about the nature of God.

Let us just lightly summarize some possible explanations to the question of why God allows what appear to be random acts of violence, death and sorrow. In the previously quoted passage of Luke 13, Jesus condemns some of the people who believed that these two tragedies were judgments from God and that all the people who died were evil. Jesus states that "unless you repent, you too will all perish". Jesus was saying, unless these people, probably Pharisees, turn from their sin of unjustly judging others they would perish. This is a reminded that after death comes judgment from God for each and every word we have spoken and every action we have made during our lifetime. The important point here is to recognize that we are to be judged individually. The men and women who died in tragic events are not judged by the disaster but by their individual sins. This brings us to some theological questions we can ask: Are there random acts of nature out of God's control? Is God truly all powerful and in control of all things? Does God have any limitations? If He does, what are they? The Bible seam to tell us that God does indeed have at least a few self-imposed, temporary limits. He allows free will and therefore allows rebellion and sin to exist. Second, God can not be in the presence of sin. Third He loves every person in the world, past and present and future and wants to have a loving, fatherly, intimate, relationship with His creation. What can God do about this dilemma? The key to understanding this mystery, somewhat, is to realize that time has virtually no meaning to our infinite God. When you consider that our father God exists outside of time, the entire course of human events passes in an instant. Also, since God can create and restore life effortlessly, suffering is almost meaningless to our Father God. So how can God understand us and our suffering? Only through the man: Jesus. "Jesus who is called Christ ... And they will call him Immanuel – which means, God with us." Mathew 1:14, 23. This is why there is a big difference between God's relationship with mankind in the New Testament as compared with the Old Testament. This changed relationship we have explored in several sections of this book. Jesus is our mediator and He alone can stand between us and the wrath of our father God. Studying the life and teachings of Jesus, is probably about as close as we can get to an understanding of the infinite mystery of God's conflict between Holiness and a desire to love His creation. Some questions that continue to put the best theologians to the test are: Why does God continue to allow evil to exist? Why do bad things happen to Christians? Why was it necessary for Jesus to die on the cross in order for us to be saved?

Let us explore the limitations of God just a little bit further. One event that is difficult to comprehend is the death of Christ on the cross. Traditional Christian theology states that Christ is God in human flesh. We have explored some of the divine characteristics of the Lord Jesus Christ. "'Anyone who has seen me has seen the Father. How can you say, 'Show us the Father?' 'Don't you believe that I am in the Father, and that the Father is in me?'" John 14:9. "I and the Father are one." John 10:30. So, how could Christ, the son of God, die? Why was His death necessary for the redemption of mankind? These are not easy questions to answer. In fact, it seams that even Jesus was perplexed with this conundrum. "My soul is overwhelmed with sorrow to the point of death. ... 'Abba, Father,' he said, everything is possible for you. Take this cup from me. Yet not what I will, what you will." Mark 14:34-36. Jesus knew the kind of death and torture he was about to endure. He knew that he was about to take on the sins of the whole world when he said this prayer. "God made him who had no sin to be sin for us, so that in him we might become the righteousness of God." 1Corinthians 5:21. Christ not only died, he was tortured and died one of the most agonizing deaths imaginable. Mel Gibson's film, The Passion of Christ dramatically illustrates this point. The film was the most accurate and graphic portrayal of the death of Christ on film to this date. However, it may not even be enough to grasp the pain Christ endure for us. "The Romans used spikes that were five to seven inches long and tapered to a sharp point. They were driven through the wrists. ... 'What sort of pain would that have produced?' I asked. 'Let me put it this way,' he replied. 'Do you know the kind of pain you feel when you bang your elbow and hit your funny bone? That's actually another nerve, called the ulna nerve. It's extremely painful when you accidentally hit it. Well, picture taking a pair of pliers and squeezing and crushing that nerve,' he said. ... 'That effect would be similar to what Jesus experienced.' ... 'Crucifixion is essentially an agonizingly slow death by asphyxiation. The reason is that the stress on the muscles and diaphragm put the chest into the inhaled position; basically, in order to exhale, the individual must push up on his feet so the tension on the muscles would be eased for a moment.'" [10.31] Why was this necessary? All we can know is that in order for the full payment for sin to be paid, Christ had to die on the cross, as prophesied in Isaiah. "Because he poured out is life unto death, and was numbered with the transgressors. Fore he bore the sins of many, and made intercession for the transgressors." Isaiah 53:12. When we go through difficult times, the Lord Jesus has given us two "model" prayers. The first one is the so called "Lord's prayer", which we discussed in the introduction. The second is the above prayer from Mark 14. When we are faced with difficult circumstances we can pray that the Lord will; "take this cup from me", and spare us from the trouble we are facing. However we must end our prayer with a yielding of our heart to do whatever is necessary for God's kingdom. "Yet not what I will, what you will." Then we ask God to strengthen us. "I can do all things in him who strengthens me." Philippians 4:13.

False Christ's

There are many cults that have developed around the world. Worldwide there are an increasing number of men claiming to be Christ, or a savior to all their people, as predicted by the word of God. "Beware of false prophets, who come to you in sheep's clothing but inwardly are ravenous wolves. You will know them by their fruits. ...So every sound tree bears good fruit, but the bad tree bears evil fruit. A sound tree cannot bear evil fruit, nor can a bad tree bear good fruit. Every tree that does not bear good fruit is cut down and thrown into the fire. Thus you will know them by their fruits. 'Not every one who says to me 'Lord, Lord,' shall enter the kingdom of heaven, but he who does the will of my Father who is in heaven. On that day, many will say to me, 'Lord, Lord, did we not prophesy in your name, and cast out demons in your name, and do many mighty works in your name?' And then will I declare to them, 'I never knew you; depart from me, you evildoers.'" -Mathew 7:15, 17-23. What was the fruit of the work of men like Charles Mansion, and other cult leaders? Death and destruction were ultimately what they offered. The rise of cult groups is an indication that we are at least approaching the last days. "The disciples came to him privately, saying, 'Tell us, when this will be, and what will be the sign of you coming and of the close of the age?' And Jesus answered them, 'Take head that no one leads you astray. For many will come in my name, saying, 'I am the Christ', and they will lead many astray. And you will hear of wars and rumors of wars; see that you are not alarmed; for this must take place, but the end is not yet. For nation will rise against nation, and kingdom against kingdom, and there will be famines and earthquakes in various places; all this is but the beginning of the birth-pangs. ... And many false prophets will arise and lead many astray. ... And the gospel of the kingdom will be preached throughout the whole world, as a testimony to all nations; and then the end will come. ... Then if any one says to you, 'Lo, here is the Christ!' or 'There he is!' do not believe it. For false Christs and false prophets will rise and show great signs and wonders, so as to lead astray, if possible, even the elect." -Mathew 24:3-8, 11, 14, 23-24. "For such men are false apostles, deceitful workmen, disguising themselves as apostles of Christ. And no wonder, for even Satan disguises himself as an angel of light." -2 Corinthians. 11:13-14.

False teachers, preachers, and cult leaders are one sign of the end times. We have only lightly touched on a few topics in Biblical prophecy. Many Christians look to the rapture as the true beginning of the end. However, we must search the scriptures to discover our role in these times. Many Christians have believed that one of the most important tasks to prepare for the last days is to fulfill the "great commission." This is to fulfill the Lords final commandment to: "Go into all the world and preach the good news to all creation. Whoever believes and is baptized will be saved, but whoever does not believed will be condemned." Mark 16:15-16. So, missionaries are sent out all over the world and Bibles are distributed in nearly every language on earth. I have come to realize more each day just how important it is to tell others about Jesus. When will the end come? It will be when the church has does its best to teach the world about Jesus. At that moment, the "great commission" will have been fulfilled and "the church" will have fulfilled its purpose. This world is filled with information. As we have stated many times, faith is dependant on your reasoning i.e. your faith depends on what makes "sense" to you. What set of information has convinced you of your faith? As more information gathers through personal research and scientific discovery, the opinions about God become more cemented in each person's faith. Soon we will have a group of devoted believers in Christ and on the other side devout critics that refuse the gospel message. Once again, we will experience conditions similar to the first century A.D. Christians. And Christians are being martyred for their faith today. People are accusing any person with religious convictions as a fanatic. Soon, I believe, all people of the world will have herd the gospel message clearly. They then have the opportunity to accept Jesus Christ as Lord and savior or reject the gospel message. At that point in time, everyone will be without an excuse and will be judged for their decision.

What are the last events to take place on earth? We have already discussed how the beast or Antichrist will rise up. He will conquer great territories and rise to power during the seven years of tribulation for the earth. God's people have been raptured, and the non-Christians and the Jewish nation will be left. The beast will make a peace agreement with Israel creating a false sense of peace in the Middle East. Two and a half years into the seven year reign of power, the beast breaks his agreement and conquers Jerusalem. He then puts his thrown in the temple of God and claims to be God. He forces the people of Israel to worship the golden image of the beast. The Jews now realize that he is the Antichrist, because of the commandments of God to worship no graven image, Exodus 20:4-5, and begin to rebel. During these events God has sent his plagues on the earth. Also, the beast is gathering forces to annihilate any further rebellion from the Jews. Then come the final events leading to the battle of Armageddon. "Immediately after the tribulation of those days the sun will be darkened, and the moon will not give its light, and the stars will fall from heaven, and the powers of the heavens will be shaken; then will appear the sign of the Son of man in heaven, and then all the tribes of the earth will mourn, and they will see the son of man coming on the clouds of heaven with power and great glory; and he will send out his angels with a loud trumpet call, and they will gather his elect from the four winds, from one end of heaven to the other." -Mathew 24:29-31. The account in Matthew about the sun darkened and the changes in the stars are repeated in the book of Revelation. "When he opened the sixth seal, I looked, and behold, there was a great earthquake; and the sun became black as sackcloth, the full moon became like blood, and the stars of the sky fell to the earth." Revelation. 6:12-13 See also verses Revelation. 8:12 and 9:2. These events announce the coming of the Lord Jesus to earth and the gathering of his army for the battle of Armageddon. "The sixth angel poured his bowl on the great river Euphrates, and its water was dried up, to prepare the way for the kings from the east. ... to assemble them for battle on the great day of God the Almighty. ... And they assembled them at the place which is called in Hebrew Armageddon." -Revelation 16:12, 14, 16. After the battle of Armageddon, Satan is captured and bound for 1,000 years. "And he seized the dragon, the ancient serpent, who is the Devil and Satan, and bound him for a thousand years, and threw him into the pit, and shut it and sealed it over him, that he should deceive the nations no more, till the thousand years were ended. After that he must be loosed for a little while. Then I saw thrones, and seated on them were those whom judgment was committed. Also I saw the souls of those who had been beheaded for their testimony to Jesus and for the word of God, and who had not worshiped the beast or its image and had not received its mark on their foreheads or their hands. They came to life, and reigned with Christ a thousand years. The rest of the dead did not come to life until the thousand years were ended. This is the first resurrection." Revelation. 20:2-5. This is the end to the history of the old world and a new beginning with a new heaven and a new earth.

According to some of the movies and books about the last days, previously mentioned, some people became Christians after the first great sign of the end of the world had taken place: the rapture of the saints. Following this event, many people accepted Christ as savior and Lord. These people had the most difficult times living with the beast ruling all countries, means of commerce and trade and the ever present insistence to take the mark of the beast. Despite these difficulties, God provided for their survival in many instances. Many of them, however, were beheaded for the faith in Christ. After Christ's return, they were given great honor for their perseverance and courage. Their reign with Christ for a thousand years is hard to imagine. A thousand years of learning from God and living in a Garden of Eden with no Satan, no sin, no temptations. Throughout the long history of mankind, God has encouraged us to grow and develop. I feel that all historical events from the first days of Adam and Eve in the Garden of Eden to the present day have been a series of tests given to us to see if we will truly honor the Lord. As this life comes to a close, and a glorious new life begins with the eternal reign of Christ, we are given a thousand years to grow and mature. Following this period, we are tested one last time. This is to test the remaining elite for their faith in Christ. "Satan will be loosed from his prison and will come out to deceive the nations which are at the four corners of the earth that is Gog and Magog, to gather them for battle; their number is like the sand of the sea. And they marched up over the broad earth and surrounded the camp of the saints and the beloved city; but fire came down from heaven and consumed them, and the devil who had deceived them was thrown into the lake of fire and sulfur where the beast and the false prophet were, and they will be tormented day and night for ever and ever." -Revelation. 20:7-10.

There are many people who are curious about what the Bible has to say about many subjects. There is a renewed interest in the claims of Christ and his ministry. I read a Newsweek article on How Jesus Became Christ. When I saw the cover, my first reaction was one of curiosity and skepticism about the article's conclusions. My thoughts were that this would be another secular article ridiculing the Christian faith. So many newspapers try to portray the birth of Christianity as simply fishermen making up stories about what Jesus said and did. This article was different. It portrayed the difficulties in explaining away the resurrection of Jesus Christ from the dead in a positive light. "Without the Resurrection, it is virtually impossible to imagine that the Jesus movement of the first decades of the first century would have long endured. A small band of devotees might have kept his name alive for a time, even insisting on his messianic identity by calling him Christ, but the group would have been just one of many sects in first-century Judaism, a world roiled and crust by the cataclysmic war with Rome from 66 to 73, a conflict that resulted in the destruction of Jerusalem. [10.32]" The article points out the many difficulties in the early church and possible explanations to how Christianity eventually became the powerful religion it is today. On of the themes is found in the Christian principles of accepting people with various differences. This concept of "unconditional love" is indeed a big part of the Gospel. However, the crucial doctrine is about the death and resurrection of Jesus Christ. The success of the faith is deeply routed in the lack of ability for the Roman Empire to destroy or discredit the Christian faith. No body of Jesus was ever recovered and those who testified to be eyewitnesses to his resurrection could not be swayed in their convictions. "I can trust the apostles' testimonies because eleven of those men died martyrs' deaths because they stood solid for two truths: Christ's deity and his resurrection. These men were tortured and flogged, and they finally suffered death by some of the cruelest methods then known. ... After the Resurrection, Peter, who had denied Christ, stood up even at the threat of death and proclaimed that Jesus was alive. [10.33]" The apostles before the resurrection were depressed, defeated men who could not understand the death of Jesus. After the resurrection they declared their faith boldly, even though it meant torture and death, see the book of

Acts chapter 5. This was an amazing transformation of not just one, but many individuals including the disciples. They were thoroughly convinced of the resurrection. For further details I highly recommend reading More Than A Carpenter by Josh McDowell.

The entire basis of the Christian faith is about the redemption of sin by Christ on the cross. If Christ did not rise from the dead, sin had victory over God. Instead, God proved by the resurrection of Jesus that we have victory over Satan and our "sin nature" through Jesus Christ. The entire Christian faith is based on this act of obedience from Jesus the Son of God, to his Father in heaven. Jesus was all about love and self-sacrifice to God. This was the message of his entire ministry and his death on the cross. I was incredible shocked when this point was over-looked by many critics concerning the film, The Passion of Jesus Christ by Mel Gibson. The reviews continued to present the film as anti-Jewish in content and said the film would provoke violence. This is the same gospel message taught, preached, and shown in every film about Jesus ever made! What made Mel Gibson's version so different? One thing, which was special about the Passion film, was it was the first time such a large amount of money was spent to make a film about Jesus. It was very dramatic and had incredible special effects. Also, it was extremely detailed and graphic on the presentation of the death of Christ. Gibson may have taken minor liberties with details on the event, but for the most part it was the most historically accurate portrayal of the death of Christ ever made. How can so many people be ignorant of the message of the film? The message was about the love Christ has towards all people of the world. The film begins with one of the Jews most treasured books, Isaiah. "For by His stripes were we healed." Isaiah 53:5. The title was the Passion of Christ indicating Jesus had a passion to give his life to God and save His people from the destruction of sin. Even by showing great love towards everyone, there are always enemies who hate you. We all have people who hate us for reasons we can not begin to comprehend. The Romans who scourged Jesus and the Jews who insisted Christ be put to death on the cross are not examples of any particular race, religion, or creed. They only belong to the group of people who hated Christ and refuse to accept Jesus as Lord. The Christians who saw the movie clearly understood the intention of the film. As we watched Christ suffer from the torture, we realized that it should have been us taking this punishment. Jesus "stood in" for us and took the punishment we deserved for each sin we have committed and will commit during our lifetime. With each blow, we understand that Jesus was taking our punishment for us. We then thanked God for the gift of His son and the great sacrifice he has made on our behalf. When we are tempted to sin, we can remember the images of the film and realize that if we sin we have caused another strike of the devices of torture on the back of Jesus. We are reminded how horrible sin is and how we must avoid all sin in our lives.

Many people fear the events described in the book of Revelation. All the battles, torment of the wicked, judgment of the wicked, tribulation, plagues, are necessary to purify the world, the universe, and the kingdoms of heaven and hell. The Christian looks at these events with optimism. Some people seam to never get past the tenth verse of chapter twenty in Revelation, quoted previously. If they read further, they would see the glorious future God is preparing for us. "I am going there to prepare a place for you. And if I go and prepare a place for you, I will come back and take you to be with me that you also may be where I am." John 14:2-3 The most wonderful place that we can imagine is found in the new heaven and new earth especially prepared for us to remain in the presence of the Lord forever. The love shown toward us throughout the Bible is fulfilled in the final two chapters of Revelation. "And the sea gave up the dead in them, and all were judged by what they had done. Then death and Hades were thrown into the lake of fire. This is the second death, the lake of fire; and if any one's name was not found written in the book of life, he was thrown into the lake of fire. Then I saw a new heaven and a new earth; for the first heaven and the first earth had passed away, and the sea was no more. And I saw the holy city, New Jerusalem, coming down out of heaven from God, prepared as a bride adorned for her husband; and I heard a loud voice from the throne saying, 'Behold the dwelling of God is with men. He will dwell with them, and they shall be his people, and God himself will be with them, he will wipe away every tear from their eyes, and death shall be no more, neither shall there be mourning nor crying nor pain any more, for the former things have passed away." -Revelation 20:13-21:4. Prepare your hearts for the coming of the Lord so you will enter the kingdom of heaven. Accept by faith, Jesus Christ as Lord. "For if Abraham was justified by works, he has something to boast about, but not before God. For what does the scripture say? Abraham believed God, and it was reckoned to him as righteousness." Romans 4:2-3. "Therefore, since we are justified by faith, we have peace with God through our Lord Jesus Christ."- Romans 5:1. "Whoever believes in the Son has eternal life, but whoever rejects the Son will not see life, for God's wrath remains on him." John 3:36. The message is the same as has been told for two thousand years. We must believe in the Lord Jesus Christ to be saved. "I tell you, he will see that they will get justice, and quickly. However, when the Son of Man comes, will he find faith on the earth?" Luke 18:8. This is the crucial question God asks of the world. Will He find the people having faith in His Son the Lord Jesus Christ? What faith will God find? Every person will be judged according to what they believe. Are you sure you have faith in the things of God? Are you sure you will be judged worthy of His kingdom? Science helps us to test and define our faith. Science teaches us many things about analyzing situations. Science often opens doors to an evangelistic presentation of the gospel as we have shown in this book. Please pray for us as we teach others about the important role the subject of science plays in a person's decision of faith in Christ. "I urge you, brothers, by our Lord Jesus Christ and by the love of the Spirit, to join me in my struggle by praying to God for me. Pray that I may be rescued from the unbelievers in Judea and that my service in Jerusalem may be acceptable to the saints there, so that by God's will I may come to you with joy and together with you be refreshed." Romans 15:30-32 Pray for the members of the Institute for Creation Research and their struggle to get more information into the hands of Christians who are tested in their faith. Pray for other ministries. Please pray for myself, my wife and my family to continue serving the Lord by writing more books. Science is all about learning and using our minds, which God has given to us, to make decisions that can affect lives around the world. Make the reasonable decision to follow the Lord Jesus by faith and read God's Holy Bible daily. Praise be to God from whom all things are made.

References for Chapter 10

10.1   Sidney I. Landau- Editor in Chief, Webster Illustrated Contemporary Dictionary, Garden City, New York, Doubleday & Company, Inc., J. G. Ferguson Publishing Company, 1982, p.45.

10.2   Tom Morris, Philosophy For Dummies, Hungry Minds Inc., New York, N.Y., 1999, p. 241.

10.3   Ibid p. 241.

10.4   Josh McDowell, Evidence That Demands a Verdict, Campus Crusade for Christ, Inc., Here's Life Publishers, Inc., San Bernardino, Ca, 1975, p. 383.

10.5   Ibid. p. 16-17.

10.6   Ibid. p. 17.

10.7   Ibid. p. 18-19.

10.8   Ibid. p. 17.

10.9   Ibid. p. 65.

10.10   Ibid. p. 68.

10.11   Josh McDowell and Don Stewart, Answers To Tough Questions skeptics ask about the Christian faith, Living Books, Tydal House Publishers, Inc. Wheaton, Illinois, 1980, p. 25.

10.12   Josh McDowell, Prophecy Fact or Fiction? Daniel In The Critics' Den, Here's Life Publishers, Inc., San Bernardino, Ca, 1981, p. 5.

10.13   Ibid p. 3.

10.14   Josh McDowell and Don Stewart, Answers To Tough Questions skeptics ask about the Christian faith, Living Books, Tydal House Publishers, Inc. Wheaton, Illinois, 1980, p. 40-41.

10.15   Popular Science Magazine, September 2005, Volume 267 #3, 'Better ... Stronger ... Faster ... Popular Science Introduces The Engineered Human' Illustrated by John MacNeil, p. 49-55. Fold out insert.

10.16   Ibid. , 'Will We Grow Babies Outside Their Mothers' Bodies?' by Gretchen Reynolds.,p. 77.

10.17   Ibid. IS ANY OF THIS A GOOD IDEA? By Robert Sapolsky, Illustrated by John MacNeil., p,97-98.

10.18   Ibid. p. 98-99.

10.19   Charles H. Dyer, The Rise of Babylon. Sign of the End Times., Tyndale House Publishers, Inc. , Wheaton, Illinois, 1991., p. 15-16.

10.20   Ibid p. 18.

10.21   Ibid p. 22.

10.22   Ibid p. 50.

10.23   Ibid p. 19.

10.24   Ibid p. 26-27.

10.25   Ibid p. 49.

10.26   Ibid p. 136-138.

10.27   Ibid p. 166.

10.28   Ibid p. 167-168.

10.29   Popular Science Magazine, May 2005, Volume 266, #5, Tsunamis, Volcanoes, Hurricanes, Landslides – The Single Certain Thing About Nature's Killers is That They will Strike Again, And Again. Our Only Defense: Even Better Prediction and Protection By Michael Behar, p. 46.

10.30   Ibid p. 48-49.

10.31   Lee Strobel, The Case For Easter, Zondervan, Grand Rapids, Michigan, 1998, 2003, p. 18-20.

10.32   Newsweek, March 28, 2005, How Jesus Became Christ, From Resurrection to the Rise of Christianity By John Meacham, p. 43-44.

10.33   Josh McDowell, More Than A Carpenter, Living Books, Tyndale House Publishers, 1977, 2004, p. 57, 63.

Illustrations for Chapter 10

10.1   Josh McDowell, Evidence That Demands a Verdict, Campus Crusade for Christ, Inc., Here's Life Publishers, Inc., San Bernardino, Ca, 1975, p.386.

10.2   Ibid p. 384-385.

10.3   Ibid p.42.

10.4   Ibid p. 43.

Back Cover Quotation

♦   Albert Einstein, Ideas and Opinions, New York, Dell Publishing Co., Crown Publishers MCMLIV, p.53.

♦   Ibid. p.55.

The Essential Scientific Knowledge Quiz
By Allen E. Hillegas
Answer all questions True or False. Answer key is at the end of the quiz.

Part 1: Astronomy / Physics

T or F 1. The basic definition of a force is any push or pull exerted on an object.

T or F 2. There are only four fundamental forces. These are the Electromagnetic Force, The Gravitational Force, The Weak Force and The Strong Force.

T or F 3. The Strong Force and Weak Force have a range limited to the size of the atom. The Gravitational Force and Electromagnetic Force are limited in field strength.

T or F 4. Sir Isaac Newton discovered three fundamental laws which apply to all physical forces. These can be described by the following equations: 1. $F=ma$, 2. $F=\ ^-F$ 3. $P=mv$. $P_{before} = P_{after}$.

T or F 5. When you apply a force to a group of objects, the energy of this system is increased. The first law of thermodynamics states that matter and energy can not be created nor destroyed but can only change form. $E=mc^2$.

T or F 6. Normally, the effective or resultant force has the same magnitude i.e. amount of energy as the applied force. The second law of thermodynamics.

T or F 7. All fundamental forces are created by an exchange of "virtual particles". EM- Photons, Gravity – gravitons, Strong – pi-mesons and gluons. Weak – Intermediate bosons.

T or F 8. Experiments at the Relativistic Heavy Ion Collider, or RHIC (pronounced "Rick") at Long Island, have produced the most accurate re-creation of the beginning of the universe. †

T or F 9. The scientists at RHIC showed that at the "Big Bang" all matter and all fundamental forces were created by numerous 'five-dimensional Black Holes' separating a "water" like "perfect fluid" composed of gluons and quarks. †

T or F 10. According to experiments at RHIC, all particles, and all objects "might really be manifestations, projections, from a higher-dimensional space". †

T or F 11. Experiments at RHIC indicate that "98 percent of the mass of protons and neutrons … doesn't come from quarks" but has originated and are sustained by the residual power of the Big Bang projected out of a "fifth dimensional black hole". †

T or F 12. Scientists now know everything about all fundamental forces and the structure of the atom. There is no longer any need for using particle accelerators to explore the inner atom.

Part 2: Scientists and Teachers

5 Main Points – Review of part 1

1) The results of Science are everywhere in our society. Ever time you watch a movie, ride in a car, use a tractor, a radio, a microwave oven. Science is an important part of our daily lives.

2) Science influences our <u>F</u>aith your personal beliefs, convictions in a positive or negative way.
Your beliefs are changed by what you accept as "true". How Much evidence does it take to change your beliefs?

3) Science explores cause-effect relationships. We ask Why things are the way they are and How things work.

4) All Physical <u>F</u>orces have limits. There are things they can and can not do.

5) Your <u>F</u>uture will depend on what you Believe to be true. Get a Big Dream, take steps to achieve it.
If you don't stand for something you will fall for anything.

Personal Testimonies.

1.   Sir Isaac Newton: "This most beautiful system of the sun, planets, and comets, could only proceed from the counsel and dominion of an intelligent and powerful Being. ... This Being governs all things, not as the soul of the world, but as Lord over all. .... The Supreme God is a Being eternal, infinite, absolutely perfect; ... for we say, my God, your God, the God of Israel, the God of Gods, and Lord of Lords. ... The word God' usually signifies Lord; but every lord is not a God. ... The true God is a living, intelligent, and powerful Being. ... He is eternal and infinite ... that is, his duration reaches from eternity to eternity; his presence from infinity to infinity; he governs all things, and knows all things that are or can be done." Source: The Mathematical Principles of Natural Philosophy (1687).

2.   Albert Einstein: "But science can only be created by those who are thoroughly imbued with the aspiration toward truth and understanding. This source of feeling, however, springs from the sphere of religion. To this there also belongs the faith in the possibility that the regulations valid for the world of existence are rational, that is, comprehensible to reason. I can not conceive of a genuine scientist without that profound faith. The situation can be expressed by an image: science without religion is lame, religion without science is blind. ... I have asserted above that in truth a legitimate conflict between religion and science cannot exist." Albert Einstein, Ideas and Opinions, Crown Publishers p. 54-55.

3.   Francis Collins (1993 Director of the Human Genome Project mapping out the 3.1 Billion bits of DNA: "Science doesn't refute God. It affirms him, and gives us new respect for the beauty of creation." Guideposts Magazine December 2006.

Part 3: Bio-Chemistry –The origin of Life.

T or F 1. The basic building block of all life is amino acids.

T or F 2. Scientists can produce amino acids from chemical reactions in the laboratory.

T or F 3. Amino acids are routinely created from chemical reactions in earth's oxygen rich environment. The conditions necessary for this processes is well-understood.

T or F 4. You can produce all 22 amino acids necessary to make a single strand of protein in a laboratory.

T or F 5. DNA has chemical bonds holding the information in place- but no bonds between the nucleotide bases. However, there is NO chemical bonding determining letter sequence of DNA instructions.

T or F 6. It has been Scientifically proven that it IS POSSIBLE to synthesize proteins from amino acids, combine proteins, chemicals, and genetic information to produce single-celled life forms.

T or F 7. Every known form of life requires some type of moisture and oxygen to survive carried by the earth's well balanced eco-system.

T or F 8. The presence of either water or oxygen aids the chemical production of life.

T or F 9. Cells require all their millions of necessary parts to remain alive.

T or F 10. We now have a complete understanding of all the basic components necessary to form the simplest single-celled life.

Part 4: The Human Mind.

T or F 1. For proper cognitive function, the brain needs healthy neuron activity. Also, you must have a stable network of neurons working together in different regions of the brain.

T or F 2. There is a great deal of difference between the neurons of animals and the neurons of human beings.

T or F 3. Science has discovered that the main difference between animal and human brains is due to a fundamental difference in their brain waves i.e. EM waves i.e. a form of light. ††

T or F 4. You could say the electromagnetic spectrum is just different forms of light instead of saying that light is only a small part of the electromagnetic spectrum.

T or F 5. Light has a particle-wave dual nature and all matter has a "wave-nature".

T or F 6. Dr. Roger Penrose, world renowned mathematician and scientist, "proposed that consciousness was a quantum computation within the brain." †††

T or F 7. In 1998 Juan Maldacena proposed a theory combining a pseudo-QCD theory with a modified string theory. This theory was essentially proven correct by the experiments at RHIC. †

T or F 8. Maldacena's Theory combining Quantum Color Dynamics and string theory which explains the beginning of the universe, could help explain the abilities of the human mind. †

Answer Key: Astronomy / Physics : 1.T 2.T 3.T 4.T 5.T 6.F 7.T 8.T 9.T 10.T 11.T 12.F
Bio-Chemistry: 1.T 2.T 3.F 4.F 5.T 6.F 7.T 8.F 9.T 10. F The Human Mind: 1.T 2.F 3.T 4.T 5.T 6.T 7.T 8. T

† Tim Folger, The Big Bang Machine, Discover Magazine, February 2007, p. 34-38.
†† R. Douglas Fields, Beyond The Neuron Doctrine, Scientific American Mind, June/July 2006. p. 22-27.
††† Jay Tolson, Is There Room for the Soul?, U.S. News & World Report, October 23,2006, p. 63.

Printed in the United States
by Baker & Taylor Publisher Services